Mark . . . is written in a extremely plain, abrupt, often unidiomatic and dogged Koine which has generally been made to seem falsely natural, even eloquent in English translations. . . . Admittedly, Mark's final effect in Greek is one of a great and spare eloquence; but that strength is seldom owing to the actual words or structure of his sentences and never to calculated effects of mellifluous rhetoric. If his eloquence has primarily linguistic origins, that power rises from the struggle between Mark's headlong intent and his gravely hobbled command of his medium. Yet a strong argument can easily be made that Mark — whoever he may have been . . . is the most original narrative writer in history, an apparently effortless sovereign of all the skills and arts of durably convincing storytelling. . . . [D]espite centuries of neglect when it was thought to be a mere summary of the longer and fuller Matthew and Luke, Mark has proved the most influential of human books. All other books from four thousand years of epics, plays, lyrics, and biographies have touched human life less potently.

Reynolds Price, *Three Gospels*

The Gospel of Mark

A Socio-Rhetorical Commentary

Ben Witherington III

WILLIAM B. EERDMANS PUBLISHING COMPANY
GRAND RAPIDS, MICHIGAN / CAMBRIDGE, U.K.

Wm. B. Eerdmans Publishing Co.
255 Jefferson Ave. S.E., Grand Rapids, Michigan 49503 /
P.O. Box 163, Cambridge CB3 9PU U.K.

Printed in the United States of America

06 05 04 03 02 01   7 6 5 4 3 2 1

Library of Congress Cataloging-in-Publication Data

Witherington, Ben, 1951-
    The Gospel of Mark: a socio-rhetorical commentary / Ben Witherington III.
        p.   cm.
    Includes bibliographical references and index.
    ISBN 0-8028-4503-7 (softcover: alk. paper)
    1. Bible. N.T. Mark — Commentaries.   2. Bible. N.T. Mark — Socio-rhetorical
criticism.   I. Title.

    BS2585.53.W58   2001
    226.3′077 — dc21

                                                                00-049472

www.eerdmans.com

Dedicated to the memory of
    Donald English and William Lane
        This Gospel left its mark on them,
            just as they did on us.

And

    dedicated to Richard Cornell,
    an excellent teaching and research assistant,
    and, one day, a great teacher

Contents

THE COMMENTARY

Abbreviations of Periodicals and Other Reference Works

ABD	*Anchor Bible Dictionary*
BAGD	W. Bauer, W. F. Arndt, F. W. Gingrich, and F. W. Danker, *Greek-English Lexicon of the NT*
BDF	F. Blass, A. Debrunner, and R. W. Funk, *A Greek Grammar of the NT*
BJRL	*Bulletin of the John Rylands University Library of Manchester*
BT	*The Bible Translator*
BTB	*Biblical Theology Bulletin*
BZ	*Biblische Zeitschrift*
CBQ	*Catholic Biblical Quarterly*
CTM	*Concordia Theological Monthly*
ET	*Expository Times*
EvQ	*Evangelical Quarterly*
HeyJ	*Heythrop Journal*
HTR	*Harvard Theological Review*
IEJ	*Israel Exploration Journal*
Imm	*Immanuel*
Int	*Interpretation*
JBL	*Journal of Biblical Literature*
JSNT	*Journal for the Study of the New Testament*
JTS	*Journal of Theological Studies*
JTSA	*Journal of Theology for Southern Africa*
MT	Masoretic Text
NedTTs	*Nederlands theologisch tijdschrift*

Neot	*Neotestamentica*
NovT	*Novum Testamentum*
NTS	*New Testament Studies*
PGM	Papyri graecae magicae: Die griechischen Zauberpapyri
PJ	*Palästina-Jahrbuch*
P.Oxy.	Oxyrhynchus Papyri
RB	*Revue biblique*
RBén	*Revue bénédictine*
TCGNT	B. M. Metzger, *A Textual Commentary on the Greek New Testament*
TDNT	G. Kittel and G. Friedrich, eds., *Theological Dictionary of the New Testament*
TLZ	*Theologische Literaturzeitung*
TZ	*Theologische Zeitschrift*
ZNW	*Zeitschrift für die neutestamentliche Wissenschaft*

Bibliography

Commentaries on Mark

Cranfield, C. E. B. *The Gospel according to St. Mark.* Cambridge: Cambridge University Press, 1972.

English, D. *The Message of Mark.* Downers Grove: InterVarsity, 1992.

Gnilka, J. *Das Evangelium nach Markus.* Zurich: Benziger, 1979.

Guelich, R. *Mark 1–8.26.* Waco: Word, 1989.

Gundry, R. H. *Mark: A Commentary on His Apology for the Cross.* Grand Rapids: Eerdmans, 1993.

Hooker, M. *The Gospel according to Mark.* Peabody, Mass.: Hendrickson, 1991.

Hurtado, L. *Mark.* New York: Harper & Row, 1983.

Juel, D. *The Gospel of Mark.* Nashville: Abingdon, 1999.

Lane, W. *The Gospel of Mark.* Grand Rapids: Eerdmans, 1974.

Lightfoot, R. H. *The Gospel Message of Mark.* Oxford: Oxford University Press, 1950.

Marcus, J. *Mark 1–8.* New York: Doubleday, 1999.

Martin, R. P., *Mark: Evangelist and Theologian.* Grand Rapids: Zondervan, 1972.

Moule, C. F. D. *The Gospel according to Mark.* Cambridge: Cambridge University Press, 1965.

Nineham, D. *The Gospel of St. Mark.* London: Penguin Books, 1963.

Oden, T. C., and C. A. Hall, eds. *Mark,* vol. 2 of *The Ancient Christian Commentary on Scripture.* Downers Grove: InterVarsity, 1998.

Painter, J. *Mark's Gospel.* London: Routledge, 1997.

Pesch, R. *Markus-Evangelium I.* Freiburg: Herder, 1976.

Plummer, A. *The Gospel according to St. Mark.* Cambridge: Cambridge University Press, 1914.

Schweizer, E. *The Good News according to Mark.* Atlanta: John Knox, 1971.

Swete, H. B. *The Gospel according to St. Mark.* London: Macmillan, 1909.

Taylor, V. *The Gospel according to St. Mark.* New York: St. Martin's Press, 1966.

Commentaries (non-Markan)

Craigie, P. *Psalms 1–50.* Waco: Word, 1983.

Marshall, I. H. *The Gospel of Luke.* Exeter: Paternoster, 1978.

Weiser, A. *The Psalms.* Philadelphia: Fortress, 1962.

Witherington, Ben, III. *The Acts of the Apostles: A Socio-Rhetorical Commentary.* Grand Rapids: Eerdmans, 1998.

———. *Conflict and Community in Corinth.* Grand Rapids: Eerdmans, 1994.

———. *John's Wisdom.* Louisville: Westminster/John Knox, 1995.

Rhetorical Studies

Blount, B. K. "A Socio-Rhetorical Analysis of Simon of Cyrene: Mark 15.21 and Its Parallels." *Semeia* 64 (1993): 171-98.

Dewey, J. "The Literary Structure of the Controversy Stories in Mark 2.1-3.6." *JBL* 92 (1973): 394-401. Repr. on pages 109-18 of *The Interpretation of Mark.* Issues in Religion and Theology 7. Edited by W. Telford. Philadelphia: Fortress/London: SPCK, 1985.

———. *Markan Public Debate.* Chico: Calif.: Scholars, 1980.

Fowler, R. M. *Let the Reader Understand.* Minneapolis: Fortress, 1991.

Hester, J. D. "Dramatic Inconclusion: Irony and the Narrative Rhetoric of the Ending of Mark." *JSNT* 57 (1995): 61-86.

———. "Socio-Rhetorical Criticism." *JSNT* 45 (1992): 27-57.

Koester, H. "Mark 9.43-47 and Quintilian 8.3.75." *HTR* 71 (1978): 151-53.

Mack, B. *A Myth of Innocence: Mark and Christian Origins.* Philadelphia: Fortress, 1988.

Meynet, R. "Qui Donc est 'Le Plus Fort'? Analyse Rhetorique de Mc 3,22-30; Mt. 12,22-37; Luc 11,14-26." *RB* 90 (1983): 334-50.

Owen-Ball, D. T. "Rabbinic Rhetoric and the Tribute Passage (Mt. 22.15-22; Mk. 12.13-17; Lk. 20.20-26)." *NovT* 35, no. 1 (1993): 1-14.

Parrott, R. "Conflict and Rhetoric in Mark 2.23-28." *Semeia* 64 (1993): 117-37.

Phelan, J. E. "Rhetoric and Meaning in Mark 6.30-8.10." Ph.D. diss., Northwestern University, 1985.

Rhoads, D., and D. Michie. *Mark as Story: An Introduction to the Narrative of a Gospel.* Philadelphia: Fortress, 1982.

Robbins, V. "Beelzebul Controversy in Mark and Luke: Rhetorical and Social Analysis." *Forum* 7 (1991): 261-77.

———. *Jesus the Teacher: A Socio-Rhetorical Interpretation of Mark.* Minneapolis: Fortress, 1992.

———. "Mark 1.14-20: An Interpretation at the Intersection of Jewish and Graeco-Roman Traditions." *NTS* 28 (1982): 220-36.

———. "The Woman Who Touched Jesus' Garment: Socio-Rhetorical Analysis of the Synoptic Accounts." *NTS* 33, no. 4 (1987): 502-15.

Salyer, G. "Rhetoric, Purity, and Play: Aspects of Mark 7.1-23." *Semeia* 64 (1993): 139-69.

Young, D. M. "Whoever Has Ears to Hear." Ph.D. diss., Vanderbilt University, 1994.

Monographs, Dissertations, Articles, and Lectures

Achtemeier, P. J. "And He Followed Him: Miracles and Discipleship in Mk. 10.46-52." *Semeia* 11 (1978): 115-45.

———. "He Taught Them Many Things: Reflections on Marcan Christology." *CBQ* 42 (1980): 465-81.

———. "Mark, Gospel of." Pages 551-53 in vol. 4 of *The Anchor Bible Dictionary*. Edited by David Noel Freedman. 6 vols. New York: Doubleday, 1992.

Adna, J. "The Encounter of Jesus with the Gerasene Demoniac." Pages 279-301 in *Authenticating the Activities of Jesus*. Edited by B. Chilton and C. A. Evans. Leiden: Brill, 1999.

Allison, Dale C., Jr. *Jesus of Nazareth: Millenarian Prophet*. Minneapolis: Fortress, 1999.

———. "Behind the Temptations of Jesus." Pages 195-213 in *Authenticating the Activities of Jesus*. Edited by B. Chilton and C. A. Evans. Leiden: Brill, 1999.

Aune, D. E. "A Note on Jesus' Messianic Consciousness and 11Q Melchizedek." *EvQ* 45 (1973): 161-65.

Baird, J. A. *Discovering the Power of the Gospel*. Akron: Hampshire Books, 1989.

Bammel, E., "Markus 10.11f. und das judische Eherecht." *ZNW* 61 (1970): 95-101.

Barrett, C. K. "The Background of Mark 10.45." Pages 1-18 in *New Testament Essays: Studies in the Memory of T. W. Manson, 1893-1958*. Edited by A. J. B. Higgins. Manchester: Manchester University Press, 1959.

———. *The Holy Spirit and the Gospel Tradition*. Philadelphia: Fortress, 1947.

———. *The Signs of an Apostle*. London: Epworth, 1970.

Bauckham, R., ed. *The Gospel for All Christians: Rethinking the Gospel's Origins*. Grand Rapids: Eerdmans, 1988.

Beasley-Murray, G. R. *Baptism in the New Testament*. Grand Rapids: Eerdmans, 1962.

Beavis, M. A. *Mark's Audience: The Literary and Social Setting of Mark 4.11-12*. Sheffield: University of Sheffield Press, 1989.

Bennett, W. "The Son of Man Must." *NovT* 17, no. 2 (1975): 113-29.

Berger, K. "Hartherzigkeit und Gottes Gesetz. Die Vorgeschichte des anti-judischen Vorwurfs in Mk. 10.5." *ZNW* 61, nos. 1-2 (1970): 1-47.

Best, E. *Disciples and Discipleship: Studies in the Gospel according to Mark.* Edinburgh: T & T Clark, 1986.

———. "Mark's Preservation of the Tradition." Pages 153-68 in *The Interpretation of Mark.* Edited by W. R. Telford. Edinburgh: T & T Clark, 1995.

———. "Mark III.20, 21, 31-35." *NTS* 22 (1976): 309-319.

———. *The Temptation and the Passion.* 2nd ed. Cambridge: Cambridge University Press, 1990.

Bilezikian, G. C. *The Liberated Gospel: A Comparison of the Gospel of Mark and Greek Tragedy.* Grand Rapids: Baker, 1979.

Black, C. C. "Was Mark a Roman Gospel?" *ET* 105 (1993-94): 36-40.

Black, M. "The Christological Use of the Old Testament in the New Testament." *NTS* 18 (1971): 1-14.

Blass, F. "On Mark xii.42 and xv.16." *ET* 10 (1898-99): 185-87.

———. "On Mark xii.42." *ET* 10 (1898-99): 286-87.

Bligh, J. "Qorbon!" *HeyJ* 5 (1964): 192-93.

Bode, E. L. *The First Easter Morning.* Rome: Biblical Institute Press, 1970.

Bond, H. *Pontius Pilate.* Cambridge: Cambridge University Press, 1998.

Boobyer, G. H. *St. Mark and the Transfiguration Story.* Edinburgh: T & T Clark, 1942.

Booth, R. P. *Jesus and the Laws of Purity: Tradition History and Legal History in Mark 7.* Sheffield: JSOT Press, 1986.

Boring, E. *The Continuing Voice of Jesus.* Louisville: Westminster/John Knox, 1991.

———. "Markan Christology: God-Language for Jesus?" *NTS* 45 (1999): 451-71.

Bornkamm, G. *Jesus of Nazareth.* New York: Harper & Row, 1960.

Brandon, S. G. F. *Jesus and the Zealots.* Manchester: Manchester University Press, 1967.

Brower, K. E. "'Let the Reader Understand': Temple and Eschatology in Mark." Pages 119-43 in *Eschatology in Bible and Theology.* Edited by K. E. Brower and M. W. Elliot. Downers Grove: InterVarsity, 1997.

Brown, R. E. *New Testament Essays.* Garden City, N.Y.: Image Books, 1968.

Brown, R. E., K. P. Donfried, and J. Reumann, eds. *Peter in the New Testament.* Minneapolis: Augsburg Press, 1973.

Bruce, F. F. "Render to Caesar." Pages 249-63 in *Jesus and the Politics of His Day.* Edited by E. Bammel and C. F. D. Moule. Cambridge: Cambridge University Press, 1984.

Bryan, Christopher. *A Preface to Mark.* Oxford: Oxford University Press, 1993.

Buby, B. "A Christology of Relationship in Mark." *BTB* 10, no. 4 (1980): 149-54.

Buechner, F. *Telling the Truth: The Gospel as Tragedy, Comedy, and Fairy Tale.* San Franciso: Harper & Row, 1977.

Bultmann, R. *History of the Synoptic Tradition.* Oxford: Blackwell, 1963.

Burridge, R. A. *What Are the Gospels?* Cambridge: Cambridge University Press, 1992.

Casey, M. *Aramaic Sources of Mark's Gospel.* Cambridge: Cambridge University Press, 1998.

Catchpole, D. "The Fearful Silence of the Women at the Tomb: A Study in Markan Theology." *JTSA* 18 (1977): 3-10.

———. "The Triumphal Entry." Pages 319-24 in *Jesus and the Politics of His Day.* Edited by C. F. D. Moule and E. Bammel. Cambridge: Cambridge University Press, 1984.

Chadwick, G. A. "The Daughter of Jairus and the Woman with the Issue of Blood (Mt. ix.18; Mk. v.22; Lk.viii.41)." *ET,* 4th ser., 8 (1893): 309-20.

Chilton, B. *Jesus' Baptism and Jesus' Healing.* Harrisburg, Pa.: Trinity Press, 1998.

Collins, A. Y. *The Beginning of the Gospel: Probings of Mark in Context.* Minneapolis: Fortress, 1992.

Cope, O. L. Matthew: *A Scribe Trained for the Kingdom of Heaven.* Washington, D.C.: Catholic Biblical Association, 1976.

Crossan, J. D. *The Historical Jesus.* San Francisco: Harper, 1991.

———. "Mark and the Relatives of Jesus." *NovT* 15 (1973): 81-113.

Cullmann, O. *Peter: Disciple, Apostle, Martyr.* London: SCM, 1953.

Dalman, G. "Vierlie Acker." *PJ* 22 (1926): 120-36.

Daube, D. "Evangelisten und Rabbinen." *ZNW* 48 (1957): 119-26.

———. "Responsibilities of Master and Disciples in the Gospels." *NTS* 19 (1972-73): 1-16.

De Bruyne, D. "Les plus anciens prologues latins des Evangiles." *RBen* 40 (1928): 193-214.

Denny, J. "The Sadducees and Immortality." *ET,* 4th ser., 10 (1894): 401-9.

Derrett, J. D. M. "Contributions to the Study of the Gerasene Demoniac." *JSNT* 3 (1979): 2-17.

———. "ΚΟΡΒΑΝ, Ο ΕΣΤΙΝ ΔΩΡΟΝ." Pages 112-17 in *Studies in the New Testament.* Vol. 1. Leiden: Brill, 1977.

———. "Law in the New Testament: The Palm Sunday Colt." *NovT* 13 (1971): 241-58.

———. "Law in the New Testament: The Syrophoenician Woman and the Centurion of Capernaum." *NovT* 15 (1973): 161-86.

———. "Mark 9.42 and Comparative Legal History." Pages 4-31 in *Law in the New Testament.* Leiden: Brill, 1974.

Dibelius, M. *From Tradition to Gospel.* London: Ivor Nicholson and Watson, 1934.

Dittenberger, W. *Orientis graeci inscriptiones selectae.* Hildesheim: Olms, 1960.

Dodd, C. H. "The Appearance of the Risen Christ." Pages 9-35 in *Studies in the Gospels: Essays in Memory of R. H. Lightfoot.* Edited by D. E. Nineham. Oxford: Oxford University Press, 1955.

————. *The Parables of the Kingdom*. New York: Scribner, 1961.

Doudna, J. C. *The Greek of the Gospel of Mark*. Philadelphia: SBL, 1961.

Drury, J. "The Sower, the Vineyard, and the Place of Allegory in the Interpretation of Mark's Parables." *JTS* 24 (1973): 367-79.

Dubrow, H. *Genre*. The Critical Idiom Series 42. London: Methuen, 1982.

Dunn, J. D. G. *Jesus and the Spirit*. Philadelphia: Westminster, 1975.

————. *Jesus, Paul, and the Law*. Louisville: Westminster/John Knox, 1990.

————. "The Messianic Secret in Mark." Pages 116-31 in The Messianic Secret. Edited by C. Tuckett. Philadelphia: Fortress, 1983.

————. "Pharisees, Sinners, and Jesus." Lecture presented at Duke University, 1986.

Dyer, K. D. "But concerning *That* Day . . . (Mk. 13.32): 'Prophetic' and 'Apocalyptic' Eschatology in Mark 13." Pages 104-22 in *SBL Seminar Papers*. Atlanta: Scholars, 1999.

Eppstein, V. "The Historicity of the Gospel Account of the Cleansing of the Temple." *ZNW* 55 (1964): 42-58.

Evans, C. F. "I Will Go before You into Galilee." *JTS* 5, no. 5 (1954): 3-18.

Falk, Z. W. "Notes and Observations on Talmudic Vows." *HTR* 59, no. 3 (1966): 311-12.

Farmer, W. R. "Palm Branches in John 12, 13." *JTS*, n.s. 3, no. 1 (1952): 62-66.

Farrar, A. *A Study in St. Mark*. London: Dacre, 1951.

Fiorenza, E. Schussler. *In Memory of Her*. New York: Crossroad, 1985.

Fish, S. *Is There a Text in This Class?* Cambridge: Harvard University Press, 1980.

Fitzmyer, J. A. "The Aramaic Qorban Inscription from Jebel Hallet et-Turi and Mark 7.11/Matt. 15.5." *JBL* 78 (1959): 60-65.

Fledderman, H. "A Warning about the Scribes (Mark 12.37b-40)." *CBQ* 44 (1982): 52-67.

Flusser, D. "The Crucified One and the Jews." *Imm* 7 (1977): 25-37.

————. "Two Notes on the Midrash on 2 Sam. 7.1." *IEJ* 9 (1959): 99-109.

Ford, D. *The Abomination of Desolation in Biblical Eschatology*. Washington, D.C.: University Press of America, 1979.

Freyne, S. *Galilee from Alexander the Great to Hadrian (323 B.C.E. to C.E. 135)*. Notre Dame: University of Notre Dame Press/Michael Glazier, 1980.

————. "The Geography, Politics, and Economics of Galilee." Pages 75-122 in *Studying the Historical Jesus: Evaluations of the State of Research*. Edited by B. Chilton and C. A. Evans. Leiden: Brill, 1994.

Furnish, V. P. *The Love Commandment in the New Testament*. Nashville: Abingdon, 1972.

Gamble, H. Y. *Books and Readers in the Early Church*. New Haven: Yale University Press, 1995.

Garrett, S. *The Temptation of Jesus in Mark's Gospel*. Grand Rapids: Eerdmans, 1998.

Gaston, L. *No Stone on Another*. Leiden: Brill, 1970.

Gnilka, J. "Das Martyrium Johannes des Taufers (Mk. 6.17-29)." Pages 78-92 in *Orientierung an Jesus. Zur Theologie der Synoptiker. Für Josef Schmid*. Edited by P. Hoffman. Freiberg: Herder, 1973.

Goodman, M. *The Ruling Class of Judea*. Cambridge: Cambridge University Press, 1987.

Grasser, E. "Jesus in Nazareth (Mark VI.1-6a): Notes on the Redaction and Theology of St. Mark." *NTS* 16 (1969-70): 1-23.

Hamilton, N. Q. "Temple Cleansing and Temple Bank." *JBL* 83 (1964): 365-72.

Harrisville, R. A. "The Women of Canaan: A Chapter in the History of Exegesis." *Int* 20, no. 3 (1966): 274-87.

Hawkins, J. C. *Horae Synopticae*. Oxford: Clarendon, 1909.

Head, P. *Christology and the Synoptic Problem*. Cambridge: Cambridge University Press, 1997.

Hengel, M. *The Charismatic Leader and His Followers*. New York: Crossroad, 1981.

———. "Entstehungenszeit und Situation des Markesevangeliums." Pages 1-45 in *Markus-Philologie*. Edited by H. Cancik. Tübingen: Mohr, 1984.

———. *Studies in the Gospel of Mark*. Philadelphia: Fortress, 1985.

———. *Die Zeloten*. 2nd ed. Leiden: Brill, 1976.

Hoehner, H. W. *Herod Antipas*. Cambridge: Cambridge University Press, 1972.

Jaubert, A. *The Date of the Last Supper*. Staten Island, N.Y.: Alba, 1965.

Jeremias, J. *The Eucharistic Words of Jesus*. London: SCM, 1966.

———. *Jesus' Promise to the Nations*. London: SCM, 1958.

———. *The Parables of Jesus*. 2nd ed. New York: Scribner, 1963.

Juel, D. *Messiah and Temple: The Trial of Jesus in the Gospel of Mark*. Missoula: Scholars, 1977.

Kebler, W. H. *Mark's Story of Jesus*. Philadelphia: Fortress, 1979.

Kee, H. C. "The Changing Meaning of Synagogue: A Response to Richard Oster." *NTS* 40 (1994): 281-83.

———. "Christology in Mark's Gospel." Pages 187-208 in *Judaisms and Their Messiahs*. Edited by J. Neusner, E. Frerichs, and J. Z. Smith. Cambridge: Cambridge University Press, 1987.

———. *Community of the New Age: Studies in Mark's Gospel*. Philadelphia: Westminster, 1977.

———. "The Transformation of the Synagogue after 70 C.E.: Its Import for Early Christianity." *NTS* 36 (1990): 117-23, 191-99.

Kennedy, G. *New Testament Interpretation through Rhetorical Criticism*. Chapel Hill: University of North Carolina Press, 1984.

Kermode, F. *The Genesis of Secrecy*. Cambridge: Harvard University Press, 1979.

Kim, S. *The Son of Man as the Son of God*. Grand Rapids: Eerdmans, 1985.

Kingsbury, J. *The Christology of Mark*. Philadelphia: Fortress, 1984.

————. *Conflict in Mark: Jesus, Authorities, Disciples.* Minneapolis: Fortress, 1989.

Kittel, G., and G. Friedrich, eds. *Theological Dictionary of the New Testament.* Translated by G. W. Bromiley. 10 vols. Grand Rapids: Eerdmans, 1964-1976.

Kurzinger, J. *Papias von Hierapolis und die Evangelien des Neuen Testaments.* Regensburg: Pustet, 1983.

Lambrecht, J. *Die Redaktion der Markus-Apokalypse.* Rome: Papstliches Bibelinstitut, 1967.

Lampe, P. *Die Stadtromischen Christen in den ersten beiden Jahrhunderten: Untersuchungen zur Sozialgeschichte.* Tübingen: Mohr, 1987.

Levine, L. "The Second Temple Synagogue: The Formative Years." Pages 201-22 in *The Synagogue in Late Antiquity.* Edited by L. Levine. Philadelphia: American School of Oriental Research, 1987.

Lewis, C. S. *Preface to Paradise Lost.* Oxford: Oxford University Press, 1942.

Lifshitz, B. "Fonctions et titres honorifiques dans les communautes juives." *RB* 67 (1960): 58-59.

Lincoln, A. T. "The Promise and the Failure: Mark 16.7, 8." *JBL* 108 (1989): 283-300.

Lohmeyer, E. *Das Evangelium des Markus.* Göttingen: Vandenhoeck & Ruprecht, 1951.

Luhrmann, D. "Die Pharisaer und die Schriftgelehrten im Markusevangelium." *ZNW* 78 (1987): 169-85.

MacArthur, H. K., and R. M. Johnston. *They Also Taught in Parables.* Grand Rapids: Zondervan, 1990.

McCall, M. H. *Ancient Rhetorical Theories of Similes and Comparisons.* Cambridge: Harvard University Press, 1969.

McHugh, J. *The Mother of Jesus in the New Testament.* London: Darton, Longman, Todd, 1975.

Mack, B. *Rhetoric and the New Testament.* Minneapolis: Fortress, 1990.

Mack, B., and V. Robbins. *Patterns of Persuasion in the Gospels.* Sonoma, Calif.: Polebridge Press, 1989.

Malbon, E. "Galilee and Jerusalem: History and Literature in Markan Interpretation." *CBQ* 44 (1982): 242-55.

Malina, B. "Assessing the Historicity of Jesus' Walking on Water." Pages 351-71 in *Authenticating the Activities of Jesus.* Edited by B. Chilton and C. A. Evans. Leiden: Brill, 1999.

Maloney, E. L. *Semitic Interference in Marcan Syntax.* Chico, Calif.: Scholars, 1981.

Mánek, J. "Fishers of Men." *NovT* 2 (1958): 138-41.

Manson, T. W. *The Sayings of Jesus.* London: SCM, 1957.

————. *The Teaching of Jesus.* 2nd ed. Cambridge: Cambridge University Press, 1935.

Marcus, J. "The Beelzebul Controversies and the Eschatologies of Jesus." Pages 247-77 in *Authenticating the Activities of Jesus.* Edited by B. Chilton and C. A. Evans. Leiden: Brill, 1999.

————. "Mark 4.10-12 and Marcan Epistemology." *JBL* 103 (1984): 557-74.

————. *The Mystery of the Kingdom of God.* Atlanta: Scholars, 1986.

————. *The Way of the Lord: Christological Exegesis of the Old Testament in the Gospel of Mark.* Louisville: Westminster, 1992.

Marshall, C. D. *Faith as a Theme in Mark's Narrative.* Cambridge: Cambridge University Press, 1989.

Marxsen, W. *Introduction to the New Testament.* Oxford: Blackwell, 1968.

May, D. M. "Mark 3.20-35 from the Perspective of Shame/Honor." *BTB* 17, no. 3 (1987): 83-87.

Meagher, J. C. *Clumsy Construction in Mark's Gospel.* New York and Toronto: Mellen, 1979.

Meier, J. *A Marginal Jew: Rethinking the Historical Jesus.* 2 vols. New York: Doubleday, 1991, 1994.

Meye, R. P. *Jesus and the Twelve: Discipleship and Revelation in Mark's Gospel.* Grand Rapids: Eerdmans, 1968.

Milton, John. *The Complete Poems of John Milton.* New York: Washington Square Press, 1964.

Morgenthaler, R. *Statistik des neutestamentlichen Wortschatzes.* Zürich: Gotthelf, 1958.

Moule, C. F. D. *The Birth of the New Testament.* London: A. & C. Black, 1962.

Myers, C. *Binding the Strong Man: A Political Reading of Mark's Story of Jesus.* Maryknoll, N.Y.: Orbis, 1988.

Nanos, M. *The Mystery of Romans.* Minneapolis: Fortress, 1996.

Neirynck, F. *Duality in Mark: Contributions to the Study of the Markan Redaction.* Leuven: Leuven University Press, 1972.

Neugebauer, F. "Die Davidssohnfrage (Mark 12.35-37 parr.) und der Menschensohn." *NTS* 21 (1974-75): 81-104.

Neyrey, J. "The Idea of Purity in Mark's Gospel." *Semeia* 35 (1986): 91-128.

Oakman, D. *Jesus and the Economic Question of His Day.* Lewiston, N.Y.: Mellen, 1986.

Oster, R. "Supposed Anachronism in Luke-Acts' Use of *sunagoge:* A Rejoinder to H. C. Kee." *NTS* 39 (1993): 178-208.

Perkins, P. *Jesus as Teacher.* Cambridge: Cambridge University Press, 1990.

Perrin, N., and D. C. Duling. *The New Testament: An Introduction.* New York: Harcourt, 1982.

Pesch, R. *Anfang des Evangeliums Jesu Christi: Eine Studie zum Prolog des Markusevangeliums (Mk. 1.1-15), Die Zeit Jesu.* Edited by G. Bornkamm and K. Rahner. Freiburg and Basel: Herder, 1970.

————. "Jairus (Mk 5,22/Lk 8,41)." *BZ* 14, no. 2 (1970): 252-56.

Peterson, N. R. "The Reader of the Gospel." *Neot* 18 (1984): 38-51.

————. "When Is the End Not the End? Literary Reflections on the Ending of Mark's Narrative." *Int* 34 (1980): 151-66.

Ramsey, W. M. "On Mark xii.42." *ET* 10 (1898-99): 232.

————. "On Mark xii.42." *ET* 10 (1898-99): 336.

Richard, Earl. *Jesus: One and Many.* Wilmington, Del.: M. Glazier, 1983.

Robinson, J. M. *The Problem of History in Mark.* London: SCM, 1957.

Roth, C. "The Cleansing of the Temple and Zechariah." *NovT* 4 (1960): 174-81.

Sanders, E. P. *The Historical Figure of Jesus.* London: Penguin Books, 1993.

————. *Jesus and Judaism.* Philadelphia: Fortress, 1985.

————. *Jewish Law from Jesus to the Mishnah.* Valley Forge, Pa.: Trinity, 1990.

————. *The Tendencies of the Synoptic Traditions.* Cambridge: Cambridge University Press, 1969.

Schaberg, J. "Daniel 7,12 and the New Testament Passion-Resurrection Predictions." *NTS* 31 (1985): 208-13.

Schaller, B. "'Commits Adultery with Her' Not 'against Her,' Mk. 10.11." *ET* 83, no. 4 (1972): 107-8.

Schilling, F. A. "What Means the Saying about Receiving the Kingdom of God as a Little Child (την βασιλειαν του θεου ως παιδιον Mk. x.15; Lk. xviii.17)." *ET* 77, no. 2 (1965): 56-58.

Schlosser, J. *Le Regne de Dieu dans les Dits de Jesus.* Paris: Gabalda Press, 1980.

Schmidt, H. H. "Semitismen bei Papias." *TZ* 44 (1988): 135-46.

Schnackenberg, R. *Jesus in the Gospels.* Louisville: Westminster/John Knox, 1995.

Sherwin-White, A. N. *Roman Society and Roman Law in the New Testament.* Oxford: Oxford University Press, 1963.

Skeat, T. C. "The Oldest Manuscript of the Four Gospels?" *NTS* 43, no. 1 (1997): 1-34.

Slingerland, H. D. *Claudian Policymaking and the Early Imperial Repression of Judaism at Rome.* Atlanta: Scholars, 1997.

Smallwood, E. M. *The Jews under Roman Rule from Pompey to Diocletian.* Leiden: Brill, 1976.

Smith, D. "Our Lord's Hard Saying to the Syro-Phoenician Woman." *ET* 12 (1900-1901): 319-21.

Smith, R. H. "New and Old in Mark 16:1-8." *CTM* 43 (1972): 518-27.

Sordi, M. *The Christians and the Roman Empire.* London: Routledge, 1994.

Sperber, D. "Mark xii.42 and Its Metrological Background." *NovT* 9, no. 3 (1967): 178-190.

Standaert. B. *L'Evangile selon Marc.* 2nd ed. Bruges: Cerf, 1984.

Stanton, G. N. "The Fourfold Gospel." *NTS* 43 (1997): 317-46.

Stauffer, E. *Jesus and His Story.* New York: Scribner, 1960.

Stern, J. B. "Jesus' Citation of Dt. 6.5 and Lv. 19.18 in the Light of Jewish Tradition." *CBQ* 28 (1966): 312-16.

Storch, W. "Zur Perikope von der Syrophonizierin Mk 7,28 und Ri 1,7." *BZ* 14, no. 2 (1970): 256-57.

Strack, H. L., and P. Billerbeck. *Kommentar zum Neuen Testament aus Talmud und Midrasch.* 6 vols. Munich: C. H. Beck, 1926-61.

Taylor, R. O. P. *The Groundwork of the Gospels.* Oxford: Blackwell, 1946.

Telford, W. *The Barren Temple and the Withered Tree.* Sheffield: Sheffield University Press, 1980.

———. *The Theology of the Gospel of Mark.* Cambridge: Cambridge University Press, 1999.

Theissen, G. *The Gospels in Context.* Edinburgh: T & T Clark, 1992.

———. *The Sociology of Early Palestinian Christianity.* Philadelphia: Fortress, 1978.

Tolbert, M. A. *Sowing the Gospel: Mark's World in Literary Historical Perspective.* Minneapolis: Fortress, 1989.

Trocme, A. *Jesus and the Nonviolent Revolution.* Scottdale, Pa.: Herald, 1964.

Tuckett, C., ed. *The Messianic Secret.* Philadelphia: Fortress, 1983.

Turner, C. H. "Marcan Usage: Notes, Critical and Exegetical, on the Second Gospel." *JTS* 25 (1924): 377-86.

Turner, N. "The Translation of μοιχαται επ αυτην in Mark 10.11." *BT* 7 (1956): 151-52.

Twelftree, G. H. *Jesus the Exorcist: A Contribution to the Study of the Historical Jesus.* Tübingen: Mohr, 1993.

Van Iersel, B. *Mark: A Reader-Response Commentary.* Sheffield: University of Sheffield Press, 1998.

———. "The Gospel according to Mark: Written for a Persecuted Community?" *NedTTs* (1980): 15-29.

Voerster, W. S. "Literary Reflections on Mark 13.5-37: A Narrated Speech of Jesus." Pages 269-88 in *The Interpretation of Mark.* Edited by W. R. Telford. Edinburgh: T & T Clark, 1995.

Watts, R. E. "Jesus' Death, Isaiah 53, and Mark 10.45." Pages 125-51 in *Jesus and the Suffering Servant: Isaiah 53 and Christian Origins.* Edited by W. H. Bellinger and W. R. Farmer. Harrisville, Pa.: Trinity Press, 1988.

Weber, H. R. *The Cross: Tradition and Interpretation.* Grand Rapids: Eerdmans, 1975.

Weeden, T. H. "The Heresy That Necessitated Mark's Gospel." *ZNW* 59 (1968): 145-58.

———. *Mark: Traditions in Conflict.* Philadelphia: Fortress, 1971.

Westermann, C. *The Parables of Jesus in the Light of the Old Testament.* Minneapolis: Fortress, 1990.

White, K. D. "The Parable of the Sower." *JTS* 15 (1962): 300-307.

Wiedmann, T. J. "From Nero to Vespasian." Pages 256-82 in *The Augustan Empire 43-69*. Edited by A. K. Bowman. Vol. 10 of *The Cambridge Ancient History*. Cambridge: Cambridge University Press, 1996.

Wilde, J. A. "A Social Description of the Community Reflected in the Gospel of Mark." Ph.D. diss., Drew University, 1978.

Wink, W. *John the Baptist in the Gospel Tradition*. Cambridge: Cambridge University Press, 1968.

Witherington, Ben, III. *The Christology of Jesus*. Philadelphia: Fortress, 1990.

————. *The Jesus Quest*. 2nd ed. Downers Grove: InterVarsity, 1995.

————. *Jesus the Sage*. Minneapolis: Fortress, 1994.

————. *Jesus the Seer*. Peabody, Mass.: Hendrickson, 1999.

————. *The Many Faces of Christ*. New York: Crossroad, 1998.

————. *Women in the Earliest Churches*. Cambridge: Cambridge University Press, 1988.

————. *Women in the Ministry of Jesus*. Cambridge: Cambridge University Press, 1984.

Wolff, C. "Zur Bedeutung Johannes des Taufers im Markusevangeliums." *TLZ* 102 (1977): 857-65.

Young, B. H. *Jesus and His Jewish Parables*. New York: Paulist, 1989.

Zeller, D. "Bedeutung und Religionsgeschichtlicher Hintergrund der Verwandlung Jesu (Markus 9:2-8)." Pages 303-21 in *Authenticating the Activities of Jesus*. Edited by B. Chilton and C. A. Evans. Leiden: Brill, 1999.

Zwick, R. *Montage im Markusevangelium. Studien zur narrativen Organisation der altesten Jesuserzahlung*. Stuttgart: Katholisches Bibelwerk GmBh, 1989.

Introduction

Without question, Mark's Gospel is one of the most exciting and intriguing of ancient Christian documents. It may then come as something of a surprise that this Gospel was neglected for many centuries of Christian history, from at least the early Middle Ages until the nineteenth century. But scholarly discourse on Mark since the last decade or so of the nineteenth century has more than made up for the earlier neglect. The study of Mark today is an ever expanding growth industry. As G. G. Bilezikian says, like "Cinderella, the Gospel has at last been discovered but not yet explained."[1] The sheer volume of recent studies, however, suggests that we are trying harder to grasp the meaning of this, the earliest of Gospels. Before we may examine the text, though, we must carefully weave through the critical minefield and answer some introductory questions that will affect our reading of it.

The Genre of Mark

"The first qualification for judging any piece of workmanship from a corkscrew to a cathedral is to know *what* it is — what it was intended to do and how it is meant to be used."[2] C. S. Lewis was quite right in this remark, and it is espe-

---

1. G. G. Bilezikian, *The Liberated Gospel: A Comparison of the Gospel of Mark and Greek Tragedy* (Grand Rapids: Baker, 1979), p. 11.
2. C. S. Lewis, *Preface to Paradise Lost* (Oxford: Oxford University Press, 1942), p. 1. I must thank Christopher Bryan, *A Preface to Mark* (Oxford: Oxford University Press, 1993), p. 9, for reminding me of this fine quote.

cially apt when dealing with either an oral presentation or a written document. Addresses to Congress should never be mistaken for funeral orations, nor should wills of real people be treated like novels. These sorts of considerations apply especially when the possibility of anachronism is a serious danger — namely, when one is dealing with ancient documents. Works of ancient history or biography or romance should each be judged by their own conventions.[3]

The word "genre" means a literary kind or type. It refers to a sort of compact between an author and his reader whereby the author, using various literary signals, will indicate to the reader what sort of document is being read and how it should be used. The genre signals in the text provide the reader with a guide to the interpretation of the text.[4] To make a genre mistake is to make a category mistake, which skews the reading of the document.

"The genre of a particular work is established by the presence of *enough* genric motifs in sufficient force to dominate,"[5] so that when the reader picks up the document he will know soon thereafter whether he may expect to derive phone numbers, definitions of words, entertainment or historical or biographical information, or even some combination of such things from the document. It follows, then, that it is important to discover just what kind of document Mark is. There have been no end of suggestions on this count, ranging from the sublime to the ridiculous. We must canvass various of these at this juncture.

From time to time it has been suggested that we should see Mark's Gospel as an example of Greek drama. Some, in fact, have gone so far as to suggest that Mark attended the theater (perhaps Herod's theater in Jerusalem?).[6] There is a certain plausibility to this suggestion. Mark's prologue has not infrequently been compared to the prologue of a Greek play.[7] But what sort of drama would

---

3. One of the major flaws in some forms of reader-response criticism is that they tend to ignore the compact between author and audience, overlook that the author had some purpose and information to convey when he wrote the document, and assume that it is the reader who can and must decide what sorts of things, including what sort of meaning, one can derive from a text. This is one reason why various reader-response approaches to the Gospels have failed so miserably to come to grips with the genre question. Historical information that would help sort this issue out is ignored or neglected. Instead, the Gospels are treated as if they were works of modern fiction.

4. See H. Dubrow, *Genre,* The Critical Idiom Series, vol. 42 (London: Methuen, 1982), p. 118, and cf. R. A. Burridge, *What Are the Gospels?* (Cambridge: Cambridge University Press, 1992), p. 53.

5. Bryan, p. 13.

6. See M. A. Beavis, *Mark's Audience: The Literary and Social Setting of Mark 4.11-12* (Sheffield: University of Sheffield Press, 1989).

7. M. Hooker, *The Gospel according to Mark* (Peabody, Mass.: Hendrickson, 1991), pp. 18-19, notes this possibility, and hints at the possibility that Mark might be seen as a drama. But she also points out that other Gospels also have prologues, and certainly it would be difficult to read Luke's Gospel as a drama.

Mark's Gospel be? It is certainly not a Greek comedy. Nor does it have the ending of a Greek tragedy. Jesus' death is transcended by the resurrection. Even if the Gospel is seen to end at Mark 16:8 (on which see below), there is still both the empty tomb and the Easter proclamation. Nor do we find in Mark the chorus that one finds in Greek drama. We do have an author who occasionally intrudes into the narrative, but that is a literary, not a drama, technique. Thus, while we grant that Mark's is a dramatic Gospel with an interesting plot and plenty of controversy and pathos leading to the death of the main character, it does not seem to be a Greek tragedy. To the contrary, it is a book of good news rather than tragedy.[8] There are, however, two other possible ancient types of literature that Mark might be said to exemplify — the historical monograph and the ancient biography.[9]

Recently A. Y. Collins suggested that Mark's Gospel be seen as some sort of historical monograph.[10] This theory has a certain plausibility because there is overlap between the characterizing features of an ancient biography and an ancient historical monograph, but when the more specific telltale signs of an historical monograph are looked for, they seem to be almost entirely lacking. For example, Mark shows no real interest in synchronisms with the events of the larger Roman world, unlike what we find from time to time in Luke-Acts. Furthermore, Mark shows little interest in historical causality or explaining the links between the various events in his narrative, with the exception of some of the material in his passion narrative. Furthermore, unlike historical monographs, Mark focuses not on a series of events and those involved, but on a singular person. People are mentioned in Mark's narrative only because of their connection or interaction with the central figure, Jesus.[11] This is even true of

---

8. But see Bilezikian, *The Liberated Gospel*.

9. It should be clear that Mark should not be compared to modern biographies of the psychological sort which analyze an historical figure in depth and in detail and chronicle a life from womb to tomb. This is clearly not what any of the Gospel writers are about. Their accounts are episodic, and they show little or no interest in the character development of the central figure. Nor does Mark work as myth either, for what ancient myth recounts the crucifixion and utter shaming of a God?

10. See A. Y. Collins, *The Beginning of the Gospel: Probings of Mark in Context* (Minneapolis: Fortress, 1992), pp. 1-38.

11. In his recent commentary, J. Marcus, *Mark 1–8* (New York: Doubleday, 1999), pp. 65-66, suggests that Mark might be more of an historical narrative because stylistically he occasionally imitates the OT historical narratives with phrases like "and it came to pass in those days." But the overlap between some features of an historical biography and a monograph can explain this similarity. He then goes on to suggest that we have a biography of a movement, but this ignores both the heavy critique of the disciples in Mark and, on Marcus's showing, the ending (since he thinks the book ends at 16:8), neither of which suggests that Mark is trying to highlight the Jesus movement. To the contrary, he is focusing on one central figure who is the paradigm for his audience — Jesus.

John the Baptist. Furthermore, when one considers Mark's portrayal of the disciples or the crowds, it seems clear that he has the sort of paraenetic purposes which more nearly and more frequently characterize ancient biographies than historical monographs.

Having dealt with the various other possible genres, we turn now to the possibility that Mark might be an example of an ancient *bios,* an ancient biography of Jesus. Once again we must remind ourselves that this possibility must not be assessed on the basis of modern biographical conventions, but rather of ancient ones.[12] Yet, determining the genre of a work means assessing not merely its form but also its content, at least to some extent. The content of Mark's Gospel is Jewish through and through. In its present form we have a document that is written in Greek and reflects various of the Greek rhetorical and biographical conventions of the era in which Mark lived. Is this sort of surprising combination possible in an ancient biography?

The one thing to keep in mind is that ancient *bioi,* like modern biographies, center on a particular person and seek to present an adequate and accurate characterization of that person. An ancient biography certainly would include information about other persons and groups of people, but the major focus throughout the work would be on the central character. What was considered revealing of that person's character and personality would be included, what was considered not revealing would likely be left out. Thus, while a biographer might well include a short story or anecdote about a person which was certainly not of any larger "historic" significance, an ancient historian was unlikely to do so.[13]

The aims of ancient biographers, such as Plutarch, were often hortatory. They sought to inculcate mimesis, of a positive or negative sort. The message was "go and do likewise" (if the biographical subject acted in a virtuous manner

---

12. This was precisely the problem with the assessments of R. Bultmann and other form critics like W. Marxsen, *Introduction to the New Testament* (Oxford: Blackwell, 1968), p. 125, who, on the basis of modern biographical considerations, complained that the Gospels reflect the "absence of everything required for a biography (sequence of events, development, Jesus' appearance, etc.)." The former two items listed were characteristics of ancient historical works, not ancient biographies. The latter is a concern of modern biographers but not necessarily ancient ones.

13. Notice Plutarch's famous remarks at the beginning of his *Life of Alexander* 2-3: "For it is not Histories I am writing, but Lives; and in the most illustrious deeds there is not always a manifestation of virtue or vice, no, a slight thing like a phrase or a joke often makes a greater revelation of character than battles where thousands fall. . . . Accordingly, just as painters get the likenesses in their portraits from the face and the expression of the eyes, wherein the character shows itself, but make very little account of the other parts of the body, so I must be permitted to devote myself rather to the signs of the soul of a person, and by means of these to portray the life of each. . . ."

or revealed a virtuous character), or in some cases "go and do otherwise." To be sure, there was some overlap of features and aims between biography and history, or between biography and moral philosophy, or between biography and encomium, but one could still tell the difference between a life and a tract of moral philosophy. The point is, as R. Burridge stresses, "Ancient βιος was a flexible genre having strong relationships with history, encomium and rhetoric, moral philosophy and the concern for character."[14]

The historian's concern was with movements, historical developments, cause and effect, synchronisms — in short, with what was historic and epoch making. The ancient biographer also drew on historical data about his central figure, but he did so with different aims and purposes. For instance, we should not be surprised that Mark seems almost unconcerned about explicating how event A was related to event B, which seems to have followed it. Rather, he sought to ask and answer the questions: Who was Jesus, what was he like, and why is he worth writing a biography about?

In evaluating Mark as a biography, one must have a firm handle on its chronological and social setting. Whatever its date, Mark was written after the beginning of the Roman Empire and during the rise of the Roman biographical tradition, following in the footsteps of the Greek biographical tradition. What the Roman tradition added to the discussion was a greater concern for family traditions, the need for the demonstration of public honor, and, sometimes in the latter two-thirds of the century, a focus on the hero's patient suffering and death under a tyrant (cf., e.g., Thrasea Paetus's *Life of Cato*). "The genre of *exitus illustrium virorum* became fashionable under oppression by Tiberius, Nero, and Domitian. Such a focus on the subject's death [often an untimely death] is an important parallel for the Passion narratives in the gospels. . . ."[15]

Mark's Gospel, which has been called a passion narrative with a long introduction, has this form in part because it was written in an environment where there would be a certain sympathy in the empire for chronicling a life that could be shown to be good or virtuous but that unfortunately suffered an untimely and unjust end at the hand of some authority figures. In fact, Mark devotes some 19 percent of his narrative to the passion narrative, compared to 15 percent by Matthew or Luke. There is, in short, proportionally more emphasis in Mark on the last week of Jesus' life than in the other Synoptics.[16]

---

14. Burridge, p. 69.

15. Burridge, p. 77. Marcus, *Mark 1–8*, p. 67, thinks Mark 16:1-8 may not be a suitable ending for a biography, and he is largely correct. This does not affect our discussion, however, if Mark 16:1-8 is not the Gospel's original ending.

16. It is useful at this point to compare Plutarch's life of Julius Caesar, where there are signs in the heaven before his tragic murder, including an eclipse of the sun, showing the gods' disapproval of this action (*Caes.* 69.3-5).

A variety of external and internal features of Mark's Gospel point us toward it being a biography of some sort. Firstly, it is the right length, and in fact is clearly much shorter than Luke or Matthew (Mark has 11,242 words, Luke 19,428, Matthew 18,305).[17] Matthew and Luke are actually at the upper limits for a biography (Luke being at the upper limits for what a single scroll could contain), but Mark is closely similar to the average length of one of Plutarch's *Lives*. Secondly, even at a glance the work is clearly a continuous prose narrative, which places it in the category of history, biography, or romance. It is clearly not a moral tract, a speech (encomium), or a play. It has a basic chronological and even geographical progression — from a largely northern ministry to a final visit to Jerusalem, from Galilee to Jerusalem. Thirdly, notice how rarely Jesus is *not* the center of attention of any given narrative in Mark's Gospel (the exception would be Mark 6 in the story about Herod, but even there Jesus is discussed at 6:14-16). Jesus or his teaching is the subject of over 44 percent of the verbs in Mark's Gospel,[18] and in almost any given narrative he is either the center of attention or of discussion, or not far from the spotlight. This book is the good news about Jesus, and it seldom strays any distance or length of time from its main subject.

Fourthly, Mark follows the ancient biographical convention of using indirect portraiture to reveal his central figure. By this I mean, Mark largely lets Jesus' words and deeds speak for themselves. He does not intrude into his story with a great deal of authorial commentary, nor do we find much first-person commentary by Jesus about himself (unlike John's Gospel).[19] Fifthly, Mark is characterized by short anecdotal stories that focus on a word or deed of Jesus, and whether we call these pronouncement stories or, more appropriately, *chreiae* (see below), the stringing together of such short condensed narratives was indeed characteristic of ancient biographies.

Sixthly, the normal subjects for an ancient biography were public figures such as emperors or generals, or literary figures such as rhetoricians or poets, or finally sages or philosophers. As Bryan suggests, it appears likely that an outsider reading Mark, but even more so Matthew, would assume the work was a biography about some sage.[20] It was not unexpected that sages would be misunderstood and would suffer at the hands of society, being treated as the nonconformist outcasts they often managed to be (see Lucian, *Demon.* 11.65). Finally, in regard to

---

17. See R. Morgenthaler, *Statistik des neutestamentlichen Wortschatzes* (Zürich: Gotthelf, 1958), table 3, p. 164.

18. See the chart offered by Burridge, p. 271, whom I largely follow throughout this section of the introduction.

19. See, e.g., the demonstration by Burridge, pp. 143-45, that direct character analysis or physical description of a figure or first-person commentary was not a sine qua non of ancient biographies. Rather, it was common to present samples of the person's words and deeds.

20. Bryan, p. 37.

Mark's somewhat rough Greek style, bear in mind that *bioi* in the first century A.D. were by their very nature popular literature. They did not need to be considered in the same league as, say, Vergil's *Aeneid* or Homer's *Odyssey*, or even as precise as a careful work of history like Thucydides' *History*. The goal was to create a lasting impression through the impact of the whole *bios*.

Two final considerations are important. Firstly, neither the superscript of the Gospel nor the first verse tells us much about the genre of the work. As Bryan says, Mark uses the term *euangelion* to refer to the content of God's saving work, just as Paul does (cf. Mark 1:1, 14; 8:35; 10:29; 13:10; 14:9 to Gal. 1:7-9; Rom. 2:16).[21] That Paul and Mark can use this same term, and always in the singular, in works of two very different literary kinds shows that it had not yet become a technical term for a certain kind of literature. This also in a small way favors the suggestion that Mark's Gospel is early. Not until at least the writing of the *Didache* is *euangelion* used for a certain kind of text or document. Notice that it is used in the plural in several sources in the second century (*2 Clem.* 8:5; Justin Martyr, *Apol.* 1.66.3; *Dial.* 10.2; 100.1).

It is important at this juncture to say in what way one can use the term "apocalyptic" of Mark's narrative, especially since, as C. Myers says, "Mark chose realistic narrative over the more highly fabricated fictions of apocalyptic." When we speak of Mark's apocalyptic rhetoric, we are referring to the fact that he operates with an apocalyptic worldview that affects the way he casts some of his narrative and the shape of some of his characterizations, including that of Jesus.[22] H. C. Kee, after pointing out how Mark seems to show more interest in Daniel than any other OT prophetic book (and in general favors excerpts from apocalyptic material found in Daniel; Isa. 24–27; 34–35; Ezek. 38–39; Joel 3–4; Zech. 9; 12–14; Mal. 3–4), and in fact quotes from every chapter in Daniel, argues that Mark adopts Daniel's narrative strategy of presenting miracle tales in the first half of his work, followed by a second-half focus on suffering and martyrdom. He further finds a series of traits in Mark that often characterize apocalyptic works: (1) dualism — the new order is opposed to the old; (2) use of the combat myth, in this case the contestants being Jesus and Satan; (3) the theme of lack of understanding unless there is revelation of the divine perspective on things;[23] (4) a narrative that is bound spatially from above by the supernatural world and temporally from beyond by the climactic eschatological events, including final judgment by the Son of Man.[24]

---

21. Bryan, p. 33.

22. See C. Myers, *Binding the Strong Man: A Political Reading of Mark's Story of Jesus* (Maryknoll, N.Y.: Orbis, 1988), p. 104; Marcus, *Mark 1–8*, pp. 71-73.

23. H. C. Kee, *Community of the New Age: Studies in Mark's Gospel* (Philadelphia: Westminster, 1977), pp. 45-66.

24. See Myers, p. 103. He is following J. Collins in this matter.

Something must now be said about the bit of the superscript which designates this work as *kata Markon,* added when more than one Gospel was circulating to distinguish this one from others. M. Hengel, sometime ago, made the
rather convincing case that at least early in the second century there was a deep
conviction that there was only *one* Gospel, presented according to several different Evangelists.[25] Especially striking is p66 from about A.D. 200, which has
the clear heading "Gospel according to John." Hengel argues that from early in
the second century there was both a collection of the fourfold Gospel and that
the "Gospel according to . . ." had become the regular title for any and all these
Gospels, in order to differentiate one from the other three. Already in the
Didache there are references to a written document, not merely an oral tradition called *euangelion* (*Did.* 8.2; 11.3; 15.3-4).

It has been suggested that the rise of the fourfold Gospel circulating together (presumably beginning not long after the writing of the Fourth Gospel)
precipitated the prevalent use of the codex in Christian circles, for no scroll
could contain even two of these Gospels.[26] There is now some manuscript evidence for a fourfold Gospel collection in the second century.[27] The implications of the circulation of the fourfold Gospel would seem to include the following: (1) the notion that one Gospel was sufficient was rejected; (2) the
notion that a harmony of the four Gospels was sufficient was rejected; (3) the
notion that other Gospels were equally valid and valuable was at least implicitly
rejected.[28] Irenaeus's defense of the idea that there was only one Gospel in only
four presentations in the latter third of the second century (*Against Heresies*
was written about A.D. 180 — see 3.11.8) reflects the prior existence and growing normativity of that collection.

But this entire process raises a pressing question about our subject. Why
was a Gospel by a somewhat obscure, nonapostolic figure like Mark accepted
into this collection, especially when Matthew already includes the vast majority
of his work? Would such a title really have been dreamed up in the second century when there was great concern to connect all foundational documents
closely with apostles? I think not, and there is further reason for thinking that
the earliest Gospel was from the beginning connected with one Mark, an early
Christian.

Mark's work is, and would have been seen as, a biography, and ancient biographies almost invariably had *known* authors, whether we think of Plutarch's

---

25. M. Hengel, *Studies in the Gospel of Mark* (Philadelphia: Fortress, 1985), pp. 64-84.

26. See the discussion by G. N. Stanton, "The Fourfold Gospel," *NTS* 43 (1997): 317-
46, here pp. 336-39.

27. T. C. Skeat, "The Oldest Manuscript of the Four Gospels?" *NTS* 43, no. 1 (1997): 1-
34.

28. See Stanton, pp. 342-44, and Skeat, pp. 32-33.

Lives, or Suetonius's narratives about the Caesars, or Tacitus's *Agricola,* or Josephus's autobiography. Though internally Mark's Gospel does not reveal the name of the author, the predication *kata Markon* very likely has some foundation in fact. We will deal with this further when we discuss the authorship question.

The Rhetoric of Mark

We mentioned that various of the pericopes in Mark, in particular in the pre-passion narrative material, take the form of *chreiae.* This in itself provides an additional good reason to see Mark as an example of ancient biography. It was precisely short, character-revealing anecdotes that biographical writers ranging from Plutarch to Tacitus were looking for in the NT era when they wrote their *bioi,* and it was also the form that was the end product of their boiling down of larger and more cumbersome accounts. In an age when papyrus and thus writing space was at a premium, there were several motivations for choosing to present the *Reader's Digest* version of someone's life.

But the use of the *chreia* form would also signal to a culture saturated with rhetoric that the author was not just interested in informing, but also in persuading. The rhetoric of Mark's Gospel, however, is of a different ilk from that found in Paul's letters, which often reach a level of considerable sophistication.[29] Even the longest continuous speech in Mark, in chapter 13, does not appear to take the standard form of a rhetorical speech. Compared to Paul, Mark's rhetoric is more elementary and is to be found primarily at the micro rather than macro level of the Gospel's material — i.e., in the individual pericopes that are in *chreia* form.[30]

Indeed, Mark's rhetoric is of the sort one finds in the *progymnasta,* the elementary handbooks. These handbooks introduced students to basic rhetorical matters before they went on to higher education, where they learned more advanced rhetorical skills, such as the composition of deliberative, forensic, or epideictic speeches. D. M. Young reminds us that "The list of progymnasta was generally the same throughout Imperial times and included

---

29. See, e.g., my *Grace in Galatia* (Edinburgh: T. & T. Clark, 1997) or my *Conflict and Community in Corinth* (Grand Rapids: Eerdmans, 1994).

30. Hopefully it does not need to be said that when rhetoric is referred to here, the term is not meant in the modern sense of what R. O. P. Taylor artfully calls "verbal stucco-work," a mere decorative art, "full of sound and fury" but "signifying nothing." Rather, the very practical and highly skillful art of persuasion is in view. See Taylor, *The Groundwork of the Gospels* (Oxford: Blackwell, 1946), p. 76 n. 1.

the following compositional exercises: fable, narrative, chreia, aphorism, confirmation or refutation, commonplace, eulogy or censure, comparison, prosopopoeia, thesis, and discussion of the law. Each of these increased over the preceding in degree of sophistication. . . ."[31] Notice that narrative, *chreia,* and aphorism, some of the most elementary exercises, are the sorts of rhetoric we find in Mark, in addition to the usual array of smaller rhetorical devices such as rhetorical questions. This strongly suggests that our author does not operate at the level of rhetorical sophistication that Paul did — as does his failure to provide us with a fluid style throughout the Gospel.[32] We may distinguish between the primary rhetoric of what Mark does with actual speech material and the secondary rhetoric in the narratives, where various smaller rhetorical devices crop up. It is also important to bear in mind that Jesus is the only figure in the entire Gospel that has discourses of any length at all. This comports with the author's biographical focus.

There is this further difference between Paul and Mark: Mark's work apparently is primarily meant to be read, while Paul's letters are meant to be declaimed and heard in the congregation. Mark 13:14 speaks of "the one reading," in the singular, thus apparently indicating something other than a public or congregational reading.[33] The rhetorical situation that generates Mark's Gospel and Paul's letters is quite different.

Mark is meant to be seen as a text, perhaps the first real Christian text, perhaps the first "book" in the later Western sense of the term, whereas Paul's letters are not intended this way. The latter are surrogates for oral communication. To push this a bit further, Mark's rhetoric is of the sort one finds in a handbook or a biography written with a knowledge of the sort of rhetoric one finds in the *progymnasta.* These are "recollections" of Jesus in written form, collected, edited, and presented as a *bios.* Mark is not meant to be heard, but rather

---

31. D. M. Young, "Whoever Has Ears to Hear" (Ph.D. diss., Vanderbilt University, 1994), p. 69. His analysis is one of the more sophisticated ones. Various of the earlier attempts were less successful, and dealt with literary devices that could be called rhetorical, but only in the broadest sense of the term (e.g., chiasmus). See, e.g., J. E. Phelan, "Rhetoric and Meaning in Mark 6.30–8.10" (Ph.D. diss., Northwestern University, 1985).

32. Notice Young's conclusion, p. 70, that since "the author was likely familiar at least with the simpler progymnasta, it is not necessary to argue that he received an advanced rhetorical education. . . ." Indeed, I would suggest it would be very difficult to prove he had done so on the basis of the prima facie evidence in Mark itself.

33. It appears there is an echo of Daniel here which also signals that this work is to be read, like Daniel, as a piece of revelatory literature, a piece of apocalyptic material, or at least a work meant to be read in light of and in close comparison with Daniel. The verse may also provide another sort of clue indicating not only that this is a document for Christian insiders, but that it is meant to be read and studied "in house" like a piece of apocalyptic literature, trying to uncover its mysteries.

to be taken in through the act of reading. Paul's letters are closer to speeches and preaching, while Mark's Gospel is intended to provide additional information about Jesus that supplements the preaching — it has catechetical and paraenetic purposes molding and shaping those who are already disciples.[34] Thus, while J. Marcus is quite right that Mark does not, for the most part, reflect the level of rhetorical sophistication of Paul, as shown not least by his frequently awkward style, this does not mean he has no rhetorical ability, interests, or aims.[35]

Thus neither Bultmann nor Dibelius was right. Mark's Gospel is not the kerygma or the sermon. It is not intended to be proclaimed as it is. It is intended to instruct as a supplement to such proclamation and, as such, presents Jesus as the Master and Teacher — indeed, the Master Teacher.[36] He is of course also presented as Messiah and Son of God (see below). Mark's Gospel is the textbook which has gathered up the memoirs or memoranda or recollections and presented them. It is of course true that Mark is not like modern history writing. The author is a partisan and is unashamedly trying to convict and convince his audience about a particular point of view. But this does not make Mark a transcript of preaching. It reveals that Mark is rhetorically sensitive and has rhetorical purposes.

An important point needs to be stressed about the *chreiae* in Mark. Despite the best efforts of B. Mack and V. Robbins to argue otherwise,[37] it is not convincing to maintain that these Markan *chreiae* are necessarily a result of boiling *up* a short narrative on the basis of mere shards of earlier tradition (if any) — an isolated saying here or a vague memory of a notable deed there. It is ironic that these authors (whose treatment of Mark's rhetoric is sometimes helpful and who are rightly strongly critical of some of the basic assumptions of earlier form criticism as practiced by Bultmann, Dibelius, and others) nonetheless carry forward the tired old form-critical theory that the Gospel writers had little material to work with and thus had in large measure to act as creators or authors of the material they included in their Gospels. Mack and Robbins then try to merge such a form-critical theory with the rhetorical practice of creating *chreiae*.

But an actual study of how ancient biographers used *chreiae* and formed their material for their works will reveal it was more often a matter of editing

---

34. See, for example, the older but still germane comments of C. F. D. Moule, *The Birth of the New Testament* (London: A. & C. Black, 1962), pp. 86-96.

35. See Marcus, *Mark 1–8,* p. 60.

36. See V. Robbins, *Jesus the Teacher: A Socio-Rhetorical Interpretation of Mark* (Minneapolis: Fortress, 1992).

37. B. Mack and V. Robbins, *Patterns of Persuasion in the Gospels* (Sonoma, Calif.: Polebridge Press, 1989).

source material *down* to *chreia* form, not creating the material out of thin air. Of course there was expansion, arrangement, rephrasing, but source material was indeed used. This was even true when *chreiae* were formed as a school exercise. Thus, for example, Aphtonius the Sophist reminds his listeners that a *chreia* is a *concise* statement of *apomnemoneumata*, which may be translated memoirs, recollections, or memoranda. The recollection is sometimes told at considerable length on its own merits because of its subject matter, but the *chreia* must be brief and pointed, referring to a particular person. The word *apomnemoneumata* is important, for it is precisely the word Justin Martyr uses for the Gospel material (*Apol.* 1.67). They are based on the apostle's memoirs or recollections, so to speak. Like the term *diegesis,* or narrative, which Luke uses (Luke 1:1-4), "recollections" can be seen as longer, less precisely formed pieces of tradition which could serve as the basis for the creation of a *chreia.*

Put another way, a *chreia* is a concise "recollection" with a specific focus and source. R. O. P. Taylor is right to say that these *chreiae,* which always are related to and about real historical persons, "were not merely a literary form, but essentially a historical statement — So-and-so who was a known historical figure, actually said or did this. . . . Actual fact was demanded. If then the Gospels had not some guarantee of this kind, if they could not be shown to be ascertained history, they would have failed in their appeal."[38] In short, the very use of this *chreia* form implies some historical claims about what Jesus actually said or did.[39] There must be a bit of narrative with a particular person in focus, and then too a *chreia* may focus on a deed rather than a maxim.[40] *Chreiae* arise from a particular situation and refer to a particular person.

But there are further problems with the approach of Mack and Robbins to this material. The form-critical assumption about the basic trend in the handling of Gospel material was that, as the first century went on, the Gospel material simply evolved and expanded. This basic assumption is refuted not only by E. P. Sanders's detailed, seminal study of how the other Gospels handle Mark,[41]

---

38. Taylor, p. 87.

39. Shorter than any of these forms would be the maxim *(gnome),* which is simply a pithy saying. *Chreiae* can include these, as can recollections or narratives, but a maxim is not a *chreia.*

40. See the helpful discussion by Taylor, pp. 78-79.

41. E. P. Sanders, *The Tendencies of the Synoptic Traditions* (Cambridge: Cambridge University Press, 1969). Sanders's careful study shows that there is no definite trend toward expansion in the later Gospels. Of course, it is true that occasionally the material is expanded by the later Evangelists. Sometimes they do add details or additional material. But most of the time they edit down their source material. There is also no definite trend from more generic to more specific as the Gospel tradition develops. Sometimes names and places are added in the later accounts (e.g., the famous case of the anointing of Jesus by Mary of Bethany), but just as often, if not more often, the narratives become more generic in character.

but also by a simple comparison of Matthew's and Luke's use of these very Markan *chreiae.*

For example, it has long been noted that Mark almost always provides longer accounts of Jesus' miracles than do Matthew or Luke. Why is this? Because Matthew and Luke are editing down their Markan source so that they can include various other sources of information. Luke tells us quite plainly in the prologue to his Gospel (1:1-4) that many have gone before him and that he has chosen to present his own account, which involved investigation, comparing, and editing of sources. Why should we assume that Mark's modus operandi is any different in handling his source material? To say that Mark is the first written Gospel is not to say that it marks the beginning of the traditions found in that Gospel.

One case that might seem to point toward Mark boiling up his source material is his account of Jesus' temptation, which is clearly shorter than that found in Matthew and Luke. But if one accepts that Matthew and Luke are drawing on Q material for this story, then this material likely existed in some form, probably oral, prior to the writing of Mark's Gospel. It is possible that Mark knew the Q material and edited it down, but even if he did not know Q, he may well have known the expanded form of the story as a free-floating tradition.[42] In short, a reasonable case can be made that even when Mark presents a shorter account, it is a result of his pruning of his sources. We will say more about Mark's use of sources and how we can identify some of them in the next section.

Do we also have examples of expansions of *chreiae,* called *ergasiae* (elaborations), in Mark? This is the contention of Mack in particular, and it requires close scrutiny.[43] For example, Mack finds an expanded *chreia* in Mark 14:3-9.[44] Theon says that to expand a *chreia,* one must first provide a brief introduction, then use the *chreia* as a thesis, then present a series of arguments in order, using elaborations, digressions, and character delineation (*Progymnasta* 215.10-15). Can we see such a pattern in the narrative in Mark 14:3-9?

Where, for example, is the *chreia* that is being expanded on? Mack sees a challenge and response story, with the challenge coming in vv. 4-5 after a brief introduction, and the response in vv. 6-9. This is fair enough, but vv. 6-9 can

---

42. I agree with Marcus, *Mark 1–8,* pp. 51-53, that the omission of the Sermon on the Mount material by Mark must count strongly against the hypothesis that Mark knew Q, for Mark certainly could have used this teaching material in his Gospel since he does wish to stress that Jesus was a teacher.

43. In fact, various scholars have followed Mack and Robbins down this road, some with more success than others, but none completely convincingly; but cf. R. Parrott, "Conflict and Rhetoric in Mark 2.23-28," and G. Salyer, "Rhetoric, Purity, and Play: Aspects of Mark 7.1-23," in *Semeia* 64 (1993): 117-37 and 139-69.

44. Mack and Robbins, pp. 92-93.

hardly be called an expansion into a series of arguments. This is but a few tele-graphic questions and statements (as Mack is forced to admit), in the midst of which comes a memorable saying ("the poor you always have with you . . .)."[45]

The question in v. 6a is not an argument, nor is there an analogy in v. 7b, nor is the reference to the woman's charitable act an *elaboration* based on an-other example (contrast the example Mack cites from Hermogenes 7.10–8.14).[46] Indeed, her act is what prompted the discussion in the first place; it is not a secondary example. We seem to have a summary of one argument or, better said, a response to a challenge centered on one saying. At most we have a slightly long *chreia* here, not really an example of the expansion of that form in a schoolboy exercise. I doubt anyone in the first century would recognize this brief narrative as something that mirrored the exercises in the *progymnasta*.

Much more promising is the analysis by G. Salyer of Mark 7:1-23, where a reasonable case can be made that we have two *chreiae* with expansions or elabo-rations of each.[47] Even here, however, it seems that Mark has edited down his source material to suit such a rhetorical pattern, not boiled up fictitious argu-ments on the basis of the *chreiae*. Thus we may say that there is a little evidence in Mark, though not much, of taking a rhetorical step beyond that of simply forming one's source material into *chreiae*.

But this should not be taken to repudiate the correct observation that various of Mark's narratives take the form of a *chreia*. This is a correct and helpful observation, and shows the level of Mark's rhetoric. We may also wish to point to Mark's use of other rhetorical devices like rhetorical questions, irony, and the like. We will point out such devices as we go, but we should be under no delusion that Mark's rhetoric is of the order or degree of complexity of Paul's or Cicero's.

Nevertheless, it is quite right to say that Mark has rhetorical aims throughout this Gospel. He wishes to persuade his audience that it is correct to view Jesus in the way that his thesis statement in Mark 1:1 suggests. There are also some subordinate themes that involve persuasion about the first disciples and Jesus' opponents as well, which we will say more about in the commentary itself.[48] For now it is sufficient to offer the judgment of R. M. Fowler: "Mark's

---

45. See Mack and Robbins, p. 94.

46. Mack and Robbins, p. 51.

47. Salyer, pp. 139-69.

48. It is important to avoid confusion when using the term "rhetoric." By "rhetoric" I mean Greco-Roman rhetoric and its various devices. I do not merely mean Mark's narrative art or literary skills. There is something to be said for Mark's skill in arranging his material, but this has more to do with narrative and storytelling skills than with the use of ancient rhe-torical devices and arguments. For examples of the looser and more modern use of "rheto-ric" to refer to most any and all literary skills, and the literary effects Mark attempts to pro-duce, see R. M. Fowler, *Let the Reader Understand* (Minneapolis: Fortress, 1991).

rhetoric is not, like Paul's, the rhetoric of oratory, with its logical arguments and emotive appeals. Rather, Mark's is the rhetoric of narrative."[49] Just so, and thus one should not expect Mark to very often mirror the rhetoric found in speeches, or even the exercises schoolboys performed to turn *chreia* material into rhetorically acceptable speech material. One need also bear in mind that if someone like Cicero had read Mark's Gospel, he would not have regarded it as composed according to the highest standards of rhetoric. For example, the mixing of languages such as we have in this Gospel (which has Greek, Hebrew, Aramaic, and Latin) was considered bad form, and a sign of an inadequate education in what is rhetorically appropriate when one is trying to persuade (cf. Cicero, *Off.* 1.111; Lucian, *Hist. conscr.* 15; Horace, *Sat.* 2.10.20-30).

This last point raises one further consideration. Was Mark's Gospel intended to be read or to be orally performed? It appears to me that while the traditions *in* Mark were certainly orally transmitted before they were written down, and Mark's style is close to an oral style, as if he is telling a story to someone, we must nonetheless take the important signal in Mark 13:14 very seriously, especially as it contrasts with Jesus' usual rejoinder of "let those with two good ears, hear." 13:14 is a warning to the *reader* of the document that when he sees such things happening as are described in chapter 13, he must act. This is not the kind of warning one gives to a person who is merely reciting a document for others. Mark does not say, "let all those who hear this read, understand." Rather he says, "let the reader understand." The document, then, is directed to a reader. In a largely oral culture, Mark has offered a written document which understands and draws on that culture's expectations, and takes into account the advice of rhetoricians as to how to deal with a narrative.

Quintilian, for example, says that while the expansive rhythms of periodic sentences are not required, what one wants in a narration of some historical subject is "a certain continuity of motion and connection of style. All its members are closely linked together . . . [like] people who link hands to steady their steps, and lend each other mutual support" (*Inst.* 9.4.129-30). Mark accomplishes what Quintilian mandates by a beguilingly simple means. He inserts motion into the story, particularly up to the passion narrative, by the prevalent use of the term ευθυς (immediately), and he connects the narratives with και again and again, much as a person writing in Hebrew would use the *waw*-consecutive. He uses repetition but without being redundant, for a second phrase amplifies on the first one (e.g., "And very early on the first day of the week, when the sun had arisen . . ." [Mark 16:2]).[50]

This comports with the advice about narrative found in *Ad Herennium*

---

49. Fowler, p. 63.
50. See the exhaustive study of this phenomenon by F. Neirynck, *Duality in Mark: Contributions to the Study of the Markan Redaction* (Leuven: Leuven University Press, 1972).

4.43.54: "We shall not repeat the same thing precisely — for that, to be sure, would weary the reader and not refine the idea — but with changes . . . in the words." Mark's rhetoric is simple but effective, especially in a largely oral culture. It is likely that the original reader of this Gospel would have read it aloud to himself, for this was the regular practice in antiquity, and so it would have an aural as well as visual effect. Thus, while I would not agree that Mark was intended for a public rhetorical performance,[51] I do think it was meant to be read. But since in antiquity this almost always meant reading aloud (even if one was only reading to oneself), there is a deliberate oral dimension to the text, as well as a rhetorical dimension. Mark seems to have believed what Milton once said about Jesus: He "held it more humane, more heavenly first / By winning words to conquer willing hearts / And make persuasion do the work of fear."[52]

Mark's Sources

If we were to take Mack's view that Mark is almost entirely a work of Greek fiction, we would not really have to concern ourselves much with the question of Mark's sources — there would be little to mention.[53] But such a view is seriously problematic, as we have already partially seen. The strong evidence that Mark is presenting a biography of Jesus means that he will have proceeded like other ancient biographers in the gathering and use of sources. The use of *chreiae*, which were always tagged to and derived from specific historical incidents and individuals, also must count heavily against such a thesis. But there are other very good reasons to think that Mark used sources to compose his Gospel.

In the first place, E. Best has carefully laid out the evidence in Mark's Gospel of small incongruities, infelicities, and inconsistencies of speech that reflect unmodified tradition and so a style other than Mark's own. In fact, Best comes to a conclusion very close to that of R. Pesch about Mark as an editor of his sources. "Faced with a piece of tradition, Mark altered it internally as little as possible. If . . . notes of time, space and audience were missing then he felt free to set those pericopae which now lacked context in new contexts but even where it would have suited his purpose to do so he has not altered their content nor has he abbreviated them by omitting logia which were irrelevant or even

---

51. But see Bryan, pp. 72-84.

52. John Milton, *Paradise Regained,* in *The Complete Poems of John Milton* (New York: Washington Square Press, 1964), p. 368.

53. See Mack, *A Myth of Innocence: Mark and Christian Origins* (Philadelphia: Fortress, 1988).

meaningless in the context he has given them. It is perhaps fair to say that in this respect he was more careful than Matthew or Luke."[54] In short, Mark appears not to have been a novelist but instead a rather conservative editor of the Christian traditions that he uses in his Gospel, having edited them down into *chreia* form and placed them in a larger literary matrix, which would suggest an ancient biographical work.[55] It is important to get the balance right here, for it is also true that Mark shows some creativity in his handling of his source material. Marcus helpfully suggests that Mark is more an assembler of a collage than a painter painting on a blank canvas.[56]

The argument that Mark used sources, indeed extensive sources, can be strengthened from another quarter as well. Recently M. Casey argued at great length that Mark's Gospel is based on one or more Aramaic sources, not merely for the logia of Jesus but for whole narrative portions of the text.[57] Casey takes core samplings from various portions of the Gospel, including the ministry accounts as well as the passion narrative, and provides a battery of arguments for seeing the rather awkward and sometimes even redundant Greek of these sections as examples of translation Greek. Specifically, he provides this sort of argument for Mark 2:23–3:6; 9:11-13; 10:35-45; and 14:12-26. One may wish to debate one or another of his arguments, but the weight and persuasiveness of the cumulative case is impressive. He has made quite clear that if one really wishes to understand the historical Jesus, a much more serious effort must be made to deal with the Aramaic substratum of the arguably authentic Gospel traditions, especially of Jesus' words.[58]

Furthermore, there is strong support for Casey's basic argument from other scholars who have carefully analyzed Mark's Greek. For example, J. C. Doudna argues that the "Semitic coloring is uniform enough to give us to suppose that in many cases the whole [Markan] story with introductory statements was composed in Aramaic and later translated into Greek."[59] To this may

---

54. E. Best, "Mark's Preservation of the Tradition," in *The Interpretation of Mark*, ed. W. R. Telford (Edinburgh: T. & T. Clark, 1995), pp. 153-68, here p. 163. Cf. R. Pesch, *Markus-Evangelium I* (Freiburg: Herder, 1976), pp. 15-32.

55. That ancient biographers had some historical concerns, along with their other interests, must be kept steadily in view.

56. See Marcus, *Mark 1–8*, pp. 59-62.

57. M. Casey, *Aramaic Sources of Mark's Gospel* (Cambridge: Cambridge University Press, 1998).

58. Of course, one may ask: Who other than a small handful of NT specialists are sufficient for such things? Still, Casey has pointed a way forward that needs to be pursued, perhaps with the help of various Hebrew Bible scholars who are well familiar with both Aramaic and also at least the Greek of the LXX.

59. J. C. Doudna, *The Greek of the Gospel of Mark* (Philadelphia: SBL, 1961), p. 136, though he goes on to conclude that Mark based his Gospel on the earlier translation of the

be added the extensive demonstration by E. L. Maloney that various of the infelicities in Mark's grammar and syntax reflect Semitic interference — the problem a translator faces when moving from one language to another, especially when there are not equivalent expressions in the receiver language.[60]

Mark's Style and Facility with Greek

A good deal has been written about Mark's style, and some of it needs to be rehearsed at this juncture.[61] This data is important not merely because it tells us something about the author, namely, that Greek was not likely his first or only spoken or written language, but also because it helps us with the Synoptic problem, for time after time it is very difficult to imagine Mark being a condensation of one of the other Synoptic Gospels. This latter suggestion would mean we have an author who has gone out of his way to use more clumsy Greek constructions, more peculiar words, and the like than his sources. The rationale for such a move is hard to fathom, especially when we also discover that the portrait of the disciples and of Jesus is more stark, scandalous, and potentially offensive in Mark than in either Matthew or Luke. It is also hard to fathom a Gospel writer who would stress that Jesus was a teacher, then choose to omit all the Sermon on the Mount to make room for mere verbal expansion of some miracle and controversy stories!

Let us list some of Mark's stylistic traits: (1) the frequent use of verbs (especially λεγω and ερχομαι) in the historical present tense ("and we go into a house, and he sees . . .");[62] (2) the use of repetition of phrases or, better said, phrases that build on each other; (3) the use of the impersonal plural verb (no subject specified) followed by a singular verb; (4) the telling of the story in the

---

Aramaic text, rather than Mark being the translator himself. One has to wonder in view of the state of Mark's text whether he made any stylistic improvements on such a translation. It is easier to suppose that Mark himself, clearly a bilingual person, was the translator, and the rough condition of the Greek is not something he inherited.

60. E. L. Maloney, *Semitic Interference in Marcan Syntax* (Chico, Calif.: Scholars, 1981).

61. Cf., for instance, the older but still helpful treatments by C. H. Turner, "Marcan Usage: Notes, Critical and Exegetical, on the Second Gospel," *JTS* 25 (1924): 377-86, and 26 (1925): 225-40, and by J. C. Hawkins, *Horae Synopticae* (Oxford: Clarendon, 1909), pp. 114ff. And much more recently J. C. Meagher, *Clumsy Construction in Mark's Gospel* (New York and Toronto: Mellen, 1979).

62. This trait is especially notable when one compares Mark to Matthew and Luke, for in the latter two Gospels the historical present tense verb is either rare (Matthew, 20 times) or very rare (Luke, only once), but in Mark we find it some 151 times.

first-person plural; (5) the use of parenthetical remarks to clarify matters for the audience (e.g., 7:3-4); (6) the use of final γαρ clauses to offer explanations; (7) whether it is a deliberate stylistic trait or not, we certainly find anacolutha at several junctures in the text (2:10; 7:19; 11:32; 14:49); (8) the consistent use of καί parataxis instead of the more polished periodic Greek style, and yet also the use of asyndeton (the absence of connecting words and conjunctions) — 89 of Mark's 105 passages begin with the word καί; (9) the use of Aramaic phrases on occasion, especially to indicate Jesus' spoken language to the reader (3:17; 5:41; 7:11, 34; 14:36); (10) the use of unusual or harsh words or constructions, including words that are hapax legomenon (e.g., σχιζομένους at 1:10);[63] (11) the use of the *chreia* form to condense narratives into a manageable size (see above).

When one takes this evidence together, and especially when one compares how Matthew and Luke deal with the same material, the argument for Markan priority becomes as close to a certainty as one can imagine in scholarly discourse. Matthew and Luke deliberately smooth out the harsh, rough edges of Mark's grammar and syntax and vocabulary and, of course, some of the content, including the christological content, of his Gospel as well (e.g., cf. Mark 10:18 to Matt. 19:17).[64] One cannot very readily imagine the process working the other way around. Mark's Greek is not elegant and his rhetoric not advanced, but we should not make the mistake of thinking that because of this the content of his Gospel and his arrangement of his material is not profound, powerful, and persuasive, for indeed it is.[65] In fact, it must have been seen that way in the early church, or Matthew and Luke would never have felt compelled to use their Markan source anywhere near as much as they in fact do, often taking over large chunks of the Markan material virtually verbatim.[66] This is all the more remarkable when Mark is likely struggling to express the Gospel in a language in which the material was not originally written in, and in which Mark himself has only basic writing skills.

---

63. See the list in Hawkins, pp. 131-34, where he provides thirty-three examples.

64. On the latter see now P. Head, *Christology and the Synoptic Problem* (Cambridge: Cambridge University Press, 1997). For some powerful arguments for Markan priority on the basis of his translation Greek, see Casey, *Aramaic Sources of Mark's Gospel.*

65. See the conclusion of J. Painter, *Mark's Gospel* (London: Routledge, 1997), p. 8: "These few pieces of evidence are indicators of the rudimentary nature of Markan *literary* style which must be set over against the overall dramatic effectiveness of the Gospel. Limited facility with syntax, grammar, and vocabulary make clear that Mark is not a work of 'high literature' and was capable of being read by those of moderate education."

66. Matthew uses some 95 percent of Mark, Luke some 53 percent; but of the percent each takes over, Luke is a bit more apt to follow Mark verbatim than Matthew is.

The Authorship and Audience of the Earliest Gospel

We must now consider both the internal and external evidence that gives us some clues about the authorship of this Gospel. It is formally anonymous, as, unlike Paul's letters, the author nowhere mentions his name between v. 1 and the end of the document. The superscript may well have been an early addition to the document, but we do not know that the author himself applied it. Originally, if Mark was written on a scroll, a tag would likely have been attached to identify the document, but whether it would have read *euangelion kata Markon* is an open question — especially since the *kata Markon* identifier likely only arose when the existence of other Gospels necessitated this way of distinguishing the earliest one. What, then, do we know about the author from the document itself?

Firstly, we know that he was a Christian. He writes this document as one who has been persuaded about the good news involving Jesus of Nazareth. He is a partisan, and he is seeking to persuade others to become partisans for Jesus. Secondly, it is highly likely that the author is a Jew. This is so not merely because he knows a good deal about Jewish customs and culture and sects, but also because he seems to be well grounded in the Hebrew Scriptures, or at least the LXX, and takes such documents as sources of God's truth, including true prophecy. He also has a knowledge of early Jewish eschatology and apocalyptic. There is perhaps a slight possibility that he was a convert to Judaism, but in view of his knowledge of Aramaic, this seems less likely than that he grew up in a Jewish family. Of the author's use of Aramaic, Hengel not only remarks on his correct use of that language, but adds: "I do not know of any other work in Greek which has as many Aramaic or Hebrew words and formulae in so narrow a space as does the second Gospel."[67] That the author must translate his Aramaic words and phrases tells us that his audience is likely of a different extraction than himself. Surely it is an audience that knows no Aramaic.

Thirdly, we know this man is a somewhat educated man, one who can read and write after a fashion in Greek. This would place him in the upper 10 to 20 percent of his whole culture in terms of education, but from a social point of view many such persons experienced considerable status inconsistency. Witness the well-educated persons taken captive by Romans, turned into slaves, and then made to live out their lives as tutors for wealthy Roman children or the like. Education was only one status indicator in antiquity, and often enough not the definitive one.

Fourthly, the author of this Gospel uses a profusion of Latinisms, both individual words but possibly also brief phrases.[68] These words do not simply

---

67. Hengel, *Studies*, p. 46.

68. See the list in R. H. Gundry, *Mark: A Commentary on His Apology for the Cross* (Grand Rapids: Eerdmans, 1993), p. 1044.

consist of military, economic, or judicial terms which might well be used throughout the empire. One should pay special attention to the explanation of Greek expressions by Latin ones at 12:42 and 15:46. The explanation at 12:42 suggests an audience which is in a place where the Latin term is known but the Greek λεπτον is not. Otherwise, why the need for explaining it in terms of the quadrans? Furthermore, Mark sometimes gives us combinations of Greek words that seem to be a rendering of Latin idioms connected with the trial in ungrammatical Greek (e.g., το ικανον ποιεω = *satisfacere;* 15:15). Or notice the explanation of the αυλη in 15:16 as meaning Praetorium.[69] This suggests that our author or his audience or both are in some sort of Roman setting, whether it be in Rome itself or in a Roman colony city where Latin would have been used, at least in official contexts and by the Romans living there.

A further clue about the author and the audience is the term "Syrophoenician" at 7:26. I agree with Hengel that the use of this term is difficult to explain if the author and/or audience is in the East — whether in Israel or Syria.[70] In Roman sources it is used to distinguish the residents of Syria from those of Carthage in Africa called Libuphoenicians (cf. Juvenal 8.159-60; Pliny the Elder, *HN* 7.201). Thus, when one combines this with the use of the Latinisms, it is more probable than not that our author resides in and writes for those in the West. No location is more probable than Rome, though we cannot be sure on the basis of internal evidence alone. Thus at this juncture we turn to the external evidence.

We have already seen the attribution of the Gospel to one Mark in the superscript. The superscript may have existed as early as the composition of the second Gospel to be written (presumably Matthew), which relies so heavily on Mark. This would mean presumably that it may have existed as early as the last two decades of the first century, and more certainly in the early second century.

A variety of sources, dating ultimately to the second century A.D., univocally indicate that this Gospel was written by a person named Mark who was an associate of Peter. The testimony of Irenaeus in *Against Heresies* 3.1.1 is as follows: "After their [i.e., Peter and Paul's] departure, Mark, the disciple and *hermeneutes* of Peter, transmitted his preaching to us in written form." The anti-Marcionite prologue to Mark's Gospel says, "Mark asserted, the one who was called stump-fingered because he had short fingers in comparison with the size of the rest of his body. He was Peter's *interpres.* After the death of Peter

---

69. See the helpful discussion by B. Van Iersel, *Mark: A Reader-Response Commentary* (Sheffield: University of Sheffield Press, 1998), pp. 33-34. His critique of the arguments for a Galilean or Syrian provenance is telling as well. As he says, Mark's stories have the local Palestinian color precisely because they are about that region and have originated in that region, not because Mark's audience is there.

70. Hengel, *Studies,* p. 29.

himself, Mark wrote down this Gospel in some part of Italy."[71] A quotation
from late in the second century by Clement of Alexandria says that Mark wrote
in Rome during Peter's lifetime, but this is only cited in the later work by
Eusebius (*Hist. eccl.* 6.14; cf. 2.15).[72]

The quotation of the famous Papias source comes from the fourth-
century work by Eusebius entitled *The History of the Church,* but Eusebius (at
Hist. eccl. 3.39.15) is in turn quoting Papias's second-century five-volume work
Interpretation of the Lord's Sayings, a document which dates to about A.D. 120-
30 and says:

> And this is what the Elder said, "Mark, who became Peter's *hermeneutes,* ac-
> curately wrote, though not in order *(taxei),* as many of the things said and
> done by the Lord as he had noted *(emnemoneusen).* For he neither heard the
> Lord nor followed him, but afterwards, as I said, followed Peter who com-
> posed his teachings according to the *chreiae* and not as a rhetorical arrange-
> ment *(suntaxin)* of the Lord's sayings. So Mark made no mistake in writing
> some things just as he recollected *(apemnemonesen)* them. For he was careful
> of this one thing, to leave nothing he heard out and to say nothing falsely.

The first thing that strikes a reader familiar with rhetoric is that this earliest attribution of Markan authorship from Papias is full of semitechnical rhetorical
terms,[73] a fact too often overlooked by commentators on this Gospel. For example, many have tried to translate the word *chreia* quite literally as "need" and
then fall into difficulties explaining what it means to compose one's teachings
according to the "needs" (plural)! This is not a problem when one realizes that
the author is saying that Peter composed his teachings according to the *chreiae*
(on which see above) — in other words, using the most elemental rhetorical
way of condensing material into a persuasive historical, biographical anecdote.
Further terms in this section with rhetorical significance are, for instance, *taxei*
(order) and *suntaxin* (arrangement). Now the issue of "order" is an important
one in rhetorical terms, and it refers not to chronological order but to what
would be a rhetorically and logically effective order.

What is especially striking is that the reference to "order" is in close conjunction with the discussion of Peter composing his narratives according to the
chreiae. Recall that in our discussion of the *progymnasta,* what is supposed to

---

71. On this text see D. De Bruyne, "Les plus anciens prologues latins des Evangiles,"
RBén 40 (1928): 193-214.

72. For an introductory discussion of all the relevant testimonies about Mark's Gospel
from the early church fathers, see now T. C. Oden and C. A. Hall, eds., *Mark,* vol. 2 of *The Ancient Christian Commentary on Scripture* (Downers Grove, Ill.: InterVarsity, 1998), pp. xxi-
xxix.

73. Rightly noted by R. Guelich, *Mark 1–8.26* (Waco: Word, 1989), p. xxvii.

follow the *chreia,* if it is used as a thesis statement, is the *taxis,* the arguments in order in an "elaboration." In short, what we are being told is that Mark would *not* compose his Gospel according to prescribed rhetorical form if he were to follow the dictates of the *progymnasta.* We do not have *chreia* as thesis statement followed by elaboration of arguments in rhetorically effective order. In other words, Papias is saying that we *don't* have what Mack and Robbins believe they have found in Mark's Gospel (and the other Synoptics). Mark's rhetoric is of a simpler order than that.[74]

We also learn that it is denied that Peter considered rhetorical *arrangement (suntaxin)* of Christ's sayings when he composed his narratives. This may mean that the material was not arranged according to the parts of a rhetorical speech or, more broadly, according to what was deemed the most persuasive way to line up one's evidence (e.g., appeal to inartificial and then artificial arguments).[75]

There is, further, the use of the verb *apemnemoneusen.* This is the verbal form of the word for recollections. We remember that "memoirs" or "recollections" are what those like Justin Martyr said apostles like Peter left the church, and that "recollections" are the larger narratives out of which *chreiae* are formed. The claim, then, is quite straightforward here. While Peter shaped his teaching in the form of *chreiae,* Mark followed his lead and took the larger recollections and accurately summarized the tradition. He made a narrative out of the individual *chreiae* and by and large did not insert large collections of Jesus' teaching, so as not to interrupt the flow of that narrative. Thus he did not testify falsely as he wrote down single items as he recalled them.[76] This is an important final statement, because Theon says the two greatest faults *chreiae* can have are either leaving out essential information or telling what is false.[77] Mark is exonerated of these charges. He wrote what he remembered of what Peter had said.[78]

---

74. See the discussion by Mack and Robbins, p. 40.

75. It is possible that Papias has in mind a comparison with the collection of the Lord's sayings we call Q, which does indeed have a rhetorically effective form of arrangement. See my discussion of this in *Jesus the Sage* (Minneapolis: Fortress, 1994), pp. 211-35.

76. See the helpful translation by Robbins, p. 66: "Peter gave his teachings in chreia form: he was not making a compilation of the dominical oracles. Therefore Mark was not wrong when he composed them in the form of an *apomnemoneumata.*" He argues that the verb here means "to write an apomnemoneumata." If this is correct, it suggests that rudimentary rhetorical considerations were involved, but not much more. It should also be noted that the verb "as he recollected them" suggests a composition made after Peter was dead.

77. See the discussion by R. P. Martin, *Mark: Evangelist and Theologian* (Grand Rapids: Zondervan, 1972), p. 82.

78. On the need for reading the Papias testimony in light of its use of rhetorical terminology, see H. H. Schmidt, "Semitismen bei Papias," *TZ* 44 (1988): 135-46, here p. 138 n. 12, and J. Kurzinger, *Papias von Hierapolis und die Evangelien des Neuen Testaments* (Regensburg: Pustet, 1983).

We come finally to the term *hermeneutes,* which must surely mean something like interpreter. Why would Peter need an interpreter? Perhaps he offered his teachings in Aramaic and Mark was required to interpret them in the receiver language. On the other hand, the Papias text seems to suggest that Mark became Peter's *hermeneutes after* Peter died, and accurately wrote down as many things as he could remember.

Yet we also recall that Paul tells of an agreement that Peter would be the apostle primarily to the Jews, including apparently the Jews in the Diaspora (Gal. 2:7; cf. 1 Cor. 1:12 and 9:5), and Paul the apostle to the Gentiles. It is possible that Peter mainly taught in Aramaic and used a translator when he traveled beyond Israel. It may be that near the end of Peter's life, Mark had already assumed such a role as translator and interpreter (see 1 Pet. 5:13). Papias is also clear that Mark had not personally followed or known Jesus, but had only followed Peter. This means that Mark was Peter's disciple for some time before Peter died.

The Papias tradition has been far too quickly dismissed from the discussion of the authorship of this Gospel by some commentators.[79] It needs to be kept steadily in view that though Papias was a Christian from Hierapolis who lived in the early second century, he claims to be citing the tradition of an earlier witness — namely, the Elder John. He is not simply conjecturing on the basis of hearsay about the origins of the Gospels. Here is not the place to get into a lengthy discussion about the Elder John, but the point to be made is that Papias is relying on first-century testimony that claims to be connected with the original apostolic testimony. Papias did not dream up the summary he offered, and indeed it is hard to imagine anyone making up the notion of Mark, a noneyewitness, nonapostle, as the author of this important and earliest Gospel. The burden of proof must lie with those who deny that some early Christian named Mark wrote this work.

But who is this Mark? Could he really be the sometime associate of, first, Paul and Barnabas, then of Barnabas alone, and later of Peter? Could he really be the son of a woman who housed church meetings at the beginning of the church age? Here we get into the realm of subjective impressions. Many scholars have recognized echoes of the Pauline letters, but also of 1 Peter, in texts like Mark 10:45, in the presentation of the Last Supper, and in the general emphasis on servanthood and suffering themes. At the level of ideas, nothing in Mark's Gospel suggests that Mark *could not* have known Paul and Peter and been familiar with their teachings, and there are some positive reasons to think he might have.

There is certainly nothing in Mark's knowledge of early Judaism or of

---

79. Gundry, pp. 1026-44, deals admirably with most of the major objections to this tradition's historical value.

Greek to disqualify him from being such a person. His knowledge of Jerusalem may well be more precisely accurate than his knowledge of the geography of the northern part of the Holy Land, but this is not surprising if the man had not personally traveled with Jesus in the north and in fact had been a resident of Jerusalem during that time.[80] The plausibility of such a thesis, however, must stand or fall on the basis of the detailed historical and exegetical study of the text of Mark itself. The reader must decide whether the exposition offered in this commentary supports such a thesis or not.

Something more can be said about Mark's relationship with Paul, however. The author of Acts is not usually given to highlighting rifts in the early church, and so we may take it as historically probable that Mark did indeed have a working relationship with Paul for some time (Acts 12:12, 25; 13:5, 13; 15:36-41), but there was a rupture in the relationship. However, Philem. 24 and Col. 4:10 suggest there was also a reconciliation. In assessing the possible influence of Paul on Mark, J. Painter says this: "Not only is there a concentration on the passion of Jesus (the cross) in Mark (see 1 Corinthians 1.17-18, 23), there is also a critique of the law more in keeping with Paul than Peter. The use of 'gospel' language and the equation of the gospel preached by Jesus (1.14-15) with the 'word' (4.33) are also features common to Paul (see 1 Corinthians 1.18). The Jesus of Mark not only does not keep the sabbath, he declares all foods to be clean (7.19) thus invalidating food and purity laws which were essential to the Jewish way of life."[81]

The Papias tradition does not, however, tell us what sort of perspective Mark brought to the construction of his Gospel, and it is perfectly possible that he brought one that is more Pauline than Petrine. But judging from Acts, Peter himself came around to the more Pauline position about food laws and the celebration of the Sabbath, and certainly there is nothing in 1 Peter, if it is by the apostle, as many scholars still think, that contradicts the heart of the Pauline gospel. There is much on suffering and servanthood there that Paul would have heartily endorsed.[82]

One further remark must be made on the connection of Mark with the apostles. I have argued elsewhere that Acts paints a rather reliable portrait of the leaders of early Christianity, including John Mark.[83] Based on this source and the data from Paul's letters and 1 Peter, the summary by R. Bauckham

---

80. On the alleged geographical blunders of Mark, see the discussion of Hengel, *Studies*, pp. 46ff., and Gundry, p. 1039. As Gundry says, the topographical notations grow clearer and denser the more the text focuses on Jerusalem and its environs.

81. Painter, pp. 5-6.

82. On the connection between Mark and Paul, see Marcus, *Mark 1–8*, pp. 73-75.

83. See my commentary *The Acts of the Apostles: A Socio-Rhetorical Commentary* (Grand Rapids: Eerdmans, 1998).

about John Mark is perfectly plausible: "John Mark, a member of a Cypriot Jewish family settled in Jerusalem and a member of the early Jerusalem church, was then in Antioch, accompanied his cousin Barnabas and Paul on their missionary journey as far as Pamphylia, later accompanied Barnabas to Cyprus, and is finally heard of in Rome, if Philemon is written from Rome, where 1 Peter also places him."[84] There is nothing in the earliest Gospel that is not compatible with this summary, and a good deal which could support it, especially the detailed knowledge of Jerusalem and its environs.[85]

A few comments on Mark's audience: First, it reads Greek, but equally it requires explanation of Jewish customs, Aramaic terms and phrases, and even some Greek terms. This supports the long-standing theory that Mark's audience is largely composed of Gentile converts to the Christian faith, and presumably Gentiles who have not first been Jewish proselytes or synagogue adherents. There is no good reason to reject the testimony of the external witnesses that this Gospel was written from Rome for Roman Christians, and certainly there is nothing that particularly favors another and more eastern locale for the audience.

Indeed, the explanation of the *lepton* and the use of the term "Syrophoenician" suggest that this Gospel comes from and is for "western" Christians. But can we go further than this, and on the basis of texts like Mark 13 deduce that Mark's audience is under fire — indeed, perhaps has already undergone some persecution and is expecting more? Should we conclude with H. Kee and J. Marcus that Mark's community is a missionary sect whose worldview is apocalyptic and is largely at odds with the dominant culture's worldview, not least because it has suffered persecution?[86] If this sort of mirror

---

84. R. Bauckham, ed., *The Gospel for All Christians: Rethinking the Gospel's Origins* (Grand Rapids: Eerdmans, 1988), p. 35.

85. Some have conjectured that the peculiar text found at Mark 14:51-52 about the young man is rather like what Alfred Hitchcock did in his own movies — make a cameo appearance for a moment in the story as a sort of signature of authorship. This is not impossible, if only because: (1) we know that John Mark lived in Jerusalem (Acts 12:12); (2) to judge from Acts, he would certainly have been a young man at the time of Jesus' crucifixion in A.D. 30; (3) the author of this Gospel is certainly a disciple of Jesus, and perhaps these verses are his way of saying that although he had followed Jesus from an early age, he too, like the Twelve, failed Jesus at the crucial hour. This would make him an eyewitness of some of the passion events perhaps, at most. But this theory also requires that we believe that the audience of this Gospel already knew the story of John Mark as a young man having this one moment of contact with Jesus. On the other hand, some have seen this as an anticipation of the young man at the tomb who bears witness to Jesus. Are we then to think of this person as an angelic figure who failed Jesus, or should we see this as some sort of allegory of failed discipleship? Since there are almost as many opinions on these verses as there are commentators, it is best not to base too much on them.

86. Kee, *Community of the New Age,* and J. Marcus, "Mark 4.10-12 and Marcan Epistemology," *JBL* 103 (1984): 557-74.

reading of the text to find out clues about the community is viable, it may suggest that Mark is writing to Roman Christians after the Neronian crackdown, in the mid-60s, which again has often been suggested by commentators on this Gospel. Mark 13:14 certainly intimates that the reader is expected to see some trials and tribulation in due course.

A fair bit can be known about what was transpiring in Rome during the late 60s, because we have the historical materials of Tacitus and others to aid us. The facts are that by A.D. 68 the support in the provinces for Nero being emperor had very seriously eroded. Indeed, there was already open rebellion against his rule in various places, and it must be remembered that the Jewish War had been going on since 66 as well. Nero had long since lost his best advisers, Seneca and Burrus, and had not been able to shake the suspicion that he had set the fire in Rome in 64. Christians had been chosen as his scapegoats for the fire, and the persecutions appear to have continued well beyond 64 (cf. Tacitus, *Ann.* 15.44), since the suspicions against the emperor himself would not die. Things came to a head in the middle of 68, and Nero took his own life, thus ending the Julio-Claudian line of emperors. The empire was in chaos, and several pretenders sought to be the next emperor — Galba, Otho, Vitellius. In fact, each was briefly emperor beginning in 68 and continuing into 69, but none could really put down all his opponents, and none had such popularity as to overcome the usual start-up problems when one seizes power. Thus it was, in 69, that General Vespasian, who had been successfully wrapping up the fight against the Jews in Israel, became the next emperor to establish a stable rule, and would be followed by his offspring, Titus and then Domitian, establishing a new family line of emperors.[87] But in 69 and 70 Vespasian was still consolidating his power and control of things, and the situation was still very unstable. There must surely have been considerable apprehension and fear amongst Roman Christians, both Jews and Gentiles, as to what the new emperor would do in Rome, having seen what he did to Jews in the Holy Land. Under such circumstances, and bearing in mind that the fall of Jerusalem seemed imminent, it is not at all surprising that Mark would choose to write a Gospel using apocalyptic rhetoric, preparing his audience for further suffering and difficulties and reminding them that their Master had already experienced such things at the hands of the Romans.

In further support of the Roman provenance of the audience, one may point to the detailed work of P. Lampe on the social makeup and level of the Christians in Rome.[88] He points to the fact that many Roman Christians were

---

87. See the very helpful, detailed discussion of all these matters by T. J. Wiedmann, "From Nero to Vespasian," in *The Cambridge Ancient History,* vol. 10, *The Augustan Empire, 43 B.C.–A.D. 69,* ed. A. K. Bowman et al. (Cambridge: Cambridge University Press, 1996), pp. 256-82.

88. P. Lampe, *Die Stadtromischen Christen in den ersten beiden Jahrhunderten: Untersuchungen zur Sozialgeschichte* (Tübingen: Mohr, 1987), see esp. pp. 37-52.

of low social status and subject to the abuses of Nero and other officials looking for people to blame for their problems. Noncitizens especially would be subject to the kinds of things described in Mark 13, especially if they were advocates of strange eastern religions, such as Jews and Christians. The "in-house" orientation of Mark when he speaks about Jesus' teaching comports well with the house church nature of Roman Christianity, especially since there seems to have been no central gathering of Christians but meetings in various homes in various quarters of Rome. Furthermore, the critique of early Judaism found in Mark comports with the tensions that existed between Jews and Christians in Rome from the late 40s (remembering the expulsion in 49; see Acts 18) right through the early 60s (see Acts 28) and beyond. Thus, while Mark is certainly not *about* Christianity in the 60s in Rome, we can only agree with C. C. Black that "we can nevertheless acknowledge an appreciable social, religious and theological congruence between the Second Gospel and first-century Roman Christianity. . . . I consider the relevant evidence strong enough to support the assumption of Mark's Roman provenance. . . ."[89]

At this juncture a new thesis about the audiences of the Gospels must be taken into account. R. Bauckham has recently proposed, in a well-argued essay entitled "For Whom Were the Gospels Written?" that the Gospels were in fact written not just for a specific, discrete Christian community in a particular locale but for all Christians in the various parts of the Roman Empire.[90] He begins by assuming the usual solution to the Synoptic problem, and then asks: If Mark was written only for a specific community, how is it that Matthew and Luke have copies of his work and use it presumably not terribly long after it was written? He then points out that the context out of which a Gospel is written and the context to which a Gospel is written should not be assumed to be one and the same. Furthermore, he contends that not all the material in a given Gospel need be there for or apply to the whole of the audience for which the Gospel is written. Bauckham objects strenuously to the attempts to take the Gospels as allegories of community struggles and issues. He stresses that a "Gospel text has to be treated as transparently revelatory of the community for which it was written because the interpretive aim of reconstructing this community would be defeated by any other kind of text."[91] He urges that the Gospels must not be treated like Paul's ad hoc letters, which certainly are addressed to particular Christian communities with specific concerns.[92]

If the Gospels are indeed ancient biographies, then one must ask whether

---

89. C. C. Black, "Was Mark a Roman Gospel?" *ET* 105 (1993-94): 36-40, here p. 39.

90. See the book he edited entitled *The Gospel for All Christians*. His essay is on pp. 9-48.

91. Bauckham, p. 26.

92. For a fresh critique of Bauckham's thesis, see Marcus, *Mark 1–8*, pp. 26-28.

ancient biographies were simply written to address the specific circumstances of a very small community of people. Bauckham thinks this unlikely; they were rather meant to be circulated more widely. He then raises the interesting question of why a Gospel writer would *write* a Gospel just for the community of which he was already a part. Couldn't he just have taught them orally? In any case, if Gospels were meant to address specific concerns, why would he want to freeze the ongoing discussion at some particular point by putting the matter into writing, when he knew matters would soon develop further? The answers to these last two questions may be: because Mark sees himself passing on the traditions once given, not merely taking part in an ongoing discussion, and furthermore he would have been justified to have concerns about the preservation of such traditions relying purely on oral memory, now that the three major apostles had recently been killed.

At the historical level, Bauckham challenges the assumption that Christian communities were isolated parochial entities that had little or no contact with each other. To the contrary, says Bauckham, we have firm evidence from Paul's letters and elsewhere that Christians had considerable social networks, and most of the major leaders of the early church are said to have traveled rather widely through these communities, binding them together to some degree.[93] Bauckham suggests that these sorts of folks, the peripatetic church leaders, are the ones who likely wrote Gospels. There is no good reason why we must see an Evangelist as like a reclusive professor in Cambridge, England, who never learned to drive and simply confined himself to his academic community and wrote to and for his students and colleagues there. Bauckham also argues that he is not merely maintaining that the Gospels were written for a larger group of specific churches than previously imagined. To the contrary, he is urging that the audience for these works was indefinite rather than definite, general rather than specific, and thus the Gospels cannot be used as hermeneutical keys to determining what was going on in some specific Christian community. The historical context of the Gospels is not a specific Christian community but the larger Christian movement of the first century A.D. They are open rather than closed texts.

We have laid out this tour de force argument at some length because it is well worth pondering especially in regard to Mark. I am convinced that Bauckham is right in a good deal of what he asserts, but I would make two or three particular caveats. Firstly, ancient biographies were indeed written for somewhat specific audiences: the educated public. Unlike some of the plays written in the first century, serious biographies had a more highbrow audience in view. The audience often began with a patron and then expanded from there. If Mark is a biography, and especially if it is a biography meant to be *read* and

---

93. On the social setting of this Gospel, see below.

not merely heard, it does have something of a specific audience, even if that audience happens to be literate Christians all over the empire.

Secondly, while I quite agree that the Gospels should not be read as allegories of early Christian community life in the middle to late first century A.D.,[94] I do think the Evangelists had some specific things and people in mind when they wrote. The Gospels are not *about* these communities, but they are written *for* them. The way I would put the matter is as follows: the Gospels are indeed written with one eye on the larger Christian public, even in places far removed from where the author is. As a part of an evangelistic religion, the Gospel writer intends for the good news to be spread, in part by the circulation of his Gospel, across the empire. But at the same time, like Luke, who writes for his patron Theophilus in the first place, the author of Mark's Gospel has in mind addressing in the first place the Christians he is with so as to persuade, encourage, and exhort them during a difficult time of suffering and persecution. A good deal of what he says will be especially pertinent for that first target audience, though it will also have relevance for the wider circle of Christian churches. This is one of the reasons the four Gospels have turned out so very differently from one another, even in the case of Mark and Matthew, the latter of which takes over 95 percent of Mark's content.

Finally, a brief word about the date of Mark's Gospel is in order. While I think Casey is likely right that there are substantial Aramaic sources behind Mark's Gospel, it does not follow from this that Mark wrote it in the 40s, though I would certainly not rule out this possibility. Indeed, a certain kind of reading of Mark 13 might even lead one to think Mark was writing during the age of Caligula in the late 30s, for Caligula really did try to set up a statue of himself in the temple of Jerusalem. In fact, in a tour de force argument, G. Theissen has argued for this point of view, suggesting that the so-called Markan apocalypse was composed around 39-40.[95] His case should not be quickly dismissed. There are, however, several problems with such an argument. It must first ignore or dismiss the external testimony that Mark wrote his Gospel after Peter's death, or perhaps shortly before it, which would give us a date no earlier than the mid-60s. One could argue that an Ur-Markus was composed in the 40s, but in fact the Mark we have appears to be a document that has not undergone polishing and refinement. That is, our current Mark appears to be Ur-Markus if there ever was one. The second problem with such an early date is the various parenthetical explanations in Mark's Gospel which suggest a

---

94. Mirror reading is precisely the problem with Marcus's (*Mark 1–8*, pp. 33-37) analysis of the provenance of this Gospel based on the assumption that Mark 13 reflects closely the experiences of some of Mark's contemporaries in Israel and nearby Syria (the locale favored by Marcus), and creatively written up after the fact.

95. G. Theissen, *The Gospels in Context* (Edinburgh: T. & T. Clark, 1992), pp. 161ff.

predominantly non-Jewish audience. Where would there have been such a Christian audience in the 40s, before Paul even began to be successful in the Diaspora? The evidence reviewed earlier for a western provenance of the document must also count against this thesis.

One further social factor needs to be taken into account. The anti-Semitism of the rulers of the Roman Empire was in evidence throughout the NT and involved unsavory actions by Tiberius, Caligula, Claudius, and Nero against Jews, which by Claudius's age affected Jewish Christians as well.[96] It seems likely to me that Mark's Gospel must have been written both during a time when Christians (and Jews) were in danger of persecution and a time when a large portion of the audience Mark is addressing were Gentile Christians. This best suits the period after the missionary work of Paul had had considerable effect. In short, it best suits a period at least a couple decades after A.D. 40. No period better suits the evidence internal and external than that of the Jewish war against Rome which led to the destruction of the temple in Jerusalem. Thus we must date this work from 66 to 70, and probably closer to the latter.

Mark in Its Social Context

There are two poles to consider when discussing the social context of Mark's Gospel: the social setting Mark is reporting on in his Gospel — Galilee and Judea in the 20s and 30s — and Rome in the 60s. Both were volatile settings for religious Jews and perhaps especially for the Jesus movement, whose members were not seeking solitude and the avoidance of controversy, but rather, by being involved in a movement to radically reform early Judaism, were the center of controversy in the 30s, and then, as a visible and openly evangelistic group in the 60s, were the victims of Nero's reprisals after the fire. In the 60s they would have attracted this sort of animus not least because they refused to participate in various facets of public life, including the worship of the emperor. More needs to be said at this point about each of these settings, which could be called seething cauldrons waiting to boil over.

These two settings in a sense overlap in the period from 66 to 70 during the Jewish War, when things were especially difficult for Jews and Christians in both places precisely because of the war. Latent and not so latent Roman anti-

---

96. See the helpful discussion by H. D. Slingerland, *Claudian Policymaking and the Early Imperial Repression of Judaism at Rome* (Atlanta: Scholars, 1997), who debunks any overly rosy pictures of the relationship between Jews and the powers that be in the Roman Empire. The relationship was always a troubled one, and there was plenty of anti-Semitism on the part of the emperors, both officially and unofficially.

Semitism rose to the surface, and things were grim for the Jewish and Christian religious subcultures. Judaism lost its temple and center of worship, Jerusalem. Christianity lost its two great apostles — Paul and Peter — and had already lost James in Jerusalem in 62 when some Jewish authorities took matters into their own hands during a period between prefects. It may indeed have been these last shocking events, more than the impending destruction of the temple, which prompted the writing of this Gospel.[97]

I have had occasion elsewhere to deal at some length with Jesus' social setting.[98] Here I must simply summarize some of my findings. Before doing so, I would like to emphasize what C. Myers also has stressed. Mark's Gospel is remarkable because it is written about mostly ordinary people who were not by and large part of the social elite. Not too many ancient biographies were written about a person of the social level of Jesus. I do not, however, think Mark's own audience will have simply been of the lowest social level. It is more reasonable to suppose that there were at least some of higher social level in Mark's audience, as was true in Paul's churches, some for instance to whom Mark could have written and whom he could have counted on being literate.

What may we say about Galilee and Judea in the 20s and 30s? It is fair to say that while the situation was not always bellicose, nonetheless it was normally far from bucolic. The image of Jesus as a gentle shepherd sitting in verdant pastures teaching enjoyable but inoffensive parables to audiences who all loved him, is far from an accurate assessment of the situation. Both the situation and the way Jesus addressed it were full of incident and danger. One must remember that in Jesus' world politics and religion were always intimately intertwined, even if one was not part of a zealot movement or a political appointee of a Roman ruler, like the high priest.

This intertwining is very evident during the time of Pilate. For example, Josephus tells us that Pilate at one point wanted to improve the water supply in Jerusalem, and so decided to confiscate funds from the temple treasury for this worthy cause. He had not anticipated that the Jews would see this not merely as theft but as a sacrilege (*Ant.* 18.60-62; *War* 2.175-77). Thus, when word got out, a mob of Jewish protesters was waiting for him when he next visited Jerusalem. One must also take into account the character of Pilate himself, which is revealed in his bloody massacre not only of Samaritans (*Ant.* 18.85-89) but also,

---

97. I agree in principle with B. Van Iersel that the descriptions of the "birth pangs" in Mark 13 seem particularly apt, not merely to the situation in Judea but also to the turbulent time in Rome immediately after Nero's death, especially taking into account the dark year of the three emperors. See Van Iersel, pp. 39-44. He is following the telling study of M. Hengel, "Entstehungszeit und Situation des Markesevangeliums," in *Markus-Philologie,* ed. H. Cancik (Tübingen: Mohr, 1984), pp. 1-45.

98. See especially the second edition of my book *The Jesus Quest* (Downers Grove: InterVarsity Press, 1995), both chap. 1 and the appendix, reviewing R. Horsley's Galilee book.

according to Luke, of Galileans (Luke 13:1). Unfortunately, Judea was considered a second-rate province, and so did not get the best governors, only prefects of equestrian rank. There was clearly danger for Jesus and his followers in Pilate's territory. But what about Galilee itself?

Galilee was of course ruled by Herod Antipas, a client king whom Rome allowed to supervise things for them. As E. P. Sanders has remarked, "Rome generally governed remotely, being content with the collection of tribute and maintenance of stable borders; for the most part it left even these matters in the hands of loyal local rulers and leaders."[99] But the leader who had been left in charge in Galilee was not only corrupt and devious and immoral, he was also of Idumean extraction (Edomite!). Furthermore, Herod Antipas pursued vigorously a course of Hellenizing the region, chiefly by building Sepphoris and Tiberias as Greco-Roman cities. So insensitive was he to Jewish feelings that Tiberias was built in part upon Jewish graveyards, which made such buildings permanently unclean. Thus Herod had to bribe people to live there! As Martin Goodman stresses, the principal means of governing throughout the regions of Israel and Judea were fear and brute force, which only engendered hostility.[100]

As Goodman goes on to say, matters were made even worse because Rome tended to rely on the local aristocracy in a country having enough clout and respect among the people to make governing possible and peaceful. But the local landed elite, whether Sadducees and others in the south or the Herods in the north, were far from widely popular. Indeed, they were apparently often despised and hated by the ordinary people, a fact made worse when their agents helped in the collection of taxes for the Romans! And in fact, the tax burden was indeed excessive. It is not a surprise under such circumstances that ordinary Jews were shocked at Jesus' dining with the Zacchaeuses of his world. There were further factors causing stress and distress for persons such as fishermen in Galilee. Since their "crop," as it were, was in a commodity that had to be sold quickly, their assets tended to be in money. They were far easier targets for the tax collectors than peasants who only had their land and usually bartered crops for goods.[101]

Peasants as well as fishermen were indeed increasingly being marginalized in Galilee, and promises of lands, houses, and new kinfolk in the dominion must have sounded not only good, but more like a political manifesto than

---

99. E. P. Sanders, *The Historical Figure of Jesus* (London: Penguin Books, 1993), p. 18.

100. M. Goodman, *The Ruling Class of Judea* (Cambridge: Cambridge University Press, 1987), p. 1.

101. S. Freyne, "The Geography, Politics, and Economics of Galilee," in *Studying the Historical Jesus: Evaluations of the State of Research,* ed. B. Chilton and C. A. Evans (Leiden: Brill, 1994), pp. 75-122.

an otherworldly dream to many of them. One must constantly reckon with the political impact of Jesus' teaching on such people. It is surely no accident that Jesus seems to have stayed away from the Greco-Roman centers of Tiberias and Sepphoris and instead focused on redeeming the ordinary people in small villages and towns. His approach was not a frontal assault on the heart of Herod's domain, but rather, according to Mark, an attack on the underlying causes of the trouble — the powers of darkness.[102] Of relevance for the discussion of Mark is the fact that in the environment described briefly above, there was good reason for Jesus not to make an open proclamation of who he believed himself to be.

The situation was hardly better in Rome in the late 60s — indeed, one can argue that it was worse than in Galilee in the 20s and 30s. The tyranny of Nero was at its height, and we have already spoken of the anti-Semitism of the Julio-Claudian emperors throughout the period in question. It cannot have been easy to be a Jew or a Christian living in Rome under these circumstances,[103] much less an evangelistic Christian, for proselytism was considered an un-Roman act "that was not usually prohibited but was discouraged and may have led to several expulsions and to conscription."[104]

Christians would have been even more vulnerable in Rome in the late 60s because Nero appears to have been the first Roman ruler to actually distinguish Jews from Christians when he singled them out and blamed them for the fire (see Tacitus, *Ann.* 15.44.2-8). Christians were no longer associated with a religion of long standing which at least officially was not prohibited or banned by Roman law. Thus it is not surprising that our sources say the main complaint about the Christians is that they were guilty of practicing a *religio nova*, and thus the charge in regard to starting the fire seemed reasonable at the time (cf.

---

102. Here I would part company with C. Myers, who follows W. Wink. They identify those powers as Herod himself and the ruling parties, not as supernatural forces. This is to misunderstand the nature of ancient apocalyptic language and the ancient world, where it was most certainly believed that there were real demons. The more nuanced view, that we are talking about demonized hierarchial governmental structures, is not much of an improvement. It is very difficult to interpret most of the exorcisms in Mark as an attack upon the imperial realm.

103. I find quite unconvincing the arguments of M. Sordi, *The Christians and the Roman Empire* (London: Routledge, 1994), pp. 7ff., that prior to Nero the Romans were entirely neutral or benevolent toward Christians, apparently being able to distinguish them readily from Jews. She also puts forward the thesis that Tiberius actually proposed an edict to name Christ a god by the Senate, but it was rejected, whereupon he imposed a veto against any future actions versus Christians! Where is the credible evidence from any texts from the first or second centuries for this view? This view hardly explains texts like Acts 18 where both Jews and apparently Jewish Christians were expelled from Rome during the reign of Claudius.

104. Here M. Nanos, *The Mystery of Romans* (Minneapolis: Fortress, 1996), p. 66, is referring to Jews in Rome, but it is equally apt of Christians.

Tacitus, *Ann.* 15.44.5-6, but Tacitus, while clearly accepting the charge of practicing a *superstitio,* rejects the charge of them being incendiaries; Suetonius, *Ner.* 16.2, says Christians were guilty of a superstition, and in chapter 38 suggests Nero started the fire). Being hauled before authorities, as discussed in Mark 13, would surely have been seen as a real possibility in Mark's day. When one takes the trouble to consider the list of prominent Roman or Greco-Roman writers who expressed strong feelings of revulsion toward Judaism or any of its offshoots that would be seen as a *superstitio,* a list which includes Cicero, Tacitus, Martial, Juvenal, Ovid, Quintilian, Seneca, and even someone like Plutarch, it becomes apparent what a widespread feeling this was in Roman culture.

Because they would not participate in public games, in public sacrifices, or willingly in the military, and because they steadfastly maintained a monotheistic approach to religion, Jews and Christians in Rome were seen as not merely antisocial and unfriendly but in fact as *atheoi* in various cases. "In summary, it is fair to say that the prevailing attitudes among the gentiles of Rome to Jews and Judaism, while no doubt mixed, was often negative. . . . Nor is it likely that all Romans overlooked the political and military problems associated with the Jews of Palestine in the development of their opinions about Jews in Rome."[105] It is this dark and dangerous context in which Mark wrote his Gospel to Roman Christians.[106]

Finally, can we say anything about the ethnic makeup of Mark's audience in Rome?[107] It would appear that, at the end of the 40s, Jewish Christians had to leave Rome for a period of time.[108] By the late 50s, when Paul writes to Rome, it appears the audience is mixed, but Gentiles appear to be dominant (cf. Rom. 11 and 16). If we move forward another decade and examine Mark's Gospel, we find him having to explain not only Aramaic words but also Jewish customs. This surely suggests that he assumes the majority of his audience is Gentile Christians. These Christians were facing not merely marginalization in their own culture but possibly even execution. Mark must explain to them the way of the cross that Jesus took, and the way the first disciples failed to follow his ex-

---

105. Nanos, pp. 67-68.

106. See the summary above, pp. 27-28, on the revolving door of emperors at the end of the 60s.

107. Perhaps one further small pointer that Mark is writing to Rome is the possible connection between Rom. 16:13 and Mark 15:21. The former text mentions one Rufus and his mother in Rome, whom Paul greets. The latter refers to Simon of Cyrene having two sons, Alexander and Rufus. Now the question is: Why mention the sons at all? Presumably because they are known to Mark's audience, and if this is the same Rufus as mentioned in Rom. 16, then there is a small confirmation that Mark's audience is in Rome.

108. See my discussion in my *Acts of the Apostles* on Acts 18, and the excursus on Claudius.

ample. The message seems clear — follow the example of Jesus and avoid the mistakes of the first disciples.[109]

The Structure of Mark's Gospel

It is possible to analyze both the micro- as well as the macrostructures of Mark's Gospel. A good example of the former would be the chiasm we seem to have in the controversy stories of Mark 2:1–3:6. J. Dewey outlines the pattern as follows:

A	2:1-12	the healing of the paralytic
B	2:13-17	the calling of Levi/eating with sinners
C	2:18-22	sayings on fasting, and on old and new
B′	2:23-27	plucking grain on the Sabbath
A′	3:1-6	healing on the Sabbath.[110]

Thus the unit is framed by healing stories, has two units of controversy involving eating, and then provides as a centerpiece a rationale for the behavior of Jesus and his disciples.

Another sort of structuring device found regularly in Mark's Gospel is the so-called sandwich technique, or intercalation — the weaving together of two stories by splitting the first story into two parts to serve as a frame around the second story. At least seven examples of this are widely accepted by scholars: (1) the Beelzebul controversy, surrounded by the confrontation between Jesus and his family (3:20-21, 22-30, 31-35); (2) the raising of Jairus's daughter as a frame around the healing of the woman with the issue of blood (5:21-24, 25-34, 35-43); (3) the sending out and return of the Twelve, in the midst of which one hears about Herod's banquet (6:7-13, 14-29, 30-44); (4) the fig tree incident surrounding the temple action of Jesus (11:12-14, 15-19, 20-25); (5) Jesus' anointing for death within the plotting against him (14:1-2, 3-9, 10-11); (6) the denials of Peter surrounding the trial of Jesus (14:53-65, 66-72; 15:1-15);

---

109. On Roman Christianity see P. Lampe, *Die stadtromischen Christen in den ersten beiden Jahrhunderten,* 2nd ed. (Tübingen: Mohr, 1988). A case can be made for Mark being as late as A.D. 71 and dealing with the problems in the aftermath not only of failed discipleship under Nero, but actual betrayals of some Christians by others. One also can only imagine the effect on Jewish Christians as well as non-Christian Jews when they saw the temple treasury items from Jerusalem marching past in Titus's triumph in the summer of 71. See Van Iersel, pp. 51-52.

110. J. Dewey, "The Literary Structure of the Controversy Stories in Mark 2.1–3.6," in *The Interpretation of Mark,* ed. W. R. Telford, pp. 141-51.

(7) the mock coronation of Jesus within the trial and execution (15:6-15, 16-20, 21-32).[111] The purpose of this technique in each case seems to be to encourage the reader to read the two stories in light of each other, with the one interpreting the other. This is most obvious in the fig tree and temple episode. Just because Mark's Greek is not sophisticated does not mean he does not have some literary skills in the arrangement of his material.

A further device that Mark uses is sometimes called doublets. Thus we have two feeding narratives (of the five thousand and of the four thousand) and two misunderstandings on the Sea of Galilee as well. These stories alternate (feeding of the five thousand in 6:30-44; sea tale in 6:45-52; feeding of the four thousand in 8:1-9; sea tale in 8:10, 14-21). There are also two major blocks of teaching material, one during Jesus' Galilean ministry (Mark 4), one during his teaching in Jerusalem during his last week of life (Mark 13). These doublings highlight the denseness of the disciples, who have not learned from previous occasions, and thus double their culpability.

Thus far we have referred only to the microstructures in Mark, about which a good deal more could be said, but our concern at this point must be for the macrostructure of the Gospel and what it tells us. Mark's Gospel is loaded with questions, both rhetorical and real, some of which go unanswered (cf. 1:27; 2:7; 4:41; 14:4; 16:3). Fowler counts some 114 in the Gospel, and posits that 77 go unanswered, or are rhetorical.[112] But not surprisingly in a biography, the big question the book raises and attempts to answer is, Who is Jesus?

Thus I would suggest that the structure of Mark's Gospel divides rather neatly into several parts. The first part emphasizes the raising of questions about Jesus, such as the following:

Mark's Questions

1:27	What is this? A new teaching with authority?	Crowd
2:7	Why does this fellow speak this way?	
	Who can forgive sins but God?	Scribes
2:16	Why does he eat with sinners?	Scribes
2:24	Why are they doing what is not lawful?	Pharisees
4:41	Who, then, is this, that even wind and water obey him?	Disciples
6:2	Where did this man get this wisdom?	Hometown folks
7:5	Why do your disciples not live by tradition?	Pharisees

---

111. See Fowler, pp. 143-44.
112. Fowler, p. 132 n. 8.

In Mark's outline he has structured his Gospel so that once the *who* question is answered, Jesus is able to reveal what his mission is. All the questions cited above are ultimately ways of questioning Jesus and trying to figure out who he is. They lead to the answering of the major question, Who is Jesus? at 8:27-30. This is a climax in the narrative and a major turning point in the story. Only after this identification do we have the explication of what Jesus' real mission is, and this point is reiterated three times in the space of three chapters — 8:31, 9:31, 10:32-34. The essence of these mission statements is that the Son of Man must suffer and be rejected, and on the third day rise. Thus we may present Mark's outline as follows:

The questions — Who and why? — 1–8:27
The who *question answered* — Peter's confession of faith: Jesus is the Christ — 8:27-30
What is the mission? — A mission of suffering — 8:31, 9:31, 10:32
Mission accomplished — The passion narrative — 11–16

This simple outline, which does justice not only to the plethora of questions raised in Mark but also to the strong stress on suffering and the space given to the passion narrative, has a few implications worth fleshing out.[113] Firstly, it supports the theory that we are dealing with a biography which has as its most basic question not ecclesiological struggles in Mark's church, nor even matters of Christian discipleship (though that is indeed an important secondary theme in this Gospel), but rather the big question: Who is Jesus? This in turn means that Mark's major concern in this Gospel is indeed theological or, better said, christological.[114] Mark seems to believe that only by first answering the christological question correctly can one truly understand why Jesus had to

---

113. Much more complicated narratival analyses have been offered by R. Zwick, *Montage im Markusevangelium. Studien zur narrativen Organisation der altesten Jesuserzahlung* (Stuttgart: Katholisches Bibelwerk GmBH, 1989).

114. Note Gundry, pp. 1045-49, who shows ably the problems with topographical or even most topical outlines of Mark's Gospel. Notice, for example, B. Standaert's outline in *L'Evangile selon Marc*, 2nd ed. (Bruges: Cerf, 1984), 1:14–6:13; 6:14–10:52; 11:1-15:47, which fails to come to grips with the climactic nature of the revelation at Caesarea Philippi. Better is that of Hooker, pp. 27-29, which does see 8:27-30 as a crucial juncture in the text, though she places it at the beginning of the fifth segment of a text divided as follows: (1) Prologue, 1:1-13; (2) Success and Opposition in Galilee, 1:14–3:6; (3) Parables and Miracles, 3:7–6:6; (4) Hard Hearts and Lack of Faith, 6:6b–8:21; (5) The Way of the Cross, 8:27–10:52; (6) The King Comes to Jerusalem, 11:1–13:37; (7) The Story of the Passion, 14:1–15:47; (8) The Epilogue: The Resurrection, 16:1-8. I am not happy with the notion that we take Mark 16 as something of an afterthought or postlude. There is a somewhat similar outline of the first half of Mark in Guelich, pp. vi-vii.

die as he did, or understand how his death should be evaluated positively. It is no accident that scholars have seen as perhaps the major motif of this Gospel the messianic secret. We must in a moment evaluate W. Wrede's theory at some length in the context of a larger discussion of Mark's Christology, but first, one other structural note needs to be made.

C. Myers has made a compelling case for seeing three pillar stories as anchoring Mark's account, each portrayed in an apocalyptic light.[115] These three stories are found at the beginning, middle, and end of the account involving Jesus' baptism, transfiguration, and death. Myers presents the parallels in this material as follows:

Baptism	Transfiguration	Crucifixion
Heavens rent	Garments turn white	Sanctuary veil rent
Dove descends	Cloud descends	Darkness spreads
Voice from heaven	Voice from cloud	Jesus' great voice
"You are my beloved Son"	"This is my Son, the Beloved"	"Truly, this man was a/the Son of God"
John the Baptist as Elijah	Jesus appears with Elijah	"Is he calling Elijah?"

These three moments are meant to focus the reader's attention on the identity of Jesus, and thus they strengthen the biographical portrayal of the author. Not all the stories in Mark have such a cast, which suggests that Mark wants to make clear that revelation breaks through the darkness only periodically. But these three moments are indeed the high revelatory ones in the account offered in support of the thesis statement in 1:1, and they stress that the King who really had the divine imprimatur was none other than Jesus, God's only Son. In short, this Gospel offers up a potentially politically dangerous thesis, especially in times when the emperorship kept changing hands.[116]

---

115. Myers, pp. 390-91.

116. I distinguish here between apocalyptic moments of revelation from above and disclosure moments in the narrative. One would have to include for example the Caesarea Philippi story and the climax of the Jewish trial as disclosure moments, along with the apocalyptic revelatory moments as key junctures.

Mark's Christology, the Messianic Secret, and Mark's Ending

In recent years the christological interpretation[117] of what most scholars believe is the earliest of the canonical Gospels has been bedeviled by both old and new factors.[118] Certainly one of the most enduring theories used to explain what we find in Mark's Gospel is W. Wrede's messianic secret theory. Another factor which has loomed larger and larger is of more recent vintage: the theory that the original ending of Mark's Gospel is 16:8, in spite of the various attempts by later scribes to add other endings, attempts we usually find in brackets or in the margins of modern translations designated as 16:9-20. It may not be immediately obvious why this discussion impinges on the subject of Christology until it is realized that if the Gospel ended at 16:8, it did not record any resurrection appearances of Jesus. This raises the question of how Mark understood what happened to Christ after his death and what its importance was for the good news about Jesus Christ, which 1:1 says he is offering to his audience.

Let us consider first the messianic secret theory, which continues to haunt the discussion of Christology in this Gospel.[119] It will be remembered that W. Wrede's theory was that Jesus' ministry was nonmessianic and that Mark or perhaps his source created the messianic secret motif to cover up or smooth over this embarrassing fact for his church audience, who believed Jesus was the Christ. There are, however, some severe problems with this theory, not least of which is that all the canonical Gospels and indeed all the NT documents suggest that Jesus did leave a messianic impression on his audiences and that the earliest Christians believed in and elaborated on this significance.

There are also problems that arise just from a close analysis of Mark. For one thing, there is no unified messianic secret motif in Mark. By this I mean that the secrecy motif does not all have to do with Christology. In 4:10-12 the secret has to do with God's dominion, and in 5:43 it has to do with miracles. In 1:24 it does have to do with Jesus as the Messiah, but in 3:11 it has to do with Jesus as God's Son. It was also always awkward for Wrede's theory that in 10:46ff. Jesus was clearly called by a Davidic royal label (Son of David) and Jesus is not

---

117. On the theology of Mark, including his Christology, see now W. R. Telford, *The Theology of the Gospel of Mark* (Cambridge: Cambridge University Press, 1999).

118. This portion of this introduction can be found in a fuller and somewhat different form in my work *The Many Faces of the Christ* (New York: Crossroad, 1998). See H. C. Kee, "Christology in Mark's Gospel," in *Judaisms and Their Messiahs*, ed. J. Neusner et al. (Cambridge: Cambridge University Press, 1987), pp. 187-208. For a rather compelling argument for Markan priority based on a study comparing Mark's Christology to that of the other Synoptics, see Head, *Christology and the Synoptic Problem*.

119. Notice how the issue still receives significant play and the theory is given fresh life by the title and the substance of books like *The Messianic Secret*, ed. C. Tuckett (Philadelphia: Fortress, 1983).

the one who silences the one calling him by this title. There is in fact a tension in this Gospel between secrecy and openness, and both tendencies must be taken into account.[120]

It was always the heart of Wrede's case that this motif could be seen in the exorcism stories in Mark. But even in these stories (cf. 5:1-20; 7:24-30; 9:14-29) the command to silence is not always found. J. D. G. Dunn, in fact, turns the tables on Wrede's argument by noting a publicity theme in the exorcism story in Mark 5 (see vv. 19-20, where the former demoniac is told to go and tell what the Lord has done for him). It is then difficult to argue that either Mark or his source consistently imposed a secrecy motif on these exorcism stories.[121] Furthermore, there is also a publicity theme in some of the healing stories (2:12; 3:3ff.), which differs from some stories where a privacy motif is brought to the fore in order to show Jesus' compassion and his attempt to protect a family from unnecessary attention (5:43).

There is also the more puzzling issue of why Mark records the disobedience to Jesus' command to silence in 1:25-28, 43-45, and 7:36-37 if he was really trying to impose a messianic secrecy motif on his material. Are we to think Mark is simply a bad editor of his source material despite considerable evidence to the contrary?[122] It is better to conclude that he was not trying to impose a messianic secret motif on his source material, for neither the healing texts that call for privacy nor the kingdom secret material really fit under this conceptual umbrella and the publicity and disobedience motifs both move in the opposite direction. Then too, the fact that the disciples are taught in private probably has nothing to do with a messianic secret motif. On the one hand, some of these texts are about Jesus revealing the kingdom's secrets to his disciples, and some are about in-house teaching of the disciples about divorce and other nonchristological issues (cf. 10:10-12). There is furthermore the too often overlooked fact that Mark is deliberately casting his Gospel in an apocalyptic vein — it is a Gospel about incomprehension without disclosure moments when revelation breaks through. It is about secrets that are revealed, but only in certain contexts and to certain persons. This motif, I believe, is in fact grounded in Jesus' own self-presentation as revealed indirectly by his chosen form of discourse and actions.[123]

Jesus' main form of public discourse was wisdom speech in the form of aphorisms, parables, riddles, and the like.[124] There is an inherent veiledness

---

120. See my discussion in *The Christology of Jesus* (Philadelphia: Fortress, 1990), pp. 261-67.

121. See Dunn, "The Messianic Secret in Mark," in *The Messianic Secret*, pp. 116-31.

122. See above the discussion about the micro- and macrostructures of Mark's Gospel.

123. On which see now my *Jesus the Seer: The Progress of Prophecy* (Peabody, Mass.: Hendrickson, 1999).

124. See pp. 13-15 above.

or indirectness to this form of metaphorical speech, and if Jesus spoke in this fashion about the coming of the kingdom, he could just as well have done so about the coming of the King. It is still easier to believe that because of the volatility of Jesus' environment, he might silence or reject certain kinds of acclamations of him to prevent misunderstanding without this implying that he had no messianic self-understanding.[125] That Jesus rejected the notion of being a political pretender does not imply that he rejected all messianic ideas when applied to himself. I thus must conclude that something else is going on in Mark's Gospel, and it does not involve an attempt to veil Jesus' nonmessianic ministry, nor to reconcile two dueling Christologies, one suggesting that Jesus became Messiah at the resurrection (something the Markan outline gives no hint of — notice the lack of titles at 16:6) and another that he was Messiah all during his ministry.

The second misleading discussion has to do with where Mark's Gospel originally ended. Some scholars have suggested that 16:8 is a perfectly appropriate ending in a Gospel that presents a semiveiled and enigmatic portrait of Jesus, and that this ending is quite possible grammatically, even if 16:8 seems abrupt to moderns who tend to expect happy endings with all loose ends neatly tied up. This sort of reasoning in turn sometimes leads to the conclusion that Mark did not see the recording of the resurrection appearances in this Gospel as crucial to the Christian faith of his audience in Jesus as Son and Christ (either they already knew about them, or they simply weren't critical in Mark's view) or that Mark thought they were not crucial to understanding or revealing Jesus' identity. There are at least four major problems with this whole line of reasoning.

Firstly, Mark's Gospel is an ancient biography. A clue to his purposes is found in examining the structure of the Gospel and its narrative flow. What is of paramount importance to Mark is shown by the very first verse of the book, where we are told that the book will be about the beginning of the good news about Jesus Christ, the Son of God. This way of announcing the subject matter of the book at the very beginning strongly suggests that we are meant to see this book as falling into the genre of ancient biographies which focused on presenting a vivid portrait through the chronicling of words and deeds of some great ancient person — in this case Jesus.[126] This in turn means that the *who* question was very important for Mark. The main character's personality and identity must be revealed in one way or another, and we would look for this to be the case especially at key or climactic junctures in the story. The story in the first half of the Gospel especially, but afterwards as well, is structured around certain key christological moments. But if 16:8 is the ending of the Gospel,

125. See pp. 49-52 below.
126. See Burridge, *What Are the Gospels?*

where is the final key christological moment where the central character one final time appears on the stage confirming the main theme of the work?

There was indeed a concern in such biographical works, especially those as encomiastic as the Gospels, to be sure the book ends on a positive note. Consider several examples from some of Mark's near contemporaries. Plutarch writes a biography of Julius Caesar, who, like Jesus, died an untimely and unjust death. At its conclusion Plutarch doesn't merely stop with the death of Caesar or the mourning of his friends. No, he must tell what happened to those who killed Caesar in order to show that Caesar had been in the right, and that the gods avenged his wrongful death. He must, in short, tie up the loose ends and not leave his audience wondering — was the death of Caesar after all just? What was the sequel, and how was he vindicated? Plutarch says this:

> However the great guardian genius of the man [Caesar], whose help he had enjoyed throughout life, followed upon him even after death as an avenger of his murder, driving and tracking down his slayers over every land and sea until not one of them was left, but even those who in any way soever either put a hand to the deed or took part in the plot were punished. Among the events of human ordering, the most amazing was that which befell Cassius; for after his defeat at Philippi he slew himself with that very dagger which he had used against Caesar; and among the events of divine ordering, there was a great comet, which showed itself in great splendor for seven nights after Caesar's murdering, and then disappeared; also the obscuring of the sun's rays occurred. (*Caes.* 69.2-5)

The account goes on briefly beyond this point, but this excerpt is enough to show that Plutarch as a biographer was very concerned to tie up loose ends, especially when some divine vindication was required. Caesar not only had to be shown to be in the right, it had to be shown that the gods had vindicated him with visible signs, appearances in the heavens. It is surely likely that Mark would have known that his own biographical work would have been incomplete if he did not provide evidence of vindication of Jesus by God. One may say that the empty tomb and the proclamation in part do that. But for an ancient, this was surely not enough, as is proved by the reaction of the women in 16:7-8! An empty tomb could be explained in a variety of ways, and few of them are positive. As for the messenger at the tomb, if he is the same young man seen earlier running away, some would doubt he was a credible witness.[127]

Consider now the end, save for a couple of postscripts, of Josephus's autobiography. Having recounted his life, presenting it in the most favorable light possible, Josephus reveals himself as a man unjustly accused of many things but finally vindicated by the emperor and by God. When one of the Jewish zealots

---

127. See above on the young man.

was brought to Rome in chains and accused Josephus of funding his operation, Josephus says: "Undeceived by this mendacious statement, Vespasian condemned him to death, and he was delivered over to execution. Subsequently, numerous accusations against me were fabricated by people who envied me my good fortune; but by the providence of God I came safely through all. Vespasian also presented me with a considerable tract of land in Judaea" (*The Life* 425-26). Once again the biographer feels the need, since there have been some apparent injustices, to show how all turned out well in the end, and that God was on his side as well as the emperor. Vindication not only came, it had its public face, with a gift of land to Josephus. Again we see the concerns of the ancient biographer to show how justice was done in the end and all turned out well.

Tacitus, as a writer of histories and biographies, is well known to have been very levelheaded, careful, even a bit cynical and satirical. One would not expect from him epideictic rhetoric or verbal hyperbole unless he felt that the conventions of the work he was writing called for such. In this light, consider what he has to say about Agricola, his father-in-law. He finishes the narrative with regret that he and Agricola's daughter could not have been at his bedside when he passed away. He then adds, "if there is any habitation for the spirits of the just; if, as wise men will have it, the soul that is great perishes not with the body, may you then rest in peace. . . . Whatever we have loved in Agricola, whatever we have admired, abides, and will abide, in the hearts of human beings, in the procession of the ages, by the records of history. Many of the ancients will be engulfed by forgetfulness as neither fame nor name were theirs. Agricola, whose story here is told, will outlive death, to be our children's heritage" (*Agr.* 46).

This is just the sort of flourish that we do not find if Mark's Gospel ends at 16:8. Indeed, it is left very much in question if Jesus' words and deeds would be remembered. It is left in doubt if the message of Easter would even be communicated to Peter and the other disciples. It is not sufficient to say that the audience knew how things turned out, so Mark did not need to abide by the conventions of ancient biographies and provide a suitable ending to the work, showing not only that Jesus was vindicated by God but that Jesus' memory would be carried forward. Judged by ancient biographical standards, 16:8 does not provide a suitable ending, and likely would not have been seen as such by Mark's audience, not least because Christianity was a missionary religion and there was always the chance that its documents or their contents would be shared with nonbelievers.

The appropriateness of modern abrupt endings to novels should not lead us to think that such an approach was equally appropriate in the case of ancient biographies. Anyone who has read Plutarch's *Lives* or other ancient biographical literature knows that it was widely believed that how a person's life ended revealed a person's true character. It must be doubted that the final impression Mark wanted to leave in readers' minds about the Jesus he believed in as Son of

God and Christ was his cry "My God, my God, why have you forsaken me?" or that the final impression of the disciples was that they were cowards, for they are depicted as either dispersed and in hiding (having betrayed, denied, or deserted Jesus — 14:50) or, in the case of the women, in fright and in flight and silent (16:8). Silence was not golden after Good Friday, as is made very clear in 16:6, and Mark's failure to flesh out what this latter text points to would have been seen as a significant omission by ancient readers of biography.

Though there is certainly some evidence for a Greek sentence or even a paragraph ending with εφοβουντο γαρ ("For they were afraid . . ."), I know of no evidence whatsoever for this being an appropriate ending for a whole document of the biographical sort that we have in Mark's Gospel.[128] Mark knew very well that there was a better way to conclude a Greek sentence that spoke of a group of persons being afraid that did not leave a *gar* dangling at the end (see 5:15; cf. 6:50), even if one wanted to use a *gar* phrase about fear to end a sentence (cf. 9:6 — εκφοβοι γαρ εγενοντο).[129]

There is also the problem of the verb tenses and structure of 16:8. The two key verbs are in the imperfect, and we have two *gar* clauses here, not one. The structure suggests that because the women were possessed with fear and trembling, they fled from the tomb, and because they were afraid, they said nothing to anyone. Both the fleeing and speaking are aorist verbs indicating a particular and punctiliar action motivated in each case by fear. The text implies that the fleeing and silence went on only for a specific period of time, namely, for the period while the women were afraid. This combination of verbs seems to set up an expectation for a sequel when the women are no longer scared to death and no longer fleeing and silent, a sequel in which they presumably are finally obedient to the angelic command. It is hard to believe that Mark wanted to leave his audience with a picture of the women's disobedience and denseness *after* Easter, whatever may have been appropriate before Easter.

If this Gospel is meant to help meet the need to proclaim the good news about Jesus the Son of God to all the Gentile nations, this ending is hardly in keeping with that aim. Mark 16:8 is not good news. As Kermode at one point says, such an ending is "either intolerably clumsy; or it is incredibly subtle."[130]

---

128. Note that F. Kermode, *The Genesis of Secrecy* (Cambridge: Harvard University Press, 1979), p. 66, likewise found no such evidence after a search.

129. I thus must disagree with my old mentor A. T. Lincoln, "The Promise and the Failure: Mark 16.7, 8," *JBL* 108 (1989): 283-300. The example from Gen. 18:15 (LXX) certainly shows that a sentence can end in this fashion, but of course the narrative goes on, and we are not in any case dealing with an ancient biography in Genesis. The examples from the philosophical treatises (Plato, *Prt.* 328C; and Musonius Rufus, *Twelfth Tractate;* Plotinus, *Enn.* 5.5) are also quite beyond the point. A philosophical discourse is not a biographical narrative, and in any case the discourses with others continue beyond the point in question.

130. Kermode, p. 68.

Modern literary critics have opted for the latter view, but it hardly comports with the rest of the Gospel where Mark is about as subtle as a sledgehammer. It must be remembered that this is the Gospel which gives us the Jesus who says "Why do you call me good? No one is good but God alone." It is the Gospel in which Peter, the greatest apostle, is called Satan by Jesus! It is the Gospel that says Jesus' family thought he was out of his mind (3:21)! It is the Gospel where pigs are invaded by demons and rush into the sea! It is the Gospel where John the Baptist's head is presented to Herod on a silver platter! It is the Gospel where in essence Jesus calls the Syrophoenician woman a bitch! This Gospel is many things — stark, powerful, dramatic, disturbing, confrontational, para-doxical, even ironic. Subtle, however, is not one of the terms that immediately comes to mind. I thus must conclude that 16:8 is not the original ending of Mark's Gospel, and that it does not reveal the christological cards Mark was playing with all along.[131]

Furthermore, it is clear enough from the textual history of this Gospel that more than one early Christian in the second century (the author of the long ending, and also the author of the so-called Freer logion) did not feel that 16:8 properly brought the Gospel to an adequate closure.[132] This fact must be taken into account, for it is far more likely that the earliest readers would un-derstand the literary conventions of documents such as Mark's Gospel than we do at almost two thousand years' remove, and that they would know when a narrative did not have an appropriate closure.

The next point has to do with the Markan outline itself. This Gospel is not just interested in silence, but also in key moments of disclosure or revela-tion in regard to Jesus' identity, as we have already pointed out. In particular, 14:28 and 16:6-7 both set up an expectation in the reader's or hearer's mind that there will be at least one appearance account at the end of the Gospel, an appearance in Galilee to Peter and the others in the inner circle of disciples. Then too, the disclosure accounts which are carefully placed at the beginning (1:9-11), in the middle (8:27-30; 9:2-8), and toward the end of the book (14:61-62) set up an anticipation in the reader that the book will close with a final cli-

---

131. In other words, I think Mark's ending is lost, probably due to the fact that Mat-thew's Gospel, a much fuller and complete Gospel, became the church's favorite by or before the second century, and since it contained 95 percent or more of Mark (and half of that is a verbatim copy of Mark), Mark's Gospel was quickly eclipsed and fell into disuse in most cir-cles. It is quite easy to see how the original ending could be lost, because ancient documents tended to be left with the end edge exposed to the elements. Even in ancient times people were lazy about rewinding things. Perhaps only one vertical column of the original docu-ment was lost, and perhaps we may see the substance of what it looked like in Matt. 28:9-10, 16-20.

132. See below, pp. 412-19 of the commentary, on Mark 16:8.

mactic disclosure of Jesus' identity to the very disciples that we are told in 14:28 and 16:6-7 will receive such a disclosure.

It is clear enough that after 14:62, keeping the messianic secret is no longer the order of the day, not even in a hostile public setting. There are in fact at least five christological disclosure moments in the narrative: (1) at the baptism at 1:9-11, but this is a private and visionary disclosure to Jesus himself that he is God's beloved Son; (2) at Caesarea Philippi at 8:27-30, where a disciple reveals and learns something about Christ's identity; (3) at 9:2-8, where the inner circle of three disciples receives a visionary disclosure of Jesus' identity as the beloved Son; (4) at 14:61-62, where Jesus is finally asked publicly and in point-blank fashion by the Jewish authorities whether he is the Christ, to which he responds with a rhetorical question but immediately qualifies his remarks by referring to his coming tasks as Son of Man, just as he did for the disciples in Mark 8; (5) the revelation of Jesus' identity on the cross, proclaimed by a Gentile centurion.[133] In short, Mark has revealed not only that Jesus' preferred self-designation was Son of Man, but that the church's belief in his being the Christ and Son of God, the two titles mentioned in 1:1, is vindicated by climactic christological disclosure moments in the story.

A failure to recognize the narrative flow of the Markan outline and the importance of the climactic christological disclosure moments has sometimes led to various skewed readings of Mark's purposes, including the theory that this Gospel presents a polemic against the earliest disciples.[134] To the contrary, the point is that no one could understand Jesus, not even the disciples, unless the secret of his identity and mission was revealed to them (cf. 4:10-12; 9:2-8 on the importance of disclosure or revelation even to the disciples). Thus we have a right to expect one final revelatory moment at the end of the Gospel where Jesus' true identity would be made known to the disciples. In short, we would expect the recounting of at least one or two appearances of the risen Jesus to the disciples.

What then happened to Mark's original ending? Has it been totally lost to us? Let us focus on the first question first. It is of course possible, as M. Casey has recently suggested, that Mark's Gospel is unfinished.[135] This possibility must be taken seriously. But if this is the case, how did it come to have a rather wide circulation and use in the early church? Someone obviously saw the docu-

---

133. I would distinguish between the epiphanic apocalyptic moments, which are three in number, and the christological disclosure moments which include the former, and add two more stories that basically lack apocalyptic coloring.

134. See, e.g., T. H. Weeden, *Mark: Traditions in Conflict* (Philadelphia: Fortress, 1971), and the response by J. Kingsbury, *Conflict in Mark: Jesus, Authorities, Disciples* (Minneapolis: Fortress, 1989).

135. See Casey, p. 135. Casey urges this on the grounds of Mark's roughness, for various of Mark's translations from his Aramaic sources are left in a rough and unrevised state.

ment as suitable for circulation and widespread use. A second possibility is that what we have really is "the beginning of the Gospel of Jesus" and that the author intended, much like Luke, to offer a second volume to talk about the continuation of the Gospel. If this is the case, for whatever reason the author apparently did not accomplish his aim, or the second volume was completely lost. This last conjecture really doesn't much help us with 16:8, for we can see from the ending of Luke's Gospel and the beginning of Acts that we should expect the first volume to be properly rounded off and the second volume to involve a brief recapitulation of that ending before carrying on with subsequent events. This is all the more the case if Mark was writing a biography in the first volume.

Let us then consider briefly whether and how Mark's ending could have come to be lost. If one studies carefully the nature and use of ancient scrolls,[136] one discovers that the ancients were no more careful in the way they treated documents than we are with modern videotapes. A moderately long scroll like Mark's Gospel, once read, would often not be rewound. This is one reason why the identifying scroll tags were placed on the end of the roll. It follows from this that the outermost edge that was exposed to the most wear and tear would be the ending of the document. Thus we need not imagine, as Austin Farrer once apparently facetiously suggested, that the rats nibbled the ending of Mark's Gospel.[137] Simple wear and tear may have accomplished the job. When Mark began to be copied frequently, presumably in the second century when there began to be interest in the fourfold collection,[138] the version being copied was the truncated version, not the version known much earlier to the author of Matthew.

It is thus not difficult to believe that Mark's original ending might well have been lost, especially *after* the vast majority of Mark, including its original ending, had been copied into Matthew's Gospel and the latter quickly became the most popular and widely circulated Gospel. It would be easy to assume, in an age when papyri were not cheap and copying of documents was a laborious and costly process, that Mark's Gospel was expendable since over 95 percent was included in Matthew's.

This leads to a plausible conjecture. Mark's ending is lost,[139] but in fact we find traces of it in Matthew. Clearly enough, Matthew is copying Mark at Matt. 28:8 and making his usual effort to ameliorate the harshness of Mark's presen-

---

136. Here I quite agree with H. Y. Gamble, in his recent helpful study *Books and Readers in the Early Church* (New Haven: Yale University Press, 1995), pp. 56-57, that it is unlikely, though not impossible, that Mark was first written on a codex and was never in scroll form. The codex form became necessary when two or more Gospels needed to be circulated together.

137. A. Farrer, *A Study in St. Mark* (London: Macmillan, 1951).

138. See above.

139. At least until we begin to find considerably earlier copies of this Gospel which may correct this problem.

tation. I would suggest that what follows this in Matt. 28:9-10 and in 28:16-18 is the redaction of what Matthew found in his Markan source. There was then a brief account of an appearance to the women, followed by another brief account of the promised appearance of Jesus in Galilee to the Eleven. Notice the Markan theme of doubt or incomprehension at Matt. 28:17, but of course Matthew has added material of his own both at 28:11-15 and probably also in 28:19-20. Notice that Luke knows nothing of this Markan ending, but rather supplies other traditions in Luke 24.[140]

The original ending of Mark must have been lost at a very early date. If this is even remotely close to correct, it then follows that we should not build vast theological and literary castles on the uncertain foundation that 16:8 *must have been* Mark's original intended ending. It will come as no surprise, then, that Mark's Christology will look a bit different to those who think Mark did end at 16:8, compared to those who think it did not. Indeed, Mark's approach to discipleship will also appear different to those who think 16:8 is an ending, compared to those who do not.

The Contours of Mark's Christology

There was a time earlier in this century when many scholars saw Mark as almost pure unvarnished narrative, with little theological profundity or depth. It is safe to say that those days are now long gone. Wherever Mark got his Gospel material, he has shaped it in such a way as to present a very striking portrait of Jesus as Christ, as Son of God and as Son of Man — the man destined to die, the beloved Son destined to save and be raised from the grave. This last point, which is clearly announced at 16:6 and coupled with the pointing out of the empty tomb, makes evident that Mark is concerned to proclaim the Easter message, but in a way that is not open to misunderstanding.[141] In particular, Mark is concerned that royal titles such as Christ or Son of God or King are not misinterpreted to suggest that Jesus was some sort of political figure and aspirant.[142]

---

140. This suggests that Luke may well have been writing at a later time than the author of Matthew.

141. See the discussion in R. Schnackenburg, *Jesus in the Gospels* (Louisville: Westminster/John Knox, 1995), pp. 17-73.

142. But Mark does wish us to see Christ as divine. See now E. Boring's helpful recent study "Markan Christology: God-Language for Jesus?" *NTS* 45 (1999): 451-71, who concludes: "The explicit use of God-language for Jesus by later NT authors and the classical creeds is in continuity with the Christology already present in Mark. . . . John, Nicea, and Chalcedon understood and developed Mark's Christology in a more profound sense than was done by either Matthew or Luke."

To fully understand Mark's use of titles like Christ, Son of God, King, and Son of Man, it is crucial to take into account the matter of point of view. As 1:1 indicates, Mark shares with his audience a Christian viewpoint about Jesus' character, but individuals within the narrative almost never (some scholars would say never) have this understanding, and even when, as in the case with Peter in Mark 8, some glimmering of comprehension breaks through, it immediately becomes clear that partial insight is still blended with partial misunderstanding requiring further correction. J. D. Kingsbury has made an excellent case that the theme of Jesus as Son of God is the red thread tying together the christological reflections of Mark in this Gospel, for the theme is announced at 1:1;[143] revealed privately to Jesus at baptism; known by demons and spirit beings; revealed to Peter, James, and John on the Mount of Transfiguration but not understood and disbelieved by Jesus' adversaries at his trial; and finally announced at Jesus' death by the centurion, a Gentile.[144]

A closer look at the way the "Son of God" phrase is used shows that in 1:11 the announcement reflects a combination of Ps. 2:7 and Isa. 42:1. What unites these allusions is the royal or kingly character and power of the one spoken about. This suggests that we should see Jesus' baptism as his enthronement by God as King, but in the Markan outline this is only revealed to Jesus himself at this point.[145]

If we compare this to what we find at Mark 9:2-9, we discover that while here Jesus is announced as God's Son to the disciples, they are told not to tell anyone until after the Son of Man rises from the dead, and clearly enough they don't understand this latter reference. Mark seems to be making clear that during the ministry of Jesus there was indeed a necessary and intentional veiling of Jesus' true identity until after Easter. Even the demons are silenced during the ministry when they call Jesus something like Son of God (1:25, 34; 3:12). The reason why is probably not disclosed before Mark 15, where Jesus is repeatedly called king. During the ministry there were certain kinds of messianic expectations that Jesus wanted nothing to do with, including particularly the more overtly political ones, and as things turned out this is seen by Mark as a wise move.

---

143. There is some textual uncertainty here since some manuscripts don't have the phrase "Son of God," but it is supported by a wide array of early and important manuscripts, including ℵ-A and B, and D, and is probably the original reading.

144. J. D. Kingsbury, *The Christology of Mark* (Philadelphia: Fortress, 1984).

145. It is not convincing to argue that the use of "Son of God" in this Gospel has no overtones of divinity because the term was used in the OT of God's chosen people as a whole (Exod. 4:22; Deut. 14:1; Hos. 11:1). This logic overlooks two important factors: (1) Jesus alone is being singled out at the baptismal and transfiguration scenes (and elsewhere) as God's unique Son in a way that echoes the material in the Psalms where the king is singled out in this fashion; (2) Jesus' disciples as a group are never called the Son of God in this Gospel.

With the command to silence, Jesus was free to continue to minister until such time as God, not popular expectations, led him up to Jerusalem to suffer as the Son of Man. Mark's Gospel is written with a knowledge of the volatile and dangerous potential of certain kinds of royal claims. Jesus is not to be publicly acknowledged as God's Son before he is lifted up on the cross; at and after that point it will be appropriate.[146] It is also right to note that the title Son of God is presented at the beginning of Mark's Gospel without definition, in order to allow the story to reveal its proper content and to critique misunderstandings of the use of the title.[147] "The title *Son of God* fulfills for Mark a summary view of the Jesus who is at work on earth, is equipped by God with the Spirit and power, yet goes his way obediently to the cross. In every realm of activity . . . the secret of the Son of God who is close to God is visible, although still veiled and incomprehensible to witnesses."[148]

The title Christ also occurs in 1:1 and crops up at crucial junctures, as we saw in our analysis of Mark's narrative structure. The first public announcement within the narrative of this title is of course at 8:27-30, but Mark stresses that on this occasion Jesus, while not rejecting the title, qualified it dramatically by speaking of the coming suffering of the Son of Man. The idea that the Christ would be immune to suffering is seen as a misunderstanding about what God's Anointed One would do and be. Indeed, the suggestion that the Christ must not suffer is seen as satanic and to be rebuked. Here in Mark 8, as in Mark 1, it must be noted how the various titles and their content flow into one another and must in the end be evaluated together for their overall impact.

"Son of Man" is the most frequently used title, and with one probable exception (2:10 — where it is apparently part of the author's aside) is found solely on Jesus' lips. There is also only one exception to this rule elsewhere in the Synoptics, so it seems clear enough that Mark is conveying an historical fact about Jesus' self-disclosure here. When we combine insights from 8:31 and parallels with what we learn from 14:61-62, we discover that the author is drawing on allusions and overtones from Dan. 7 (this is particularly clear in Mark 14) and that the roles assigned to the Son of Man in Dan. 7:13-14 are in fact royal roles — he will have dominion, glory, and kingship.

In other words, Mark does not see Son of Man terminology as an alternative to royal phrases being used of Jesus, but as another way of putting the point about Jesus' kingship with some new nuances and connotations. Jesus is a king all right, and Peter's confession is not to be rejected, but it must be qualified three times in 8:31, 9:31, and 10:32 to make clear that he is to be a suffering king, a Son of Man who must go up to Jerusalem and die. Notice too how the

---

146. See the discussion of P. J. Achtemeier, "Mark, Gospel of," in *ABD*, 4:551-53.
147. See Earl Richard, *Jesus: One and Many* (Wilmington, Del.: M. Glazier, 1988), p. 117.
148. Schnackenburg, p. 52.

allusion to Dan. 7 in Mark 14:62 is combined with an allusion to Ps. 110:1 — the Christ who is also the Son of Man will be first seated at the right hand of God before he comes on the clouds. "Thus Jesus' public confession in Mark points to the equivalence of the three titles used, Christ, Son of God, and Son of Man, with their one common element the reference to kingly power."[149]

This overall royal impression is only further confirmed by a text like Mark 10:46-52, where Jesus is publicly addressed as Son of David, and not Jesus but the disciples silence the man.[150] Also important in a text like 10:45 is that we see that the Son of Man theology includes both Jesus' humility during his ministry, coming to serve others, and his self-sacrifice, ultimately coming to present himself a ransom for many.[151]

Schnackenburg has urged that we see in 14:61-62 a summary or condensation of Markan Christology. Mark presents the two titles Son of God and Son of Man as coming together at this juncture with both being affirmed, but Son of Man being used to correct or further define what an affirmation of being the Son of God means.[152] "Jesus answers the high priest affirmatively, but at the same time his answer corrects the Jewish concept of Messiah: he is the one sitting at the right hand of God and the Son of Man coming on the clouds of heaven (14.62). Here the 'Son of God' appears in yet another light. He is the one exalted to God and the Son of Man coming again in power. The Son of God Christology is connected with Son of Man Christology."[153] However, as we shall point out in our discussion of 14:61-62, it is not completely clear that Jesus answers the priest affirmatively.[154]

While the conjunction of these two titles comes at the climax of Jesus' ministry as he makes his final public utterances, it is also illuminating to consider what we find at the beginning of the ministry as well. As is well known, Mark does not record the substance of Jesus' temptation by Satan in the wilderness, only the fact of it, and he alone mentions that Jesus was with the wild beasts (1:13). Mark also goes on to affirm that angels waited on him. This has suggested to Schnackenburg that Mark is portraying paradise restored with Jesus being an Adam who did not succumb to temptation and so humankind's place in the hierarchy of being is restored — ruling over the animals and served by the angels. This is a possibility, but Mark does not make much of the matter,

---

149. Achtemeier, p. 553.

150. I personally would not see Mark 12:25-37 as evidence that Mark thought Jesus denied that he was David's Son, but rather he is denying a false understanding of that sonship that considers the Messiah only David's human heir and not also someone much greater than David.

151. See Schnackenburg, pp. 58-59.

152. Schnackenburg, p. 39.

153. Schnackenburg, p. 52.

154. See pp. 383-86 below.

and in fact the text does not say that Jesus subdued or ruled over the animals while in the wilderness, but that he is simply with them.[155]

It should not be seen as puzzling that the title king does not appear until Mark 15. Our author has been carefully nuancing the christological discussion up to this point so that his audience would not misunderstand what was meant when Jesus is repeatedly called king at the end of his life.[156] We have a clear case of Markan irony here for, while the acclamation is true, it is equally clear that Pilate and others misunderstand what it really means when applied to Jesus. A crucified king would seem a contradiction in terms to the authorities, but not to Mark. Pilate asks Jesus point-blank if he is the king of the Jews (v. 2), and then uses the phrase again at vv. 9 and 12.

At 15:18 the title King occurs on the lips of the Praetorian Guard, and both here and already in vv. 9 and 12 we have a public announcement of Jesus as the king of the Jews which is set down in a sort of legal proclamation on the *titulus* or placard that was to go on Jesus' cross (15:26). It is in all these cases Gentiles who speak of Jesus this way, even though they are insincere. This is finally followed by what appears to be the climactic confession by a human being in this Gospel, again by a Gentile who sincerely recognizes Jesus in his noble death as Son of God in some sense (15:39). Before this juncture perhaps only Peter has been given this sort of insight that leads to a true confession, but notice that unlike Peter, the centurion is not silenced or rebuked. In this way Mark makes evident that it was not until after Jesus' death, and by precisely reflecting on that death, that Jesus was seen to be who he really was — Christ, Son of God, Son of Man, and even king of the Jews.

This is why even the disciples in the Markan story never quite get things completely right before Easter. This is also why it is unlikely that 16:8 was Mark's original intended ending. The post-Easter acclamation and even the empty tomb, if not also accompanied by post-Easter appearances, did not in Mark's view transform the disciples into true Christians, and Mark is writing to a Christian audience that would have needed confirmation that the original disciples, like Mark's audience themselves, had indeed been so transformed, not left out of the kingdom as those who feared and fled, or denied, deserted, or betrayed Jesus. This Gospel is not just about how the proclamation of Jesus as Christ and Son of God was the good news for Mark's disciples, but also about

---

155. But see Schnackenburg, pp. 48-49.

156. Richard, pp. 110-11, rightly points out that in Mark there are only two instances where "Son of Man" is used of Jesus as he acts in the present on earth, while the vast majority of instances have to do with the coming suffering of the Son of Man or his future return from heaven. This must count against the suggestion that the earliest form of the Son of Man sayings was noneschatological in character and was simply an oblique form of self-reference, or meant something like "a person in my position."

how it came to be good news for the first disciples as well. Mark's attempt at biography means that by and large he is happy with a narrative Christology that is revealed indirectly through the words and deeds of Jesus, but occasionally also in moments of divine disclosure.

It seems probable that Mark's Gospel, as the earliest Gospel, retains a key historical element from the actual ministry of Jesus, namely, that Jesus' self-disclosure came in an indirect manner in general, and involved hiddenness and yet revelation as well in places and only to certain persons. Occasionally the light partly dawned during the ministry, though rightly Mark suggests there were no full-fledged Christians before the death of Christ.

At the end of the day, there is something to be said for a messianic secret (or Sonship secret) being both Markan and historical. Jesus was an enigmatic and forceful figure, and Mark, probably more than any other Gospel writer, has given us the flavor of what it might have been like to encounter him in a world with a wide variety of hopes and dreams about redeemer figures. He did not wish to be defined by others, but rather to redefine the christological categories. Mark would also have us know that spiritual things are spiritually discerned — only by revelation can the Christ be truly comprehended, but once comprehended, he could be confessed with a variety of royal titles — Christ, Son of God, Son of Man, King, Son of David.

Mark on Discipleship

There are basically two camps of scholars when it comes to analyzing the portrayal of the disciples in Mark. The first says that in the early part of the Gospel the portrait is largely favorable, but in the second half they are increasingly portrayed as not comprehending and, in the end, as deserters. The second school of thought suggests that the portrait is, almost from the outset, unrelentingly negative and polemical. Much, however, depends on whether one insists that only the Twelve are portrayed as disciples in Mark. The response to this last suggestion must be no for three reasons: (1) The women are portrayed as disciples, particularly in Mark 14 (the anonymous anointer), 15:40-43 (they followed him in Galilee), and Mark 16 (having been last at the cross, they are first at the tomb). The only negative thing said about their discipleship is at 16:7-8, and as we have suggested, this is unlikely to be the end of Mark's tale. Basically, as the men become worse and worse examples of following Jesus, the women replace them as images of what disciples ought to do and be. (2) There are also isolated figures, such as Bar-Timaeus, who are likewise portrayed as being prepared to follow Jesus even to Jerusalem (10:46-52). (3) To be sure, the crowd is not portrayed as disciples or followers of Jesus, but a careful analysis of texts such as

4:10 suggests that Mark has in mind more than the Twelve when he uses the term μαθητης. Let us now consider several of the more influential treatments of this matter.

There is firstly the approach of T. J. Weeden that sees Mark as offering a deliberate polemic against the earliest disciples.[157] This view has been echoed by a variety of other scholars with some variation.[158] Yet the majority of scholars reject this severe assessment, and most suggest some variation on the theme that the "misunderstanding" motif has some pedagogical purpose. E. Best suggests, I think rightly, that the disciples to some extent act as a foil for Jesus.[159] But are we then to think of Jesus' family as also a foil to the portrayal of Jesus? They also come in for some heavy weather, especially in Mark 3. Some would take Mark's point to be a more pastoral one. His community is facing persecution. He wishes to warn of the dangers to keeping the faith that lurk ahead and to make the strong point that Jesus, and not the early disciples as they behaved at the end of Jesus' life, is the model of the way of the cross, the way of faithfulness to the end.[160] This is a plausible conclusion.

Perhaps the clearest attempt to do damage control on Mark's portrayal of the disciples is by J. Kingsbury.[161] He stresses that there are two sides to the portrayal of the disciples — commitment on the one hand and incomprehension on the other. Eventually, by the end of the story the latter leads to the abandonment of the former, but this does not vitiate the fact that the disciples are portrayed as having initially responded properly to the call to discipleship, and indeed are portrayed as successfully emulating Jesus' acts of healing and teaching to some degree. This is true enough, and to this point one may add the portrayal of people like Bar-Timaeus and, to some degree, the women, which serves as something of a counterbalance to the failure of the disciples known as the Twelve.[162]

Thus it is unlikely that we should see a polemic here against the disciples, but there is indeed a sharp criticism of their failures and incomprehension. Mark does not gild the lily when it comes to this matter, and the Twelve do, especially in the passion narrative, serve as a foil to Jesus and his faithfulness to the end. Even the three could not watch with him in the garden for one hour. He must hang

---

157. See, e.g., T. H. Weeden, "The Heresy That Necessitated Mark's Gospel," *ZNW* 59 (1968): 145-58.

158. Cf. W. H. Kelber, *Mark's Story of Jesus* (Philadelphia: Fortress, 1979); J. D. Crossan, "Mark and the Relatives of Jesus," *NovT* 15 (1973): 81-113; M. A. Tolbert, *Sowing the Gospel: Mark's World in Literary Historical Perspective* (Minneapolis: Fortress, 1989).

159. E. Best, *Disciples and Discipleship: Studies in the Gospel according to Mark* (Edinburgh: T. & T. Clark, 1986).

160. See E. Schweizer, *The Good News according to Mark* (Atlanta: John Knox, 1971).

161. In *Conflict in Mark*.

162. On the portrayal of the women at the end of Mark's Gospel, see my *Women in the Ministry of Jesus* (Cambridge: Cambridge University Press, 1984).

alone, abandoned on the cross at the end. Thus it is important to do justice to the various nuances of the portrayal of the disciples in Mark. Since this work is a biography, however, it is a mistake to think it is chiefly about the disciples, whether in Jesus' day or in Mark's. To the contrary, the focus is christological, even to the extent that Jesus ends up being the model of following the way of the cross. Nevertheless, since this matter is exceedingly complex, a full discussion will be given to Mark's discipleship language at the end of this commentary.[163]

Mark as Story

It has been in vogue for some time to treat Mark's Gospel as a story, and apply modern literary critical tools to it so as to analyze Mark's plot, characters, and the like. There is nothing in principle wrong with such an attempt, for certainly what Mark is presenting is a compelling and persuasive narrative. Many good insights into Mark's compositional art and arrangement of material have come from some of the close readings done of Mark as story, including some of those produced by the advocates of reader-response criticism and structuralism.[164] There is certainly a plot involving the controversies Jesus was embroiled in which eventually led to his death. Indeed, one might say that Mark stresses that from the first there was a plot not merely involving Jesus but against Jesus (3:6). There is no question but that Jesus is the central figure in the drama, and that there are few other well-rounded characters. One might at most point to Peter, or the composite pictures of the opponents or the crowd. The spotlight never strays far from Jesus.

However, some presuppositions that are often brought along in such an exercise need to be challenged. Firstly, Mark is not a work of ancient or modern fiction, and this means that some things which apply especially to modern fiction do not apply to Mark. For example, there is no gap between the implied author and the real author in this work. This is not just because the implied author is a reliable narrator, but because the author is composing an ancient biography whose author would be known, as was the case with Plutarch's *Lives* and other such documents. Secondly, there is no such thing as an omniscient narra-

---

163. See the detailed appendix to this commentary on Mark's use of the terms "disciple" and "the Twelve."

164. We have already had occasion to refer to Fowler, *Let the Reader Understand*, and one must also add the very influential treatment by D. Rhoads and D. Michie, *Mark as Story: An Introduction to the Narrative of a Gospel* (Philadelphia: Fortress, 1982). Structuralism also has some insights to share; see E. Malbon, "Galilee and Jerusalem: History and Literature in Markan Interpretation," *CBQ* 44 (1982): 242-55.

tor in Mark's Gospel. Mark is drawing on sources that indicated that Jesus, and indeed some of his disciples when they received the Holy Spirit, had prophetic insight into human character and also revealed sometimes to others what the Spirit had revealed to them about various matters and people. Having prophetic insight into a human character was regularly asserted about ancient prophetic figures.[165] Thus, when we come to texts like 5:30, we should not jump to the conclusion that the narrator of this ancient document is acting like the narrator of a modern work of fiction, for he is not.

Thirdly, there are serious problems with the theory of meaning that undergirds reader-response criticism. While it is certainly true that readers, especially active readers, bring expectations, thoughts, interests to the reading of documents, it is not true either that "meaning is merely in the eye of the beholder" or that "meaning is merely an event that happens between the reader and the text." It is of course possible for people to read all kinds of things into texts that are not in fact there. Doubtless it is possible to treat a text like an abstract painting. But one must be able to make a distinction between meaning, which does indeed lie in the text and has been encoded there by the author, and significance.

A text may well have a significance for a person that goes well beyond the author's original and intended meaning. Indeed, it may even go against what the author intended. But it is rank solipsism to suggest that the author is unimportant, or that all we have is texts (ignoring of course other forms of historical evidence such as artifacts, coins, and the like), or that we do not need to respect the author of the document and enter into a dialogue with him (trying to find out what he had in mind), or that the compact between author and audience that sets up the genre of the work and provides the author's clues as to how it should be read can be safely ignored.

The ultimate disconfirmation of such theories of meaning is that they are inherently self-defeating and even their advocates cannot live with their implications and consequences. It is striking that even the gurus of such theories, like S. Fish, have been willing to object that they have been misquoted or misunderstood at times and that we must think in terms of interpretive communities which guide our reading.[166] But no complaints about being *misunderstood* can be allowed to stand unless one has intended some specific meaning in the first place which was misheard or misinterpreted. And why should we need interpretive communities if the meaning simply happens between the reader and the text?

Unfortunately, such "underdetermined" theories of meaning have led to some peculiar readings of Mark's Gospel, making him a master of modern literary techniques, a master of modern angst and irony, which are in fact traits

---

165. See now my *Jesus the Seer*.

166. See, e.g., S. Fish, *Is There a Text in This Class?* (Cambridge: Harvard University Press, 1980).

more appropriately predicated of certain modern readers than of Mark. It is not surprising that such readings are essentially self-referential when one has given up any respect for the original author and abandoned the time-consuming task of doing historical research and trying to find out what the author would have been like and what the text would have meant in its original historical and social and religious context.

None of this vitiates the fact that there is also much to be learned from reading Mark as a story and applying various narratological techniques to help us understand the text. It is just that one needs to be clear about the limits of such approaches in order to be able to avoid anachronism in the interpretation of Mark. One also needs to be fully cognizant of what sorts of theories of meaning one is bringing to the table when one seeks to interpret an ancient text, written when very different theories of knowing and meaning applied and were exercised.

Lastly, texts such as Mark's Gospel are most definitely not "autonomous cultural objects" or self-contained systems of symbols and signs. To the contrary, the text is constantly referential to the outside world of the first century A.D., and in particular to the time of Jesus of Nazareth's ministry in Israel. To be sure, Mark's story is not simply a news report of events that happened in the first century A.D., but it is closer to that sort of written document than it is to a self-contained work of fiction, whether ancient or modern. There was indeed a real world beyond the narrative world that Mark intended to speak about and also to speak to. He was quite innocent of modern notions that narratives and language need not be referential.

It is interesting to note that ideological readings of Mark contain a strong critique of the "formalist" approach to this Gospel. For example, C. Myers suggests that the formalist attempt to strip the text from its historical and economic and political matrix is a false move, a bad strategy for reading the text, not least because the meaning of the text can only be determined when one sees how the text is embedded in its original social context.[167] An ahistorical approach is not merely docetic, it is naive, for it has consciously or unconsciously substituted its own ideology and politics of interpretation for the ancient one of Mark's. In other words, formalism is an approach that arises out of a certain modern literary culture and tradition that has its own agendas and ideology. This stands in contrast to Myers's observation that "Mark believed he was reworking traditions about real (not make-believe) events, sayings, and personalities, and put each detail in his narrative for a reason. . . . I will go still further, and contend that Mark is an authoritative and therefore fully reliable interpreter of the original ideology of Jesus and his movement."[168] This commen-

---

167. See Myers, pp. 25-26.
168. Myers, p. 31.

tary finds this view much nearer the mark, and nearer to Mark, than some formalist readings of the text.

Point of View

Recent literary criticism of the Gospels has stressed the importance of determining point of view. This may be seen as a key to deciphering an author's purposes in writing a Gospel. From a literary critical standpoint, an author tries to place the reader in the shoes of one or another character in the story so that the reader views matters from that character's point of view. This sometimes involves revealing that central character's innermost thoughts about various others in the story. If the portrait of the central character is a winsome one, the reader is usually beguiled into accepting that character's view of things.[169] For example, it is hard for the reader to really identify with the disciples when the central character Jesus says to them, "Why are you afraid? Have you still no faith?" (4:40). Such remarks, if accepted at face value, put a distance between the reader and the disciples and at the same time bind the reader even more firmly to Jesus' point of view, which, not incidentally, is the author's. In Mark's Gospel, only Jesus is really presented as an example for the audience to follow, while the disciples to some extent serve as a foil warning of the pitfalls of discipleship with the not so subliminal message being, "You see how the first disciples failed him under pressure and facing persecution. Go and do otherwise."

There is, however, another dimension of point of view, and that is how the author chooses to cast his material. Mark has chosen to present the story and its central character from what I would call an "apocalyptic" point of view.[170] By this I do not mean that Mark's Gospel is an apocalypse, though most assuredly Mark has been influenced by such literature in his presentation. Not even Mark 13 really qualifies as an apocalypse, despite its often being called so. It is rather an eschatological discourse with a bit of apocalyptic imagery. In what sense, then, is Mark's point of view apocalyptic? In this respect — Mark sees the world very much as John of Patmos saw the world.

From Mark's point of view, the world is a battleground between good and evil, between Satan and God, between humans and demons. If the world is to be freed from being in thrall to Satan, it must be liberated. The strong man must be

---

169. See Fowler, pp. 66-69.

170. On this see J. M. Robinson, *The Problem of History in Mark* (London: SCM, 1957); N. Perrin and D. C. Duling, *The New Testament: An Introduction* (New York: Harcourt, 1982); J. Marcus, *The Mystery of the Kingdom of God* (Atlanta: Scholars, 1986); and most recently Collins, *The Beginning of the Gospel*.

overthrown by a stronger one. In a world that is dark and dangerous, it is not a surprise that even the disciples don't understand. It requires radical change for a person in such a world to really know and be what God wants a person to know and be. It requires revelation breaking into a realm of ignorance and the ignoring of God. It requires grace that not merely informs but also transforms a person. In such a world it is not a surprise that God's message comes to people in the form of parables and riddles, meant, as C. H. Dodd said long ago, to tease the mind into active thought. It is not a surprise that such a metaphorical speech needs to be explained, its secrets unveiled to the lost. But even when unveiled, it can still be misunderstood or even rejected by those who have lived in darkness so long that their eyes have difficulty adjusting to the light.

Thus Mark presents Jesus as one who must cast the truth like a stone through a plate glass window. Even though he teaches in parables, he has no time to mince words or soft-pedal the Gospel. Mark's Jesus can be harsh and argumentative. The time has come for God's saving activity to break into the midst of God's people, and like a man going around a village yelling "Fire!" the Gospel must be vigorously proclaimed to wake people up. But Jesus is also an exorcist. We see him do battle with Satan's minions and win. We see him best his adversaries in verbal combat. And then, paradoxically, we see him deliberately go up to Jerusalem and submit to an unjust trial and execution at the hands of these adversaries. Mark's world is full of paradox, full of the least, the last, and the lost becoming the most, the first, and the found. It is a world where children, not wise adults, are the model of how to enter God's dominion. It is a world full of surprises and reversals.

Perhaps the greatest surprises come in the revelatory moments in the Gospel — at Jesus' baptism when he hears the voice, at Caesarea Philippi, on the Mount of Transfiguration, at the trial, at the cross, at the tomb. In all these places the light breaks through, but one knows if God had not chosen to make himself known in and through Christ, penetrating the darkness, all would still be lost. Salvation is of God. This message could hardly be clearer than in Mark, where the disciples are only saved in spite of themselves and their denseness in the end. Mark does not offer his audience a human self-help program. With the possible exception of a few stories at the beginning of the Gospel, the disciples are not really held up as positive models for the audience. But in a dark and dangerous world, one expects disaffection, disappointment, desertion from the true way. It is hard to follow the light when it seems the thunderclouds are much larger and more powerful, and the light seems to only break through them on rare occasions.

As Joel Marcus has rightly stressed, there is a certain epistemology connected with apocalypticism which Mark reflects in texts like 10:42, which, read literally, refers to "those who are thought to rule over the nations." "Those who are commonly thought to be rulers are not, from the apocalyptic view point, the real rulers of this world. Behind them stand the real rulers, God and Satan, each with a host of servants."[171] The apocalyptic mind-set believes that it is what happens behind the canvas of history, or at least with the invisible forces working both in the spiritual and material realms, that really explains why things are as they are in this world. It is thus the job of the apocalyptic seer to unveil the secrets, peel back the curtain and reveal the underlying and overriding forces that control what happens in the human sphere.

The epistemology that goes along with this mind-set is that true knowledge of such things comes by having them revealed to a recipient. Such knowledge is not obtained by native brilliance or diligent scholarship. Such knowledge is a gift of God. This includes knowledge of who Jesus is and why he had to die. "Knowing is connected with God's act of bringing in his kingdom: thus the scribe in 12.34 who speaks *nounechōs* ('intelligently') is 'not far from the kingdom of God.'"[172] Thus Mark's concern with secrets in Mark 4 reflects the notion that essential truths about God, Jesus, the dominion, and life are only obtained by revelation. In this Mark is much like what we find in Daniel, or in the apocalyptic material from Qumran.

There is also this further similarity. This knowledge is only revealed, or at least only revealed fully, it would appear, to insiders. It is only to the disciples that the dominion's mysteries are unveiled. This comports with what we hear in *2 Bar.* 48:2-3: "you do not reveal your mysteries to many." But even with the inner group, full knowledge does not come until the end (cf. 1 Cor. 13:12). This sheds light on the Markan theme of the disciples' incomprehension. In part they do not understand because in fact the most essential bit of knowledge — the meaning of Jesus' death and resurrection — will not come until after Easter, when the dominion will have been well and truly inaugurated. In fact, the influence of either supernatural good or evil is so powerful that it can even control a person's thoughts. Thus Marcus notes Mark 8:33, where Jesus says to Peter, "Get behind me, Satan," indicating that Peter's thoughts come from his being under the influence of the Prince of Darkness. Further, he points to the phrase "he who has ears — let *him* hear" as an indicator that only some have the equipment to receive and believe Jesus' message. This may be pushing things too far, though the analogy with the seed falling on good soil as opposed to unreceptive soil may suggest he is right.[173] What is clearer is the noted contrast between the demons and the crowd — the demons know quite clearly who Jesus is. There is no messianic secret being kept from them. The crowd, on the other hand, has to contend with parables and being on the outside of such knowledge. Yet there is a further reversal once Jesus dies and is raised from the grave. At that point, as J. Gnilka says, while Jesus com-

---

171. J. Marcus, "Mark 4.10-12," p. 558.

172. Marcus, "Mark 4.10-12," p. 559.

173. Marcus, "Mark 4.10-12," p. 562.

manded secrecy and open proclamation was disobedience during his ministry, after Easter the command is proclamation and secrecy is disobedience.[174] It may in fact be Mark's view that after Easter the dominion of God has come more fully and one has gotten beyond the age when secrecy and the dark clouds of evil rule the day and arrived at "the age of full disclosure."[175] Perhaps he believed, as another NT writer did, that "greater is he who is in you than the forces extant in the world." Yet clearly from texts like Mark 13, the only place in Mark where the audience's future is really addressed, he still believes persecution and suffering and also false messiahs loom on the horizon.

Yet another facet of an apocalyptic point of view is that Mark is concerned to make clear that justice will be done in the end (Mark 13), and in fact already has been done in the case of egregious error and sin in regard to Jesus, whom God vindicated when he raised him from the dead (16:6-7). It is this very mentality that leads John of Patmos to make sure to end his work with a portrait of triumph in Rev. 20–21, and this is one of the factors that make it unlikely that Mark would have ended his Gospel at 16:8. For the apocalypticist, it is not enough to announce that someday justice may be done. Rather it must be seen to be done, and that victory must be depicted in advance for those who are suffering and being persecuted. Mark 16:8 would be cold comfort for Christians under fire. It would not steel them to face the steel or the animals in the arena. As we turn now to the commentary itself, we need to bear in mind that an apocalyptic mind-set informs the way Mark shapes his narrative. It is one of the features of this Gospel which most distinguishes it from the other three.[176] It is also one of the features that makes this Gospel in various respects the closest to the historical Jesus and his own orientation.[177]

---

174. J. Gnilka, *Das Evangelium nach Markus* (Zürich: Benziger, 1979), 2:344.

175. Marcus, "Mark 4.10-12," p. 574. Notice the way Marcus's reading of the post-Easter situation is rendered less telling and convincing because he thinks the Gospel ended at 16:8: "the Gospel ends with the rising of the sun, the empty tomb (its door thrown open!), the splendid messenger, the amazing message. True the women run away terrified and tell the message to no one. Yet even this last act of human disobedience, this last shadow of cosmic darkness, cannot defeat God's purpose, for Mark has transmitted the tale that the women kept to themselves. Somehow the news has leaked out; it could not remain hidden." But in fact, Paul tells us very well how the news leaked out — through the appearances of the risen Lord to various of the disciples (1 Cor. 15), and Mark twice leads us to expect him to recount such a conclusion to the story (14:28; 16:7).

176. To give but one example from each other Gospel — John has no exorcisms, Matthew presents Jesus' baptism as a public rather than a private revelation of who Jesus is, and Luke deliberately de-emphasizes future eschatology, instead focusing on the unfolding progress of salvation history.

177. On Jesus as seer, see my *Jesus the Seer,* chap. 8.

THE COMMENTARY

I. The Superscript

Though not a part of the original text of this Gospel,[1] this superscript tells us three important things. Firstly, it suggests that by the time this superscript had been added the word ευαγγελιον had become almost a technical term for a particular kind of Christian literature about the life of Jesus, such that it could equally well be applied to works by several different authors. Secondly, the use of κατα (according to) strongly suggests that there were various different readings of the story of Jesus. This was just one among several. There was not one Gospel, but rather several different ones which were considered valid interpretations of the Christ event. It is possible the κατα clause first arose when Mark's Gospel was bound together with another Gospel, presumably Matthew's, perhaps toward the end of the first century A.D.[2]

Finally, the attribution of this Gospel to someone named Mark, even if this is John Mark, is not likely an example of pseudonymity. John Mark is not portrayed as an apostle or a major figure in the events of the earliest days of the Christian movement either in Acts or in the epistles. Thus, though the Gospel does not mention the name of the author within the parameters of Mark 1:1 to the end of the Gospel (and so the document is formally anonymous), it seems very likely that there must be some significant historical reason for this attribution. It is not sufficient to say that the traditions in the NT generated this attribution due to Mark's association with Peter, for in fact Mark is hardly ever associated with Peter in the NT; rather he appears in the Pauline circle far more often. As M. Hengel has recently suggested, it is doubtful that this Gospel ever

---

1. See pp. 20-30 above in the introduction.
2. See the discussion, pp. 25-32 above.

circulated *without* an ascription of authorship of some kind, especially since it was intended to be an ancient biography.[3]

3. M. Hengel, *The Four Gospels and the One Gospel of Jesus Christ* (London: SCM Press, 2000), pp. 8-115.

II. News of New Beginnings (1:1-15)

The opening scenes of the Gospel of Mark remind one of minimalist theater, collapsing a world of meaning into a few concentrated images, or of a chiaroscuro painting, with vivid profiles etched in a dark, obscure backdrop. Punctuated by divine voices offstage and human cries at center stage, the prologue narrates the story of an invasion, throwing existence-as-usual into sharp relief. Prophetic muses, long silent, suddenly sing again. A messenger is announced and in turn heralds the advent, at long last, of one strong enough to wrestle the world away from the death grip of the powers. This leader appears on the horizon of history, and in a dramatic symbolic action declares himself an outlaw. This immediately provokes a challenge from the prince of the powers himself, who takes the leader deep into the wilderness, where he disappears. . . . In this prologue Mark wields the scythe of apocalyptic symbolics, clearing narrative space from among the weeds so that the seeds of a radically new order — to borrow the author's own metaphor (4:7) — might be pressed into the weary soil of the world. This subversive story is what Mark entitles *good news*.[1]

TRANSLATION — 1:1-15

Beginning of the good news of Jesus Christ, of the Son of God.
As it has been written in the prophet Isaiah, "Behold, I am sending my messenger before your face, who builds your road. A voice crying: 'In the wilderness make ready the road of the Lord, make straight his beaten track.'" John the

---

1. C. Myers, *Binding the Strong Man: A Political Reading of Mark's Story of Jesus* (Maryknoll, N.Y.: Orbis, 1988), p. 91.

Baptizer[2] came into the wilderness proclaiming a baptism of turning back/change of heart for the forgiveness of sins. And all the Jews of the region and the Jerusalemites were going out to him, and they were baptized by him in the Jordan, publicly confessing their sins. And John was clothed with camel's fur and a girdle made of leather around his waist, and he was consuming locusts and wild honey. And he proclaimed saying, "One stronger than me follows me, of whom I am not worthy stooping down to unlace the thong of his sandals. I baptize you in water, but he himself will baptize you in the Holy Spirit." And it happened in those days that Jesus came from Nazareth of Galilee and was baptized in the Jordan by John. And immediately coming up from the water he saw the rending of the heavens and the Spirit like a dove descending upon him, and there was a voice from heaven [saying], "You are my Son, the Beloved, on whom I rest my favor." And immediately the Spirit cast him out into the wilderness. And he was in the wilderness forty days being tempted by the Satan, and he was with the wild beasts, and the angels provided for him. But after John was handed over, Jesus [came] into Galilee preaching the good news about God, and saying, "The time is fulfilled and the dominion of God is at hand, change your hearts and believe in the good news."

There is debate as to how far the prologue of this Gospel extends. I would suggest, agreeing with J. Painter, that we pay close attention to the *inclusio* that links 1:1 and 1:15, namely, that both verses speak about the good news.[3] But is this the good news about Jesus or the good news that Jesus himself proclaims? Are we dealing with objective or subjective genitives with such phrases? If we connect 1:1 and 1:15, it would appear that what is meant is the news Jesus proclaims about the inbreaking dominion, news which can also be called the good news about God and what God is doing (1:14). Yet of course, this news about the dominion is also news about the One who not merely proclaims its coming but brings it in through his ministry.

From a narrative point of view, we need to see that in fact Mark 1 recounts a time of transition of a threefold nature. The Evangelist tells of the transition from John to Jesus, from a ministry at the Jordan and in the wilderness to a ministry in the villages and countryside of Galilee, from a ministry of baptism connected with repentance to one of proclaiming and bringing in the good news.[4] The beginning of the good news is about the changing of the guard, the passing on of one era and the dawning of another, eschatological one. Thus, as Marcus points out, vv. 1-8 deal with John, vv. 9-15 with Jesus.[5]

---

2. The original reading here is more likely Baptizer than the more common Baptist (Mark 6:25; 8:28). See Metzger, *TCGNT,* p. 73.

3. J. Painter, *Mark's Gospel* (London: Routledge, 1997), p. 35.

4. Painter, p. 33.

5. J. Marcus, *Mark 1–8* (New York: Doubleday, 1999), p. 138.

Notice that the term "good news" (ευαγγελιον) occurs frequently in Paul (59 times, counting the later Paulines) and in Mark (7 times) but rarely elsewhere in the NT (4 times in Matthew, none in Luke, twice in Acts, and twice elsewhere in the NT). Similar statistics link Mark and Paul in regard to the term κηρυσσω (19 times in Paul, 12 in Mark, 9 in Matthew, 9 in Luke, 8 in Acts, twice elsewhere in the NT).[6] Mark's and Paul's concept of the character of the message and of the act by which the message is conveyed is closely similar.

The first chapter of Mark begins with the word αρχη, and of course the reader is reminded of Gen. 1:1 (see the use of αρχη at Mark 10:6). Here, however, the subject is neither the beginning of creation nor even, as in John 1, the beginning of the Son of God, but rather the beginning of the good news about Jesus of Nazareth. In other words, it is about the beginning of the spreading of a message about Jesus, the beginning of an historical phenomenon. This way of starting this work is perfectly appropriate if this is an ancient biography, for it was crucial to inform the audience at the very outset who the biography was about and, secondly, what the character of the work would be.

The first verse, then, signals that what follows, however stark and full of suffering and sorrow, is paradoxically not bad news or a tragedy, but rather good news, like the announcement of a birth or a major success of an emperor. Consider, for example, the famous Priene inscription about Octavian which dates from 9 B.C.: "Because providence has ordered our life in a divine way . . . and since the Emperor through his epiphany has exceeded the hopes of former good news (ευαγγελια), surpassing not only the benefactors who came before him, but also leaving no hope that anyone in the future will surpass him, and since the birthday of the god was for the world the beginning of his good news [may it therefore be decreed that]. . . ."[7]

Notice particularly the last line of this inscription. The emperor is called a god, and we are informed that his birth or advent on the human scene already augurs good things for the world. If Mark has in mind such familiar inscriptions (which became increasingly common throughout the empire as the emperor cult spread in the first century A.D.), then it would appear that he is making a parallel claim about the divinity of Jesus. The combination of the reference to "beginning" plus "good news" plus the reference to the coming of a "god" finds clear analogies in Mark 1:1, especially if the phrase "Son of God" is original here, which seems highly likely.[8] Only a god is really able to bring

---

6. See Painter, p. 24.

7. W. Dittenberger, *Orientis graeci inscriptiones selectae* (Hildesheim: Olms, 1960), II, no. 458, pp. 48-60, here lines 40-42.

8. See the discussion in Metzger, *TCGNT*, p. 73. The combination of ℵ-A B, D, L, W, and other manuscripts, as well as Irenaeus, in support of reading "Son of God" here is a strong one and suggests that this is the original reading. The omission by several manu-

world-changing and lasting good news and benefaction and hope. Mark, then, from the outset, is announcing not merely a coming of a teacher or even just a human messianic figure (though that is also part of the truth), but the epiphany or advent of a deity who will reveal himself in various and sundry ways during his time on earth. This latter is surely how a largely Gentile audience would have heard this opening salvo, since it so clearly echoes the more familiar inscriptions like that quoted above. The form of 1:1 would also have clearly suggested to the audience that this work is about events of considerable historical significance. The secular usage was always about a significant past event, as is the focus in this telling of good news as well. Very few verses in this Gospel deal with events which would have been in the future for Mark's audience (but cf. below on Mark 13 and a few other texts).

The birthday of the emperor was celebrated throughout the empire and was the occasion of festivals called *evangels*. What is different about this announcement is that Mark wishes to begin with Jesus' coming on the public scene as a significant historical figure, not his actual birth. Other, later Gospels (Matthew and Luke) felt it important to go even further back to Jesus' birth and perhaps, especially in Luke's case, to even further heighten the parallels with such announcements about the emperor.

We must ask at this juncture, however: *What* does Mark refer to as "the beginning of the good news about Jesus Christ, the Son of God"? Is this a reference to the whole Gospel, or alternatively, is Mark telling us that the brief narration about John the Baptist is the beginning of Jesus' story and the good news? If the former, it might suggest that Mark anticipated writing another volume, as Luke did.[9] On the other hand, if we follow M. Hengel's suggestion that we take seriously the tradition of the association of Mark with Peter, it is noteworthy that at Acts 10:37 Peter begins the telling of the good news about Jesus with the reference to John the Baptist baptizing Jesus.[10]

But why should a biography clearly focusing on Jesus begin with the story of John the Baptist? Probably the answer is that John figured prominently in Jesus' life prior to his independent public ministry (cf. John 3:22–4:3).[11] Jesus'

---

scripts, including a*, Θ, and 28, can be attributed to a scribal oversight due to the similar endings of the sacred names. There is also the further factor that "Son of God" is clearly a crucial title for Mark, perhaps even the crucial title that helps tie this Gospel together from start to finish for its largely Gentile audience (cf., e.g., Mark 15:39).

9. See pp. 3-9 above in the introduction.

10. M. Hengel, *Studies in the Gospel of Mark* (Philadelphia: Fortress, 1985), pp. 2-14.

11. There are, of course, numerous debates among scholars about the historical substance of this or that verse of Mark, often grounded in certain literary or form-critical approaches to both the narrative and sayings material of Mark. In this commentary, as previously in my Acts commentary, I have attempted to deal with some of the larger issues primarily through the excursuses. Since R. H. Gundry has recently provided a very detailed

public ministry grew out of and in fact was set in motion in various ways by the prior ministry of the Baptist.[12] Thus we should likely see 1:1-8, or perhaps more likely 1:1-15, as the prologue to this Gospel, with v. 15 the transition from the prologue to the account of Jesus' ministry itself. It is not just John the Baptist's ministry which is the beginning of the good news about Jesus, but also Jesus' baptism and temptation as part of this beginning. Nevertheless, what this beginning means in part is that a portion of John's story has been subsumed within the story of Jesus.

At v. 2 we have a composite quotation initially attributed to Isaiah the prophet.[13] Though this may mean that this is the most familiar source of the quotation, it is by no means the only source. The first phrase is verbatim from Exod. 23:20a in the LXX, combined with Mal. 3:1 and finally Isa. 40:3. The combination may have been pre-Markan, as there is evidence from early Judaism that these texts were associated with an Elijah figure that was to come, one who would be like Moses. This combination may have been taken from a *testimonium* — a collection of OT texts used to demonstrate the divine character of the Gospel story by portraying it as a fulfillment of various scriptural oracles. W. Lane sees the wilderness as the theme of this entire section.[14] The wilderness is the place where John is and Jesus must go. Furthermore, it is the place where God's people must go if they wish to hear God's word to them. To sum up the gist of the scriptural fragments: they focus on the herald, the Lord, and the wilderness. John is the one seen as preparing or paving the way for Jesus to come on the scene. At the beginning of Mark's narrative a figure goes before others preparing the way (John), and again at the end another figure does this for the disciples (Jesus — 16:7).[15]

There is a question as to where the comma should be placed in the quote in v. 3a. The Isaiah text itself would suggest we read the phrase as follows: "a voice crying: 'in the wilderness make ready the way of the Lord, make straight his beaten track.'" That this is the right reading of Isaiah is made evident by the second member of the phrase, which says, "make straight in the wilderness his path." I would suggest this is also the way Mark wishes us to read the text. Thus the emphasis is on making the way straight in the wilderness, not on the voice

---

response, verse by verse, to some of the more extreme skepticism about Mark's historical substance, and since I agree with much of his argument, I see no pressing need to reiterate most of these sorts of arguments in this study. See R. H. Gundry, *Mark: A Commentary on His Apology for the Cross* (Grand Rapids: Eerdmans, 1993).

12. See the discussion of such matters in J. Meier, *A Marginal Jew: Rethinking the Historical Jesus*, 2 vols. (New York: Doubleday, 1991, 1994), 2:100-196.

13. Marcus, *Mark 1–8*, p. 139, points out that each of the first five pericopes of Mark's Gospel has a strong connection with Isa. 40–55.

14. W. Lane, *The Gospel of Mark* (Grand Rapids: Eerdmans, 1974), pp. 39-45.

15. Myers, p. 124.

crying there. This may suggest that the focus is not on John but on those responding to him. We are then told that John the Baptizer was in the wilderness, preaching a baptism of repentance for forgiveness of sins. This latter provides the clearest point of continuity with the preaching of Jesus as summarized at 1:15. It is also true, as Origen once suggested, that Mark is seeking to show that the beginning of the Gospel is intrinsically connected with the Old Testament and its prophecies (*Against Celsus* 2.4).[16] Though Jesus' coming is a new thing, it is not unanticipated or without advance warning.

There would appear to be something radical about John's message. He seems to have been offering forgiveness without sacrifice being offered in the temple. He was offering remission of sins without connection to the hierarchical system in Jerusalem. Is this why so many Jerusalemites came to check out John's message? Was John suggesting, like those at Qumran, that the temple in Jerusalem was hopelessly corrupt and one must look elsewhere for means to reconcile oneself with a holy God?

How John's water rite should be evaluated is much debated. It does not appear to be a repeatable ritual like many of the lustrations at Qumran.[17] On the other hand, there is a question whether Gentile proselytes to Judaism were already being baptized at this time. The discussion by Meier suggests they were not,[18] and in any case John's rite was not transferring one ethnic group into fellowship with another, for John performed his rite on Jews. John's baptism had to do with the restoration of Jews and their preparation for the judgment which was to come. Its connection with repentance and forgiveness by Mark is likely authentic, as it is not probable that the church would have invented the notion that Jesus underwent such a baptism. Finally, proselyte baptism appears to have been self-administered, whereas John's rite had to be sought from John's own hand. He came to be called the baptizer or immerser for good reason. All of this suggests an eschatological thrust to the ministry of the Baptist. It is in part this eschatological message of John and Jesus' indebtedness to him that makes very unlikely a noneschatological interpretation of Jesus and his ministry. In fact, John's baptism only makes sense when we understand his eschatological role as the one who prepares for the final act of God's revelation or activity — the coming redemptive judgment that comes first upon the household of God. Repentance was urgently needed because one must prepare for the final act of his-

---

16. Here and elsewhere in this commentary I am indebted to T. Oden and C. Hall for making it easy to find and find out what the Fathers thought of various Markan passages. See their *Ancient Christian Commentary on Scripture*, vol. 2, *Mark* (Downers Grove, Ill.: InterVarsity, 1998).

17. See the helpful discussion in B. Chilton, *Jesus' Baptism and Jesus' Healing* (Harrisburg, Pa.: Trinity Press, 1998), pp. 1-29.

18. Meier, 2:49-52.

tory which involved both judgment and the pouring out of God's Spirit. There is a sense in which this final act happens to Jesus first — he undergoes a repentance baptism and receives the Spirit through his encounter with John at the Jordan.

It has often been suggested that John's locale, his diet, and his message may mean that he was at one point associated with the Qumran community, who also made much of the quote about preparing the way in the wilderness. This may well be so, but when we meet him in Mark he appears to have broken away from them and is taking his message to the people, not selecting a few holy ones to join the commune of the elect and await the coming end. Israel was called by John to come out to the wilderness, turn from their sins, and so renew the covenant with God and thus renew their sonship status.[19] Yet, ironically it is Jesus who is portrayed as heeding this summons and receiving the assurance that he himself was God's Son. Thus it appears that Mark wants us to see Jesus as being portrayed as true Israel here.

We are further told that John attracted a crowd from the whole Judean countryside and even from among the Jerusalemites. This is of course a hyperbolic remark, but its rhetorical purpose is to indicate John's great popularity. People walked great distances to hear him, perhaps because there had not been a prophet quite like him in Israel in a very long time. They came to be baptized, acknowledging or admitting (εξομολογουμενοι) their sins. V. 6 appears to be a deliberate attempt to make clear that John is that Elijah figure Israel was looking for as a forerunner of God's eschatological action. The text here should be compared to 2 Kings 1:8, where we are told of Elijah's garment of hair and his leather girdle or belt. The diet is precisely what might be found in the wilderness, and of course, locusts were a clean food according to Lev. 11:21f. We know that desert nomads didn't hesitate to eat insects.

But John did not merely baptize; he proclaimed that there was a stronger one coming after him for whom he was not even fit to be a servant (for such is the likely meaning of the metaphor about not being fit to unlace someone's sandals). The term "stronger one" suggests a comparison, but also a social position. John portrays himself as inferior in both regards. Notice that v. 7 calls Jesus the one coming after him. This could be taken to mean "the one who is following me," which would suggest that Jesus was a follower or disciple of John. More likely, Mark at least understands this to mean the one who chronologically comes after John, which is what v. 14 suggests. The contrast between John and the Coming One is punctuated by contrasting their immersions — one with water, one with Spirit. It is difficult to know whether to take εν in v. 8 in a locative sense (i.e., "in the Spirit") or as a preposition followed by the specification of means ("by the Spirit"). One is proba-

---

19. See Lane, pp. 47-51.

bly meant to hear an echo of Joel 2:28-29 (3:1-2 in the Hebrew). One should not press the metaphorical language here about the Spirit too far. For example, Mark is probably not suggesting that spirit is a substance like water which one can get in several doses.

V. 9 is to be contrasted with v. 5 — one particular individual instead of all the people, an individual from Galilee and not from Judea, is the one who truly responds to John's summons. Indeed, this individual came from an insignificant village in Galilee all the way to where John was at the Jordan to be baptized. At v. 10 we have the first occurrence of one of Mark's favorite words, ευθυς (immediately), which will occur some forty more times in this Gospel. The term often functions rhetorically to give the narrative a sense of pace and movement, and often is not meant literally. The repetition of the term gives the reader a sense of things happening at a breakneck or breathless pace.

The narrative of Jesus' baptism uses language that suggests a visionary experience.[20] "The rending of the heavens is a common feature of apocalyptic thought, the underlying idea being that of a fixed separation of heaven from earth only to be broken in special circumstances"[21] (cf. *Apoc. Bar.* 22:1; *T. Levi* 2:6; 5:1; 18:6; *T. Jud.* 24:2; Rev. 4:1; 11:19; 19:11). In addition, the voice from heaven speaks only to Jesus. This is a private experience and revelation (contrast Matt. 3:16-17). It is only Jesus who is said to see the Spirit coming down. Notice also that nothing is said about the reception of the Spirit by means of the water ritual. Rather, it is when he is coming up out of the water, or just after the baptismal act, that the Spirit and the voice are encountered. The phrase suggesting the analogy ("descending like a dove") is surely not meant as a description of the form the Spirit took when coming down, but rather the manner of the descent, like a dove coming gently down for a landing.[22]

---

20. See now D. C. Allison, "Behind the Temptations of Jesus," in *Authenticating the Activities of Jesus,* ed. B. Chilton and C. A. Evans (Leiden: Brill, 1999), pp. 195-213, and compare my *Jesus the Seer: The Progress of Prophecy* (Peabody, Mass.: Hendrickson, 1999), chap. 7.

21. V. Taylor, *The Gospel according to St. Mark* (New York: St. Martin's Press, 1966), p. 160.

22. J. Marcus, "The Beelzebul Controversies and the Eschatologies of Jesus," in *Authenticating the Activities of Jesus,* pp. 247-77, has made the interesting suggestion that the baptismal event was a "watershed" event in Jesus' thinking about matters eschatological. By this he means that the futurist eschatology witnessed in the Beelzebul controversy reflects Jesus' prebaptismal belief that Satan was still Lord of the cosmos, whereas after his baptism Jesus believed that Satan had been dethroned and was progressively being despoiled of his victims through Jesus' ministry. But where is the real or hard evidence of Jesus having a prebaptismal ministry, much less a controversy with religious leaders over Satan prior to his baptism? Realized eschatology by no means rules out future eschatology in any case. However, Marcus is right about one thing — Jesus was in all likelihood an apocalypticist. The question is — What sort? Cf. my *Jesus the Seer.*

Here there is a clear echo of Isa. 64:1, where the prophet prays that the heavens be rent and God come down so that the mountains might quake at God's presence. Mark, then, is suggesting that what is happening to Jesus is an earthshaking event. Jesus is anointed by the very presence and power of God, such that wherever Jesus goes and whatever he does, the presence and power of God dwells in him and empowers his words and deeds. He has in a sense what the sociologists call derived authority and power, but once invested, it becomes an inherent authority and power which people recognize in Jesus (see Mark 1:27). It may be debated whether we should see the voice from heaven as being like the later notion of the *bath qol*, the so-called "daughter of a voice." There is nothing derivative about this voice; it is God's own. The visionary and indeed apocalyptic character of this scene suggests the proper analogy is with voices that accompany visions, not the *bath qol*.[23]

V. 11 is again a composite Scripture citation combining Ps. 2:7 with Isa. 42:1. The language is covenantal, denoting a special relationship between God and his Son. The word αγαπητος literally means "beloved," but it can connote "unique" or "only" on occasion. As God's special Son, Jesus receives God's special favor, including the full endowment of God's Spirit, equipping him for ministry. What we see here is the confirmation given to Jesus of who he is in relationship to the heavenly Father. In the Markan scheme of things, it is no accident that it is only after this occasion that Jesus is both tested and then begins his ministry. The baptismal event equips him for both of these subsequent matters. Jesus must know who he is before he can do what God has assigned him to do, just as we will see later that the disciples must first know who Jesus is before they can understand about Jesus' mission to Israel. It is probable that Ps. 2:7 was originally used as a coronation ode when a Jewish individual was elevated to the throne.[24] Whatever one makes of the OT quotation here, it is interesting that Origen sees in this scene a tableau involving the Trinity — the Father bore witness, the Son received witness, and the Spirit gave confirmation (*Against Celsus* 2.72). It was perhaps reflections of this sort about Jesus' baptism story that led some early Christian authors to the sort of trinitarian stress and formulae associated with Christian baptism (Matt. 28:19).

Vv. 12-13 should not be separated from v. 11. No sooner had the Spirit come upon Jesus than it cast or drove him out into the wilderness.[25] Jesus must experience the full wilderness experience of God's people and, in a sense, the

---

23. See my discussion of this entire passage in *The Christology of Jesus* (Philadelphia: Fortress, 1990), pp. 148-55.

24. See P. Craigie, *Psalm 1–50* (Waco: Word, 1983), pp. 62-69; A. Weiser, *The Psalms* (Philadelphia: Fortress, 1962), pp. 108-16.

25. E. Schweizer, *The Good News according to Mark* (Atlanta: John Knox, 1971), pp. 42-43.

full consequences of their sin.[26] Thus he is endangered by wild beasts and tempted by a powerful adversary — the Adversary (Satan). In other words, Jesus' adversities were both physical and spiritual in nature. The wilderness was not merely the place of Israel's testing (Ps. 95:7-11), it was also the place of demons (Isa. 34:14; cf. Deut. 32:17).[27] But it is also true that, like the experience of Elijah, the angels of God minister to Jesus while he is in the wilderness. Here Jesus first experiences the wilderness character of a fallen world. In various places in the OT the wilderness is associated with the place of the curse. It is not a place anyone would want to dwell, and is fit only for wild and ferocious animals. Note how the wild beasts are linked with Satan in *T. Iss.* 7:7 and *T. Naph.* 8:4. It seems unlikely, then, that we should see an Edenic motif in the reference to the beasts.[28] If the Lukan and Matthean presentations of this same story are any guide, then it seems likely that Mark has to some extent cast his narrative with Ps. 91:9-14 in mind, believing Jesus' experience fulfilled what the psalmist said:

> For he will command his angels concerning you
>   to guard you in all your ways.
> On their hands they will bear you up,
>   so that you will not dash your foot against a stone.
> You will tread on the lion and the adder,
>   the young lion and the serpent you will trample under foot.
> Those who love me, I will deliver;
>   I will protect those who know my name. (NRSV)[29]

The difference, of course, between Jesus and Israel is that he passes the tests he undergoes there and so is allowed to leave the wilderness and reenter the Promised Land, indeed minister there. There is in this narrative the announcement of a major theme of this Gospel, namely, Jesus' battle with the

---

26. S. Garrett, *The Temptations of Jesus in Mark's Gospel* (Grand Rapids: Eerdmans, 1998), p. 59, stresses "that it was (the spirit of) God who put Jesus into the wilderness to be tested. God has declared Jesus to be his son, and now God arranges for Satan to test Jesus to see whether he is worthy of that assessment. From this context, I infer that *the test was a real one*, in which Jesus was free to choose whether he would follow God's way or not, and in which his obedience could not simply be assumed. Otherwise the test would not have achieved its purpose of proving Jesus to be righteous."

27. For the motif of struggle with supernatural evil in the wilderness, see Marcus, *Mark 1–8*, pp. 169-70.

28. Yet the association of wilderness, animals, and temptation, coupled with the term "beginning," makes such a connection a possibility. If Genesis is the story Mark is echoing here, then Jesus is being portrayed as the latter-day Adam who passed the test. Is this a connection between the Markan and Pauline Christology? See Marcus, *Mark 1–8*, p. 170.

29. See Garrett, p. 57.

powers of darkness. It would appear that we must think of this episode as the account of Jesus binding the strong man (cf. Mark 3:27), even though the Markan version is brief in comparison to the Q version.[30] Yet Mark's account is elliptical, for the nature of the test is not revealed (was it mainly physical and emotional suffering or mainly seduction which constituted the test?). It is the fact of the testing rather than its nature that is Mark's concern.

One could read the Markan account of the temptation story in another way. There is a story in Daniel about a king who wanders in the wilderness with wild beasts, and mention is made there of angelic attendants as well (see Dan. 4:28-37). In addition, the issue in the story in Daniel is that Nebuchadnezzar had claimed to have built his kingdom by his own might and so is being given a lesson in humility, being shown that in fact it is God who bestows kingdoms and titles. There is also the intriguing reference to Nebuchadnezzar being bathed with the dew of heaven, a sort of natural immersion (v. 33). But once Nebuchadnezzar comes to his senses in the wilderness, having been informed about who really rules the world, his majesty and kingdom are restored to him (4:36). After Jesus' experience in the wilderness, he goes forth proclaiming the coming of God's dominion. This entire episode, especially when coupled with the baptismal scene where Jesus is spoken to in the same terms David was, suggests that Jesus is being portrayed as a king, only one who is wiser than Nebuchadnezzar.

At v. 14 we are told what Jesus decided to do once John was arrested — he went out preaching the gospel of God. This must surely mean the good news about God, with the content of the good news spelled out in v. 15: "the time is fulfilled and the dominion of God is at hand (or is near)." The people must turn and believe in this news. Saying the time is fulfilled suggests a view of God having a plan for human history which has set times and seasons (cf. Isa. 60:22). The period of time determined by God in advance that had to elapse before these events could transpire is completed. It also likely means that the time is right and the waiting is over. The dawning of the eschatological age is at hand, the climactic and most decisive age of human history.

We have here a summary statement by Mark meant to suggest what characterized the early preaching of Jesus, and his continuity with the Baptist's ministry and message. As such it seems to be a summary in advance for the entire unit 1:1–3:6.[31] The use of the language "the time is fulfilled" conjures up an image of Jesus as a prophetic herald (cf. Isa. 56:1; Ezek. 7:3, 12).[32]

---

30. See the helpful discussion by E. Best, *The Temptation and the Passion*, 2nd ed. (Cambridge: Cambridge University Press, 1990), pp. 28-60.

31. See Taylor, pp. 165-67.

32. See the discussion by R. Pesch, *Anfang des Evangeliums Jesu Christi: Eine Studie zum Prolog des Markusevangeliums (Mk. 1.1-15), Die Zeit Jesu,* ed. G. Bornkamm and K. Rahner (Freiburg and Basel: Herder, 1970), p. 135.

There has been considerable controversy over how to render the verb ἤγγικεν. The Aramaic equivalent is likely to be *qrb*. Despite the repeated arguments of C. H. Dodd, ἤγγικεν normally refers to the approach or drawing near of something in time or space.[33] Notice how in the LXX this verb is regularly used when the nearness of God or of his judgment is the subject (Deut. 4:7; Isa. 41:21; 48:16; 51:5; 56:1; Jer. 23:23). It is thus unlikely that we should translate the text here "the dominion of God has come," as Dodd argued. This does not mean that the reference is to something in the remote future. Rather, as J. Schlosser suggests, the reference is to something imminent or near.[34] In view of the use of this verb in Rom. 13:12, James 5:8, and 1 Pet. 4:7 (cf. Luke 21:18, 20), a translation such as "has drawn near" best captures the sense here. This is especially likely if this verse is no more than a summary of Jesus' early preaching, when there still seems to have been influence by the Baptist. 11QMelch (especially lines 15ff., which offer a pesher on Isa. 52:7), which suggests that it is the task of God's anointed one or *mashiach* to bring good news about God's impending action for his people, may be of relevance here.[35] It may be suggested that Jesus could say the dominion of God was near precisely because he was near to those hearing this message. In short, Jesus saw the reign of God as being manifested in his life, and when others came under that reign there began to be a realm, a community where the dominion was manifest. An analogy with Mark 13:28 is perhaps apt.

Much debate has also raged over the term βασιλεια. Does it refer to a realm or a reign, a state or a divine activity? I have suggested elsewhere that the term behind this use of βασιλεια, namely, the Aramaic term *malkuta*, allows several nuances as determined by the context in which the term is used. In general it seems to refer to an activity, in this case God's divine saving activity, when used of something happening in the present. The concept involves the idea of God taking control of a human being or human situation such that his reign becomes manifest and his intentions become fulfilled on the human scene. When it refers to something in the future, it appears to also have additional connotation — namely, a place or a realm where such a divine reign is manifest. When Jesus speaks of entering, obtaining, or inheriting the dominion in the future (cf. Mark 9:47; 10:15b; 14:25), not merely a condition but a place seems entailed.[36]

---

33. But see C. H. Dodd, *The Parables of the Kingdom* (New York: Scribner, 1961), pp. 29-30.

34. See the detailed discussion in J. Schlosser, *Le Regne de Dieu dans les Dits de Jesus* (Paris: Gabalda Press, 1980), pp. 91ff.

35. See D. E. Aune, "A Note on Jesus' Messianic Consciousness and 11Q Melchizedek," *EvQ* 45 (1973): 161-65.

36. See my discussion in *The Christology of Jesus*, pp. 194-98.

The way Mark has cast his material suggests that Jesus' ministry in Galilee really began in earnest after John was arrested and off the scene. What John 3–4 suggests is that Jesus had a ministry while John was still free, but perhaps not in the region of Galilee. Putting matters this way seems to indicate that Jesus is the successor of John, who had simply paved the way for Jesus to come as the Lord on the Lord's road. At the historical level, there is every indication that Jesus had great respect for John's ministry, and it may be that he would have waited to begin his Galilean ministry so as not to interfere with John's work, or at least so as not to confuse the issue about the importance of what John was doing. For our purposes it is important to note that Jesus' ministry is bracketed by temptation (here and in the garden) and by baptisms of Jesus — here and on the cross. One can also argue that it is bracketed by empowerment by God — here Jesus receives the Spirit, at the end of the story he is raised from the dead and empowered to be alive forever as the Risen One. The prologue of this Gospel prepares us quite well for what is to follow, for both the triumphs and seeming tragedies.

Bridging the Horizons

In evaluating the opening to Mark's Gospel, it is important to keep in mind the difference between what Mark's readers know on the basis of what Mark tells us, and what the characters within Mark's story know. These are clearly two different matters. The reader knows right from the outset that Jesus is the Christ, the Son of God, but the characters in the story have to have this truth revealed to them along the way. What may seem obvious to us will not seem at all obvious to the characters in the story, for they do not operate from the outset with the same sort of inside information. For this reason, among others, we should not be so hard on the disciples in Mark's story. They do not know what the reader knows. Seeing the narrative with the benefit of hindsight is a wonderful thing.

Mark himself, and apparently his audience, lived in a scripturally textured world. Even when Mark is not directly quoting Scripture, it is Scripture that informs how he presents things, even things as mundane as the apparel of John the Baptist. Recognizing the scriptural allusions and contexts is one of the keys to understanding the text of this Gospel. For example, John is seen as a preparer on the basis of juxtaposing several OT texts with the account of John's activities. We will see in due course that the main character of Mark's story, Jesus himself, keeps pointing to the necessity of exegeting life and particularly Jesus' activities by means of Scripture. "Mark's Jesus will repeatedly appeal to the Hebrew Bible to justify his practice. He deploys it offensively (11.17) and defen-

sively (2.24ff.). . . . His challenge to the ideological competence of his ideological rivals often has a bitter rhetorical edge: 'Have you never read what David
did . . . ?' (2.25); 'Have you not read in the book of Moses . . . ?' (12.26)."[37]

It will pay us to closely consider in what way Mark thinks John the Baptist
paved the way for the coming of Jesus. Did he perhaps prepare the hearts of
God's people to hear the good news by humbling them with the threat of judgment and calling them to repentance? Should we see repentance as the prepara-
tory step for having faith in the good news? Probably this is in part what Mark
would have us think. But on another level, John's announcement of imminent
judgment brought by the stronger one who would baptize with the Spirit prepared God's people for an eschatological message such as Jesus offered. Though
it is an old cliché, it bears asking: If you knew for a certainty you would face
God's judgment very soon, what would you do in the short time before then?
Would you amend your life? Would you turn from the things that fall short of
God's highest and best for you? Or would you take the opposite approach of in-
dulging in every excess you could think of before time ran out? It may well have
been fear rather than faith that motivated many to come and hear John and respond to his call for repentance and baptism.

Two important distinctions need to be made when discussing temptation
and sin. First, the Greek terms πειρασμος/πειραζω can be translated either
temptation/tempt or test. It is an old but valid distinction that God tests us but
Satan tempts us. The difference is not necessarily in the substance of what happens to the person undergoing trial, but in the intent behind the trial. God puts
us to the test to strengthen our moral character, like a workman tempering steel
so it will be strong and not alloyed with impure substances. The devil, on the
other hand, puts us to the test in order to destroy our good character. Yet there
is a further paradox, which the Markan account especially brings to the fore. It
is God's Spirit who casts Jesus out into the wilderness to be tempted. God certainly allows human beings to be tempted, and indeed, may even place them in
a locale where they will necessarily be tempted. This phenomenon may explain
the petition in the Lord's Prayer which says to God, "lead us not into temptation," or as another translation has it, "do not put us to the test/time of trial."

The distinction between temptation and sin is also crucial. Put simply, to
be tempted is not the same as to sin. A person who is tempted but successfully
resists the temptation has not sinned. Nevertheless, temptation indicates our
human vulnerability. If a person had no inclination to ever sin, he would be immune to temptations. The concept implies that a person is capable of being en-
ticed to do what he knows he ought not do. This tells us something significant
about Mark's portrait of Jesus as a human being. Jesus was truly human and so
not immune to real temptations. The Markan portrayal of things with tempta-

---

37. Myers, p. 97.

tions framing Jesus' ministry suggests that Jesus' temptations especially had to do with God's call on his life and what God wanted him to do. This is also often the case with those called into various forms of ministry today. One is often tempted to take the easy or comfortable road rather than the wilderness road which is the high calling of God on a person's life. As D. Bonhoeffer once said, when Christ calls a person, he calls him to come and die — die to self and selfish desires and to a self-directed course of living. A life lived out of a call from God is the antithesis of a life lived on the basis of self-centered career planning.

The portrayal of Jesus' time of trial involves both danger and assistance. There are wild beasts in the wilderness, but there are also angels. We are not told elsewhere in Mark's Gospel that angels assisted Jesus (though we may think that the transfiguration story in Mark 9 is about the OT saints assisting Jesus), but we are told that here in the first chapter. It reminds us that in the hour of need, God provides extra help, extra sustenance, extra strength so that we may persevere through the trial. Here no doubt there is an echo of a similar scene involving Elijah in 1 Kings 19:4-6. God may put us to the test, but he gives us the resources to persevere through that test. It is probable that no person can judge in advance what sorts of trials or temptations he could endure, precisely because one cannot gauge how much grace or what resources God will make available at the time of the trial in order to overcome it.

Finally, notice that the summary of Jesus' message implies three things: (1) The coming-near of God's dominion must be announced. Its appearance is not immediately evident to all and sundry. (2) In order to appropriately relate to the inbreaking divine saving and ruling activity, one must turn around or turn back. One must repent. (3) Not only must one divest oneself of certain past orientations, but one must face the future in a new way — one must believe the good news about this dominion. Without faith, the dominion of God may come, but one may get no personal benefit or help from that coming. In other words, each person must respond to this coming as an individual. This is precisely what we will see happening in the next section of Mark with the initial calling of individuals to discipleship. It must never be forgotten that Peter and the others could have rejected the call. They could have failed to respond in faith to it. That they did respond positively shows that they at least wanted to believe the good news.

III. The Call of the Fishermen (1:16-20)

This unit deserves to be treated independently of what precedes and follows it, as it takes the form of a call narrative. In fact, one could argue that we have two call narratives compressed together here at 1:16-18 and 1:19-20. There is a further such narrative at 2:14. These narratives establish from the outset that Jesus was doing something distinctive, for other Jewish teachers apparently did not go fishing for followers or disciples.[1] The tone of the narratives is positive in Mark 1, as Jesus is with friends and neighbors. It is only when we turn to Mark 2 that we begin to find conflict narratives. Furthermore, it appears that we are dealing with the Capernaum chronicles here, for most of the stories are set there, have indications of time, and call Peter "Simon" (1:16, 29, 30, 36).[2] Here a good case can be made for a Petrine source.

A literary analysis of 1:14-20 by V. K. Robbins has led to the suggestion that our author is combining Mediterranean preacher-teacher traditions with Jewish traditions, but this suggestion seems to be based on the assumption that the author has not created this pericope on the basis of a substantial historical tradition about what Jesus' itinerant ministry was actually like. Furthermore, it was not just Hellenistic preachers and philosophers who went on travels and taught and performed miracles as they went. The Jewish tradition also had itinerant leaders and prophets, whether one thinks of Abraham, Moses, or Elijah. Nor does there seem to be anything particularly "rhetorical" in the Greco-Roman sense of the term in the pattern — move to a new region and announce the summary of one's mes-

---

1. J. Marcus, *Mark 1–8* (New York: Doubleday, 1999), p. 177, notes three commissioning narratives in 1:16-20; 3:13-19; 6:7-13. These three narratives follow a summary of Jesus' activities in 1:14-15; 3:7-12; and 6:6b.
2. Marcus, p. 177.

sage, interaction with some listeners, the summons to discipleship or activity.[3]
The teacher/discipleship model revealed here seems in any case closer to Jewish
models than Greco-Roman ones. Jesus is actually looking for followers, not just
learners or dialogue partners. Marcus puts matters this way: "It is thus not principally the brothers' detection of some special quality in Jesus that leads to their becoming his followers, as in the typical disciple-teacher relationship . . . but *his* perception of *them*, his prophetic vision of what they will become under the impact
of his presence (cf. 1:17 'I will make you . . .')."[4]

TRANSLATION — 1:16-20

*And passing alongside the Sea of Galilee he saw Simon and Andrew, Simon's
brother, casting a circular net in the sea for they were fishermen. And Jesus said to
them: "Come on after me, and I will make you to be fishers of human beings." And
immediately leaving the nets they followed him. And going on a little he saw Jacob
the son of Zebedee and John his brother, and they were in the boat mending the
nets, and immediately he called them. And leaving their father Zebedee in the boat
with the hired man, they came after him.*

According to the Markan account, Jesus calls two pairs of brothers to be his first
disciples, all four of whom are fishermen. Notice that they are not called upon
to repent and believe but rather to leave their nets and follow. The social situation is one of the recruitment of disciples for new tasks, not, or at least not primarily, the conversion of the lost, but one may also add that by so recruiting
and training them Jesus is de facto establishing a new social entity, a new community.[5] Though we are accustomed to thinking of these men as poor, the social indicators in the text may suggest otherwise. The Zebedees could afford
both a boat and a hired man. Furthermore, we know that fishermen were indeed the regular targets of tax collectors since they had to sell their product
quickly and so dealt more often in money rather than relying on the bartering
system. If it is true that the Sea of Galilee was famous for being teeming with
fish, it would appear that one could have had a reasonably prosperous business
as a fisherman. The social situation described here is typical, for in both cases
we are dealing with family businesses, which in the case of the Zebedees involved two generations working together, plus extra help. Peter and Andrew
would seem to have had a more modest business, as they are not said to have a

---

3. See V. K. Robbins, "Mark 1.14-20: An Interpretation at the Intersection of Jewish
and Graeco-Roman Traditions," *NTS* 28 (1982): 220-36.

4. Marcus, p. 183.

5. See J. Painter, *Mark's Gospel* (London: Routledge, 1997), p. 35.

boat but rather were using a circular net with weighted edges to trap fish near the shore and perhaps to gig them. "The fishing trade is accurately represented: we see an independent artisan class, distinct from day laborers, whom they could afford to hire (1:20)."[6]

Jesus' call is only quoted once in this pericope, and in essence it is to come and fall in line behind him (οπισω in vv. 16 and 20). They are called to break ties with the past, but also to take up a new trade that in some way would be analogous with their old one. This is a call for total dedication to the mission. It is significant that though they respond to the call here, they do not fully take up the tasks entailed for some time. They must first be "made" fishers of human beings — shaped and molded and trained in the requisite skills. And of course, human beings are a hard species of creature to catch. The text says they responded "immediately" to the summons, and commentators have often speculated whether this suggests the authoritativeness of Jesus' summons[7] or whether, as John 3–4 may suggest, they had known something of Jesus' message and methods prior to this summons. There is a brief indication of the degree of sacrifice involved — namely, the Zebedees left father, boat, hired man, nets behind and got in line behind Jesus. "The point here is that following Jesus requires not just assent of the heart, but a fundamental reordering of socio-economic relationship. . . . This is not a call 'out of the world,' but into an alternative social practice."[8] But renunciation does not seem to be absolute, for we find the disciples back in their own homes soon thereafter, reminding us that it is likely that they had a home base (apparently Capernaum) from which they regularly went with Jesus to various parts of the region, only to return (see Mark 1:21; 2:1; etc.).

A survey of all the OT passages which use the analogy with fishing (cf. Jer. 16:16; Ezek. 29:4-6; 38:4; Amos 4:2; Hab. 1:14-17) shows there is an ominous overtone here in this word of Jesus, for always this metaphor is used in the context of a discussion about judgment.[9] What Jesus seems to be asking these disci-

---

6. C. Myers, *Binding the Strong Man: A Political Reading of Mark's Story of Jesus* (Maryknoll, N.Y.: Orbis, 1988), p. 132.

7. So, for example, Jerome, who says there must have been something divinely compelling in the face of the Savior, otherwise these men would not have acted so irrationally as to follow a man they had never seen before. His very countenance must have seemed irresistible (*Homily* 83). See T. C. Oden and C. A. Hall, eds., *Mark*, vol. 2 of *The Ancient Christian Commentary on Scripture* (Downers Grove, Ill.: InterVarsity, 1998), p. 20. If this were actually the case, it is hard to explain the widespread rejection of Jesus even by his own hometown folks. Cf. Marcus, p. 185, who stresses the overwhelming power of Jesus' word: "all human reticence has been washed away because *God* has arrived on the scene in the person of Jesus, and it is *his* compelling voice that speaks through Jesus' summons. . . ."

8. Myers, p. 133.

9. On the authenticity of this saying, see my work *The Christology of Jesus* (Philadelphia: Fortress, 1990), pp. 129-32.

ples to do is rescue some in the face of the coming eschatological judgment, lest all be lost, or rescue some out of the clutches of the powers of darkness. Various texts suggest that water was seen as a symbol of evil or loss, indeed of chaos (see, e.g., Ps. 74:13). From such waters one needed to be rescued. "In the background of Jesus' picture of 'fishers of men' it is therefore necessary to see that the waters . . . are the underworld, the place of sin and death. To fish out a [person] means to rescue him from the kingdom of darkness, out of the sphere which is hostile to God and remote from God."[10]

Because Jesus had come, and with him the inbreaking dominion of God, now was the time to rescue the perishing. Since the hour of decision was upon God's people, it was imperative to have fishers of human beings immediately. The disciples following Jesus, having given up much (including a normal life) to do so, served as visible symbols that the time for repentance or turning or change of direction had come. They demonstrated by their actions how to respond to the announcement that the dominion of God was at hand. A radical announcement requires a radical and total response. All prior claims on a person lose their urgency. This text is in various ways paradigmatic for the rest of this Gospel as per its teaching on discipleship (cf. 3:13-19; 6:7-13). It also stresses the distinctiveness of Jesus' approach to ministry among God's people. "There are no rabbinical stories of 'calling' and 'following after' analogous to the pericope in Mark and Q, nor did the summons 'follow me' resound from any rabbinical teacher in respect of entry into a teacher-pupil relationship."[11]

---

10. J. Manek, "Fishers of Men," *NovT* 2 (1958): 138-41, here p. 139.

11. M. Hengel, *The Charismatic Leader and His Followers* (New York: Crossroad, 1981), pp. 50-51.

IV. The Sabbatical Plan (1:21-28)

"Verses 16-20 have exhibited the authority of Jesus' word in calling disciples. Verses 21-28 now exhibit the authority of his word in teaching and exorcism."[1] The presentation of Jesus as an authority figure is clearly one of the major goals Mark wants to accomplish in the early part of his narrative. But is the issue primarily his authority or his power? The term εξουσια can be translated either way, and so we could translate the text "A new teaching with power?" This, however, does not suit most uses of the term in Mark, and so "authority" is a better translation.

Capernaum was a fishing village on the northwest side of the Sea of Galilee, and apart from the more explicit reference in Matt. 4:13, it would appear even from the Markan account that we are meant to think of this town as something of a headquarters for Jesus' Galilean campaign. This is not a surprise if Jesus took his own advice of accepting hospitality where it was offered, for we know that both Peter and his family and James and his family lived in this village. It is believable that he was a regular visitor in the homes of his first four disciples.

This story has a twofold emphasis on Jesus as a teacher and exorcist. The former emphasis, however, does not yet include revealing the content of the teaching other than that it was of a sort not encumbered with the citation of various external authorities and traditions to give it force and make it compelling. The worship of Jesus' day seems to have centered on prayer, the reading of Scripture, a sermon which exposited the text, and benedictions. If the Scriptures were read in Hebrew, there may have been summary translations in Ara-

---

1. R. H. Gundry, *Mark: A Commentary on His Apology for the Cross* (Grand Rapids: Eerdmans, 1993), p. 73.

maic (the reading of a targum?) or possibly even in Greek. Whether such worship services were held in a purpose-built building or a general assembly hall is uncertain (but cf. the excursus below). What actually made a place a religious assembly was not the building or its shape but rather whether a quorum of ten Jewish males was present.[2] It needs to be emphasized that the worship service was not led by clergy but rather by laypersons, perhaps especially those who had some expertise in the Scriptures, namely, the scribes. This may be why Jesus' teaching is here compared to that of the scribes. Jesus was able to teach in various synagogues precisely because it was a time before the dominance of ordained rabbis.

It is helpful to compare and contrast the first synagogue teaching of Jesus as presented in Mark and Luke. "In one sentence Mark moves Jesus from the symbolic margins to the heart of the provincial Jewish social order: synagogue (sacred space) on a sabbath (sacred time)."[3] Mark begins with a story where the response seems to be open or even positive to Jesus' synagogue message. Luke, on the other hand, in chapter 4 presents his version of the rejection in the Nazareth synagogue, a story Mark does not recount until chapter 6.[4] The net effect of this is that Mark's account seems to suggest that Jesus was setting out on a rather promising ministry in Galilee, whereas Luke highlights the difficulties, even with those one grew up with, right from the outset.

Synagogues in the Time of Jesus?

Were there purpose-built buildings for Jewish worship in Galilee or elsewhere in the Holy Land in the time of Jesus? This issue has been heatedly debated of late, and is especially pressing in regard to the synagogue remains in Capernaum.[5] It is true enough that the beautiful synagogue which now stands in Capernaum dates no earlier than the third century A.D., but there are clearly foundational remains from earlier buildings underneath the third-century structure. Furthermore, clear remarks by rabbis in the second century mention synagogues as religious buildings. Thus Abba Benjamin remarked: "One's prayer is heard only in the synagogue" (b. Ber. 6a), and R. Judah the First and R. Yohanon are mentioned as having studied in front of the large synagogue in Sepphoris, only a few miles from Jesus' hometown (y. Ber. 5.1.9a).

---

2. Women could not be counted among the quorum due to periodic uncleanness.

3. C. Myers, *Binding the Strong Man* (Maryknoll, N.Y.: Orbis, 1988), p. 141.

4. See J. Painter, *Mark's Gospel* (London: Routledge, 1997), p. 41.

5. For the debate see, e.g., H. C. Kee, "The Transformation of the Synagogue after 70 C.E.: Its Import for Early Christianity," *NTS* 36 (1990): 117-23, 191-99; R. Oster, "Supposed Anachronism in Luke-Acts' Use of *sunagoge*: A Rejoinder to H. C. Kee," *NTS* 39 (1993): 178-208; and Kee, "The Changing Meaning of Synagogue: A Response to Richard Oster," *NTS* 40 (1994): 281-83.

The lintel of the synagogue in Corinth which reads "synagogue of the Hebrews" seems to give us more secure evidence from the second century. If we work back to the evidence in Josephus, who spent considerable time in Galilee and was in a position to know if there were synagogues there and elsewhere in the first century, we find positive evidence for such religious buildings in *Jewish War* 2.285-91 (Caesarea Maritima), 7.43-44 (Syrian Antioch) that dates to at least A.D. 80 if not earlier. The inscription from the African city of Berenice dating from the mid-50s A.D. is best explained as a reference to a place (for it refers to the repair of the "synagogue"). The chief archaeological evidence from the Holy Land comes from Masada, the Herodium, and Gamala; the last particularly has features which suggest a building built specifically for religious meetings (e.g., it has an adjacent *mikvah;* Second Temple iconography on the lintel; the size of the hall makes clear it is not a household room, or a remodeling of such a room).[6] In the face of this evidence, the references to synagogues in various parts of the NT, including the Synoptics, Acts, and John, must be taken quite seriously, and this includes the ones in Mark, our earliest Gospel. It cannot plausibly be argued that Mark's references to synagogues as places reflect the post–A.D. 70 Jewish reality. Mark's references are, in various cases, clearly to a building, which Jesus and others can enter (Mark 1:21, 23, 29; 3:1; etc.). This reflects the fact that there was a well-organized religious life and focus even in various Galilean villages, as well as in the larger towns. It is a mistake to underestimate the profoundly religious character of the Galilee in which Jesus operated.

TRANSLATION — 1:21-28

And they went into Capernaum. And immediately on the Sabbath entering into the synagogue he taught. And they were awestruck by his teaching, for he was teaching them as having [inherent] authority and not as the scribes. And immediately there was in their synagogue a person with an unclean spirit, and he cried out saying, "What have we to do with you, Jesus of Nazareth? Have you come to destroy us? We know what you are — the Holy One of God." And Jesus rebuked him saying, "Be silent and come out of him." And the unclean spirit convulsed him and crying out with a loud cry he exited from him. And everyone was amazed, so that they debated with each other saying, "What is this? A new teaching with authority? And he commanded the unclean spirits and they obeyed him."[7] And the hearing of him went immediately everywhere unto the whole surrounding countryside of Galilee.

---

6. See L. Levine, "The Second Temple Synagogue: The Formative Years," in *The Synagogue in Late Antiquity,* ed. L. Levine (Philadelphia: American School of Oriental Research, 1987), pp. 201-22.

7. There are numerous textual variants in this verse, with the most well-supported alternative being the text which adds οτι before the reference to authority in C, K, Δ, Π, and various other texts. But the reading which best accounts for the others is the one rendered in the translation above. See Metzger, *TCGNT,* p. 75.

V. 22 tells us that people were astonished or overwhelmed by Jesus' teaching, and especially by the fact that it manifested an innate rather than a derived authority. Mark is placing an emphasis on the manner rather than the matter of Jesus' teaching. The γραμματευς were not in the main scribes, but rather those who were literate, could read and write, and so could quite naturally become the authorities in the Law, responsible for its interpretation and application. There was indeed a vast array of oral traditions and expansions of the written Law which the scribes were also cognizant of. Their authority was based on their learning, whereas Jesus' seemed to be like that of a prophet — someone who had received a word of God without study. It is interesting, as D. Luhrmann points out, that the scribes are linked closely with the theme of authority, in particular Jesus' authority, throughout Mark's narrative (cf. 1:22; 2:6, 10; 3:15, 22; 11:27-29, 33).[8] Jesus' exercise of power and his authoritative teaching that was independent of scribal traditions were a direct threat to the scribes' power and authority over the people.

While Jesus was teaching, a man with a spirit that made him ritually unclean entered the synagogue. He should not have been present since he was ritually unclean, and thus we should probably see his entry into the synagogue while Jesus is there as a deliberate provocation. The unclean spirit will be confronted and challenged by its opposite — the Holy One of God. Notice that Jesus' focus is on teaching and his teaching is interrupted, and only then does he respond by healing the possessed man. This is a regular pattern in Mark's Gospel. Healings seem mostly to happen in response to a pressing need, not as part of a program Jesus set out to follow. Notice that it is the spirit in the man that initiates the conversation. It is not accidental that Mark presents an exorcism as the first miracle in this Gospel. He wishes to make evident that Jesus has come to destroy the powers of darkness. His ministry involves waging war on these powers.[9]

The words of the spirit must then be seen as hostile. They should also be seen as an attempt, by a naming ritual, to get control of the situation. This defensive maneuver required that a correct name or title be used for Jesus in order to try and gain control.[10] The OT parallels to the phrase "what to me and to you" (cf. Judg. 11:12; 2 Sam. 16:10; 19:22; 1 Kings 17:18) mean something like: What do we have to do with you, or what do you want with us, or why are you meddling with us? The spirit rightly feels threatened and so is hostile, even though Jesus has done nothing yet to warrant such verbiage. Yet it is a paradox that Jesus encounters evil not merely on the Sabbath but in the synagogue right

---

8. D. Luhrmann, "Die Pharisaer und die Schriftgelehrten im Markusevangelium," *ZNW* 78 (1987): 169-85, here p. 182.

9. See J. Marcus, *Mark 1–8* (New York: Doubleday, 1999), p. 195.

10. See Gundry, p. 76.

at the beginning of his ministry. The demon seems to be suggesting that by his teaching there, Jesus had invaded the territory of this spirit.[11]

It is uncertain whether we should see v. 24b as a statement or as a question ("you have come to destroy us" or "have you come to destroy us?"). In either case an ongoing battle is indicated, not a battle with an isolated demon but with "us." Jesus' attack is on the whole community or realm of evil. Here, as elsewhere in Mark, only God, or supernatural beings, or humans who have received revelation from above know who Jesus really is.[12] In Mark ordinary sick individuals call Jesus names like teacher (9:17) or Son of David (10:47-48) or master (10:51) or good sir ("lord" with a little *l*), while by contrast the demons address Jesus as the Holy One of God (here cf. John 6:69) or the Son of God (3:11) or the Son of the Most High God (5:7). It is possible that this naming is to be seen as an attempt by the spirit to gain control over Jesus.[13] In short, they identify Jesus as more than a teacher, indeed as a unique and even supernatural figure who is recognizably part of their world and capable of doing battle with them. It is important to stress that in Mark a distinction is made between those who are sick or have a disease or fever and those who are possessed. This suggests that our author does not see possession as just another disease.[14]

Jesus rebukes the demon, as he does not wish to be confessed by the powers of darkness. Though the reader knows this is a true confession, it comes from a bad source. The command to be silent is in a sense the way the exorcist takes or exercises control over the demon. As PGM IX.4, 9 shows, this was a normal way to start an exorcism ritual, coupled with the command to come out (cf. PGM IV.1243, 1245, 3013). It is thus not at all clear that we should see this particular command to silence as part of a messianic secret motif. Nor is Jesus being depicted here as a magician. He uses no adjuration, incantations, physical manipulation, or appeal to a deity to accomplish this exorcism. The emphasis is

---

11. Mark's use of the primitive phrase "unclean spirit" rather than "demon" is another clue to the Jewish provenance of the author and his source material.

12. The reaction of the church fathers to this story is interesting. Ambrose says we are not to believe the demons even when they tell the truth. Augustine says the crucial difference between this confession by the demon and Peter's is that the former was offered out of fear, the latter out of love. See T. C. Oden and C. A. Hall, eds., *Mark*, vol. 2 of *The Ancient Christian Commentary on Scripture* (Downers Grove, Ill.: InterVarsity, 1998), p. 21.

13. See Myers, p. 143, and compare the converse of this process — see Mark 5:9.

14. It is also interesting that one study that W. Lane, *The Gospel of Mark* (Grand Rapids: Eerdmans, 1974), pp. 73-76, cites makes the following "modern" distinctions between psychoses and the reports of exorcisms here and elsewhere: (1) symptoms of possession are arbitrary, whereas psychotic syndromes are fixed; (2) the possessed react to religious matters and the supernatural but are indifferent to profane matters; (3) exorcism produces unique psychic phenomena such as supernatural knowledge which ceases once the exorcism is over.

entirely on Jesus' simple, effective command, and so on his innate authority in the situation.[15]

The possessed man is then convulsed, there is a loud shriek, and the demon leaves the man just as Jesus commanded. It is characteristic of the first half of this Gospel that Jesus' deeds of power draw wows from various observers. Astonishment, however, must not be mistaken for faith in the Markan scheme of things. In fact, Myers stresses the following: "The terms at the start and finish of this episode that describe their reaction (ekplesso, thambeomai) are strong, and are used by Mark almost always in relation to Jesus' teaching (6:2; 10:24, 26, 32; 11:18). They connote not just incredulity but a kind of panic associated with the disruption of the assumed order of things."[16] In fact, Mark uses six different words to describe the reactions of astonishment to Jesus' mighty works. "Mark wishes us to know that Jesus constantly filled people with a mixture of wonder, awe, and fear at what he said and did (1.27; 2.12; 4.41; 5.15, 20, 33, 36, 42; 6.50, 51; 9.6, 15, 32; 10.24, 32 (twice); 11.18; 12.17; 15.5, 44; 16.5ff., 8)."[17]

Jesus' powerful acts are unsettling and often prompt questions about who Jesus might be. Notice we are told that the crowd debates this matter, which means it is not a foredrawn conclusion. The wonders in themselves neither force a faith response nor clearly indicate the character of the one performing them. The latter comes only through a word of revelation.

Mark's Theology of Miracles

Mark's theology of miracles would seem to entail the following: (1) They can perhaps create an openness to true faith in Jesus but do not create faith. "On the one hand the healing narratives attract men to Jesus; on the other, they do not reveal his true nature and the real claim he makes on them; this only comes from the cross. Hence Mark's ambivalent attitude. So he retains the miracles but sets them within the framework of a story dominated by the passion."[18] (2) A belief in Jesus' ability to perform miracles is a true but inadequate faith in him. (3) Lack of faith can hinder or prevent Jesus from performing all the miracles he might in a given locale (see 6:5). (4) Miracles can strengthen the faith of someone who already believes in Jesus. (5) Miracles are not the main thrust of Jesus' ministry. He does not normally set out to perform miracles, but rather does so on request, providing a sort of crisis intervention service in this regard. Almost all of Mark's miracles are clustered in the first half of his Gospel, the stories about them making up about 47 percent of that half,

---

15. See rightly Gundry, p. 77.

16. Myers, p. 142.

17. D. English, *The Message of Mark* (Downers Grove: InterVarsity, 1992), p. 54.

18. E. Best, *Disciples and Discipleship: Studies in the Gospel according to Mark* (Edinburgh: T. & T. Clark, 1986), p. 190.

with the most frequently represented miracle being exorcism (cf. 1:32-34; 3:7-12; 6:53-56; 8:14-21). Mark wishes to stress the supernatural war that Jesus is taking part in, but it is hard to find any redactional evidence that Mark is interested in heightening the miraculous aspect of his source material.[19] C. K. Barrett is surely correct that the Markan miracle stories themselves are commonplace enough, but it is their christological and eschatological context and interpretation which set them apart from either Jewish or Greco-Roman miracle tales about figures such as Honi the Circle Drawer or Apollonius of Tyana.[20]

Notice that Jesus, unlike other exorcists,[21] uses no chants, spells, incantations in performing his exorcisms. He simply speaks a word of power and the exorcism transpires. P. Achtemeier is on the right track when he says about 1:21-28: "Here, plainly, Mark wants us to be clear on the fact that the power inherent in Jesus' teaching is precisely the power that enables him to overcome demonic forces. . . . The Jesus who performed mighty acts is the Jesus who is preeminently the teacher. . . ."[22]

V. 27b is difficult to punctuate. Should we read "What is this new teaching with authority? He even commanded the unclean spirits . . ."? Or should it read "What is this? A new teaching with authority he even commanded . . ."? Most scholars take the term εξουσια with what precedes, and so modifying the term "teaching," particularly because a powerful teaching has already been referred to in v. 22. Against this, however, Mark may intend to indicate that like the teaching, the exorcism was also a powerful happening. In any case, we are told that the news of this event rapidly spread throughout the region. Yet Mark in his elliptical account does not here tell us what the content of the new teaching is. The focus is on Jesus as the authoritative teacher, not on his subject matter. In short, the focus is christological, not pedagogical.

In regard to the command to silence, it appears that we are to see this as simply part of the exorcist's ritual to gain control of the demon, rather than a part of Mark's messianic secret motif. Does Mark wish us to think that Jesus did not want to gain a reputation as an exorcist or healer because he had come primarily to proclaim the gospel of God? In view of the narratives that follow, should we think that if Jesus got a reputation as a healer he might be prevented from accomplishing his main task of proclaiming the good news about the inbreaking dominion of God? These questions must be kept in mind as the story progresses.

Whatever else one may say, Mark is careful to warn his audience that mir-

---

19. Best, p. 182.

20. C. K. Barrett, *The Holy Spirit and the Gospel Tradition* (Philadelphia: Fortress, 1947), p. 57.

21. On which see my work *The Christology of Jesus* (Philadelphia: Fortress, 1990), pp. 164-66.

22. P. J. Achtemeier, "He Taught Them Many Things: Reflections on Marcan Christology," *CBQ* 42 (1980): 465-81, here pp. 478-80.

acles could be ambiguous, for: (1) they lead Pharisees and Herodians to oppose Jesus (3:6); (2) they cause scribes to think of Jesus as possessed (3:22); (3) they leave his hometown folks unimpressed (6:2-3); (4) they cause Herod to erroneously think John the Baptist is back from the dead (6:14-16); (5) they do not eliminate the disciples' misunderstanding (6:52; 8:17-21). At the same time, miracles are neither dismissed by Mark nor denied nor demythologized, but simply presented in a larger eschatological and christological context.

Bridging the Horizons

In a compelling book entitled *The Irresistible Urge to Preach,* Dr. William Myers chronicles the "call" narratives of various African-American preachers who felt led to pursue a pulpit ministry. The common element in all these stories is that they felt "called" by God to do this. It was not simply a matter of career planning; indeed, in many cases it went quite against such planning. This is why Myers entitled a subsequent work dealing with this subject *God's Yes Was Louder Than My No.* In reading Mark 1:16-20, it needs to be borne in mind that this is not primarily a summons to salvation, but rather a story of a call to ministry offered by one devout Jew to other devout Jews. The disciples could not have known in advance how costly pursuing such a call would be, and yes, pursuing it would change their spiritual orientation as well, but the focus is on the call and the future ministry ("becoming fishers of human beings").

The cost of pursuing the call is ably summarized by John Wesley in his covenanting service created in the 1740s for his growing Methodist movement: "This taking of His yoke upon us means we are heartily content that he appoint us our place and work, and that He alone be our reward. Christ has many services to be done; some are easy, others are difficult; some bring honour, others bring reproach; some are suitable to our natural inclinations and temporal interests, others are contrary to both. In some we may please Christ and please ourselves, in others we can not please Christ except by denying ourselves. Yet the power to do all these things is assuredly given us in Christ, who strengthens us."

When one talks about being called by God, one is recognizing that the initiative is with God and not with us. Sometimes a call is a matter of being recalled back to a service that one had already been involved in and committed oneself to. George Herbert describes some of his own struggles in the poem "The Collar." In this poem he cries out to God that he has had enough and wishes to take the clerical collar off. He complains that his friends are all having fun and enjoying life, whereas he is bearing various burdens and responsibilities. He would rather be saying *carpe diem* than *carpe Deum.* But in the midst of his protest to the Almighty, he says he heard a voice saying to him, "Child," to which he responded, "my Lord." Like the psalmists who cry out to God in the midst of pursuing a called existence, Herbert rightly took his complaint to the highest court of appeal, which is a way of saying he left it in the right hands to resolve the issue. The call of God leaves an indelible mark on a person, but whether that mark is a blessing or a curse depends on how one responds to it.

It is right to link the exorcism stories with the larger assault by Jesus on disease, decay, and death. Notice that the NT shows little interest in demons except when the discussion is about exorcisms, namely, when the powers of darkness impinge on human life. Mark's Gospel does not seek to distill esoteric knowledge meant to satisfy pious curiosity about the great unknowns in regard to the existence of evil in this world. It is not an exercise in early Gnosticism. What Mark does seek to do is offer saving knowledge to those who need help and healing.

Donald English, in his balanced treatment of the subject, stresses that while on the one hand one certainly does not find a demon under every rock in the NT, even in its apocalyptic literature, on the other hand the authors of the NT certainly affirm the reality of supernatural evil, and that this evil has a personal face — involving intention, will, power, and other traits of a personal being.[23] I agree with his conclusion that perhaps the greatest mistake one could make is to fall for the ultimate deception perpetrated by the powers of darkness — the deception that there is no such thing as Satan or supernatural evil. On the other hand the NT, including even Mark, does not absolve human beings of moral responsibility for their actions simply because there are supernatural beings involved in the human drama. To the contrary, the degree of ethical rigor and accountability called for in the Synoptics is very high indeed. The major focus even in Mark is on how human beings can and do (or don't) respond to the ministry of Jesus. Even in the case of the demon possessed, much is expected once he returns to his right mind.

Lessons are also to be learned from the fact that the ancients, including Mark, tended to treat human beings as psychosomatic wholes, such that the person's spiritual condition could affect his physical or emotional or mental condition, and by the same token any of these other areas of human personality could affect each other. There were of course social consequences to being ritually unclean as well, such that one became an outcast from society. This is poignantly illustrated by the story of the Gerasene demoniac who was forced to live in what Jews considered the most unclean of all spots — a graveyard. There are of course modern analogies to how society treats someone with a deadly contagious disease such as HIV/AIDS.

What one notices about Jesus' behavior is that he is never worried about

---

23. English, p. 56.

becoming unclean or sick by fraternizing with or touching the spiritually or physically or morally unclean. Indeed, he seems to have gone out of his way in some cases to minister to them. Not surprisingly this behavior offended those who were part of the holiness movement of that day — the Pharisaic movement. The question a text like Mark 1 raises for us is: Are we more concerned with public opinion and with not offending some people by being compassionate to society's outcasts, or are we more concerned with helping those in the greatest need in our society? The answer to this question in Jesus' case seems obvious from the very outset in Mark. Jesus did not particularly care whom he scandalized if he believed he was doing God's work and helping to bring in God's dominion. He was also more concerned with who got the cure than who got the credit.

V. Healings at Home and on the Road (1:29-45)

In Mark 1:21-39 the Evangelist presents a portrait of a day in the life of Jesus, beginning on the Sabbath morning with the healing in the synagogue (1:21) and continuing through sundown (1:32) and into the early morning of the next day (1:35). The social settings of this day include the synagogue, a house, and a deserted place — "there is a public/private dialectic in Jesus' movement, with the former consistently exerting pressure on the latter."[1] 1:28 should be compared to 1:39, which makes clear that Jesus' public face is becoming increasingly visible and well known during the early ministry period in Galilee. Yet Myers suggests that we must contrast Capernaum, which was a (small) city that stood close to the highway that ran northward into Syria, with the country villages or market towns which Jesus decides to frequent after being "crowded" in Capernaum.[2] There is of course the further difficulty that John 1:44 tells us that Peter and Andrew were from Bethsaida, but it is not impossible that, since they were commercial fishermen, they had more than one residence.[3] In any event, Mark 1:29-31, 32-34, and 35-38 look like three pieces of traditional material to which Mark has made minimal redactional modifications.[4]

1:29-45 involves two somewhat longer stories of healing (Simon's

---

1. C. Myers, *Binding the Strong Man: A Political Reading of Mark's Story of Jesus* (Maryknoll, N.Y.: Orbis, 1988), p. 149.

2. Myers, p. 150. He also notes that once Jesus is driven out of Capernaum at 3:6, he does not enter a polis again until he comes to Jerusalem. His is clearly not an urban strategy of ministry.

3. See R. Guelich, *Mark 1–8.26* (Waco: Word, 1989), p. 62.

4. Guelich, p. 66.

mother-in-law and the man with the skin disease) which frame two shorter notices about Jesus being a healer and an exorcist and about Jesus, the hunted man, seeking an isolated place to pray. It is important to see the social significance of especially the first of these stories. All the stories show Jesus acting in ways that could lead to his marginalization in Jewish society, but the story of the touching and healing of a sick woman on the Sabbath would clearly have been the most troubling. It can be no accident that Mark chooses to highlight the fact that Jesus' first two miracles (an exorcism and a healing of a disease) both occurred on the Sabbath. Jesus is established as a very controversial figure from the outset of this biography.

Though there are later stories of rabbis taking the hand of another man and healing him, there are no such stories of rabbis doing so for a woman, and especially not for a woman who was not a member of the healer's family (*b. Ber.* 5b). In addition, there is the fact that Jesus performed this act on the Sabbath. Thus, while touching a nonrelated woman was in itself an offense, and touching one that was sick and therefore unclean was doubly so, performing this act on the Sabbath only compounds the social offense. But this is not all. The service of Peter's mother-in-law to Jesus (and the others) itself could have constituted work on the Sabbath, depending on what was done (e.g., preparing food). In any case, later Jewish traditions suggest that women should not serve meals to male strangers.[5] The important point about Jesus, however, is that he does not see the touch of a woman, even a sick woman, as any more defiling than the touch of the man with the skin disease. Jesus' attitudes about ritual purity differed from those of many of his fellow Jews.

Jesus' command to the man with the skin disease to present himself to the priest suggests another aspect of his social agenda. For those who were not becoming his disciples and following him, Jesus tried to reintegrate the healed back into normal Jewish village life. The purpose of the command was not to suggest that Jesus still believed all such rules were mandatory on all Jews, but rather it was an act of compassion on Jesus' part, helping the healed recover a normal existence.

TRANSLATION — 1:29-45

And immediately coming out from the synagogue he went into the house of Simon and Andrew with Jacob and John. But the mother-in-law of Simon was laid up being feverish, and immediately they speak to him concerning her. And coming in he raises her grasping the hand; and the fever left her and she served them. But it

---

5. See my discussion in *Women in the Ministry of Jesus* (Cambridge: Cambridge University Press, 1984), p. 172 n. 125.

was early evening, when the sun set, they carried to him all those having illness and those being demon-possessed. And there was the whole of the city collected before the door. And he cured many sick having various diseases, and many demons he cast out, and he did not allow the demons to speak, because they knew him.[6]

And rising up in the very early evening Jesus went out and entered into a deserted place and there he prayed. And Simon and those with him hunted him down. And they found him and they say to him, "All are seeking you." And he says to them, "Let's go elsewhere to the next market town so that I might even preach there, for I have come forth for this purpose." And he went preaching into their synagogues in the whole of Galilee and casting out demons.

And a man with a dreaded skin disease comes to him crying out and falling on his knees[7] saying to him, "If you will, you are able to cleanse me." And being angry,[8] extending his hand he touched him and says to him, "I will, be clean." And immediately the skin disease left him and he was clean. And being enraged Jesus sent him back immediately and says to him, "Say nothing to anyone, but go show yourself to the priest concerning your cleansing as Moses commanded as a witness to them." But going out he began to preach a great deal and spread about the word, so that Jesus was no longer able to openly enter into a city, but rather was outside in the deserted place. And they came to him from everywhere.

A. A Miracle for a Mother-in-Law (1:29-31)

The pericope in 1:29-31 is apparently meant to be an account of an event which happened shortly after the synagogue occurrence mentioned just previously in the chapter. It has been conformed to the typical pattern of such miracle stories, highlighting the key elements of: (1) the touch of the healer; (2) the sudden cure; (3) the action by the cured person demonstrating he is well once more.

---

6. Some manuscripts add "to be the Christ" here, which seems surely to be a later expansion.

7. Some important manuscripts omit the phrase "falling on his knees," including B, D, and W. In view, however, of the parallels in Matt. 8:2 and Luke 5:12, which both indicate that the man knelt, it would seem likely that their Markan source contained such an idea. See Metzger, *TCGNT*, p. 76.

8. There is considerable controversy as to whether the original reading is "having compassion" (supported by a good spread of good manuscripts, including ℵ, A, B, C, K, and others) or "being angry" (supported by D, it, Ephraem). Clearly the latter reading is more difficult and perhaps is to be preferred. On the other hand, two other Markan texts refer to Jesus as angry (3:5; 10:14), and no copyists felt compelled to emend them. There is a possibility that the two renderings represent different readings of an Aramaic original for *ethraham*, which means "he had pity" in Syriac, while *ethra'em* means "he was enraged." The two terms could have been mistaken for each other. See Metzger, *TCGNT*, pp. 76-77.

Here in v. 29 it is made quite clear that Peter is married (cf. 1 Cor. 9:5), and so we see some of the cost of discipleship for him here as well. This healing, like the exorcism, takes place on the Sabbath, and it is important to understand the theology of the Sabbath in Jesus' day. The Sabbath had become a symbol of the eschatological rest or shalom that God would one day provide for his people when, as the Pharisees thought, Messiah came and brought in the age to come. The longed-for Sabbath was the coming of the dominion of God. Thus Jesus' beginning his healing work on the Sabbath should be seen as a deliberate attempt to bring in that final Sabbath rest, a time when creation would be relieved not just of the toil and turmoil of a fallen world but of disease, decay, and death as well. From this perspective, there was no better time to heal a person than on the Sabbath as an indicator that the ultimate Sabbath was coming.

Yet unfortunately, what Jesus did would be seen and was seen as a violation of the Sabbath, indeed as work on the Sabbath. Such a response to Jesus' miracle reflects a failure to understand what the Sabbath is for, to give persons rest from what ails them or wearies them, as well as the further failure to recognize that the Lord of the Sabbath was in their midst — the one who had authority and power to bring in the Sabbath rest.

We are told in v. 30 that Peter's mother-in-law had a fever. This was an all-encompassing designation, and was in some cases even seen in antiquity as a disease itself rather than a symptom of some other malady. Jesus lifts up the hand of the woman, "immediately" the fever leaves her, and she serves Jesus and his entourage. The word used in v. 31 is διακονεω. It often has the semitechnical sense of to serve food or to wait tables, and could certainly mean that here, though it could also have the broader sense of "to serve." Notice that in 9:33-37 and 10:43-45 the essence of discipleship is described in terms of service. This may suggest that we are meant to see Peter's mother-in-law as giving the proper response of a disciple to Jesus, serving the Master as she was able.

This story is typical of the sorts of short narratives or characteristic anecdotes that one would expect in an ancient biography. In view of the fact that Mark will go on to recount numerous other stories of a more impressive nature, it seems likely that this story was preserved because of whose mother-in-law was involved. This is the only tale in Mark's Gospel which tells of Jesus helping the family of one of his disciples.[9] Schweizer also emphasizes that the phrase "with Jacob and John" "is noteworthy because it may stem from an old Petrine tradition formulated in the first person: 'We came with. . . .'"[10]

---

9. See J. Painter, *Mark's Gospel* (London: Routledge, 1997), p. 45.

10. E. Schweizer, *The Good News according to Mark* (Atlanta: John Knox, 1971), p. 53.

B. Night Work (1:32-34)

Vv. 32-34 are a summary statement of the response to these first Sabbath miracles. Here the crowds wait until after the Sabbath, until early evening on Saturday, presumably because they were fearful that carrying the sick to Jesus on the Sabbath would be a violation. Marcus rightly points out that this shows that devotion to traditional Jewish religious practices could coexist with reverence for and dependence on Jesus.[11] The response was overwhelming, so much so that there was a huge crowd at the door of the house where Jesus was (Peter's mother-in-law's?). We are told he healed many with various and sundry diseases. The point of the remark seems to be that Jesus' power was so great that no disease was untreatable for him. Again we are told that demons, when they were cast out, were not allowed to speak. This time we are informed why that was — because they knew him.

Here, I think, one can perhaps refer to a messianic secret motif. Obviously Jesus doesn't want demons to be the ones to reveal his identity to God's people. The command to silence of the demons has a different social function than the command to silence of the man with the skin disease, for the latter is ordered to allow Jesus to continue to freely pursue the reasons he undertook his ministry in the first place. We must beware of reading vv. 32-34 as simply a success story. The people are not coming to Jesus for the reason he wants them to come. They come for relief from physical ailments, but Jesus came to preach the dominion of God. The reader may be meant to think that the crowds did not see the exorcisms and healings as Jesus did — as victories in the conflict with Satan, and as examples that the dominion was breaking in. The crowds may have seen them as only a temporary respite from their woes.

C. Embarking on a Mission (1:35-39)

It is possible that v. 35 is meant to suggest that the pressure was already getting too great on Jesus, or things were not going as he would wish. "Prayer was an essential part of his service and continually guarded that service from overactivity as well as from indolence. It was at the same time a refuge from an enthusiastic recognition on the part of the individuals who did not desire to become disciples."[12] Jesus thus slips away to the desert, or chalk wilderness, to pray. Only three times in this Gospel do we hear of Jesus praying: (1) here at the beginning of the ministry; (2) in the middle of the ministry at the feeding of the multitude; (3) in the Garden of Gethsemane. In other words, these references

11. J. Marcus, *Mark 1–8* (New York: Doubleday, 1999), p. 200.
12. Schweizer, p. 56.

appear at crucial junctures, at crisis moments in the narrative. Notice that there are five references in Mark to "uninhabited places" (1:35, 45; 6:31, 32, 35).

We must bear in mind the symbolic character of the "desert" or wilderness. It is the place of contact with the supernatural, both for endowment when the contact is with God and for conflict when it is with Satan. The point here is that Jesus went to a solitary place to pray, to be alone with the deity. In each praying episode Jesus' retreat is preceded by a demonstration of his great power and preaching. If Gethsemane is any clue, Jesus is seeking guidance from the Father about what he should do in view of the responses he is getting to his ministry.

As is not infrequently the case in Mark, Peter is depicted as seeking out Jesus. Indeed, the verb here conveys a sense of urgency, and the translation "pursued" would not be inappropriate. He takes the lead among the disciples in following Jesus wherever he goes, and he speaks for the disciples when he addresses Jesus. Cranfield suggests plausibly that we have here in 1:29ff. a series of episodes based on Petrine reminiscences.[13] Peter informs Jesus in v. 37 that all are seeking him, but apparently we are to think they are seeking Jesus for the wrong thing and the wrong reason. Jesus' response is apparently to be seen as surprising. He says let's go somewhere else where I can continue preaching, for that is the main reason I have set out on this ministry. This saying should be compared to the other remarks which identify Jesus' purposes for his ministry (cf. 1:24, 38; 2:17; 10:45). As Marcus says, a case can be made that Jesus is being presented as a divine envoy, sent by God as a herald to proclaim a message (cf. Amos 7:14-15; Dan. 9:21-23; Josephus, Ant. 3.400).[14] Thus v. 39 informs us that Jesus implemented his plan, making the preaching circuit of Galilean synagogues in market towns, but also continuing to cast out demons. These were the two main thrusts of his attack on the powers of darkness. It is interesting that in Mark 1 the real emphasis is on Jesus' preaching, but thereafter it is on his teaching.

D. The Maladies of Skin and Sin (1:40-45)

At vv. 40-45 we have the story of a man with a dreaded skin disease coming to Jesus. As Hooker suggests, the story is presented in a fashion which intimates that we are to think of this man as having an apparently incurable disease who is driven by desperation to violate the social codes in order to find a cure.[15] Ac-

---

13. C. E. B. Cranfield, The Gospel according to St. Mark (Cambridge: Cambridge University Press, 1972), pp. 81-84.

14. Marcus, p. 204; cf. E. Lohmeyer, Das Evangelium des Markus (Göttingen: Vandenhoeck & Ruprecht, 1951), p. 43.

15. M. Hooker, The Gospel according to Mark (Peabody, Mass.: Hendrickson, 1991), p. 78.

cording to Levitical law (Lev. 13:45), such a person was to go about crying "Unclean, unclean" so that no one would approach him and be contaminated. He knew of Jesus' power, for he says, "If you will, you can make me clean." Notice that the primary concern is with being clean so that he can reenter Jewish society, being a whole person. This is a very Jewish way of looking at disease, by focusing on its ritual effects, whereas a pagan would have simply said, "If you will, you can make me well."

The term λεπρος (from λεπειν, meaning to scale or peel off) in antiquity covered a whole gamut of skin diseases, and it is difficult to say what this man had. The disease we know as leprosy appears not to have existed in Jesus' time and region. In any event, the disease made the man perpetually unclean (see Lev. 13:45-47) and must have caused deep anguish, for it prevented normal relationships and fellowship with one's neighbors and friends. This was doubly so because such a disease was often seen as a divine punishment for serious sins (see 2 Kings 5:7). Thus cleansing is uppermost in the man's mind, for he would like to lead a normal life.

In this story we see a definite contrast between Jesus, who can make someone clean, and the priest, who can only declare someone to be clean. Clearly Jesus is seen as superior. Later rabbinic literature suggested that such skin diseases were as difficult to get rid of as raising the dead was to accomplish.[16] Thus this miracle takes on significance as a deed of great power. The seriousness with which Jews took this disease is clearly shown by the fact that they believed that someone who came in contact with a person with such a disease may as well have touched a corpse. A man with this disease was among the living dead — untouchable (cf. Num. 12:12; Job 18:13; 11QTemple 45.17-18).

V. 41 has a serious textual difficulty. Should we, with most manuscripts, read that Jesus was deeply moved with compassion, or is the more difficult reading "he was angry" to be preferred? It is difficult to understand why a scribe would ever substitute wrath for compassion if the latter was the original reading. But if we accept the minority reading, we must ask, Angry at what? Possibly we are to think that Jesus is angry at the ravages of the disease, or some have even suggested that prophetic foresight is involved here. Jesus is angry because he knows what the man is about to do — namely, disobey Jesus once he is healed, and ignore the command to silence. The former suggestion finds some support in the healing scene in Mark 7:34, and one may compare John 11:33, 38. "Therefore, Jesus' anger is a 'righteous anger' that recognizes the work of the Evil One in the sick as well as the possessed. . . ."[17] This makes good sense in light of the use of the term "cast out," which also occurs in this narrative.

Jesus heals the man anyway, and we are told quite specifically that he

---

16. See Schweizer, p. 57.
17. Guelich, p. 74.

touched him, which stands in contrast to what we find in 2 Kings 5:10. This would certainly render Jesus unclean, but the issue of Jesus' view of the Levitical laws is not really fully broached until Mark 7. One could argue that Jesus was willing to incur uncleanness in order to help others, but this seems an inadequate assessment because we are nowhere told that Jesus, like the man he heals, ever went through ritual cleansing after this encounter. What Mark will suggest in chapter 7 is that Jesus believed that with the inbreaking of God's dominion these rules about clean and unclean, and indeed also various Sabbath rules, were obsolescent. Such rules had fulfilled their purpose, but now the Holy One of God had appeared and a new state of affairs was at hand.[18]

Jesus sternly warns the man to say nothing to anyone (vv. 43-44). The double negative used here in the Greek makes this statement emphatic. Instead, the man was to simply show himself to the local priest in order to receive a clean bill of health.[19] This was to fulfill what the Mosaic Law said about priests having to witness and vouch for the person's healthy condition. Hooker is probably right about the use of the verb εκβαλλω here, that it indicates the urgency with which Jesus sends the man to the priest, commanding him not to stop along the way and speak to people.[20] Instead, the man does his own free-lance witnessing to what has transpired (notice the mention of preaching and spreading the word around openly). Unfortunately he bore witness about the wrong thing in the wrong way. The results of this ill-advised witnessing were also all wrong. Jesus was made unable to come openly into a Galilean city because of his burgeoning reputation as a healer. Thus Jesus goes out once more to the desert or wilderness area to escape the throng. But this time not just the disciples but the crowds follow him. The man who came to bring in God's shalom and rest was himself to have no rest or peace.

---

18. See Marcus, p. 211: "Our passage, then, foreshadows both Jesus' eschatological freedom vis-a-vis the Law and his insistence that he upholds it."

19. It is possible to read the text to mean "to bear witness against them," which might refer to Jesus providing evidence to the authorities, which counts against the conclusion that he was one who disregarded or broke the Law. See Guelich, p. 76. But nothing in the story itself suggests such a conclusion. Hooker, p. 82, debates why Mark should say "them" when only one priest is actually mentioned, but then concludes, rightly I think, that the one priest stands for the entire group. It is unlikely that we are to see this phrase as referring to a witness against Jesus' opponents (Pharisees, scribes), who have yet to really appear in the story, but it is believable that this story is meant to make us think of Jesus as one who respects Torah, in view of the controversies that are to arise in Mark 2–7 over Jesus and the Law.

20. Hooker, p. 81.

Bridging the Horizons

In this section of Mark 1 we have seen a portrait of Jesus as both compassionate and angry, as on the one hand prepared to heal and help the mother-in-law of a disciple, and yet upset at being overly pressed to perform miracles and then angry when confronted with the ravages of the illness of a man with skin disease. Mark does not offer us a one-dimensional picture of Jesus, nor does he just highlight Jesus' humanness, though he certainly does the latter perhaps most effectively of all the Evangelists.

Consider for a moment Jesus the man of prayer, who is especially depicted as such in Mark during a time of crisis or at a crucial juncture in his ministry. It is a clear indicator of his true humanness that Jesus feels a need to withdraw and speak with his Father in heaven to gain perspective and direction, and perhaps also reassurance. Prayer is the posture of a human as he approaches his God. It is a matter of supplication, not a forcing of a reluctant deity to do something God might not otherwise have done. Jesus prayed because he needed to do so, for he was truly human. From the Christian point of view which also affirms that Jesus is divine, Jesus' praying did not mean that Jesus went off and talked to himself, but rather he had communion and communication with another member of the triune Godhead.

Prayer, of course, in the Judeo-Christian tradition, is also not a matter of informing an ignorant deity of what needs to be said or done. Indeed, it is not a matter of informing God about anything. God already knows all realities and all possibilities. Prayer is for the benefit of the one who prays. It is a tool for God to use to better inform us, better direct us, better help us be conformed to God's will. Notice how Jesus in Gethsemane quite deliberately asks one thing but then makes the proviso "but not what I want but what you want" (14:36). Prayer is a time in which our wills are not merely to be expressed but also conformed to God's will. But God in his mercy also has chosen to use prayer as one means by which the divine plan is indeed to be carried out. God has chosen to implement the dominion agenda by means of human beings and their prayers. Prayer, then, is not empty words or useless talk; it is God's tool to bring about the divine will. It may also be stressed that prayer is the means by which the divine-human encounter is enhanced and the divine-human relationship gains greater intimacy.

It has been said that the capacity for righteous anger is essential to being a minister or servant of God. We may think of anger against injustice, but the story of the leper presents us with a Jesus who is angry with the ravages of sin and disease. There are three Greek words in this tale ("angry"; εμβρειμησα-μενος, which literally means snorting, referring to great internal agitation; and finally the verb "cast out") that suggest very strong emotion on Jesus' part. The Markan portrait of Jesus does not fit the image of a Jesus who was never stern or emotional or angry or even abrasive. Yet one must ask what Jesus was angry about.

Properly directed, a righteous anger, an anger caused by not settling for "the way of the world," can be a very good thing, indeed a catalyst for necessary change in the world. Whether it is the civil rights marchers in the 1960s in the United States with their nonviolent expressions of righteous anger, or the abolitionists of the eighteenth and nineteenth centuries on both sides of the Atlantic, or even doctors and scientists who have become so frustrated and angry with diseases that have taken away friends and family members that they have worked even harder to find cures, we can all think of examples where righteous anger has produced good fruit. This in turn means that a bland submission to or tolerance of all worldly conditions should not be seen as a virtue. There are indeed some things worth combating in this world, and no Gospel more aptly presents Jesus as a battler against the forces of evil than Mark's. As such, the Markan Jesus stands at odds with the stereotype of a Jesus who was always so meek and mild that he never said a discouraging word, never got angry, never condemned anyone or anything, and so was generally innocuous.

There is, according to the theology of our earliest Evangelist, some kind of connection between faith and healing, but what kind of connection? On the one hand, a lack of faith seems to definitely impede the healing of people (6:5-6). On the other hand, faith, whether on the part of the diseased person or as exercised by those connected with the diseased person, seems to make healing more possible or feasible (cf. 1:40 to 2:5). The man with the skin disease says to Jesus, "You can make me whole, if you will." Although it is not faith itself but rather Jesus who heals, faith seems to be a vehicle or vessel through which healing more easily or readily comes to a person. There is of course mystery involved in all of this. Not every sick or injured person who believes Christ can heal him is in fact healed. Paul, a man of great faith, asks for some sort of healing and is told that he will be instead given grace to endure his condition since God's power is often most fully revealed or perfected in the crucible of human weakness (2 Cor. 12:7-10).

This suggests that when we evaluate the Markan perspective on maladies and malignancies and malformations, we must consider first that on the one hand Mark stresses that Jesus came to combat all the forces of evil, spiritual and physical and emotional. On the other hand, Jesus knew that the only lasting cure for physical ailments was not the temporary reprieve of a healing now (only to die of something else later), but resurrection — the putting of humankind into a condition where they are immune to disease, decay, and death and no longer subject to the ravages of sin, suffering, and sorrow. This is perhaps in part why Jesus is presented as saying in this very first chapter that in the main he came to proclaim the good news of the inbreaking of God's dominion, not primarily to give temporary respite from a human condition that is eventually terminal anyway. Jesus is certainly not a reluctant healer, but on the other hand healing is not the focus of his mission.

Another dimension of this mystery involves Jesus himself. From at least Mark 8 onward, Jesus is presented as the man who came to die, as the suffering Son of Man. In other words, Jesus is presented as one who is fully human and, as a human, did not himself fully experience the everlasting life God intends for all his human creatures until he had died and was raised from the dead. Only then did he have a physical and personal condition immune to disease, decay, and death. It is perhaps Jesus' firm belief in resurrection that in turn makes him take a more limited view of the value of temporary cures for creatures who will one day die in any case.

This is not to say that healing in this life is not a very good thing. It is simply to say that it is at most a foreshadowing, not really a full foretaste, of the life to come. Jesus the healer of temporal illnesses and difficulties, according to the earliest Evangelist, must be exegeted in the context of Jesus the proclaimer of something greater than temporary solutions — the inbreaking of the dominion of God. And nowhere is the meaning of that inbreaking clearer than on Easter morning, where we hear in Mark 16: "He has been raised; he is not here. Look, there is the place where they laid him." The eternally living one cannot be found amongst the dead, because resurrection is not just one more form of temporary healing or a partial reversal of the universal human condition. It is rather an entire new creation. The one who proclaimed the inbreaking new creation was in fact the one who first experienced what it truly meant for a human being to be in God's dominion permanently, the dominion of the one who is Life.

VI. The Controversial Christ (2:1–3:6)

Traditionally this section of Mark has been labeled controversy dialogues, and this is certainly appropriate. The rhetoric of this entire unit is basically judicial in character and involves attack and defense, though it does not conform in detail to the conventions of judicial speeches, as Jesus and his disciples are being challenged to defend their actions. Jesus uses a variety of arguments, including inartificial appeals to sacred texts (the Hebrew Scriptures), to make his case.[1] He regularly places his opponents on the defensive by requiring them to answer questions about the Law or reflect on their ignorance of an OT precedent. This style of argumentation only works in an environment where there is great respect for the authority of sacred texts and traditions and persons.

The social milieu out of which these controversies arise is pedagogical. Certain assumptions about the relationship between a master-teacher and his disciples come into play regularly. "A person who is a disciple has accepted a social position of subordinance for the purpose of learning through imitation and instruction. It is the responsibility of the Master to teach and encourage good actions and thoughts and correct and discourage bad actions and thoughts."[2] Notice that in none of these stories does Jesus correct his disciples, but he does challenge his opponents and their ignorance and obduracy. The challenging of the ignorance and obduracy of the disciples comes later in Mark.

Mark 2:1–3:6 as a literary unit appears to have been carefully constructed, as J. Dewey has shown, in a concentric or chiastic pattern of A, B, C, B', A' (2:1-

---

1. See, e.g., G. Kennedy, *New Testament Interpretation through Rhetorical Criticism* (Chapel Hill: University of North Carolina Press, 1984), pp. 18-19.

2. B. Mack and V. Robbins, *Patterns of Persuasion in the Gospels* (Sonoma, Calif.: Polebridge Press, 1989), p. 111. Here they are following D. Daube's reflections (cf. below).

12; 2:13-17; 2:18-22; 2:23-28; 3:1-6).[3] Thus the stories of the healing of the paralytic and the healing of the man with the withered hand are parallel in form (cf. the Greek of 2:1 and 3:1), content, and some detail (in-house healings), and both deal with the issue of the Sabbath controversy. These two stories, unlike the other three in the cycle, are healing stories. The other three have to do with food, or abstinence from food. Thus B and B′ deal respectively with eating with tax collectors and plucking grain on the Sabbath by the disciples, while C has to do with fasting. In these middle three pericopes the cast of characters is consistent — Jesus, the opponents, and the disciples. In the miracle stories we find Jesus, the one being healed, and the crowd, which in the lattermost story is said to include Pharisees. It is possible, but uncertain, that this cycle of stories is pre-Markan and has simply been taken up by Mark and lightly edited (see, e.g., the parenthetical remark in 2:10a). There are some catchword connections between this story and the cleansing of the man with the skin disease in Mark 1 (e.g., cf. 1:45 to 2:1-2 — τον λογον, ωστε μηκετι . . . εισελθειν), which suggests that whatever the source of this material, Mark has made it his own.[4] Recently Marcus critiqued this analysis, suggesting that 2:13-17 and 2:23-28 do not really correspond to one another, and he is largely correct. He also rightly points out that even more important is the rising tide of opposition in these pericopes, such that the opponents first question Jesus silently (2:7), then question his disciples about him (2:16), then question Jesus about his disciples' behavior (2:18, 24), then seek a legal reason for condemning him (3:2), then plot his murder (3:6).[5]

Mark is probably using this collection "to show how the authority of Jesus was rejected by the Jewish authorities. . . . [I]t is this refusal to accept Jesus' authority which leads to his rejection and ultimately to his death, a fate foreshadowed in 2.20 and 3.6. This chapter therefore is not simply a collection of 'conflict stories' but a demonstration of Jesus' authority and the refusal of the Jewish religious authorities to recognize it."[6] In short, the real drama and pathos of Mark's account begins to surface in these narratives. D. Rhoads and D. Michie are correct that while Jesus is the immediate cause of the conflicts in these stories, ultimately God and the inbreaking dominion are the origin of the actions and events that transpire. "God's rule challenges every other claim to power. The conflicts that result occur in part because of what God is doing; in part the conflicts occur, too, because people do not recognize God's rule or submit to it. The result is the power struggle between Jesus and those who resist or

---

3. J. Dewey, "The Literary Structure of the Controversy Stories in Mark 2.1–3.6," *JBL* 92 (1973): 394-401.

4. See J. Dewey, *Markan Public Debate* (Chico, Calif.: Scholars, 1980), pp. 117-18.

5. J. Marcus, *Mark 1–8* (New York: Doubleday, 1999), p. 214.

6. M. Hooker, *The Gospel according to Mark* (Peabody, Mass.: Hendrickson, 1991), p. 83.

oppose him."[7] Yet God's rule is hidden. The issue is presented in a way much like what one finds in apocalyptic literature. God's will and way is not evident to all, and even when miracles signal the coming of the dominion, the way to interpret the event is not clear without revelation, in this case from Jesus, who unveils the secrets of the dominion. Further, the power struggle is not just on the human level but in the invisible realm and involves the powers and principalities, the latter having their tentacles around the human authorities, according to Mark's worldview. Jesus is accused of being in league with Satan. Jesus in turn suggests that his opponents are the ones in his thrall. Unless one is fully cognizant of the transcendent component and factors in the story, one cannot understand the plot.

A goodly portion of this section, namely, 2:23–3:6, has been used as a test case by M. Casey to see if one could argue that there is an Aramaic substratum, and thus likely an Aramaic source behind at least some of Mark's Gospel.[8] Casey makes a formidable case by retroverting the Greek text back into Aramaic. If he is correct, this means that Mark did not simply compose his Gospel in Greek as a free-form literary exercise. Rather he was at least to a very significant degree constrained by the sources he used when he wrote. It also makes it likely that Mark's source material here was in some written form very early on, Casey suggesting as early as the 40s. All other things being equal, this increases the likelihood that this material is in close touch with the Jesus of history and his ministry, as Casey also argues.[9]

TRANSLATION — 2:1–3:6

And entering again into Capernaum, after some days it was heard that "he is in house." And many were gathered together so that there was no longer room not even space near the door, and he was speaking to them the Word. And they come bringing to him a paralytic carried by four. And not being able to bring him to Jesus because of the crowd, they unroofed the roof where they were, and making a hole lower the litter on which the paralytic lay ill. And Jesus seeing their faith says to the paralytic, "Child, your sins are sent away."[10] But some of the scribes were sit-

---

7. D. Rhoads and D. Michie, *Mark as Story: An Introduction to the Narrative of a Gospel* (Philadelphia: Fortress, 1982), pp. 74-75.

8. M. Casey, *Aramaic Sources of Mark's Gospel* (Cambridge: Cambridge University Press, 1998), pp. 138-92.

9. The difficulty, of course, is that in the present state of New Testament studies, precious few NT scholars are competent to evaluate the validity of Casey's retroversions and so of the very heart of his arguments.

10. There are three different readings as to what the main verb is here. B, 28, 33, 565, and some others have αφιενται, ℵ; A, C, D, K, L, W, and various others have αφεωνται; and a

ting there and questioning in their hearts, "Why does this man speak like this? He blasphemes; for who is able to send away/forgive sins except one — God." And immediately Jesus having discerned in his spirit that they were questioning in their hearts says to them: "Why do you question this in your hearts? What is easier to say to the paralytic, 'Your sins are sent away' or to say 'Rise and take up your litter and walk'?" [But in order that you may know that the Son of Man has authority to send away sins upon the earth] — He says to the paralytic, "To you I say, arise, take up your litter and go unto your house. And he arose and immediately taking his litter went out before them all, so that all were beside themselves and glorified God saying, "We have never seen anything like it (before)."

And he went out again beside the sea, and all the crowd came to him and he taught them. And in passing he saw Levi the [son] of Alphaeus[11] sitting at a custom house, and he says to him, "Follow me." And arising he followed him. And Jesus reclined at his table in his house, and many tax collectors and sinners dined with Jesus and his disciples, for they were many and they followed him. And the scribes of the Pharisees[12] seeing that he eats with the sinners and the tax collectors said to his disciples, "[Why is it] that he eats with the tax collectors and sinners?" And hearing Jesus says to them [that] "Those who are strong do not have need of a doctor, but rather those having illness. I did not come to call the righteous but rather the sinners."

And the disciples of John and the Pharisees were fasting. And they come and they say to him, "Why do the disciples of John and the disciples of the Pharisees fast, but your disciples do not fast?" And Jesus said to them, "The sons of the bride chamber are not able to fast when the bridegroom is with them. As long as they have the bridegroom with them they are not able to fast. But days will come when the bridegroom will be taken away from them and then they will fast in that day.

"No one sews patches of unshrunk cloth upon an old outer cloak. But if he does the piece added tears away from it, the new from the old, and there is a worse tear. And no one pours new wine into old wineskins — but if he does the wine bursts the wineskin, and the wine is lost and the wineskin — but new wine [goes] in new wineskins."[13]

---

few manuscripts, including 1009 and 1010, have αφεονται or some form of this verb. The perfect tense (have been forgiven) is well supported and in fact is found in Luke's parallel at Luke 5:20. Mark, however, has a penchant for the present tense, and Matt. 9:2 suggests that this was Mark's original reading (see Metzger, *TCGNT*, p. 77).

11. Some Western and Caesarean texts, perhaps influenced by Mark 3:18, have Jacob of Alphaeus.

12. This more unusual phrasing is to be preferred to the texts which read the more common "scribes and Pharisees." Mark reflects here a knowledge that while some scribes were Pharisees, not all Pharisees were experts in the Law.

13. There are various textual variants in this verse, meant to alleviate Mark's difficult syntax and grammar. See Metzger, *TCGNT*, p. 79.

And it happened on the Sabbath they were passing through the crops, and his disciples began to make a way pulling ears of grain. And the Pharisees said to him, "Look, why are they doing what is not permitted on the Sabbath?" And he says to them: "Have you never read what David did when he had need and he himself and those with him felt hunger? How he entered into the House of God at Abiathar's high priesthood,[14] and he ate the bread of the presence, which no one was permitted to eat except the priest, and he gave it even to those who were with him?" And he said to them, "The Sabbath was made because of human beings, not human beings because of the Sabbath (so that the Son of Man is lord even of the Sabbath)."

And he entered again into the synagogue. And there was there a person having a withered hand. And they were watching him closely [to see] if he would heal him on the Sabbath, in order that they might accuse him. And he says to the person having the withered hand, "Stand up in the middle." And he says to them, "Is it permitted to do good or to do evil on the Sabbath, to save life or to kill?" But they were silent. And looking around at them with anger, being grieved at the hardening of their hearts, he says to the person, "Extend your hand." And he extended it and his hand was restored. And going out the Pharisees immediately took counsel with the Herodians concerning him, how to destroy him.

A. The Healing of Forgiveness (2:1-12)

Mark 1 was notable in that it gave samples of Jesus' variety of ministry (preaching, teaching, healing, exorcising) and of the response, especially to the teaching and exorcism. The question continually pressed was one of authority. By what right or power did Jesus do and say these things? In Mark 1 Jesus' words and deeds raised questions, and then in Mark 2 the matter is taken a step further. In Mark 1 Jesus' fame as a wonder-worker grows, but in Mark 2 we see how his opposition grows. Here we have real debate, growing hostility, culminating in a decision mentioned at the climax of this section (3:6) to find a way to eliminate Jesus.

This section might be called "Jesus Meets His Critics in Galilee." The five pericopes in 2:1–3:6 indicate the nature and scope of the issues Jesus was being challenged on — forgiveness of sins, fellowshipping with the unclean and immoral, fasting, healing and working on the Sabbath. These controversies are not by and large the sort that characterized the early church in Mark's day or locale,

---

14. According to 1 Sam. 21, Ahimelech was the high priest when David ate the bread of the presence. D, W, and others omit the phrase about Abiathar to avoid this problem, and so conform the text to Luke 6:4 and Matt. 12:4. Other witnesses add the Greek word του before "high priest" to suggest it was in the time of Abiathar, but not necessarily during his tenure as high priest. See Metzger, *TCGNT,* p. 79, and the commentary below.

so far as we can tell. Rather they are thoroughly Jewish in character. This is another telltale sign that we must take seriously the fact that Mark is trying to convey some historical and biographical information, not merely trying to relate to contemporary crises in his own church situation.

There is no reason to think that all these incidents happened in the exact sequence that Mark presents them, not least because they are introduced in very general ways ("on one Sabbath . . ." or "again he entered the synagogue"). Rather this is a topical arrangement involving controversy dialogues. It is important to note that we get five more controversy dialogues in 11:27–12:37, but in these the setting is Jerusalem. Mark is making the point that Jesus was controversial wherever he went. The radically new situation that Jesus introduced into Israel stirred up serious debate, even conflict, and in due course, even Jesus' death. In the very first controversy dialogue the charge of blasphemy is raised. This is a very serious charge which, if proved, could result in death. Then again, Sabbath violation, if witnessed and with the correct procedures of warning, could also lead to death for the offender. Thus it is fair to say that a person doing the sorts of things Jesus was doing, in not merely a Jewish environment but in a milieu in which a holiness reformation was in progress (led by the Pharisees), could reasonably expect a premature death.

The setting for the healing of the paralytic is Capernaum once again. Notice that Jesus is teaching "in the house" (one of his disciples' homes perhaps?). Gundry suggests plausibly that this could be the house of Simon and Andrew "and reflects Simon's standpoint in telling the story, which Mark may have heard from him (see Eusebius *H.E.* 3.39.15 . . .). The forward position of the phrase gives the news that Jesus is at home a note of excitement."[15]

The people were so plentiful that not only was the house full but people were crammed in the doorway. Jesus was not at the time healing but doing what he saw as his primary mission, speaking τον λογον to people. A paralytic is brought to Jesus, carried by four men. They are unable to get through the crowd, and so they apparently go up the staircase on the side of the house and onto the flat mud roof and then begin to pull back the straw covered with mud, or perhaps the tiles if it was a more well constructed house. The text simply says these men unroofed the roof, made a hole, and lowered the man into the presence of Jesus. The term used for the "stretcher" that bore the man is κραβαττον, which is in fact a Latinism usually used to describe a poor man's mattress or even a spartan bedroll of a soldier.[16] It must also be noticed that it is "their" faith which causes Jesus to respond as he does to the paralytic. Their daring ac-

15. R. H. Gundry, *Mark: A Commentary on His Apology for the Cross* (Grand Rapids: Eerdmans, 1993), p. 110.

16. See C. Myers, *Binding the Strong Man: A Political Reading of Mark's Story of Jesus* (Maryknoll, N.Y.: Orbis, 1988), p. 154.

tion in disassembling the roof presumably is what we are meant to think demonstrated their faith. They dared to do the difficult, the dangerous, the controversial in order to bring their friend into the presence of Jesus. And Jesus' response to the man is equally shocking. He says, "My child, your sins are forgiven." Now, this is a surprising utterance. We might have expected a simple healing as before, a "stand up and walk," and the story would have been over.

We have a textual problem at v. 5 in regard to the verb. Should we read the present passive αφιενται (are sent away/forgiven) or the perfect passive αφεωνται (have been forgiven/sent away)? Probably the present tense is to be preferred, which would mean forgiveness is conveyed at that very moment,[17] but there is also a question of how literally we should translate the verb. Is the OT notion of the scapegoat, on whom a person's burden of sins could be laid and then sent away into the wilderness, being conjured up? This is possible, but in any case notice that Jesus does not say "I forgive your sins." The passive voice of the verb allows one to conclude that the sins are forgiven either by God or by Jesus, the former if the verb represents the divine passive.[18] Thus, perhaps the reason for the stir in the hearts of the theological lawyers is Jesus' presumption in announcing what only God could know or a priest could announce (e.g., at Yom Kippur). The question is whether Jesus is guilty of a presumption of knowledge or of divine prerogatives and power.[19]

There is certainly an emphasis in this narrative on Jesus knowing what was in the hearts of people — in this case, of the legal experts. They were suggesting that Jesus' words were blasphemy, for only God can either forgive sins or know without a doubt that they have been forgiven. "This will ultimately be the charge for which Jesus is condemned to death at the end of the story (14.64). Though here it is not yet pressed, it is no accident that the next time the scribal authorities appear it is in the person of government investigators from Jerusalem (3.22)."[20] As Gundry says, Jesus' pronouncement, coupled with the scribes' response, "set the stage for an implied claim to deity on Jesus' part. Thus it is no ordinary man, much less a criminal who will die on the Cross. He is a divine figure unrecognized as such by those who will put him there."[21] Part of the lawyers' problem was that they did not know the hour of their visitation. Notice the possible contemptuous tone of ουτος — "this fellow."[22] They didn't realize that God's saving activity, the

---

17. See V. Taylor, *The Gospel according to St. Mark* (New York: St. Martin's Press, 1966), p. 195.

18. But see Marcus, p. 216.

19. Marcus also suggests that the scribes may have been priests or of the priestly line, in which case they had a vested interest in who could pronounce forgiveness. See Marcus, pp. 523-24.

20. Myers, p. 155.

21. Gundry, p. 112.

22. See Gundry, p. 112.

eschatological work of redemption, was happening already in their very midst. We are told quite clearly in v. 8 that Jesus discerned their internal attitudes and confronted them — "why are you disputing/debating in your hearts about this matter?" Indeed, we are told that Jesus knew what was in their hearts "immediately," not needing to figure out what they were thinking.

Vv. 9-12 should be seen as a two-pronged query raised by Jesus. The question is not only which is easier to say, but also which is easier to do. Obviously it would be easier to say a person's sins were forgiven because there was no objective way of telling if this was true or not, unlike healing a cripple, where the evidence would either stand up for and support the pronouncement or not.[23] But in regard to which was easier to do, without question it was the healing of the body. Various OT prophets and others had been able to perform such miracles, but only God could send away sins. As Hooker remarks, "there is nothing in Jewish literature to suggest that any man — not even a messiah — would have the authority to forgive sins (see Tg. Isa. 53.5b). It is also true that nothing is said in Jewish literature about such authority being given to the Son of Man, but it would certainly be appropriate for a figure who acts as God's representative on earth and shares in his judgement to be given this power."[24] But Irenaeus rightly queries this sort of conclusion, saying, "How can sin be rightly remitted unless the very One against whom one has sinned grants the pardon?" (*Against Heresies* 5.17). Mark's portrayal here is christologically focused, and one of the things he wishes to convey is the divine character and authority of Jesus; otherwise, ironically if Jesus had merely been God's agent, the charge of blasphemy would have been correct. Yet "Jesus not only forgave sins, but showed he had also another power that belongs to God alone: the power to disclose the secrets of the heart" (Chrysostom, *Homily on Matthew* 29.1).

A great deal of the debate about this text has centered on v. 10a, because elsewhere in this Gospel Jesus is very secretive about who he is when in public and not simply in the presence of his disciples. The question becomes: Would Jesus have really asserted that he had the power to forgive sins on earth as the Son of Man in the presence of these skeptical scribes, who then logically should have taken up stones against him? This seems unlikely. Jesus' utterance would initially have sounded rather like that of Nathan to David in 2 Sam. 12:13 — a prophetic utterance saying "The Lord has forgiven your sins." Probably for Jesus to go beyond that would be quite out of character, especially considering the Markan way of portraying Jesus at this stage of his ministry in front of such an audience.

The considerable awkwardness of the grammar at this point suggests that we should take seriously the likelihood that we have a parenthesis inserted by

---

23. Gundry, p. 114.
24. Hooker, p. 88.

Mark here and directed to his own audience ("but so that you may know that the Son of Man has the authority to forgive sins . . ."). In fact, Lane suggests that a "purpose clause can sometimes in Greek be used to introduce an independent proposition, and here it likely does and should be translated 'Know that the Son of Man has authority . . .' rather than 'in order that you may know. . . .'"[25] But it seems more likely that we have a transition to an editorial comment here where the author addresses the audience as "you." Parenthetical remarks are not uncommon in Mark (cf. 2:15, 28; 7:3-4, 19; 13:14).[26] The Evangelist in fact had no choice, if he wanted to make an explanatory remark to his own audience, but to put it in the text, since there were no footnotes. This means we should likely see v. 10a as Mark's own comment and not as a saying of Jesus, which makes it an unusual statement, for the title Son of Man is usually recognized as something the early church, especially a church largely populated by Gentiles, did not use to speak of Jesus (cf. the phrase's total absence in Paul's letters).

The narrative continues with the healing of the paralytic, who rises up in their midst, picks up his bedding, pushes his way through the crowd, and goes home, with the usual amazement and astonishment of the crowd (as well as their glorifying of God, not of Jesus) being the result. The parting remark, "we've never seen anything like this before," is so typical of these sorts of stories where the reaction of the crowd is stressed at the close of the tale.

Sickness and Sin and the Ministry of Jesus

Without doubt the Jews of Jesus' day believed there was a connection between sickness and sin. This can be seen clearly in the somewhat later pronouncement of the Talmud: "No one gets up from his sick-bed unless all his sins are forgiven" (*b. Ned.* 41a). If a person's body was not whole, either that person himself or, if it was a birth defect, his parents had sinned.[27] Such a person very readily became socially ostracized not only because of the Levitical purity codes but also because of the assumption that he had been cursed by God because of his own or his family's sin. And of course, the doors to full participation in the life of the synagogue or normal social events were also closed to such a person.

Elsewhere in the Gospel tradition (e.g., Luke 13; John 9), Jesus (without denying that a serious sin can lead to a guilty and thence to a sick person) denies that a one-to-one correlation between a particular sin and a particular sickness can normally be made. About the man born blind, it is said in John 9 that neither he nor his parents sinned. In a sense, what these Gospel texts suggest is that Jesus dismissed facile assumptions about the

---

25. W. Lane, *The Gospel of Mark* (Grand Rapids: Eerdmans, 1974), pp. 97-98.

26. Marcus, p. 218, suggests an echo of phrases from Exod. 8:22 and 9:14, in which case it is to be pointed out that these "so that you may know" sayings in the OT all involve divine speech.

27. See rightly Myers, p. 155.

118MARK

association of sin and sickness. But in the story before us, some sort of connection between sin and sickness, or at least forgiveness and wellness, seems assumed. It may be that the man Jesus was dealing with was not unlike the woman M. Hooker cites, "who was totally paralysed for two years. When questioned, it was discovered that she had succumbed to the paralysis immediately after witnessing on television a violent killing, which had by chance been broadcast as it took place. Reassurance that she was in no way responsible for the crime resulted in a cure as instantaneous and dramatic as the paralysis. While such cases are undoubtedly rarer than popular imagination supposes, the fact that they happen at all confirms the likelihood that a sense of guilt could cause paralysis, and that the assurance of forgiveness could bring a cure. Jesus' response then is by no means unnatural or digressionary, and is not in itself sufficient reason for supposing that two stories have been joined together. Certainly for Mark, healing and forgiveness belong together."[28] Of such a person Augustine once said, "You have been a paralytic inwardly. You did not take charge of your bed. Your bed took charge of you" (On the Psalms 41.4).

Perhaps one could argue that Jesus' priorities in this story are to heal the human heart or spirit, a much more difficult task than healing the human body, though Jesus does not fail to do the latter as well from time to time. The story could be said as well to be an example of how Jesus took a holistic approach to healing — the whole person must be ministered to for it to be truly well. But frankly, forgiveness and spiritual salvation are seen as the key things which Jesus says he has come to proclaim and administer to people. Only secondarily and as an outward witness to this ("so that you may know . . .") does he also heal. Jesus' own theology in regard to disease, decay, and death may have entailed a belief that these things existed in the world as a result of the Adamic fall from grace, though our text does not make this clear. In any event, he had come to bring in the eschatological reversal of such conditions and maladies. He had come to create a community of faith where the content of one's character and the reality of one's faith rather than the condition of one's body were what determined one's status among God's people.

B. Levi's Genes (2:13-17)

Though this pericope is brief, it in fact appears to be composed of two different stories that have been condensed and edited together — a call narrative and the story of a dinner in the house of a toll collector, or at least with sinners and toll collectors.[29] The two stories were brought together because of the mention of toll collectors. It is possible they were put together because they also both involved a toll collector named Levi, though he is not mentioned by name in 2:15-17. Certainly Luke drew this conclusion, mentioning Levi in both stories (see Luke 5:27 and 29).

---

28. Hooker, pp. 86-87.
29. Note E. Schweizer, The Good News according to Mark (Atlanta: John Knox, 1971), p. 63: "Vs. 14 speaks with the conciseness of a woodcut in which everything is reduced to essentials, and in this respect is very similar to 1.16-20." This astute observation could be made of Mark's technique in handling his sources in general, boiling them down rather than boiling them up. See pp. 16-18 in the introduction.

Much ink has been spilled by commentators trying to determine whether Levi is in fact the same person as Matthew. The name Levi for a disciple occurs only here and in Luke 5:27-32. Mark tells us he is "son of Alphaeus," which suggests that Mark does indeed have a specific historical person in mind. Levi is not mentioned in Luke's list of the Twelve (Luke 6:12-16), but James son of Alphaeus is, and furthermore Matthew does not mention Levi in his list of the Twelve, but the First Evangelist does list Matthew the tax collector right before James the son of Alphaeus (Matt. 10:2-4). With this data we might conclude that Levi and Matthew were definitely two different tax collectors, except that Matt. 9:9-13 presents the story of Levi as the story of the call of Matthew. It is certainly possible that Levi and Matthew are two names for the same person, as various ancients, including early Jews, had more than one name, though usually the second name of a Jew was a nickname (e.g., Simon and Cephas). There are perhaps a few clues in these various traditions that Levi and Matthew are the same person: (1) the first two sets of disciples called by Jesus were two pairs of brothers — Peter and Andrew, and Jacob and John; (2) it is thus quite possible that Levi and Jacob, both said to be sons of Alphaeus, are also brothers;[30] and (3) this would explain why in the First Gospel, Matthew's and Jacob's names are adjacent in the list of the Twelve, as is also the case in Acts 1:13 (while Luke, perhaps writing his Gospel a bit later than the First Evangelist, mentions Thomas in between Matthew and James son of Alphaeus — Luke 6:13-16).[31] (4) The First Evangelist, using Mark, quite clearly believes Levi is the same person as Matthew (cf. Matt. 9:9-13 to Mark 2:13-17). (5) Mark has presented the call of Levi in the same form as the call of the first disciples (cf. 1:16-20).

Yet Mark himself does not make clear that this is the case, for he lists Matthew among the Twelve in 3:15-19 and does not place his name adjacent to James son of Alphaeus in the list, nor does he ever clearly associate the name Levi with the name Matthew.[32] In fact, some early Christian scribes felt they should solve these dilemmas by substituting the name James for Levi here (thus D, Θ, Origen, Ephraem, and a variety of other witnesses).[33] Thus it cannot be proved beyond a shadow of a doubt that Matthew and Levi are one and the same person, though several clues suggest that this is the case.[34] One wonders if

---

30. See Hooker, p. 94.

31. It is my view that Acts preserves an earlier tradition of the list than Luke's Gospel does. What we have in the Gospel is a second edition or smoothed-out edition of the Third Evangelist's work. See my discussion of the relationship of Luke and Acts and their additions in my work *The Acts of the Apostles: A Socio-Rhetorical Commentary* (Grand Rapids: Eerdmans, 1998), pp. 31-68.

32. But see Lane, p. 100 n. 29, on alternate names.

33. See Metzger, *TCGNT*, p. 78 — chiefly it is Western and Caesarean texts which have the reading James.

34. See Gundry, pp. 127-28.

there were also other pairs of brothers amongst the Twelve, and whether choosing pairs of brothers was one of Jesus' strategies to bind the Twelve into a family unit. What one can say with some assurance is that the importance of this pericope to Mark is not whether Levi was one of the Twelve or not, but rather that he was a tax or toll collector whom Jesus called and befriended. In other words, Mark includes the story to present another side of Jesus' controversial activities which were in due course to get him in hot water. Mark's interests are primarily biographical, and so he presents traditions in a way that sheds light on Jesus' character and mission. He was sent to minister to the least, the last, and the lost.[35]

V. 13 is transitional, and Lane thinks he sees here the back-and-forth motion noted before where Jesus goes away from the city and crowds and then returns to them.[36] In this case the crowd comes to Jesus and he teaches them by the sea. The call of Levi would presumably occur in or near a city, depending on whether he was a toll collector sitting on the border between two regions or a tax collector who lived in a city or village and engaged in tax farming. A crucial point to mention is that a τελωνιον is not a "publican" — he did not collect income tax or poll taxes, nor was he likely involved in census activities. Rather he was some sort of customs official placed at bridges, canals, and on state roads, or a tax farmer collecting from the farms in the region. Such persons were Jews, and were especially despised and considered traitors by their fellow Jews, because not merely were they associated with Gentiles but in fact often worked for them — helping to collect funds for the Roman oppressors. In the Talmud such tax collectors are lumped together with murderers and thieves. It needs to be understood that they made their living from the extra they charged people on top of the taxes actually owed Rome and/or its client kings. The rulers did not usually care how much extra they charged, so long as the rulers got the specified cut they had demanded. The potential for corruption and extortion was high. The way one got such a job in the first place was by paying for it — by outbidding others for the privilege of collecting taxes! If Levi was a tax collector in Capernaum, then fish were indeed one of the commodities regularly taxed in the region. In that case, he probably was already well known and despised by Simon and Andrew, Jacob and John.

Jesus is said to attend a banquet with controversial guests. The phrase "to recline at table" indicates that this is a meal taken in the Greco-Roman style, which had been adapted and adopted by Jews well before Jesus' day.[37] "The context implies that Levi arranged a banquet to celebrate his call to disciple-

---

35. On the considerable historical substance of this pericope, see my work *The Christology of Jesus* (Philadelphia: Fortress, 1990), pp. 76-78.

36. Lane, pp. 99-100.

37. See Schweizer, p. 65.

ship."[38] Tax collectors are mentioned in v. 15 together with sinners, which suggests that the latter is a definable, separate, though associated category of persons.[39] In fact, these two groups are mentioned together in a variety of Gospel sources (besides here in Mark 2, cf. Luke 15:2; Matt. 11:19 and par.). There has been no little debate about who is meant by the term αμαρτωλοι. Is this a reference to the "people of the land" (the ʿam haʾaretz),[40] or should we follow E. P. Sanders's suggestion that the term refers to the "wicked" *(resaim)* — those who sin willfully in major ways without repenting?[41] This broader term would include tax collectors and other notable sinners such as harlots. According to Sanders, this group of people is not to be associated merely with the poor, downtrodden, or meek. Nor is Jesus being accused of merely associating with the ritually unclean or with those who were not as ritually observant as the Pharisees. Rather he is banqueting with the bad. This behavior is seen as objectionable not least because of what the OT says about the wicked (cf. Pss. 10:15; 141:5, and especially Prov. 2:22; 10:30; 14:9 — "God scorns the wicked, but the upright enjoy his favor"). How could Jesus be a godly man, much less sent by God, if he acted contrary to what the Scriptures said about the wicked and God's attitude toward them? Sanders argues that Jesus did not require what was normally taken as the tokens of repentance — sacrifice, restitution, returning to law observance.[42] What Jesus stressed was hearing and heeding the good news and participating in his mission. J. D. G. Dunn has objected to Sanders's views and has contended that the Pharisees did indeed classify other Jews who were not necessarily notoriously immoral as "sinners."

But the question is whether Jesus or Mark would have accepted such a definition of sinners as the Pharisees may have offered and simply repeated it here.[43] I think not. The contrast in Mark 2:17 suggests a moral contrast between the category wicked and the category righteous. Thus it seems likely that this reference is to the notoriously immoral, not merely the ritually negligent. The term "sinner" could be used by early Jews of Gentiles not merely because they were thought to be unclean but also because they were considered immoral. It is in any case understandable, if the historical Jesus fraternized with

---

38. R. Guelich, *Mark 1–8.26* (Waco: Word, 1989), p. 101.

39. Lane, pp. 100-102, objects that had the immoral been meant by "sinners," the text would read "tax collectors and *other* sinners." But the phrase is a coordinate one, and thus immorality in both cases is probably implied by the frequent grouping of the two together. Tax collectors are one category of the larger group called sinners.

40. See my discussion on the later use of this term in *The Christology of Jesus*, pp. 73-77.

41. See E. P. Sanders, *Jesus and Judaism* (Philadelphia: Fortress, 1985), pp. 188-99.

42. Sanders, *Jesus and Judaism*, p. 75.

43. J. D. G. Dunn, "Pharisees, Sinners, and Jesus" (lecture given at Duke University, 1986).

immoral as well as unclean Jews, how having fellowship, including table fellowship, with Gentiles could be seen as a natural extension of this. Under these circumstances it is very believable that the Pharisees bore considerable animus toward Jesus and his mission — he seemed to be undoing what they were trying
to do, or moving in the opposite direction to them in regard to holiness.

As was true normally in the ancient Near East, to have a fellowship meal
with people, to recline at table with them, implied that you accepted them in
your company. Here the basis of such fellowship appears to be forgiveness,
which allowed sinners to come into the presence of someone like Jesus. We are
told that many of these sorts of people followed Jesus, and so Jesus' entourage
must have seemed to many a motley crew — involving ordinary men, women,
and some of the notable and the notorious (cf. Luke 8:1-3). But in fact, notice
that Mark in vv. 15b-16 distinguishes between the disciples and the sinners and
tax collectors. Presumably we are to see the latter as prospective disciples.[44]

At v. 16 we hear of the scribes of the Pharisees, a phrase that occurs elsewhere also at Acts 23:9, which indicates that Mark understands that not all
Pharisees were scribes, and indeed that the Pharisees had particular need of
such experts in the Law. They especially who best knew the Law and the oral
tradition would find Jesus' behavior particularly offensive. This is not surprising since table fellowship seems to be one of the most characteristic concerns of
the Pharisees and their Law experts.[45] These scribes protest to Jesus' disciples
and Jesus hears of it. His response is to first quote a conventional or proverbial
saying (cf. *Mekilta Exod.* 15.26; Pausanias ap. Plutarch *Apophthegmata Laconica*
230F). This saying, however, gives us a rather clear view into how Jesus viewed
his ministry — like a doctor whose task is to help those who are ill or in need of
treatment. This same image of Jesus as a doctor is found in another layer of the
tradition as well — Luke 4:23, where it is once more paired with a conventional
saying. The saying suggests that Jesus believed that to recover the wicked for
God, he had to be willing to abrogate or transcend certain provisions of the OT
Law. Thus an inherent by-product of Jesus' ministry was that strict observance
of the written, much less the oral, Torah was an impossibility. But Jesus was no
mere pragmatist. He believed that the new eschatological action of God demanded such an approach, but equally clearly those who did not see the signs
of the times would indeed have seen Jesus as a lawbreaker.

---

44. On the presentation of the disciples in Mark, see the appendix below, pp. 421-42.
45. Myers, p. 158. Their focus on dietary concerns is a reflection of this concentration on
table fellowship and its accoutrements. Myers adds: "Thus in the repetitive rhetoric of 2.16,
Mark is 'elaborating' the Pharisaic symbolics of the meal to reveal their real concern: not the
welfare of the masses, but their own class status." I would suggest that the issue is not class status, but rather purity concerns. The stricter Pharisees, or *haberim*, especially seem to have seen
very strict table fellowship rules as essential to renewed holiness among God's people.

V. 17b is a programmatic statement by Jesus, but should we see it as ironic or tongue in cheek or take it straightforwardly? If it is ironic, then the term "righteous" would mean something like "the so-called righteous." In some texts, however, Jesus seems to allow that the Pharisees did maintain a laudable standard of righteousness (Matt. 5:20), but plenty of material suggests the contrary as well (Matt. 23:1-7; Mark 12:38-40). For our purposes, it is crucial to stress that Jesus is claiming that his ministry has a specific focus — the least, last, and lost. The term "sinner" should not be understood here to have its broader and later Christian sense of all fallen human beings (cf., e.g., the use in Paul and in Luke 13:1-3, or in *Pss. Sol.* 17:21-22). Here the term means something like what it means at Luke 24:7 — immoral people.

What, then, does it mean to call sinners? Painter suggests it means to call them to repentance rather than to be disciples, but this is based on the erroneous view that only the Twelve are called disciples in this Gospel.[46] Presumably this means to invite them to become disciples, as the story about Levi which opens this pericope suggests. It may also entail summoning them to repentance in the moral sense of that term. What is nonetheless striking is that Jesus appears to not require repentance in advance of having table fellowship with sinners and tax collectors. This comports with various Gospel traditions' suggestions that a variety of people from the fringes of society were in the wider circle of Jesus' followers — a tax collector, a Zealot, some fishermen, some women, some sinners. Notice also that Jesus' vision of the messianic banquet seems to have included such people (see Matt. 8:11-12/Luke 13:29). Possibly Jesus saw such meals with the bad as a foreshadowing or foretaste of the banquet in the dominion of God. Perhaps he saw such meals as a dramatization of the coming dominion. More clearly, Jesus saw his ministry as something distinctive and special, and its positive results as something worth celebrating.

C. Fasters and Feasters (2:18-22)

At 2:18-22 Mark presents us with another controversy narrative, in this case about fasting. It is possible to see 2:18-20 as a *chreia*, with the saying in v. 20 being the focus and climax of the unit. It seems likely then that, as with the previous section, we are actually dealing with the combination of two sets of material, here condensed and then combined (2:18-20, 21-22). The sayings in vv. 21-22 were deemed similar enough due to the theme of incongruity or inappropriateness to connect them with the bridegroom saying.[47] The biographical focus

---

46. Cf. J. Painter, *Mark's Gospel* (London: Routledge, 1997), p. 59, to the appendix, pp. 421-42 below.

47. See Hooker, pp. 97-98.

of a *chreia* needs to be borne in mind, and so the appropriate question to be asked about 2:18-20 is what it tells us about Jesus, his character and his roles. The answer in part must be that he saw himself as the focus of a celebration, as one who brought something new to the scene which made regular fasts inappropriate for his disciples. The story seems to have come from a time after the death of John the Baptist when his disciples were mourning and fasting, and its placement here is due to the theme of controversy.[48]

Both John's disciples as well as the followers of the Pharisees fasted (the latter doing so with regularity on Mondays and Thursdays; cf. Luke 18:12; *m. Ta'an.* 1.4-5; *b. Ta'an.* 10a). There was, of course, the annual fast which most Jews would share on the Day of Atonement (Lev. 16:29; see Acts 27:9) and also a fast on Rosh Hashanah (New Year's Day), but here the question pertains to a much more regular practice of fasting week by week. The question then asked is why Jesus' disciples are not following suit with the sort of frequent fasting engaged in by John's disciples and the followers of the Pharisaic teaching.[49] The assumption in this segment is that a teacher is responsible for the behavior of his disciples, which in turn implies that Jesus was recognized as a notable teacher with followers even by those who objected to his behavior.[50]

Jesus then draws on an analogy with a wedding, and apparently we are meant to think of Jesus as the bridegroom and his disciples as the "sons of the bridal chamber." The latter are likely groomsmen,[51] and more particularly groomsmen who had the responsibility of guarding the bridal chamber when the bride and groom entered it, protecting and guaranteeing as witnesses that the marriage had been properly consummated. At such a time feasting and joy rather than fasting and solemnity were in order.

Jesus goes on to speak of a day when he will be taken away and fasting will be appropriate. This strikes a jarring note. Bridegrooms are not taken away from weddings; guests leave such events. The verb implies the use of force (cf. Isa. 53:8), but Mark is deliberately vague about when that might be. Thus we have a contrast between death, funeral, mourning, and life, wedding, celebration.[52]

We have here what can be called the first parable in Mark. It seems to be grounded in material such as we find in Isa. 54:4-8; 62:5, or Ezek. 16:7ff., where God is depicted as a bridegroom. There may then be an implicit claim that Je-

48. See my *Christology of Jesus*, p. 71.
49. While Pharisees themselves did not have followers, probably Mark has in mind the great Pharisaic teachers or scribes who did indeed have disciples. See Painter, p. 60.
50. See D. Daube, "Responsibilities of Master and Disciples in the Gospels," *NTS* 19 (1972-73): 1-16.
51. See Guelich, p. 110.
52. Guelich, p. 112.

sus now fulfills for Israel, or at least for his own disciples, the role previously predicated of God. The relationship between parable and allegory needs to be dealt with briefly at this juncture, for it is simply not true that there was a hard-and-fast distinction between the two in early Judaism.

Parable and Allegory in Early Judaism and in the Ministry of Jesus ————

The term *mashal* is a broad one, and the range of material it can refer to includes riddles, aphorisms, proverbs, extended analogies, full-fledged narrative parables, and even allegories or at least parables with allegorical elements. The term, then, which is later translated as παραβολος in the Greek, refers to metaphorical speech in a broad sense.

The parables of Jesus need to be seen in their original historical context, without the encumbrance of various modern theories of metaphor and meaning which are not really appropriate for analyzing the historical phenomena in question.[53] If we wish to consider the category of metaphor as understood by the ancients, then Aristotle's dictum that a metaphor is when a single aspect of A is related to a single aspect of B needs to be taken into consideration (*Art of Rhetoric* 2.20ff.). Yet this definition shows that parables, which frequently have several points of comparison with reality, were more than just metaphors, though perhaps we might call them extended metaphors. We must remember that in early Jewish and Jewish Christian literature, metaphors and parables were by no means self-contained units creating their own literary sphere or realm. Rather the issue was regularly the matter of *tertia comparationis*, with the assumption always being that they referred in some way to some reality outside themselves.[54] Parables are comparisons in the form of an analogy or story. Jesus' parables in particular were both timely and historical in character and were meant to provide his audience with various sorts of comparisons between what God's dominion and its inbreaking were like in comparison to familiar early Jewish life experiences.

Though Jesus was certainly notable because of the frequency with which he used the parabolic form, and in some cases the subject matter he used the form to speak about (God's inbreaking dominion), he was not unique in his use of the form, and recent studies of other early Jewish parables, many of which clearly have allegorical elements and some of which could simply be called allegories, have made clear that Jesus was a practitioner of a well-known art.[55] But of importance is the fact that narrative *meshalim*, which seem to be Jesus' most preferred form, were not characteristic of sages whose work made it into the OT, but rather seem to have been a prophetic phenomenon, a prophetic modification of a Wisdom form (cf. 2 Sam. 12:1-4; Ezek. 17:3-10; Isa. 5:1-6). Basically they are comparisons elongated into short narratives. It is fair to say that Jesus cast his teaching into a recognizable sapiential form (riddles, aphorisms) or the prophetic adaptation of such a form (the

---

53. On this see my *Jesus the Sage* (Minneapolis: Fortress, 1994), pp. 147-50.

54. See C. Westermann, *The Parables of Jesus in the Light of the Old Testament* (Minneapolis: Fortress, 1990).

55. See R. E. Brown, *New Testament Essays* (Garden City, N.Y.: Image Books, 1968), pp. 320-23; B. H. Young, *Jesus and His Jewish Parables* (New York: Paulist, 1989); and H. K. MacArthur and R. M. Johnston, *They Also Taught in Parables* (Grand Rapids: Zondervan, 1990).

narrative parable, often with allegorical elements). In either case, he speaks by various means of figurative speech, choosing to address his audience indirectly. The evidence suggests that narrative *meshalim* were becoming increasingly popular in Jesus' era.[56]

When one analyzes such material, it becomes clear that one needs to be able to distinguish between (1) allegory, (2) allegorical elements in what is otherwise not an allegory, (3) and allegorizing of nonallegorical material produced either by altering the original text or by means of allegorical interpretation of the text (e.g., such as the medieval treatments of various of Jesus' parables).[57] Whatever the merits or problems of medieval interpretation of Jesus' parables, it has no bearing on the question of the relationship of parable and allegory in Jesus' day. It must also be stressed that parables in early Judaism regularly came with explanations or interpretations appended, and of seventy-one or so possible parables in the Synoptics, forty-two, or the majority, have some sort of explanation attached.[58] It thus must not be automatically assumed that an explanation attached to a parable must have necessarily been added later by the church. It may be a later addition, but this must be judged on a case-by-case basis.

Some features of Jesus' use of *meshalim* seem to make them stand out from the figurative speech forms offered by other early Jewish practitioners: (1) Jesus' riddles and aphorisms seem to be of a counterorder variety, not confirming preexisting notions about order and society but rather undermining and challenging such notions. They reflect not collective wisdom but individual wisdom. (2) Jesus almost never uses *meshalim* to interpret Scripture or clarify some law or rule. Halakic questions do not arise in Jesus' *meshalim* by and large. (3) Jesus' parables are not about sapiential matters (folk wisdom, keys to living a happy or healthy or wealthy life), but are rather about eschatological matters which challenge all conventional assumptions. "In order to show people how radical the challenge is, he often uses images that are extreme or even paradoxical. Unlike the commonplaces of much wisdom tradition, which says the world will go on as a place where fools repeat the same mistakes, Jesus sees the coming of the Reign of God as an opportunity for radical change."[59]

Both the analogy with the bridegroom and the two which follow are meant to show the incongruity of juxtaposing two things which do not fit. In each case the metaphor indicates that Jesus has initiated a new state of affairs and that the old and new cannot be mixed together.[60] Just as it would be incongruous to fast at a wedding feast, so it would be incongruous to sow unshrunken cloth on an old garment or put new wine in old wineskins. New wine requires new wineskins, an old garment requires an old patch.[61] Jesus'

56. Brown, pp. 320-23.

57. See my discussion of A. Julicher's errors and overreaction to medieval hermeneutics in *Jesus the Sage,* pp. 159-60.

58. See J. A. Baird, *Discovering the Power of the Gospel* (Akron: Hampshire Books, 1989).

59. P. Perkins, *Jesus as Teacher* (Cambridge: Cambridge University Press, 1990), p. 44.

60. Painter, p. 61.

61. Hooker, p. 100.

ministry has to do with the new, which requires new forms, not a grafting of the new onto an old form. Likewise it would be incongruous and inappropriate for Jesus to insist that his disciples fast when he is present. Rather it was time to celebrate, a time of joy. Presumably we are meant to think of the banquet with the tax collectors and sinners as an example of the sort of behavior which was appropriate as the dominion was breaking into human history. It is possible also to connect this material with the Q saying in Matt. 11:16-19/Luke 7:31-35, which may contrast the asceticism and mourning of John's approach to the partying and celebratory mode of Jesus' ministry.

It is possible that the wedding metaphor was meant to conjure up the notion that a new covenant was being initiated with new rules about what behavior was and wasn't appropriate.

At several points in the OT, particularly in Hosea, God's relationship with Israel is seen to be analogous to a marriage. Very clearly Jesus is seen here as the center of the disciples' joy such that they will fast and mourn when he leaves (on fasting and mourning going together, see 1 Sam. 31:13). Since there is no evidence that the bridegroom image was used of messianic figures (though the wedding image was used of the messianic age) in early Judaism, even in literature later than the NT, the notion must have originated either in the teaching of Jesus or in the early church's reflection about Jesus (cf. Eph. 5:22-32; 2 Cor. 11:2; Rev. 19:7, 9; 21:2, 9; 22:17). Notice that here in Mark Jesus is not directly called the bridegroom, which fits in general Jesus' allusive and indirect manner of referring to himself and distinguishes our text from the aforementioned early Christian texts.

Vv. 21-22 refer to two inappropriate actions. The connection between these two sayings and what has come before may be that wine and new clothes are both regular items at weddings.[62] Holding on to the old, or trying to sew the new onto or pour it into the old, just wouldn't work. Jesus had come to make all things new. The Pharisees had assumed that the way to hasten and prepare for the coming of the new age was through stricter adherence to the old covenant. They did not seem to see that the coming of the new age was a gift of God's grace, not a response by God to Israel's faithfulness. If you put an unwashed piece of cloth on an old garment, when the new whole is washed the new piece shrinks and leaves a bigger tear in the old garment than existed before. If you put new wine in an old wineskin — wine not yet fully fermented that will ferment while in the skin — it will burst the skin. These images convey the dynamism in Jesus' ministry and the new thing he was doing.

62. See Gundry, p. 134.

D. Sabbatical Patterns (2:23-28)

Another Sabbath controversy story appears at this juncture.[63] The controversy is not over the disciples gleaning and eating a little grain, for that was allowed to the stranger or the poor by law (Deut. 23:25). The issue in this text has to do with reaping, a form of work. This was an activity prohibited on the Sabbath at Exod. 34:21 and listed in the Mishnah explicitly as one of the things one must not do on the Sabbath. Notice the technical language in v. 24: Why do Jesus' disciples do what is not legally permitted? There is good reason to think that behavior on the Sabbath was one of the Pharisees' major litmus tests of proper piety. Jesus' response is clever but not entirely clear, not least because the account is compressed and only a part of the dialogue is reported.

In regard to rhetoric, one may see in these controversy stories the use of judicial rhetorical motifs, but there is no clear conforming of the speech material here to that of a judicial oration.[64] Rather the story here, like these other controversy stories, is being conformed to the *chreia* pattern, with v. 27 seen as a maxim which leads to the conclusion of the pericope in v. 28.[65]

This Sabbath story has been subjected to detailed analysis of late by M. Casey, who has also shown how this Greek text can be retroverted back into an Aramaic original. He is able to explain various oddities in the text as translation phenomena (e.g., the use of the plural τα σαββατα when speaking of a sin-

---

63. For an attempt to analyze this pericope as a *chreia* elaboration, see R. Parrott, "Conflict and Rhetoric in Mark 2.23-28," *Semeia* 64 (1993): 117-37. The problem is in part that the normal *chreia* pattern order is not found in this story, as Parrott admits, and his attempt to find two forensic speeches in this small passage is unconvincing. Parrott himself is right to wonder "whether the Markan passage is really an elaboration, or simply has common rhetorical elements which also happen to occur in the elaboration" (p. 125), especially when the essential thesis statement seems lacking in this pericope, or if it is v. 28, then we have no elaboration of the thesis, for v. 28 concludes and rounds off the discussion. No, at best we may call this another *chreia* with a concluding memorable saying.

64. Even the detailed analysis by Mack and Robbins, pp. 107-29, is not able to show a clear following of deliberative or judicial patterns here. There are, for instance, no proofs or arguments by the Pharisees to support their accusation. Mark's concern is not detailed rhetorical argumentation. Rather he seeks to portray an important historical figure in a biographical format that is rhetorically sensitive — the *chreia*. Mack and Robbins also make some false steps (p. 115) in analyzing Jesus' argument. For example, Jesus does indeed use innuendo in rebutting the Pharisees here (they are ignorant of the Scriptures, particularly the implications of the story of David), but this does not reflect epideictic rhetoric. To the contrary, it reflects the judicial pattern of *insinuatio*, which, according to Quintilian, is to be used if the case is vulnerable. See Quintilian, *Inst.* 4.1.42-45, and *Rhetorica ad Herennium* 1.6.9-11, and the helpful analysis by Parrott, here pp. 128-32. One could even argue for the use of an *altercatio* sort of approach here. What we do not likely find here, however, is the elaboration of a *chreia*.

65. See B. Mack, *Rhetoric and the New Testament* (Minneapolis: Fortress, 1990), p. 52.

gle particular Sabbath). He shows that the issue in this text is the system of Peah (cf. Lev. 19:9; 23:22), a sort of social security system for the poor and hungry which allowed them to pluck grain in other people's fields. "Hunger had to be mentioned explicitly by Jesus, and by our source at 2.25, to make sure that the David incident was a clear exemplum,"[66] and the example assumes that Jesus' disciples were likewise hungry and in need. It was at the edges or fringe of a field, and so beside a path, where the grain was to be left ungleaned so the poor and hungry could pick it.

E. P. Sanders has objected at length to the likelihood that Pharisees would have been in Galilee scrutinizing Jesus' disciples as they walked through fields of grain, and I have dealt with his objections elsewhere,[67] but now we have also the following helpful comment from Casey:

> Firstly, orthodox Jews who lived in Capernaum were liable to join the Pharisees, and any Pharisees who did live in Capernaum were perfectly entitled to go for a stroll on the sabbath, just like Jesus and his disciples. . . . Nor is it too coinciden-tal that they should meet Jesus' disciples doing something they disapproved of. They perceived themselves as guardians of the Law at a time when we can verify the increase in sabbath Law in which they themselves played a significant part, while Jesus took his prophetic message to the people of the land. That was suffi-cient to make conflict inevitable. . . . There is a second reason why the Pharisees may have been there: they were quite free to go and see whether Jesus was teach-ing in accordance with the Law. . . . Jesus' lifestance was significantly different again. He came from the prophetic wing of Judaism, and the centres of his life were God himself and love of one's neighbour. He did not share the concern of the Pharisees and others to defend Judaism by means of expansion of regula-tions. Thus he observed the sabbath, but he vigorously defended his right to heal on that day, and he was not shocked that people who were hungry and in need should pluck corn in order to have enough to eat on that day: rather with prophetic authority he defended their right to satisfy their most basic needs on the day which God had created for them to rest on and to enjoy.[68]

Pharisees checking up on Jesus and his disciples is all the more likely if this plucking-grain event took place after Jesus had already established a track record of doing controversial things on the Sabbath. As Casey says, the only really plausible *Sitz im Leben* for a dispute about plucking grain is during the ministry of Jesus in the context of disputes with other Jews. It is not a matter the early church was likely to have debated.[69] Myers brings out well the social

---

66. Casey, p. 141.
67. Cf. Sanders, *Jesus and Judaism*, pp. 263-68, to my *Christology of Jesus*, pp. 66-67.
68. Casey, pp. 145, 148.
69. Casey, p. 150.

dimensions of the clash between Jesus and the Pharisees. "In all three episodes in which the Pharisees figure, Mark has focused upon some aspect of food consumption. First Jesus defended his (and his disciples') right to break bread with the socially outcast. Then he asserts their freedom to ignore ritual noneating practices; such piety, after all was a luxury for the affluent, not the poor for whom hunger was an involuntary and bitter reality! Now Mark escalates his attack: he justifies the disciples' right to break the law by procuring grain on the Sabbath in a situation of hunger. Mark is doing more than simply deflating the Pharisaic holiness code. He is implicitly raising a political issue of criticism by identifying the Pharisees with issues of 'land and table.'"[70] This characterization is telling, and it comports with what we know of Pharisaic interests from later Jewish sources such as the Mishnah and Talmuds. But it is perhaps better to speak of the Law being superseded in light of the eschatological situation, or alternately the Law being reinterpreted and things being reprioritized in light of the Law's chief aims and tenets.

Jesus appeals to an haggadic example from the life of David and his men. There is a certain appropriateness to this analogy since, according to 1 Sam. 21, David and his men were in need and on the run from Saul. We have a serious problem in v. 26 because it appears to say that Abiathar was priest when David was doing this deed, but in fact it was his father according to the Hebrew Scriptures who was involved. Much hinges on how one interprets the επι, which is idiomatic usage on any showing. If επι with the genitive means "at the time when . . . ," then we have a mistake here.[71]

Casey, however, suggests that the Aramaic original read "in the day (time) of Abiathar the high priest" and suggests that the translator failed to leave in the article before "high priest," which left the text open to the suggestion that Mark had made a mistake. He also argues that "Abiathar was much more important than Ahimelech, and his presence may reasonably be deduced from the narrative in 1 Samuel."[72] Other meanings are given in later manuscripts of this verse to correct the problem, for example, by inserting a του before the words "high priest," and note that Matthew and Luke omit the offending words altogether. Casey is also able to point out examples from early Judaism which assume that David's eating of the showbread did indeed transpire on a Sabbath (cf., e.g., b. Menaḥ. 95b, where the showbread is said to be baked just before the Sabbath on Friday; and Yalqut Shim'oni II.130). Thus the assumption of an incoherence in Mark's account of Jesus' appeal to David's example falls to the ground.[73]

---

70. Myers, p. 160.

71. See BDF 234.8.

72. Casey, p. 151.

73. Casey, p. 155, versus J. D. G. Dunn, Jesus, Paul, and the Law (Louisville: Westminster/J. Knox, 1990), pp. 22-23.

Jesus' point in any case is that the Pharisees have their priorities all wrong. V. 27 enunciates the basic argument supporting such behavior. The Sabbath was set up to benefit humankind; human beings were not created in order to observe the Sabbath.[74] The idea of the Sabbath being a gift from God to human beings is common both in the OT and in early Jewish literature (Exod. 16:29; *Jub.* 2:17; *Mekilta* 109B on Exod. 31:14). More broadly there is also the notion that the world and its institutions were to be managed by human beings, not the other way around (2 Esd. 6:54). Notice specifically *2 Bar.* 14:18: "And you said that you would make for your world a son of man as the manager of your works, to make it clear that he was not made for the world, but the world was made for him." Casey urges: "Mark 2.27-28 makes perfect sense against the background of a standard Jewish theology of creation, and the use of the words for 'man' is all the more natural in the context of a dispute which hinges partly on the importance of bodily needs which are common to all people."[75] Yet this assumes that the phrase "Son of Man" does not distinguish Jesus from the group of other humans but rather stresses the connection between him and humanity in general (cf. below). Some confirmation that Jesus was likely to use the sort of argument found in v. 27 can be found in Matt. 12:11-12/Luke 14:5 (cf. Luke 13:15-16), where the superiority of humans over beasts forms the basis of Jesus' arguments (cf. also Matt. 6:26).

What the disciples were doing could then be seen as an appropriate activity on the Sabbath — the taking of nourishment and refreshment, for the earth and the fullness thereof belongs to them. More importantly, what is behind the story is the implication that new occasions teach new duties, and a new state of affairs was in existence with the coming of God's dominion, such that the old Sabbath rules no longer applied. One should be paying attention to what God was now saying and doing.

V. 28 may be taken as another Markan parenthetical remark in which the author presses beyond the general maxim about the Sabbath and humankind and, in light of Jesus' actions here, concludes that Jesus, the Son of Man, is lord even over the Sabbath and its regulations. Thus Jesus understands the original intention of the Sabbath and is bringing that into focus — providing true rest and restoration for his disciples. He has the power and authority to declare that the old ways are no longer applicable in view of the inbreaking eschatological action of God.

There are several reasons not to see v. 28 as the enunciation of a principle true of all human beings: (1) In Jesus' day it was widely believed that the Sabbath was given to Israel in particular for its shalom. No stress was placed on its

---

74. For a considerably more detailed treatment of vv. 27-28, see my *Jesus the Sage*, pp. 167-69.

75. Casey, p. 160.

being given to humankind in general. (2) More importantly, while it was agreed that the Sabbath was a gift from God (see above), the available evidence does not speak of humans ruling the Sabbath or overruling some Sabbath regulations. It was certainly not believed by early Jews that all and sundry, being lords of the Sabbath, had the right to determine what was appropriate behavior on that day. (3) V. 28 is a ωστε clause. This particle can introduce an absolute proposition (BDF 391.2), but more frequently it establishes a link between two different propositions. In either case, the particle is unnecessary if v. 28 simply further explicates a general principle already enunciated in v. 27. Rather here, as elsewhere in Mark, such a clause enunciates the *conclusion* Mark is drawing from what has preceded; it is not simply reiterating in another way what has already been said. A good example of a final result clause in Mark which is a comment of the narrator is found in 15:5, where Mark states that the result of Jesus' failure to speak was that Pilate was amazed, or 2:12, which states that the miracle precipitates the crowd's reaction.

As Fowler notes, ωστε clauses regularly point out an inside view, not something known to the characters in the story itself other than the spiritually perceptive such as Jesus (cf. Mark 1:27 to 2:28).[76] It is thus natural to see this as a parenthetical remark and conclusion of the Evangelist, whose concern is biographical and who thus wants to make clear what the story reveals about Jesus in particular. The Sabbath was indeed made for human beings, but only one human being, the Son of Man, was lord over the Sabbath such that he could declare healing and other debatable activities appropriate on that occasion. This is because, as Dan. 7 makes evident, only the Son of Man was given authority over all humankind and human kingdoms and human institutions.[77] "In Mark's presentation, this . . . response . . . centres on the status of Jesus and underlines his authority."[78] "If the sabbath was made for man (i.e., for Israel), then it is to be expected that the Son of man (representing obedient Israel, restored to dominion in the world) should be Lord even of the sabbath. . . ."[79]

E. The Withered Hand and the Withered Heart (3:1-6)

3:1-6 concludes the first major section of the Gospel in which subjects Jesus taught on or matters he dealt with caused controversy or conflict. The repeated theme in this section has been that controversy centered on what Jesus said and did on the Sabbath. These matters come to a boiling point at 3:6 where, so

---

76. R. M. Fowler, *Let the Reader Understand* (Minneapolis: Fortress, 1991), pp. 103-4.
77. See my *Jesus the Sage*, pp. 168-69.
78. Hooker, p. 105.
79. Hooker, p. 105.

threatening is Jesus to the status quo, or at least the Pharisaic and Herodian agendas, his demise is plotted by these two disparate groups. We are presumably meant to think that Jesus was such a threat that even groups not normally allied banded together to do away with him.

As Guelich points out, this story does not fit neatly into any of the traditional form-critical categories, for it is a mixture of controversy, healing, and biography.[80] It does, however, meet the requirements for a *chreia*, which in this case primarily focuses on an action rather than a pithy saying of Jesus as a means of revealing his character — manifesting righteous anger and compassion. The biographical elements (vv. 5-6) need not be seen as later additions if Mark was compressing his source into the *chreia* form in the first place.[81] It is also true, as Casey demonstrates, that this story, like the others in this cycle, best suits a situation in the life of Jesus rather than one in the life of the early church. The early church, so far as we know, did not have disputes about plucking grain or healing on the Sabbath.[82]

3:1 begins with Jesus once again going into an unspecified synagogue, but the definite article may suggest that it was the Capernaum synagogue again. We are told there was a man with a "dried up" (i.e., withered) hand there. At this juncture the Pharisees and the Herodians are watching Jesus closely, to see what he would do. Their intent was to catch him in some illegal action so that they could denounce or accuse him and so discredit him.

Jesus tells the man to stand up in the middle of the synagogue, and then puts the ball in his adversaries' court. He tells the man to "rise up in the middle" of the synagogue, and then he asks the onlookers, "Is it (legally) permitted on the Sabbath to do good or to do evil, to save life or to kill?" As in the later story in 12:35-37, Jesus takes the initiative in this controversy, as though deliberately trying to force the issue and bring to light the true attitudes of the hearts of the adversaries. In this case, as in the story which began this cycle in Mark 2, the illness of the man is not life-threatening, and thus the rule that it was okay to do good on the Sabbath when a life was at stake or seriously in danger did not apply. *M. Yoma* 8.6 says explicitly: "Whenever there is doubt whether life is in danger this takes precedence over the sabbath."

Notice that Jesus is not posing a hypothetical question here, but rather

---

80. Guelich, p. 131.

81. This brings up an important point, which is rightly stressed by Robbins in *Jesus the Teacher: A Socio-Rhetorical Interpretation of Mark* (Minneapolis: Fortress, 1992). If we are going to do form-critical analysis, then we need to ask what ancient forms an ancient writer may have used to present his data, rather than inventing more modern categories like controversy narrative or pronouncement story and then complaining that the ancient story doesn't fit a Procrustean bed of our own devising.

82. Casey, pp. 160-92, here p. 192.

pressing an issue that stands before the audience in the person of the man with the withered hand. In essence Jesus is posing the awkward question to the residents about one of their fellow villagers whether it is all right to help him on this occasion. But Jesus' adversaries refuse to respond.

L. Hurtado points out that this healing's real significance is that it permits this man to fully participate in the worship of God, for Lev. 21:16ff. had stipulated that such persons in this man's condition were forbidden to enter the temple and worship there. Notice that Jesus uses nothing but a word to heal this man, unlike many another ancient wonder-worker. The adversaries do not doubt or dispute that Jesus has the power to heal, but the question is what the origin and nature of this power might be.[83]

Mark's presentation suggests that Jesus knows that his adversaries' silence does not imply their consent to what he does. He knows what is in their hearts, and he is angered and grieved at their hard-heartedness. They have not perceived that the Sabbath is for the refreshment and restoration and relief of humanity. Nor do they see that Jesus is bringing in the eschatological Sabbath conditions, when there will be ongoing relief from such maladies. The adversaries have missed God's purpose and compassion in giving the Sabbath in the first place — it was to be a time when those things that wearied or worried or plagued a person ceased. Hardening of the spiritual arteries is a repeated theme in Mark's Gospel (cf. this passage to 6:52; 8:17; 10:5), with sometimes the adversaries and sometimes the disciples as the subject. What we discover is that, wherever Jesus goes, he provokes a crisis of faith. It is impossible to cling to the status quo and accept Jesus at the same time. Jesus even forces the issue of decision making with his own disciples.

There is a sense in which he asked each group in Israelite society to give up what was most dear to them in order to embrace him. To the disciples the challenge meant giving up family and job, to the Pharisees it meant giving up their position of chief religious figures of their age, to the scribes it meant giving up being the providers of the correct interpretation of the oral and written Torah, for Sadducees and priests it was to mean giving up a certain kind of temple-centered approach to Judaism, for ordinary Jews it meant giving up certain attitudes about the moral outcasts and the diseased in society. The wonder is not that Jesus was eventually rejected by all these groups, but that he was not rejected and killed sooner.

Myers stresses that this synagogue episode is carefully staged political theater. Jesus could have healed the man in another place and at another time (a few hours later), especially if this event transpired in Capernaum. He could have healed the man quietly without challenging the observers, and so in essence shaming them in public. The man himself never asks for healing — Jesus

---

83. L. Hurtado, *Mark* (New York: Harper & Row, 1983), p. 35.

brings the matter up by commanding him to stand in the midst of the congregation. "He paraphrases the watershed question of Deuteronomic faith (Dt. 30.15ff.): 'Is it lawful on the Sabbath to do good, or to do evil?' (3.4). He then adds bitterly, 'To save life or to kill?,' drawing a sharp contrast between his messianic intentions and those of his opponents (*apokteinai* is always used in Mark in reference to political execution; see 6.19; 8.31; 12.5; 14.1)."[84] Of course, as Gundry points out, it was never permitted to do harm or kill on the Sabbath, and so, in the end, those who would contemplate such things were the real Sabbath violators.[85] Notice how Jesus controls the scene with aggressive speech and here, as at 2:9, has an advantage, for he gives his audience only two choices as to what should be done.[86] He does not for instance give them the option of saying that on the Sabbath it is lawful and proper to do nothing in this case. He is clearly forcing the issue. The authoritative manner in which he operates throughout 1:14–3:6 is shown by a series of commands he issues to both actual and potential disciples and to those being healed (1:15, 17, 38, 41, 44; 2:11; 2:14; 3:3, 5).[87]

As Robbins stresses, neither the actions nor the words of Jesus in this first part of Mark are like those of other early Jewish teachers. But one may add, neither are his actions or words and authority much more like Greek teachers such as Socrates. Jesus does not engage in long dialogues which slowly lead an audience to a proper conclusion. Rather Jesus, speaking authoritatively, seems to have forced the issues rather quickly with a citation of Scripture or proverbial wisdom to support what he said or did. In fact, there is no dialogue or debate at all in this particular story, just implacable opposition which does not or cannot respond to Jesus' questions.

Here we have a portrait of Jesus as not merely a healer but as an agent provocateur.[88] A. Trocmé has called this Markan episode the turning point of Jesus' public ministry,[89] and while this is saying too much, it can be said to be the straw that broke the camel's back and set in motion the forces which were eventually to lead to Jesus' demise. Jesus had crossed the line. If we see this story as the sequel to the Capernaum synagogue episode (cf. 1:21 to 3:1) and to the story found at the end of Mark 2, then Dewey is right that we may see 2:24 as the legal warning before actual prosecution on a charge would be set in motion, and at 3:2 the opponents are observing so that if Jesus acts illegally again on the Sabbath, he is liable to arrest. "The claim of Jesus in 2.28 prepares the reader for

84. Myers, p. 162.
85. Gundry, p. 151.
86. See Robbins, *Jesus the Teacher,* p. 112.
87. Robbins, p. 111.
88. See Painter, p. 64.
89. A. Trocmé, *Jesus and the Nonviolent Revolution* (Scottdale, Pa.: Herald, 1964).

the higher level of hostility and the greater stakes involved in 3.1-6."[90] It is also correct to stress that the charge of blasphemy which crops up at 2:7 will reappear at the trial in 14:62-64, as does the portrayal of Jesus having authority as the Son of Man to do various things elsewhere predicated of God.[91] The focus of the story is biographical and christological, not casuistic or medical.[92] Once the man is healed, he disappears from the story, but the controversy goes on, for its focus is Jesus, not the healed man. The question of whether healing might be seen as a form of saving a life is not pressed any further. Yet if one were to press the matter, it needs to be noted that Jesus heals here by means of speaking only. He does not do anything else. It would be hard to conclude that speaking could qualify as work, even on its strictest early Jewish definition.[93] There is then no open objection to Jesus speaking.

The story ends with the man's hand being healed "immediately" and unnatural allies taking counsel as to how to destroy the one who was a threat to what they held dear. The language of "decision" and "destroy" will crop up again in the passion narrative (see 15:1 and 11:18), and the combination of Pharisees and Herodians will be seen again at 12:13.[94] It also ends with Jesus being extremely angry and grieved when he looked around in the synagogue and saw the hardness of heart displayed there. Apparently a similar situation prompts a similar response of Jesus when he gets to the temple (11:11). The terminology used here in v. 5 for rage (μετ οργης) has no real parallel elsewhere in the NT. But Jesus is not merely angry, he is also very sad, even grieved (συλλυπουμενος). This combination of emotions is interesting, and it portrays Jesus not merely as a person of righteous anger, but also of compassion even for the hard-hearted. The story is laden with irony. "By bringing the new life of God's rule to bear, Jesus risks losing his own life."[95] Jesus, the one who comes to

---

90. Dewey, *Markan Public Debate*, p. 100.

91. See Hooker, p. 106.

92. See my *Christology of Jesus*, pp. 69-70, on how the narrative implies that Jesus is more than a prophet and teacher.

93. See E. P. Sanders, *Jewish Law from Jesus to the Mishnah* (Valley Forge, Pa.: Trinity, 1990), p. 21.

94. The Herodians are to be conceived of as Herod's spies or possibly representatives of his retainers or aristocracy who kept their finger on the pulse of what was happening in Galilee and reported back to Herod. They may even have been "royalists" wanting Herod made king of all the Holy Land, like his father. We get a glimpse of the sort of people Mark has in mind in 6:21. See R. Pesch, *Markus-Evangelium I* (Freiburg: Herder, 1976), p. 195; Gundry, p. 152. See especially the discussion now by Casey, pp. 186-89. He rightly points out that if Herod had worries about and surveillance on John the Baptist, the same is likely to be the case with Jesus. He also provides an extensive rebuttal to Sanders and Meier, who wrongly conclude that 3:6 is not grounded in any situation in the life of Jesus. See Casey, pp. 190-91.

95. Guelich, p. 139.

do only good, is, because he does do good on the Sabbath, being plotted against by those who should be upholding the moral order but instead are seeking to do harm, even on the Sabbath, to a healer like Jesus!

If anywhere, one would expect compassion to be displayed in the presence of God — that is, in the midst of worship in the place of worship. Yet what we find is "stubbornness of heart," a phrase that probably in the main means mental obtuseness and obduracy, for the heart was the center of thought in Semitic anthropology.[96] An interesting pattern begins to emerge, namely, that either when Jesus is mobbed due to the miracles or when he is rejected as here in the synagogue, he tends to withdraw and regroup, and in this case he regroups by commissioning his followers to go out in his place, as we shall see in the discussion of the next section of Mark (cf. 3:13-19 to 6:1-13). A crisis prompts a retrenchment and a fresh approach or a second effort.[97] But a dark cloud now hovers on the horizon, and the lightning will soon strike, though the first major victim was to be the Baptist.

Bridging the Horizons

We are well accustomed in our era to touting the accomplishments of modern medicine, and rightly so, but the first story in our cycle of stories reminds us that ministering to a mind or heart diseased is far more difficult than healing a body. When we consider the major causes of war and family breakdown and general social chaos, only rarely is the primary cause something like the bubonic plague. Much more often are the causes of major social dysfunction found within the depths of the human heart, wherein lie hatred, prejudice, lust, greed, false pride, envy, and a host of other spiritual and emotional and mental maladies. Though there is irony in the story, it is nonetheless true that only God can really forgive sin and deal with the root causes of most human misery. Jesus, in seeking to deal with such root causes, implicitly assumes the divine role in this story. In Mark 2:1-12 Jesus does not respond to the disbelief of some of the observers, nor to the amazement of the crowd. He responds to faith. His motives for healing have nothing to do with trying to impress people into the dominion of God or proving by miracles who he is. He is concerned that the paralytic get the cure, and most importantly that he know that the root cause of his even deeper problems has been dealt with. Thus we might say that Jesus was an early practitioner of holistic healing.

It has been said that the love of God is not like a heat-seeking missile di-

---

96. See Hooker, p. 107.
97. See Myers, p. 161.

rected toward a target because of something inherently attractive and attracting in that target audience. Rather God's love is self-giving and other-directed, not based on some inherent loveliness in its object. It does not look for loveliness or worth; it bestows them both. We see something of this pure graciousness in the calling of Levi and the other disciples. Mark says and indeed suggests absolutely nothing about any of these men being chosen because Jesus thought they had potential. To the contrary, to judge from what we are told of their character and spiritual perceptivity, they are more like the Dirty Dozen than the Magnificent Twelve. This description is perhaps especially apt for a Levi, who had chosen to aid a tyrant like Herod and/or the Romans by bilking his own people. Jesus had surely not picked him because he had good business skills and high moral character! The issue here was not what he was, but what by grace Jesus was calling him and would instruct him to become.

Jesus was prepared to have table fellowship with a Levi and indeed with notable and notorious sinners in order to bring them back to God. He was more concerned about reaching them for God than about protecting his reputation. Rather than them making him unclean, he believed he could sanctify and cleanse them and reintegrate them into normal Jewish society. Yet this did not mean that he condoned their immoral and unethical behavior. But his way of approaching the matter was by practicing forgiveness in action as an open door to invite them to amend their lives. A person who has not sinned does not need forgiveness, and clearly Jesus believed all sorts of people needed forgiveness, including the sexually immoral. Jesus was not like some moderns who think the Christian approach is to baptize people's sins and call them good and healthy, a matter of lifestyle choice rather than ethical considerations. Jesus found a way to strike the balance between loving sinners and even fellowshipping with them while not endorsing their sin. Here is another case where Jesus is a tough act to follow. But some have managed it. There once was a brilliant young Englishman who was extremely rich. His name was C. T. Studd. Under the conviction of Christ's words and example, he gave away most of his fortune in order to go out to the forests of Africa and reach some for Christ. He put his life philosophy as follows: "Some like to dwell / Within the sound / Of church and chapel bell. / But I want to run a rescue shop / Within a yard of Hell." This appears to aptly sum up Jesus' approach as well.

Knowing and seizing the moment, and knowing what is appropriate at a given moment, is what the Bible calls wisdom. It involves a sense of time and timing and a willingness to do what is appropriate on the occasion. Jesus, when he offers the small parable about the bridegroom, suggests that mourning and fasting are basically not apropos now that the dominion of God is breaking in and Jesus is present. It is rather time for feasting and joyful celebration. I once pastored a man who was an alcoholic. He spent a good deal of time drinking to try and forget that he had missed his golden opportunity in life. He had been an excellent baseball player and had an opportunity to sign a pro contract, but his father would not allow it. The opportunity passed and he spent the rest of his life doing blue-collar jobs and feeling sorry for himself. It was Shakespeare who suggested that there is a tide in the affairs of humankind which, if taken at the flood, leads on to great things. Jesus was suggesting that his audience needed to seize the moment, for the divine saving activity was breaking in to human history.

The illustration about new wine and old wineskins suggests not merely that the new could not be confined by the old forms and ways of doing things, but also that new forms were necessary to contain and sustain the new wine. A new wineskin is more flexible than an old one and can expand with the fermenting juices. Jesus, then, is not suggesting that no forms or rules are necessary, but that some flexibility about such matters is necessary in view of the new thing God is doing in their midst. New occasions teach new duties and generate new forms of worship and fellowship.

Jesus, like all other pious early Jews, appealed to Scripture to explain or justify his behavior. This, of course, presupposes not only the authority of the Hebrew Scriptures but also a considerable knowledge of those Scriptures, and not merely the legal parts. In the story in Mark 2:23-28, Jesus appeals to a story in the life of David to justify the behavior of his disciples in plucking grain on the Sabbath. He seems initially to be on the defensive, but in fact he immediately challenges his questioners whether they knew the Scriptures or not. Apparently he believed that the best defense is to go on the offensive and put one's opponents on their heels. Yet he accepted the implicit challenge of the Pharisees that he should be able to explain and should be responsible for the behavior of his disciples. He considered himself answerable for their actions. The disciples were hungry, and Jesus did not see plucking some grain as any sort of work which was prohibited by the Sabbath laws. Even if there was such a prohibition in some oral tradition, Jesus believed the need to provide rest and restoration overrides such a rule and that the Sabbath was an especially appropriate day for such actions. It would be worthwhile to ponder what actions we may deem inappropriate on Sunday and ask ourselves why we think so. We would need to probe deeply and ask what are the real aims and purposes of Sunday for a Christian. Do we consider Sunday a Sabbath, or do we think the OT sabbatical rules do not apply to the Lord's Day? These are the sorts of questions one can raise on the basis of this story.

The Scriptures say "be angry, but sin not," and in 3:1-6 we see the sinless one very angry indeed. It reminds us that anger itself is not a sin; indeed, one could even say that righteous anger is a prerequisite for ministry, for a person who has no capacity for righteous anger at the things that destroy humankind is a person who fails to be truly compassionate. Notice the combination of emotions predicated of Jesus here — anger at hard-heartedness but also sadness at the lack of compassion. Anger without compassion results in censoriousness. Compassion without righteous anger results in the tolerance of the very things that destroy humankind. Augustine put it this way in his great classic *The City of God*, book 14: "If angry emotions which spring from a love of what is good and from holy charity are to be labeled vices, then all I can say is that some vices should be called virtues. When such emotions as anger are directed to their proper objects, they are following good reasoning, and no one should dare to describe them as maladies or vicious passions. This explains why the Lord himself . . . was guilty of no sin whatever as he displayed these emotions openly when appropriate." Another way of assessing Jesus' behavior here is this: "Here is no sword-wielding rebel worthy of a Roman cross but a man who grieves deeply over his enemies . . . and who gets angry to save life, not kill, to do good, not harm."[98]

Perhaps better than anyone else, D. English has aptly summed up the overall biographical and christological portrait of Jesus embedded in Mark 2:1– 3:6. It is, as English stresses, a portrait of a human being who is also divine and so deems it appropriate to take on the roles of God as forgiver, bridegroom of God's people, great physician, Lord:

> Hidden within these four pronouncement stories are claims of Jesus about himself which are not to be missed. In the story of the paralytic it is his claim to forgive sins which so offended the teachers of the law (2.7). They know that only God could forgive sins. Just so! In 2.17, to explain his presence among the acknowledged sinners of Levi's company, he uses the doctor-patient analogy which shows that he is the soul doctor who comes to heal the sick-sinners. In 2.19, 20 he is the bridegroom, an Old Testament picture of God in relation to his people. In 2.25 he is the lord of the Sabbath. Since God gave it, who else could be lord of it? The points are so subtly made by Mark's presentation, though they would be offensive to the religious leaders of the day, that we might miss them. We mustn't for Mark's point is that one group after another was missing the real understanding of who it was who stood in their midst. When will they see? (And when will we see?)[99]

---

98. Gundry, p. 151.
99. D. English, *The Message of Mark* (Downers Grove: InterVarsity, 1992), p. 100.

VII. Preview and Review (3:7-12)

This brief section is transitional in nature, linking what comes before with what comes after, and though it is a Markan summary and should be compared with other Markan summaries (e.g., 1:14-15, 32-34, 35-39, and especially 6:53-56), it has enough awkwardness and unique terms to suggest that Mark is using some source material even here. The vocabulary of 3:9-10, with four hapax legomena, prepares us for what we find in the miracle cycle of stories which follows in 4:35–6:56. It has even been suggested that this summary immediately preceded those stories in Mark's source; however, it has a retrospective quality as well.[1] If we view this material from the perspective that Mark is writing an ancient biography, then it is in order to point out that "3.7-12 brings together Mark's portrait of Jesus' ministry from 1.16 to 3.6"[2] with a clear focus on Jesus being the Son of God, which can be said to be one of, if not *the*, most important of Mark's christological titles (1:1, 11; 9:7; 15:39). While it is now generally recognized that the older arguments that Jesus is portrayed as a Hellenistic "divine man" figure (θειος ανηρ) in Mark are extremely weak, nevertheless Mark is stressing in his Gospel that Jesus is the divine Son of God for whom even the powers of darkness are no match. Indeed, after this transitional passage it is fair to say that "this section presents Jesus increasingly as an epiphany of God himself: he stills the unruly waters, walks upon the sea, and identifies himself with the formula 'I am' as God

---

1. See R. Guelich, *Mark 1–8.26* (Waco: Word, 1989), pp. 142-46; V. Taylor, *The Gospel according to St. Mark* (New York: St. Martin's Press, 1966), p. 225; C. E. B. Cranfield, *The Gospel according to St. Mark* (Cambridge: Cambridge University Press, 1972), p. 124; R. Pesch, *Markus-Evangelium I* (Freiburg: Herder, 1976), pp. 201-2.
2. Guelich, p. 144.

himself does in the Old Testament (4.35-39 cf. 6.45-52)."[3] Yet, though Jesus is revealed as the appearance of the God of the exodus, it is also true that the re-action to his miracles is no more perceptive than that of Pharaoh and others to the great signs performed in Egypt. The supernatural world knows well who Jesus is but does not wish to acknowledge him unless forced to, while mere mortals still do not really know who Jesus is even though he has per-formed great miracles and even though they are impressed by his mighty works and follow him around.

TRANSLATION — 3:7-12

And Jesus, with his disciples, withdrew to the sea, and a large crowd from Galilee [followed] and from Judea, and from Jerusalem, and from Idumea even beyond the Jordan [Perea], and from Tyre and Sidon, a large crowd, hearing what he did came to him.[4] And he spoke to his disciples in order that a small boat might stand by him because of the crowd in order that they not crush him. For he healed many, with the result that they fell upon him in order to touch him whoever had a scourge, and the unclean spirits, whenever they saw him fell down before him and cried out saying, "You are the Son of God." And he rebuked them many times lest they make him known.

There is a sense in which 3:7-12 can be seen as an appropriate Markan intro-duction to the second major section of this Gospel. Like 1:14-15, which intro-duces the first major section, we begin with a summary followed by the choos-ing of disciples (cf. 1:16-20 to 3:13-19).[5] Both summary statements have something of a programmatic character. We are being told emphatically and re-peatedly that Jesus ministered by healings and exorcisms and chose disciples to become involved not only in this ministry but also in proclaiming the advent of God's dominion and so bring it in by word and deed.

Vv. 7-8 are meant to make clear that Jesus' fame as a miracle worker as well as a preacher was spreading throughout the region — indeed, to a wider region than did John's fame — apparently due to the miracles. Notice that two regions are notable by their absence in this list — Samaria and Decapolis. Com-

---

3. J. Marcus, *Mark 1–8* (New York: Doubleday, 1999), p. 256.

4. This awkward sentence produced many textual variants, and in this case it seems likely that we should follow B, L, l, and 565 for our text, as the other readings can be ex-plained on the basis of the one found in these manuscripts. The major issue is whether the verb "follow" is a part of the original text, and if so whether it is in the singular or plural. Probably the absence of the verb from Western and Caesarean witnesses is due to oversight. But see Metzger, *TCGNT,* pp. 79-80.

5. See W. Lane, *The Gospel of Mark* (Grand Rapids: Eerdmans, 1974), pp. 127-28.

mon to the regions mentioned is their heavy concentrations of Jews. In due course Jesus will go on a preaching tour of each of these regions except Idumea, which is ancient Edom, south of Judea. The point of these geographical references seems to be to make clear that people were coming from north, east, south, and west to reach Jesus.[6]

Despite Jesus' successes, he withdraws to the sea, which some have seen as the place of temptation and chaos and demonic forces. Hooker suggests that the withdrawal mentioned in 3:7 should be seen in light of 3:6, in which case it could be attributed to the plot against Jesus, and in fact this is how Matthew understands the matter (Matt. 12:14-15).[7] Once again we hear of the demons crying out a title which described Jesus' very identity.

The press of the crowd seeking healing was so overwhelming that Jesus required the disciples to ready a boat to escape in as a safety valve. In v. 10 we find the word μάστιξ, which literally means scourge. Are we to think of Jesus healing wounded persons who were oppressed and had been beaten by some authorities? This is not impossible, especially in view of the preceding reference to plotting involving Herodians and the story which will follow about the Baptist's demise in Mark 6. Against this conclusion is the only other use of the term in 5:29, 34, where it refers to a woman who was hemorrhaging. It may be possible, however, that Mark is using the term in a way which reflects the common theology that such maladies were seen as divine chastisement.[8]

This crowd is not "following" Jesus as disciples. The verb "to follow" here has none of its more pregnant theological connotations. Rather they are chasing after and tracking down Jesus. They seem to have a magical view of Jesus, believing if they just touch him they will be well. But Jesus does not wish to be treated as some sort of reservoir of magical powers. The crowd nearly crushes Jesus, yet despite this Jesus still takes time to heal many. He does not simply retreat without helping anyone.

The mention of the boat, however, brings to the surface another possible pedagogical technique of Jesus the teacher. If Jesus were to teach from the boat, then people would not be able to crowd and crush or even touch him, providing he was just far enough out in the water so he could not be easily reached. In fact, 4:1, 34-35 suggest that Jesus used this technique not merely to get away from the press of the crowd but so that he could concentrate on preaching and teaching, which he saw as his primary mission (see 1:38), rather than healing.

The cry of the unclean spirits is correct but unwelcome. The text says Je-

6. See C. Myers, *Binding the Strong Man: A Political Reading of Mark's Story of Jesus* (Maryknoll, N.Y.: Orbis, 1988), p. 163.

7. M. Hooker, *The Gospel according to Mark* (Peabody, Mass.: Hendrickson, 1991), p. 109.

8. See Hooker, p. 110; Cranfield, p. 125; Marcus, p. 258.

sus "subdued" (which apparently means silenced) them even though they prompted their hosts to bow down before him. Why was their confession unwelcome? Hurtado conjectures it is because the naming of Jesus by the unclean spirits is an attempt to gain control over Jesus and does not arise out of commitment or discipleship to Jesus.[9] By contrast, Guelich suggests that the problem is simply that the timing of the confession is all wrong.[10] This seems a less convincing explanation than that Jesus did not want a confession from such a dubious source.

There is irony in the fact that the wrong beings, indeed the ones Jesus came to combat, say the right things about Jesus. Jesus will be accused of being in league with Satan and his minions, perhaps in part because of these acclamations. Yet Jesus is possessed and driven by the Holy Spirit, not unclean ones. Augustine conjectured that what was wrong with the demons' confession was that it did not exhibit love or personal commitment to Jesus. The demonic confession is simply the truth, but not a truth those who made it wish to embrace or trust, for these are the same beings who said to Jesus, "What have we to do with you?" (*Letter to Sextus* 194). "The human and demonic reactions to Jesus are linked by the use of similar verbs: the human sufferers *fall upon* him in their agitation to touch him, and the unclean spirits *fall before* him blaring out his divine identity . . . the knees of both earthly and unearthly creatures are beginning to bow before Jesus, and even the mouths of the demons are confessing his eschatological lordship."[11]

---

9. L. Hurtado, *Mark* (New York: Harper & Row, 1983), p. 42.
10. Guelich, pp. 148-49.
11. Marcus, pp. 258-59.

VIII. The Creation of a Ministering Community, the Forsaking of Family and Neighbors (3:13–6:6a)

This second major section of the Gospel of Mark seems in the main to have been constructed on the basis of a collection of parables (Mark 4) and a collection of miracle tales, plus some memorabilia about Jesus' relationship with his family and disciples. In an ancient biography we would expect a discussion of the central character's relationship, however strained, with his family, and Mark does not disappoint us, as comments on the family basically frame this section of the Gospel. But what becomes clearer as this section develops is that Jesus is misunderstood not merely by his adversaries or the crowds but even by his family, and in fact by various of his disciples. In other words, the central character in this drama begins to look increasingly like a tragic figure. It is also in this section that Mark emphasizes once more that Jesus was a teacher, finally giving us a substantial sample of Jesus' public teaching in Mark 4, as well as a miracle worker. Yet miracles fail to make completely clear who Jesus is. They cause various people to raise the question about his identity, but they do not provide the answer. Answers come, whether about the mysteries of the dominion or the identity of Jesus, by means of revelation. Otherwise, such things would remain apocalyptic secrets about the eschatological realities.[1]

---

1. See R. Guelich, *Mark 1–8.26* (Waco: Word, 1989), pp. 152-53.

TRANSLATION — 3:13–6:6

>   And he goes up onto the mountain and he calls to himself those he wanted, and they came to him. And he made twelve (who were also designated apostles), in order that they might be with him and in order that he might send them to preach and to have authority to cast out the demons, [and he made twelve][2] and he imposes a name on Simon, Peter, and Jacob the son of Zebedee and John the brother of Jacob, and he imposed on them the name Boanerges, which is Sons of Thunder. And Andrew and Phillip and Bartholomew and Matthew and Thomas and Jacob the son of Alphaeus and Thaddeus and Simon the Cananean, and Judas Iscariot, who also handed him over.

>   And he comes into the house; and the crowd again comes with him, so that they were not even able to eat. And those close to him[3] hearing, they came out to take charge of him for they said that he was beside himself. And the scribes who were from Jerusalem coming down said that he has Beelzeboul and that by the ruler of the demons he casts out the demons. And calling them together he spoke to them in parabolic speech: "How is Satan able to cast out Satan; and if a dominion should be divided against itself, that dominion is not able to stand: and if a house should be divided against itself, that house will not be able to stand. And if Satan has risen up against himself and is divided, he is not able to stand but rather he is finished. But no one is able, entering a house of the powerful, to plunder his goods unless first the powerful one is bound up, and then the house can be plundered. Amen I say to you that all the sins of the sons of humankind will be forgiven and whatever blasphemes they blaspheme, but whoever speaks blasphemy unto the Holy Spirit is not forgiven forever, but is guilty of an eternal sin" — because they said, "He has an unclean spirit."

>   And his mother and his brothers come and they are standing outside, they sent for him, calling him. And a crowd was sitting around and they say to him, "Look, your mother and your brothers [and your sisters][4] out there they seek you." And answering them he says, "Who is my mother and my brothers?" And looking around at those sitting in a circle around him he says, "See my mother and my brothers. [For] whoever does the will of God, this one is my brother and sister and mother."

---

2. This clause is probably original, as it is needed to carry on what was said in v. 14. See Metzger, *TCGNT*, p. 81.

3. The criterion of embarrassment clearly comes into play here. Some scribes found the reading οι παρ αυτου, "his relatives," or less probably "his friends," too embarrassing, so that in D, W, and other manuscripts we read "when the scribes and the others had heard about him, they went out to seize him. . . ."

4. The shorter text, which omits sisters, may be original at this point, though certainly they are mentioned thereafter. See Metzger, *TCGNT*, p. 82, and particularly Metzger's own judgment in disagreement with the committee.

4   *And again he began to teach beside the sea. And a huge crowd gathered together around him, so that he, getting on board a boat he sat in the sea, and all the crowd were on the ground by the sea. And he taught them in many parables and he spoke to them in his teaching: "Listen. Look, a sower went out to sow. And it happened in the act of sowing that on the one hand it fell along the path, and the birds came and ate it up. And on the other hand it fell upon the stony ground, which did not have much earth, and immediately it sprang up because it did not have depth of earth. And when the sun shone it was scorched, and because it did not have roots it dried up. And on the other hand other seed fell into the thorns and the thorns grew up and choked him, and it did not give fruit. But other seed fell upon the good earth, and it gave fruit rising up and increasing and bearing in thirty and sixty and a hundred fold." And he said, "Whoever has ears let them listen so as to hear."*

And when it happened he was alone, those surrounding him with the Twelve asked him about the parable. And he said to them, "To you the mystery of the dominion of God is given, but to those outside it is all given in parables in order that 'Seeing they see and do not perceive, and hearing they hear but do not understand, lest they turn and it is forgiven to them.'"

And he says to them, "Do you not know this parable, and how will you know all the parables? The sower sows the word. But this is the word sowed along the path and when they hear about it immediately Satan comes and takes the sown word from them. And this is the seed sown on stony ground which when they hear the word immediately with joy they receive it, and they do not have roots in themselves, but they are temporary; then when suffering or persecution happens because of the word immediately they are caused to stumble. And the others are as the seed falling on thorns. These are those listening to the word, and the worries of the age and the deception of wealth and the intervening of cravings for other things suffocate the word, and it is unfruitful. And the other is like that which is falling upon good earth, these listen to the word and welcome it and bear fruit thirty, sixty and a hundred fold."

And he said to them, "The light is not brought in order to put it under the peck measure or under the couch is it? Is it not brought in order to put it on the lamp stand? For it is not hidden except in order to be made evident, nor is there a secret but in order that it might become clear. If any have ears, let them listen so as to hear."

And he said to them, "Take note of what you hear! In the measure you measure, it will be measured to you and it will be added to you. For whoever has, will be given it; and whoever does not have, even what they have will be taken from them."

And he said, "Thus is the dominion of God as a person throwing the seed upon the earth. And he sleeps and rises night and day, and the seed sprouted and grew, how he knows not. By itself the earth bears fruit, first the blade, then the ear, then the full wheat in the ear. But when the crops allow immediately he sends out the sickle, because the harvest has come."

And he said, "To what shall we compare the dominion of God, or in what parable shall we represent it. Like a mustard grain, which when it is sown in the earth, being the smallest of all the seeds upon the earth, and when sown, it rises up and becomes the greatest of all the vegetables and makes great branches, so that the birds under its shade may roost."

And in many of such kinds of parables he spoke the word to them, just as they were able to hear. But without parables he did not speak to them, but privately he explained everything to his own disciples.

And he says to them on that day, being early evening: "Let us cross unto the other side," and sending the crowd away, they took him along as he was in the boat and other boats were with him. And there was a squall with a great wind, and the waves broke over the boat, so that the boat was indeed filling up. And he was in the stern upon the pillow sleeping. And they aroused him and said to him, "Teacher, is it not a concern to you that we are perishing?" And he rebuked the wind, and said to the sea, "keep silent, be still." And the wind dropped, and there was a great calm. And he said to them, "Why are you cowardly? Do you not yet have faith?" And they were frightened with a great fear, and they said to one another, "Then in light of this, who is this that even the wind and the sea obey him?"

5   And they came unto the other side of the sea into the region of Gerasa[5] and as he was coming out from the boat immediately a person with an unclean spirit met him from the tombs, who had his dwelling in the tombs, and not chains nor anyone was able to bind him, because the same often with fetters and bonds would be bound and having burst the fetters and binds that bound him, no one was able to subdue him. And through all the nights and days in the tombs and in the mountains he was crying out and bruising himself with stones. And seeing Jesus from afar he ran and knelt before him, and crying out in a loud voice he says, "What to me and to you, Jesus, son of the most high God? I adjure you by God, not to torture me." For he said to him, "Come out from the person, unclean spirit." And he asked him, "What is your name?" And he says to him, "Legion is my name, because we are many." And he begged him urgently in order that he not send them from the region.

But there was on the mountain a great herd of pigs grazing. And they begged him saying, "Send us into the pigs, in order that we may go into them." And he allowed them. And coming out (of him) the unclean spirits entered into the pigs and the herd rushed over the cliff into the sea, about two thousand, and they drowned

---

5. Early witnesses of both the Alexandrian and Western text types suggest this is the correct reading here rather than Gadara, which may be an assimilation to Matt. 8:28. Gergasa seems to be a later correction by a scribe, and Origen may have been the first to propose it. See Metzger, *TCGNT*, p. 84.

in the sea. And the pig herders fled and reported unto the city and to the country-side, and they went to see what had happened. And they came to Jesus, and they saw the demoniac sitting clothed and sane, the one who had had the Legion, and they were greatly afraid. And they described to him, those seeing how it happened to the demoniac and concerning the pigs. And they began to beseech him to leave from their region. And getting him into the boat, the demoniac begged him in or-der that he might be with him. And he did not permit him but says to him, "Go back into your house to your family, and report to them all the Lord has done for and had compassion on you." And he went and began to preach in the Decapolis what Jesus had done to him and all were amazed.

And Jesus crossing over [in the boat] again into the region a great crowd gathered together around him, and he was by the sea. And he comes upon the syn-agogue leader named Jairus,[6] and seeing him the latter fell down at his feet, and begging him a great deal saying, "My daughter is at the end, in order that coming you might lay hands on her in order to save and enliven her." And he went with him.

And a great crowd follows him, and crowds around. And a woman suffering a flow of blood for twelve years. And having suffered much from many doctors and having spent all that she had and having not benefited but rather came into a worse condition, hearing about Jesus, coming in the crowd from behind she touched his garment. For she said, "If only I might touch his garment I will be saved." And immediately her fountain of blood became dry, and recognizing this in her body, that she was finally cured from the scourge. And immediately Jesus per-ceiving in himself that from him power had gone out turned to the crowd and said, "Who touched me?" And he looked around to see the one who had done this. But the woman, in fear and trembling knowing what had happened to her, came and prostrated herself before him and told him all the truth. But he said to her, "Daughter, your faith has saved you. Go into peace, and be healed from your scourge."

While he was speaking some from the synagogue ruler come saying, "Your daughter has died. Why then trouble the teacher?" But Jesus overhearing the word they were speaking says to the synagogue ruler, "Fear not, only believe." And he would not permit anyone to go in with him except only Peter and Jacob and John, Jacob's brother. And they come into the house of the synagogue ruler, and they see uproar and weeping and much wailing, and entering in he says to them, "Why be in an uproar and weep? The child is not dead but sleeping." And they ridiculed him. But he casting out everyone takes along the father of the girl and the mother and those with him, and went within where the child was. And grasping the hand

---

6. Though a few Western manuscripts omit the name Jairus, which is also not found in the Matthean parallel, the preponderance of evidence supports its inclusion here as original to the text.

of the child he says to her, "Talitha cumi,"[7] which translated means "Little girl, I say to you, arise." And immediately the little girl arose and walked around, for she was twelve. And [immediately] they were astounded in great ecstasy. And he ordered them much in order that no one would know this, and he said to give her something to eat.

6   And he went out from there, and comes into his hometown, and his disciples followed him. And being the Sabbath he began to teach in the synagogue. And many hearing were astounded saying, "Where does he get this? And what sort wisdom is this one given, and what power are these things done through his hands? Is this not the carpenter,[8] the son of Mary and brother of Jacob and Joses and Jude and Simon? And are not his sisters here with us?" And they were scandalized about him. And Jesus says to them, "A prophet is not without honor except in his own hometown and among his kin, and in his own household." And he was not able to do any mighty works there except laying hands on a few sick he cured them. And he marveled at their unbelief.

A. Appointment on the Mountain (3:13-19)

This text provides us with a traditional list of the Twelve, about which there are various enigmas. The setting for this appointment is "the mountain," which presumably is meant to be reminiscent of the setting at which Israel was constituted a people (Exod. 18–19).[9] We are told at v. 13 that Jesus called unto himself those whom he wished to call,[10] and they responded. The concept of election seems clear here, and note that he chose twelve from among Israel. "The use of

---

7. A few manuscripts (W, 28, 245, 349, and a few old Latin manuscripts) read Tabitha here without the word κουμ, undoubtedly a scribal mix-up with the proper name found in Acts 9:40. We also have in this verse a variation between κουμ and κουμι which reflects the difference between genderized forms in the Aramaic of the imperative singular (κουμι is feminine and likely the original). Here we have not only evidence that our author knows some Aramaic, but also that Jesus spoke in Aramaic, and lastly that at least the sayings of Jesus were likely transmitted first in Aramaic, if not the Markan narratives as well. On this see M. Casey, *Aramaic Sources of Mark's Gospel* (Cambridge: Cambridge University Press, 1998).

8. A few witnesses, including p45, assimilate the text here to Matt. 13:55, which simply calls Jesus the son of a carpenter. This reading, however, cannot override the testimony of all the uncials, many minuscules, and various important versions which present Mark 6:3 as we have rendered it above. See Metzger, *TCGNT*, pp. 88-89.

9. J. Marcus, *Mark 1–8* (New York: Doubleday, 1999), p. 266, plausibly suggests an echo of Exod. 19.3ff., which continues with a prophecy of Israel being God's prized possession.

10. J. Painter, *Mark's Gospel* (London: Routledge, 1997), p. 66, suggests that the Markan account intimates that Jesus picked the Twelve out of a larger bunch of disciples. I personally do not think Mark 3 implies this.

the intensive pronoun αυτος clearly accentuates that the choice was Jesus' alone based on his own desire. One cannot help but hear a faint echo of the OT references to God's sovereign call or selection of his own."[11] There can be little doubt that the number chosen is deliberate and is meant to allude to the twelve tribes of Israel. But are the Twelve meant to be Israel, or are they simply chosen to be Jesus' emissaries to Israel? They can't be representatives of ancient Israel, for in Jesus' day there were only two and a half tribes left, but they could symbolize the eschatological restoration of all Israel which was expected at the end (cf. Isa. 49:6; Ezek. 45:8; Sir. 36:10; 48:10; *Pss. Sol.* 17:26-32; *Sib. Or.* 2:170-76; *T. Jos.* 19:1-7; Josephus, *Ant.* 11.133).[12] At the least, the Twelve would seem to reflect Jesus' claim on Israel. We will say more on this shortly. V. 14 says Jesus made twelve. In Mark the Twelve are referred to ten times (3:14; 4:10; 6:7; 9:35; 10:32; 11:11; 14:10, 17, 20, 43). In an appendix to this study, we have dealt with the argument that Mark intends to limit the disciples to the Twelve.[13] We found this argument unsatisfactory, especially in view of texts like 4:10 and 10:32, and in view of the concept of the family of faith we find in a text like 3:34. There is, however, no doubt that there is a focus on the Twelve as the main group of disciples in Mark's Gospel, and as such they are regularly contrasted with the crowd (cf. 10:46; 12:41, 43). Their preparation for ministry is stressed up to about 10:45, but others are not excluded from Jesus' instruction or from being his followers.

Notice that in v. 14 we are told that Jesus appointed the Twelve to be with him. This is part and parcel of the portrait of the fully human Jesus in this Gospel — in this case he needed a support group, he longed for fellowship. He lives as a person in community, not as an isolated prophet. These were not merely to be Jesus' pupils (remembering that the word "disciple" actually means learner), but his friends and coworkers. They are appointed for fellowship as well as for witness, being sent to teach and cast out demons.[14] It is also said in v. 14 that the Twelve were named apostles, but this seems to be a parenthetical comment of Mark's. In view of 6:30, it seems clear that Mark understands the term to refer to those who have been sent out by someone as authorized agents.

Simon is given first mention, as is his nickname — Cephas (see Matt. 16:18), or in Greek πετρος, which as of yet is unattested in the era before Jesus as a Greek personal name. It is not clear whether we are meant to see this nick-

11. Guelich, p. 157.
12. Some have suggested that in fact there were portions of the remaining tribes left, but the evidence, in regard to the northern tribes, seems insubstantial. See Marcus, *Mark 1–8*, p. 267.
13. See pp. 421-42 below.
14. Notice that Mark has two pericopes, one about the appointment in Mark 3 and another in Mark 6 about the sending out of the Twelve, whereas in Matthew 10:1-15 the two stories are found together.

name as a double entendre or not (the rock, or rocky), and in fact the word *cepha* primarily means stone rather than rock. Notice that the nickname Peter is used from this point on in Mark (3:16; 5:37; 8:29, 33; 9:2; 11:21; 13:3; 14:29, 31, 33, 66-67, 72; 16:7), except that Jesus returns to his formal name, Simon, in the Gethsemane scene, which may reflect the seriousness of the occasion and Jesus' disappointment (14:37).[15] It has been suggested that the renaming be viewed like the renaming of the patriarchs (e.g., Abram to Abraham, noting that Abraham is called the rock in Isa. 51:1-2),[16] in which case Jesus may be bringing about the eschatological rebirth of Israel with new patriarchs.

Nor do we know why the Zebedees are called the Sons of Thunder, though there have been various conjectures that it referred to their fiery temperament or the like (cf. Mark 9:38 to Luke 9:54). This naming seems different from Peter's because it is applied to both brothers, and in fact does not amount to a change of name, for they retain their names throughout the Gospels.[17] Half of the Twelve may well have been made up of pairs of brothers, that is, if Jacob and Levi/Matthew of Alphaeus were brothers and Levi was one of the Twelve.[18] The traditional nature of the list seems clear from the fact that Levi is not mentioned here, at least by that name. Bartholomew is not a name but a patronymic, meaning son of Thalmai, so we do not know this man's personal name. There is difficulty with the name Thaddaeus as well; it does not occur in Luke, but rather in its place we have Judas the son of Jacob (Luke 6:14-16; Acts 1:13). "Simon the Cananean" (which does not likely mean Canaanite) presumably refers to Simon the zealous one or patriot. He may have been, at least formerly, involved in revolutionary circles. Judas is identified by the fact that he handed Jesus over. The term "Iscariot" might mean a person from Kerioth, a town possibly in Idumea, possibly in Judea (cf. Josh. 15:25 near Hebron, Jer. 48:24 in Moab, but in either case he is not a Galilean), but it is also possible that this label indicates he was one of the *sicarii* or dagger men, the extreme faction and hit men among the revolutionary party.[19] This latter view seems to be supported by the variant reading Σκαριωθ at Mark 3:19; Matt. 10:3; Luke 6:16 in D, it, and Vg.[20] If Kerioth in Idumea is correct, then, like Herod the Great, Judas may not have been a full-blooded Jew, or at least not a native of Israel.

The overall impression one gets is that the Twelve was a socially diverse group including both fishermen and their nemeses the tax collectors, and

---

15. See Painter, p. 67.
16. Marcus, *Mark 1–8*, p. 268.
17. See Guelich, p. 162.
18. On which see pp. 118-20 above.
19. See my book *The Christology of Jesus* (Philadelphia: Fortress, 1990), pp. 96-98.
20. See Guelich, p. 163.

both a tax collector and those who opposed paying any taxes to Rome or the overlords, indeed those who had supported opposing such oppressors even by violent means. In any event, though the list begins in good fashion, it ends in depressing fashion. One of the handpicked Twelve is remembered for one thing only — betraying Jesus. "There is a warning to the reader not to expect too much of these disciples."[21] At the outset these men are enlisted in the war against the powers and principalities, yet there is enough dark undercurrent to already prompt a worry that they may become casualties in that apocalyptic war.

B. Meanwhile, Back on the Home Front . . . (3:20-35)

We should probably recognize at vv. 20ff. the first clear example of Mark's use of intercalation, or the sandwich technique (cf. 6:7-13/30-32; 9:37/41; 11:12-14/20-26; 14:1-2/10-11; 14:54/66-72), wherein he inserts a story into the midst of two parts of another story so that they may interpret each other, perhaps in part due to related subject matter. Also, from a narratological standpoint a delay is required in various of the first stories, and the second story gives the first time to reach its culmination. "The form functions to establish a fundamental relationship between the two elements, represented by two charges: 1. And his family . . . said, 'He is out of his mind.' 2. And the scribes . . . said: 'He is possessed by Beelzebub.' The Capernaum campaign ends with this double counterattack upon Jesus: to his extended family he is deluded, to his political opponents he is demonic."[22] Both Jesus' family and his opponents think he is not in full possession of his mental faculties (cf. 3:21, 30).

If, however, we consider the narrative from a rhetorical point of view, it is possible to see this unit 3:20-35 as coherent and purposeful, involving the following chiasm:

A		Jesus and the crowd — v. 20
	B	Jesus' family appears — v. 21
		C The accusation of the scribes — v. 22
		C′ Response to the scribes — vv. 23-30
	B′	The family reappears — v. 31
A′		Jesus and the crowd — vv. 32-35[23]

---

21. Painter, p. 69.

22. C. Myers, *Binding the Strong Man: A Political Reading of Mark's Story of Jesus* (Maryknoll, N.Y.: Orbis, 1988), p. 164.

23. See D. M. Young, "Whoever Has Ears to Hear" (Ph.D. diss., Vanderbilt University, 1994), pp. 94-95.

One of the things binding this rhetorical unit together is a series of accusations — the first apparently by Jesus' family,[24] then by the scribes, to which Jesus must respond. Though this material likely comes from two different sources of stories, Mark has molded his material into a coherent unit. Young finds the rhetorical pattern of exordium (3:23) followed by *probatio* (3:24-27) involving comparisons and an enthymeme (Satan cannot stand if divided against himself) in the minispeech of Jesus to the scribes.[25] Though there is some merit in the analysis of the *probatio*, 3:23 surely cannot be both the exordium and the *propositio*, as Young claims. In addition, the speech is too short to contain all the requisite parts of any sort of rhetorical speech, be it judicial, deliberative, or epideictic. Better to simply note that the comparisons and the enthymeme show knowledge of the art of persuasion in the way the material has been edited.[26]

The phrase οι παρ αυτου is important and should be contrasted with οι περι αυτου. The former in this Gospel refers to Jesus' physical family (cf. Prov. 31:21 LXX; Sus. 33; Josephus, *Ant.* 1.193), whether nuclear or extended is not clear, while the latter is a term for the family of faith or for Jesus' circle of disciples (v. 34; cf. 4:10).[27] Many controversies have arisen in regard to v. 21. Could Mary and Jesus' family really have so badly misunderstood Jesus that they could have tried to come and cart him off, thinking he was crazy?[28] There is an interesting set of emendations centering on the word εξιστημι. While most manuscripts present us with some form of this verb, Θ, 565, and others read εξεσταται, which means "he escaped," and D and it add to this the verb αυτους, so the text would read "he escaped from them." W and 28 remove all references to insanity by having εξηρτηνται αυτου, "they were adherents of his." All these variants reflect a concern to protect the image of the holy family, and also the image of Jesus. This in turn tells us that at an early date οι παρ αυτου was quite rightly taken to refer to Jesus' family. "In both the LXX and contemporary colloquial Greek it meant 'relatives' or 'friends.'"[29]

---

24. On Jesus' family not responding positively to Jesus in Mark's Gospel, see J. D. Crossan, "Mark and the Relatives of Jesus," *NovT* 15 (1973): 81-113.

25. Young, p. 109.

26. Young, p. 112, attempts to argue that we do have Aristotle's necessary parts of a speech, but he wants to see 3:33-35 as the epilogue, and this will not do since it is part of a separate speech and discussion. On Aristotle's short form for a rhetorical speech (*prooimion*, statement of facts, the proof epilogue), see his *Rhetoric* 3.13.

27. Interestingly, in Hellenistic Greek the usual meaning of the former phrase is adherents or envoys, but in the LXX it can mean family.

28. Notice how D, W, and some old Latin manuscripts change the text to read "the scribes and the rest" because of their discomfort with this unflattering portrait of the holy family. See Marcus, *Mark 1–8*, p. 270.

29. M. Hooker, *The Gospel according to Mark* (Peabody, Mass.: Hendrickson, 1991), p. 115.

It appears likely, recognizing Mark's sandwich technique, that we are meant to see οι παρ αυτου as being explained in v. 31, where we have the clear reference to his mother and brothers. Some have tried to argue that the subject of the verb ελεγον in v. 21 is indefinite, but this is unlikely not only because elsewhere Mark's use of this verbal form is definite (cf. 5:31; 6:15), but also because the immediate context provides us with the natural plural subject of οι παρ αυτου.[30] Thus, at a minimum, we must conclude that Mark in vv. 20-21 is presenting the unflattering picture of Jesus being misunderstood by his own family. They either thought he was unbalanced or, at least, not in control of the situation he was precipitating. If the latter, then they may be trying to protect Jesus rather than remove him from the public scene because of the shame and controversy he was bringing on his family. Yet the verb here, which occurs again in 6:17 and 12:12, is a strong one and refers in those texts to attempts to arrest Jesus. Here it must mean at least that they have come to restrain Jesus, a forceful action.

On the basis of the honor challenges Jesus had been issuing to the authorities, it is understandable why his family might think he was courting disaster and had taken leave of his senses and that strong measures were called for. "Since madness was often regarded as due to possession by a demon, it is arguable that their judgement on the situation was close to that of the scribes in the next verse."[31] Seen from the perspective of honor and shame conventions, it is possible to see the action of the family as an attempt to protect their own family honor rather than protect Jesus in particular. They did not want him to disgrace the family.[32] There may also be this further connection between the family passage and the passage about the scribes — the reference to a house divided against itself could in fact be taken as an allusion to Jesus' own household.[33]

Furthermore, this unflattering reading of Jesus' family's understanding seems confirmed in vv. 31-35, where Jesus contrasts his physical family with the family of faith.[34] In its Markan context, this latter contrast between the two

---

30. E. Best, "Mark III.20, 21, 31-35," *NTS* 22 (1976): 309-19, here p. 313, is right to point out that the clauses would have been reversed if in fact the verb "they said" was meant to be taken impersonally. In other words, the sentences would have read "and they were saying, 'He's out of his mind'; and his relatives . . . went out to seize him."

31. Hooker, p. 115.

32. See B. Buby, "A Christology of Relationship in Mark," *BTB* 10, no. 4 (1980): 149-54, and especially D. M. May, "Mark 3.20-35 from the Perspective of Shame/Honor," *BTB* 17, no. 3 (1987): 83-87.

33. Young, p. 127: "η οικια is moved to an emphatic position, serving to highlight the 'divided house,' likely underlining what appears to be Jesus' own divided house which gave rise to the entire episode."

34. The contrast is made even more vivid in Matt. 12:49, where Jesus actually points to or places his hands on his disciples and says they are his family.

families would have no real force if Jesus' family did not at least share the opinion expressed in 3:21. The door is left open for Jesus' physical family to join the family of faith in 3:35 ("whoever does the will . . ."), but Mark does not suggest that the family, even later, walked through that door, nor does Mark 3 suggest that Jesus actually granted his physical family an audience on this occasion. In fact, Mark 6 continues the picture of misunderstanding and rejection — a prophet lacks honor even in his own home.[35] 3:21 was clearly too offensive for either Matthew or Luke, who both omit it.[36]

The story as told in 3:22ff. suggests that Jesus was attracting so much attention that scribes were coming down all the way from Jerusalem to check out this new teacher. Could they have been official emissaries of the temple hierarchy or the Sanhedrin? Either is possible, especially if the charge of blasphemy had reached their ears and it was known that Jesus' influence with the crowds was growing. A rhetorical analysis of 3:19b-35 has been undertaken by V. K. Robbins, who suggests that in the argumentation of Jesus we find a high degree of epideictic rhetoric.[37] But the rhetorical situation, as presented by Mark, seems far more a judicial situation with Jesus being accused of being in league with the devil. The rhetoric we find here is that of attack and defense, not of praise and blame. It is, however, correct to say that we do find some standard argumentative forms here, such as an argument for implausibility based on analogy ("if a kingdom is divided against itself . . . and if a house is divided against itself . . ."), argument for falsity from a contrary ("but no one can enter a strong man's house and plunder his goods unless he first binds the strong man . . ."), and argument from a judgment ("all sins will be forgiven . . . but whoever . . .").[38]

Initially it is said in v. 22 that Jesus has Beelzeboul, which is to say he himself is possessed, to which we may compare v. 30, where it is said he has an unclean spirit.[39] This was to become a repeated accusation thrown at Jesus. In fact, this accusation is independently attested in John (John 7:20; 8:48, 52; 10:20). Such a charge of madness was not uncommon for a healer or exorcist, presum-

---

35. It does not appear that Mark is referring to Jesus' mother at 15:40 and 16:1 (the second Mary).

36. On all this see my *Women in the Ministry of Jesus* (Cambridge: Cambridge University Press, 1984), pp. 86-88.

37. See V. K. Robbins, "Beelzebul Controversy in Mark and Luke: Rhetorical and Social Analysis," *Forum* 7 (1991): 261-77, especially pp. 261-67. On the entire subject of Jesus as an exorcist and its importance to the early Synoptic tradition, see G. H. Twelftree, *Jesus the Exorcist: A Contribution to the Study of the Historical Jesus* (Tübingen: Mohr, 1993).

38. See Robbins, "Beelzebul Controversy," p. 264. This analysis is quite helpful and on target.

39. Does this accusation have anything to do with Jesus being a northerner and so living closer to what had been the cult centers for Baal?

ably based on a guilt by association kind of thinking.[40] The function of such a charge was to discredit Jesus and distance the general populace from him.[41] The word "Beelzeboul" is a combination of the name for the Canaanite storm god Baal and the epithet *zeboul,* which possibly means "house." Jesus' use of the house-divided metaphor, then, may have been especially apt. There was a deliberate parody of this name in the Vulgate and in some Syriac manuscripts in the form Beelezebub, which means the lord (Baal) of the flies (cf. 2 Kings 1:2). By Jesus' day this Canaanite god's name was used for the prince of darkness — Satan.[42] It is also charged that Jesus casts out demons by means of the power he has from the devil, presumably under the assumption that since Satan can control his underlings, others who do so must be in league with Satan. The language used here needs to be seen in light of other literature which is affected by apocalyptic notions and perspectives. For example, in *1 Enoch* 85–90 when Israel lost its political independence, we are told that God allowed fallen angels, the subjects of Satan, to rule over the land. We are meant to think of Jesus dealing with a situation where it was widely believed that the powers and principalities were in control of much of what went on in the land, and any powerful figure, whether it be a Roman ruler or Jesus, was suspected of being in collusion with such powers. The apocalyptic version of the combat myth underlies the discourse here.

Jesus responds to these charges by using figurative speech, simple similes or analogies, which is what the term "parable" refers to here. The term literally means a setting of something beside (something else). Riddles, aphorisms, proverbs, and narrative parables could all be referred to by this terminology.[43] Jesus appeals to logic here. He asks what sense it makes to say that Satan casts out Satan. If Satan were battling himself, his kingdom would be crumbling. Since it is taken as obvious that this is not the case, then it is concluded that Jesus' power source for exorcism must obviously not be what the scribes thought it was. But as Hooker says, there was another way for a kingdom to fall other than by crumbling or division from within, namely, by invasion from without, and Jesus explains that this is his role.[44] Jesus explains he is the one who binds the strong man and thereafter plunders his possessions, in this case his captives. This is meant to indicate that Jesus is the ad-

---

40. See Marcus, *Mark 1–8*, p. 271.

41. For the literary analysis of Mark 3:22-30, see R. Meynet, "Qui Donc est 'Le Plus Fort'? Analyse Rhetorique de Mc 3,22-30; Mt. 12,22-37; Luc 11,14-26," *RB* 90 (1983): 334-50. This is not, however, really a rhetorical analysis of this material. It does not, for example, interact with what the rhetoricians say about parables and the like.

42. Could this sort of word association between Satan and a pagan god be one reason that Paul and others associated the table of pagan idols with the table of demons?

43. See the discussion, pp. 125-26 above.

44. Hooker, p. 116.

versary, not the ally, of Satan.[45] On Jesus as the stronger one, we may compare 1:8. Again one must ask, who is stronger than Satan? Surely the answer is God, and so once again Jesus is depicted as one with a plenitude of divine power and authority. In any case, Jesus is using daring imagery here to describe his ministry. It is depicted as a form of criminal activity — breaking and entering and stealing. But one may wish to ask when Jesus bound the strong man. If the exorcisms are indeed taken as a sign that the strong man is already bound, then one perhaps looks to the encounter of Jesus in the wilderness with the devil before he embarked on his ministry. This is the only juncture in the Markan outline which suggests such an encounter, even though Mark does not make as much of it as the other Synoptic writers.

At v. 28 we have the first instance of the phrase "Amen, I say to you" in Mark. This phrase seems to have been characteristic of Jesus, and suggests that he felt free to vouch for himself and the truth of his own word without requiring external human testimony to his truthfulness. The latter, of course, was the normal Jewish way of establishing the truthfulness of someone's remarks. The prepositive use of "amen" with a verb of saying is not found anywhere else in the NT other than on Jesus' lips, and it is found in all the layers of our Gospel sources: (1) thirteen times in Mark, (2) nine times in Q, (3) nine times in M, (4) nine times in L, (5) twenty-five times in a doubled form in John. Outside the Jesus tradition the word "amen" in the NT is always used to attest to the truthfulness of someone else's words (1 Cor. 14:16; 2 Cor. 1:20; Rev. 5:14; 7:12). Jesus, unlike a mere prophet, could attest to his own truthfulness and the authority of his words in advance of uttering them.[46] J. D. G. Dunn best sums up the significance, for our understanding of the historical Jesus, of his use of the prepositive "Amen" followed by "I say to you . . .":

> His authority was charismatic also in the sense that it was immediately received from God, or rather *was the immediate authority of God*. This is the clear implication of Jesus' "emphatic *ego*" and "Amen" — a style of speaking expressing a consciousness of transcendent authority. . . . When others in the tradition in which Jesus stood expressed immediacy of their authority, they prefaced their words with "Thus says the Lord." But Jesus said "Amen, I say to you." . . . It is this charismatic nature of Jesus' authority, the immediacy of his sense of authority together with the *conscious self-reference* of so much of his teaching, which seems to set Jesus apart from other men of comparable significance in the history of religions.[47]

---

45. Were the scribes suggesting that Jesus was possessed by Satan, that he was unclean because something impure had invaded his body? See May, pp. 85-86. It appears more likely they were claiming that Jesus was in league with Satan.

46. See my *Christology of Jesus*, pp. 186-90.

47. J. D. G. Dunn, *Jesus and the Spirit* (Philadelphia: Westminster, 1975), p. 79.

There is a sense in which v. 28 is a sentence of great hope. All sins are forgivable save one — blasphemy against the Holy Spirit. Blasphemy was of course normally a capital offense in early Judaism (Lev. 24:16; *b. Pesaḥ.* 93b; *m. Sanh.* 7.5), and this saying of Jesus reflects how seriously Jews took such an offense against God. What Jesus is talking about is no accidental sin but a willful perversity which calls the work of God's Spirit the work of the devil. The scribes, by accusing Jesus of being in collusion with Satan, were in danger of committing this sin, precisely because the works which Jesus performed, including the exorcisms, were performed by means of the power of the Holy Spirit resident within Jesus. Clearly this whole discussion is about something which could only be true during Jesus' ministry, for we are not talking about blasphemy against the risen Lord, but rather against the Spirit who empowered Jesus to act while on earth.[48]

But notice that Jesus warns even the scribes against this sin, which suggests that they were not yet past the point of no return and Jesus did not wish for them to commit a spiritually fatal error. According to Lane, "blasphemy against the Holy Spirit denotes the conscious and deliberate rejection of the saving power and grace of God released through Jesus' word and act."[49] Jesus' implicit claim here is that his words and deeds are the words and deeds of God in the person of the Holy Spirit, which is in effect another way of saying that the dominion of God is breaking in where God's Spirit in plentitude is at work changing lives. Jesus is the one through whom this is happening, and to reject Jesus is to reject the eschatological saving activity of God. Mark makes clear that this is indeed a fatal error.

Vv. 31-35 present Jesus' vision for a new community where spiritual kinship and not physical relationship is the fundamental basis of family. "We find here a redefinition of family akin to Jesus' teaching on discipleship in Mark 10.29."[50] The story appears to be condensed into the form of a *chreia*, with the saying at the end being the focal point and main reason for the preservation of the story. The upshot was that Jesus' natural family at this point had no part in Jesus' movement or ministry, and in any case that family and friends had no special advantages in the dominion which was coming.[51] This concept can only be called radical in a traditional patriarchal culture where blood is seen as thicker than water or any other substance. "Jesus' challenge to the traditional authority structures of Palestinian society is now complete. He has repudiated

---

48. See Guelich, p. 180.

49. W. Lane, *The Gospel of Mark* (Grand Rapids: Eerdmans, 1974), p. 145. It is worth noting that the form of the discussion found in *Gos. Thom.* 44 must surely be later, for it speaks in explicitly trinitarian terms contrasting blasphemy versus the Father or Son as opposed to blasphemy versus the Spirit.

50. Guelich, p. 182.

51. Painter, p. 75.

the 'old fabric' (2.21), in order to make way for the new order. The fundamental unit of 'resocialization' into the kingdom will be the new family, the community of discipleship." Nevertheless, this is not to say that Jesus sets out here to deliberately discredit or dishonor his physical family. The "resolution of this narrative tension is found in the legitimating norm of 'doing God's will.' When he places the honor of God above his family, Jesus does not dishonor his family and is shown at the same time to be even more honorable."[52] With the final climactic saying, Jesus retreats to the sea to reflect upon the fortunes and future of his messianic mission. The Markan account seems entirely unconcerned about matters that later exercised early church fathers, such as whether Mary remained a virgin after Jesus was born, and so whether these brothers and sisters were children of Joseph by a previous marriage or cousins.[53]

C. Sow Far, Sow Good (4:1-20)

We have already noted that Mark stresses that Jesus is a teacher, yet up to this point in our narrative there has not been a significant block of teaching material.[54] The importance of Mark 4 for the Evangelist can hardly be overestimated, for here Mark's apocalyptic rhetoric about mysteries and secrets, his christological focus, and his views on disciples and opponents all converge in one place.[55] Speaking about the parable of the sower and the parable in Mark 12 about the vineyard, M. A. Tolbert stresses that "The two parables in Mark present in concise summary form the Gospel's view of Jesus: he is the Sower of the Word and the Heir of the Vineyard. The first emphasizes his task and the second his identity; together they make up the Gospel's basic narrative Christology."[56] Hooker, in fact, suggests that these two parables taken together "encapsulate the whole story of the ministry."[57] Thus, here we see explicated Jesus' role as the teacher, but not only so, for we discover why people respond to Jesus as they do, with more cases of rejection than acceptance, and we also learn of the role the Adversary and his minions play in this process. This parable then

---

52. May, p. 86.

53. See my discussions in *Women,* pp. 89-92.

54. Myers, p. 170, stresses the need to compare the two major blocks of teaching in Mark 4 and Mark 13. In one the repeated exhortation is to listen, in the other it is to watch. Aural attention is stressed in the former, visual attention in the latter.

55. It needs to be kept in mind that *meshalim* are regularly found in apocalyptic material such as *1 Enoch,* thus the use of parables should be seen as part and parcel of the portrayal of Jesus as an apocalyptic seer and sage.

56. M. A. Tolbert, *Sowing the Gospel: Mark's World in Literary Historical Perspective* (Minneapolis: Fortress, 1989), p. 122.

57. Hooker, p. 122.

provides a comprehensive overview of the ministry of Jesus and the roles played by Jesus, disciples, crowds, and opponents, the major characters in Mark's narrative.

But this view of Mark 4 of course assumes that the parable of the sower or, better said, the parable of the different soils is a detailed analogy, or as we might call it, an allegory. It is certainly carefully constructed, following the rule of three, and thus we have two sets of three seeds (4:4-7, 8), three adverse conditions (path, thorns, rocky ground), three degrees of productivity.[58] The standard view of the matter is that while we have an allegorical interpretation of the parable in 4:13-20, this explanation is alien to the character of the parable itself and is a later imposition by either the Evangelist or his source. A *mashal* could well have allegorical elements or virtually be an allegory, for there was no hard-and-fast distinction between parable and allegory in early Judaism.[59] Thus, while it does appear that Mark has contextualized or pointed up his source material, it is doubtful that the old distinction between the parable of the sower and its alien allegorical interpretation will hold up. Mark was simply explicating or expanding on a process already encouraged and inherent in the parable itself.[60] Thus, while 4:13-20 does reflect Mark's reaudiencing and editing of the material, it is probably based on an application that came with the parable itself.

Greco-Roman Rhetoric and παραβολαι[61]

It is fair to say that ancient writers and readers in the Greco-Roman world treated parables as comparisons or comparative illustrations that could be used for rhetorical purposes, that is, for the purpose of persuading someone about something.[62] This raises the question as to whether Mark, writing to rhetorically aware Gentiles, might have edited and used some of Jesus' parables in a rhetorically adept manner. It is Aristotle, apparently, who took the step of using parables as a subclass of a particular kind of proof, the so-called paradigm (παραδειγμα), which makes its point indirectly or inductively through comparison or illustration (*Rhetoric* 2.20.1ff.). Aristotle distinguishes such illustrations taken from everyday existence from those taken from historical examples (exempla, called by Aristotle

---

58. Guelich, p. 190.

59. See pp. 125-26 above.

60. One point which probably shows that Mark has made his contribution is the stress on sowing "the Word." One might have expected Jesus to talk about sowing the good news of the coming dominion of God rather than the "Word."

61. I am indebted to Young, pp. 117-19, for pointing out the salient issues in the following discussion.

62. M. H. McCall, *Ancient Rhetorical Theories of Similes and Comparisons* (Cambridge: Harvard University Press, 1969), pp. 1-22.

πράγματα προγεγενημένα). "Parables" are also to be distinguished from comparisons that in essence draw on fables (*fabella* or λογοι).

Quintilian, in his discussion of "parables," basically agrees with Aristotle that they are one form of paradigm drawn from common experience. His view is that they are most effective when their referents are apparent and immediate and so lack the opaqueness of a metaphor (*Inst.* 5.11.22-30). A metaphor is just a stylistic device, rhetorically speaking, but a parable can be an actual inductive proof. Note that Quintilian commends the use of animals and inanimate objects in "parables." A good example is his use of sowing a seed as a comparison or illustration for conveying culture to the mind of a student (*Inst.* 8.3.74-75).[63]

Let us consider, then, Mark 4 from a rhetorical point of view, first noting that it is normally deliberative speeches which use "paradigms" (including parables) to perform an act of persuasion (*Inst.* 3.8.34). This was also the view of Isocrates at an earlier juncture in time (*Ad Demon.* 34), as also Aristotle (*Rhetoric* 3.17.5). What, then, is Mark's audience being shown by Mark 4 that is useful or beneficial to know in deciding on their future course of action? We shall see in a moment that the parable of the sower is an attempt to persuade an audience about the issues and outcomes of persuasion about the gospel of the dominion.

In deliberative oratory, it is indeed the speaker's authority which carries the greatest weight (Quintilian, *Inst.* 3.8.13). The authority is made clear in the setting of this parable not just by stressing that Jesus was the great public teacher, and also the private mentor of his own disciples, but by the authoritative pronouncement "Whoever has two good ears, better listen." This is the pronouncement of an authority figure.

The parable of the sower itself must be taken as the rhetorical unit or speech proper.[64] The issue or exigence that the parable seems to be dealing with is the discouragement a sower (read proclaimer or persuader) faces when so many do not, or do not for long, respond positively to the message implanted in their minds. The parable is realistic in the sense that it makes evident that there will be both unreceptiveness, shallow reception, temporary reception which is squeezed out by competition, and finally good fruit, a real harvest. In fact, as Young says, we have not one but four comparisons here, which might explain the reference to "parables" (plural) in v. 10.[65]

The rhetorical situation addressed is that Mark's audience faces a world that is in large measure unreceptive to the gospel. Mark must persuade this audience to continue to share the gospel in spite of this fact. He does so by stressing that those who do have ears and hear respond in a far more profound way than one might ever expect. There has *not* been a failure on the part of the sower or because the seed was defective. Rather, what determines the outcome of the matter is the differences in the soils. This is useful for the proclaimer to know, and will affect his future decision making and actions. He can take heart knowing that there will be good results, and knowing that the apparent failures are not necessarily because of his own shortcomings. The way the parable is framed suggests that

63. See below on Mark 4.

64. Young, p. 169, tries to include the private explanation, but this is stretching things too far. Mark 4:11-12 is not the proposition of the parable itself, it is the explanation of who will and won't understand this parable, and why (some are insiders to whom the secrets of such a discourse is revealed, some are not).

65. Young, pp. 174-77.

Mark's audience needs the encouragement to go on sharing the good news in a hostile environment.[66]

There is little dispute that the parable of the soils goes back in some form to Jesus[67] and suits the milieu in which he operated (cf. the parable in 4 Ezra 8:41), but then the question must be asked, How personal is this parable? Is this in fact a commentary by Jesus on the failures and successes of, the opposition to and support of, his own ministry? J. Jeremias has suggested that it is.[68] The parable then suggests failure, some ephemeral successes with some, and finally some lasting results with some. We must keep steadily in view that Jesus' parables are indeed about the dominion of God, and his own role in bringing it in. They are not merely stories or illustrations of general moral truths nor illustrations of the preaching of Jesus, but rather they are examples of his preaching.[69] In this particular case the debate between whether the focus is on the seeds or on the soils misses the point that the parable is about the seed merging with the soil to produce a crop. The focus is not just on one or the other.[70]

The effectiveness of a parable depends not so much on its aptness as an illustration (though the analogy must be close enough to seem fitting) as on how well it produces the desired response in the audience. Those who have two good ears must listen and respond appropriately. But we must bear in mind that as a form of counterorder wisdom, Jesus' parables are intended to be unsettling, disturbing, sometimes even ominous and shocking. They are not told to reinforce the status quo like so many traditional proverbs are. Rather they alert people to the new and disturbing thing God is doing in their midst which involves reversal of expectations, values, social standing, roles in society. C. H. Dodd's suggestion that parables were meant to tease a person into active thought is also correct, which suggests that their application would not always be immediately apparent or crystal clear. Normally in early Jewish parables there are clear con-

---

66. I am unpersuaded that we can dissect this parable into the specific parts of a rhetorical speech. It is a comparison in the form of a narrative, and as such is not like a syllogistically driven speech. We must look more generally at its overall rhetorical function and purpose.

67. Notice also that there are no major textual problems in the first thirty-four verses, which may suggest little controversy about the meaning or thrust of this material among the scribes.

68. J. Jeremias, *The Parables of Jesus* (New York: Scribner, 1963), p. 151.

69. See rightly T. W. Manson, *The Teaching of Jesus,* 2nd ed. (Cambridge: Cambridge University Press, 1935), p. 65: "It is emphatically not a mere sermon illustration for the purpose of stating some abstract proposition of ethics or theology in a simple pictorial form for the benefit of the unlearned. It is the word of God itself. . . ."

70. See Tolbert, p. 153 and n. 42.

trasts between good and evil, wise and foolish, moral and immoral, but this is not always the case with Jesus' parables. He can, for instance, use a particular attribute of an immoral and unscrupulous character (the wicked judge) to illustrate a characteristic of God and his dealings with and saving activities on behalf of humankind.

Yet, something also needs to be said about the placement of this material. If Painter is right, we should see these parables as Jesus' response to the public challenge to his authority. "The parables are instruments of judgement to those opposed to Jesus. But the parables are also told in a context emphasising the need and importance of hearing and responding to Jesus, assuring the *hearers* of the certainty of the dawning of the kingdom."[71] Parables to outsiders and explanation of meaning to the insiders (4:10-20, 33-34; 7:17-23) — this is how Jesus responds to the challenge to his authority. But this presupposes a certain kind of reading of 4:10-12 (on which see below). Myers as well has suggested that Mark has deliberately placed the two major blocks of teaching after blocks dealing with controversy and conflict, so that the teaching appears as a reflection after the fact on the conflict.[72] "Jesus relies upon parables when faced with intense ideological controversy."[73]

The setting of this teaching session is once more beside the Sea of Galilee (cf. 2:13). The crowd is once again huge (cf. 3:8-10), indeed so huge that Jesus is backed into the boat. V. 1 says literally that Jesus got into the boat and sat on the sea. Sitting is the posture in Jesus' culture of the teacher, and so even under awkward circumstances he assumes the posture of the teacher. We are told explicitly at v. 2 that Jesus deliberately taught the crowd in parables, indeed in many parables. This suggests that Mark only wishes to give us a small sampling of such teaching. He is editing his material down, not boiling it up. Jesus begins in v. 3 with an exhortation to listen intently, for it would require open ears and a sympathetic hearing, not to mention some faith, to understand what he is saying. Apocalyptic rhetoric in the form of parables requires open ears and an open mind to comprehend, and some are simply not ready or able to hear (4:33).[74] There can be little doubt that Mark intends us to see the parable of the sower as paradigmatic in some way, telling us something crucial about Jesus' ministry. J. Marcus is likely right that the reference to the sower "going out" is

---

71. Painter, p. 76.

72. Myers, p. 170.

73. Myers, p. 172.

74. The exhortation to listen which both precedes and follows the parable suggests that the meaning of a parable is not to be seen as perfectly evident to everyone. It may rather be more like a two-way mirror. If looked at from one side, one can see through it to the reality on the other side. However, if viewed from the other side, one only sees one's own reflection. Hooker, p. 120, suggests that parables are somewhat like crossword puzzle clues, which are clear to some and opaque to others.

meant to echo the language of Mark 1:38, 2:13, and 2:17,[75] and thus it is Jesus who is seen as the sower in this parable.[76]

Some have sought to locate the focus of this parable on the sowing,[77] but this cannot be the whole truth, for what makes the difference in the story is the different types of soil. Notice that the sower, the seed, and the method of sowing are the same in each case. This strongly suggests that the point has to do with the reception of the seed — whether one is hard-hearted, softhearted, distracted, or attentive will affect how and whether one receives the message that Jesus is proclaiming.

The parable is true to life in several respects. Firstly, it is true that a small landholder would likely plant on all the ground he had available to him, whether it had good soil or not. Secondly, there is clear evidence that sowing seed could and did precede plowing in Israel in this era (cf. *Jub.* 11:11; *b. Šabb.* 73b; *t. Šabb.* 7.2). The parable is about three sorts of failure and three degrees of success, and at least part of its point seems to be that no matter how much failure there is, it is the sower's job to continue to sow in hope and leave the results in God's hands. But there is also reassurance that there would be notable successes.

It is not clear from the grammar of v. 4 that Mark means that seed was strewn on the path, for the Greek here would normally be translated alongside of or beside the path, the point being that all available arable land would be used.[78] The picture painted by Jeremias in regard to vv. 6-7, of a farmer throwing seeds even among existing thistles, is challenged by the parable itself, which says that thistles sprang up and choked the seed.[79] Marcus helpfully suggests that we should notice that each of the failures occurs at a different stage in the maturation process — the first seed scattered doesn't even germinate, the second withers away as soon as it sprouts up, the third grows but seems to produce no fruit.[80]

V. 8 deserves close attention. A tenfold harvest would be considered a very good one, but most scholars have suggested that a thirty-, sixty-, or hundred-fold one would be nothing short of miraculous.[81] As Jeremias points out, this

75. J. Marcus, *The Mystery of the Kingdom of God* (Atlanta: Scholars, 1986), pp. 37-39.

76. There are various awkward aspects to Mark's telling of the story, including some redundancies in the descriptions of what happens to the seeds, and the version in *Gos. Thom.* 9 seems much more symmetrical. But precisely for this reason it is likely to be the later, more well edited form of the story. See Guelich, p. 194.

77. See, e.g., Lane, pp. 146-52.

78. See K. D. White, "The Parable of the Sower," *JTS* 15 (1962): 300-307; J. Drury, "The Sower, the Vineyard, and the Place of Allegory in the Interpretation of Mark's Parables," *JTS* 24 (1973): 367-79.

79. Cf. Hooker, p. 124, to Jeremias, *The Parables of Jesus,* pp. 11ff.

80. Marcus, *Mystery,* p. 22.

81. G. Dalman, "Vierlie Acker," *PJ* 22 (1926): 120-36, however, disputes this, pointing

suggests that the eschatological harvest is in mind. Now is the time of sowing and initial response to the sowing, not the final harvest. The parable ends with an *inclusio* — let those who have ears listen attentively.

In vv. 10-11 we hear for the first time about the secrecy motif so far as it involves the disciples. The idea of private teaching is part of the secrecy motif. The mystery or secret of God's inbreaking dominion is given to the inner circle of followers. Thus, are we to see the parables as protecting the incognito of Jesus when he speaks in public, at least until the time comes for public disclosure of the truth about him? This would seem to be the case.

Much ink has been spilled on the interpretation of the quote from Isa. 6:9-10. If Lane is right that the formulaic introduction to the quote with ινα means "so that" rather than "in order that," the point would be that Jesus' parables have the effect, rather than the purpose, of concealing the truth from those not ready to perceive, and perhaps revealing the truth only to those who are (which depends on what type of soil they are). Notice what vv. 33-34 say. Whether this is directed to the crowd or refers to the private explanation to the disciples, the purpose of Jesus is said to be communication at the level his audience is prepared to receive.

But Lane's sort of explanation overlooks the apocalyptic imagination of our author and the conceptual thought world out of which he operates. For example, consider the closing lines of Daniel — "I heard, but I did not understand. . . . 'None of the wicked shall understand, but those who are paying attention will understand'" (Dan. 12:8-10).[82] Jesus is unveiling apocalyptic secrets about the coming of God's eschatological reign. To understand such mysteries requires close attention and an open heart. Such an interpretation as Lane's also overlooks how both in Isaiah and in Ezek. 12:1-2 (which is closely similar to our text), God is commanding a prophet to speak to his hard-hearted, rebellious people in a way that will make clear to them that they do *not* understand. Parables or allegories in such a circumstance have a judicial function and reveal the people's distance from God, much as uninterpreted tongues are said to do with the unbeliever in 1 Cor. 14. Hooker thinks there is no doubt that these verses reflect the fact that Israel had largely rejected Jesus' ministry, and Mark is explaining that that was within the scope of God's knowledge and

---

out that individual grains were known to produce thirty-five kernels on average, with sixty being not unusual and a hundred not unheard of. This may mean that our parable is talking about an extrodinarily good harvest but not one that strains the story beyond verisimilitude. Yet Jesus' parables frequently use hyperbole or exaggeration precisely at the point where they want to say something about God or the dominion or grace. See, e.g., the parable of the woman and the leaven in Matt. 13:33/Luke 13:20-21, where an enormous amount of dough is used.

82. See rightly Myers, p. 172.

plan all along. The parables, then, were to mainly serve as stones of stumbling deliberately placed in Israel's path.[83]

There is perhaps some truth to this explanation, for it was necessary for the church to explain why so many of Jesus' own fellow Jews rejected the gospel, but it must not be overlooked that Jesus operated in a context in which John the Baptist had already come and warned that judgment would fall on Israel unless it repented. At least some of the parables could have been fashioned by Jesus to serve the same purpose — for instance, the parable of the vineyard. The quotation of Isa. 6:9-10 in v. 12 is closer to the Targum than to the LXX, which suggests it goes back to an Aramaic source, and quite possibly to Jesus himself. One must conjure with Jesus himself soberly reflecting in this parable and with this OT citation on how many of his fellow Jews had not listened so as to hear and heed the good news he brought.

Other ameliorating interpretations of the use of Isaiah here have involved, for example, suggesting that μηποτε, normally translated "lest" or "otherwise," is in fact translating the Aramaic word *dilema* with the meaning "unless."[84] The point then would be that they will hear and not understand unless they repent and receive forgiveness, at which time the light dawns. Yet, if this is the original meaning, it seems unlikely that the translator or Mark got the point when the term μηποτε was chosen to render the text. Another ameliorating approach suggests that Jesus is being sarcastic here, and thus the text is to be read: "and so hearing they will not understand, lest (perish the thought) they should repent and be forgiven." This, however, hardly seems to suit the context, and nothing suggests that the Isaiah quote is being used to convey a meaning that different from the way it had meaning in its original context.

The purpose of such apocalyptic rhetoric was not simply to be mysterious or enigmatic but to communicate in a way that would elicit whether one was responding in faith or not. "The parables were designed so that no response meant no perception, no understanding, no forgiveness."[85] The parables give insight to the open-minded but come as a judgment on the obdurate. A survey of the "perception" vocabulary of Mark shows that listening intently is closely associated if not equated with understanding and knowing. Put another way, when dealing with a matter of new revelation, listening intently is the necessary prerequisite to understanding because no one has this knowledge already within him (cf. 4:13; 7:14; 8:17, 21).[86] Notice that v. 34 tells us that Jesus explained all things to his disciples, which means of course that they needed such an explanation. V. 33 seems meant to tell us that parables were Jesus' dominant

---

83. Hooker, p. 126.
84. Jeremias, *The Parables of Jesus*, p. 17.
85. Painter, pp. 80-81.
86. See Myers, p. 182.

form of public teaching, but it was also a way for the disciples to learn from him. It is interesting that, so far as we can tell, they did not seem to follow Jesus in the practice of creating parables.[87]

V. 13 suggests that understanding the parable of the sower is crucial for understanding any or all of the parables, or at least any of the seed parables. It may imply that if you can't understand the clear seed parable, you are not likely to understand any of the rest of them. Yet the sower parable is the only one to which is appended a real explanation or interpretation.

Vv. 14-20 could perhaps be seen as a long Markan footnote for the benefit of his own audience, not unlike the shorter explanations of Jesus' parabolic speech in Mark 7. Yet, whatever the source of this explanation, which may in some form go back to Jesus, the application makes quite good sense. In its present form, this explication and application seems to reflect the language of the early church, using words not elsewhere found in the teaching of Jesus, but rather in the epistles (e.g., λογος in the sense of gospel, cf. Gal. 6:6; 1 Thess. 1:6;[88] προσκαιρος, 2 Cor. 4:18, in the sense of short-lived; μεριμναι, meaning cares, cf. 1 Pet. 5:7; η απατη, Col. 2:8, seduction).[89] V. 15 refers to the active work of Satan and perhaps reveals to us something of Mark's view of the cosmic warfare that is going on in regard to the spread of the gospel. The activity of Satan is then likened to the activity of a scavenger bird (cf. *Jub.* 11:11), and as Pesch says, the failure here is blamed not on the seed, nor even primarily on the soil, but on the external intruder that comes and takes away the seed.[90] This is typical of the apocalyptic perspective which stresses the role of the supernatural players in the human drama. V. 17 would certainly be appropriate for a congregation under the Neronian gun and facing persecution. We are told that these people are scandalized (σκανδαλιζομαι), that is, they stumble over their commitment to the gospel when trouble or persecution arises. Here again we probably have a clue to the sort of context in which the Evangelist believes his audience is operating (cf. below on Mark 13), but the description could also apply to Jesus' own disciples during the latter stages of his earthly life and ministry. Tolbert suggests that the disciples and in particular "Rocky" are represented by the rocky ground, for in the end they deny, desert, and betray.[91] Vv. 18-19 refer to those, perhaps like the rich young ruler, who are overcome by worldly

---

87. There is precious little evidence outside the Gospels of parables in the NT, though a couple of Paul's allegories in 1 Cor. 10 and Gal. 4 probably qualify.

88. And note that this is the only place in Mark where the phrase "the Word" appears on Jesus' own lips; indeed, it is the only place in the Synoptics that we find it on his lips.

89. See the balanced discussion by Guelich, pp. 217-18.

90. R. Pesch, *Markus-Evangelium I* (Freiburg: Herder, 1976), p. 243.

91. Tolbert, p. 154, noting that the disciples fail Jesus precisely at the point when his persecutions begin at 14:43-50. She also argues plausibly that the scribes, Pharisees, and Jewish leaders are those represented by the path from which the seed is extracted immediately.

cares and the desire for wealth and so are not really able to truly become Jesus' disciples (cf. Matt. 6:24-25). The explanation ends in v. 20 with a reminder that there are two possible responses to the Word, and only one of them involves hearing so as to bear fruit.[92] The dominion of God is given to those who do so. The overall effect of this material on our evaluation of the disciples themselves suggests anomaly or tension. The disciples on the one hand are recipients of special knowledge, but on the other hand they lack spiritual insight and understanding. We see these two things juxtaposed throughout the Markan narrative (cf. 4:40-41; 6:52; 7:18; 8:14-21; 9:5-6; 10:24; 14:40), and this suggests that the disciples are being used as examples for Mark's audience, but not always, indeed not often, positive ones.

D. Hidden Lights and Seedy Characters (4:21-34)

Mark has grouped together separate groups of sayings here, presumably because of some thematic connection. Each new unit is signaled by "And he said to them," at 4:21, 24, 26, and 30. That we should treat this material as separate sayings is probably also shown by the scattering of this material in Matthew and Luke (Matt. 5:15; 7:2; 10:26; 13:12; 25:29; Luke 6:38; 11:33; 12:2; 19:26). It is not clear who the "them" being addressed by these parables is within the Markan narrative — the crowds or the disciples. In any case, Mark is addressing the parables to his own audience. In his exposition of the parable of the lamp and the lamp stand, Lane suggests and Hooker agrees that the lamp here is a figure for Jesus himself, just as the sower was in the previous parable. This would be the Markan way of saying Jesus is the light of the world.[93] This comports nicely with the apocalyptic image in Zech. 4:2, though it is not impossible to interpret the light to be a reference to the dominion which is also said to come (cf., e.g., the Lord's Prayer). The purpose of the coming of the light is not to be put under a bushel basket (or a bushel measure?) or a dining couch, but rather to be set up so it is visible to all. The Greek term ο μοδιος refers to a measure for grain which could hold about two gallons. Obviously an empty "peck measure" is meant. The lamp is not lit for the purpose of being hidden or concealed. The

---

92. Guelich, p. 223: "In each of the previous expressions [of the language about hearing], the aorist tense in the oblique mood (subjunctive, participle) indicating punctiliar action has described the situation; here the present tense in the indicative mood characterizes the continuing reality of hearing the word." Forms of the verbs for hearing appear some thirteen times in 4:1-34, making clear that this is where the emphasis lies in regard to Jesus' teaching.

93. Lane, pp. 165-66. He points out that the verb "comes" rather than "is brought" suggests a reference to a person who is the light. Notice also the continual present active tense of the verb. See Hooker, p. 133.

implication of v. 22 (cf. Matt. 10:26; Luke 12:2; *Gos. Thom.* 5, P.Oxy. 654, 4) seems to be that there is an appropriate time for some secrets to come to light — in particular the time for the revelation of the truth about the enigmatic Son of Man. Here we learn something about the "messianic secret." Things are indeed hidden and concealed, but for a purpose — in order that they might be revealed at the proper juncture or time. This is also true of Jesus during his ministry. There are disclosure moments, such as at Caesarea Philippi. Thus we see how Mark's apocalyptic conception of time and revelation affects his presentation of Christology and related matters. The light did not come ultimately to be hidden, but it may be concealed for a time until the appropriate hour or venue or audience appears. In Jesus' case the ultimate disclosure does not come until the crucifixion and resurrection.[94] Tolbert puts the matter thusly:

> The kingdom of God is a secret, but a secret that can not be hidden. Mk. 4.10-12 is balanced by 4.21-22: "Is a lamp brought in to be under a bushel, or under a bed, and not on a stand? For there is nothing hid, except to be manifest. . . ." The secret of the kingdom of God, given to insiders who do the will of God, can remain a secret only for a brief time, for nothing is "secret except to come to light." Neither Jesus himself, nor his powerful healing word, nor those of the good earth who bear fruit can remain secret or be hidden, for secrecy is only for the purpose of bringing to light. All the apparent secrets in the Gospel — Jesus' identity, his healing miracles, his control over evil spirits — have as their goal the revelation of the kingdom, but only for those with the ears to hear it will hear it.[95]

Vv. 24-25 have nothing to do in this context with judging other persons, but rather with how one weighs the revelation of the dominion, particularly as revealed in Jesus and his ministry. This saying seems to have been joined to the lamp saying because of catchword connection — in this case having to do with measuring things. As you receive this revelation, so shall you be weighed or received in the future dominion, and even more will be added. V. 25 may mean that the receptive person is given more than the unreceptive one, and the latter will ultimately have taken from him any chance to receive and know, especially if he has rejected the initial approach of the light. The eschatological judgment lurks not too far in the background of this parable (cf. Matt. 7:2 and Luke 6:38).

Mark 4:26-29 is the only section in this Gospel without some sort of parallel in either Mathew or Luke. We are explicitly told at the outset that this is a parable about God's dominion. But are we to compare the dominion to the farmer or to the seed, or to the interaction between the seed and the soil? The

---

94. See Hooker, p. 134.
95. Tolbert, p. 161.

farmer, of course, plays an important role: he casts the seed on the ground and then observes the ground and watches the seed sprout and grow. The reference to his doing so evening and morning reflects the Jewish way of reckoning the day, which begins at sunset and continues until the next evening (see Gen. 1:5). Yet the farmer does not know how the growth occurs. At the end of the process he also plays a crucial role, harvesting the crop. V. 28 says that "automatically," or more literally, without visible cause (αυτοματη), the seed grows, and means in this case growth without human effort, and as we have already been told, without human understanding. V. 29 has a clear allusion to Joel 4:13 (MT) in the phrase "puts in the sickle," a reference which seems to allude to the eschatological harvest. But should we see this as a reference to eschatological judgment (see Matt. 13:24-30) or to the harvesting of the saved? The metaphorical purpose statement used earlier, "I will make you fishers of human beings," suggests rescue in the face of the wrath to come, if sowing and reaping are the means by which the dominion comes. Painter sees this parable as admirably suiting the context, and Mark's theme for the point is that though the dominion of God seems largely hidden during the ministry of Jesus, yet the seeds have been sown and they are growing imperceptibly.[96] Growth is not something the sower can force to happen.

The parable of the mustard seed in vv. 30-32 is perhaps one of the most familiar of Jesus' parables and seems clearly to be a contrast parable rather than a growth parable, comparing tiny beginnings with enormous results.[97] There is little dispute that it goes back to Jesus in some form, and in fact is the only parable attested in Mark, Q (Matt. 13:31-32/Luke 13:18-19), and also *Thomas* (*Gos. Thom.* 20). The extreme smallness of the mustard seed was proverbial in the region of Israel, though in fact it was not the smallest of all seeds on earth, but Mark's readers apparently would not know of this proverbial smallness, so he offers an explanatory clause for his western audience.[98] Painter again suggests that this parable is a response to a challenge to Jesus' authority.[99] Though the dominion seemed to be small and ineffectual at present, it will eventually blossom into something enormous, even attracting those far off. It is usual to apply the reference to the birds to the people of the Gentile nations (cf. Ezek. 17:23; 31:6; Dan. 4:12, 14, 21). Myers, in a creative move, sees the mustard bush as a reference to the upstart Roman Empire, which Israel, being like other small

---

96. Painter, p. 84.

97. Tolbert, p. 162, however, denies this conclusion, saying that the parable is about the powerful generative earth, not about a contrast between small beginnings and large results.

98. See R. H. Gundry, *Mark: A Commentary on His Apology for the Cross* (Grand Rapids: Eerdmans, 1993), p. 229. The clause is entirely absent in Luke.

99. Painter, p. 84.

birds, was dwelling in the shadow of.[100] But where is the story of the dominion's growth or development in such an analysis?

It is far better to follow the suggestions of J. D. Crossan[101] and D. Oakman, who point out the following: (1) If this was a simple parable about the eventual triumph of God's people who started small but became big and indeed became world rulers, then the image of the cedar of Lebanon, as in Ezek. 17:22-24, is a far more likely candidate to have provided the image here. (2) In fact, the mustard bush, whether domesticated in a garden or wild in a field, was an extremely noxious and dangerous plant, as it threatened to take over whatever area its seed finally took root in. Pliny the Elder says of it, "Mustard . . . with its pungent taste and fiery effect . . . grows entirely wild, though it is improved by being transplanted: but on the other hand when it has once been sown it is scarcely possible to get the place free of it, as the seed when it falls germinates at once" (*Natural History* 19.170-71). The point, then, is that the mustard bush, which never grows into a tree like the cedar of Lebanon, but rather into a large unpleasant bush, is not seen as something desirable. (3) "It is hard to escape the conclusion that Jesus deliberately likens the rule of God to a weed."[102] The dominion that Jesus was proclaiming, which called home various unwanted birds to live[103] (the sinners and tax collectors? the Gentiles?), was a threat to the existing garden or field of early Judaism. If Jesus' proclamation took root, it stood in danger of subverting existing kingdom visions and power structures in Israel. Though the dominion appeared small like a seed during Jesus' ministry, it would inexorably grow into something large and firmly rooted,[104] which some would find shelter in and others would find obnoxious and try to root out.

Mark 4:33-34 brings this small collection of parables to a close. The verb of speaking in these verses is in the imperfect tense, which suggests he habitually spoke this way to the crowds, and indeed the text says he spoke many such parables to them.[105] The summary here clearly distinguishes between parables offered to the crowds (but of course, the disciples also necessarily heard them) and private explanation of such teaching to the disciples. The clause "just as they were able to hear" stresses that the response to Jesus' teaching was limited by the audience's willingness or readiness to hear and understand what he was saying. "Right hearing is attentive, committed, determined, obedient hearing

---

100. Myers, p. 180.

101. J. D. Crossan, *The Historical Jesus* (San Francisco: Harper, 1991), pp. 277-79.

102. D. Oakman, *Jesus and the Economic Questions of His Day* (Lewiston, N.Y.: Mellen, 1986), p. 127.

103. The verb κατασκηνουν means literally "to live." Cf. Matt. 13:32; Luke 13:19.

104. Hooker, pp. 136-37.

105. See Painter, p. 85.

which bears fruit."[106] Mark also stresses that Jesus did not speak without parables to the crowds. This was perhaps his almost exclusive practice when he dealt with the crowds, at least in Galilee.[107]

We must keep steadily in view that there was not an impermeable boundary between outsiders and insiders, but rather, the outsiders who heard and heeded the word would become insiders. Indeed, this was the goal, and the purpose of the parables was not obfuscation but revelation. But part of what the parables revealed was something about the audience. Part of the audience was receptive, able to hear, and part of it was not. The nonreceptive received the revelation of the dominion as a sort of judgment on their hard-heartedness, a revelation that they were unprepared to enter that dominion. The insiders also got the information in the form of parables, but, as Schweizer stresses, real understanding of the dominion comes not merely through the transfer of information but through being in ongoing fellowship with the One who spoke these parables in the first place, and all the more so since the dominion is best spoken of in figurative speech and apocalyptic rhetoric, which invariably requires some assistance from the speaker to fully understand.[108] It is also possible that, comporting with the secrecy-during-the-ministry theme, the "parables are seen as the appropriate form of speech during the period when the full meaning of Jesus had not been shown, and indeed, *could not* be shown."[109]

E. *"Break on through to the Other Side"* (4:35-41)

This passage is a miracle tale which leads to a salient pronouncement in the form of a question by the disciples in the boat. The story is littered with Semitisms and other signs that make it likely that it was originally told in Aramaic and came from the earliest Christian circles.[110] We see once more in this story that while miracles can unsettle a person's worldview and prompt the raising of questions about Jesus' identity, they cannot provide the answer to such questions. This passage is also transitional as Jesus is depicted as crossing over into foreign, indeed pagan territory — a land where pig herding is acceptable and demons mass in legions. It is of course true that there were Jews and Gentiles on

---

106. Painter, p. 85.

107. On the possible difference in dominant modes of discourse when Jesus spoke to crowds in Galilee as opposed to when he spoke in Judea, see my *Jesus the Seer: The Progress of Prophecy* (Peabody, Mass.: Hendrickson, 1999), chap. 8.

108. E. Schweizer, *The Good News according to Mark* (Atlanta: John Knox, 1971), p. 106.

109. L. Hurtado, *Mark* (New York: Harper & Row, 1983), p. 63.

110. Guelich, p. 262.

both sides of the sea, but Mark is using the story symbolically to suggest the crossing over into a largely pagan realm, and indeed this is the first of several crossing stories of this sort. W. Kelber suggests the following schema: first voyage to the other side, 4:35–5:1 (storm); return, 5:21 (no storm); second voyage to the other side, 6:45-53 (storm); return, 8:13, 22 (no storm).[111] Kelber expands these observations to suggest a whole cycle of material for each (symbolic) side of the sea:

Events	Jewish Side	Gentile Side
inaugural exorcism, fame	1:21-28	5:1-20
popular ministry	1:29-39	6:54-56
symbolic healings	5:22-43	7:24-37
wilderness feedings	6:32-44	8:1-10
noncomprehension of loaves	6:51f.	8:14-21

Whether one accepts all the particulars of this schematization or not, it has enough merit that it is probably right to conclude with Myers that the purpose of this sort of arrangement is to suggest symbolic action on Jesus' part.[112] He is not just the healer of Israel. There may be some echoes of the story in Jonah 1, Jonah being another prophet to foreigners, particularly in the detail about the sudden calming of the sea.[113]

The transition from 4:34 to 4:35 is not abrupt, but we do turn here to a different sort of material, having left behind the block of teaching material. In fact, in 4:35–5:43 we have a sequence of three dramatic miracle narratives that appear to be selected to demonstrate Jesus' power over: (1) the natural elements, (2) the demonic forces, and (3) death. These were seen in antiquity as the gamut of nonhuman forces that most threatened human life. It is characteristic of Mark's portrait of Christ that, compared to the other Gospels, he appears the most human here, and yet in some ways the most divine and mysterious at the same time. Yet, as Hooker stresses, the major point of the story for Mark is the divine power at work in Jesus, "a power which was experienced by the disciples during his ministry and affirmed by subsequent generations of men and women who had faith in him."[114]

The pericope begins with Jesus getting in the boat, presumably to get away from the crowds by crossing the Sea of Galilee. Several features in the story suggest an eyewitness account — the superfluous reference to other boats, the harshness of the rebuke of Jesus by the disciples, the picture of the boat fill-

---

111. See W. Kelber, *Mark's Story of Jesus* (Philadelphia: Fortress, 1979), pp. 30-33.
112. Myers, p. 189.
113. See Schweizer, p. 108.
114. Hooker, p. 139.

ing with water and the rising panic of the disciples.[115] At v. 37 we are told that a great squall of wind arose, and the waves became so high that they started splashing over the bow of the boat, filling and swamping the boat. The Sea of Galilee is in a depression between various hills, and because it is a relatively small body of water in a basin, a storm and wind can arise and quickly change the character of the lake.

One must remember that these men, at least the fishermen among the Twelve, had sailed this lake for some time, so one must surmise that, for these veteran sailors to react as they did, this must have been an extraordinarily severe storm. Surprisingly, during the commotion Jesus is asleep in the stern on a cushion, and he appeared to the disciples unconcerned about their fate. How could he sleep through this storm and through the foundering of the boat? Wouldn't a great and prescient person have immediately sensed danger?[116] This is the only mention in the NT of Jesus sleeping.[117] Mark wishes to make clear the fully human character of Jesus, especially right before the miracle he is about to relate.

According to v. 38, the disciples arouse Jesus and call him "Teacher,"[118] and as the story progresses it becomes clear that they do not understand how much more than a teacher Jesus is. They say, "Teacher, is it not a concern to you that we are perishing?"[119] These are, apart from 1:37, the first words addressed by the disciples to Jesus in this Gospel, and they had too strong a tone to suit Matthew or Luke, who soften them down in one way or another. As Guelich says, the similarities between Jesus asleep in the boat in the midst of a raging storm and the case of Jonah in Jon. 1 are too strong to overlook, not least because it would be the behavior of the prophet when notified which would result in the calming of the storm in each case.[120] In each case the captain of the boat rouses the person in question

---

115. See V. Taylor, *The Gospel according to St. Mark* (New York: St. Martin's Press, 1966), p. 272.

116. On the other hand, Hooker, p. 139, remarks: "For Jesus to sleep in these conditions suggests confidence in his disciples' seamanship, but to sleep when surrounded by danger is also a sign of trust in God (e.g. Ps. 4.8), and no doubt Mark interpreted Jesus' sleep in that way." As to the former suggestion, Painter, p. 87, says: "Such a psychological interpretation has no place in Mark." Painter suggests that Mark sees Jesus' sleeping as a test of the disciples, to reveal their faith or lack thereof.

117. "He was tired — yet his is the 'rest' of the weary and the burdened." Gregory Nazianzen, *Oration to the Son* 29.20.

118. Notice how Matthew changes this to κυριε.

119. Gundry, p. 239, suggests that the construction ου plus the verb in the indicative implies that the disciples don't doubt that Jesus cares, and so we should translate the sentence: "You care that we are perishing, don't you?" Against this is not only the subsequent behavior of the disciples but the way the other Synoptic writers seem to have handled their Markan source at this point.

120. See Guelich, p. 266.

with a charge of dereliction of duty (cf. Jon. 1:6). In addition, the verb "to die" is the same here as in Jon. 1:6, 14 and 3:9. But one prophet is seeking to escape his mission, the other surely is not. One prophet is encouraged to pray to God for help, the other simply acts in divine fashion.

V. 39 says Jesus rebuked the wind, which, since it is the same verb and same form as in 1:25, has reminded many commentators of the fact that Jesus rebuked the demons. Notice the other texts where Jesus rebukes something or someone (1:25; 3:12; 7:18; 8:17-33; 9:19). Is Jesus treating the sea like a personified force of evil, or at least as in the grip of such a force? It is true that in ancient mythology the sea was seen as a sometimes malevolent deity, but in Jewish ways of thinking it was seen as a natural dwelling place for demons and spirits (cf. below on 5:1-20). The disciples, then, may have seen Jesus' action here as another demonstration of his authority and power over the forces of darkness, but if so, Mark does not dwell on this point. "Between the *great* storm of wind (4.37) and the *great* calm (4.39), the dynamic word of Jesus interposed."[121]

According to v. 39, Jesus tells the sea to keep silent or be still (literally "be muzzled"), in addition to rebuking the wind. In short, he addresses the forces of nature in a personal way, apparently assuming that a personal agency controls or is behind them. Now the miracle would be evident not so much in the sudden ceasing of the wind, but rather in the sudden calmness of the sea, which by all rights should be choppy for some time after a storm passes. The response to Jesus' commands was instantaneous — the wind dropped and a great calm came over the sea. The portrayal of Jesus here certainly suggests his divinity and may be contrasted with 2 Macc. 9:8, where Antiochus Epiphanes attempts to command the sea to demonstrate his divine power. According to Job 26:11-12; Ps. 104:7; Isa. 51:9-10, the commanding of the sea is something only God can do.

V. 40 must be allowed to have its full effect. Jesus accuses the disciples of being cowards and says, "Have you not yet faith?" This makes clear that they do not yet have the requisite faith, but it may also suggest that Jesus was expecting them at some point to have such faith.[122] One may contrast Jesus' trust in this situation with the disciples' panic.[123] Jesus' miracle, however, does not produce this faith even in those who are already disciples. Instead, we are told that they respond rather like the crowd in the face of the supernatural. It says literally, "they feared a great fear," a Semitic form of expression that echoes Jonah 1:10 (LXX). They were terrified and asked one another in the light of this happening, "Who is this fellow, that even wind and sea obey him?"[124] Here and in 5:36

---

121. Painter, p. 88.

122. See Marcus, *Mark 1–8*, p. 334.

123. Hooker, p. 141.

124. The answer, in light of Ps. 89:8-9, is that God does so, and once more the casting of Jesus in a divine light is an important part of Mark's purpose.

fear is seen as the opposite of faith. The focus again is on the fact that miracles raise the question about Jesus but do not give the answer or key to his identity.[125] As we argued in the introduction, this is one of the main functions of all the narratives leading up to the Caesarea Philippi episode in Mark 8. Mark, conforming his account to the requirements of an ancient biography, presents stories meant to focus on the issue of the identity and nature of the central character, Jesus.

The question this and other such narratives raise in a tale full of secrets, mystery, veiled discourses, and apocalyptic rhetoric is — "Who is this masked man?"[126] This sort of response by the disciples may be called situational irony, for the character in the story seems oblivious to something the reader knows is true.[127] "For Mark, the key point is that the man who will later be crucified is the man who without prayer to God or adjuration in God's name successfully commands the wind and the sea. He is a divine man who represents the one true God."[128]

As for the disciples, they have acted like the crowd elsewhere in Mark, even though they are insiders in the same boat with Jesus. Mark is perhaps almost as concerned about revealing the discipleship secret, the clues to what makes for a real disciple, as he is the messianic secret. Awe or even terror in the face of the divine is not enough, as not only this story but also others in Mark will reveal.[129] Yet Mark does not treat these disciples as simple outsiders. They have not rejected Jesus, they have simply failed to understand him, and the upbraiding of their lack of faith assumes that they should by then have had more faith than a member of the crowd.[130]

---

125. Schweizer, p. 109: "Here is where we find the purpose of the storyteller. He places believing in contrast to faintheartedness, so that believing is not simply intellectual agreement to certain statements; it embraces the whole of life. Therefore, to believe means to rely upon God and his might in such a way that one positively expects to encounter this might again and again in Jesus."

126. Prudentius, in *Hymn on the Trinity* 656-59, says, "Who would command the stormy gales: 'Be still, Your strongholds keep and leave the boundless sea,' except the Lord and maker of the winds? . . ." See Ps. 106:9.

127. See Tolbert, p. 101.

128. Gundry, p. 241. Gundry does not have in mind the old θειος ανηρ concept here.

129. Not least of which is the story about the women at the tomb in Mark 16:6-8.

130. On the extensive parallels with the Jonah stories, see O. L. Cope, *Matthew: A Scribe Trained for the Kingdom of Heaven* (Washington, D.C.: Catholic Biblical Association, 1976), pp. 96-97.

F. A Legion of Demons, a Herd of Swine (5:1-20)

Mark 5 provides us with the most graphic of all the exorcisms, indeed, in many regards the most graphic of all the miracle tales, and in some ways the most disturbing as well. This story has more elaboration than any other tale prior to the passion narrative, which may suggest that it had particular importance for Mark's largely Gentile audience. It has been called the second inaugural exorcism by Myers, due in part to the close similarities of language to the exorcism tale in Mark 1 (cf. 1:21ff. to 5:1ff.).[131] Yet one of these exorcisms takes place on sacred soil in sacred space (the synagogue), the other in an unclean land in an unclean place. This suggests that Mark saw this story as particularly revealing of the identity of the subject of this biography. It is not at all clear if we are to see this tale as the immediate sequel to the storm at sea, but in any case Jesus and the disciples go across the Sea of Galilee to a region called the Decapolis, the Ten Cities. These cities formed a defense league about A.D. 1 to protect themselves, and there was a trading agreement as well. The cities, except for Scythopolis (Beth Shean), lay to the east and south of the Sea of Galilee. There can be little doubt that most of the population was non-Jews, and our story makes plain that Jesus is in Gentile territory by mentioning the herd of pigs. No practicing Jew would have had such a herd, nor for that matter would they have been found residing in a graveyard. Isa. 65:4, in fact, shows God's displeasure with Jews

> who sit inside tombs,
>   and spend the night in secret places;
> who eat swine's flesh,
>   with broth of abominable things in their vessels. (NRSV)

It is then quite likely that Mark's largely Gentile audience would have understood this story to suggest that while Jesus did not inaugurate a full-fledged Gentile mission himself during his lifetime, he did provide certain precedents for that sort of mission.[132] On the other hand, Painter sees this passage as foreshadowing 7:24–8:10, where he thinks we see Jesus' mission into largely Gentile territory.[133] On closer inspection, that particular portion of Mark does not

---

131. Myers, pp. 192-93. Yet most of the similarities of language have to do with the schematized way Mark presents exorcism tales — the demons shout, they name Jesus, Jesus responds with a command, the demons are called unclean spirits, the response is fear and amazement.

132. See the still valuable discussion by J. Jeremias, *Jesus' Promise to the Nations* (London: SCM, 1958).

133. Painter, pp. 89-90. Or does he? Later he speaks merely of the foreshadowing of the Gentile mission. He is probably right to say that Mark wants to stress that the Gentile mission was a direct and legitimate consequence of Jesus' own mission (p. 92).

present Jesus preaching or teaching or recruiting disciples, but rather only meeting people's physical needs when he is approached to do so while outside the sacred zone of Israel seeking to avoid being pursued. Thus, while we may talk about that section of Mark presenting Jesus as ministering while in Gentile territory, we should not talk about a mission to Gentiles.

Indeed, if one reads our story closely, one sees that Jesus commands the former demoniac to go back to his family and friends and report all that the Lord has done for him. This must not be overlooked in light of the commands to silence we have already heard in Jewish territory. This contrast may suggest that, though Jesus did not see it as his main task during his earthly ministry, he was willing to help or reach out to Gentiles, even if the good news was for the Jew first. Notice also the contrast in our story between the Gentiles who want Jesus to leave and the Jews who can't get enough of the miracle-working Jesus, even though they do not respond in true faith; this may suggest that we are meant to think that Jesus' disclosure of who he was (κυριος, v. 19) in Gentile territory would not lead to the same misunderstandings that such a title or claim would in Israel, where messianic claims were politically charged. On the other hand, "Lord" here may refer to God rather than Jesus, as it does in 1:3 and 12:36-37, and in the Lukan parallel to our tale Luke has changed the wording to "God" (Luke 8:39).

J. Adna has suggested a three-scene structure to this passage: (1) introduction, presenting the two main figures, vv. 1-2; (2) scene 1, vv. 3-9 — the encounter between Jesus and the demoniac; (3) scene 2, vv. 11-13 — the episode with the herd of pigs; (4) scene 3, vv. 14-19 — the result of the exorcism and its effects on people.[134] This structure roughly conforms to the usual structure of a miracle tale. Notice that a new set of persons is introduced in each new scene.

One further important piece of information that Adna highlights needs discussion before we look at the story in detail. By Jesus' day the pig had become in a sense the symbol of paganism (cf. Matt. 7:6; Luke 15:15-16; 2 Pet. 2:22), and as such something to be avoided, whether it was alive or already someone's food, at all costs. This, in part, is because Torah classifies the pig as an unclean animal and so forbidden for food (Lev. 11:7-8; Deut. 14:8; cf. Isa. 65:4; 66:17). It is more a reaction to the strong-arm tactics of the Seleucids, in particular Antiochus Epiphanes (r. 175-163 B.C.), who attempted to force Jews to sacrifice and eat pigs, an action Jews vigorously rejected (1 Macc. 1:47; 2 Macc. 6:2-5; 6:18–7:42). This story must be read in light of these facts.[135]

At 5:1 we have a textual problem which deserves close attention.[136] Is the name of the place Jesus visited Gerasa, Gadara, or Gergesa? Gerasa was a city of

---

134. J. Adna, "The Encounter of Jesus with the Gerasene Demoniac," in *Authenticating the Activities of Jesus*, ed. B. Chilton and C. A. Evans (Leiden: Brill, 1999), pp. 279-301.

135. Adna, p. 293.

136. Marcus, *Mark 1–8*, pp. 341-42.

the Decapolis probably to be identified with modern Jerash, which is thirty-seven miles southeast of the Sea of Galilee. The pigs could certainly not run into the sea from there! But might Mark mean that Jesus was in the region of Gerasa rather than at or near the city itself? Gadara, on the other hand, is only five miles southeast of the Galilee lake and had territory that extended to the sea itself. In terms of the text criticism, it is clear that the prevailing text in Matthew's parallel had Gadara,[137] but this is much less sure in the Markan text, where Gerasa seems to be the original reading. On the other hand, Luke 8:26 and 37 appear in the earliest and best manuscripts of Luke's Gospel to refer to Gergesa.

Yet the matter is made more complex by the fact that Gadara was the capital of a toparchy, so what the First Evangelist may have meant was "in the Gadarene region." If Gerasa is the correct reading in Mark, then Mark or an early copyist made a mistake, or we should place the stress on the fact that the text actually reads "in the territory (vicinity?) of Gerasa."[138] It may be relevant that near the modern town Kursa (Kursi) is a steep slope that runs down to within forty yards of the sea, and two miles beyond that are some cave tombs which may have been used as dwellings at some time. This location has been touted by various scholars as the original locale of this occurrence and to be identified with Gergesa.[139] If we are dealing with a translation of an Aramaic original, it is easy to see how Gergesa, Gerasa, and perhaps even Gadara might all have been translators' attempts to deal with the Semitic original, especially if it had a radical something like KRS or GRS. Origen is worth quoting here: "Concerning Palestinian place names the Greek copies are often incorrect, and one might be misled by them."[140] He seems to identify the site as Gergesa, which may well be the same as the modern city of Kursi.[141]

---

137. See Metzger, *TCGNT,* pp. 23-24 and 84.

138. See Adna, pp. 294-95.

139. See Taylor, p. 279; C. E. B. Cranfield, *The Gospel according to St. Mark* (Cambridge: Cambridge University Press, 1972), p. 176; Lane, p. 180; J. Gnilka, *Das Evangelium nach Markus* (Zürich: Benziger, 1979), 1:201, all following the original suggestions of Dalman. On the entire dilemma and debate see Guelich, pp. 274-77.

140. This is found in Origen's commentary on John 6:24 as quoted in T. C. Oden and C. A. Hall, eds., *Mark,* vol. 2 of *The Ancient Christian Commentary on Scripture* (Downers Grove, Ill.: InterVarsity, 1998), p. 67. Origen goes on to add his view that the original text referred to Gergesa, which was a village near the Sea of Galilee and had a hill such as that described in the story. He points out that the name of that village means "dwelling of one who drives out" and suggests that the city may have been prophetically named (or more likely, received such a name after this incident, in which case it had another name before then).

141. Contrast Hooker, p. 142, who thinks we do not know where this city is, to Gundry, p. 256, who suggests the locale and recent archaeological work favor both the identification of Gergesa with Kursi and in turn with the original locale of this story. I agree with Gundry that it is much easier to see why the little-known town of Gergesa would be replaced in the manuscript tradition with two more familiar cities in the Decapolis as time went on.

At v. 2 we are told that no sooner had Jesus and the disciples disembarked than they were met by a man with an unclean spirit from the tombs. To a Jew he would be unclean merely by frequenting the tombs, since corpses and cemeteries were considered unclean, especially Gentile ones. The phrase "unclean spirit" must mean a spirit which makes a person ritually unclean. This spirit (or spirits) is not called a demon in this tale, though clearly that is how Mark views the matter. The stress is on how the spirit affects the man. He was obviously in great misery and seen as a threat to many, for the various attempts to bind him or chain him somewhere failed, so great was the power of evil in him. He was like a wild animal on the loose. "So powerful was the possession that chains could not bind the man. All night long he cried out and cut himself with stones. His behavior was anti-social and self-destructive."[142] Yet this strong man, possessed by the Strong Man's Legion, was about to be dispossessed by the Stronger Man.

Notice too how the spirit had taken over the man's personality and was seeking to destroy it, even speaking through him without his consent. The man was no longer in control of his faculties. He is what most would call mad. Lane makes much of the fact that the very function of the unclean spirit was to distort and destroy the image of God in a person, which was accomplished by reducing the man to animal status. We may even be meant to think that he was impelled to be involved in satanic rituals (slashing oneself with rocks?), and the capacity to communicate and relate to God on a personal basis was taken away. We are told that the man night and day cried out and bruised or cut himself with rocks. He was so little in control of himself that he could not keep from injuring himself.

Probably not too much should be made of the fact that the man comes and kneels before Jesus, for it is likely an indication that the demons are in control of him and recognize in Jesus a superior power who is a threat to them. The man cries out in a loud voice, "What to me and to you, Jesus, son of the most high God?" The latter phrase was the familiar terminology for the chief god of the pagan pantheon (cf. Acts 16:17; Heb. 7:1), but even in the earlier OT period, in a polytheistic setting, Yahweh could be referred to in this manner by a non-Jew or at least in a Gentile context (Gen. 14:18ff.; Num. 24:16; Isa. 14:14; Dan. 3:26; 4:2; or even where Yahweh is contrasted with pagan deities as in Ps. 79:9). The phrase "what to me and to you" appears in settings where some hostility is expressed and seems to connote "What do we have to do with each other?" or "Why do you interfere with me?" (cf. John 2:4), with the possible implication of a threat — "Mind your own business" (cf. Josh. 22:24; Judg. 11:12; 2 Sam. 16:10; 19:22; 1 Kings 17:18). The entire phrase is not language a Jew or Christian would use of God, and so it is probably incorrect to suggest that the demon is making a true confession about Jesus or God.

---

142. Painter, p. 90.

In any case, these words are followed by an oath: "I adjure you by God not to torture me." This is the demons rather than the man speaking, but they ironically are the ones torturing the poor man.[143] Equally ironic is the fact that they are adjuring Jesus by the name of the one who is Jesus' Father, as if that could give them power over Jesus![144] The demons appear to fear that Jesus will torture or destroy them, and to be sure, that is his long-range goal — to destroy the works of the devil. Schweizer remarks that our author believes that demons would see it as torment simply to be in the presence of Jesus.[145] Here he does not destroy them but rather transfers them to a less valuable host, the pigs, which in turn are destroyed by the demonic power driving them into a frenzied act. It is possible that originally this story was meant to be humorous — unclean spirits destroy unclean animals! From a Jewish point of view this might produce a wry smile in Jesus' original audience, but Mark's audience would likely focus on the power struggle between Jesus and the demons and the implications about Jesus' identity.[146] In any case the story, as we have it now, emphasizes Jesus' concern to help the man return to normal life.

At v. 9 the demons are asked to name themselves, but it is hard to know what to make of the reply. Clearly Luke believed in the concept of a person being possessed by multiple demons (Luke 8:2). At first glance "My name is Legion, for we are many" seems a curious response. In an exorcism ritual, naming is a crucial part of trying to gain control of the demon, and it is possible to see this response as an attempt to avoid giving Jesus the power of the personal name over these spirits. A legion in Roman military terms was six thousand foot soldiers, but it is doubtful a specific number is meant (though notice that about two thousand pigs are said to be destroyed). The military metaphor is used presumably to indicate that many demons were involved, acting like a military force which had taken captive the man's spirit and being. J. D. M. Derrett rightly points out the use of military language in the rest of this passage. For example, the term for herd (αγελη — 5:11) is inappropriate for pigs, who do not move together in herds, but is often used of a band of military recruits. Also the phrase "he dismissed them" is reminiscent of a military command, and likewise

143. Note Marcus, *Mark 1–8,* p. 350: "There is an element of burlesque comedy when the demons, as part of their negotiations with Jesus, plead with him not to torment them and back up this plea by invoking God himself. . . . Very religious demons indeed, and very brazen, to plead for mercy when they have shown none; like typical bullies, they can dish it out but they can not take it."

144. See Guelich, p. 279. The demons assume the position normally taken by the exorcist who does the adjuring, but in the end they must negotiate a settlement with the Stronger One.

145. Schweizer, p. 112.

146. Schweizer, p. 112.

having martial overtones is the reference to the pigs' "charge" into the water (5:13).[147]

Some commentators have suggested that this story is something of a political allegory. Jesus has come to cast the unclean Roman presence out of the region or out of the Holy Land. The problem with this conclusion is of course that Jesus is not in the Holy Land when this encounter occurs, nor is he rescuing a Jew. But perhaps it is a satire on the Roman presence in the entire region, a suggestion made more plausible when one notes that the wild boar was in fact the emblem of the Roman legion stationed in Palestine.[148] In any event, the focus should be on the fact that Mark is characterizing Jesus' struggles with demons as part of the larger war between the supernatural forces of good and evil during Jesus' ministry, or Jesus the Stronger One binding the Strong Man. Of no relevance to the study of this passage are references in Josephus to a military action during the time of Vespasian (i.e., after Mark wrote his Gospel) against the city of Gerasa (but cf. *War* 4.9.1).[149] Hooker is correct that the explanation of the term "Legion" by "for we are many" surely suggests that it is not the Roman association that Mark is making something of, but rather the fact that the term suggests a vast number.[150] V. 15, which refers to the man who has "the legion," also suggests that this is not taken as a personal name but as a description.

V. 10 seems even stranger. Why did the demons not want to be sent out of the region? Is it because Gentile territory is more demon-friendly and they could more easily hold sway in such a place? "What follows is a negotiation by the spirit(s) to ensure survival."[151] Hooker may be correct that this negotiation reflects the idea that demons are associated with particular localities (Luke 11:24-27).[152]

Some people have even gotten upset with this story because it involves the destruction of animals, but here it is a matter of priorities. A human life is seen as more important than a herd of pigs, even though the Gentiles who came afterward to see Jesus seem more concerned with the lost pigs than the restored man. Both Jerome and Chrysostom dealt with this issue and stressed that it was for the greater good of eliciting faith and attesting God's power that the pigs were slain.[153] Jerome stresses that no one would have believed so many demons came out of the man unless a similarly large number of swine had been afflicted

---

147. J. D. M. Derrett, "Contributions to the Study of the Gerasene Demoniac," *JSNT* 3 (1979): 5ff.

148. Marcus, *Mark 1–8*, p. 351.

149. Against Myers, p. 191.

150. Hooker, p. 143.

151. Painter, p. 91.

152. Hooker, p. 145.

153. See Oden and Hall, pp. 66-67.

thereafter (*Life of Saint Hilarion* 32). The pig herders were the ones who spread the tale in the towns and villages of what Jesus did (v. 14).

Notice that the man for whom nobody had been able to do anything, not even chain him down so he wouldn't hurt himself, is now said to be clothed, sitting, and sane — things no one who had known him expected to see him do or be again. Once more Jesus' miracle working causes a great fear to come on the people — fear of the awesome supernatural power Jesus must have in order to do what he did to the demons and the pigs, a power even greater than a legion! Schweizer speaks of the irresistible majesty of Jesus in this episode.[154] There is a rather sad point and counterpoint between the Gentiles who want Jesus to go and the restored man who wanted to go with Jesus. Instead Jesus tells him to return to his village and resume a normal life, except that in addition he is to be a witness. "Jesus' answer shows how impossible it is to have a stereotyped definition of discipleship. One person is taken away from home and family (1:16-20), another is sent back to them contrary to his own wishes."[155] There can be little doubt that the man did indeed wish to be a disciple, not only because of what follows in v. 20 but also because the description of his longing to be "with Jesus" is a deliberate echo in the Greek of the earlier description of what would be true of Jesus' inner circle (cf. v. 18 to 3:14 — ινα . . . μετ αυτου in both cases).

At v. 20 we hear of the obedient response of this man. He went and preached (κηρυσσειν) in the Ten Cities about what Jesus had done for him, and all were amazed. Again notice that amazement and fear do not equal full or true faith in Jesus. Jesus would have been perceived in this region, and perhaps by parts of Mark's own audience, as another Hellenistic wonder-worker that wowed the people like a Simon Magus or an Apollonius of Tyana. But the ability to impress a crowd and the ability to call out and make disciples are not one and the same.

G. Women in Need, Jesus on Call (5:21-43)

Though it seems clear enough from other examples in Mark that Mark uses the literary device of intercalation, or the sandwich technique, where two stories are combined, with the first story being divided in half and the second story being inserted in the middle, it may be doubted that we find this device here, for as both Dibelius and Pesch pointed out, the delay caused by the healing of the woman is integral to the Jairus story.[156] Furthermore, we have the unusual case

---

154. Schweizer, p. 114.

155. Schweizer, p. 114.

156. M. Dibelius, *From Tradition to Gospel* (London, 1934), p. 72; R. Pesch, "Jairus (Mk 5,22/Lk. 8,41)," *BZ* 14, no. 2 (1970): 252-56. See also the discussion in Guelich, p. 292.

here of a Jewish official who has substantial faith in Jesus, perhaps another mark of the historical character of the tale.[157] Mark 5:21-43 has many interesting details that are unique to this story (e.g., the command in Aramaic, the messengers' skeptical attitude about Jesus' ability to help), and if it is historical in character, it is likely to be based in the reminiscences of one of the inner circle of the Twelve, particularly Peter, James, or John, who would have been in a position to say what happened in Jairus's house. In favor of the essential historicity of our narrative is the fact that we find stories about Jesus helping women in a variety of sources (Mark, special L, special M, John). Pesch has made a good case for the view that Jairus's name is an original part of the story but was later omitted by Matthew and the Western text of Mark.[158] In fact, if one compares the Matthean and Markan versions of the story carefully, one finds a textbook example of how a vivid Markan tale has been shortened and generalized by the later Evangelist who produced Matthew:[159] (1) the name Jairus is omitted, as is the Aramaic command; (2) he uses the more general term for Jairus — αρχων; (3) he telescopes the whole story by omitting the messengers altogether; (4) he adds a generalizing conclusion (Matt. 9:26; cf. Luke 7:17); (5) he neatly summarizes the woman's illness by simply using the term αιμορροουσα.[160] The social significance of the story should also not be overlooked, for we see Jesus aiding both a male of high status (Jairus) and a woman who was an outcast and marginalized because of her physical condition.[161] This, however, must tell us that Jesus was prepared to help anyone, though he was especially concerned for the vulnerable and marginalized.

---

157. See Hooker, p. 147.

158. Pesch, "Jairus (Mk 5,22/Lk. 8,41)," pp. 255-56. The textual tradition strongly favors the conclusion that the name is original — p45, ℵ, A, and B all have it. See Metzger, *TCGNT*, pp. 85-86.

159. Which means that we must reject V. K. Robbins's ("The Woman Who Touched Jesus' Garment: Socio-Rhetorical Analysis of the Synoptic Accounts," *NTS* 33, no. 4 [1987]: 502-15) analysis of this pericope. He sees it as an elaborated *chreia*, with perhaps the Matthean form of the *chreia* being closer to the original form of the story, and perhaps all three Synoptic versions being based on some common unknown original. Yet the vast majority of scholars think we have good reason to think that Matthew regularly edits down the longer Markan form of various of these miracle stories (in this case Mark has 374 words, Matthew 138, and Luke 280). Furthermore, it may be doubted whether this story can be called a *chreia* at all, if by that one means a story that represents a rhetorical elaboration based on some original memorable saying of a famous person. Can we really say with Robbins that "Daughter, your faith has made you well, go in peace and be healed from your ailment" is such a saying (see Robbins, p. 510)? It seems unlikely that such a saying would generate a *chreia* or be the cause of elaborating some nodal story into *chreia* form. A better case can be made with a saying like "The Sabbath was made for human beings. . . ."

160. On Mark's own editing of his source for these stories, see my *Women*, p. 72.

161. See rightly Myers, pp. 202-3.

The story itself builds from the healing of one person to the raising of another, and it includes an intriguing contrast between the elicited testimony from the woman with the flow of blood and the command to silence in regard to the daughter of Jairus. The passage illustrates the way the gospel reaches both those at the bottom of the social scale (an impoverished unclean woman) and those at the top (Jairus and his family).

The narrative begins in v. 21 with Jesus once again being surrounded by a crowd once he has landed on the Galilean side of the lake. Jesus is approached by a synagogue president[162] who, because of his daughter's desperate situation, forgets his position and pride and falls on his knees before Jesus, begging for aid. The term προσεκυνει is found in the Matthean but not in the Markan version of the story, and while it can at times refer to worship, it probably does not in this instance. Rather the First Evangelist seems to be suggesting that respect and a special sense of urgency seem to prompt the self-forgetful act.[163] Mark uses the idiomatic phrase εσχατως εχει to describe the girl's condition, which means something like "at the point of death (end)." Matthew, apparently due to compressing the account, probably suggests that the girl had just died.[164] Jesus is requested to come and lay hands on the young girl (v. 42 tells us she is twelve).[165]

Jesus agrees to the request, and as he goes to Jairus's house, a considerable crowd presses in on him such that we are meant to think of various people jostling and bumping into Jesus.[166] In this crowd is a woman suffering with a twelve-year flow of blood.[167] Mark includes a comment derogatory toward physicians in v. 26, which Luke interestingly omits.[168] The doctors had not

---

162. This is probably what αρχισυναγωγος means, though it could be simply an honorary title. See B. Lifshitz, "Fonctions et titres honorifiques dans les communautes juives," *RB* 67 (1960): 58-59.

163. On the other hand, it could be Matthew's attempt to introduce a more christologically focused approach to the story. Compare Matt. 28:9.

164. On the other hand, G. A. Chadwick, "The Daughter of Jairus and the Woman with the Issue of Blood (Mt. ix.18; Mk. v.22; Lk. viii.41)," *ET*, 4th ser., 8 (1893): 309-20, here p. 310, suggests that a person full of anxiety might say "she is dead by now" and in fact mean "she is at the point of death."

165. The explanation is perhaps given because of the use of the diminutive θυγατριον, which might suggest a younger girl if a true diminutive. This means that the mention of the age is probably not extraneous information which caused these two stories of healing to be linked by the catchword "twelve."

166. Mark uses the milder term "to press" (συνθλιβω), but Luke has the more dramatic "to choke, suffocate" (συνπνιγω).

167. Twelve may be a round number indicating an illness of very long standing. See Taylor, p. 290.

168. However, Schweizer, p. 117, cautions against seeing here a polemic by Christians against doctors. Rather the point is to stress the severity of the illness.

made her better, and in fact during their treatment she had become worse and had lost her financial security in the bargain. "In contrast, the true physician (2.17) will cure this woman without charge."[169] We are probably also to consider this woman as perpetually unclean due to her illness, which appears to be vaginal bleeding, and so she is a social outcast (see Lev. 15:25-30).[170] With hopes of a cure, she touches Jesus' outer garment (ιματιον). In one of the rare minor agreements of Matthew and Luke over against Mark, the other two Synoptic writers add that the woman in fact touched the tassels on Jesus' garment, which any Torah-observant Jew would have (cf. Num. 15:38-40; Deut. 22:12) and which Mark elsewhere tells us Jesus did have (Mark 6:56).[171]

Mark 5:28 (cf. Matt. 9:21) suggests that the woman had a magic-tainted belief about Jesus, thinking that even a touching of his garments would transfer enough holiness or healing power into her to make her well. But perhaps her approach was simply based on the magic-tainted comments she had heard from others.[172] Here, as elsewhere in the Synoptics, the verb "saved" does not have its fuller Christian sense, but rather means healed (so probably in v. 34 as well). Yet in its larger Markan context we must also see a reference to God's eschatological deliverance from the powers of darkness.[173] V. 29 stresses that immediately the woman's blood flow did stop and she was instantly aware of the fact. Equally quickly, we are told that Jesus was aware of power going forth from him. V. 30 says he turned to the crowd and asked, "Who touched my clothes (outer garment)?" (Mark and Luke only). The Markan presentation of the story stresses that while Jesus is spiritually aware that something has happened beyond a simple jostling by the crowd, yet he is unaware of who has touched him in a special way. There is, then, a stress on Jesus' supernatural though limited knowledge, and the grammatical construction here makes Jesus' supernatural power and what has happened with it the object of this knowledge.[174] It is possible that we are meant to think that Jesus asks the question in order to elevate the woman's faith beyond the level of thinking there might be magical power in the holy man's garments.[175] Jesus apparently wants the woman to bear witness to the crowd about her faith and the cure she received. In other words, Jesus wishes to make an example of her in the good sense of that phrase.

---

169. Myers, p. 201.

170. See Hooker, p. 148.

171. Since Mark does have this information elsewhere, we should probably think of the addition by Matthew and Luke as not a fortuitous coincidence, but rather as a retrojection of the information found later in the Markan source into this appropriate spot.

172. See Hooker, p. 148.

173. See Marcus, *Mark 1–8*, p. 366.

174. Gundry, p. 270.

175. Against Robbins, "The Woman," pp. 510-13, who apparently thinks the woman exhibits fully exemplary faith in Jesus.

V. 31 indicates that the disciples are not as spiritually perceptive as Jesus; indeed, they appear a bit stunned that Jesus should ask who touched him in the midst of such a crowd. Notice how the First Evangelist spares the disciples from looking dense by omitting Mark 5:31. The portrait of the disciples in Mark is clearly less forgiving than in Matthew.[176] The woman had taken a risk in touching Jesus, as she might have been condemned or further ostracized for daring to be in a crowd full of ritually clean Jews, never mind touch a holy man. Thus her response in v. 33, that she comes to Jesus in fear and trembling and falls before him confessing all, is historically plausible.[177] The text says she told Jesus "the whole truth," which suggests that she understood that she had not approached the Master or dealt with this problem in a proper manner. She had perhaps hoped to slip away quietly, but was afraid when she was found out. Yet Jesus seizes the moment, and according to v. 34 says, "your faith has saved you, go in peace, and be healed of your affliction" (cf. John 5:6, 9, 11-15; 7:23).[178] In the light of this saying, this brief narrative has been seen as a *chreia*.[179] She had had enough faith to believe that Jesus might help her, but she had been superstitious enough to think that a personal transaction between herself and Jesus was not necessary, only a touch of a garment.

Jesus chooses to explain to her and to all that it was not a garment but her faith in him that was the means through which she received healing. By contrast, the disciples are seen to be not spiritually perceptive about Jesus or what was going on in this situation. As was apparently often the case, Jesus' apparently simple words "Who touched me?" carried more meaning than the superficial interpretation the disciples suggested. Notice that Jesus not only explains to the woman what has transpired and why, but suggests that God's peace or wholeness now rests upon her and so she can be reintegrated into society. The last phrase, "be healed of your disease," may suggest that Jesus understood there was more to healing than just the restoration of the body.[180] Health, after all,

---

176. See pp. 421-42 below in the appendix.

177. Robbins, "The Woman," pp. 509-10, is quite right that Mark's version of the story focuses on the perceptions of the woman and the perceptions of Jesus, the emotions of the woman and the reaction of Jesus to being touched in this way. "Instead of controlling the healing through the logic of naming, he controlled the feelings and thoughts of the woman by calling forth 'fear,' 'trembling,' 'obeisance,' and 'a full confession of the truth.' . . . the Markan version explores the emotional dynamics of allegiance to Jesus in a world containing pain, suffering, and loss." Just so, and what this means is that Mark's biographical focus has led him to emphasize the personal nature of such a story. It is the biographical drive, not a desire to create a *chreia*, that explains the Markan shape of this miracle tale.

178. The reference to going in peace may refer to her restoration to right relationship with the God who grants shalom. See Guelich, p. 299.

179. See rightly Painter, p. 95.

180. Robbins, "The Woman," p. 510, suggests plausibly that the way Jesus' final remark

was the condition she was seeking after she was rescued by Jesus from the mal-ady.[181] Many times a person who has become physically well still carries mental and emotional scars. Jesus is perhaps suggesting that she needs to know and ac-cept that she is now whole again.

It is at this juncture in both the Markan and Lukan accounts that the messengers arrive to report to Jairus that his daughter is dead, and they ask, "Why trouble the teacher further?" V. 36 indicates that Jesus overhears this con-versation and, seeking to allay Jairus's fears and prevent him from despairing, says, "Fear not, only keep on believing." The verb πιστευω is in the present con-tinual tense. When Jesus arrives at Jairus's house, he allows only Peter, Jacob, and John among the nonresidents to enter the house with him, leaving the crowd and other disciples and onlookers outside. These three serve as the wit-nesses to the miracle which transpires, as representatives of the disciples. Wit-nesses were important in an environment where Jesus could be accused of nec-romancy, having already been accused of being in league with Satan (cf. Mark 3). Jesus will now attack the ultimate tool of the powers of darkness and the "last enemy," death.[182]

Once Jesus has entered the house, he sees the confusion, weeping, and much wailing and asks those present why they are acting as though the girl were dead. Jesus says succinctly, "She is not dead but sleeping." The response to this pronouncement is derisive laughter, and perhaps we are to think it comes from the paid mourners who would normally be present with a well-to-do family to carry out the extended ancient Near Eastern rites of mourning. If we are to think the laughter is from relatives, perhaps it is intimated that they thought Je-sus' remark was stupid or flippant and insensitive. They apparently interpret his remarks to mean that the girl continues to live, and it is just possible that the Markan narrative is about a girl in a coma, but Luke seems clearly to view the Markan story as a raising from the dead (cf. Luke 8:53, 55).

In any case, Jesus puts these people out of the house and takes only the parents of the girl and the three in to where the child is. Mark is probably not using the word καθευδει as a metaphor for the condition of the deceased, since the text does not say "Yes, she's dead, but death is like sleep." Rather here, as in 1 Thess. 5:10, "sleep" is the term a person uses for death when one believes in resurrection (cf. John 11:4-14; Dan. 12:7 LXX; Ps. 87:6 LXX; *Gen. Rab.* 96.60-61). Probable is the view that the ουκ . . . αλλα contrast lies in who Jesus is and what he is about to do — namely, raise the girl. The girl is dead and her death is

---

is framed has been made to appear like both a common Jewish and Hellenistic valediction (the former involving the word "shalom," the latter being "take care of yourself so that you remain healthy").

181. See Hooker, p. 149.

182. See Marcus, *Mark 1–8*, p. 372.

not merely like sleep, but in Jesus' presence it is sleep rather than a terminus of life, for the girl will come back from it after the miracle both healthy and hungry.[183] It is not the end of her life, but an interim condition.[184]

As in the case with Peter's mother-in-law, v. 41 says Jesus took the girl by the hand, and Mark and Luke include the command, "Girl, I say to you, arise," but only Mark records the transliteration from Aramaic ταλιθα κουμ.[185] The translation by Mark not only suggests that he does not expect his audience to know Aramaic while he does, but also that he does not want his audience to think Jesus used some magical formula to raise the girl.[186] Luke's omission of the transliteration probably suggests that both Luke and his audience are further removed than Mark from the original source. I would suggest that the Aramaic reflects a Petrine remembrance, not an attempt by Mark to add local color to the story, and this occasion marks the first of three times in this Gospel that Peter, Jacob, and John will share a special moment with Jesus (cf. 9:2; 14:33; and see 13:3). To aid the return to normalcy Jesus commands that the girl's physical needs now be attended to, since she is back from death.

Both of these narratives make clear Jesus' attitude about the Jewish laws about ritual purity. It seems unlikely that we are to think that Jesus was prepared to incur ritual impurity on behalf of the woman and the girl, a problem he would later have remedied. To the contrary, as the Evangelist will tell us later at 7:15 and 21, Jesus' operative principle seems to be that in the existing eschatological situation with the dominion breaking into history, uncleanness is a matter of human character, a matter of the heart, not a matter of the physical condition, and this means that even corpses are not untouchables as far as Jesus is concerned.

This attitude of Jesus was bound to affect the marginalized of society in a positive way, including especially women. If a woman with a flow of blood is neither defiled or defiling, then the reason for not requiring a woman to fulfill all of the law's positive commandments, and not permitting her to be counted on for the periodic feasts and functions of the faith, is by implication rejected by Jesus. The way is cleared for women to participate more fully in their faith.

As I have said elsewhere: "In both stories [in Mark 5] faith is a key com-

---

183. See Taylor, p. 295, and cf. Augustine, *Sermons on NT Lessons* 48, who says she is asleep only in relationship to Jesus, who alone was capable of waking her (in Oden and Hall, p. 77).

184. See Schweizer, p. 119.

185. The reading in W, 28, 245, 349 is due to scribal confusion with the name Tabitha found in Acts 9:40. See Metzger, *TCGNT*, p. 87. D and several other Western manuscripts have κουμι here, which is Hebrew, and this reading is supported by the translators of the RSV. The reading κουμ has better support, being found in A, B, C, and others. See Lane, p. 195 n. 57.

186. See rightly Painter, p. 94.

modity which the healed woman is as capable of possessing as Jairus. Since this
is also the commodity which is the basis of association in Jesus' community, the
woman, and perhaps to a lesser extent Jairus, become examples to the Gospel
writers' audiences. Certainly, the healed woman is made an example by Jesus
when He calls her to centre stage and speaks of her faith. In Mark's presentation
of the event, the woman appears in a more favourable light than the exasperated disciples."[187]

Finally, we do find the Markan secrecy motif here, but it may only be related to the fact that Jesus wished for the child to have the opportunity to return
to a normal life without unnecessary outside prying and attention. Hooker argues that "the child's cure must not be announced to those who are unable to
comprehend it — which include, of course, all Jesus' contemporaries. The miracle of resurrection can only be understood by those who believe in the one
who has himself been raised from the dead."[188] But Jesus' resurrection is not at
issue here. What we may find, however, is Jesus' attempt to avoid encouraging
magic-tainted faith in both these tales. In the first case he does so by bringing to
light the connection between faith and healing, and in the second case by limit-
ing the witnesses to those who have faith in Jesus. Even in the second story we
are talking about a witnessed secret, or better said, a secret revealed quite intentionally to a limited receptive audience. There is a going back and forth in this
Gospel between veiling to those outside and disclosure to those inside.[189]

H. A Painful Homecoming (6:1-6a)

This text is a rather classic example of a *chreia*, a short narrative about an historical figure climaxing with a memorable saying (6:4). Mark concludes his second major division of his narrative with the rejection of Jesus, just as he concluded the first major division (3:6).[190] But it is not an ideal scene which was
generated out of the famous saying, for the saying does not suggest the sort of
narrative about Jesus' relatives that we actually have here.[191] As Cranfield says,
the story "contains elements which it is particularly hard to imagine the early
Church inventing: the statement in v. 5, the reference to Jesus' kinfolk in v. 4

---

187. Witherington, *Women*, p. 75.
188. Hooker, p. 151.
189. Lane, p. 198.
190. Schweizer, p. 122.
191. Notice how Dibelius, p. 110, cf. p. 43, parts with the earlier judgment of R. Bultmann, *History of the Synoptic Tradition* (Oxford: Blackwell, 1963), pp. 30-31, that it is an arti-
ficially constructed ideal scene. From the Markan point of view, one must note that Mark's
interest in Jesus' family seems slight (Mark 3:21, 31-35). There is, for instance, nothing like
John 19:26-27 in this Gospel.

which was discreditable to people who had become prominent in the Church, and probably also the designation of Jesus as 'Son of Mary.'"[192] It is worth stressing from the outset that the family is apparently not present on this occasion in the synagogue (or only his sisters were; cf. below), but they are mentioned first by Jesus' listeners and then by Jesus himself. 6:1-6 is connected with 3:21, 31-35 in that both texts suggest the idea that Jesus' physical relationship to his family proves to be a stumbling block for his family to see Jesus as he truly is. There is furthermore the connection that Jesus places his relatives and even his own household in a category other than that of believer or disciple.

The story begins by speaking again of Jesus leaving one place and entering another, in this case "his own country." The term πατρίδα means literally "fatherland" and refers to the specific region where his family lived, in this case Nazareth and its environs. The disciples are described in v. 1 as following along behind Jesus. Nothing is said about what he did there until the Sabbath occurs, and then we are told in v. 2 that he began to teach in the synagogue, presumably the only such meeting place in this small village.

The result of Jesus teaching in the synagogue is not accolades but astonishment; or, as the Greek verb means literally, they were "knocked out" by what he said and had done.[193] They ask in essence where he had gained this learning, what was the wisdom that had been given to him, and what was the meaning of the mighty works performed through his hands. Notice that they neither dispute that he has wisdom or that he performs mighty works; they are just dumbfounded that it comes from a hometown boy like Jesus. More than just a matter of familiarity breeding contempt, this comes from the ancient mentality that geographical and heredity origins determine who a person is and what his capacities will always be. They see Jesus as someone who is not merely exceeding expectations but rather is overreaching. This will in fact be the last time in Mark that we find Jesus in a synagogue and is the last mention that Jesus taught[194] (though here with no explication as to its content), and once more he is embroiled in a controversy in that locale which is supposed to be sacred space.[195] The issue seems to be suspicion about Jesus' character — "uncertain origin implies uncertain character."[196]

In v. 3 we are confronted with a textual problem. Some important manuscripts (p45, and f13, 33 among others) have the reading "the son of the carpenter, the son of Mary" rather than the more widely supported reading "the carpenter, the son of Mary," with the former perhaps being a case of assimila-

---

192. Cranfield, p. 88.
193. Gundry, p. 289.
194. See Guelich, p. 308.
195. See Myers, p. 212.
196. Gundry, p. 291.

tion to Matt. 13:55. On the principle that the reading which best explains the others is likely to be original, the latter rendering calling Jesus a carpenter is to be preferred. Furthermore, if this Gospel did have as its primary audience Gentiles, it is more probable that the change would be made to "son of the carpenter" because, unlike in the Jewish world, Greco-Roman persons, in particular the more elite among them, saw such manual labor as demeaning. Celsus, for example, in his polemic against Christianity, sneers that this religion was founded by a carpenter (see Origen, *C. Cels.* 6.34, 36). In addition, it is hardly likely that the phrase "the son of Mary" would have been added later to this text, yet some texts have simply "of the carpenter, the son."[197]

The phrase "son of Mary" may reveal one reason why Jesus' words, however wise, were not immediately received by the audience. How could a child of undistinguished or even dubious origins (was Joseph really the father?) be able to interpret the Torah like this? It is Mark alone who records that Jesus placed his own family among those who stumbled over his apparently ordinary or abnormal origins.[198] More importantly, the phrase "son of Mary" may itself be intended as a slur (cf. Judg. 11:1-2).[199] Or it may simply indicate that Joseph is deceased, although it was a regular Jewish practice to continue to identify a child by the name of his deceased father, using the patronymic (see *b. Yoma* 38b).[200] It is then likely that we are dealing with a slur here.

Only in Mark 6:3 and Matt. 13:55 are Jesus' brothers referred to by name. There have been three views concerning the relationship of these brothers and his sisters to Jesus. The most widely held view in the Western church was that of Saint Jerome, which he promulgated in 382 in a treatise against Helvidius where he asserts that the Lord's brothers are cousins, being the children of a sister of Mary. The prominence of this view in later church history was largely due to the fact that both Jerome and Augustine advocated it, though in their own times the matter was hotly debated. The view of Helvidius which prompted Jerome to speak was that they were Jesus' flesh and blood brothers, being the children of Mary and Joseph after the time of Jesus' birth. This view was also held by Tertullian and several minor figures from before the time of Helvidius (e.g., Bonosus in Sardica and Jovinian in Milan). Finally, there was the view put forth in 376-77 by Epiphanius, who held that these were children of Joseph by a previous marriage, a view also put forth in the *Gospel of Peter* and the *Gospel of*

---

197. Metzger, *TCGNT*, pp. 88-89. Interestingly the Palestinian Syriac simply has "the son of Mary."

198. Knowing the later reverence for the holy family, it is not plausible that Christians would have invented this saying.

199. Myers, p. 212; Taylor, p. 299.

200. See Schweizer, p. 124. On the likelihood of there being a slur here, see Marcus, *Mark 1–8*, pp. 374-75.

the Hebrews and the *Protevangelium of James*, and by Clement of Alexandria. It is hard to doubt that the views advocated by Jerome and Epiphanius arose because of the growing belief in the notion of the perpetual virginity of Mary as well as because of the increasing asceticism of the early medieval church.

The burden of proof must rest on those who wish to argue that the term "brothers" here means cousins, in view of the fact that: (1) the noun αδελφος seldom if ever is used to mean cousin (ανεψιος; cf. Col. 3:10) in the NT or in classical literature; (2) the view of Jerome has the further problem of entailing the belief that James the brother of the Lord = one of the Twelve = James the Less, son of Alphaeus, but this contradicts the plain sense of Mark 3:21, 31-35, which distinguishes Jesus' physical family members from the Twelve; (3) Jerome's view also involves the questionable assumption that John 19:25 is referring to two sisters in one family with the name of Mary such that Mary of Clopas was the sister of Mary the mother of Jesus.[201] The Epiphanian view labors under the difficulty that if Joseph previously had other sons, Jesus could not legally be his firstborn or first in line for the Davidic throne, and it also depends on very dubious and weak church traditions. The view of J. McHugh that these brothers are first cousins, being the children of Joseph's sister and brother, is more plausible but still labors under the difficulty that nothing in the text suggests such is the case. The phrases "the son of Mary" and "a brother of James . . ." are perfectly natural in view of the fact that James had other brothers than just Jesus and Jesus is *the* son of Mary in question in this particular discussion.[202] In fact, it could be argued that since there is only the one article in the phrase "the son of Mary and brother of James . . . ," Jesus had the same sort of relationship to both Mary and the brothers and sisters. There is little evidence to tell us whether or not the brothers in 6:3 and the men mentioned in 15:40 are different or the same; but James and Joses were very common names in the period and thus could easily be two different sets of brothers. I would suggest that Mark calls the James of 15:40 "the little" in order to distinguish him from the James previously mentioned in 6:3.

There is, of course, also a reference here to Jesus' sisters being there with them, which might mean present in the room. The verse concludes by saying that the audience was deeply scandalized by his remarks. The verb εσκανδαλιζοντο can be said to refer to a deep religious offense.[203] It is in the imperfect, suggesting an ongoing condition — they were taking offense, or were

---

201. For a detailed discussion of these issues, see my *Women*, pp. 88-90, and the notes there.

202. But see J. McHugh, *The Mother of Jesus in the New Testament* (London: Darton, Longman, Todd, 1975).

203. See E. Grasser, "Jesus in Nazareth (Mark VI.1-6a): Notes on the Redaction and Theology of St. Mark," *NTS* 16 (1969-70): 1-23.

being scandalized by him. It could perhaps also be translated "they were being caused to stumble" or "they were finding him to be a stumbling block."[204]

The "kinsmen" in v. 4 is perhaps to be taken as a reference to a wider circle of Jesus' kin than those just mentioned in v. 3. Thus we should see the saying in v. 4b as referring to groups ever diminishing in size — one's heredity territory, one's wider kinship group, and the members of one's own household. V. 4 is of interest to Mark in part because it reveals to us Jesus characterizing himself as a prophet, even if he is quoting a traditional maxim here (cf. John 4:44 and also the variant in *Gos. Thom.* 31 and P.Oxy. 1.5, which conflates this saying with the physician saying). Mark emphasizes that the lack of acceptance of Jesus involves not only his hometown but even the members of his own family. The saying also stresses that Jesus is operating in an honor and shame culture where one's public honor rating and the "face" one has in one's own home territory is important. Yet paradoxically Jesus must labor in a situation where those very persons who should most honor him give him the least "face." This must have cast a considerable cloud over Jesus' ministry in a culture where kinship ties and affirmations by one's kin were considered all-important, and where honoring parents involved accepting their evaluations of one's self and work.

V. 5 stresses that such was the unbelief in his hometown that Jesus was unable to do any mighty work there except lay hands on a few sick persons and heal them. The focus, then, is not so much on Jesus' inability as on the amazing lack of faith, but clearly Mark sees a connection between faith and healing, as the previous stories in the second half of Mark 5 show. We may perhaps put it this way — lack of faith limits the reception of help readily available from Jesus.[205] "Jesus was not free to exercise his power *in these circumstances.*"[206] The story ends in v. 6, as they so often do, with amazement or wonder, only uniquely in this case it is said not to be the crowd but Jesus who is amazed at the unbelief he encountered in what should have been a friendly environment. If the story in Luke 4 is in fact a different record of this same occasion, then it is in order to point out that the reaction to Jesus in Nazareth was more hostile than even Mark suggests. In any event, the second major section of Mark's Gospel ends like the first with the rejection of Jesus, and also like the first instance, Jesus responds by withdrawing, spending time with the Twelve, and as we shall see, commissioning them to go forth on their own, two by two.

---

204. See Hooker, p. 153.
205. See Painter, p. 97.
206. Lane, p. 204.

Bridging the Horizons

Mark 3:7-12 is an interesting summary passage on several accounts. For one thing it reveals a Jesus who, while certainly a healer, apparently does not see that as the real focus of his ministry. He will be depicted as repeatedly trying to get away from crowds clamoring for a miracle so that he can focus on preaching and teaching, usually at his next stopping place. This presentation, however, should not lead us to minimize the miraculous in these stories, including the presentation of exorcisms. It is interesting that in a postmodern age there is now less resistance to and more curiosity about the notion of the reality of supernatural evil and supernatural good than in the four decades preceding the nineties. Television shows and movies involving angels, extraterrestrials, God, the devil, demons, witches, and the like are not uncommon. Filmmakers are even braving the subject of heaven and hell in films like the Robin Williams movie *What Dreams May Come.*

Thus the presentation of Jesus' confrontation with supernatural evil may not only warrant close scrutiny, but may garner a good deal of interest if taught and preached on today. One of the main things that Jesus' confrontation with demons suggests is that the value of character references depends on the character of the referee. The naming of Jesus by the demons reveals some of the truth about Jesus, but he is not keen to have that source accredit him. Could it be that rumors of these sorts of encounters are what prompted the Jewish authorities to suggest that Jesus was in league with the devil? After all, if both the demons and Jesus' disciples acclaim Jesus to be the same thing, what are outsiders to think? It is worth reminding ourselves that Mark operates with an apocalyptic outlook on life, which means he believes that the major players affecting human lives, human history, even human governments are supernatural. If we were to adopt this viewpoint, how would it change the way we evaluate such matters today?

In the presentation of the appointing of the Twelve, D. English noted three features of Mark 3:13-19 that deserve comment: (1) Jesus called his disciples away from ordinary life to a place where they could be apart and alone with him; (2) Jesus picked those he wanted; and (3) they actually came.[207] The narrative suggests but does not clearly state that there was a larger crowd of followers out of which Jesus picked the Twelve, a conclusion Luke 6:13 supports. Notice the stress in the Markan account on Jesus choosing the Twelve so that they might be *with* him. Mark's presentation of Jesus reveals a flesh and blood human being who had needs for human relationship just like the rest of us. Besides the task of being with Jesus, the Twelve also had the tasks Jesus had, though the best manuscripts do not add that they, like Jesus, had the job of

---

207. D. English, *The Message of Mark* (Downers Grove: InterVarsity, 1992), p. 83.

healing the sick. The disciples are named, and there is something foreboding about a list which begins with someone who would deny Jesus three times (Peter) and ends with the one who would betray him (Judas), as the text here already makes clear. The inner circle hardly looks like a perfect circle of friends. While this presents us with a gloomy picture, it could be seen as a sort of good news, namely, that if Jesus can pick this lot, he can also use us, as imperfect as we may be.

Here in 3:21, 31-35, and again at the beginning of Mark 6, we confront a very difficult issue. We are dealing with the inability of people who ought to understand Jesus to do so. In particular, we are dealing with members of Jesus' own family badly misunderstanding him. There is independent confirmation of this lack of understanding and faith in Jesus by members of his family in John 7:5. Perhaps many of us have encountered a similar difficulty with some member or members of our own family, though perhaps not to the degree Jesus experienced it. From the narrative in Mark 3, the problem may have been exacerbated by the fact that Jesus said his true or real family was whoever did the will of God, whoever was his true disciple.

In our age many churches are emphasizing that they are "family" churches, by which is meant churches which nurture the nuclear family. Jesus, however, offers us a different set of priorities. The family of faith, not the nuclear family, must come first. If the nuclear family is part of the family of faith, then well and good, one may concentrate in the first instance on one's obligations to one's physical family as part of one's commitment to the family of faith. But if this is not the case, the coming of Christ into one family member's life may cause division rather than unity when the Christian tries to put Christ and Christian priorities first. At one point Jesus' disciples, at Mark 10:28-31, remind Jesus that they have had to leave their families behind to follow him. Jesus tells them they have brothers and sisters and other relatives aplenty in the family of faith, and indeed in the age to come. Jesus' point is that with the dominion of God breaking in, it is the forever family of God, not the physical family (which is a temporal institution), that should be first priority. This is, of course, not the message many Christian family counselors are offering up today, but that is in part because the church has left behind the vital eschatological outlook of Jesus and focused instead on the things of this world and this age.

If being called "mad," likely by family members, was not galling enough, 3:22-30 confronts us with the fact that some of Jesus' interlocutors saw him as possessed and in league with the devil. It is hard to know whether this charge was meant absolutely seriously or whether it was rhetoric employed by his opponents to prevent people from becoming Jesus' adherents. In any case, these opponents are not neutral about what Jesus is doing, and it is hard to doubt that this accusation in large measure arose out of Jesus being an exorcist. C. S. Lewis, in his famous *Screwtape Letters*, remarked that it is the great trick or smoke screen of the devil to convince intelligent people that he does not exist. Yet it is hard to doubt that evil beyond mere human devising exists when one considers some of the atrocities that were perpetrated in the so-called "modern, civilized" twentieth century, for example, during WWII against the Jews in the concentration camps.

It is possible to get to a point where one calls evil good and good evil, and Jesus warns his audience sternly against calling the work of God's Spirit the work of some evil spirit. Blasphemy is defined not as saying this or that sort of curse formula or swearword, but of actually attributing the work of God to the devil. Helpfully, Marcus says: "Pastors who counsel such troubled souls that, if they are worried about having blasphemed against the Holy Spirit, they probably have not done so, have good biblical grounds for their position. In the Markan context blasphemy against the Spirit means the sort of total, malignant opposition to Jesus that twists all the evidence of his life-giving power into evidence that he is demonically possessed (see 3.22, 30); those guilty of such blasphemy would not be overly concerned about having committed it."[208]

English says about such an action: "There is no forgiveness here because such an attitude is incapable of seeking it. What makes it worst of all is that these are the informed and educated religious leaders."[209] His conclusion about what we may learn from this story is equally apt: "Intellectual grasp and academic ability are not of themselves signs of saving faith or perceptive spirit. They can equally provide ample skill to deflect the challenge of gospel truth."[210]

The parable of the sower in Mark 4 is a classic example which makes clear that sharp distinctions between parable and allegory regarding early Jewish *meshalim* are just not possible. We may, however, distinguish between allegorical elements in a parable, allegorizing methods of interpreting nonallegorical parables, and finally proper allegories. It is the first of these that we seem to have in Mark 4. What is remarkable about this likely authentic parable is that it paints a painfully honest picture of Jesus' ministry. There were many failures and some very notable successes. Even more to the point, the parable reminds us that in each case the sower and the seed are the same, so what makes the difference in the results is the soil the seed falls into. In other words, the recipients and their condition determine the reception.

This is a humbling truth, for as much as those of us who are teachers and preachers would like to think that it is the sower or the way he plants or presents the seed that determines the matter, this is basically not the case. The parable also makes evident that initial positive responses may be superficial ones, and furthermore that there are cares and concerns that can crowd out the good

---

208. Marcus, *Mark 1–8*, p. 284.
209. English, p. 89.
210. English, p. 91.

effects of the seed. Once the seed is sown, the good results do not thereby become automatic. Finally, we must always bear in mind that Jesus' parables are about the inbreaking of God's saving reign into human history. They are not lessons in agriculture or even in human culture, and the places in the parable that seem least lifelike are probably where the major theological and ethical points are being made. Yet these parables do bear witness to the social realities that Jesus had to deal with.

Ostracism on the basis of illness or possession was a common phenomenon in antiquity, and still is today. Witness the case of Ryan White, a young man who lived in the midwestern United States who had contracted AIDS through a blood transfusion. Not only was he shunned for fear that the illness was easily communicated to others, but even those who had been his friends stopped going to school with him, and the reaction of the church was hardly better. Fear, not faith, ruled the behavior of many of those around him. It was suggested that the boy be confined or quarantined. It was no different with the Gerasene demoniac. He had been forced to live in a cemetery. People had tried to chain him down, but he had been too strong for them. Yet, of course, this was not Jesus' reaction to the demoniac. He was not worried about being contaminated, harmed, or made unclean, but was concerned about the man getting the cure he needed. He was not concerned about his reputation or how his actions would look. He was indeed the Great Physician. He did the right thing, which was in this case the controversial thing.

There are two further major stories in Mark 5, one about Jairus's daughter and one about a woman with a flow of blood, which continue to show where Jesus' primary concerns lay. Jesus' relationship with women, even unknown and unclean women, is one of the things which most sets him apart from various of his Jewish male contemporaries, as I have stressed at length elsewhere.[211] It is no surprise that Jesus raised the eyebrows and the ire of a patriarchal culture in the way he related to women, often with flagrant disregard for customs about not having contact with nonfamily members who are female, and not just customs, for Jesus also violated various of the taboos about ritual impurity. Furthermore, we have no evidence that Jesus ever observed the rules for being cleansed of ritual impurity. These stories provide an acted-out parable of the teaching of Jesus found in Mark 7, in which Jesus declares that only what comes from the heart makes someone impure. Both his actions and his words suggest that Jesus believed that new occasions teach new duties, that God's inbreaking realm had changed the rules of the game.

The old saying "familiarity breeds contempt" seems to have been coined for just such an instance as is recorded in Mark 6:1-6. Jesus is not appreciated for the prophetic figure he is by those who ought by rights to most appreciate

---

211. See my *Women in the Ministry of Jesus.*

him — his family and hometown folks. The problem with hometown folks is that they know both too much and too little about a person. What they know has to do with their memories of what a person was like while growing up and becoming an adult. Once one has left town and gone elsewhere, they know little about what is or is not true about the person over that period of time. Therefore they continue to evaluate the person on the basis of old information. The reaction to Jesus' preaching assumes that Jesus couldn't possibly know more than the other locals about the Scriptures, since he received the same sort of synagogue training they did. He is also judged on the basis of his lineage, indeed, on the basis of his possibly questionable lineage. In a world where gender, geography, and generation were thought to determine one's identity, Jesus' audience is offended that he seems to be claiming he knows more than they do, more than he ought to on the basis of his family and geographical heritage. Notice that the lack of faith in Jesus affected the degree to which he was able to help them, presumably whether by teaching or by miracles. While faith in itself does not necessarily produce a miracle, unfaith can impede one from happening, it appears.

IX. The Tests of Discipleship; the Trials of God's Anointed One (6:6b–8:38)

The third long section of Mark's Gospel focuses on a period of time in which Jesus sent out his disciples as his agents and saw John the Baptist taken off the scene, and perhaps consequently also on a time when Jesus performed the same sorts of tasks as before, only now chiefly beyond the borders of Galilee.[1] As such, we are perhaps meant to sense the rising tide of opposition against Jesus, having now been rejected not only in Galilee but even in his own home territory. Mark 6:6b must be seen as transitional, and the next major section actually encompasses 6:7–8:26, leading up to the climactic utterances at Caesarea Philippi, which in turn are followed by the announcement of the coming passion.

Each of the three major sections in the first half of Mark (1:16–3:12; 3:13–6:6; 6:7–8:26) opens with a story about the disciples (1:16-20; 3:1-19; 6:7-13), and each draws to a close with a tale about the negative response to Jesus' ongoing ministry (3:1-6; 6:1-6a; 8:14-21). There is a summary or transitional statement as well that reminds us of the character of Jesus' ministry at the end of each section or, one could argue, at the beginning of the following section (3:7-12; 6:6b; 8:22-26). But since it is transitional, it points both ways.[2]

From a biographical point of view, Jesus will continue to be the central character in this section, for even the longer story about the demise of the Baptist is prompted by a connection with Jesus and serves as a foreshadowing of the violent end that is in store for Jesus, and also provides the rationale for Jesus' leaving the Galilean region for a more extended period of time. It must be re-

---

1. See W. Lane, *The Gospel of Mark* (Grand Rapids: Eerdmans, 1974), p. 210.
2. See R. Guelich, *Mark 1–8.26* (Waco: Word, 1989), p. 316.

membered that within the narrative itself, the question of Jesus' identity, as raised by his deeds and words, has still not been definitely answered even for the disciples, a climax that will not come until 8:27-30, and it is only after that point that Mark can begin to explain why Jesus must die.[3]

Some have been concerned about the redundancy of some of the stories in this section (e.g., the feeding of the four thousand after the feeding of the five thousand), but repetition was an important pedagogical and rhetorical device and was often used in ancient biographies, not least because they would be read aloud and only by repetition would their major themes be remembered or made clear. Also, we are meant to see Jesus addressing a somewhat different audience in this section of the Gospel. If the parable of the sower is indeed paradigmatic for the Gospel, then we are seeing the Sower scatter seed in different soil in this section of Mark. Perhaps one can argue that the story of "the Gerasene demoniac and his preaching (5.1-20) may have set the stage for Jesus' healing of the Deaf Mute (7.31-37) and a second Feeding (8.1-9) in the area of the Decapolis preceded by a journey through Tyre (7.24-30) and Sidon (7.31 cf. 3.8) that clearly put Jesus in touch with Gentiles (cf. 7.26, 'a Greek'; 8.3, 'from afar'). These stories all follow a critical discussion (7.1-13; 14-23) about the nature of the purity laws, the social boundaries that set off Jew from Jew and not least Jew from Gentile."[4] Jesus, then, is seen as not merely one who crosses boundaries, but as one who does so on principle. The coming of the dominion of God has made obsolescent the boundary-defining rules found in the Levitical code. This undoubtedly would have resonated well with Mark's largely Gentile audience, even though Jesus does not so much evangelize the Gentile world in Mark as he paves the way for such contacts to be made by helping various Gentiles in need.[5]

The detailed analysis by J. E. Phelan finds a concentric structure in 6:30–8:10 as follows:

A   Feeding of the five thousand (6:30-44)

  B   Walking on water/Healing the sick (6:45-56)

    C Conflict on tradition (7:1-23)

  B′   Syrophoenician woman/Healing of deaf and dumb man (7:24-37)

  A′   Feeding of the four thousand (8:1-10)

---

3. See pp. 36-37 above in the introduction.

4. Guelich, p. 317.

5. I would suggest that Mark is indeed, as an ancient biographer, trying to avoid historical anachronism, while at the same time building a bridge between the historical Jesus' efforts and his own work as an Evangelist to reach Gentiles through this Gospel. He does so by showing Jesus' willingness to help non-Jewish Semites, and even Gentiles.

As Phelan notes, in such a chiastic or concentric structure the outer elements in a sense help exegete each other, but the central, or C, element provides as it were the key theological rationale for Jesus' going forth into Gentile regions and dealing with non-Jewish people — if all foods are clean, then by extension all persons may be as well, at least through contact with Jesus.[6] Another, similar way of analyzing this section also emphasizes an intricate structure of parallel narratives. There is the feeding of the crowds twice (6:32-45; 8:1-10), disputes with Pharisees (7:1-23; 8:11-13), and private healing narratives (7:31-37; 8:22-26).[7] One may suspect that this arrangement serves a pedagogical purpose of some kind, hammering home by repetition the kinds of things Jesus did.

Marcus is right that the overall tone of this section of Mark's Gospel is positive. But while the disciples actually accomplish a good deal in these stories, they also demonstrate a low spiritual IQ at various junctures, asking dumb questions and even manifesting the sort of hard-heartedness previously only seen amongst the Pharisees.[8]

TRANSLATION — 6:6b–8:38

And he went around the circuit of the villages teaching. And he called the Twelve and began to send them two by two and he gave to each one power/authority over the unclean spirits. And he charged them in order that they would not take [anything] on the road with them except only a staff — not bread, not a bag, not a money belt, but wearing sandals and wearing two cloaks. And he said to them, "Whenever, if you enter in to a house, remain there until you leave there. And whoever in that place does not receive you nor is listening to you, as you are leaving there shake off the dust under your feet as a witness unto them." And going out they preached in order that they would repent, and they cast out many demons, and anointed with oil many sick persons and healed.

And King Herod heard, for his name was well known, and said that "John the Baptizer is raised from the dead and because of this the power was at work within him." But others said that he is Elijah. But still others said that he was a prophet like one of the [old] prophets. But Herod hearing said, "John the one I myself beheaded, has been raised." For the same Herod sending arrested John and bound him in prison because of Herodias the wife of Philip his brother, because he married her. For John said to Herod that "It is not permitted to have the wife of your brother." But Herodias

---

6. See J. E. Phelan, "Rhetoric and Meaning in Mark 6.30–8.10" (Ph.D. diss., Northwestern University, 1985), pp. 207-10.

7. See below and see M. Hooker, *The Gospel according to Mark* (Peabody, Mass.: Hendrickson, 1991), p. 154.

8. J. Marcus, *Mark 1–8* (New York: Doubleday, 1999), p. 381.

resented him and wished to kill him, and was not able. For Herod feared John, know-
ing he was a righteous and holy man, and he kept him safe, and hearing him was
much puzzled, [but] gladly heard him. And a suitable day came about when Herod
for his birthday made a dinner for his nobility and the senior officers and the first cit-
izens of Galilee. And coming in and dancing, the daughter of Herodias⁹ pleased
Herod and those dining with him. The king said to the girl, "Ask me whatever you
wish, and I will give it to you." And he took a strong oath. "Whatever you ask me I
will give you, up to half of my kingdom." And going out to her mother she said,
"What shall I ask?" But she said, "the head of John the Baptizer." And immediately
entering in with haste she asked saying: "I wish that at once you give me upon a dish
the head of John the Baptizer." And being deeply distressed the king, because of the
oaths and those reclining with him did not wish to break his word to her. And imme-
diately the king sending a courier commanded him to bring his head. And entering in
he beheaded him in the prison and brought his head upon a dish and he gave it to the
girl and the girl gave it to her mother. And hearing about it his disciples went and
took his body and buried him in a tomb.

And the apostles gathered together around Jesus and reported to him every-
thing that they did and that they taught. And he says to them, "Come away alone
with me to a deserted place and rest a little." For there were many coming and go-
ing and they did not have time even to eat. And they went in the boat to a deserted
place alone. And they saw them going and many recognized them, and on foot they
ran from all the cities to there and arrived before them. And coming out [of the
boat] he saw a great crowd and he had compassion on them because they were like
sheep not having a shepherd, and he began to teach them much. And already it was
very late, [so] the disciples coming to him said: "This is a deserted place, and al-
ready many hours have passed. Send them away in order that entering into the
surrounding fields and villages they may buy themselves something to eat." But
answering he said to them: "You give them something to eat." And they say to him:
"Shall we go spend 200 denarii for bread and give it to them to eat?" But he says to
them, "How much bread do you have? Go see." And knowing they say, "Five, and
two fish." And he commanded them to make them all recline in groups on the green
grass. And they sat down in groups by hundreds and by fifties. And taking the five
loaves and two fish, looking up into heaven he blessed and broke the loaves and
gave to the disciples in order that they might serve them, and the two fish he di-
vided among all. And all ate and were satisfied. And they took twelve basketfuls of
fragments and scraps of fish, and those eating were five thousand men.

---

9. Various manuscripts seem to identify the daughter as Herodias, but v. 24 makes
quite clear that the girl is the daughter of Herodias, and in any event we know from other
sources the daughter's name was Salome. This is one of those cases where the more difficult
reading (with αυτου) is in fact too difficult to be original, despite good external support with
A, B, D, and others. But see Metzger, *TCGNT*, pp. 89-90.

And immediately he compelled his disciples to get into the boat and go ahead unto the far side, to Bethsaida, while he himself dismisses the crowd. And saying farewell to them he went up unto a mountain to pray. And when evening came the boat was in the middle of the sea, and he alone upon the land. And seeing them straining in the rowing, for the wind was contrary to them, he comes to them during the fourth watch of the night, walking upon the sea; and he wished to pass them. But they, seeing him walking upon the sea, thought he was a ghost (phantasm) and screamed. For everyone saw him and they were troubled. But immediately he spoke with them and says to them, "Courage, it's me; do not fear." And he went up into the boat to them and the wind dropped. And they were very astounded within themselves, for they did not understand about the bread, but their hearts were hardened.

And crossing over they came unto the land at Gennesaret and anchored. And coming out of the boat immediately they were recognizing him and running about that whole country and they began [to bring] upon stretchers the ill, having to carry them where they heard he is. And wherever he entered into villages or cities or farms, they laid the ailing in the marketplace and begged him in order that they might touch even the fringe/edge of his outer garment, and those who touched him were made well.

7 And the Pharisees gather around him and some of the scribes coming from Jerusalem and seeing some of his disciples who had "common" hands, that is unwashed, they ate the bread (for the Pharisees and all the Jews unless they wash diligently[10] their hands, they do not eat, keeping the traditions of the elders, and from the marketplace unless they wash they do not eat [anything], and many other are the traditions they keep e.g. washing wine cups and vessels and copper utensils [and beds][11] —) and the Pharisees and scribes asked him, "For what reason do your disciples not live according to the traditions of the elders, but eat the bread with common hands?" But he said to them: "Well did Isaiah prophesy concerning you actors as it is written 'This people honor me with lips but their hearts are far away from me. In vain do they worship me, teaching as [solid] teachings the commandments of human beings.' Neglecting the commandment of God you keep the traditions of human beings." And he said to them, "How well do you annul the commandment of God, in order to uphold your traditions. For Moses said, 'Honor your father and your mother' and 'The one speaking evil words about father or mother, let him be put to death.' But you say, 'If a person says to father or mother,

---

10. The word πυγμη means literally "with a fist," but we seem to be dealing with an idiom meaning in effect diligently (or as we would say, "two-fisted"). The metaphorical sense was not understood by various copyists who omitted the word. See Metzger, *TCGNT,* p. 93.

11. Various copyists could not understand the logic of adding beds at this point, perhaps unaware that, for instance, menstrual blood had to be cleaned from a bed or it was ritually unclean. Cf. Lev. 15 and see Metzger, *TCGNT,* p. 93.

Corban (which means Dedicated), whatever you might have benefited from me'
you do not permit him to do anything for father or mother, annulling the word of
God with your tradition you have passed on, and many similar such things you
do."

And speaking again to the crowd he said to them, "Listen to me everyone and
understand. Nothing from outside a person entering into them is able to make
them common (unclean). But that coming out from within a person defiles the
person." And when he entered into the house from the crowds, his disciples asked
him about the figurative saying. And he says to them, "Are you also without understanding? Do you not know that every outside thing entering into a person is not
able to make him common/unclean, because it does not enter into his heart but
into the stomach and then goes out into the latrine?" (Thus making clean all
foods.) But he said, "That which comes out from a person makes that person unclean. For from inside, from the heart of humans comes forth evil thoughts, sexual
sins, thefts, murderers, adulteries, various forms of greed, various kinds of mali-
ciousness, deceit, indecencies, the evil eye, blasphemy, arrogance, folly. All this evil
comes out from inside and defiles the person."

But rising up he went from there unto the area of Tyre and entering into a
house he wished no one to know, and he was not able to escape. But immediately a
woman hearing about him, whose daughter had an unclean spirit, came, she fell
down at his feet. But the woman was a Gentile, Syrophoenician by birth. And she
asked him that he cast the demon out of her daughter. And he said to her, "Permit
the children to be fed first, for it is not good to take the bread of the children and
throw it to the dogs." But she answered and says to him, "Sir, even the dogs under
the table eat from the crumbs of the children." And he said to her, "For this saying,
you may go, the demon is cast out from your daughter." And leaving the house unto
her home, she found the child lying on the bed and the demon had gone out.

And again coming out from the region of Tyre he went through Sidon unto
the Sea of Galilee between the region of the Decapolis. And they brought him deaf
and dumb, and they entreated him to lay his hands on him. And taking him aside
from the crowd alone he put his fingers in his ear and spitting touched his tongue,
and looking into heaven he groaned and he says to him, "Ephatha" (which means
be opened). And [immediately] his ears heard and the ligament of his tongue was
loosened, and he spoke properly. And he commanded them in order that they not
say anything. But however much he commanded them, that much more they proclaimed it. Beyond measure they were astounded, saying, "He does all things well,
even making the deaf to hear, and the dumb to speak."

8   In those days there was again a large crowd having nothing to eat, calling
the disciples to himself he says to them, "I am deeply moved by the crowd because
already three days they stayed with me and they have not anything to eat. And if I
send away the hungry into their houses they will faint in the road. And some of
them have come from afar." And his disciples answered him, "How will we be able

to satisfy them here with bread in the desert?" And he asked them, "How much bread do you have?" They said, "Seven [loaves]." And he orders the crowd to recline on the earth, and taking the seven breads, giving thanks, he broke it and gave it to his disciples in order that they might distribute and serve food to the crowd. And they had a few fish. And blessing them he said to also distribute them. And they ate and were filled, and there was a surplus of seven basketfuls of pieces. But there were about four thousand. And he dismissed them. And immediately he got into the boat with his disciples, he went into the region of Dalmanutha.[12]

And the Pharisees came and began to dispute with him, seeking from him signs from heaven, testing him. And groaning in his spirit he says, "Why does this generation seek a sign? Amen I say to you, if ever a sign will be given to this generation." And he left them again getting into [the boat] he went to the other side.

And they forgot to take bread, and they only had one loaf with them in the boat. And he instructed them, saying, "Beware, look out for the leaven of the Pharisees and the leaven of Herod."[13] *And they discussed among one another, "We have no bread." And knowing it he says to them: "Why are you still dialoguing about not having bread? Do you neither perceive nor understand? Have you hardened your hearts? Having eyes do you not see and having ears do you not hear? Do you not remember when I broke the five loaves for five thousand people, how many baskets of pieces did you collect?" They say to him, "Twelve." "When the seven [were given] to the four thousand how many baskets of pieces did you collect?" And they say to him, "Seven." And he said to them, "Do you not yet get it?"*

And they come into Bethsaida. And they bring to him a blind person and entreat him so he will touch him. And taking hold of the hand of the blind he led him outside the village, and spit on his eyes, laying his hands on him, he asks him, "Do you see anything?" And looking up he said, "I see people, that look like trees walking around." And again he put his hands upon his eyes, and he saw clearly, and was restored, and he saw everything clearly. Then he sent him away to his home, saying, "Do not even go into the village."

A. Mission Possible (6:6b-13)

It is difficult to know whether 6:6b-13 should be taken with what precedes or, more probably, with what follows (see above). It makes sense that Jesus might

---

12. Clearly enough various scribes were puzzled by the reference to Dalmanutha, and still today it is a place of uncertain locale. This is why a few copyists substitute a different location such as Magdala in Θ. See Metzger, *TCGNT,* p. 97.

13. At an early date, perhaps as early as the third century (see p45, W, cop[sa]), some copiers changed the reading to the Herodians, presumably because they had been mentioned earlier in 3:6 and come up again at 12:13. See Metzger, *TCGNT,* p. 98.

take on a preaching tour in the surrounding areas to Galilee, having been rejected at home. Notice that we are told he went around teaching, which goes
very well with what follows about the commissioning of the disciples to do
ministry. Here we do indeed have an example of intercalation, for the true sequel to 6:6b-13 is found in vv. 30ff. Many scholars have noted the various parallels between the second and third sections of Mark. Notice that 3:1-6 parallels
6:1-6 in speaking about the rejection of Jesus, and in both cases this is followed
up by a statement about ministry to a wide variety of people and the empower-
ing of the Twelve (cf. 3:7-12 and 3:13-19, the latter of which is paralleled in
6:6b-13). At 6:7, as at 3:15, the disciples are given authority or power (εξουσια)
over unclean spirits. The Twelve are clearly seen as an extension of Jesus' own
ministry. They are his authorized agents.[14] It is worth stressing, especially in
view of the frequent negative comments about the disciples that increasingly
crop up after this point, that 6:6b-13 makes clear that the disciples did do some
positive things in obedience to Jesus' commissioning. They seem to be better at
doing the ministry than understanding what it is all about. In Mark 3–5 we see
the fulfillment of their calling to be with Jesus, and in Mark 6 we see the fulfillment of the calling to go forth and act like Jesus (cf. 3:14-15).[15]

It was customary to send messengers in pairs because of the OT law requiring the testimony of two witnesses to validate the truthfulness of any statement (cf. Deut. 17:6; 19:15; Num. 35:30; b. Sanh. 26a and 43a). Another reason
Jesus sent the disciples out in pairs may have been because there were certainly
two and possibly three pairs of brothers among the Twelve. Hooker points out
that v. 11 indicates the pair would be called upon to give formal testimony that
those who refuse to hear are under judgment.[16] As it stands, the text reads as
though we are to see in this commissioning a foreshadowing of the eventual
post-Easter roles of the disciples, but this commission during the ministry was
apparently unique and limited in scope. Thus the provisions about clothing
and eating were never taken in the early church to be generally applicable to all
missionary ventures.[17]

14. See pp. 150-53 above and L. Hurtado, *Mark* (New York: Harper & Row, 1983), pp.
81-85.

15. See C. Myers, *Binding the Strong Man: A Political Reading of Mark's Story of Jesus*
(Maryknoll, N.Y.: Orbis, 1988), p. 213.

16. Hooker, p. 156.

17. See Lane, p. 207. But Marcus, p. 383, points to Acts 13:1-3. On the whole Lane
seems to be right on this point.

Wandering Itinerants and Warranted Emphases

Much has been made of G. Theissen's theory that there were something like two subsets to the Jesus movement. The one was the radical itinerants for whom the radical advice found in Mark 6 (and elsewhere) applied, the other was the more sedentary supporters who aspired to less spiritual athleticism.[18] This theory has been critiqued in various ways, but here it is in order to consider Myers's critique. In the first place, he points out that the advice given here to the Twelve is not unique to this mission or this group of missionaries. Rather it is for the "way," which is to say for the discipleship lifestyle in general (6:8). The proof of this is of course that Jesus makes equally radical demands of those not among the Twelve in this Gospel (see 10:21-22).[19] Myers goes on to stress that heroic asceticism (à la medieval mendicants) is also not what Jesus is calling his disciples to here. They are not renouncing food and clothing in general but rather relying on the hospitality of their hosts wherever they go. Jesus' own fellowshipping with various sorts of people also must count against any theory of his inculcating radical itinerant asceticism. Rather, what is happening here is the Twelve, "like Jesus who has just been renounced in his own 'home' are to take on the status of a sojourner in the land. We might note that the 'donning of sandals' [i]s a Markan metaphor for discipleship (. . . 1.7)."[20] What this narrative does suggest to the Markan community is that both itinerant ministry and hospitality, both evangelism and fellowship, are crucial to the survival of the community as a social entity.

But it is not just this narrative in Mark 6 by which Mark reveals his true sociological colors. One may also profitably read the story of the beheading of John as Mark's political parody of the corrupt government in Galilee, revealing what the corrosive influence or leaven of Herod is really all about. Here again Myers is on target when he says: "Mark accurately describes the inner circle of power as an incestuous relationship involving governmental, military, and commercial interest."[21] The guest list for the birthday party reveals the court and its web of power extending into the military and into the commercial sector.[22] The parody of course comes when Mark reveals that in the midst of all these powerful men the Baptist's fate is determined by a dancing girl and a foolish oath made to her.[23] "A more sarcastic social caricature could not have been spun by the bitterest Galilean peasant! Yet it stands well within the biblical tradition that pits arrogant kings against truth-telling prophets."[24]

Yet, what Myers overlooks is that the basis of this parody is Mark's apocalyptic outlook, an outlook on Roman government and its client rulers not much different from that found in Revelation. Those earthly kings and kingdoms are so corrupt that, like Israel under Ahab, they are fit only to be destroyed and/or replaced. And what will replace them in Mark's theology is the dominion of God which prophets like John and Jesus make clear is

---

18. G. Theissen, *The Sociology of Early Palestinian Christianity* (Philadelphia: Fortress, 1978).

19. Myers, p. 213.

20. Myers, p. 213.

21. Myers, p. 216.

22. See A. N. Sherwin-White, *Roman Society and Roman Law in the New Testament* (Oxford: Oxford University Press, 1963), p. 137.

23. Myers, p. 216.

24. Myers, p. 216.

breaking in, for which pains they lose their lives. Myers puts it this way: "the political destiny of those who proclaim repentance and a new order is always the same. Now we can understand why the John story has been inserted into the narrative of the apostles' mission: insofar as they inherit this mission, they inherit its destiny."[25] Thus this intercalation of the sending and return of the Twelve with the story of the Baptist's death is not a haphazard thing at all. Those who go out proclaiming that God is coming to rule are as likely to be shunned or come back dead as they are to come back alive (witness the Baptist). The ominous clouds of an apocalyptic darkness through which is breaking in only the light that comes from heaven characterize this narrative. Thus in the end Mark offers up neither a mere radical ethic or a call to radical politics, but an eschatological and apocalyptic scenario in which God's messengers can expect to suffer and die for the message. This is an extremely appropriate message if Mark is writing during or just after the Neronian persecutions to those Christians who are still in Rome.

We are told at v. 7 that Jesus began to send them out two by two. The word "apostle" is not used here, but the verbal equivalent is. The verb εδιδου is notable for it is third-person singular, which suggests a translation "he gave to each one individually authority over unclean spirits." It is interesting that this is mentioned first, but perhaps the reason is that this, more than the preaching, manifested that the kingdom had come in power, and Mark's concept of the inbreaking of the eschatological time is dynamic, not merely a matter of proclamation. The control of demons was to be central to both Jesus' and his agents' ministries.[26]

The disciples are allowed to take a staff and sandals but not bread or money belt, nor two tunics, nor a bag (which may refer to the beggar's bag).[27] The point then would be that there was to be no begging of money or food by the disciples: they were not to be like various itinerant Greek philosophers or rhetors (nor like the later begging mendicants). The reason for the distinctions here seems to be that Jesus is saying take only what is absolutely necessary, like a staff for fending off bandits or wild animals, and sandals and a basic tunic. "Short distances between Galilean towns make unnecessary the taking of bread for roadside nourishment, of a bag in which to carry the bread, and an extra tunic for warmth while sleeping outdoors between towns and cities. Hospitality in the towns will provide bread and bed and thus eliminate the need of small change for purchasing bread and staying at inns (cf. Acts 9.30; 16.15, 40; 17.5-7; 18.1-3)."[28]

A possible parallel to this instruction can be found in *m. Ber.* 9.5, where a

25. Myers, p. 217.

26. Hooker, p. 156.

27. The χαλκον refers to copper money and thus small change.

28. R. H. Gundry, *Mark: A Commentary on His Apology for the Cross* (Grand Rapids: Eerdmans, 1993), pp. 307-8.

person is forbidden to enter the temple mount with staff, or sandals, or wallet, or dust on his feet. T. W. Manson suggested that Jesus' restrictions then reflect that he is sending them on a sacred errand.[29] More probably, the point was that the disciples were to rely on the standing system of ancient Near Eastern hospitality. We do not then find here a call to an ascetical lifestyle for the Twelve. M. Hengel has suggested that we have here an intentional parody of the frugality demanded by the Cynic itinerant preachers, for even they allowed taking bread and the beggar's bag. Possibly early Christianity saw itself as competing with other movements and here distinguishes itself from them.[30] But there are also interesting parallels with OT materials, for example, in Exod. 12:11 and Deut. 29:5-6.[31] V. 10 means they were not to take a better offer after already accepting hospitality in a home, perhaps from a poorer person. This would make clear that they were not in it for the money or perks. Schweizer also reminds us that Josephus seems to have known about Jewish cities and villages having what amounts to a social welfare worker providing food and clothing for wanderers (*War* 2.125).[32]

At this juncture we must face a serious problem for those who feel that harmonizing the various Gospel accounts is important. Matt. 10:9-10/Luke 9:3 both seem to prohibit even the sandals and the staff.[33] Thus the three accounts of this pericope differ in detail. At this juncture there does not seem to be any way to resolve this issue, and even from just an intertextual point of view it is hard to understand why both the First and Third Evangelists would have added such a further, more stringent demand.[34] Were their texts of Mark different from the earliest and best text we can now construct? This is certainly possible. The second tunic would be used to cover a person or to serve as something to sleep on if one were out in the open. But clearly Jesus envisions not a camping trip, but a reliance on the available hospitality.

Jesus says in v. 11 that if anyone doesn't welcome them or listen to them in a given region, they are to shake off the dust from under their feet as a witness to them. But what does this symbolic gesture mean? We know that it was customary for Jews to shake foreign dust off their clothes when they had been traveling outside the Holy Land (cf. *m. Ohol.* 2.3; *m. Tohar.* 4, 5l; *b. Šabb.* 15b).

29. T. W. Manson, *The Sayings of Jesus* (London: SCM, 1957), p. 181.

30. See M. Hengel, *The Charismatic Leader and His Followers* (New York: Crossroad, 1981), p. 28; cf. Guelich, p. 322.

31. Marcus, p. 389.

32. See the discussion by E. Schweizer, *The Good News according to Mark* (Atlanta: John Knox, 1971), p. 130.

33. For a close comparison with the Q material on the same subject, see now Marcus, pp. 386-89. In general, Mark's version of these instructions seems more lenient, though he is more pessimistic about the outcome of such ventures.

34. See Lane, pp. 207-8.

Thus perhaps the point is to treat such inhospitable people as foreigners, subject ultimately to God's judgment (cf. Acts 13:51; 18:6). It is interesting that manuscript A and a few others interpret this act in light of the Sodom and Gomorrah story, and so clearly see it as a symbolic judgment ritual. The point here seems in the main to be about not having any more to do with that region, an implicit judgment since this would also mean they would never again hear the good news about the dominion of God. "Jesus' words read ominously, coming so soon after the story of his own rejection in his home town."[35]

Notice that v. 12 says the apostles preach so that people would repent. Jesus' disciples, like their Master and the Baptist, seem to be involved in the same sort of eschatological preaching that requires repentance and turning back to God. They are also said to cure many sick and cast out demons. Demon possession and sickness are distinguished here, and notice that they require different sorts of remedies. Mark, it would appear, does not see demon possession as just another form of physical or even mental illness.

B. A Gruesome Banquet (6:14-29)

To some scholars this story about the fate of John the Baptist seems an odd historical interlude, or in this case a retrospective, that digresses from the story of Jesus' ministry, but this is not quite correct. It is the only story in the Gospel of any length that is not about Jesus, proving once more the author's clear biographical intent in this work. Had this been an historical monograph, there would surely have been more episodes such as we find here. What prompts this story is that, as we are told at v. 14, some thought Jesus was John the Baptizer redivivus.[36] As Painter suggests, this may mean that Jesus was relatively unknown until the Baptist was off the scene, and initially stood in the Baptist's shadow.[37] This story then clarifies matters for the Markan audience by distinguishing between the two men, while at the same time foreshadowing the sort of violent end that Jesus would also come to. 8:27ff. is, in addition, prepared for in this story, as is 9:9-13, which is in a sense the commentary on 6:14-29. Thus we would do well not to see this as some colorful digression but rather as a story which sets forth the theme that righteous persons often meet untimely ends in a dark and dangerous world. It also provides an historical explanation for Jesus' withdrawal to a solitary place for a while on more than one occasion when things got tense.

---

35. Hooker, p. 157.

36. As Gundry, p. 311, says, these inadequate identifications prepare us for the correct designation in 8:27-30.

37. J. Painter, *Mark's Gospel* (London: Routledge, 1997), p. 100.

In other words, this is the sort of tale that a biographer would want to tell to sharpen the historical focus of his narrative and prepare the reader for the events involving Jesus that would begin to be predicted in Mark 8. We may also surmise that in historical fact the death of John had a very significant effect on Jesus' ministry and view of himself and his future.[38] In any event, the Evangelist has done his best to highlight the similarities between this episode and the later violent death of his main character, Jesus, as C. Wolff has shown through the following parallels in the two stories and their sequence: (1) arrest, 6:17/14:46; 15:51; (2) death plot, 6:19/14:1; (3) fear, 6:20/11:18, 32; 12:12; 14:2; (4) innocent man executed under pressure, 6:26/15:10, 14-15; (5) burial, 6:29/15:45-46.[39] We may also note the parallels with other martyrological tales in 2 Macc. 6:18-31 and 4 Macc. 5:1–6:30.

Notice that in v. 14 Herod is called king, surely an ironic twist because, though Antipas ruled Galilee from 4 B.C. to A.D. 39 and had pretensions to be a king, it was precisely the request to be called king by Rome and everyone else, the request for the title, that eventually got him sent into exile in 39 by a paranoid Caligula. In fact, he was tetrarch of the region of Galilee and Perea. Antipas must not be seen as a good Jew. Besides his forbidden marriage to Herodias, his brother's wife,[40] which was prohibited according to Lev. 18:13 while the brother was still alive, Antipas also built his capital Tiberias on top of a pagan cemetery, something an observant Jew would never sanction. A good Jew would never even enter the city due to its uncleanness. In many ways he was a chip off the old block, being a son born to Herod the Great and his Samaritan wife Malthace in 20 B.C.[41]

It is clear from this story that Herod in fact does not know Jesus, though he knows something about him. He has heard the rumor that Jesus was John come back from the dead, a rumor that apparently originated in an attempt to explain where Jesus' power came from. The theory was that this power was at work in Jesus because he had come back from the dead. This way of putting things ("these powers are at work in him") is especially apropos for a Greco-Roman audience which believed in certain humans as conduits for divine power.

Notice that the other theories are that Jesus is Elijah or the eschatological prophet or one of the other prophets. There was indeed popular speculation, in

---

38. Notice that the story is told in the imperfect and aorist, not with the usual Markan historical present, suggesting the use of a source here. See Marcus, pp. 397-98.

39. C. Wolff, "Zur Bedeutung Johannes des Taufers im Markusevangeliums," *TLZ* 102 (1977): 857-65.

40. There is some dispute over this matter, for while Josephus says Antipas was married to Herodias, he also says Philip was married to Salome (*Ant.* 18.5.2).

41. See Guelich, p. 329.

light of Mal. 3:1; 4:5-6, that Elijah would return to announce the Day of the Lord. This latter description in some ways better suits the Baptist than Jesus and may explain why Jesus may have suggested that John was that Elijah figure (Matt. 11:14). It is worth pointing out that since Elijah was considered the patron saint of the poor and needy, this may be why some speculated that Jesus was Elijah.[42] But the portrait of John here as one who criticizes an improper marriage suits the characterization of John as an Elijah figure (cf. 1 Kings 19:1-2). As Painter remarks, the phrase "a prophet like one of the prophets" affirms that Jesus stands in a prophetic line and tradition found in the OT. This is as opposed to distinguishing him from the earlier prophets.[43] The point is that people with their own speculations were not coming up with the notion that Jesus was Messiah or Lord, and in a biography this story about the Baptist is crucial, for it clears up once and for all that Jesus is not John, who predeceased him, and indeed Jesus' disciples are not the same as John's (see v. 29). It also, coupled with what has come before in this Gospel, makes clear some of the similarities and differences between Jesus and John. This was not an unimportant issue because, judging from the writings of Josephus and Tacitus, there must have been a tendency in the Gentile world to lump Jewish prophets and messianic figures together, and Mark has as one function of his biography distinguishing Jesus from other such Jewish figures. Thus we remember that Mark had told us that Jesus' ministry, properly speaking, did not really get under way until John was imprisoned (1:14), a fact which distinguishes the two figures from the outset. In terms of the logic of the story, if indeed Jesus had arisen into the public eye once John was off the scene, it is understandable how Herod might think, "The one I beheaded has come back to haunt me."

At v. 17 the actual retrospective begins, and notice the emphatic αυτος at the outset. Herod said what he did because he *himself* had sent and had John arrested for protesting Herod's sinful relationship with Herodias.[44] But v. 17b indicates that ultimately Herodias was behind this action because John's polemic had angered her personally and she was looking for an opportunity to do him in. But in fact, she was unable to do so directly, and so the imprisoning of John apparently was a compromise measure taken by Herod to placate Herodias. This seems historically likely, as imprisonment was in general not in itself a form of ancient punishment but a way of holding a person until his case had been cleared up or judgment had been rendered. According to Josephus, John was imprisoned east of the Dead Sea in the fortress of Machaerus (*Ant.* 18.5.2).

---

42. See Guelich, p. 330.

43. Painter, p. 101.

44. On the structure of the narrative and its characterizations, see J. Gnilka, "Das Martyrium Johannes des Taufers (Mk. 6.17-29)," in *Orientierung an Jesus. Zur Theologie der Synoptiker. Fur Josef Schmid*, ed. P. Hoffmann (Freiburg: Herder, 1973), pp. 78-92.

But it would appear that the banquet recounted here is in Tiberias, since it is Galileans who attend it.[45] Perhaps Herod had John moved to Tiberias at some juncture, though clearly the journey from the Machaerus to Tiberias would take longer than an overnight trek (see Josephus, *Ant.* 18.5.2). On the other hand, some have suggested that the banquet was actually at Machaerus.[46]

We are also told clearly that Herod feared John, but he was apparently also fascinated with him — drawn to his preaching but not convicted enough to change his life. In short, we have here the portrait of a weak and vacillating man. Mark says clearly that Herod thought John a righteous and holy man. Hooker notes the parallel with Mark 15:14, where Pilate thinks Jesus is innocent but has him executed anyway.[47] Though Herod listened to him gladly, he puzzled much over what John said. At v. 20 the preferable reading is "puzzled much," for "he did many things" would be pointless here.

V. 21 depicts Herod throwing a birthday party to end all birthday parties with all the notables of Galilee, as well as Herod's inner circle of "great men," and the local military commanders (possibly even Roman officers, though they could be Herod's local militia commanders). That this is a banquet done in a fashion bound to offend the religiously scrupulous is shown by the fact that Herodias's daughter dances apparently a lascivious dance meant to arouse Herod and make him vulnerable to suggestion. Mark does not tell us the name of this daughter,[48] but Josephus says it was Salome. If so, it is Herodias's child by previous marriage. But a textual variant suggests that the child is also named Herodias, which would make her the daughter of Herodias by Antipas, the daughter of the incestuous union that John had condemned. It is easy to understand why she also would have had enmity against John.[49] Vv. 23-24 make evident that Herodias is elsewhere (with the women's group at the party?) biding her time. She was already about forty when she married Herod Antipas, whereas Salome is called a κοσαριον, which presumably means a teenage girl.

In the spirit of, and on the spur of, the moment, Herod offers the girl who has danced in such alluring fashion up to half his kingdom, presumably not really expecting her to take him up on the offer. Indeed, the girl has no strong feelings about the matter, as she goes and asks her mother what to ask for. Herod in addition foolishly swears a solemn oath, indeed multiple oaths (v. 23a), that he will give her whatsoever she asks for, up to half his kingdom.

---

45. Schweizer, p. 132, agrees, pointing out that the size of the banquet was such that it must have been held in the Herodian palace in Tiberias.

46. H. W. Hoehner, *Herod Antipas* (Cambridge: Cambridge University Press, 1972), pp. 146-48.

47. Hooker, p. 161.

48. See above, p. 204, on the textual problem.

49. See Painter, p. 103.

The story may owe something to Esther 5:1-8 at this juncture, particularly the midrash on the story found in *Midr. Esther* 1:19-21, where Vashti's head is brought to the king on a platter.[50] But when she asks for John the Baptist's head on a dish — a gruesome final course to a sumptuous feast — Herod goes from being very pleased to being very distressed. He does not want to appear to be an oath breaker before the notables he had regular dealings with, so he sends a courier to get John's head.[51]

There are certainly some difficulties with Mark's account of this affair when compared with Josephus's, though they are for the most part reconcilable.[52] Of this gruesome event, Chrysostom remarks: "He cut off the head but he did not cut off the voice. He curbed the tongue but he did not curb the accusation" (*Baptismal Instruct.* 10.27). At the end of the tale (v. 29) we are told that "the disciples" come and take the body of John away and bury it, and this seems likely to refer to John's, not Jesus', disciples. This may well suggest that they are the source of this story, for we know that John's disciples continued to exist as a definable group well into the first century A.D. and long after John's death (see, e.g., Acts 19:1-12).

Hurtado makes the following insightful comparison, suggesting that Mark is setting this up at this juncture. Just as John's ministry has foreshadowed Jesus', so does John's death, for: (1) Jesus, like John, will be executed by civil authorities; (2) Herod, like Pilate later, hesitates to execute the person in question but then does so; (3) Herodias, like the chief priests later, finally gets her way through scheming and pressure; (4) the disciples come and bury John, like Joseph of Arimathea is to do for Jesus.[53] This tale then serves as an ominous warning about the fate of Jesus. The cross looms in the background from this point on in the narrative. This becomes even more evident when one notes that the same word for body (το πτωμα) is used of the Baptist here as of Jesus in 15:45, and the same word for tomb is used in both cases as well (cf. 15:46; 16:2).[54]

---

50. But Gundry, p. 313, is surely right that our story has not simply been created out of such a story, as is corroborated by a somewhat different account in Josephus.

51. "The going out of the daughter to ask her mother what to request (v 24) shows that the dance was not planned with a view to John's beheading" (Gundry, p. 321). The dance also need not have been lascivious, but it probably was.

52. See Lane, pp. 216ff. It is interesting that Eusebius says that Josephus said Herodias was first the wife of Philip, then of Antipas (*Hist. eccl.* 1.11), which would appear to conflict with what is in the text of Josephus we have.

53. Hurtado, pp. 82-83.

54. See Hooker, p. 162.

C. A Grand Feast (6:30-44)

Mark has a way of juxtaposing stories, and in this chapter two major meals are juxtaposed. One foreshadows the demise of Jesus, the other the rise of the eschatological feast in the dominion of God. Unlike Herod, who thought of himself as a king over part of Israel but simply indulged himself and was immoral, Jesus will be presented here as Israel's true shepherd king who feeds the flock, meeting their needs as Moses did in the wilderness. There can be little doubt how important the story of the feeding of the five thousand was to the Gospel writers, for it is the only ministry miracle recorded in all four Gospels. It is quite clear that this event was understood to mean much more than various other miracles Jesus performed. From the biographer's viewpoint, it is meant to give a particularly clear insight, serving almost as an epiphany, into who Jesus is. It is not accidental, then, that Mark spends so much time on the story; in fact, even though overall his Gospel is the shortest, his account of this story is the longest in the NT. There are, of course, two such feeding narratives in Mark, but we will reserve our discussion of whether one is a doublet of the other for when we reach Mark 8.

One possible way to get at Mark's unique perspective on this story is to notice the ways his account differs from the three other Gospel accounts. Thus Mark alone tells us that this event transpired in a lonely or deserted place (6:31, 32, 35), which intentionally brings to mind the story of the feeding of Israel in the wilderness in Exod. 16. The reference to Israel being like sheep without a shepherd also serves as an intertextual echo meant to recall what was said of the wilderness-wandering generation at Num. 27:17 (cf. Ezek. 34:1-31). Even the organizing of the seating of the crowd in hundreds and fifties may recall Moses' organizing of Israel at Exod. 18:21. Yet there are also clear echoes from the Elisha material in 2 Kings 4:42-44, and one may compare the Elijah story and its vocabulary in 1 Kings 17:8-16.[55]

V. 30 returns to the subject matter of 6:7-13, so that the Baptist story becomes the middle section of a Markan sandwich. But while some connections can be seen between the Herod and the Baptist story and the missionary work (public figures who go forth proclaiming can incur the anger of the ruler), the connections between the two meals seem more telling (see above). Here the disciples are called apostles, apparently in the straightforward sense of those who were sent out and are now reporting back.[56] The report refers to both what they

---

55. Marcus, p. 415.

56. In classical Greek the term refers to a military or naval expedition. More germane is the fact that the LXX uses the term "apostle" to translate the Hebrew *saliah,* an authorized agent, empowered to act with the full authority of the one who sent him but with a limited commission. This latter is surely far closer to the sense here.

have done and what they have taught. Their ministry seems to have the same scope as that of Jesus, and the focus is on both words and deeds.

At this juncture Jesus bids the Twelve to come away with him to a deserted place. Once again we see the sequence of dramatic action followed by withdrawal for rest and recuperation. V. 31 suggests that Jesus does not want his emissaries' lives to be all work and no rest. So many people had been coming and going that the disciples, like Jesus earlier, had not even had time to eat. The impression one gets from vv. 32-33 is that Jesus and the disciples were unable to escape from the crowd who followed them around the rim of the lake on foot to meet them when they arrived on the other shore. They were so eager they ran and got there before the boat had docked. We are told the crowds came from all the cities, presumably all the surrounding cities, but the rhetorical point of this somewhat hyperbolic remark seems to be the same as similar expansive remarks in the summaries in 3:7 and 6:53-56, namely, that Jesus drew a lot of attention.[57] Indeed, Jesus attracted so much attention that he had to regularly flee from it in order to focus on the teaching and preaching.

We are told at v. 34 that when they got out of the boat, Jesus saw the great crowd and was deeply moved. He felt compassion for them because they were like sheep without a shepherd. This verse is indeed crucial for interpreting the miracle that follows, for it suggests that Jesus is to be seen as the new Moses who leads and feeds God's people. First, however, Jesus taught the crowd many things or, if we take πολλα adverbially, "much" (i.e., at length).[58] Yet it is obviously the fact rather than the content of that teaching which is important to Mark here, as he does not reveal the content at all. To be sure, Jesus would not provide the same sort of sumptuous meal that Herod had, but he would provide a far more palatable and satisfying one in various ways. One could say we have simple food for simple folks, and this turns out simply fine.

The story indicates that the day was waning and the disciples came to Jesus asking him to send the crowd away to buy themselves something to eat in the nearby cities and towns and countryside. Quite clearly the disciples are not expecting a miracle, or for Jesus somehow to provide for the crowd. Jesus, however, surprises everyone by telling the disciples, "You give them something to eat." They object because of the high expense — two hundred denarii would be two-thirds of a year's wages for a day laborer who made one denarius a day (Matt. 20:2).

An ordinary loaf of bread would have been about an inch thick and eight inches across. The disciples' response is to be seen as either a cross or sharp retort, perhaps an instinctive one at the end of a long, wearisome day. The disciples evidently just wanted to get away from the crowd, and that had initially

---

57. Guelich, p. 338.
58. Hooker, p. 166.

also been Jesus' intent. Notice, however, that Jesus wants the disciples to continue to be extenders of his ministry, to continue to be on duty as his agents even though they have returned to him. Now they are being asked to be shepherds of the people just as Jesus is providing for them and not just preaching to them or healing them. Perhaps one could call this on-the-job training.

Notice that throughout this story the focus is on the bread; the fish are sort of an afterthought (mentioned after the fact at v. 41b). It should be stressed that the story is about bread and fish, not bread and wine, and so it is doubtful that Mark had any intent in portraying this as a eucharistic meal.[59] To the contrary, it was a very filling and satisfying normal supper, and Mark uses the term "blessed." The word ευχαριστεω in fact does not occur in this story. This tale is to be seen in light of OT parallels, not NT ones.

Jesus orders the disciples to go see how much food they have. Five loaves, presumably of barley bread, and two fish is the tally. Jesus commands the disciples to make the crowds recline on the grass in groups of hundreds and fifties. The term used for "companies," συμποσια, when combined with the command to recline for a meal, would have suggested to a largely Gentile audience a dinner party involving a special sort of bond among the guests. It is possible that the arranging of them in groups of fifties and hundreds echoes Exod. 18:25 (Num. 31:14), where Israel is arranged in groups of a thousand, five hundred, one hundred, and ten under their respective leaders.[60] It is right to note that these same OT texts were taken as a model for the eschatological groupings of Qumranites, and specifically in 1QSa 2.11-22 it is seen as a blueprint for the messianic banquet.

Though a deserted place, this is no desert, for we are told of the lush green grass (thus also indicating a time in the spring when the previous fall's grain supplies would be low at best). Jesus looks up into heaven (is he praying for a miracle?), a gesture which may suggest his close relationship with the Father, for normally a Jew would bow his head and pray. Perhaps Jesus prayed something like the traditional Jewish blessing: "Praise unto thee, O Lord, our God King of the world who makes bread to come forth from the earth."

Notice that it is the disciples' food that is being used to produce this miracle. They must provide for the crowd as well as serve the food to them, for v. 41 says that when Jesus broke the bread, he gave it to the disciples "in order that they might serve them." Notice that there is no focus on the how of the miracle. Presumably it transpired as the food was distributed, but Mark does not focus on the mechanics of the miracle. There is furthermore no clear indication that the crowd knows a miracle has transpired, though the disciples clearly do. The event, then, was to reveal to the disciples Jesus' true character, and also their true calling to serve the people.

59. But see Marcus, p. 410.
60. See Guelich, p. 341.

The crowd ate and was satisfied — indeed, twelve baskets full of scraps of bread and fish were left over. God's provision was more than abundant, and the food was collected so it would not be wasted. A κοφινος was a small wicker basket used to carry a light lunch or odds and ends. Some have sought to make something of the number of baskets, but probably we are simply talking about the Twelve's own small baskets that they would carry things in. But nonetheless, this Twelve had symbolically served the people of God in the wilderness, and they should have recognized from this miracle that someone was in their midst who was more than an ordinary prophet. Indeed, a latter-day Moses had arrived. They should have also seen this as yet another indication of God's eschatological dominion breaking into their midst. There may also be an echo of 2 Kings 4:42-44, where a hundred persons are fed on twenty loaves and there are leftovers. Whatever stories the disciples should have used to help them interpret this event, unfortunately they failed to draw the right conclusions. If the crowd had been thinking of Jesus as among the northern prophets, certainly the similar story about Elisha would have come to mind.

We are told that some five thousand men ate at this messianic banquet in the wilderness, which was indeed an enormous crowd, and all the more so if women and children were also present, as is likely (cf. Matt. 14:21). In fact, this would have well exceeded the population of the city of Capernaum (about two thousand people at that time). Perhaps we should think, as Lane suggests, that Isa. 25:6-9, which refers to the messianic one feasting with his people in the wilderness, is echoed here.[61]

D. Walking on Water (6:45-52)

Here we have the second sea miracle, though this one is even more mysterious than the previous one.[62] Just as soon as the crowd had been fed and the food leftovers collected, Jesus compelled the disciples to get into the boat and head toward Bethsaida. He would stay behind and dismiss the crowd. It is possible that the Moses paradigm continues with this story, for we are told that after dismissing the crowd he went up on to the mountain to pray. Meanwhile evening had arrived and the disciples were toiling against a fierce gale in the middle of

---

61. Lane, p. 232.

62. For an interesting, but at the end of the day unpersuasive, reading of this story as an account of Jesus or the disciples experiencing altered states of consciousness, see B. Malina, "Assessing the Historicity of Jesus' Walking on Water," in *Authenticating the Activities of Jesus*, ed. B. Chilton and C. A. Evans (Leiden: Brill, 1999), pp. 351-71. Nevertheless, some of Malina's arguments for the authenticity of this story are telling — for example, the fact that this tale appears in at least two sources, Mark and John. In my view his approach would have borne better fruit if applied to the transfiguration story.

the lake. Sometime between three and six in the morning Jesus finished his praying and saw the disciples "harassed in the rowing," and so he came to them on the sea.[63] Schweizer suggests that here in v. 46 Mark explains, in fashion similar to 1:35, that Jesus wanted to be alone to pray, and so "[i]n this way Mark wants to show where the source of Jesus' authority is to be found."[64] But if this is Mark's point, he does not make it explicitly, and elsewhere when Jesus prays it is for guidance, more than as a demonstration of the source of his power or authority. Still, Schweizer may be correct.

The description of the toiling disciples surely implies that his motive for coming was to aid them or at least encourage them. V. 48c, "he intended to pass them by," could perhaps mean, as Hurtado suggests, that he intended to show himself to them to let them know he was with them, revealing his power and protection — for if he could walk on water, why should they fear the waves under his feet?[65] There is, however, another possibility, namely, that this is another echo of the Moses saga, with Jesus in this case playing the role of God passing by while Moses watches, or even Moses crossing the Red Sea.[66]

It has often been pointed out that walking on water is something that only God can do in the OT (Job 9:8; Ps. 77:19), which means that we should indeed see this scene as an epiphany revealing the divine character of Jesus, an appropriate focus in a biography.[67] Thus v. 48 probably does not mean that Jesus intended to pass by the disciples and keep on going, for they were after all the reason he went out on the water in the first place. Unfortunately, instead of bolstering their faith, Jesus' act instilled fear. They thought Jesus was a phantasm, a ghost, perhaps even a sea demon, since it was believed that demons dwelt in such places. Their response then was not to shout hooray but to scream in panic. All of them saw Jesus and were deeply troubled. Jesus responded to this crisis immediately, saying, "Courage, εγω ειμι. Do not fear," after which he went up and joined them in the boat. It is certainly possible that εγω ειμι here means no more than "It is I myself" or "It's me." There was indeed the issue of identity raised at this juncture, since the disciples thought they were seeing a ghost. However, as Lane has pointed out, Pss. 115:9ff.; 118:5f., Isa. 41:4ff., 13ff.; 43:1ff.; 44:2ff.; 51:9ff. suggest that such words cou-

---

63. Notice that Mark says "around the fourth watch of the night," reckoning according to Roman time, for Jews only had three watches in the night. Here is yet another clue to the Western provenance of this Gospel. See Guelich, p. 349.

64. Schweizer, p. 142.

65. See Hurtado, pp. 90-91.

66. See Hooker, p. 170, and Marcus, p. 426.

67. Interestingly, it is Wisdom of whom this ability to walk on water is predicated in Sir. 24:5-6, and it can be said with certainty that the portrayal of Jesus as the incarnation of divine Wisdom is a very early christological move. See my *Jesus the Sage* (Minneapolis: Fortress, 1994), passim, and Marcus, p. 432, on the stress in this narrative on Christ's divinity.

pled with an admonition to take heart or have no fear appear to make up a formula of divine self-revelation. Furthermore, remembering the Moses paradigm our author is pursuing, at Exod. 3:14 God reveals himself to Moses as *eyeh asher eyeh*. Then too, the walking on the water points us to the more theophanic interpretation of these words.[68] Yet, when all is said and done, one must conclude that while the disciples in the story simply take the words as Jesus' way of identifying himself (and so again show their spiritual imperceptivity), nonetheless Mark's audience was likely supposed to take these words as of a more pregnant ilk.

Taken together, all of this suggests that we are to see this story as theophanic in character, yet the only response the disciples show is astonishment. Mark adds that this inadequate response is because they had not understood about the bread or, more aptly from the feeding miracle, that they were in the presence of more than just a wonder-worker. Painter says even more pointedly that they failed to make the connection between the miraculous provision of bread and the walking on water (Ps. 78:13-25), which should have made clear that they were in the presence of both a latter-day Moses figure[69] and yet at the same time one who could manifest the qualities of Moses' God. Indeed, as Mark says, their hearts were hardened and so not open to this truth yet, which is also precisely the complaint about Jesus' opponents (cf. Mark 3:5 and 10:5). There is irony here, for this harks back to the treatment of the outsiders by means of the quote of Isa. 6:9-10 in Mark 4:10-12, but it is also reminiscent of the use of that terminology in the exodus material.[70] Very clearly Mark does not pull his punches when speaking about the disciples' negative traits.[71]

E. Gennesaret Gets a House Call from the Great Physician (6:53-56)

This brief passage summarizes a period of ministry in the area of Gennesaret involving a vast amount of healing. People were lining up in the marketplaces and elsewhere to be touched by Jesus. In an age lacking modern medicine, we can imagine the desperation to get near Jesus. Again, some appear to have magic-tainted faith, believing if they could only touch a tassel on Jesus' garment they would be healed. If κρασπεδου means tassel, this may suggest that on occasion Jesus followed some of the smaller points of the Jewish Law (cf. Num. 15:37-41; Deut. 22:12). However, it is also possible that the term means no more than the edge or hem of Jesus' garment, which, at the end of the sleeves,

---

68. Guelich, p. 351.
69. Painter, p. 108.
70. Painter, p. 108.
71. For an overall perspective see pp. 421-42 below.

was within easy reach of passersby.[72] Whoever touched Jesus was made well. Thus, even if magic-tainted, we see here a form of faith in Jesus, and more to the point, Jesus responds to it, however inadequate the faith may have been. The story in Mark 5:21ff. provides a fuller version of this sort of encounter,[73] and in both cases Jesus' garment is seen to be an extension of his personality or to radiate his aura or power.[74]

F. Making a Clean Break with the Past (7:1-23)

Mark uses the clean/unclean discussion as the introduction and in effect the explanation for Jesus' willingness to help even a non-Jewish woman, as recorded in 7:24-30. Some have seen Mark 7 as the beginning of a new section of the discussion, and it is fair to say that this material could have been placed with the controversy narratives in Mark 2–3. Yet its placement is apt as the rationale explaining Jesus' ministry to non-Jews in three episodes that follow 7:23.

A rhetorical analysis of the entire section 6:53–7:23 has been undertaken by D. Young with mixed results.[75] On the one hand Young is quite right to emphasize the polemical rhetorical situation. Jesus and the behavior of his disciples (and his own behavior) are on trial, and forensic rhetoric would be in order. The charge is violating the religious traditions of the elders in regard to clean and unclean. Furthermore, it does appear that we do have an enthymeme in short form in Jesus' argument about Corban which concludes in v. 13. The expanded enthymeme or logical argument would look like this: (1) God's word commands persons to care for their parents; (2) the scribes and the Pharisees forbid persons who have invoked the Corban rule to care for their parents; (3) therefore the scribes and Pharisees reject God's word by their tradition. (4) Since (3) is so, their tradition must be wrong; (5) therefore Jesus' disciples have not committed any crime by not washing their hands, nor are they ritually unclean.[76] It needs to be remembered that at the level of elementary rhetoric, enthymemes were considered the strongest form of proof (Aristotle, *Rhetoric* 1.2.10-11), and thus Mark has shaped his source material accordingly to persuade his audience about this important matter. But in regard to Young's macrorhetorical analysis which tries to bring Mark 6:53-56 into the picture and make 7:6-8 both an exordium and a *propositio*, and then 7:9-19 a *probatio* with

---

72. See Marcus, p. 437.

73. On which see pp. 184-91 above.

74. Hooker, p. 172.

75. See D. M. Young, "Whoever Has Ears to Hear" (Diss., Vanderbilt University, 1994), pp. 236-71.

76. Young, pp. 257-58.

narrative interruptions followed by an epilogue in 7:20-23, this argument is less than persuasive. The material in Mark 7 involves not just one speech of Jesus, but apparently several, and Mark does little to hide this fact. There is, however, as Young rightly notes, a double defense offered by Jesus, which Mark has structured into a sort of chiasm:

A   Purity of heart is what God seeks (v. 6).
 B   Human teachings are worthless (v. 7).
 B′   The teaching of the elders nullifies God's word (vv. 9-13).
A′   Only evil from the heart defiles (vv. 14-23).[77]

The way Mark connects this material, including the quote from Isaiah, is through the external/internal or external/heart contrast. A better attempt at rhetorical analysis on a smaller scale can now be mentioned.

As with some of the other speech material in Mark (e.g., Mark 13), we have here the clearest evidence that Mark has arranged some of his material according to the rhetorical conventions of his day. G. Salyer has made an impressive case that we have in this section two *chreiae* (7:6-7 and 14-15), and that Mark has edited the rest of this section so that it would appear to his Gentile audience to be elaborations of these *chreiae*.[78] What is especially striking about the first *chreia* is that it entails a citation from Isaiah, an authority Jesus' opponents recognize. It is also crucial to the argument of the whole passage, in which Jesus will play off the prophetic word against Pharisaic tradition about washing of hands and similar traditions.

Mark 7:1 begins with what appears to be an official delegation of Pharisees and some scribes from Jerusalem coming to investigate what Jesus is doing. Yet the bone is picked with Jesus' disciples, who eat with "common" (κοιναις) hands, by which is meant unwashed, and so ritually unclean, hands. The issue, however, really has to do with Jesus, who is seen as responsible for the behavior of his followers. It was Pharisaic practice to wash diligently before eating. In order to understand the Pharisees, one must recognize that they attempted to apply the Levitical laws for the cleanness of priests to everyone (see Exod. 30:19; 40:13). They in a sense believed in a real priesthood of all believers, and therefore all Jews were called to priestly cleanness. V. 3 is an editorial remark, of which this section has several, and must not be taken overliterally, as of course many Jews did not follow such strict hygienic rules, some because their trade did not permit it (e.g., tanners of hides). Notice in the second half of v. 3 that we are told that this amounted to a keeping of the traditions of the elders.

---

77. Young, p. 253.
78. G. Salyer, "Rhetoric, Purity, and Play: Aspects of Mark 7.1-23," *Semeia* 64 (1993): 139-69.

Mark, then, does not say it is a keeping of Torah. Rather he sees it as a matter of the oral traditions the Pharisees had added to the Torah, or had particularized or expanded the Torah with. Strictly speaking, the washing of hands was only required before the breaking of bread. The practice involved washing with a handful of water. This likely explains the use of πυγμη, which is omitted in some manuscripts. Literally the term means with the fist but has a metaphorical sense of diligently, and so some scribes (א, W, and others) substituted the term πυκνα (frequently). Marcus has suggested that the phrase in question means they washed with their hand shaped like a fist (cf. *m. Yad.* 1.1; 2.3).[79]

V. 4 refers to the practice being followed after one had bought food at the marketplace. Mark says once they buy it, the Pharisees will not eat it unless they wash. This leads to a comment on how they also practice the washing of wine pots, vessels, copper utensils, and, some manuscripts add, beds (A, D, W, K, X, et al.). It is easier to see how this reading might have been omitted than how it might have been added at a later date.[80] The point of the washing is to remove uncleanness, and of course uncleanness could be found on a bed due either to menstrual blood or semen or human waste. Jesus is then asked why his disciples do not follow the halakah that the Pharisees follow.[81]

At 7:6 Jesus responds with a stinging rebuke, quoting a prophecy from Isa. 29:13. This is the only occurrence in Mark where the word υποκριτης is used of anyone, but it frequently crops up in Matthew. The contrast in the quote is between those who give lip service to God but whose hearts are far removed from him. Their worship is in vain, for they teach as divine doctrine the commandments of human beings. Doubtless it is the latter part of the quote that Jesus is focusing on. The point of the quote seems to be: the Pharisees, in their concern for external observance, had substituted the observances for heart religion, which amounted to substituting the traditions of human beings for God's word.

The danger was that mere human traditions or interpretations of God's word would be taken as the word itself and one would be categorized a bad Jew if one did follow this halakah. Thus Jesus accuses them of neglecting the actual commandments of God to keep their own commandments. This amounted to more than just neglect. It amounted to annulling (αθετειτε) the commandment of God. What happens in such cases, according to G. Bornkamm, is that the Law has been separated from God himself and has become the real authority. Thus ironically the Law becomes an obstacle to real encounter with God, because the means have been mistaken for the end.[82] Sometimes humans of vari-

---

79. Marcus, p. 441.

80. Metzger, *TCGNT,* pp. 93-94.

81. Notice that there are other similar discussions recognizing that Jews practiced hand washing. Cf. *Epistle of Aristeas.*

82. See G. Bornkamm, *Jesus of Nazareth* (New York: Harper & Row, 1960), p. 104.

ous religious traditions, including the followers of Jesus, have been able to hide behind legal observance and assume that this establishes their righteousness and God's indebtedness to them.

Jesus then gives an example that justifies his charge against his interlocutors involving the matter of Corban. The material in 7:9-13 has a good chance of being authentic, not least because the early church is not likely to have been concerned about the issue of Corban, especially once the temple was destroyed. V. Taylor, for example, says, "There can be no reasonable doubt that the words were spoken by Jesus and illustrate his attitude to the oral law."[83] What is important here is that Jesus is affirming the essence of a Mosaic commandment at the expense of legislation which vitiated something that was at the heart of the Law — honoring parents. In this case Jesus appears to be attacking the misuse of the practice of making something Corban to someone. He reminds his listeners that they are to honor both father and mother, which may be especially significant since some early Jewish teachers said the father was to be honored more than the mother (see *m. Ker.* 6.9). J. D. M. Derrett has shown that the term "honor" was often taken in early Judaism to mean providing financial support (Prov. 28:24).[84] Notice that Jesus also asserts the negative form of the commandment to honor, saying that the one who does the opposite of honoring by speaking evil of one's parents should be executed. It is truly hard to imagine a more strongly worded way of enforcing the obligations of children to their parents, especially of dependent parents.

In Jesus' era it was indeed possible to declare by means of a vow using either the term "Corban" (which means "dedicated") or κοναμ that one's parents were proscribed from benefiting from some piece of property or material asset because it had been set aside for other purposes (for example, dedicated to the temple treasury). But in fact, this procedure had come to be used in Jesus' day to simply place property out of the reach of parental use, without the pious intent to set it aside for some religious purpose.[85] Indeed, the term "Corban" may already have begun to have the force of an imprecation in Jesus' day, which would explain the reference to cursing one's parents in this text. There is furthermore the problem that oaths were taken so seriously in

---

83. V. Taylor, *The Gospel according to St. Mark* (New York: St. Martin's Press, 1966), p. 339.

84. J. D. M. Derrett, "ΚΟΡΒΑΝ, Ο ΕΣΤΙΝ ΔΩΡΟΝ," in *Studies in the New Testament*, vol. 1 (Leiden: Brill, 1977), pp. 112-17.

85. See the discussion in J. A. Fitzmyer, "The Aramaic Qorban Inscription from Jebel Hallet et-Turi and Mark 7.11/Matt. 15.5," *JBL* 78 (1959): 60-65, and *m. Ned.* 5.6; *Babba Kamma* 9.10. Corban was not originally an imprecation formula but a technical term in an oath. Cf. J. Bligh, "Qorban!" *HeyJ* 5 (1964): 192-93; Z. W. Falk, "Notes and Observations — on Talmudic Vows," *HTR* 59, no. 3 (1966): 311-12. See also Philo, *On the Special Laws* 2.16; Josephus, *Ant.* 4.73.

Jesus' social setting that it was difficult if not impossible to repent of something said using an oath, even if it was said in haste or in a moment of anger (see, e.g., 6:23). Some early Jewish teachers believed that if one broke an oath, one's life would be forfeited and indeed one would stand in danger of the judgment of God on the last day (Philo, *Hypothet.* 7.3-5). Thus Jesus complains that "you do not *permit* them to do anything for father or mother." The duty to fulfill a vow had been allowed to take precedence over the duty to parents. Jesus, however, takes the opposite view, strongly affirming the traditional obligation to honor parents, including providing them with financial support, and removing obstacles to doing so. Note also that Jesus elsewhere warned against taking oaths at all, perhaps precisely because in an honor and shame culture it was next to impossible to take back or renege on an oath, even if it was a shot fired in anger (see Matt. 5:33-37).

It is entirely possible that the Corban pericope originally belonged in some other context, for 7:14-23 seems to follow smoothly from the material in 7:1-8, providing Jesus' response to the original question about his disciples' hand washing, or rather, lack thereof. Mark then will have grouped material from several controversies together, as we also saw in Mark 3. Jesus makes clear here that what his disciples did was no accident, nor was it a result of laxness. Rather it was grounded in principle. V. 15 states unequivocally: "Nothing from outside a person that goes into him can defile him. Only those things that come from the heart defile." If indeed one takes this statement in a straightforward manner, it means that Jesus saw a significant portion of the Levitical law code as no longer applicable now that God's divine saving activity, his eschatological dominion, was breaking into human history. Jesus' approach to holiness was not going to focus on the ritual part of the holiness code.

One might say that the Jesus movement and the Pharisaic movement were both holiness movements, but they disagreed on the proper approach to creating a holy people of God. Mark understands well the implications of what Jesus is saying, but he assumes his audience or some part of it may not, so he inserts the editorial remark "thus he declared all foods clean." This remark likely intimates that Mark assumes a significant portion of his audience will not understand the legal niceties of Jewish disputes about clean and unclean. In other words, this surely suggests that Mark assumes his audience is mostly Gentile, and not even God-fearers who know the Law, at that. Jesus, then, is not merely declaring Pharisaic halakah defunct or invalid. He is declaring at least some portions of Leviticus obsolete as well. When all is said and done, Jesus believes not physical things but moral attitudes defile a person.

Mark 7:15 and the Radical Jesus

While the majority of commentators have concluded that 7:15 likely goes back to Jesus in some form, the dispute over what form shows no sign of abating. In one important monograph, R. P. Booth has argued that the tradition history of Mark 7 suggests that in its original form 7:15 involves a relative, not an absolute, contrast. Thus what Jesus actually said was: "There is nothing outside a person which *cultically* defiles him as much as the things coming from a man *ethically* defile him."[86] There are several problems with this conclusion: (1) This is certainly not how Mark understands the saying, for his parenthetical editorial comment indicates that he assumes that an absolute contrast is made. "Thus he declares all things clean" would in fact be a false conclusion if Booth is right about the original sense of the saying. (2) The contrast in the saying seems to be between that which enters a person from without and that which comes forth from within the person, not between two different kinds of defilement. (3) While a relative reading of the ου . . . αλλα is possible, one would expect some sort of signal in the context that "not . . . but" means "not so much . . . but." In other words, one would expect some sort of contextual signal that a relative comparison rather than a real contrast is meant. Such signals are entirely lacking in the context; indeed, the editorial remark of the Evangelist points in the opposite direction. The criterion of double dissimilarity also suggests the authenticity of the more radical reading of this saying.

Precisely because of some of the above sorts of considerations, J. D. G. Dunn has taken a different tack in approaching this radical saying.[87] His view is that indeed this is a radical saying in its present form, but that the *original* form of the saying was otherwise.[88] He urges that the Matthean form of the saying ("what goes into *your mouth* does not make you 'unclean' but what comes out of your mouth, that is what makes you 'unclean'" — Matt. 15:11) is likely closer to what Jesus actually said, in which case the original contrast was between what one eats and what one says. The food laws would be a subset of the larger body of Levitical laws about impurity, and Jesus would simply be declaring obsolete some of the food laws. Dunn also reckons with the possibility that the ου . . . αλλα structure involves a "dialectical negation" meaning "more important than ritual impurity is moral impurity."[89] Yet despite such reasoning, Dunn in the same discussion later admits: "But the radical character of a saying which set inward purity antithetically against ritual purity is fully of a piece with Jesus' teaching as a whole. Jesus is generally remembered as one whose teaching on the law and on human relations as governed by the law was characteristically searching and radical in one degree or another."[90] I quite agree with this conclusion, in which case it is perfectly possible that the Markan rather than the Matthean form of this saying is more likely to be original.[91] There are other problems with Dunn's

---

86. R. P. Booth, *Jesus and the Laws of Purity: Tradition History and Legal History in Mark 7* (Sheffield: JSOT Press, 1986), p. 214.

87. J. D. G. Dunn, *Jesus, Paul, and the Law* (Louisville: Westminster, 1990), pp. 37-60.

88. He rightly critiques Booth's conclusion that Jesus' original saying was simply about cultic impurity. If that were the case, it is hard to understand how the early church could have ever adopted the viewpoint expressed by Mark himself.

89. See Dunn, p. 51.

90. Dunn, p. 52.

91. Hooker, p. 179, takes a view similar to Dunn's, but she rightly points out that Jesus is at the very least challenging the notion that all commandments of the Law should be

reasoning as well: (1) The appeal to putative oral tradition which Matthew might have used to present an earlier form of Jesus' saying than that found in Matthew's Markan source is an argument from silence. It is possible, but there is no very good reason to think it is true, not least because Matthew takes more than 90 percent of his Markan source in the material they share in common, including over 50 percent of Mark's exact words. (2) Matthew's dependence on, and softening of, the harsh edges of his Markan source is too well known to need demonstration. (3) Is it really more probable that Mark and his community took a more radical stance on ritual impurity than Jesus did? Why should Mark's community need Mark's parenthetical explanation about declaring all foods clean if they themselves already held such a view, or if Mark had already taught them such a tradition? Was a largely Gentile congregation really arguing about food laws in the 60s or 70s? (4) The more traditional Jewish portrait of Jesus as a sage and upholder of a good deal of the Law in Matthew's Gospel is clearly a redactional agenda of the First Evangelist.[92]

Another sort of attempt to blunt or vitiate the radical character of 7:15 as an utterance of Jesus is that found in Guelich's commentary on Mark. Following R. Pesch and D. Luhrmann, he suggests that Jesus is not speaking programmatically but rather prophetically here. He is not abrogating or even reinterpreting the Law; he is simply summoning God's people to do God's will from the whole person. "Instead of attacking the ritual or ceremonial law of purity, Jesus calls for total purity, the sanctification of the whole person, as anticipated for the age of salvation. . . ."[93] If this conclusion is correct, it is hard to understand why the Pharisees might ever be depicted as disagreeing with Jesus, for they too were concerned with the purity of the whole person and not just with ritual purity. Equally, this conclusion completely fails to grasp the fact that Jesus was perceived as having negated some of the Law, or as having taken the Law into his own hands and changed things. Jesus' ministry is consistently portrayed in the Gospels as arising out of a context of social controversy, indeed a variety of controversies. Furthermore, the eschatological tenor of Jesus' teaching is ignored by Guelich's conclusion. Jesus believed that the eschatological reign of God was *already* breaking into human history through his ministry and that new occasions taught new duties. New wine could not be poured into old wineskins. A major difference between the holiness movement known as Pharisaism and the holiness movement that was the Jesus movement was not so much the goal (both wanted God's people to be holy unto the Lord) but the means by which this was to be achieved. One followed a program of Levitical reform, applying such laws to all Jews. The other taught that God himself was already intervening and changing people from the inside out through Jesus' ministry, and thus the gospel according to Leviticus was a message which had had its day and was no longer appropriate to the times. In short, the various attempts to whittle off the hard edges of Jesus' teaching should be resisted. The more difficult and even offensive the saying, the more likely that the church did not invent it, for even after the split between the synagogue and the church, the evidence shows that the church was still interested in sharing the gospel with Jews. The odds are that the radical Markan Jesus is closer to the

---

treated as equally important. As such, she rightly notes, Jesus stands in the prophetic tradition which speaks of that which is more central or more important among the commandments (cf. Jer. 7:22-23; Hos. 6:6). In other words, Jesus is not contrasting mere human tradition with the Law. His hermeneutic is more radical than that.

92. See my discussion in *Jesus the Sage*, pp. 335-68.

93. Guelich, p. 376.

original historical figure than the less offensive versions we find in the later Gospels of Matthew and Luke.

At v. 17 the in-house teaching-of-the-disciples motif we saw, for instance, in Mark 4 reappears. Again at v. 18 the disciples are charged with lacking understanding. Food only goes into the stomach and then passes on into the latrine (αφεορωνα). "Jesus' point is that food, which enters a person, is not 'dirty'; i.e. people do not eat physically dirty things. Instead, it is one's excretion which is considered 'dirty'; what comes out of a person is what is unclean. The simple point of the comparison is the contrast between the 'cleanness' of food versus the 'filthiness' of excretion. The actual interpretation of the comparison will be given in the following verses."[94]

The sorts of things that do defile a person are listed beginning at vv. 21ff. Here the heart is seen as the source and center of human action, determining its character. This catalogue of vices has been shown by Cranfield to be thoroughly Jewish and traditional.[95] Here are listed twelve items — evil thoughts, all sorts of sexual immorality, thefts, murders, adulteries (these words are in the plural), malice, deceit, indecencies, the evil eye (Deut. 15:9), blasphemy, arrogance, folly — to which the similar list in 1QS 4.9-11 should be compared. J. Neyrey suggests that the list of vices in Mark is based roughly on the Ten Commandments, and this is basically so, though the evil eye concept would be an exception.[96] The idea of the evil eye is well known in earlier Jewish literature (cf. Sir. 14:6, 8; Wis. 4:12), and it is very common in the papyri as well (cf., e.g., P.Oxy. 2.292 [12] and P.Oxy. 6.930 [23]). The concept is that certain persons (or animals, or demons, or gods) have the power of casting an evil spell on others or causing something bad to happen to them by looking at them. It was believed that the eye was the window on the heart or soul and the channel through which one's thoughts, desires, intentions could be conveyed. Chiefly this concept was connected with envy, jealousy, greed, or stinginess (see Plutarch, *Quaest. conv.* 680C-683B). In Mark's first-century world there was considerable fear of the evil eye, which was seen as a form of sorcery, and people would use curses, amulets, and spitting to ward it off.

Notice that some of these things are attitudes and some are attitudes that issue in actions with the focus on the deed. Jesus was not one who bifurcated attitudes and actions or suggested that only one or the other mattered. He could never have said, "It's the thought that counts." Both attitudes and actions

---

94. Young, p. 262.

95. See C. E. B. Cranfield, *The Gospel according to St. Mark* (Cambridge: Cambridge University Press, 1972), pp. 242-44.

96. J. Neyrey, "The Idea of Purity in Mark's Gospel," *Semeia* 35 (1986): 91-128, here p. 121.

counted and both manifested what one's orientation was. Jesus in his own way heightens the demand for purity beyond what the Pharisees expected, but his approach involves strict moral purity. Personal sin, not physical impurity, is what now defiles, rendering one unfit for fellowship with God or other humans. This teaching would of course have been crucial for Mark's audience, for it meant one could be a follower of Jesus without practicing ritual food laws or undergoing circumcision. It is not surprising that Mark emphasizes this material and then, beginning in 7:24, gives examples of its implications — namely, that Jesus could help, heal, even fellowship with Gentiles, because their ethnic customs did not render them inherently unclean.

Finally, Marcus suggests that Mark presents Jesus' radical teaching here as performative in nature, which is to say that "Jesus in our passage is not just holding a mirror up to nature, depicting what has always been the case, but actually *changing things* by his apocalyptic pronouncement that all foods are (now) clean."[97] Such a pronouncement is not unlike what we find in Gen. 9:3, where before the Mosaic Law but after the flood all animals could be eaten.

G. Beyond All Bounds (7:24-30)

The story of the Syrophoenician woman presents us with one of the hard sayings of Jesus, a saying it is nearly impossible to believe a largely Gentile church would invent. "If the Evangelist were to yield to the temptation to reconcile his narrative with the current situation, it would certainly have been in this instance. The fact that he did not attests to his having kept faith with the tradition."[98] In this story we see Jesus crossing a variety of boundaries — geographical, ethnic, gender, theological. This is the only passage in Mark where the healed person is definitely a Gentile pagan, and we may expect to learn something of Jesus' view of Gentiles, indeed of Gentile women, in this passage.[99]

The story begins with a desperate woman hearing that Jesus was in the area, and immediately she takes action, coming to implore Jesus to exorcise an unclean spirit from her daughter.[100] The woman falls at Jesus' feet in a gesture

---

97. Marcus, p. 457.

98. R. A. Harrisville, "The Woman of Canaan: A Chapter in the History of Exegesis," *Int* 20, no. 3 (1966): 274-87, here p. 274. On the likely authenticity of the essence of this story, see my *Women in the Ministry of Jesus* (Cambridge: Cambridge University Press, 1984), p. 63.

99. It is possible that Luke found this story too offensive for his Gentile audience and so, unlike Matthew, omitted it.

100. Notice that though this very chapter shows that Mark believes Jesus himself does not think that things or illnesses defile a person, nevertheless he still calls demons "unclean spirits." This must surely tell us something about Mark's own background in early Judaism, where there was a deeply ingrained concern about this sort of ritual pollution.

of supplication and pleads her case. Mark at this juncture stresses the woman's political and national identity (Ἑλληνίς, Συροφοινίκισσα τῳ γένει). Matthew calls her a Canaanite, which would seem to focus on her religious affiliation. Mark's way of putting the matter stresses that she is a non-Jewess and that he views her ethnic identity from a western-end-of-the-empire perspective.[101] After her request, the Markan account proceeds directly to the saying of Jesus about the children and their food, while Matthew relates a three-part response. The net effect of the Matthean additions is to stress Jesus' Jewishness.[102] The response found in both Matthew and Mark is harsh: "It is not good to take the food of the children and throw it to the dogs." Regardless of whether one thinks the term κυνάριον is a diminutive or not, the use of the term is likely an insult or slur, especially when spoken by a Jew to a Gentile.[103] It is not impossible that there is a reference here to the practice of giving unwanted bread which was not worth saving to the dogs.[104]

Insulted or not, the woman is not put off by Jesus' remark, perhaps because she is so desperate for aid, or possibly we are to think there is something in the way Jesus put the matter that invited a rejoinder. Thus she enters into the test by, in a sense, accepting Jesus' judgment on her: "Yes sir, and the dogs eat from the crumbs."[105] This implies submission to Jesus' categorization of her, and even to his apparent refusal to help. Her inventiveness lies in her accepting the categorizing as a dog but finding a way for even an outsider, even a dog, to obtain what it needs in the bargain. Notice that in Jesus' final response to her it is *what* she says, not how she says it or the cleverness of it, that he mentions as the reason she gains what she wants from him.[106] It is possible the woman is quoting a well-known proverb (see Philostratus, *Life of Apollonius of Tyana* 1.19). It may be germane to recognize that whether or not early Jews had dogs as house pets, there is no evidence that they were prepared to feed them, and thus the woman here would seem to be asking for pure grace, showing that there was a way that even dogs could be fed.

---

101. See pp. 20-30 in the introduction.

102. E.g., he is called Son of David, he says to the disciples, "I was sent only to the lost sheep of Israel," perhaps putting them and the woman to the test.

103. Diminutive forms are fairly frequent in Mark (see, e.g., 5:41; 7:25, 28), and there are examples of diminutives of contempt as well as diminutives of endearment. See D. Smith, "Our Lord's Hard Saying to the Syro-Phoenician Woman," *ET* 12 (1900-1901): 319-21; Derrett, "Law in the New Testament: The Syrophoenician Woman and the Centurion of Capernaum," *NovT* 15, no. 3 (1973): 161-86.

104. *m. Hal.* 1.8. It is not certain, however, that Jews domesticated dogs in this period.

105. Judg. 1:7 may provide a partial background to this passage. In each case we are talking about a person in a desperate situation searching for the means of surviving.

106. W. Storch, "Zur Perikope von der Syrophonizierin Mk 7,28 und Ri 1,7," *BZ* 14, no. 2 (1970): 256-57.

The woman achieves her desire not so much by a witty remark as by a faith that goes on beseeching the One who can help until the aid is granted. Her trust is manifested by the conclusion of the story where, when Jesus says "your daughter is healed," she trusts it is so and leaves in that confidence. Matthew's account makes explicit what is implicit in the Markan account when it has Jesus say, "O woman, great is your faith." In any event, it is clear that this story, perhaps building on the pronouncement about cleanness earlier in the chapter, is about transcending a certain approach to Jewish particularism.[107]

H. Deaf and Dumb in the Decapolis (7:31-37)

In this brief passage Jesus passes from one region full of non-Jews (Tyre and Sidon) to another of a similar ilk which he had visited before — the Decapolis.[108] At v. 32 the term μογιλαλον, a hapax legomenon, does not mean totally unable to speak but having a speech impediment, speaking with a stutter or some other severe difficulty.[109] It is possible, as Lane has suggested, that this pericope provides the end of a cycle of material portraying Jesus as the fulfiller of OT promises, in this case Isa. 35:5-6. Lane suggests that Mark 8:1 is the beginning of the next cycle, which, like this one, begins with a feeding miracle and climaxes with a confession in 8:27-30, as here at the end of Mark 7,[110] which suggests a theological rather than chronological or primarily geographical arrangement of materials by the Evangelist. Consider the following chart:

> Feeding of the Multitude — 6:31-44/8:1-9
> Crossing of the Sea and Landing — 6:45-56/8:10
> Conflict with the Pharisees — 7:1-23/8:11-13
> Conversation about Bread — 7:24-30/8:13-21
> Healing — 7:31-36/8:22-26
> Confession of Faith — 7:37/8:27-30[111]

---

107. Marcus, p. 466.

108. Some have complained (see Schweizer, p. 154) of Mark's lack of knowledge of regional geography, for Jesus would have had to go north from Tyre to go through Sidon on the way to Galilee. But as Hooker says, there is no reason why Jesus may have not taken a roundabout route, nor is there a good reason to deny that Mark may have envisioned Jesus doing so. See Hooker, p. 185. Painter, p. 116, rightly adds: "After all, Jesus was engaged in a mission, not attempting to travel as quickly as possible from A to B."

109. This rare term may have been chosen because Mark was familiar with the promises in Isa. 35:5ff. So Hooker, p. 186.

110. Lane, pp. 270-72.

111. Marcus, p. 476, concentrates on the close similarities of language between the healing of the deaf man in this text and of the blind man in 8:22-26. He then suggests an echo

This particular man appears to have gone deaf later in life, for had he been born deaf and mute he would not have learned how to speak in the first place. As Hooker points out, this is the first occurrence of the healing of a deaf person in this Gospel.[112] The man was brought to Jesus for the laying on of hands, which may suggest that he was a Jew, since laying on of hands was a Jewish practice. For reasons not specified in this healing story and in the parallel in Mark 8 where spittle is used in the healing of a blind man (see below), the deaf and dumb man is taken away from the crowd before Jesus performs the miracle. Jesus puts his fingers in the man's ear and spits and touches the man's tongue. Spittle was thought in both the Jewish and Greco-Roman world to have healing properties. Notice that Jesus does not attempt to perform the miracle on his own, but rather looks into heaven for help, groans deeply, and then commands, "Be opened." Is this groan from the strain of healing? Does it reflect heartache over the ravages of disease? Should we think it a sign of deep heartfelt prayer? Gundry suggests that it reflects the technique of a healer. He exudes his life force to give power to the words spoken so they will accomplish their task. This at least seems to be how a Gentile audience might have understood this text.[113]

In regard to the word *eppatha,* it is hard to know whether it should be seen as Hebrew or Aramaic. It could certainly be either. Jesus, unlike some wonder-workers, is not using gibberish or unknown words or syllables to perform a healing, but rather his own intelligible native speech. Nor does Jesus perform any incantations. The miracle here is that the man was restored to normal hearing and speech. V. 35 speaks of a ligament of the tongue being loosed so the man could speak properly. Despite Jesus' charge not to tell anyone, the more he gave such imperatives, the more they were breached. "The people disregard the command in proportion to Jesus' insistence on it."[114] This miracle absolutely overwhelmed those who heard of it and led to the saying, "He has done all things well, even to the point of making the deaf to hear and the dumb to speak." Mark apparently sees this as a very amazing miracle.[115] Thus with this allusion to Isa. 35 the connection with an action only God is said in the OT to be able to perform is made clear. It is probably not accidental that the remark about doing all things well seems to echo Gen. 1:31, which is a comment on the goodness of God's work in creation.[116]

---

in these two texts of the promise in Isa. 35:5-6 about the blind and deaf being healed in the eschatological situation.

112. Hooker, pp. 184-85.

113. See Gundry, pp. 383-84. The issue of life force being breathed into a diseased or dead or dormant person or object was at the heart of various ancient rituals, as the magical papyri show.

114. Guelich, p. 396.

115. See Hooker, p. 186.

116. See Guelich, p. 397.

I. Fed-up Gentiles (8:1-10)

The high degree of similarity between this particular feeding story and the one in 6:34-44 has led the preponderance of scholars to suggest that there was only one such event, reported in various forms. There is normally reference to 8:4, where the disciples make absolutely no mention of a previous feeding of this ilk, and it is difficult to believe they would have so soon forgotten a miracle of that magnitude and nature. On the other hand, Mark himself (and Matthew, who follows Mark in this) seems quite clearly to believe there were indeed two feedings. For instance, in Mark 8:19-20 Jesus actually reminds the disciples of the two feedings. Then too, one must remember that in the telling and retelling of the stories of the Jesus tradition, stories of a similar ilk took on similar formal features when they were repeated in the teaching and preaching. Indeed, there was, not surprisingly, some cross-fertilization of details between originally different stories, for example, the two different anointing stories in the Jesus tradition (cf. below on Mark 14:3-9 and par. and Luke 7), which are sufficiently different to make it unlikely that they go back to one tale. The question then becomes whether the differences are sufficient between the feeding stories in Mark 6 and 8 to posit two different stories at the beginning of the tradition, which stories Mark or his predecessor have edited so as to highlight the parallels for the sake of some point Mark wishes to make.[117]

In the first place, elsewhere Mark is quite careful in his selection of pericopes, and the structure we have noted above of this entire portion of Mark suggests a carefully thought-out plan of presentation. It is difficult to believe that someone with that degree of literary finesse would not have recognized the duplication, and yet 8:19-20 suggests that he doesn't see the tale that way. Thus we must place at least equal emphasis on the differences as on the similarities between the two feedings, as the differences are more than just the fact that two different audiences are involved (one predominantly Jewish, one predominantly Gentile).

Very clearly the first feeding indicates Jesus manifesting himself to Israel as the new Moses, but in Mark 8 there is no allusion to Moses or David. There the compassion of Jesus involves his concern about the crowd's physical hunger and does not involve his teaching, as in 6:34. It is true that both stories take place in an isolated or deserted location, an allusion perhaps to manna in the wilderness, but as Hurtado points out, at v. 3 it is stressed that some have come from far off, a phrase often used to speak of Gentile foreigners from distant lands (Isa. 60:4; Jer. 46:27; and material found only in the Greek version of Jer. 26:27 and 38:10).[118]

---

117. For an extended discussion of the doublet theory and arguments against the theory in this particular case, see Gundry, pp. 398-400.

118. Hurtado, pp. 109-10.

The emphasis in Mark 8 is quite clearly on Jesus feeding Gentiles, though of course the audience is mixed since it also involves some of the disciples. Notice also that a different word is used when Jesus gives thanks for the bread here (ευχαριστησας — the traditional meal grace word) than in Mark 6, the more Jewish emphasis on blessing God for the bread. This can hardly be accidental. Perhaps, indeed, Mark intends for us to see here a foreshadowing of the Christian eucharistic meal in which both Jew and Gentile participate.

It is uncertain whether we should make much of the numbers involved here, but seven and seventy are numbers associated with Gentiles (cf. Gen. 9:1ff. — seven commandments in the Noahic covenant; Gen. 10 — seventy Gentile nations). Another interesting difference in the two feeding stories is the different word used for baskets to pick up the scraps (cf. 6:43 and 8:8). In 6:43 the word used is for a small basket commonly used by early Jews to carry a variety of things such as lunch. 8:8 refers to a much larger basket, familiar in the wider cultural setting. Indeed, it could be a rope or mat basket large enough to carry a human being (Acts 9:25). One other conundrum raised by this text is where Dalmanutha was. Some commentators have suggested it might be Magdala.

In the feeding in Mark 8 Jesus takes the initiative, and there is no dialogue with the disciples about what to do with the crowds, unlike the story in Mark 6. But in both stories the Twelve are enlisted to distribute the food, and one wonders if Mark saw in this a foreshadowing of the mission of the church to the Gentiles.

J. The Tests and Leaven of the Pharisees (8:11-21)

Following on the heels of the great feeding miracle, especially vv. 11-12 come across as extremely ironic. The Pharisees come and dispute with Jesus about what he is saying and doing, and then they test him (or tempt him, depending on how one chooses to translate πειραζοντες). The test takes the form of requesting a sign from heaven, but Jesus has just performed such a sign, like unto the manna-from-heaven miracle in the OT. As, however, Lane points out, the Pharisees did not recognize Jesus' miracles as signs, and they appear in any case to be asking for a validating sign from heaven, not an act of compassion on earth.[119]

Notice that Mark, unlike the Fourth Evangelist, never calls Jesus' miracles "signs." It is then not a matter of the Pharisees refusing to believe that Jesus performed miracles; rather they doubted their godly origins and wanted confirmation from above. Jesus, of course, refuses to perform such a sign, not least because it is a request from those who refuse to have faith and would not likely gain faith if

119. Lane, p. 277.

they saw one. It is debated what should be made of the term αναστεναξας. While it certainly refers to some deep emotional reaction, should we see it as parallel to Jesus' anger in Mark 1:41 (cf. John 11:33), caused by the profound lack of faith of the Pharisees in relationship to Jesus, or should we see this as reflecting the sort of deep movement of the Spirit within a prophetic person who is about to speak an oracle? Though Guelich opts for the latter, both the context and the lack of oracular utterance following the use of this word, which occurs only once in the NT, speak against this conclusion.[120] It would appear that Jesus reacts very emotionally to the lack of faith of those around him, whether they be his adversaries or the crowds, or his friends, or even his disciples.

As Lane says, the call for a sign amounts to a radical denial of the summons to have faith. Jesus characterizes the Pharisees as being part of this generation, by which he means a generation characterized by wickedness, spiritual blindness, perversity. In the end Jesus simply leaves them standing without giving them what they desire. "Built into the perception in the ancient world is the recognition that powerful people can perform mighty deeds. The more powerful the person, the mightier the deeds. This understanding avoids many aspects commonly assumed in the discussion of 'miracles,' which is a relatively modern concept."[121] The use of the term "generation" or even "this generation" deliberately echoes the OT theme of Israel's sin of doubting God in spite of the miracles God had performed for her, especially for the wilderness-wandering generation (cf. Ps. 95:8-11; Deut. 32:5; Exod. 17:2; Num. 14:10-23).[122]

In 8:14-21 Jesus warns his disciples of the leaven of the Pharisees and of Herod.[123] Leaven was in various contexts a synonym for corruption (cf. 1 Cor. 5:6-8; Gal. 5:9), and was not identical with yeast, which was rare in antiquity.[124] Here Jesus seems to be referring to the subtle corrupting power of the Pharisees and Herod (presumably the latter, mainly because of John the Baptist's fate).[125] "Perhaps it is also its infectious, continuous operation which is referred to here (cf. Matt. 13.33 . . .)."[126] In Matthew leaven seems to be equated with false teaching, while in Luke it is equated with hypocrisy.[127] Again the disciples are

---

120. See Guelich, p. 414.

121. Painter, pp. 120-21.

122. See Hooker, p. 192.

123. This combination seems so strange that some few manuscripts (p45, W, cop^sa) have Herodians rather than Herod at this point, perhaps due to the influence of Mark 3:6 and 12:13.

124. Marcus, p. 506.

125. Painter, p. 122, however, suggests: "The leaven of Herod is Herod's evaluation of Jesus as John risen from the dead, which underestimated the significance of Jesus, as the disciples now did also."

126. Schweizer, p. 161.

127. See Hooker, p. 194.

seen to be quite obtuse, for they start talking about bringing too little bread with them on the boat trip. They are thinking purely on the physical level. Yes, they remember well the details of Jesus' miracles of feeding, but they do not understand beneath the surface what such a miracle signified. For them it was just an act "full of sound and fury, signifying nothing." Their privileged position and in-house teaching should have led to understanding, but instead they are still spiritually deaf, dumb, and blind. They are without understanding and are suffering from spiritual hardening of the arteries. It may be doubted that there are any eucharistic overtones to this story. Rather the subliminal message in a biography such as this one has to do with Christology, how the miracles reveal, though opaquely, who Jesus is.[128]

K. Blessing at Bethsaida (8:22-26)

Very clearly, the miracle recorded at 8:22-26 is meant to be seen in light of the spiritual blindness of the disciples just mentioned. Jesus is the one who opens the eyes of the blind. It is what Hooker calls an acted parable of the miracle of faith.[129] This miracle visually demonstrates the spiritual malady of the disciples. But note that it, unlike others, occurs in two stages, and so too in what follows in 8:27ff. The disciples' understanding of who Jesus is and his ministry likewise occurs in two stages. The placement of this particular miracle here is not accidental, but rather a visible parable of what was, and what was to come in the psyche of the disciples. Note too that this story, like the previous story involving spittle, is found only in Mark, and may accordingly tell us something about his unique purposes and methods.

Careful comparison with the story of the deaf mute in 7:32-37 shows some of Mark's compositional technique.[130] Though these two stories are not likely doublets, we do have the following identical phrases in the two tales — "they brought to him," "and begged him to," "and he spat." The request for Jesus to touch the infirm person, his response, the taking of the victim aside, and the request for secrecy are also closely similar.[131] This suggests that Mark wanted his hearers to notice these parallels and draw similar conclusions about what such stories could reveal about Jesus and his methods of performing such deeds.

Perhaps the reason for the privacy of healing here is because it parallels

---

128. Hooker, p. 196.

129. Hooker, p. 198.

130. Schweizer, p. 163, however, thinks it more likely that the two stories were linguistically and stylistically assimilated in Mark's source.

131. Rightly noted by Hooker, p. 197.

the privacy of enlightenment that happens to the Twelve when they are alone with Jesus. Once again it is crucial to bear in mind that there are no OT narratives of the giving of sight to the blind. There is some evidence that some teachers in early Judaism saw the giving of sight to the blind as a more difficult miracle even than raising the dead, and one that only God or his Anointed One could perform.[132]

Tacitus, *Hist.* 4.81, tells the story of how Vespasian cured a blind man in Alexandria by wetting his eyes with spittle. Thus presumably the two-stage process illustrates the difficulty of performing such a miracle. The difficulty may also explain why in this story alone Jesus asks about the success of his actions. The reference to the man seeing people looking like trees walking around not only indicates partial healing, but presumably that this man had not always been blind, for how would he have known what trees looked like otherwise? Finally, the man is able to see clearly, and Jesus sends him home, telling him not to go into the village, so the word will not be spread that Jesus is a wonderworker. Painter suggests that this story is a parable of hope about the disciples — now they see in part, in due course they will see more clearly, which leads us to Caesarea Philippi and the revelation given there.[133]

L. Credo at Caesarea (8:27-30)

There is little question but that this little pericope is the pivotal point in the Gospel up to this juncture. There are some interesting parallels between this story and the healing at Bethsaida: (1) the situation — 8:22/8:27; (2) partial sight — 8:23-24/8:27-28; (3) sight — 8:25/8:30; (4) injunction to silence — 8:26/8:30. Here, for the first time since 1:1, Jesus is designated the Christ. After that recognition comes, a dramatic change in tone happens in the story. From then on the focus is on Jesus as the suffering Son of Man or Messiah, and thus on Jesus going and dying. Thus after Caesarea Philippi we are focusing on preparation for the passion narrative and its significance. The theology of the cross, of suffering, of glory dominates the rest of this Gospel. That which was only previously hinted at is now shouted about.

Notice that human beings, left to their own musings, never come up with the idea of Jesus as Messiah. A prophet yes, even John the Baptist back from the dead, but not the Messiah. It is not completely clear whether the questions being raised about Jesus concern whether Jesus is *like* one of the great prophets or is one of the great prophets returned from the dead. In view of 2 Esd. 2:18, which speaks of Jeremiah and Isaiah returning at the end, it seems likely that

---

132. See Guelich, pp. 429-31.
133. Painter, p. 123.

the second interpretation is correct. Notice in Mark 8:29 the emphatic position of the υμεις — "but *you,* what do *you* say?" Myers rightly points out that the opinions of the disciples here almost exactly echo the editorial report in 6:14-15.[134] The point to note, then, is that the disciples seem to have little more insight into who Jesus is than "some" among the crowds who were saying these things, which things Herod had gotten wind of.

Peter here begins to act the part of the spokesman for the Twelve, a role he will continue to play in later chapters (cf. 9:5; 10:28; 11:21; 14:29). Peter is indeed the representative of the Twelve, but he represents both their insight and their blindness, with this pericope revealing both sides of this reality. By calling Jesus Messiah, Peter sees Jesus as God's anointed, and so most blessed, one. But there appears to have been little or no expectation in early Judaism that Messiah would come and suffer. Peter obviously doesn't understand Jesus' messianic vocation yet, and Mark, for his part, wants to make evident that until one understands *who* Jesus is, one cannot understand why he had to die. Thus Peter's confession, while true, is not the whole truth about Jesus.

But a key clue to understanding this whole crucial scene is being aware of the importance of the social setting of this event. Caesarea Philippi was a major Hellenistic city built in the far north of the land near Mount Hermon by Herod Philip in honor of Augustus. It had in ancient times been called Paneas in honor of the god Pan, who had a shrine there, but now there was a shrine for the emperor cult. In addition, it had been previously a site where the god Baal had been worshiped. Thus, in the midst of a city dedicated to false gods, Jesus' true identity is revealed.[135] The implications include that here we see the real divinity, indeed a divinity come in the flesh and countering the claims of emperors to being gods walking upon the earth, and paradoxically enough this divinity will insist on the title Son of Man.

The exhortation by Jesus not to tell anyone he was Messiah implies that he accepted the title but did not want it published abroad to all and sundry, lest it lead to gross misunderstanding. The verb επιτιμαω was also used at 1:25 and 3:12 to silence the unclean spirits who also made something of a true confession about Jesus. In fact, Schweizer says, "Peter's reply shows that he has no better understanding than the demons in 3.11 and 5.7, who gave a far better answer."[136] A title without a context of interpretation, especially the new interpretation Jesus wanted to give it, was worthless. "If Jesus commands secrecy, this is because the truth about his identity can be grasped only by those who are his disciples."[137] But there is more to the narrative than this. Jesus' identity is an

---

134. Myers, p. 242.
135. See Taylor, p. 375.
136. Schweizer, p. 174.
137. Hooker, p. 203.

apocalyptic secret which only the insiders at this point have any chance of understanding, and even they understand only in part. But the apocalyptic coloring of the narrative increases dramatically in the last pericope of this half of Mark's Gospel.

M. *The Passion Prediction (8:31-38)*

"The initial declaration that Jesus was God's beloved Son (1.11) was followed 'immediately' by his temptation by Satan in the wilderness. Now the drama is played out again at a human level. Peter's declaration that Jesus is the Messiah is followed by another attack attributed to Satan, this time working through Peter."[138] In fact, Mark has structured his narrative so that he stresses that Jesus faces a severe temptation at the three most crucial turning points in the narrative: (1) the beginning of the ministry; (2) at Caesarea Philippi where he is partially "unmasked" by a disciple; and (3) at the Garden of Gethsemane. In each case the nature of the temptation is to try and avoid what God wants Jesus to do and be.

In this material we begin to hear of the necessity of Jesus' suffering. The use of δεῖ here indicates divine necessity probably. The point is both that Jesus' future is part of God's predetermined plan and also that his suffering and death is not optional. Furthermore, this language is apocalyptic in character. "The theological emphasis in this assertion is to strengthen the faithful in times of frightful suffering. This is the way δεῖ is used in Mark 13:7 and also in Revelation. . . . The reader is to understand that the sufferings of Jesus were a crucial part of the eschatological drama."[139]

This may explain Jesus' strong response to Peter's rebuke.[140] Peter was acting the part of Satan and tempting Jesus to go against the specific divine will that Jesus must go the route of the cross. Garrett aptly sums up what is transpiring in this narrative when she says that here Mark gives us a glimpse of the forces that threaten to lead Jesus astray. "The severity of Jesus' rebuke of Peter in Mark 8:33 corresponds to the magnitude of Jesus' temptation here: the rebuke is sharp because the temptation is profound. Although Jesus knows where God's path for him leads — through suffering, rejection, death, and resurrection . . . he is sorely tempted to follow Peter in departing from this path. Jesus

---

138. Hooker, p. 205.

139. W. Bennett, "The Son of Man Must," *NovT* 17, no. 2 (1975): 113-29, here pp. 128-29.

140. Hooker, pp. 206-7, thinks what Jesus means is "get out of my sight," while Gundry, p. 433, suggests that he means "get back in line with the other disciples who are following behind me." There is, in any event, a stress in Mark on the disciples keeping a respectful distance (cf. 1:17-18, 20; 2:14; 6:1, 31; 8:34; 10:21, 28, 32, 52).

perseveres on the straight and narrow in spite of temptation, but one senses that his endurance is hard-won."[141]

Mark 8:31 is the first of three similar prophecies, about which we must first present a comparative chart and then analyze in detail.

The Passion Predictions

8:31	9:31	10:33-34
Son of Man must suffer, be rejected by elders, chief priests, scribes	Son of Man to be betrayed into human hands	Son of Man will be handed over to chief priests, scribes, who will condemn him to death,
be killed	they will kill him	hand him over to the Gentiles who will mock, spit upon, flog, kill him
after three days rise again	after three days rise again	after three days rise again.

It is immediately apparent that the third is the fullest and most specific of the three predictions, and the only one to mention Gentiles specifically. This may be because Gentile Christians largely constituted Mark's audience and he did not want to overemphasize a point which would be painful for that audience. Some scholars have suggested that there was originally only one passion prediction and that all three of these iterations go back to it. This is not impossible, but it would appear likely that some form of the prediction is authentic, for several reasons: (1) Notice that there is no reference to crucifixion, only that Jesus is killed. A later Christian creation would surely have wanted to use the language about Christ being crucified. (2) Each of these passion predictions speaks of the Son of Man, and we know that this was not the preferred terminology of the early church or even of Mark for Jesus. (3) The concluding clause does not match up exactly with the passion narrative account of a death on Friday and a resurrection on Sunday, unless one sees this phrase as meaning something like "after a while" or "after a couple days."[142] Gundry, however, suggests that we must see the Jewish reckoning of time here, which counts parts of days as whole days (cf. Gen. 42:17-18; 1 Sam. 30:1, 12-13; 2 Chron. 10:5, 12; Esther

---

141. S. Garrett, *The Temptations of Jesus in Mark's Gospel* (Grand Rapids: Eerdmans, 1998), p. 82.

142. Which in fact the phrase certainly can mean. Notice that both Matthew and Luke use the "on the third day" phrase, as does Paul at 1 Cor. 15:4. This is a more specific form of expression. See Painter, p. 125; Hooker, p. 206, says Mark's phrase means "a short while later."

4:16–5:1).[143] (4) We do not find here the later atonement theology of the church; rather, at most Jesus is portrayed as a martyr to the cause. It would not have taken an especially prescient person to conclude that he would meet a violent death, considering what Jesus did and the volatile environment in which he did it, especially in light of what happened to Jesus' friend the Baptist.[144]

It also needs to be noted that in fact the three passion predictions do not simply duplicate but supplement one another, none of them telling the entire tale. Only the first mentions the rejection by the authorities explicitly; only the second mentions the betrayal; only the third mentions the condemnation to death, the scourging, mocking, and spitting by Gentiles. Together they gradually reveal to the reader or hearer an ever fuller portrait of the passion narrative.

V. 32 indicates that Jesus spoke these words with complete frankness and openness. As Schweizer says, the phrase "he made this very clear to them" should be compared with the similar phrase in 2:2 and 4:33.[145] The emphasis in the phrase is on the importance of the remark just made or about to be made. Peter's response to the first passion prediction indicates he understands quite well what Jesus is saying — he just doesn't like it. There is no more time for veiledness or parabolic speech — Jesus is now explaining openly his mission and its means of fulfillment. The messianic secret, if we can even speak of such in this Gospel, is about to become an increasingly open secret, until on the cross the full revelation of the character of the Messiah transpires. As Peter had rebuked Jesus, so Jesus rebukes him, saying, "Get behind me" (presumably meaning "take the place of a disciple following me and my example"). Far from protesting Jesus' destiny and getting in the way of the trip up to Jerusalem, he ought as a disciple to follow in Jesus' footsteps, taking up his cross and following him. "Peter's assertion of authority in relation to Jesus was inappropriate for a disciple."[146] It is, of course, possible to see the use of the term "Satan" here as generic, simply meaning adversary, but the apocalyptic character of the narrative suggests a stronger reading. While Peter is not possessed, he is influenced by the forces of darkness to think in a merely human manner about the future of Jesus. So Peter unwittingly serves as Satan's tool here, ironically at the precise moment when he also has gained a partial insight into Jesus' identity. Like the blind man healed, he sees, but through a glass darkly, and so is easily misled.[147]

It is intriguing that the very same phrase οπισω μου occurs in both v. 33 and v. 34. In the first instance, when coupled with a strong verb, it means "get behind me" or even "get out of my sight," but in the second case it means what

---

143. Gundry, pp. 432-35.
144. See Hooker, pp. 204-6.
145. Schweizer, p. 173.
146. Painter, p. 126.
147. See Garrett, pp. 77-79.

it normally means elsewhere in Mark, namely, "after me," which, when coupled with the verb "to follow," means "to follow after me" (i.e., "be my disciple, follow my example") or even "get in line behind me."[148] Peter has a choice — he can either be a hindrance or obstacle serving Satan and so be something Jesus must leave behind on the way to the cross, or he can be a follower of Jesus, in which case he gets in line behind Jesus, takes up his own cross, and prepares for suffering as Jesus is doing. Myers sums up the episode as follows:

> Peter: Jesus is Messiah.
> Jesus silences Peter (8:30).
> Jesus: Son of Man must suffer (8:31).
> Peter silences Jesus (8:32).
> Jesus silences Peter (8:33).
> Jesus silences Peter as Satan's spokesman.
> As he earlier did the demons.[149]

Notice, though, that at v. 34 the call of discipleship and cross bearing is directed to all, including the crowd. As Hooker suggests, the crucial divide is not so much between those who do and don't confess Jesus as between those who do and don't follow him.[150] It is worth noting that Plutarch reminds us that "Every criminal who is executed carries his own cross" (*De sera* 9.554b). This is important for, as Lane avers, it means that this great cost is for all followers of Jesus, not just for the inner circle of the Twelve, and it involves great shame, even potentially public shaming.[151] Gundry suggests that "take up your cross" means be prepared to be ridiculed, spit on, be seen and treated as a criminal, be thought to be guilty of shameful things.[152] There is, however, no reason why Jesus could not have in addition meant this remark rather literally — be prepared to die a shameful death by public execution. V. 34 would not have sounded like a flowery metaphor to first-century persons. Rather it would be seen as an invitation to come and die, an invitation to martyrdom. True enough, Jesus does not inculcate a martyrdom complex, he does not insist his followers lose their lives, but he does insist they deny themselves and be prepared to die if that should be required to remain true to their faith in and following of Jesus. If indeed the reference to the cross is original, then it could even be said that Jesus invited his followers to take a walk on the wild side, for only criminals and revolutionaries and slaves were crucified. Crucifixion was justly called the extreme penalty and was reserved for the most hard-

---

148. See Hooker, p. 206.
149. Myers, p. 244.
150. Hooker, pp. 206-7.
151. Lane, pp. 306-7.
152. Gundry, p. 435.

ened criminals and those committing treason against the state. Thus Jesus' exhortation would not be seen as an appealing call to discipleship in its original setting. The exhortation means that the disciple in principle gives up his right to his own life up-front. He would be affirming a willingness to give all, even his very life, in order to follow Jesus.

V. 35 deals with the paradox involved in this sort of call to discipleship. This saying appears in four variations in the Gospels (cf. this verse to Matt. 10:39; Luke 17:33; John 12:25), and was obviously important to the early church. Those who want to preserve their life (ψυχη here has its Jewish sense of life, rather than soul) ultimately must give it up anyway, and in fact wanting to preserve one's life now has the opposite effect at the eschaton — one loses it then. Possibly we should see v. 35 as an editorial word of encouragement by Mark to his Gentile audience under fire. Whoever loses his life for Jesus' sake or for the sake of the gospel shall be saved. Here του ευαγγελιου likely means the good news about Jesus, its later Christian sense, not the good news Jesus himself proclaimed about the incoming dominion of God.

Then v. 36 speaks of the futility of gaining all worldly goods but losing one's life. There is nothing worth the price of life, no one could ever give an equivalent to it (could this be an indirect comment against slavery and the buying of humans?). Here Jesus may have had Ps. 49 in mind. V. 38 must be seen as a Semitic parallelism, indicating the identity of Jesus and the Son of Man who would come in glory. How one reacts to Jesus now will determine how the Son of Man reacts to that person on Judgment Day. Owning Christ leads to being owned by him, being ashamed of Christ will lead to him not recognizing a person on the final day, when he comes with his angels. Thus Jesus' ministry and life is the anvil on which one's metal will be tested. How one reacts to him will determine one's ultimate fate. Yet there is a very different way one may read 8:38 and its reference to messengers, if one reads it in conjunction with 9:1. But we will reserve that discussion for the treatment of 9:1, the beginning of the second half of this Gospel.

Bridging the Horizons

Teaching or preaching narrative material can be tricky business. It is often hard to know when the author is simply being descriptive and when he is also being prescriptive. A second order of discourse sometimes clarifies this matter. For example, in Mark 6:6b-13 we begin to get a feel for how much Mark thinks discipleship really entails the following of Jesus' example, for here we have explicit instructions given to the Twelve as to what they are to do, missionally speaking. What is both interesting and odd about this passage is that the disciples are told how to behave, but nothing is specified about the content of their preaching or teaching. It becomes clear that orthopraxy was as important to Jesus as orthodoxy, the witness of the life as crucial as the witness of the lips. But notice that Mark is not just concerned about the disciples making a good impression as embodiments of the message and even embodiments of God in Christ's reaction to the rejection of the message. This is probably what the shaking of the dust from the feet signifies, or as Jesus puts it, those who reject his agents reject him, and even the One who sent him, and the result is being left behind by God.

Another very interesting feature of this story is that Jesus never sends out any of the disciples alone. Rather he sends them out two by two, perhaps mainly because it took the testimony of two witnesses to confirm the truth of something in Jewish culture. Yet it may also be that he thought they were not ready for doing ministry alone, or that they needed the moral support of a companion, *koinonia*, while on the road. It has been pointed out that Jesus endows these disciples with authority and power over all sorts of evil. This meant they did not need to fear anything or any force they came up against.[153] Notice too that these disciples were not to go forth as beggars or like Cynic philosophers. To the contrary, they were to go forth and give rather than going forth to get.

Note also that Mark characterizes this early pre-Easter kerygma as stressing repentance, just as the Baptist and Jesus, perhaps under John's influence, did. This in turn suggests that Jesus was convinced there was something seriously wrong with the soul of God's people. Sometimes the first step toward better health is a recognition that one is sick. The mention of the casting out of demons and healing also speaks to the state of Israel's soul.

One of the interesting suggestions in Myers's *Binding the Strong Man* is that the political situation in a nation so affects its soul that its psyche is open and vulnerable to all kinds of bad influences. A nation under occupation or siege is a nation with a siege mentality, so to speak. Having personally spent time in post-Communist Russia recently and listening to the stories there, I can vouch for the fact that spiritual and political oppression are indeed closely interwoven. It's a matter of wrestling not just with flesh and blood but also with principalities and powers. An apocalyptic situation of oppression leads to an apocalyptic mentality about things. But one must hasten to add that Mark really believes that all this talk about unclean spirits and the devil is not merely an issue of psychoses, but rather a description of an actual force extant in the world that bewitches, bothers, and bewilders God's people and others as well.

As if to punctuate the intertwining of the spiritual and the political, Mark follows the brief comments about exorcism with the grisly tale of the beheading of John the Baptist. But how does one approach the proclamation of this material? It seems more suitable for the tabloids than for the pulpit in some respects. I

---

153. Pointed out to me by a pastor, Ray Stedman, some twenty-five years ago.

can't really imagine a church drama made of this grisly tale. Yet there is indeed a serious purpose to the tale beyond merely informing us about a tragic set of events. It serves as a warning about what happens to a society's prophets. More often than not they are marginalized by the powerful, and almost as often they die prematurely. The story serves as a foreshadowing of what will happen to Jesus. But John is more than just a foreshadowing, he is a prototype of Christ.[154] This text also serves as a warning to disciples who would take up their own crosses and follow Jesus. As Dietrich Bonhoeffer once said, when Christ calls a person, he calls him to come and die. As such, it serves as a corrective to a portrait of discipleship that suggests it is merely a matter of devoted study to the teacher's words, or of praising him for his miracles, or of confessing the truth about the Master.

So, should one speak about the cost of being faithful to God? Should one preach on corruption in high places? Would a moralistic teaching about the dangers of making rash oaths suffice? I have even heard an unfair use of this text to generalize about the wiles of women. But if this text has anything to tell us, it's not so much about the machinations of women caught in a corrupt patriarchal system as about the way power corrupts and ultimate power corrupts ultimately, especially weak men in power such as Herod. We are told that Herod knew John to be a righteous and holy man and that he even protected him, until of course he concluded it was more important to protect his own reputation, his honor rating in the eyes of his sycophants, than to be a person of integrity. This story also however raises a serious moral dilemma: Is it more important to be a just and righteous and fair person or to be a person whose word is his bond? Would the less evil thing have been for Herod to violate his rash oath and save John's life, or not? Mark does not tell us his opinion on this subject, as there are no editorial asides at this juncture. While being a promise keeper is often a good thing, it in part depends on what sort of promises one has made, and whether they are in accord with God's will in the first place.

Mark 6:30-44 tells us of the first occasion the Twelve became apostles, that is, sent-out agents of Jesus. As English says, it is not their own status or authority that is the basis of their actions, but rather the authority and power and status of the one who sent them.[155] They must return to Jesus after the assigned task is done to report and go apart and be refreshed with him. There is a pattern in Mark of both Jesus and the disciples alternating between advance and retreat, between ministry and recharging the spiritual batteries. There is something to be learned from this rhythm of work and renewal. This text also reminds us that the Twelve were called apostles because they functioned as such — as Jesus' special agents. The term indicated the function, and only secondarily if at all their status.

---

154. D. English, *The Message of Mark* (Downers Grove: InterVarsity, 1992), pp. 130-31.
155. English, p. 132.

The feeding of the crowds in Mark 6, followed immediately by the miracle of walking on the water, reminds us that this is not a story about mundane affairs. To be sure, the human element is there in all parts of the story, but the focus is clearly on the extraordinary and even at times on the superhuman. No one in the ordinary course of human affairs can feed five thousand people on a single McDonald's Happy Meal, nor can ordinary mortals walk on water in the course of their normal activities. This Gospel is about what happens when there is a divine-human encounter, when God is loose upon the earth. Thus, after a brief interlude, the biographical focus returns to the narrative with the stories about the feeding of the five thousand and the walking on water. Both stories are intended to reveal certain things about Jesus, but also about the disciples. They are more personally rather than principally focused.

One lesson to be learned from the feeding of the five thousand is that it is not enough for a preacher to draw a crowd. The question is what one will do with the crowd once it has assembled. Jesus believed he had a moral responsibility to feed the crowd, both physically and spiritually. He saw that as a crowd they were not a community — they were like sheep without a shepherd. This brings up the important point that in order for there to be community, there needs to be a focus and a purpose. The focus of the Christian community is of course Christ, and when a community loses sight of that fact it loses its sense of purpose. Notice that Jesus does not immediately feed the crowd; he first exhorts his followers to do so. In the end they only distribute the food and take on the role of servants of the crowd — waiters as it were (which was usually seen as the task of slaves in the Greco-Roman world).

The danger in dealing with this very familiar material is that one will either be trite or strive too hard to find something new to say about the stories. There is also something elemental about these stories, both involving what are usually called nature miracles. In both these stories it is appropriate to speak of the divine. The question raised by such miracle narratives is whether they are meant to suggest that the laws of nature have been violated, or would it be better to speak about them being transcended by the Transcendent One? It seems odd to speak of the divine Christ as violating laws that according to the Christology of the early church he helped set up in the first place.

There are certainly a variety of ways the feeding of the five thousand should not be preached or taught. (1) It should not be presented as a story about everyone chipping in and doing their part so that as a result everyone is surprisingly fed. There is no indication of any contribution from the crowd other than the initial five loaves and two fish. Trying to provide naturalistic explanations for miracle stories is an exercise in futility rather than fertility. (2) Equally unhelpful is the classing of miracle stories with myths, presumably in order to justify demythologizing the tale. But these tales have no other substance than the telling of a miracle, and their primary function is to inform the listener about some aspect of the truth about Jesus, and to a lesser degree about the disciples or crowds. (3) Equally unhelpful is the attempt to treat such stories as the residue of primitive cultures which tells us something about the belief systems of the ancients but nothing about reality. In some individual cases this might be correct about a particular story, but the miracle stories cannot be written off in this fashion any more than all the exorcism stories can be convincingly read as stories about mentally ill persons.

One of the possibly important goals of teaching and preaching such material must be to confront the modern secular world with the issue of whether miracles do or do not transpire in human history. In other words, we must not remove the offense of supernaturalism from the stories, for in the end the offense we are talking about is whether or not there is a transcendent God who dynamically intervenes on behalf of needy humankind. A nontheological reading of these stories is usually at the end of the day reductionism and a violation of the spirit in which they were written. A simple way to approach these stories is to ask a series of questions about them: (1) What do they tell us about Jesus? (2) What do they tell us about the disciples or the crowds? (3) What do they tell us about the interrelationships between these individuals and/or groups?

It is apropos when dealing with the walking-on-water story to highlight some of its often neglected elements. For example, one could see the story as one about the testing of the disciples and how they would do when faced with a problem without Jesus present. If that is what the story is partly about, they failed the test. The story shows a verisimilitude in the way it exegetes the character of Christian life in general. It so often happens that when trouble comes, God or Christ seems so very far away. But we should take comfort from the fact that up on the hill there is One praying for us. The story, following hard on the heels of the feeding of the five thousand, reminds us that when our needs have been provided for by God, then God does indeed send us forth to labor in his vineyard and be tested by the realities of this world, but he will come to us in our hour of need.

In this episode the disciples are once more confronted by a crisis. Just as they did not know how to handle the crowd, so they did not know how to deal with the sea. The latter must have been somewhat humiliating since many of the Twelve were fishermen. If they should have learned something from the first miracle on the sea when Jesus calmed the storm, it appears they had forgotten that lesson — namely, that with Jesus nearby all would be well. It is hard to know what to make of the remark that Jesus was about to pass them by, walking on the sea. Was he putting them to the test? The belief in the sea being the resting place of spirits of the departed and of demons may come into play in this story and may help explain the disciples' terror. The Son had been mistaken for an unholy ghost. In any event, these disciples are people we can at least relate to. They are fallible, but to Jesus they were also lovable. He did indeed come to their rescue in the hour of need. In the feeding of the five thousand we see his compassion on the crowds; in the walking on water we see his compassion on his followers. And the truth is, we need it just as much as those outside the circle of disciples.

Mark 7 presents various quandaries for those who don't live in cultures with strong ritual boundaries. Nevertheless, every culture has its own concepts of what amounts to dirt and what amounts to dirty. Dirt has been defined by the cultural anthropologists as matter out of place. Similarly, becoming unclean amounts to a process whereby something or someone clean comes into contact with something out of bounds or out of place — for example, a living person touching a dead person, a healthy person touching a sick person. The sick and the dead are seen as persons on the margin of society and in some cases out of bounds altogether. An outcast is by definition someone who has been placed or has placed himself outside the circle of the clean, the acceptable, the normal. At the root of this entire way of thinking is the basic concept that the abnormal is aberrant and therefore must be defined as unclean or inappropriate. Only in this way can the normal know what normalcy is. At the root of all this in the Hebrew way of thinking is the belief that God demands perfection — perfect sacrifices, perfect behavior, entire holiness of his children. There is also a theology of creation that says God made everything very good, and if a person or thing is no longer in that condition, it has strayed from God's intended purpose for such a thing or person. Anything imperfect thus is seen as unclean, even in some cases unholy if the issue is moral imperfection. In this context, the discussion by Jesus in Mark 7 begins to make a good deal of sense. Jesus is suggesting that the world is not in itself the zone of contamination. Thus food, flesh, trees, objects are not in themselves unclean. No, the zone of contamination has been contracted to the sinful human heart, and what comes out of that is or can be very unclean. Herein we can begin to understand the differing strategies of Jesus and the Pharisees. Both were leading holiness movements.

The Pharisees' view of how to right the ship of Israel was to really create a priesthood of all believers. Everyone needed to live by the rules previously reserved for Levitical priests. Jesus took a very different tack. His view was that everyone needed to be transformed from the inside out. Israel needed a heart transplant, a new heart, before it could receive new marching orders. The Pharisees' solution placed the emphasis on a new degree of rigor in orthopraxy. Jesus placed the emphasis on human character transformation. Both were concerned with deeds as well as attitudes, but Jesus believed the kingdom was coming in and God was actually changing people. The Pharisees apparently did not. It was God's activity, not human activity, much less human tradition, that was the starting point for the blueprint for the new people of God.

The good news involves both the transformation of the mind and the healing of the body. It also involves the leaving behind of some cherished traditions; often the greatest force of opposition to renewal is not the evils of this world but a clinging to past goods. It has been said that the good is often the worst enemy of the best, and it is so in this case. It was no bad thing for God's people to set themselves apart and strive to be scrupulous about the observance of the Law, even the ritual Law, in order to be holy before God. But when God has done a new work of grace, the old becomes obsolescent. In the dawning eschatological age when God comes to reign in the lives of his people, it is God in person, and not merely the doing of rituals, that purifies the people of God. By the same token, since God can indwell the human life, it is those internal things that dwell in the heart that need to be dealt with, and only God's power and cleansing force, not ritual purification, can deal with such internal matters. The question of Shakespeare's Macbeth — "Who can minister to a mind diseased?" — is appropriate at this juncture, and the answer is the God who takes up residence in the midst of his people.

"It is important to distinguish between adherence to tradition and obedience to God. . . . Denominational and theological rivalries have been fuelled by concentration on the traditions and practices of others — in worship or organization or life style — to the neglect of the deeper question of whether they follow God's word or whether they are marked by spiritual integrity."[156] Tradition in itself is not necessarily a bad thing. But following it is no substitute for obedience to the heart of the gospel.

Mark 7:24-30 presents an uncomfortable tale about Jesus and a non-Jewish woman. In some respects it is hard to read the story of the Syrophoenician woman without wincing, because of the apparently abrasive portrait of Jesus it seems to convey. Jesus appears to be a racist and a misogynistic person. Yet in fact, this impression is more conveyed by the later Matthean version of the story than the Markan one. Notice how in Mark Jesus says, "*first* let the children of God be fed," suggesting that others could be fed later. Furthermore, notice that the woman accepts the honor challenge of Jesus, which places her in the category of a dog but nonetheless gets her what she needs from Jesus. In Mark the focus is on the aptness of the woman's verbal reply. She has passed the honor challenge and is rewarded for her good answer. Thus the scene needs to be seen as Jesus testing a foreigner, not as Jesus merely reflecting the parochialisms of his day.

The story, then, on the surface, bristles with features that are certainly not politically correct. Jesus calls a woman a dog. He suggests that foreigners have no right to eat at the same table with Jews (or at least that Jews, God's chosen people, must be fed first). The woman obtains what she desperately needs by a wise or witty reply. The picture of Jesus in Mark's Gospel is without doubt stark and hard-edged. But the ready way that Jesus does respond to the woman when she accepts the testing strictures he places on her suggests that perhaps all along

---

156. English, p. 147.

there was something in Jesus' voice that indicated that he was willing to act if she pursued the matter in faith. The very fact that Jesus was in foreign territory and prepared to entertain foreign company already suggests that it would be wrong to see this as a story about a xenophobic Jesus. Jesus' being in the home region of this woman tells us clearly that he probably did not share the views of many of his Jewish contemporaries about unclean lands and unclean persons. Nonetheless, the story makes clear that Jesus saw it as his first responsibility to feed and help God's people, but the good news is that he was also prepared to help others who came to him. We cannot really talk about a Gentile mission during Jesus' life, but we can talk about Gentiles who were helped and healed by Jesus, a precedent for the later mission of non-Jews.

The story of the blind man at Bethsaida who is healed in stages shows that the Markan Jesus is not looking for publicity, especially not in regard to his miracles, which lead people to follow Jesus for the wrong reasons, and without becoming disciples. This story raises the question whether some who currently claim to be followers of Jesus are in it for the fringe benefits. One could also address the fact that even some miracles take a bit of time. In a world of instant everything, not all good things can be had immediately, especially when we are talking about healing. Even Jesus didn't always produce instant miracles on demand.

Mark 8:27-30 presents a major climax of this Gospel. There comes a time when one is put on the spot, and what one says on that occasion makes a world of difference in one's own life and perhaps even in those of others. Such an occasion is a wedding, or an interview for a job, or an oral examination for a doctoral degree. I remember well the day I was called upon in a doctoral seminar to translate a bit of the *Didache* and explain it. Sitting on my left was the former archbishop of Canterbury, Lord Michael Ramsey. Around the rest of the table were world-renowned scholars and a few doctoral candidates. I knew what I would say on that occasion would be closely scrutinized, perhaps criticized, and so I chose my words very carefully. Yet afterwards I was asked by my mentor C. K. Barrett: "And what precisely do you mean by that?" My temptation was to fade into the woodwork, saying meekly, "Honest, I didn't mean anything really." One wonders if Peter felt that way after he spoke about who Jesus was on that day at Caesarea Philippi. Certainly we are meant to realize that he said more than he knew or, more likely, what was true, but less than what was fully adequate to describe Jesus, for Jesus goes on to speak about the Son of Man and his mission.

The story of Peter's confession raises the important point of what significance should be given to a true but nonetheless inadequate confession of who Jesus is. Couldn't we say that, in a sense, almost all confessions about Jesus are inadequate if he indeed was and is both divine and human? The story and its sequel remind us that the confession of Jesus as the Christ without the addition of "and him crucified" fails to get at the heart of the matter. Mark makes quite clear that the passion predictions tell us something essential about Jesus. The way these stories are arranged reminds us that one cannot understand why the passion of Christ was necessary without having some sense of who Jesus was. The *who* question must be answered before one can understand why Jesus had to die. From a theological point of view this is an important point. The personal encounter with Jesus and a recognition of his identity must come prior to a real understanding of soteriology, or in particular atonement theology. One may think, for example, of the threefold account in Acts 9, 22, 26 of Saul's conversion, where the primary or first-order question asked by Saul is, "Who are you?" In pursuing a seeker-friendly church, one needs to keep these things in mind.

Yet it is important to stress that Jesus' death is the heart of the matter. It was what was necessary for Jesus to do if humankind was to be ransomed from the realm of darkness. This raises profound questions about the nature of God. What sort of God would require that his Son sacrifice himself on a cross? If Jesus' death was the one necessary and sufficient means of human salvation, then one can understand this demand and plan. But if this is not the case, in what sense can God be called a loving parent, much less a loving parent of his only-begotten child? What sort of parent would demand such a thing of an only child? We are dealing with a profound mystery here, and what needs to be said is that Mark believes that Jesus came to serve and lay down his life as a ransom for many. This was indeed the only way God could be both righteous and the righter of fallen humanity, both just and the justifier of sinful people. It was the only way God could express his love without becoming an unrighteous God, or conversely express his holiness without being an unloving God. Behind the scandal of the cross is the scandal of a God who is holy love — not one without the other. This God also demands in our behavior not unholy, infinitely indulgent love which simply passes over or even indulges sin, nor unfeeling holiness that makes no room for forgiveness, but that balance of justice and mercy that we see in the famous story about the woman caught in adultery where Jesus says, "neither do I condemn you," but adds, "go and sin no more."

The end of Mark 8 includes a call to discipleship in the form of Jesus suggesting that his disciples must take up their own crosses and follow him. It needs to be borne in mind that Jesus is not talking about ordinary, or even extraordinary, human burdens that we sometimes bear but that have no direct connection with discipleship to Jesus. For example, an illness may be a thorn in the flesh, but it is not our cross to bear. An injury may be a worrisome thing, but it is not our cross to bear. A difficult relative or a troublesome friend may be a problem, but it is not our cross to bear. "Cross-bearing as a follower of Jesus means nothing less than giving one's whole life over to following him. And here comes another surprise. This is the way of total freedom. If you clutch your life wholly to yourself, protecting it against all others, asserting all your rights, needs and privileges, you lose it because it isn't life any longer. If, however, you acknowledge that life is not yours by right, that all is privilege, and that it is to be lived in the love that the gospel story reveals, self-giving love, then you possess it wholly. There is now nothing to lose and everything to gain."[157]

In the end of Mark 8, Jesus tells his disciples that there are not merely many things worth living for, but some things worth dying for. Notice that he does not suggest that there are some things worth killing for. Jesus does have a theology of martyrdom, but he reflects no theology of a just war, perhaps chiefly because of his theocratic vision of reality. The kingdom of God is already breaking in to human history and God is king and judge. God will attend to the sorting out of such matters. Indeed, God is attending to the sorting out of those justice issues by Jesus' death on the cross. There is also the timely reminder to our own materialistic era that it profits nothing to gain the whole world and lose one's soul. Some years ago archaeologists discovered the tomb of Emperor Charlemagne of France. When it was opened for the first time in many centuries, the usual treasures of the kingdom were found, but in the center of the vault was a great throne, and upon it sat the skeleton of the ruler himself with an open Bible in his lap. His bony finger had been made to point to a certain verse of Scripture — in fact, the one just referred to: "For what shall it profit a person if he shall gain the whole world and lose his own soul?" It is a timely reminder that our Western society needs to hear over and over again.

---

157. English, p. 161.

X. Transfigured Glory and Transformed Disciples (9:1–10:52)

This section of the narrative can be seen as something of an interlude between the confession of who Jesus is and the first announcement of the passion, on the one hand, and the relating of the passion narrative on the other. Mark uses it to reinforce the earlier pictures of Jesus as a human and yet divine figure, as a radical teacher and yet much more than a teacher, as a healer and yet much more than a healer.

TRANSLATION — 9:1–10:52

9 *And he says to them: "Amen I say to you that some are here of those standing who will definitely not taste death until they have seen the dominion of God having come with power." And after six days Jesus takes along Peter and Jacob and John, and he leads them up onto a high mountain apart, alone. And he was transformed before them and his garment was glistening so very white that an earthly bleacher is not able thus to whiten it. And Elijah and Moses appeared to them, and they were talking with Jesus. And Peter responding says to Jesus, "Rabbi, good it is that we are here, and let us make three shelters, one for you, one for Moses, one for Elijah," for he did not know what he was saying, for he was terrified. And there was a cloud enveloping them, and there was a voice from the cloud: "This is my Son the Beloved One, listen to him." And suddenly looking around they no longer saw anyone but Jesus alone with them. And as they were coming down from the mountain he ordered them in order that they not recount what they saw to anyone until the time when the Son of Man rose from the dead. And they kept the word to themselves discussing what is the* resurrection from the dead. And inquiring they say to him, "Why do the scribes say that Elijah must come first?" But he says to them, "Elijah comes first to restore all things, and how it is written about the Son of Man that he suffers much and must be treated with contempt, but I say to you that Elijah has come and they did to him whatever they wished, just as it is written about him."

And coming to the disciples he saw a large crowd surrounding them and scribes discussing with them and immediately all the crowd seeing him were amazed, and running up they greeted him. And he asked them, "What are you discussing with them?" And one from the crowd answered him, "Teacher, I brought my son to you, having a dumb spirit, and wherever it seizes him it dashes him down, and he foams and grinds his teeth and he becomes rigid. And I spoke to your disciples in order that they might cast it out of him, and they were not able." But responding to them, he says: "O faithless generation, how long will I be with you? How much longer must I put up with you? Bring him to me." And they brought him to him. And seeing him the spirit immediately convulsed him, and falling down upon the earth, he rolled about foaming. And he asked his father, "How long have things such as this happened to him?" But he said, "From childhood. And often it casts him even into fire and into water in order to destroy him. But if you are able to do anything, help us, have compassion upon us." But Jesus said to him, "If you are able? Everything is possible to those who believe." Immediately the father of the child crying out said: "I believe. Help my unbelief." But Jesus, seeing that the crowd was running together, rebuked the unclean spirit, saying to him, "Dumb and deaf spirit, I command you, come out from him and never reenter him." And crying out and with many violent spasms it came out. And he was as dead, so that many said that he died. But Jesus grasped his hand, raised him, and he stood up. And when he had entered the house his disciples inquired of him privately, "Why were we not able to cast it out?" And he said to them, "This kind is not able to be exorcised except through prayer."[1]

From there, they went on, passing through Galilee, and he did not wish anyone to know, for he taught his disciples and he said to them, "The Son of Man will be delivered into the hands of human beings, and they will kill him, and having been killed, he will rise after three days." But they failed to understand the matter, and they were afraid to ask him.

And he entered into Capernaum, and when he was in the house he asked them, "What were you arguing about on the road?" But they were silent, for they argued on the road with one another about which one was greater. And having sat down, he called the Twelve and he says to them, "If anyone wishes to be first, he must be last of all, and servant of all." And taking a child, he stood him in the

---

1. A variety of witnesses, including many very important ones (p45vid, ℵ, A, C, D, K, et al.), add "and fasting." It is probably true that this reflects the fact that fasting became an important practice in the early church, which caused some scribes to add the phrase. See Metzger, *TCGNT*, p. 101.

midst of them and embracing him he said to them, "Whoever welcomes one child of this sort in my name, welcomes me; and whoever welcomes me, welcomes not me but the one who sent me."

John said to him, "Teacher, we saw someone in your name casting out demons, and we tried to stop him, because he was not following us."[2] But Jesus said, "Do not hinder him, for no one who does a mighty work in my name will also be able to quickly speak evil of me. For whoever is not against us, is for us. For whoever gives you to drink a cup of water in the name, because you are of Christ, truly I say that that one will not lose his reward. And whoever causes to stumble one of these little ones of those believing [in me], better it is to him if he put an asses' millstone around his neck and cast himself into the sea. And if your hand scandalizes you, cut it off. Better it is to enter into life disabled than having two hands be cast into gehenna, into the unquenchable fire. And if your foot scandalizes you, cut it off. Better it is to enter into life lame than having two feet to be cast into gehenna.[3] And if your eye scandalizes you, cast it out. Better it is for you to enter into the dominion of God one-eyed than having two eyes be cast into gehenna, where the worm does not die and the fire is not quenched, for all will be salted with fire. Salt is good. But if salt becomes insipid, how can you season it again? Have salt in yourselves, and live in peace among one another."

10 And rising up from there he comes into the region of Judea beyond the Jordan and again the crowds flock to him, and as he was accustomed, again he taught them. And Pharisees coming to him inquired of him if it was permitted for a man to divorce his wife, testing him. But he answering said to them, "What did Moses command you?" But they said, "Moses allowed a certificate of divorce to be written and to divorce." But Jesus said to them, "For your hard-heartedness was this commandment written to you. But from the beginning of creation 'male and female he made them'; for this reason a man leaves behind his father and mother, and sticks to his wife[4] and the two shall turn into one flesh, so that they are no longer two but rather

---

2. There is considerable confusion about the original form of the text at this juncture. The principal variants are: (1) "and we forbade him, because he was not following us"; (2) "who does not follow us, and we forbade him"; (3) "who does not follow us, and we forbade him, because he does not follow us." The last is surely a conflation of earlier readings, and so not the original form of the text. Probably we should prefer the first reading, which has a bit better manuscript support (A, B, Δ, et al.). See Metzger, *TCGNT,* p. 101.

3. On the basis of v. 48, apparently, some manuscripts add what we call v. 46 here, "where their worm does not die, and the fire is not quenched." It is probably not original at this point in the text. See Metzger, *TCGNT,* p. 102.

4. This last clause is missing in A, B, and several other important witnesses. This may have simply been an oversight of a scribe which was perpetuated in later manuscripts, but one could argue that the clause was added on the basis of the parallel in Matt. 19:5. On the whole, however, in view of the reference to "the two" in v. 8, it seems more likely that the clause is original. See Metzger, *TCGNT,* p. 104.

one flesh. What then God joined together let no one put asunder." And in the house again the disciples asked him about this. And he says to them, "Whoever divorces his wife and marries another woman commits adultery against her. And if a woman divorcing her man marries another man, she commits adultery."

And children were being brought to him in order that he might touch them but the disciples rebuked them. But Jesus saw this and was indignant and he said to them, "permit the children to come to me and do not hinder them, for of such is the dominion of God. Amen I say to you, whoever does not receive the dominion of God as a child, will not enter into it." And taking her into his arms he was blessing her placing his hands on her.

And he set out into the road and running up and falling on him one asks him, "Good teacher, what shall I do in order to inherit eternal life?" But Jesus said to him, "Why do you call me good? No one is good except one — God. You know the commandments 'Do not murder, do not commit adultery, do not steal, do not bear false witness, do not defraud,[5] honor your father and mother.'" But he said to him, "Teacher, all these I observed from my youth." And Jesus looking attentively at him loved him and said to him, "One thing you are lacking, go sell whatever you have and give to the poor, and have treasure in heaven, and come follow me." But that one looked gloomy upon this word, he left saddened, for he had much possessions. And looking around Jesus says to his disciples, "With what difficulty those having wealth will enter the dominion of God." But the disciples were amazed at this word. But Jesus again answering says to them, "Children, how difficult it is to enter into the dominion of God; for it is easier for a camel to pass through the eye of a needle than for a rich man to enter into the dominion of God." But they were even more overwhelmed saying to each other, "and what one is able to be saved?" But Jesus looking straight at them says, "For humans it is impossible, but not for God, all things are possible for God." Peter began to say to him, "Look we left everything and we followed you." But Jesus said, "Amen I say to you, no one who has left houses or brothers or sisters or mother or father or children or lands for me and for the good news will fail to receive a hundredfold now and in that time houses and brothers and sisters and mothers and children and lands with persecutions, and in the age to come eternal life. But many who are first shall be last, and the last first."

But they were on the road going up to Jerusalem, and Jesus was going in front of them, and they were astonished, but those following were afraid. And taking aside again the Twelve he began to tell them what was going to happen to him. "Look, we are going up to Jerusalem, and the Son of Man will be given up to the high priests and the scribes and they will condemn him to death and hand him

---

5. A number of manuscripts omit this last clause (B*, K, W, et al.), but there are also strong witnesses for its inclusion, including ℵ, A, C, D, and others, and it should probably be retained.

over to the Gentiles and they will mock him and spit on him, and scourge him and they will kill, and after three days⁶ he will rise."

And Jacob and John, the sons of Zebedee, came to him, saying to him, "Teacher. We wish to ask if you would do something for us." But he said to them, "What do you wish to ask me to do for you?" But they said, "Give us, that we might sit one on your right and one on your left in your glory." But Jesus said to them, "You don't know what you are asking. Are you able to drink from the cup which I drink, or be baptized with the baptism which I will be baptized with?" But they said to him, "We are able." But Jesus said to them, "The cup which I will drink you will drink, and the baptism which I will be baptized with you will also be baptized with, but the sitting on my right and on my left it is not given to me, but is for those for whom it has been prepared." And the ten hearing began to be indignant with Jacob and John, and calling them to himself Jesus says to them, "You know that those who seem to be thought of as leaders of the Gentiles lord it over them and the great among them wield authority over them. But not thus is it among you; but whoever wishes to be great among you is servant of you all, and whoever wishes among you to be first, is slave of you all. For the Son of Man did not come to be served but to serve and to give his life a ransom in place of many."

And they came into Jericho. And as he and his disciples and that crowd were setting out from Jericho the son of Timaeus (bar-Timaeus) a blind beggar sat at the side of the road. And hearing that Jesus of Nazareth is [here] he began to cry out and say, "Son of David, Jesus have mercy on me." And many speak to him sharply in order that he will be silent. But even much more he cried out, "Son of David, have mercy on me." And stopping Jesus said, "Call him." And they called the blind man saying to him, "Take courage, get up, he calls you." But throwing off his upper garment springing up he came to Jesus. And Jesus answered him and said, "What do you wish I should do?" The blind man said to him, "Rabbouni, in order that I might see again." And Jesus said, "Go, your faith has saved you." And immediately he rose up and followed him in the way.

A. Transfixed and Transfigured (9:1-13)

The second half of Mark's Gospel begins much like the first, on an apocalyptic note, only this time we have a private revelation (complete with numinous cloud and divine voice from the cloud), not just to Jesus about his identity but to the inner circle of the Twelve about Jesus' identity. Myers suggests the follow-

---

6. Some manuscripts have "on the third day," like the parallel in Matt. 20:19 and Luke 18:33, but the rendering in the translation above is strongly attested by A, B, C, D, and others and should be retained. Clearly Mark prefers the rendering "after three days" (see Mark 8:31; 9:31, and elsewhere of Jesus' resurrection; only at Matt. 27:63).

ing helpful comparison between the first and second major apocalyptic moments in this Gospel:

Theme	1st Apoc. Moment	2nd Apoc. Moment
Gospel	1:1, 15	8:35
Jesus as Messiah	1:1	8:29
The way	1:2	8:27
Peter, James, John	1:16-18	9:2
Kingdom	1:15	9:1
As it's written	1:2	9:13
Angels	1:13	8:38
John = Elijah	1:6	8:28; 9:12
Call to follow	1:16	8:34
John's fate	1:14	9:13[7]

In a biography done in an apocalyptic mode, we would expect the focus of the revelations to be on the central character, and when we examine this story carefully we find confirmation of that expectation. Like the appearance to Daniel of the man in shining apparel (Dan. 10:5-8; cf. Dan. 7:9), so Jesus appears transfigured much like the description in Rev. 1:9-18,[8] but ominously this bright white apparel was also the garment of martyrs (cf. Rev. 3:5, 18; 4:4; 6:11; 7:9, 11). But Jesus is also in a sense transfixed, for he neither speaks nor acts in this narrative. The story is about him, but it is from the point of view of God, who does the transfiguring and descends in a cloud to speak. This revelation builds on the discussion at Caesarea Philippi, part of which was about the popular perception that Jesus might be one of the prophets, perhaps even Elijah. The point here is not to rank Jesus with such company but to distinguish him from them, for only he is left standing after the transfiguration and the divine voice points the disciples' attention squarely to him. The disciples clearly enough, as represented by Peter, are still in the mode of ranking Jesus with the prophets, for the proposal is to build three booths, not one throne. It is also clear that this revelation is all along meant for the disciples' benefit. Jesus' transformation takes place "before them," and the two OT figures are said to appear "to them." Could it be that the disciples, like Moses and Elijah, go up the mountain at a time of great discouragement (in their case, over the word about Jesus' suffering) and receive an epiphany and instruction about what they are to do?[9] More will be said about these matters momentarily.

---

7. Cf. B. Van Iersel, "The Gospel according to Mark: Written for a Persecuted Community?" *NedTTs* (1980): 15-29, here pp. 28-29, and C. Myers, *Binding the Strong Man: A Political Reading of Mark's Story of Jesus* (Maryknoll, N.Y.: Orbis, 1988), p. 251.

8. See L. Hurtado, *Mark* (New York: Harper & Row, 1983), p. 135.

9. See Myers, *Binding the Strong Man*, p. 250.

This section, which leads up to the passion narrative, continues some of the major themes and types of stories already noted in Mark's presentation of things. The previous section is bound together with this one by means of the close connection between 8:38 and 9:1, and this is all the more the case if the interpretation we are about to suggest for 8:38 is correct. The following observations are in order: (1) 8:38 may in the first instance be a parousia prediction, and it is possible to take the transfiguration as a preview of the coming parousia of the Son of Man. (2) The term αγγελοι can of course mean simply messengers, without a particular reference to angelic messengers, or at the very least it could be a double entendre here, with one referent being to Moses and Elijah (cf. Rev. 11:3-14). (3) The key phrase in Mark 8:38 can certainly be translated "whenever/as often as he may come (aorist subjunctive) in the glory of his Father with the holy messengers." If this translation is correct, then the connection with 9:1 is made very clear and is not artificial. (4) Gundry goes so far as to suggest that since high mountains were seen as suburbs of heaven, this is the sort of place where one would go to talk not merely with God but even with deceased saints such as Moses and Elijah.[10] (5) It is clear enough that Mark links 9:1 and 9:2, thus despite the protest of some commentators, Mark at least did not see it as banal to refer to a prediction of Jesus and then immediately turn around and record its fulfillment. One must conjure with the possibility in any case of Mark juxtaposing the originally separate two verses to make clear the fulfillment. This shows the accuracy of Jesus' words, that they quickly come to pass, and as Gundry admits, lends credence to the other predictions Jesus had just made about his death and resurrection.[11] (6) The "some of those standing here will not die before they witness . . ." phrase is of course a dramatic way of putting things if the fulfillment came quickly, but again obviously Mark did not see it as banal to connect 8:38, 9:1, and 9:2ff. in this manner. Furthermore, Matthew and Luke, likely writing in the last third of the first century, also did not see the connection as banal. If they had understood this to be a failed prophecy of Jesus in Mark 8:38–9:1, would they have actually retained it in their Gospels? I think not. (7) If the above reasoning is largely correct, then the transfiguration, in the Markan view, is a preview not of the resurrection but of the Son of Man's parousia.[12] Let us now consider the particulars of the text.[13]

---

10. R. H. Gundry, *Mark: A Commentary on His Apology for the Cross* (Grand Rapids: Eerdmans, 1993), p. 457.

11. Gundry, pp. 456-58.

12. See M. Hooker, *The Gospel according to Mark* (Peabody, Mass.: Hendrickson, 1991), p. 215; G. H. Boobyer, *St. Mark and the Transfiguration Story* (Edinburgh: T. & T. Clark, 1942).

13. On the background of the text in general, see D. Zeller, "Bedeutung und Religionsgeschichtlicher Hintergrund der Verwandlung Jesu (Markus 9:2-8)," in *Authenticating the Activities of Jesus*, ed. B. Chilton and C. A. Evans (Leiden: Brill, 1999), pp. 303-21.

Mark 9:1 begins with a strong advance confirmation of the truth of what is about to be said. A distinctive of Jesus' utterances was that he often punctuated his words with an initial "Amen" or, as it is often translated, "Truly" (cf. 3:28; 9:1, 41; 10:15, 29; 11:23; 12:43; 13:30; 14:9, 18, 25, 30). The saying is even more strongly punctuated as a true word by the emphatic use of the double negative "certainly not" or, as I have rendered οὐ μη above, "definitely not."[14] Notice that this saying is about the dominion of God having come in power, whereas 8:38 is about the Son of Man "appearing in his Father's glory." That last phrase seems to point rather clearly to the transfiguration where Jesus is transformed by the Father and his clothing becomes radiantly white. The connection between 8:38 and 9:1 would seem to be this — the place where one can see the dominion of God in power or the saving activity of God in action is in the life of Jesus. The transfiguration reveals the kingdom by unveiling the king. The phrase "taste death" is a Semitic idiom (4 Ezra 6:26; Heb. 2:9), and suggests a setting where there is danger and potential martyrdom looming for at least some of Jesus' disciples. The verb "having come," a perfect participle, speaks of completed action and makes evident that Jesus did not just talk about a future coming of a dominion of God, for it was coming already in a powerful way.

Jesus goes off to a high mountain,[15] taking only the inner three of the Twelve. The time reference in 9:2 of after six days is quite specific and unusual for Mark's pre-passion material. This may mean that it has some specific symbolic significance: (1) it alludes to Exod. 24:16f., where six days designates the time of preparation for revelation from Sinai, (2) or is modeled on the time period between the Day of Atonement and the Feast of Tabernacles. This might explain Peter's reaction to the transfiguration (cf. below).

There is little doubt but that the transfiguration, as portrayed in Mark, is primarily for the disciples' benefit. We are never told what Jesus is discussing with Elijah or Moses, but the disciples are addressed directly by God. Furthermore, 9:2 says this happened "before them," and in v. 4 we are told that Moses and Elijah appeared "to them." As Lane admits, the Feast of Tabernacles in Jesus' day had come to have a clear association with the final deliverance promised by God, though there may be some attempt here to see this as a new Sinai-type theophany (or Christophany in this case).[16] The comparison of this event to a misplaced resurrection story seems misguided, for the following reasons: (1) Jesus says absolutely nothing in this story, unlike in the resurrection narratives; (2) all the resurrection stories begin with Jesus being absent, and then appearing, but here he is present from the outset; (3) the presence of Moses and Elijah are inexplicable if this was

14. J. Painter, *Mark's Gospel* (London: Routledge, 1997), p. 128.

15. Some have conjectured Mount Hermon in the north of the land, which is 9,000 feet high. This is a reasonable conjecture if Jesus had just been at Caesarea Philippi.

16. W. Lane, *The Gospel of Mark* (Grand Rapids: Eerdmans, 1974), pp. 317-18.

originally a resurrection narrative; (4) the lack of recognition of Jesus' true significance by Peter (he calls Jesus only "rabbi" here) is uncharacteristic of the way resurrection stories resolve themselves; (5) we are told at v. 5 that something dramatic but not permanent happened to Jesus. The verb used is μετεμορφώθη,
which surely means here a change of outward appearance or form, not of inward
nature. This accounts for the focus on the appearance of his clothes.[17] It is just
possible, however, that what is meant is a change that is outwardly visible. This
tale, however, has nothing to do with the Hellenistic concept of metamorphosis,
for Jesus is not transformed into something he was not before. He is simply revealed in the glory that is proper to him. More precisely, since the glory pertains
to his clothes and is bestowed from without, it should be clear that the author
wishes to distinguish this event from Hellenistic concepts.[18] The messianic secret
could be said to be unveiled here. But as Hooker suggests, the command not to reveal what was seen "suggests that the vision of Jesus which the disciples have
shared is of the glory which belongs to him after the resurrection."[19]

Possibly there is significance to the fact that Elijah is mentioned first here
(but not in the Matthean and Lukan parallels), for he was the forerunner meant
to remind one and all that the eschatological time of fulfillment is at hand. The
appearance of Moses may also point to the eschatological situation in view of
Deut. 18:15. In fact, the voice of God echoes this text when we hear the command to listen to Jesus, suggesting that Jesus must be seen as the final eschatological prophet whom Moses predicted would come. It is interesting that Bede
thought that the "figures of Moses and Elijah embrace all who are finally to
reign with the Lord. By Moses, who died and was buried, we can understand
those who at the judgment are going to be raised from the dead. By Elijah, on
the other hand, who has not yet paid the debt of death, we understand those
who are going to be found alive in the flesh at the judge's coming" (*Homilies on
the Gospels* 1.24).[20] This is quite different from the early Jewish tradition because not only did early Jews believe Elijah went up into heaven without dying,
but many apparently believed that Moses did so as well, in spite of what Deut.
34:5 says (see Josephus, *Ant.* 4.8.48).

As a result of all this, Peter's response is hardly a surprise. Notice that we
are told that Jesus' outer garment glistened very white, indeed so white that
even the best early expert in bleaching could not obtain such a result. Peter
thinks the dominion has indeed come in power, and now is the time to build
booths to have the final Feast of Tabernacles celebration. The word σκηνή is

---

17. On this not being a retrojected resurrection narrative, see Hooker, p. 214.
18. See Gundry, p. 477.
19. Hooker, p. 215.
20. See T. C. Oden and C. A. Hall, eds., *Mark,* vol. 2 of *The Ancient Christian Commentary on Scripture* (Downers Grove, Ill.: InterVarsity, 1998), p. 119.

used to translate booth *(sukkah)* at Lev. 23:42f. (LXX), and so the translation "booth" is probably appropriate here. Usually such booths were made of intertwined branches, and were not in fact tents of cloth or leather. But they were also seen as a reminder of the tents used during the wilderness-wandering period, and apparently some thought that in the messianic age God's people would again live in tents and the theocracy would exist once more with God dwelling and ruling directly in their midst.[21]

In the OT a cloud is often a symbol of God's presence and protection (cf. Exod. 16:10; 19:9; 24:15-16; 33:10). Here it separates the disciples from the three who are participating in the transfiguration. In this case we are meant to see the cloud as a sign of the theophany, or divine endorsement of Jesus, as at the baptism, where we also have the presence of God coming down (in the form of the Spirit) and a voice from heaven giving endorsement to Jesus. It is the kind of scene one might expect to find in Revelation.

Peter obviously speaks without really knowing what to say, or even what he is saying. Nor does he know what he ought to do. The cloud overshadows Jesus, Moses, and Elijah, so they have no need for booths to protect them.[22] Thus the exhortation to listen to the Son, God's beloved, is necessary. Note what Jesus first says after this command from heaven. They are not to relate this event until after Jesus' resurrection. Notice that we also have a passion prediction bound up with an explanation about Elijah. This is the message that the disciples must most especially get straight — that the Son of Man must suffer. This is, however, also the one message they least wish to hear, the one which confuses them most. V. 10a seems to mean that they kept Jesus' word by remaining silent about the transfiguration. Here is the only time in Mark that a clear time limit is placed on the silence. Presumably the exhortation is necessary lest all the disciples think in terms of glory without the cross and resurrection. Since they did not understand the suffering until after the fact, they also could not understand the character of the glory until then.

The disciples are clearly depicted here as still lacking understanding. "Just as Peter had failed to grasp the teaching in 8.32-33, so Peter, James, and John failed to grasp it here."[23] Indeed, one gets the sense that they had made no significant progress in their understanding, at least in regard to Jesus' coming suffering, dying, and being raised. One suggestion about the focus of their puzzlement is that of course they were not anticipating the raising of a particular individual in the midst of history, but rather the resurrection of the righteous in general at the end of days. What could Jesus mean by referring to the Son of Man dying and rising in isolation from others? There are in fact three transla-

---

21. See Hooker, p. 217.
22. Painter, p. 130.
23. Painter, p. 130.

tions possible of v. 10. One is "and they seized on this word, discussing among themselves. . . ." A second would be "and they observed the word (i.e., Jesus' commandment), discussing among themselves (but not with the public) . . . ," or finally "and they kept the matter to themselves, discussing what. . . ." The second and third translations come out in about the same place in regard to their meaning, but it is hard to pick between the three.

V. 12b is meant to make clear that John's suffering did not disqualify him from being this Elijah figure. Of course, v. 13 indicates that it was written of Elijah that he *would* suffer. This was only true if it refers to the suffering Elijah did during his ministry to Israel. The point here is that it was part of God's plan for both the Elijah predecessor figure and the Son of Man who followed him to suffer. It must have been confusing enough to hear about a suffering messianic figure, never mind also a suffering Elijah figure.

Nowhere is there in all the Jewish speculation about Elijah anything about a suffering that must happen first. Elijah is seen as the one who comes and restores Israel to their proper state of repentance and faith (cf. Mal. 3:1; 4:5-6), and then the end is to follow. Jesus' shocking assertion that he must suffer is accompanied by the equally shocking idea that Elijah has already come and suffered. The reference to the people doing as they wished with Elijah, "as the Scriptures say," is perhaps an allusion to the death threat against Elijah by Jezebel in 1 Kings 19:1-3. "Herodias has succeeded in doing to the second Elijah what Jezebel tried to do to the first."[24] W. Wink has pointed out the paradox here: "The identification of John with Elijah [involved] the quite offensive paradox that the heavenly Elijah (who did not taste death) should be the captive murdered prophet — a dead Elijah."[25]

B. "If at First You Don't Succeed, Pray, Pray Again" (9:14-29)

Jesus and the three come down off the mountain and back to the old reality of insufficient faith on earth. We are told at v. 14 that the disciples, surrounded by a crowd, are discussing with the scribes various matters. Could the scribes be gathering information in order to accuse Jesus of something? In any event, this is the only episode in Mark where the disciples are clearly portrayed as impotent, un-

---

24. See Hooker, p. 221. M. Casey, *Aramaic Sources of Mark's Gospel* (Cambridge: Cambridge University Press, 1998), pp. 111-37, argues persuasively that an Aramaic narrative and use of Scripture lies behind some of the complexities of this passage, in particular in regard to its use of Scripture. This source believed that various of the prophecies in Malachi and Isaiah were fulfilled in the ministry of John the Baptist.

25. W. Wink, *John the Baptist in the Gospel Tradition* (Cambridge: Cambridge University Press, 1968), pp. 15-18.

able to do something Jesus had previously empowered them to do. Yet it is hard to doubt that the lack of power must be related in some way to the lack of understanding or faith. In this case, they do not know that the power of exorcism bestowed on them (cf. 6:13) is in fact not theirs to use at liberty. Jesus informs them that they have failed because this type of exorcism requires prayer, which is to say constant reliance on the source of power! The power is conveyed through communion with the Almighty; it is not inherently resident in the disciples on an ongoing basis without such communion. This is interesting because in early Judaism it was sometimes thought that the recitation of the Shema (Deut. 6) and of Pss. 3 and 91 were means of dealing with evil spirits. Perhaps the disciples had thought the gift of exorcism was, once bestowed, in their control, and did not require further reliance on God. It is interesting that once again Mark finds a way to continue his biographical focus — the contrast between Jesus' mastery and the disciples' impotence once again places the spotlight clearly on Jesus — in the longest of all the Markan exorcism tales. One can also say that the struggle for belief is an important theme that helps unify the story, with both the father and the disciples being shown as examples of those who are struggling.[26]

It appears that the disciples were being quizzed on the exorcisms, or in this case the lack of them, by the scribes. The whole ethos of this passage reminds us of the apocalyptic context of Mark's Gospel. The battle with the powers of darkness is ongoing and involves both Jesus and his agents. Lane suggests that as the Markan narrative moves along the resistance of Satan to Jesus becomes more and more severe, until Satan's power will finally be broken by Jesus' death on the cross.[27] This may perhaps be corroborated by 10:45, which suggests that Jesus came to ransom those who were in some kind of bondage by giving his life. The severity of this case may be seen from the fact that after the exorcism, Jesus apparently also has to raise the boy from the dead (but cf. below).

Notice that at v. 15 the crowds see Jesus, are amazed, and run out to greet him. As Hooker says, it is odd that the crowd reaction comes at the beginning of the story, unlike most other examples in Mark where the astonishment ends the tale.[28] It may be, however, that we should let the verb εκθαμβεομαι have its full force, expressing strong emotion (cf. 14:33; 16:5, 6), in which case perhaps we are meant to see Jesus coming down off the mountain like Moses did, trailing clouds of glory (see Exod. 34:29-30), so to speak, which astounds the audience who sees him.[29]

The crowd is receptive to him though they do not understand him. It is also important to note how the father of this child addresses Jesus, namely, as

---

26. Myers, *Binding the Strong Man,* p. 255.
27. Lane, pp. 329-31.
28. Hooker, p. 222.
29. Hooker, p. 222. Cf. Painter, p. 132, and especially Gundry, pp. 487-88.

Teacher, not as Savior. The father sounds rather exasperated: "I brought you my son who has a dumb spirit . . . but your disciples weren't able to cast it out." The description of what the spirit did to the boy has led more than one scholar to think that epilepsy was involved. This is certainly possible, and notice that the description that the boy has a spirit of dumbness is the father's, not Jesus', and no doubt the father has only the knowledge of his time about diseases. However, v. 18 may suggest an actual case of possession, for it seems that there was some purpose to where the boy was caused to fall — in both fire and water. The demon was trying to destroy the boy. The condition was all the more difficult to cope with because it rendered the boy both deaf and dumb.[30]

Notice at v. 19 how Jesus characterizes even the disciples as part of "this faithless generation." Jesus is himself exasperated. "How long will I bear with you?" is no idle rhetorical question. It suggests Jesus may already be realizing that he is near the end. The scene is yet another example of a dismal failure of Jesus' closest followers. First the three fail to understand on the mountain, then the nine fail to carry out the sort of ministry Jesus has previously authorized and empowered them to do.

The possessing spirit is called a dumb spirit (v. 20), which perhaps explains why it does not speak during the exorcism.[31] The boy has had the disease or condition since childhood, which leads one to think that possession can come on the unsuspecting, without any dabbling in the black arts. In this regard v. 25 is most intriguing. Jesus commands the spirit to leave the boy and never to reenter him again. This suggests that repossession was possible.

The crux of the matter centers on the faith of the father. Things come to a head when he pleads for Jesus' help and compassion, saying, "Help, if you can." Jesus takes the "if" as a sort of honor challenge, and the reading in A and B of the broken-off phrase in v. 23, which has caused some textual difficulties, should likely be followed — Ει δυνῃ followed by a dash line, or in English a question mark. Jesus' response is astonishment that anyone would question his ability, but perhaps, as Hooker suggests, the father has doubts due to the failure of Jesus' disciples.[32] V. 23b says all things are possible for those who have faith. At v. 24 we get to the nub of the problem. The father does believe, but inadequately. His cry has been seen as a poignant one speaking for all partial believers ever since: "I believe, help my unbelief." Here and elsewhere Jesus readily responds to faith, not to doubt or simply to a challenge, much less to a demand for a miracle.

---

30. Myers, *Binding the Strong Man,* p. 254, notes that there is one element or term from each of the previous exorcisms or healing stories found in this one. This suggests that this story is one that Mark composed himself, not one he got from a source.

31. Hooker, p. 224.

32. Hooker, p. 224.

As a result of v. 26, various scholars have thought we are being told that the boy was dead after this exorcism. Indeed, he appeared to be dead and people were saying he was dead, and in v. 27 the verb ηγειρεν is used followed by ανεστη, very similar to the language used to describe the raising of Jairus's daughter (5:39-42). However, due attention must be given to the term ωσει in v. 26, which means "as if" or "like." He appeared to be in a comatose state but likely was not. We have again at the end of the story the in-house motif with the private teaching of the disciples. Probably the original text only spoke of prayer, not prayer and fasting, being necessary to perform this sort of exorcism (cf. above on the textual variants), although various of the church fathers thought otherwise. Tertullian, for example, says, "Fasting is the weapon of choice for battling with the more dreadful demons. Should we be surprised if the expulsion of the spirit of iniquity requires the indwelling of Holy Spirit?" (*On Fasting* 8.8).[33] But as Schweizer says, these later copyists who added "and fasting" misunderstood this passage, thinking "prayer alone seemed too simple. They were not able to perceive that what is simplest and most taken for granted is really most important, since it causes one to cease looking at himself, and look to God. . . . Mark wants to proclaim that this kind of discipleship does not result from the effectiveness of one's own piety but only from the action of God."[34]

C. On the Road Again (9:30-37)

Once again we are told that Jesus is passing through Galilee, but on this occasion he is beginning his final trip to Jerusalem and does not wish to be slowed down, nor does he wish people to know. We have here the second and least detailed in the series of passion predictions, and here for the first time we are told that Jesus will be handed over into the hands of men. Hooker says this is a paradoxical way of putting the matter because the Son of Man in Dan. 7 is given authority over human beings, even over other human authorities.[35] The verb παραδιδωμι can have the special meaning of betrayed (so 3:19 and 14:18-21), and thus this could be the first allusion to the act of an insider working against Jesus.[36] On the other hand, the more generic sense of the verb "delivered" makes good sense here, and as Hooker says, we would have expected a reference to the priestly authorities here and not just "men" if Mark wanted to be specific and refer to the betrayal. It is, after all, God who is actually delivering Jesus up into the hands of human be-

---

33. Oden and Hall, p. 125.
34. E. Schweizer, *The Good News according to Mark* (Atlanta: John Knox, 1971), pp. 189-90.
35. Hooker, p. 226.
36. So Painter, p. 135.

ings, and probably the divine and human actors in the process are being referred to here in a general way. There may be something to the suggestion that the prediction here is grounded in Dan. 7:25, which speaks of being delivered into the hands of rulers, and perhaps also Dan. 12:2, which refers to the resurrection of the just.[37] This raises the interesting prospect that Jesus, who repeatedly identified himself as the Son of Man, read his own destiny out of some of the stories in Daniel.[38] This connection makes even more plausible the argument that Jesus himself could have predicted his own fate in these very terms (noting the imprecision of "hands of men" and "killed").

Once more the disciples fail to understand, and indeed are so frightened by Jesus' remarks about suffering that they are afraid to even ask him about it. The irony is quite clear when in the next segment, in vv. 33-37, the disciples are caught jockeying for position in the eschatological dominion and debating about who is the greatest. The truly Great One has just said that the route of self-sacrifice, not self-aggrandizement, is the route to go, but the disciples are heading full speed in the other direction![39] Painter notes how after each passion prediction there is a clear portrayal of one or more of the disciples failing to really understand or be disciples. After the first passion prediction in Mark 8 Peter rebukes Jesus; after or even during this second passion prediction the disciples are debating who is the greatest; and after the third passion prediction in 10:33-34 James and John request to sit on the right and left hand of Jesus in glory. "This arrangement can be no accident. In each case, just when the Markan Jesus has made his most profound and revealing teaching to his disciples, they show themselves to be blind and devoid of any understanding of Jesus' vocation as Son of Man and how this should involve them."[40]

It would appear that we have two *chreiae* juxtaposed here, one in vv. 33-35 and another brief one in vv. 36-37, for we have two pithy sayings which end each of these segments, each of which could clearly stand on its own as a pericope. The link between v. 37 and what follows appears to have been by means of the key phrase "in my name" (vv. 37, 38, 39, 41). The reference to children, rather than lesser community members, in the second pericope probably speaks for the earliness and authenticity of this story and saying. There seems to be no compelling reason to doubt that the two pericopes vv. 33-35 and vv. 36-37 go back to incidents in the life of Jesus.

---

37. See J. Schaberg, "Daniel 7,12 and the New Testament Passion-Resurrection Predictions," *NTS* 31 (1985): 208-13, here pp. 210-13.

38. See my demonstration that it is the Danielic Son of Man concept and its later developments that seem to be the basis of Jesus' self-understanding in *The Christology of Jesus* (Minneapolis: Fortress, 1990), and see now my *Jesus the Seer: The Progress of Prophecy* (Peabody, Mass.: Hendrickson, 1999).

39. Rightly Myers, *Binding the Strong Man,* p. 260.

40. Painter, p. 137.

At v. 34, when Jesus asks them about their debate along the road, they are sheepish and silent, not wanting to admit what they were talking about. Jesus presumably asks precisely because he has a good idea of what they were talking about. As Painter suggests, the disciples' dispute "should not be understood as an 'academic' debate about facts. Rather it is an expression of the will, the desire to be first, to be greatest."[41] Vv. 35 and 36 should be seen as object lessons for the disciples in true greatness. The pedagogical posture and setting which is important to Mark should be noted: (1) Jesus is in the house; (2) Jesus is seated; (3) Jesus calls the Twelve to himself and instructs them. The difference between this and, say, 8:33 would seem to be that this is a formal teaching setting. Jesus will give an object lesson to those who would desire to be first (or greatest). If Jesus spoke in Aramaic, then there may also be a deliberate wordplay, for the word for child is the same as the word for servant in Aramaic — talya. If one wants to be first, he must be last of all and the servant/child of all. The term παιδίον usually refers to someone between infancy and young adulthood.

At v. 37 Jesus so identifies himself with the child that he says, "whoever receives (i.e., serves) such a one, receives/serves me." To be servant of all means to be servant even of children. The reference to servant here perhaps prepares us for the teaching about Jesus the servant in 10:45. The verb "receive" is often used in contexts of warm hospitality, the welcoming of a guest (cf. Matt. 10:40; Luke 10:16). Because a child was not seen in the early Jewish or Greco-Roman world as a religious model for adults, this teaching is striking. To the contrary, if one reads Proverbs or some Greco-Roman literature, the child is seen as willful, subject to various possible bad influences, and requiring instruction and regular discipline.[42]

Jesus, however, is saying to his disciples, his representatives, that they are to receive and so serve a child such as the one present for his sake. In serving the child they are in fact serving Jesus, and this of course reverses the ancient protocol where slaves and children, indeed all the subordinate members of the household, were to serve the male head of the household. Jesus is not only identifying with the helpless or most vulnerable family members so that they may be helped, he is trying to get his disciples to humble themselves, rid themselves of the usual hubris and power struggles for dominant position, and serve, even serve a child, a humiliating task in the minds of some ancients. It is clear from a passage such as this and the one we will discuss shortly (see below on 10:13-16 and par.) that Jesus did not share some of the negative opinions about children that seem to have been prevalent in his world.

---

41. Painter, p. 136.
42. See the discussion in my *Women in the Ministry of Jesus* (Cambridge: Cambridge University Press, 1984), pp. 13-15.

D. The Unknown Exorcist (9:38-41)

This brief passage presents the interesting tale of the unknown exorcist.[43] There appears to be an intertextual echo between this text and Num. 11:27-29. Moses, of course, was dealing with unofficial prophets, and we may contrast Joshua's request, "Moses, forbid them" (Num. 11:28 LXX), with our text, which puts the very same verb on Jesus' lips in Mark 9:39: "Do not forbid him." Moses' retort could easily have been that of Jesus to his disciples: "Are you jealous?" (Num. 11:29). "The arrogance in John's objection lies in its attempt to erect boundaries around the exercise of compassionate ministry 'in Jesus' name.' He equates exorcism with the accrual of status and power, and wishes to maintain a monopoly over it. This is especially ludicrous in light of the disciples' lack of exorcism power, which we have just witnessed (9.14-29)."[44] If this were not bad enough, the disciples seem to want to be "followed" by such a person!

Much debate exists as to whether this unknown exorcist is just someone using Jesus' name in magical fashion or an actual disciple of Jesus. Notice again that even John here calls Jesus "Teacher." The disciples tried to hinder (inceptive aorist verb) him "because he did not follow us." Is "us" here the Twelve, or Jesus and the Twelve? Jesus, perhaps not surprisingly, says don't hinder such a person because the one who does things in Jesus' name will not soon be able to speak evil of Jesus — "for whoever is not against us is for us."

Lane suggests that this person may have been a real disciple, just not one of the Twelve, and if so the point of the challenge seems to have been not about his discipleship status but whether he had the same authority and power as the Twelve had been granted, especially since he wasn't following them.[45] In short, this passage may tell us more about how the Twelve saw themselves as the only ones authorized to do such things than about the unknown exorcist.[46] There is a textual problem at v. 40. It may have originally read, "On the ground that you are mine," not least since Jesus seems not to have openly used the term "Anointed One" of himself during the ministry. The saying may be proverbial (cf. Cicero, *Or. Pro Lig.* 11, and in reverse form Matt. 12:30; Luke 11:23). V. 41 makes a slightly different point. Those who treat Jesus' agents well are in fact treating Jesus well, since in the early Jewish way of thinking "a man's agent is as himself" (cf. the appendix below). Jesus adds that such hospitable treatment will not lose its reward.

---

43. It is not at all clear why one should expect this story to be more likely about an event in the early church than in the ministry of Jesus. There is a similar story in Acts 19:13-17, but this only proves that human beings are often jealous and possessive about their own status and power.

44. Myers, *Binding the Strong Man*, p. 261.

45. Lane, pp. 343-44.

46. On the Markan disciples seeing themselves as an exclusive club, see Painter, p. 138.

E. On Salt and Other Savory Matters (9:42-49)

Mark 9:42-49 is something of a grab bag or collection of assorted sayings of Jesus grouped together by catchword connection (e.g., by the term "salt" and perhaps by the verb "stumble"). The catchword aided memorization, and movement from one saying to the next came by remembering the key term which
carried over. It is by no means clear that v. 42 continues the thought of v. 41, but
if it does then the point would be, as Lane suggests, that one should not be a
stumbling block to the unknown exorcists or others on the fringe of the circle
of the disciples.[47] V. 42 would not necessarily have been seen as dramatic hyperbole in Jesus' day, as some had been drowned using such methods as punishment for certain serious offenses.[48] An ονικος is a large millstone used for
grinding grain, not for a hand mill but of the sort turned by a donkey. Trial by
water ordeal was known in antiquity, and the particular horror for a Jew of the
millstone trial would be that the corpse would sink and be unable to be recov-
ered for burial.[49] Josephus tells of an occasion when Galileans turned on some
of Herod's entourage and drowned them in the Sea of Galilee (Ant. 14.15.10).
Likewise, in vv. 43ff. the punishments listed were well known in that day — cutting off the hand for theft, plucking out the eye for voyeurism, cutting off the
foot of a runaway slave (cf. Josephus, Life 34, 35; War 2.21.10).[50] The point,
then, is that even these drastic remedies would be better than sinning and going
to hell. Hooker suggests that we have here an echo of Job 31:1, 5, 7, where Job
speaks of the purity of eyes, foot, and hands.[51]

At v. 44 we hear of gehenna. This term comes from the Valley of Hinnom
south of Jerusalem, where infants were formerly sacrificed to Molech (cf. Jer.
7:31; 19:5f.; 32:35). Josiah desecrated this pagan site during his reforms and
consigned to it the burning of animal entrails and then garbage or waste. It appears that it was still used for the latter purpose in Jesus' day. At a burning garbage dump the maggots existed aplenty, feeding on carcasses, and the flame

---

47. Lane, pp. 344-45.

48. See especially J. D. M. Derrett, "Mark 9.42 and Comparative Legal History," in Law
in the New Testament (Leiden: Brill, 1974), pp. 4-31.

49. Could such practices have caused the response of the disciples to Jesus when he
walked on water — the sea being the locale where there were the spirits or ghosts of various
unburied dead?

50. H. Koester, "Mark 9.43-47 and Quintilian 8.3.75," HTR 71 (1978): 151-53, points
out the parallel in Quintilian's Institutes: "As the physicians cut off the members of the body
which are estranged (from it) through sickness, thus also evil and corrupting people, even if
they are related to us through bonds of blood must be cut off" (8.3.75). This intimates that
the metaphor could be used to suggest a particular approach to community discipline, but
this differs from Mark's approach, which has to do with individual salvation.

51. Hooker, p. 232.

kept smoldering and burning. During the intertestamental period, what went on at this site began to provide stock images for hell (cf. *1 Enoch* 27:2; 90:26f.; 4 Ezra 7:36), so Jesus was following an established practice. Needless to say, Jesus does not depict hell as an inviting prospect, though of course it is uncertain how far one should press this vivid imagery. Suffice it to say that Jesus believed hell to be an horrific and painful place. "The punishment of Gehenna is described in terms of unquenchable *fire*.[52] Thus fire becomes the new catch word,"[53] and so the connection between the two sayings in vv. 48-49.

Some have seen v. 49 as a reference to purgatory, where "all will be salted with fire." Far more likely is the idea that Jesus was suggesting that disciples would be tested by trials or persecution. It may even refer to the wiles of the devil, the one associated with gehenna, who torments the disciples. The expression "salted with fire" comes from the Hebrew Scriptures, from the practice of pouring salt on the sacrificial flame presumably to purify it (Lev. 2:13; Ezek. 43:24). Thus the meaning of this saying may be close to Rom. 12:1 — disciples are to see themselves as sacrifices. This saying might have had special significance for Roman Christians who were, quite literally, under fire. Schweizer suggests, however, that there is a connection between salt and fire here, namely, "the fire of God (the affliction of persecution, or the end-time . . .) preserves from decay like salt (with which meat is cured)."[54] This then suggests that the saying has to do with how trials can actually strengthen or preserve Christian character, not merely test it. Finally, it may be of some relevance that in 1 Cor. 3:10-15 Paul uses the image of testing by fire. For "the purificatory process may destroy, but it can also preserve."[55]

V. 50 is another unrelated saying connected to what precedes by the catchword "salt." Salt, of course, was already a preservative in the world of Jesus' day, but if mixed with gypsum when brought from the Dead Sea, it would be flat and insipid and would not serve the purpose people wanted to use it for. The disciples, then, are seen as the world's salt, a preservative in the dying carcass of a world. If they lose their savor, the world truly stinks and dies. Salt that loses its pungency is worthless; it no longer preserves anything. Saltiness, then, seems to refer to the radical commitment to discipleship that stands above personal honor or preferences. Thus the closing saying means to preserve that character of disciplined life, of being servant of one another, preferring the other, and so being at peace with one another. Here we find something of an *inclusio* with vv. 33-37 with the repetition of the theme of the disciples as being status conscious. But it is just possible that Schweizer might be correct that this

---

52. Hooker, p. 232, suggests that it is the fire, not the torment, that is unending.
53. Painter, p. 139.
54. Schweizer, *Mark,* p. 199.
55. Hooker, p. 233.

saying could be about being ready to be sacrificed, just as salt is thrown into the fire. For it is only the true, pure salt that is used for such a sacrificial ritual.[56]

The suggestion that the disciples should have salt in themselves and be at peace with one another likely draws on Lev. 2:13b: "Do not let the salt of the covenant of your God be lacking from your cereal offering." See too Num. 18:19, which speaks of a covenant of salt. Thus to share salt with someone is to share fellowship or even to have a covenant relationship with someone.[57] Thus the point of "have salt in yourselves" would be that the disciples must stop disputing and have true covenantal fellowship among themselves. We have thus come full circle from the beginning of this passage, which mentions the disciples' disputing in vv. 33-37. The construction of even passages like this portion of Mark 9, where a variety of sayings are joined, is not wholly artless, but centers on a series of interrelated themes that keep coming up in differing ways as the passage goes on.

F. Family Matters (10:1-31)

The material in roughly the first half of Mark 10 deals with family matters including marriage, divorce, children, and the effect of discipleship on family obligations and family possessions as well. The net effect of all of Jesus' teachings on these matters is to make clear that the cost of discipleship and of living by dominion principles is high, indeed too high for some (such as the rich young man) to accept. The setting of this teaching material (note the emphasis on teaching at the end of v. 1) is said to be the region of Judea and "across the Jordan." It is not completely clear whether Mark is already describing Jesus' final journey up from Galilee to Judea or some sort of ministry in Judea and Perea which he elsewhere has not highlighted.[58] At the least the point would seem to be that Jesus continues to feel free to reach out to those beyond the Holy Land as well as those within it (see above on the Syrophoenician woman). Traditionally the material in 10:2-12 and par. (Matt. 19:3-9) has been seen as a pronouncement story. But in fact, it seems more like a combination of a controversy dialogue and a pronouncement story, and it is likely we should see the "in-house" addendum to the story in vv. 10-12 as a brief *chreia*. Thus it would appear that Mark has welded together several traditions here.

The narrative begins in 10:2 with Jesus being confronted with a group of Pharisees who are seeking his opinion on whether it is legally permitted for a man to divorce his wife. But the questioning is done to trap Jesus in what he will say. In

---

56. Schweizer, *Mark,* p. 199.

57. See Myers, *Binding the Strong Man,* p. 264.

58. See E. E. B. Cranfield, *The Gospel according to St. Mark* (Cambridge: Cambridge University Press, 1972), p. 318.

other words, Jesus is once more being put to the test. Thus in a sense, the Pharisees need not be confronting Jesus with a live possibility in his setting. Like the Sadducees questioning Jesus about the woman who married a bevy of brothers in sequence, the Pharisees' question could have been hypothetical and offered to flush out Jesus' real thoughts on the matter. As Hooker points out, however, there is evidence from this era of a stricter attitude toward divorce than that espoused, for example, by Shammai or Hillel (cf. CD 4).[59] According to D. Daube, this passage follows a traditional pattern of early Jewish debating in which there is (1) a question by an opponent (10:2); (2) a public response sufficient to silence the inquisitor, but which states only part of the truth (10:5-9); and (3) private explanation given to one's followers in a fuller way (10:10-12).[60]

There has been much discussion among scholars about the differences between the Matthean and Markan forms of this discussion, for in Matthew the question has to do with what legitimate causes there are for divorcing (with the privilege of divorce itself simply assumed) and the response of Jesus takes into account at least one exception to the no-divorce rule, whereas in Mark nothing is said about an exception. In Mark the discussion is clearly about the legitimacy of divorce itself, not its grounds. In view of 1 Cor. 7:10-11, it seems reasonably clear that Mark is closer in form to the original teaching of Jesus than Matthew in this matter. As early as the 50s it was clear to Paul that Jesus' teaching was that two (believing) people joined together by God should not divorce. This, to say the least, was a radical teaching, even within early Jewish circles, and thus we need to consider Mark 10 in more detail.

Firstly, it needs to be said that separation of a married couple without divorce was not a legal possibility in early Judaism.[61] Secondly, it seems clear that Matthew has emended his Markan source here to make it more apt for his own, more Jewish Christian audience. Thirdly, divorce in Jesus' setting was almost without exception a male privilege. Thus there is some justice to E. Schüssler Fiorenza's remarks that

> Divorce is necessary because of the male's *hardness of heart,* that is, because of men's patriarchal mind-set and reality.... However, Jesus insists, God did not intend patriarchy but created persons as male and female human beings. It is not woman who is given into the power of man in order to continue "his" house and family line, but it is man who shall sever connections with his own patriarchal family and "the two persons shall become one *sarx.*" ... The passage is best translated as "The two persons — man and woman — enter into

---

59. Hooker, p. 235.

60. D. Daube, *The New Testament and Rabbinic Judaism* (London: Atholone Press, 1956), pp. 141-43.

61. See my *Women,* pp. 2-6.

a common human life and social relationship because they are created as equals."[62]

In Mark 10, v. 3 asks, "What did Moses command you?" Jesus does not dispute the authority of Mosaic Law, but he sees it as concessionary in nature, introduced because of human weakness.[63] In v. 4 the Pharisees respond that Moses permitted a man to write a bill of divorce and to divorce. Jesus in turn rejoins that Moses wrote this commandment to them because of their hardening of the spiritual arteries.[64] This raises an interesting hermeneutical issue, namely, what force should divine laws have which were originally written, in Jesus' view, as concessions to human fallenness? It appears that Jesus was prepared to appeal to God's original pre-fall intentions for marriage over against the Mosaic requirements of Deut. 24:1-4.[65] Specifically a bill of divorce was required to be given to the woman, to make clear that she was no longer married. Jesus seems to suggest that the Mosaic provision was meant to limit a problem, not license a practice that in essence goes against God's original intentions for marriage.

In the Markan form of the discussion, Jesus goes immediately from the remark on hard-heartedness to a partial quoting of Gen. 1:27, 5:2, and 2:24 in vv. 6-7. The creation order is that from the beginning of creation God made human beings male and female. Because of this duality of the sexes, a man will leave his father and mother and cleave to his wife.[66] V. 8 says the two will become one flesh.[67] "The implication is that the one flesh union becomes more constitutive of a man and a woman's being than their uniqueness. Only two can become one, and when they do they are no longer two."[68] This is not to say that the marriage

---

62. E. Schüssler Fiorenza, *In Memory of Her* (New York: Crossroad, 1985), p. 143.

63. See rightly Hooker, p. 236.

64. On the history and use of the term σκληροκαρδια, see K. Berger, "Hartherzigkeit und Gottes Gesetz. Die Vorgeschichte des antijudischen Vorwurfs in Mk. 10.5," *ZNW* 61, nos. 1-2 (1970): 1-47.

65. In view of the fact that the disciples are regularly depicted in this Gospel as either dense or hard of heart, Painter, p. 141, may be right to suggest that we should connect this with difficulties in Mark's own community where Roman law allowed divorce fairly readily whether one was a man or a woman.

66. There is considerable doubt about whether or not the original form of the Markan text had the phrase "and cleave to his wife." The phrase is omitted entirely by important witnesses such as A, B, Ψ, and others. On the other hand, while it could be an addition based on the text of Matt. 19:5 and Gen. 2:24, it appears likely that the phrase is needed to make sense of the Markan text because otherwise the antecedent of "the two" would be the parents! See Metzger, *TCGNT*, p. 104.

67. Schweizer, *Mark*, p. 203, rightly points out that the Hebrew of Genesis simply says "they will become one. . . ." It is the LXX where the phrase "the two" first appears, which makes clear that monogamy is the goal.

68. Witherington, *Women*, p. 26.

could not be broken up by some third party. Notice that the text says "*what* (i.e., the union) God has joined together, let no one put asunder." The verb here actually means "to separate" and is used in the Greek papyri to mean divorce.[69] Could Jesus be suggesting to officials that they ought not grant a legal divorce in such a situation? More clearly, it needs to be observed that Jesus is only talking about believing persons whom God has joined together. He says nothing about pagan marriages, nor does he suggest that God joins all marriages together, for he objected to relationships such as that of Herod Antipas and Herodias. The qualifiers Jesus makes in his remarks need to be taken seriously.

Jesus' argument, then, seems to be as follows: God in creation made two distinct but complementary human genders. God then also brought the two complementary genders together in marriage. No third party is allowed into this relationship. Anyone who seeks to divide those who share such a marriage and one-flesh union attacks not only the marriage and the two united in it, but God who brought them together as well. The Creator and the creation order both undergird marriage. If in fact a couple so joined together do divorce, they must not remarry anyone else because to do so would be adultery. Painter is right that the upshot of the teaching here is that while Jesus recognizes the reality of divorce, he does not think this legitimizes remarriage if the original couple were joined together by God in the first place.[70]

Mark 10:11 is a teaching apparently independently attested in Luke 16:18a. Mark seems to have added to the original form of the teaching the phrase επ αυτην, which could either be translated "against her" or "with her." Early Jews apparently never spoke of a man committing adultery against his own wife, and thus N. Turner and B. Schaller have suggested that the phrase be translated "with her" (i.e., with the second woman).[71] Thus v. 11 could mean "Whoever divorces his wife and marries another commits adultery with the other." This makes good sense, for adultery is by definition an act committed by a married person with a third party. But there are good reasons to favor the translation "against her."[72] Certainly the verse reflects the spirit of Jesus' views, for only Jesus, or someone just as radical, was likely to go against the grain of patriarchy to the degree of redefining adultery *not* as an act committed against another man who has a wife, but in terms of infidelity either against one's own wife or with another's wife.[73] What is interesting about this whole verse is not

---

69. See Painter, p. 141.

70. Painter, p. 142.

71. N. Turner, "The Translation of Μοιχαται επ αυτην in Mark 10.11," *BT* 7 (1956): 151-52, and B. Schaller, "'Commits Adultery with Her' Not 'against Her,' Mk. 10.11," *ET* 83, no. 4 (1972): 107-8.

72. See Gundry, p. 533.

73. Gundry, p. 533.

just the strictness of it, for Jesus seems to assume that the first one-flesh union is still in force even after the divorce, hence the second marriage is seen as an act of adultery, but that, against the normal use of the term in antiquity, it is the man who is called an adulterer.

One could argue that Mark 10:12 is Mark's adaptation of Jesus' radical teaching on divorce to a Greco-Roman setting, since Jewish women basically did not have the power or legal permission to divorce their husbands in Jesus' locale and era. Josephus says, "For it is (only) the man who is permitted by us to do this, and not even a divorced woman may marry again on her own initiative unless her former husband consent" (*Ant.* 15.259). Yet as E. Bammel has shown, there is some evidence that even some Jewish women in Palestine could both write out the bill of divorce and even pronounce the divorce formula. Some Jewish women of high rank such as Herodias did divorce their husbands, but this could be seen as the exception which proves the general rule (for the social elite often did not play by the normal rules).[74] This raises the possibility that 10:12 is Jesus' own comment on the famous case of Herodias (see also Luke 13:31-32). The conclusion of D. Juel about this whole passage is apt: "[Jesus'] forbidding of divorce is clearly a statement about the status of women in society. They are to be safeguarded as vulnerable members of society. . . . Crucial to their survival has always been economic support. Easy divorce of women with young children means abrogating responsibility for caring for the most important members of society at a time of maximum vulnerability. The community that forms around Jesus will be an alternative community."[75]

Very few scholars have disputed the authenticity of the material found in Mark 10:13-16 and par. M. Dibelius, in fact, includes this narrative in the category of a paradigm he sees being in nearly its original authentic condition.[76] There is, however, some debate as to whether v. 15 originally was a part of the pericope. If judged as a *chreia*, it is worth pointing out that normally a *chreia* would be formed around one particular saying or action of the hero figure, and so it may well be true that v. 15 has been added here by Mark because of the common subject matter. In support of v. 15's originally separate origins is also the fact that it is found in another context in Matthew (Matt. 18:3).

The narrative begins in v. 13 with the remark that "they" (perhaps parents) were bringing παιδια, a word usually referring to young children (cf. John 16:21 to *Gos. Thom.* 22; but in Mark 5:39-42 it refers to a twelve-year-

---

74. E. Bammel, "Markus 10.11f. Und das judische Eherecht," *ZNW* 61 (1970): 95-101. For additional evidence in favor of seeing this as Jesus' teaching about a famously scandalous situation, see my *Women,* p. 149 n. 144.

75. D. Juel, *The Gospel of Mark* (Nashville: Abingdon, 1999), pp. 131-32.

76. M. Dibelius, *From Tradition to Gospel* (London, 1934), p. 43.

old), that he might touch them.[77] But the disciples scolded or rebuked those bringing the children. This may reflect a typical ancient attitude that young children were less important than adults, and that important teachers shouldn't be bothered by them. There are early Jewish texts which stress the immaturity of children (cf. *m. 'Abot* 3.11 and 4.20). The disciples' action causes Jesus to be indignant with them, and in essence he rebukes the rebukers. They had not remembered the lesson about receiving the little ones in Jesus' name (Mark 9:36-37).[78] He says, "Permit the young children to come to me and do not hinder them, for των . . . τοιουτων is the dominion of God." The Greek phrase quoted in the previous sentence seems to mean "these children who are brought to Jesus and those others who are of this sort." G. R. Beasley-Murray rightly remarks: "Many normal occasions of the use of τοιουτος are intended to denote a class, of which the one mentioned in the context is an example. . . . it is impossible to make the primary reference of τοιουτοι a comparison with other individuals."[79] In other words, this text cannot simply refer to those adults who are childlike to the exclusion of actual young children being brought to Jesus. It can refer to both. "With an authority such as only God can claim, he promises the Kingdom to those whose faith resembles the empty hand of a beggar."[80] Notice that Jesus says nothing about building or accomplishing the dominion or making it happen, but only of receiving or entering it. Hooker is right that Jesus is not romanticizing children or childhood as a time of innocence. His point is that children are content to receive something as a gift, and this is the proper way all persons should receive the dominion or divine saving activity of God.[81]

After this saying, which climaxes the original *chreia*, there is appended an additional word of Jesus found in Mark and Luke (cf. Matt. 18:3) which says, "Amen I say to you, unless you receive the dominion as a child, you shall not enter it." Notice the way this saying suggests there is both a present ("receive") and a future dimension ("enter") to God's dominion.[82] It is unlikely that this means "unless you receive it during childhood," but it is just possible that what is meant is receiving the dominion in like fashion to which one should receive a little child — unconditionally and with open arms, as Jesus did.[83] Notice that

---

77. On blessing being conveyed by touching, see Gen. 48:14.
78. Painter, p. 142.
79. G. R. Beasley-Murray, *Baptism in the New Testament* (Grand Rapids: Eerdmans, 1962), p. 327.
80. Schweizer, *Mark*, p. 207.
81. Hooker, p. 239.
82. Hooker, p. 239.
83. See F. A. Schilling, "What Means the Saying about Receiving the Kingdom of God as a Little Child (την βασιλειαν του θεου ως παιδιον Mk. x.15; Lk. xviii.17)," *ET* 77, no. 2 (1965): 56-58.

Jesus gives a warm embrace to children in both 9:36 and 10:16.[84] This novel suggestion intimates that we are to treat the dominion as if it were a child.

The usual reading of the aphorism, however, is that Jesus means we should receive the dominion in the same fashion that children receive it, a more probable reading in view of 10:13-14, and 16, which recounts how Jesus received children, texts which speak to the issue of the place of children in the dominion. The point, then, is that the dominion is made up of children and those like them, not that the dominion is like a child in some manner. "Thus those commended become role models, while those corrected become warnings."[85] Perhaps making the child's behavior a model for adult behavior was so counterintuitive in Jesus' setting that the strong assertion of Jesus' personal authority ("Amen, I say to you . . .") was required to back it up.[86] In context there is a notable contrast between the ease with which children enter the dominion of God and the difficulty with which rich adults do so.

The pericope closes in v. 16 with an action of Jesus which indicates clear acceptance of the children and of the intentions of those who brought them. Jesus goes beyond touching the children to hugging them.[87] Thus it can be said: "Jesus uses the smallest member of the physical family as a model for members of the family of faith and gives children a place in the Kingdom. The evidence of Jesus' positive attitude toward children, their place in the Kingdom, and how they might serve as models for disciples and be served by disciples seems to imply a positive estimation of a woman's role as child-bearer and mother (as well as a positive estimation of the father's role)."[88] Of course, this text is also a parade example demonstrating Jesus' great concern for and compassion on the weak and most vulnerable members of society. Myers rightly asks:

> Why should not the child represent an actual class of exploited *persons*, as does every other subject of Jesus' advocacy in Mark? . . . [Mark is] concerned to unmask the realities of domination within community and even within kindred relationships. Indeed, from the narrative world of Mark we have cause to suspect that all is not well for the child in first-century Palestinian society. For where do we meet children in the Gospel? In every case, it is in situations of sickness and oppression: the synagogue ruler's daughter (5.21ff.), the Syrophoenician's daughter (7.24ff.), the deaf dumb son (9.14ff.). . . . The social signification of such consistent narrative portrait suggests that Mark understands the child as victim.[89]

---

84. See Painter, p. 143.
85. Painter, p. 143.
86. See rightly Gundry, p. 545.
87. Gundry, p. 545.
88. Witherington, *Women*, p. 16.
89. Myers, *Binding the Strong Man*, p. 268.

Indeed, the previous two passages show Jesus to be the protector of both women and children, the most vulnerable members of society. In the first instance he protects women by forbidding divorce, thus giving them more social and economic security. In the second instance he protects children by showing them to be valid and valuable members of God's domain who should be welcomed with open arms.[90]

Though the issue of entering God's dominion has just been broached in the children passage, it can be said that 10:17-31, which seems to be a single unit, distills Jesus' essential teaching about entrance into the realm of God's divine saving activity. The unit has something of a concentric structure, as Myers has pointed out:

A   Question about eternal life (v. 17)
   B   Rich man cannot leave possessions and follow
      C   Jesus' explanation, disciples' reaction (twice)
   B'   Disciples have left possessions and followed
A'   Answer to eternal life question (v. 30)[91]

This unit is relatively free of textual problems, with the one exception of v. 19, where various manuscripts omit the phrase "do not defraud" (an echo of Exod. 20:17 or Deut. 24:14 [LXX] or Sir. 4:1), since it seems not to be part of the Ten Commandments. Matthew and Luke also omit the phrase (cf. Matt. 19:18 to Luke 18:20), which is all the more reason to think it might be original. It is supported by good witnesses (ℵ, A, B, C, D, and others) and should likely be retained.[92] The phrase could even be said to be an extrapolation from the eighth or ninth commandment. In any event, the story as a whole has the earmarks of authenticity, for Jesus seems to imply that he might be neither good (with a capital *G*) nor God (with a capital *G*), and surely the early church would not have created a saying such as Mark 10:18b. Notice how both Matthew and Luke have modified the saying to make it less offensive precisely at this point.

The story begins with Jesus continuing in his trek up to Jerusalem when someone comes running up to him, falls on his knees, and calls him "Good Teacher." This form of address seems basically without parallel either in the Hebrew Scriptures or in early Jewish literature. Only God, of course, was called good in the ultimate sense in early Judaism.[93] It is hard to say whether one should see

---

90. See Juel, p. 131.

91. Myers, *Binding the Strong Man*, p. 272.

92. See Metzger, *TCGNT*, p. 105.

93. It is interesting to see how later Christian commentators got around the scandal of Jesus' utterance here. Hilary of Poitiers, for example, suggests that Jesus only rejects the address of the young man because it is put to him as a mere teacher of the law. "He would not

v. 17 as flattery or as a sincere remark. It may be that an Oriental custom is at the root of this interchange, for if the remark is flattery, then the man is setting up a reciprocity exchange in which he expects a flattering remark in return. "Jesus is repelling the man's hopes for return ingratiation. Instead comes a reproof. . . ."[94] Notice also the form of the question asked — "What must I *do* to inherit eternal life." V. 18 may well be Jesus' attempt to make clear to the inquirer that human achievement could not make a person good, and only God was categorically good. Perhaps we are meant to think that this man believed he and Jesus were good men because of their deeds, and notice how Jesus responds in terms of deeds. As Hurtado says, v. 18 is a rebuke to the idea that human beings can be called good because of their deeds, or that the ultimate good in life (eternal life) can be had by doing.[95] It is interesting that the term "me" is in an emphatic position in Jesus' response ("Why do you call *me* good . . . ?").[96]

At v. 19 Jesus lists some of the commandments. It is perhaps most significant what he does not list — namely, the Sabbath commandment. This deliberate omission may reflect Jesus' view that now that the eschatological age was dawning, keeping a particular day as the Sabbath was no longer obligatory, for all days would now be holy unto the Lord. Gundry suggests that the reference to defrauding may well be given in place of the commandment about coveting because Jesus is dealing with a wealthy person, who might not covet another's goods but nonetheless may engage in defrauding as a matter of normal business (cf. Mal. 3:5 LXX).[97] The man replies that he has kept these commandments since youth, perhaps a reference to his becoming a "son of the commandments" at adolescence when he assumed the full yoke of adult obedience (see *m. Nid.* 5.6).

V. 21 gives us a tender touch, saying that Jesus looks straight at the man and loves him, the only time in this Gospel that he is specifically said to love someone. There is perhaps an earnestness about him that Jesus sees as salutary. But Jesus apparently knows that there is one major obstacle to his offering total devotion to God — his many possessions. Thus Jesus says the young man lacks one thing, and so issues a command that he sell whatever he has and give to the poor.[98] Instead of such possessions, the man is to have treasure in heaven and to

---

have rejected the attribute of goodness if it had been attributed to him as God" (*On the Trinity* 9.16). Origen (*On First Principles* 1.21.3) suggests that Christ was making the point that the goodness that the Son and the Spirit have is derived from the one font of all goodness and divinity, the Father. Thus he was not denying he is good or God, but affirming the source from which he derived such attributes.

94. Myers, *Binding the Strong Man*, p. 272.
95. Hurtado, p. 151.
96. Gundry, p. 553.
97. Gundry, p. 553.
98. The text does not say give *all* to the poor, though this may be implied.

come and follow Jesus. Augustine encapsulates the truth about a world fixated on possessions — "One who gives up both what one owns and what one desires to own, gives up the whole world" (*Letter to Hilarius* 157). It appears that the young man had thought that as long as he lived a good life and obeyed the major commandments, he was in good shape so far as eternal life is concerned. But keeping commandments can lead to a false sense of security, a sense that God owes one something. There is no substitute for obedience when God calls one to do something more than obey the Ten Commandments. Mark is making clear that the demands of discipleship to Jesus go beyond the demands of the Law. The ultimate test of obedience, then, is seen as the willingness to assume the yoke of discipleship to Jesus.[99]

There may have been many early Jews in the position of Saul of Tarsus, who claims that in regard to obedience to the Law he was "blameless," which must mean having committed no willful violations of a known Mosaic law, so that he could not be accused of being a lawbreaker. Perhaps this young man fell into the same category. But not having broken a known law and being innocent or faultless are of course two different things. It is yet another thing to talk about being righteous, for it is to a higher righteousness that Jesus calls the young man.[100]

In Judaism, almsgiving was one of the three pillar virtues, but it presupposes one having assets from which to share. What Jesus says amounts to a rejection of conventional Jewish piety that said it was all right to be wealthy so long as one was also generous. Notice the examples from somewhat later Jewish literature where rabbis forbade selling all of one's property so one would not be reduced to poverty and dependency on others (*m. 'Arak.* 8.4; *b. Ketub.* 50a). Jesus is clearly enunciating a new Jewish ethic here, and it is not surprising that the young man looks gloomy when he hears about it. The bar has just been raised on what being a good or godly person entails, much less being a disciple of Jesus. The young man leaves saddened, and only at this juncture in the story are we told that he has much possessions. Notice that he is not called by Mark a rich young ruler.

V. 23 is important and must be translated carefully. "With what difficulty will those who have wealth enter the dominion of God." Jesus does not say it is impossible. V. 24 says something a bit different — "Children, how difficult it is to enter the dominion of God."[101] The disciples are addressed as children in spiritual

---

99. Schweizer, *Mark*, p. 213, rightly reminds us of the later account of this story in the *Gospel of the Nazarenes*, which involves two rich men. In that version Jesus challenges the right of one of them to say he has fulfilled the Law and prophets if he is not also prepared for discipleship to Jesus.

100. See Lane, p. 366 n. 45.

101. This is the only place within the Synoptic Gospels where the disciples are called children (cf. John 21).

knowledge. Jesus intimates that it is difficult for anyone to get in, but it is particularly difficult for the wealthy. Jesus' metaphor about the camel going through the eye of the needle has some precedents in early Judaism, in which we find phrases about an elephant going through the eye of a needle.[102] This aphorism is not to be rationalized by some reference to a nonexistent needle gate in the city of Jerusalem.[103] Some later scribes actually altered κάμηλος to κάμιλος, the latter meaning "rope," in hopes of making a deliberately hyperbolic remark seem less outlandish.[104] Jesus is contrasting the largest animal and the smallest hole that an early Jew in Israel would likely think of. The point is that salvation is not obtainable through even strenuous human effort, trying to squeeze into God's dominion. The disciples for once understand this implication of Jesus rather clearly, and so ask who then can be saved. This may mean "If a pious person whose wealth is a sign of God's favor will not be saved, what hope of deliverance from hellfire does someone without that sign have?"[105] In any case, this verse suggests the disciples have the same vision of salvation through human obedience or effort as the young man. Jesus then indicates that while salvation is impossible for humans by means of human effort, it is possible for God to give it to humans as a gift.

But Peter still obviously does not understand, for he starts to enumerate all the sacrifices he and other disciples have made to follow Jesus.[106] Jesus indicates that no such sacrifice goes without its reward, though the reward is not salvation itself but rather family and nurture within the dominion of God. Getting into the dominion means accepting a free gift. There may be a bit of deliberate irony here in that Jesus may be alluding to the fact that the disciples would have to get their food and shelter from many others who would take them in as family and offer them hospitality as they traveled. It is, of course, very unlikely that Jesus is enunciating here a get-rich-quick-through-Christian-sacrifice schema. The list of persons and things he offers is very revealing about ancient social values — relatives and basic property (house and land) were the very basis of survival and existence. To cut oneself off from all family and property was to endanger one's very existence.[107]

---

102. This, however, comes from a later period in Jewish literature, but see H. L. Strack and P. Billerbeck, *Kommentar zum Neuen Testament aus Talmud und Midrasch*, 6 vols. (Munich: C. H. Beck, 1926-61), 1:828.

103. As a note in a ninth-century commentary on Mark once suggested.

104. See Hooker, p. 243.

105. Gundry, p. 557.

106. Hooker, p. 243, rightly notes the appropriate nature of the contrast between the rich young ruler who does not give up everything and the disciples who do. This reminds us that however blockheaded and spiritually imperceptive the disciples may appear at times in this Gospel, they have made the commitment of true disciples to follow Jesus and have paid the price to do so. They are very imperfect disciples, but nonetheless real ones.

107. See Gundry, p. 558.

Near the mark about the meaning of Jesus' saying are the words of John Cassian: "you have each left but one father and mother and home, and as you have done so you have gained without any effort or care countless fathers and mothers and brothers, as well as houses and lands and most faithful servants, in any part of the world to which you go, who receive you as their own family, and welcome, and respect, and take care of you with the utmost attention" (*Conferences* 3.24.26). It is worth pointing out that this new family of faith is both affirming of gender equality (made up equally of brothers and sisters, fathers and mothers) and inclusive of children and others of the "least among you."[108] Notice also that with the blessings of the family of faith and Christian hospitality comes persecution — something Mark's Roman audience could especially relate to. It is indeed possible that Mark has added the phrase "with persecutions" to the original word of Jesus to contemporize the text, just as "for the sake of the Gospel" may also be an addition. In any event, the renunciations Jesus is referring to do not mean he is offering an ethic of asceticism. "Poverty serves evangelism, not private sanctification."[109]

V. 30 bears witness to traditional Jewish two-age theology, the age to come being the eschatological age. Jesus is bringing in a foretaste of this age, inaugurating the age to come in the midst of this age. Nevertheless, the chief blessing of the age to come, namely, eternal life, apparently is only to be had in the future. V. 31 seems to be an isolated saying that was simply attached here, though it suits the discussion on wealth. The verse deals with the matter of reversal of status and standing and so also a reversal of human expectations. Many of the first will be last in the dominion, and many now considered least, last, and lost will be first in the dominion. "While the call to become part of Jesus' group of disciples seems, at times, to be a call to be part of his mission, here it also seems to be an essential condition for eternal life."[110]

G. Sacrifice, Self-Aggrandizement, and Sight (10:32-52)

At vv. 32-34 we have the third and last passion prediction by Jesus. V. 32 is difficult grammatically. Are there two groups with Jesus — those who were amazed and those who were afraid? Perhaps so, because we do have a δε separating the two verbs.[111] Notice that once again the announcement of the passion is given to the inner circle of disciples, the Twelve. Here for the first time Jesus says

---

108. So rightly Myers, *Binding the Strong Man*, p. 276.
109. Myers, *Binding the Strong Man*, p. 276.
110. Painter, p. 146.
111. See below in the appendix on the implications of this for understanding Mark's view of discipleship and apostleship.

plainly that he is going up to Jerusalem, and here we learn that he will be handed over by his own people to the Gentiles.[112] This will make very clear the contempt the authorities have for Jesus and how far they are from seeing him as Messiah, for they would only hand the worst of their race over to the despised Romans. Every detail of this prediction is depicted as coming to pass in Mark 14–16, and it is not surprising that this is the most detailed of the predictions, being in closest proximity to the events themselves.[113] "In the light of this teaching the urgent hurrying of Jesus to reach Jerusalem is truly awesome and frightening."[114] It may also be significant that all the passion predictions are offered while Jesus and his disciples are on the road, or better said, on the way to Jerusalem and therefore Golgotha (cf. 8:27; 9:33-34).[115] This is but one more indicator that this Gospel is about the way of the cross, both as an expression of Christology and also of discipleship.

Once again the irony is so thick one can cut it with a knife. No sooner has Jesus told the disciples he is going to make the ultimate sacrifice than Jacob and John come asking for the chief seats in the dominion. Casey has now reconstructed a plausible Aramaic original of this story, and he is right to relate it to the Q saying about the Twelve judging Israel in the eschaton (Matt. 19:28/Luke 22:30).[116] This puts the Zebedees' request in a proper perspective. They are asking for seats of honor when the Twelve, rather than even the patriarchs, will be seated in judgment of Israel. Vv. 35-45 indicate clearly how very far away from Jesus' way of thinking about true greatness Jacob and John are, despite all the time and special teaching Jesus has given them. These brothers could be seen as classic examples of blind ambition. They "masked their request and sought to get Jesus to agree to do whatever they were about to ask him. The form of this question implies that those who asked thought they had some claim on Jesus, but because they could predict the answer Jesus would give (see 9.35) they masked the actual question."[117]

Notice again at v. 35 that they call Jesus "Teacher." They come to Jesus with a special request — to sit at the right and the left when Jesus comes into his glory.[118] Perhaps the journey up to Jerusalem has given them the idea that Jesus is about to set up his kingdom.[119] It is not completely certain whether they are asking for the best seats at the messianic banquet or for thrones on

---

112. See pp. 241-42 above.
113. On being whipped and spit upon, see Isa. 50:6.
114. Painter, p. 147.
115. See Hooker, p. 245.
116. Casey, pp. 193-218.
117. Painter, p. 148.
118. Notice how Matthew, in his usual way, tries to spare the disciples a bit by having the mother of the Zebedees make the request — cf. Matt. 20:20-28.
119. See Hooker, p. 246.

either side of the King when he is enthroned as eschatological judge (cf. 13:26 and Luke 22:30). The seats on the right and the left of the host were of course the chief seats of honor at a banquet (see 1 Kings 2:19; Ps. 110:1; 1 Esd. 4:29; Sir. 12:12; Josephus, *Ant.* 6.11.9),[120] and as a second possibility this might be what the request is about. Lane makes the interesting suggestion that the disciples are asking for the seats in the dominion which they already enjoy when the disciples dine (but cf. John 13:23-25).[121] On the whole, the connection with suffering suggests that a scene of judgment is in view, as Casey has suggested.

V. 38 presents Jesus as saying that Jacob and John have no clue what they are asking for. He will tell them that the road to such glory must go through suffering, and so he must ask if they are willing to pay the price to get to the position of glory. "Leadership belongs only to those who learn and follow the way of nonviolence — who are 'prepared' not to dominate but to serve and to suffer at Jesus' side."[122] The saying about drinking from the cup Jesus will drink, and being baptized with the baptism he will be baptized with, is loaded with OT allusions. The cup is surely a reference to the cup of God's wrath poured out on sin (cf. Ps. 75:8; Isa. 51:17, 22; Lam. 4:21; *Mart. Isa.* 5:13 — "for me only God has mingled the cup [of martyrdom]"). Baptism is an image of being overwhelmed by disaster or danger (cf. the analogy with the flood in 1 Pet. 3). John's baptism was of course associated with God's wrath and repentance, but in a different way. Some have seen in baptism the equivalent to the oath curse sign in some earlier covenants, namely, circumcision. Circumcision was the symbol that God would cut off his people or their progeny if they failed to keep the covenant. Similarly, baptism would also be a symbol of an oath curse if one associates it either with the flood or with a trial-by-water ordeal. Clearly water is an image of calamity or disaster in the OT (Ps. 42:7; Isa. 43:2). In any case, the images are images of suffering and death.

Jacob and John say rather glibly that they are prepared to drink of such a cup and be baptized with such a baptism. Are they thinking of undergoing John's baptism and drinking of the Passover cup? V. 39 was taken early on in church history to mean that these two would be martyred, and it may well imply that, when Jesus says they will undergo such a baptism and such a drinking, but at a minimum it implies that they will suffer for their allegiance to Jesus (cf. Acts 12:2). V. 40 indicates that seats in the dominion are assigned not by Jesus but by the Father, and will be given to those for whom they are prepared. This may intimate that God already has someone else in mind for these seats. Natu-

---

120. Since this is a joint request, it is apparently left in Jesus' hands which side Jacob or John would get. See Painter, p. 148.

121. Lane, pp. 378-79.

122. Myers, *Binding the Strong Man,* p. 278.

rally the other disciples are indignant at this self-aggrandizing action of Jacob and John, for in their view it amounted to an attempt to grasp at positions of power and authority. They were angry "perhaps not because their own attitudes were any different but because the two brothers had stolen a march on them."[123]

Jesus then tells a brief parable to indicate what sort of leaders he wants in God's dominion — servant leaders. Jesus' vision of leadership is not of a person who lords it over others or wields authority like a great one, but rather one who is the servant and slave of all. V. 45 is in many ways the key verse in Mark so far as understanding the theology of the cross in this Gospel is concerned. Jesus comes not as a glorious one, but as a humble Son of Man, one who comes to serve rather than be served. His example of leadership is diametrically opposed to the examples set by secular authorities. But in fact, Jesus comes not merely to offer just any sort of service but rather to offer the greatest service of all to humankind — to give his life (ψυχη clearly means life here, not soul) as a λυτρον αντι πολλων. This last phrase deserves close scrutiny. I agree with those who say it seems very likely that Isa. 53 lies in the background here, but a more detailed comment is in order at this juncture.

Echoes of Isaiah 53 in Mark 10:45?

While it is not possible to enter fully into the debate about the relationship between Isa. 53 and Mark 10:45, the following considerations lead to the conclusion that Isa. 53 is very likely alluded to in this Markan text. (1) The servant language in Mark 10:45, especially in view of the phrase about the one who serves many in Isa. 53:11, seems to be an echo of Isa. 53. It is not sufficient to argue that different terms for servant are used in Mark and in Isaiah, since by Mark's day there was clearly overlap in the meaning of δουλος and διακονος. (2) The contrast both in Isa. 53 and here in Mark 10:45 is between the one who suffers and the many he suffers for, not between many and all (cf. below). (3) While Hooker is quite right that the word *asam* in Isa. 53:10 refers to a sin offering, not a ransom,[124] the concept of a substitutionary sacrifice is indeed connoted by the noun λυτρον and its verbal cognate in texts like Exod. 13:13-16 (LXX) and probably carries the same connotation in Mark 10:45. In view of the text in Exodus, it is certainly wrong to suggest that substitutionary sacrifice is a later idea that could not stand in the background of the material in both Isaiah and Mark 10:45. One must conjure with echoes not just of Isa. 53 in Mark 10:45 but also of other texts about sacrifice in the OT. Furthermore, since Yahweh's redemptive work for Israel is indeed described in terms of a λυτρον throughout Second and Third Isaiah (35:9; 41:14; 43:1, 14; 44:22-24; 52:3; 62:12; 63:9), it seems forced to suggest that the author had no such notions in mind in regard to Yahweh's servant as described in Isa. 53. Is not Yahweh redeeming his people through the ser-

---

123. Hooker, p. 247.
124. See Hooker, pp. 248-49.

vant as described in Isa. 53?[125] (4) The concept of a ransom paid by one party for the sins committed by another is certainly already present in some of the Maccabean literature (see especially 2 Macc. 7:37-38; 4 Macc. 6:27-29; 17:21-22). (5) The notion of vicarious atonement for sin by means of the death of the righteous is also found in other early Jewish literature of the period (cf. 1QS 5.6; 8.3-10; 9.4; and *y. Yoma* 38b; *b. Ben.* 3.8). What this means is that the idea of such a substitutionary atoning death is certainly possible on the lips of the historical Jesus, as well as in the mind of the earliest Evangelist. (6) I have elsewhere dealt with the traditional arguments against the authenticity of this utterance and shown them to be quite weak. These arguments are usually taken to also show a lack of connection between Mark 10:45 and Isa. 53.[126] (7) It is clear that elsewhere in Mark some of the servant material is alluded to (see, e.g., Isa. 40:3 in Mark 1:2-3; Isa. 42:1 in Mark 1:11; Isa. 49:24 used in Mark 3:27; Isa. 56:7 in Mark 11:17).[127] (8) R. E. Watts has shown that the absence of clear linguistic parallels when the OT is alluded to is characteristic of explanatory statements in Mark (see Mark 14:24). (9) Even though λυτρον is used only here in Mark, the ideas associated with it seem to be present in the cup saying in Mark 14:24, especially in light of the OT texts which refer to ransom or ransoming back life (cf. Exod. 30:12; Num. 18:15; Lev. 25:51-52; and on substitution, Isa. 43:3ff.). (10) It must be kept steadily in view, then, that this whole saying is thoroughly Semitic, and S. Kim has shown that it can be readily retrojected back into Aramaic.[128] (11) C. K. Barrett was right to stress that the basic idea here is of substitution of something of equivalent value, a notion quite clear in the famous parallel in Josephus, *Ant.* 14.107.[129] (12) Both J. Marcus and Watts have shown that the Second Isaiah imagery pervades not only Mark's opening chapter but subsequent chapters as well, as Mark draws on the concept of the new exodus in Second Isaiah.[130] In particular, the presentation in Mark 10 of Jesus being on the way up to Jerusalem is shaped by the Isaianic notion of the way of the Lord. Even more strikingly, "Just as Yahweh's promise to lead 'blind' Israel along a way it does not know (Is. 42.16) indicates that Israel's deliverance will not be in keeping with its expectations, so in Mark the 'blind' disciples are led along a 'way' they do not understand as indicated by their response to the three passion predictions."[131] (13) Watts has now mounted a strong argument that Mark 9:12 has as its background (when it refers to the suffering of much) primarily Isa. 53, not Dan. 7, which does not directly refer to the Son of Man figure suffering. He also contends plausibly that the passion predictions in Mark 8, 9, and 10 also allude to both Dan. 7 and Isa. 53 (and perhaps Isa. 50 also).[132] (14) It is generally recognized

125. See R. E. Watts, "Jesus' Death, Isaiah 53, and Mark 10.45," in *Jesus and the Suffering Servant: Isaiah 53 and Christian Origins,* ed. W. H. Bellinger and W. R. Farmer (Harrisburg, Pa.: Trinity Press, 1998), p. 141.

126. See my *Christology of Jesus,* pp. 252-53.

127. See now the discussion by Watts, pp. 125-51.

128. S. Kim, *The Son of Man as the Son of God* (Grand Rapids: Eerdmans, 1985), p. 39.

129. See Barrett's earliest essay on the subject, "The Background of Mark 10.45," in *New Testament Essays: Studies in Memory of T. W. Manson, 1893-1958* (Manchester: Manchester University Press, 1959), pp. 1-18, here p. 6.

130. See J. Marcus, *The Way of the Lord: Christological Exegesis of the Old Testament in the Gospel of Mark* (Louisville: Westminster, 1992), and the article of Watts cited above, which summarizes some of his doctoral dissertation.

131. Watts, p. 130.

132. Watts, pp. 131-36.

that the phrase "gives his life" in Mark 10:45 is a reasonably clear echo of Isa. 53:12, and perhaps also of Isa. 53:10b, especially since there is no evidence that Mark was working with a text of Isaiah that did not contain either the concept of the life force or the notion of it being offered up in these verses, and since the LXX rendering contains these ideas found in the Hebrew text as well. (15) In the immediate Markan context, servant and slave are basically synonyms and the verb "to serve" does link this passage with the Isaianic material. (16) Other evangelists found the connection between Isa. 53 and Jesus' suffering a natural one (see, e.g., Acts 8:32-35), and there is no reason why Mark may not have done so as well. Not all these arguments are of equal weight, but taken cumulatively they weigh heavily in favor not only of Mark 10:45 being about a substitutionary redeeming death for "the many," but also of the notion that at several points Isa. 53 stands in the background of this saying and informs its semantic field. Mark has combined Isaianic and Danielic material here to speak of the vocation of the Son of Man to suffer and ransom many.

Mark 10:45 in a sense brings to a climax the passion predictions that come during the public ministry of Jesus. This one is in fact the only singularly focused passion prediction, for it includes no mention of the resurrection. Here, as Painter points out, unlike in the earlier passion predictions, we have not merely a statement of what will happen to the Son of Man but a statement of the purpose for his coming.[133] The purpose is stated both negatively and positively. The Son of Man came not to be served but to serve, and indeed to give his very life in that service. This links Jesus' own vocation with what was said in 10:43 to be the disciples' vocation. The term λυτρον is a mercantile term. It should be translated "ransom" and refers to the deliverance by purchase of a slave or prisoner of war or of some object one wants back (see Lev. 25:47-55). Very clearly the idea of equivalence, a quid pro quo, is in the background here. Furthermore, the preposition αντι should likely be taken to mean "in place of" or "as a substitution for." Here we have enunciated the notion of substitutionary atonement. Jesus came to set people free from the wrong sort of servitude so that, like himself, they might become free servants of God, exchanging all false masters for a true one. There may be here an allusion to being ransomed from the power of Satan, in view of the focus in Mark's Gospel on exorcisms.

While it is possible that the phrase "the many" is a technical term for "the elect," as it seems to have been used at Qumran (see 1QS 6.1, 7-25; CD 13.7; 14.7), it is doubtful that Roman Christians, who were largely Gentiles, knew Qumranite theology about the many. More likely Mark is simply contrasting the one who made the sacrifice with the many for whom he was the substitute. This in turn means the contrast is not between "many" and "all," as if Christ died only for some, but rather between the "one" Christ and "the many" benefi-

133. Painter, p. 150.

ciaries.[134] There are of course two senses in which it is true to say that Christ did not die for all: (1) he, being the substitute, did not die for himself or his own sins; (2) ultimately, since only some accept the benefits of his suffering, he died for them. Elsewhere in the Gospel tradition we learn that a minority of people enter by the straight gate.

Vv. 46-52 provide us with the last positive miracle tale in Mark (the cursing of the fig tree being a punitive miracle). In some ways it is one of the most significant miracle tales in Mark because, other than exorcisms, the one miracle Jesus performed that is not recorded in the Hebrew Scriptures is the giving of sight to a blind person. This miracle is referred to in some of the Isaiah material that deals with the restoration of the kingdom to and in Israel, and that material was later seen as messianic in character by some early Jews.

The name of the blind man is bar-Timaeus, the son of Timaeus (a patronymic like bar-Jonah in Simon's case). Notice that Mark gives both the Aramaic and the Greek equivalent of the name. The man is a blind beggar who sits at Jericho's city gate,[135] a phenomenon you can still see today in various Near Eastern cities. The name of the city is perhaps mentioned to indicate that Jesus is now not far from Jerusalem (about fifteen miles) and so nearing his goal.[136] It may be very significant that only here, just before going up to Jerusalem, is Jesus called Son of David. There is some evidence that this may be a messianic title (see 4QFlor 1.10ff.),[137] and if so, then the messianic secret is not to remain secret for much longer as the passion draws near, when Jesus will be fully revealed for who he is. Notice that the term "Son of David" in *Pss. Sol.* 17–18 refers to a militaristic figure like the original King David. But this Son of David bar-Timaeus cries out to is one who comes with mercy, not wrath, and will enter Jerusalem on a donkey, not a war charger. He fulfills the Isaianic promises about healing and deliverance (cf. Isa. 29:18; 32:1-3; 35:1-10; 61:1-4).[138] V. 48 indicates that the crowd saw this man's bellowing for help as annoying, but the man was persistent. Here the stern charge to be silent comes not from Jesus but from the annoyed crowd (cf. 1:25; 4:39; 8:30, 32).

When Jesus indicates he will see the man, some apparently change their tune and tell bar-Timaeus to have courage, get up and go to him. The man acts with reckless abandon, throwing off the outer garment, which he may have laid on the ground over his feet to catch coins. He springs up and comes to Jesus. The man quite clearly believes Jesus can heal and calls him "Rabbouni," used only here and in John 20:16 by Mary Magdalene. It means "my Master" or "my Teacher."

---

134. See rightly Schweizer, *Mark,* p. 222.

135. The first city mentioned by name since the reference to Capernaum in 9:33.

136. See Hooker, p. 252.

137. See Lane, p. 387.

138. As rightly noted by Painter, p. 151.

Jesus tells the man that his faith has saved him, and the man then commits himself to following Jesus to Jerusalem. Perhaps the use of the verb ακολυθει here indicates he was now a disciple. Certainly this appears like a call narrative, and Bar-Timaeus's persistence could be seen as exemplary. It is interesting that 2 Sam. 5:6 seems to indicate that taking away the blind was a prerequisite for David entering Jerusalem. If so, then Jesus, that latter-day Son of David, has removed the blindness rather than the blind as he goes up to the Holy City.

Painter perceptively compares this story to the one about Jacob and John earlier in the chapter. In both stories we find the response of Jesus: "What do you want me to do?" (cf. 10:36 to 51). In both stories Jesus is addressed as a teacher (called "Teacher" by Jacob and John and "Rabbouni" by bar-Timaeus). The disciples make an illegitimate request, whereas bar-Timaeus exemplifies the right sort of thing to ask of the Great Physician, seeing the Son of David as the one to fulfill texts like Isa. 35:4-5 or 61:1-4 about the blind receiving sight. Certainly in v. 51 bar-Timaeus's request "that I might see again" and the repetition of the verb αναβλεψω in v. 52 seem to be an echo of Isa. 42:18 LXX, where it occurs in the promise to the blind.[139] The story is full of irony, for it is the blind man in this crowd who can see Jesus for who he is, and not the disciples.[140] This is perhaps because we are meant to see bar-Timaeus as the paradigm of the disciple, and like a disciple he is said to "follow Jesus on the way" (cf. v. 32), even though that way involved going up to Jerusalem.[141]

It can be no accident that other than Peter at Caesarea Philippi, bar-Timaeus is the only human figure that addresses Jesus with a messianic title.[142] Like the title Christ, the title Son of David will prove to be true but inadequate to fully describe Jesus (see 12:35-37). There is a possible contrast between bar-Timaeus and the rich young man, for unlike the young man who was unprepared to leave his wealth behind and follow Jesus, we are told in v. 50 that bar-Timaeus, who had his beggar's cloak on the ground to receive alms, pushes it aside, springs up and follows Jesus, leaving the cloak and everything else behind.[143] "Bartimaeus rather than the twelve, has become the image of the true disciple. It was no accident that Mark portrays a blind man as the first person to perceive that Jesus was the son of David. His persistent (double) confession of Jesus as such is the first use of the title in the Gospel, preparing the way for the

139. See rightly Schweizer, *Mark*, p. 225.

140. See Painter, p. 152.

141. See P. Achtemeier, "And He Followed Him: Miracles and Discipleship in Mk. 10.46-52," *Semeia* 11 (1978): 115ff.

142. So rightly Hooker, p. 252.

143. On this see C. D. Marshall, *Faith as a Theme in Mark's Narrative* (Cambridge: Cambridge University Press, 1989), pp. 141-42. On abandoning everything to be a follower, see 1:18, 20; 2:14; 10:21, 28, and Myers, *Binding the Strong Man*, p. 282.

interpretation of this title in the next incident (11.9-10)."[144] Mark's contrast between bar-Timaeus and the brothers Zebedee, between the new disciples and the older ones who thought they deserved privileged positions in the dominion, could hardly be more clear or provide a more devastating critique of those who think that longevity in discipleship entitles one to certain perks from the Lord.[145]

Bridging the Horizons

I was recently talking to a student from the university I graduated from many years ago. She was enthralled with the combination of beauty and religion that she found at a Vivaldi concert at Saint Chapelle in Paris. It was for her an epiphanic experience that made her see the Christian faith in an entirely new light. Alas, the story at the beginning of Mark 9 suggests that though the inner circle of the Twelve went to the mountain and saw the vision glorious, they came back down to earth with a thud, being no wiser thereafter. Though their heads had been in the clouds, they still unfortunately had feet of clay, and more to the point, the rarefied air had not cleared but rather seems to have clouded their thinking. Shortly thereafter they would debate what Jesus could mean by being raised, and then two of them would ask Jesus for the box seats in the kingdom!

Sometimes in the midst of extraordinary situations we make total fools of ourselves. Mark indeed has a fine sense of the comic when he tells us that Peter spoke but in fact did not know what to say because he and Jacob and John were so frightened. As D. English wryly comments, "It would not, evidently, have occurred to Peter not to say anything!" But he rightly adds that perhaps many of us at various times have acted on the same instinct reflected in Peter's words, trying to capture or preserve a unique moment forever.[146] It has also been said that there are only two kinds of speakers — those who have something to say and those who have to say something! Peter in this case would seem to fall into the latter category.

Another telling aspect of this story is the encounter with Moses and Elijah. Sometimes we are apt to say that if we could only meet the great heroes and founders of our faith, then we too could be great persons of faith and would finally understand what all these spiritual things are about. But the truth is, the disciples were no better off after meeting the three greatest figures of their faith than they were before. In fact, they seem to have been more bewildered after

---

144. Painter, p. 153.
145. Myers, *Binding the Strong Man,* p. 282.
146. D. English, *The Message of Mark* (Downers Grove: InterVarsity, 1992), p. 165.

than before. Sometimes sight does not necessarily clarify faith. Sometimes proximity does not necessarily clarify persons and their significance. Such was the case with Jesus and the three on the mountain. Indeed, in the end they had to be lectured like little schoolchildren by God to listen closely to Jesus. It is sobering and yet reassuring to think that the founders of our faith, such as these three, could have foundered that badly, and yet come back to be great leaders of the new Jesus movement.

The discussion that follows in 9:9-13 is also revealing in various regards. The disciples are puzzling about: (1) what rising from the dead could mean if it referred to something that would happen to Jesus alone; (2) why some were saying that Elijah must come first and restore all things before the Messiah came (cf. Mal. 3:1; 4:5). It appears that they assumed that when the Messiah showed up, he would not be coming to do the dirty work but rather to rule a people and a land already restored and made ready to receive him. They couldn't imagine that the Messiah would need to do the variety of things Jesus was doing (healing, exorcising, exhorting), much less that Messiah would need to suffer and rise before the dominion could fully come. Jesus' activities suggested that Elijah had not yet come and restored everything, or else why did Jesus' ministry and his prediction about himself have the character they did? Jesus, of course, will surprise them by suggesting that Elijah, in the guise of the Baptist, had shown up, but he received the same sort of rough treatment Jesus anticipated for himself. Sometimes it is possible to have a dream or set notions about something that will happen that are so strong that when the reality turns out to be different we can't imagine that the two are in fact one and the same. What the disciples believed about eschatology and the Messiah was getting in the way of their applying such concepts to Jesus and his ministry.

The story about the deaf-mute seems on the surface to be the kind that would be user-friendly in a skeptical age. After all, has not the phrase "I believe, help my unbelief" almost become the mantra of the agnostic of our culture? And the story could in fact be read in several ways. For example, English points out that when Jesus says "Everything is possible for him who believes," postmoderns might well ask whether Jesus is referring to his own faith that enables him to help the man and his child or to the man's faith. Or yet again, is Jesus really saying "everything is possible for the one who has faith in me and what I can do for him," placing the stress on the relationship being the basis of all this?[147] I agree with English that the third option is most likely, for elsewhere the Jesus tradition stresses that if one has even a mustard seed–sized faith in the right object of faith (namely, Jesus), then amazing results are possible. The emphasis, then, is not on the quantity of a person's faith but on its object — is it faith placed in the right person?

---

147. English, p. 168.

One of the great tragedies of modern culture is that it mistakes over and over again earnestness for honesty, and zeal for the real. But one can have ever so much zeal for the wrong cause, place ever so much faith in the wrong object, and be none the better for all one's devotion. Though indeed there are degrees of faith, any real faith in a true object of faith avails far more than great devotion to and trust in something less than the real God. The same can be said about prayer. It is not prayer or great faith that is powerful, it is the object of prayer and faith. True prayer and true faith is prayer and faith properly directed to the Source from which all blessings flow. "The emphasis then is not on the quality of our faith but on the power of the Master with whom we are joined by faith."[148] If we ask what was wrong with the disciples' faith or approach, it may be that they had come to have faith in a process of exorcism, rather than placing their confidence in God.

In a world that confuses meekness with weakness, humility with humiliation, it is not surprising that the exhortations Jesus makes about children (as contrasted with the debates among the disciples about who is the greatest) fall on deaf ears. The disciples, to say the least, were only partially socialized followers of Jesus, and they brought into that following a lot of the views and values of their age and of their gender. Children were not seen as models of discipleship nor as paradigms for adult behavior. The concept of reversal of expectations and of values plays a major role in Jesus' teaching — the last being first, the least being most, the lost being found. Jesus believes this is what the coming of God's eschatological reign on earth will bring about. But Jesus goes beyond this: he actually puts himself in the place of the child and says whoever receives the child is receiving him. Jesus' followers are to treat the least, last, and lost as they would treat Jesus, whom they love and follow. Ray Stedman once preached a sermon on true greatness, contrasting many modern concepts of greatness with that found in our text. He stressed that the first mark of true greatness is to learn to be no respecter of persons, to welcome people simply because they are people, regardless of age or stage of life, regardless of race or gender, regardless of whether they can do something for you or cannot.[149]

O. Henry, whose short stories filled my childhood since he grew up within a few miles of my birthplace in North Carolina, tells the tale of a little girl whose mother had died when she was small. Her father would come home from work each day, fix their meal, then sit down with a paper and a pipe, put his feet up and read. When the little girl would come and ask her daddy to play with her, he would say no, he was too tired or busy, and then he would say, "Go out in the street and play." This went on for year after year until finally the little

---

148. English, p. 168.

149. The sermon was entitled "The Child in Our Midst" and was delivered March 2, 1975.

girl had grown up as a street person, indeed as a streetwalker, a prostitute. Eventually she died and went to the gates of heaven and presented herself to Peter. Peter said to Jesus, "Shall we send her to hell? She was a prostitute." Jesus' reply was "No, no, let her in. But go find the man who refused to play with her and send him to hell."

Some of the material at the end of Mark 9 raises the whole issue of hell, a topic most, even in the church, would rather not discuss. It is interesting to me that there are more verses in the Synoptics where Jesus talks about hell than where he talks about heaven. The metaphorical description of hell being, like the Hinnom valley, a noxious place full of decaying garbage and human waste is vivid and has led to some quite vivid works of art (e.g., some of the paintings of Hieronymus Bosch). Granted that Jesus is speaking in metaphorical terms, nonetheless it seems clear that he, like many other early Jews, believes hell is a real and really unpleasant place, which one ought at all costs to avoid visiting. Whatever else one may wish to say on the subject, it would seem that hell is the place where one experiences the absence of God's loving presence forever, knowing for all eternity that one has blown it and there is no remedy (such seems to be the message of the parable of the rich man and Lazarus). Jesus, then, believes that this life is the place of moral decision which determines our eternal destiny. We may wish to protest or find this concept offensive, but we must resist the all-too-human tendency to whittle off the hard edges of Jesus' message. Indeed, Jesus is even prepared to say that it is better to enter the dominion of God badly maimed than to go to hell with a whole body. The gospel not merely comforts the afflicted, it also afflicts the comfortable.

The devilishly difficult issue of divorce is treated in Mark 10, and Jesus is presented as a rigorist, it would seem. Whatever differences he has with the Pharisees on other issues, on this one he appears to make them look moderate and lenient by comparison. There is, however, a reason for this, and it has to do with Jesus' evaluation of the age he is living in, namely, the age when the dominion of God is breaking in. Jesus believes that in previous times God made provision for human hard-heartedness, but that now is the time to call people to a higher righteousness.

Yet one needs to be aware of the context in which Jesus is operating. He is talking to committed monotheists, and primarily to his followers. He is talking to an audience that marries within the community of faith and sees itself as accountable to God for its behavior. More to the point, he is talking about a relationship which he believes God is actively bringing about. It is God who is said to be the one who joins the couple together. This is an important theological point, for it is clear from Jesus' commentary on other relationships that he believes that not all such unions are joined together by God. In fact, in view of Matt. 19:11-12 it would appear that he is actively suggesting that more Jews should consider the option of not marrying at all, a radical teaching since many early Jews believed that the commandment "be fruitful and multiply" was an imperative intended for every able-bodied Jewish person.

Notice the phrase at the end of Matt. 19:11 — where Jesus says not everyone is able to receive his radical teaching on permanent, lifelong marriage, but "only those to whom it is given." The same applies to radical singleness. Jesus has turned marriage as manifest destiny into marriage as a calling for those to whom it is given. The effect of his radical teaching is, in effect, more options for women and men beyond marriage and more security especially for women within marriage, for they could not be divorced.

The key reason Jesus approaches the issue of marriage and divorce as he does is his view of the nature and meaning of the creation order. Jesus dates the original separateness of male and female to the beginning of creation. Neither Jesus nor the Pharisees nor Mark presuppose androgyny in the Genesis story. Marriage is not a recapturing of the unity of an original androgynous being. Adam didn't start out bisexual. Jesus' creativeness is seen in making the one-flesh union the reason why someone shouldn't divorce one's mate. The two become one, and remain one even if there is a formal act of divorce. This is why the subsequent remarriage is seen as adultery. Jesus may also be novel in suggesting that a man commits adultery against his own wife.

The upshot of this teaching, if it were heeded, would be a whole lot fewer broken families. But it needs to be added that the church especially needs to do a better job of promoting singleness as a viable life calling. One of the very reasons why too many marriages within the church are ending in divorce is because many not really equipped or prepared for marriage have been pressured into marriage by well-meaning people. Human beings are perfectly capable of coupling themselves together in marriage quite apart from the will of God. In fact, it happens all the time, and indeed it happens within the church. Thus it needs to be reiterated that Jesus' strict teaching of "no divorce" applies to those that God has joined together. D. English offered these words of wisdom on this difficult issue:

> Yet any who have experience of pastoral care for married people will know that, sadly and tragically, people do choose badly, make mistakes, change dramatically, fall out of love. To one happily married, or to one not married at all, these may seem to be inconceivable developments. . . . Yet the fact is that marriages do lose their inner core of meaning. People do feel trapped. Deteriorating relationships do destroy the participants. Society's pressures, increasing mobility, non-Christian standards and life styles all militate against stable marriage. In such a situation the Christian church must find a way to hold up, teach, prepare people for, and sustain couples in, the original divine purpose of one man, one woman for life. Yet at the same time it has to find ways of showing the deep compassionate sympathy and under-

standing of Jesus towards those for whom life has not turned out according to the highest ideals.[150]

The story of the rich young man has captured the imagination of many, including F. Buechner, who once offered the following modern paraphrase of Jesus' famous camel-and-needle saying: it is harder for wealthy North Americans to enter the kingdom "than for Nelson Rockefeller to get through the night deposit slot of the First National City Bank."[151] It is a daunting saying, and it often leads to a whole series of attempted qualifications and a whole lot of shuffling of feet. But this misses the point entirely. Salvation is not a human self-help program, but even so there are some things one can say or do or be that make it more difficult to receive salvation as a gift. Human impossibilities are not divine impossibilities, although it can be said that there are even some things God cannot or will not do (such as go back on his word or be unfaithful to his promises).

We need, however, in this chapter to focus on the contrast between the blind beggar who gladly leaves his coins behind and follows Jesus and the rich young man who turns sadly away. It is interesting that it is the latter that the text says Jesus loved. Herein lies the inherent tragedy in such tales. That Christ loves someone is no guarantee that he will love him back, much less follow him.

The rich young man has all the advantages in life; the beggar is destitute. There is a sense in which the lyrics of Bob Dylan are true of the latter man — "when you have nothing, you have nothing to lose." Nonetheless, it is always surprising to see who best responds to Jesus' call on their lives, and bar-Timaeus turns out to be the best paradigm of a disciple that Mark offers us in this entire part of the Gospel. So it will behoove us to consider the qualifications that make him a paradigm: (1) He knows he needs Jesus' help. (2) He persistently calls on the Lord for that help and will not be put off by those who try to silence him. (3) He knows that Jesus owes him nothing, for he asks for mercy, not for something he thinks is owed to him (contrast Jacob and John and the seats in the dominion). (4) He recognizes the truth about Jesus — he is indeed the messianic one, the Son of David. (5) He literally leaps at the chance to come close to Jesus and receive help. He does not wait for Jesus to come to him. (6) He asks plainly and directly for his wants and needs — to be able to see again, which of course means he had been sighted at some previous point in time. In short, he knows quite well what he is missing, and wants it back. (7) It is his faith in the right object of faith, Jesus, that heals and rescues him from the darkness. (8) Instead of being satisfied to be

---

150. English, pp. 174-75.

151. F. Buechner, *Telling the Truth: The Gospel as Tragedy, Comedy, and Fairy Tale* (San Francisco: Harper & Row, 1977), p. 63.

blessed and going back to ordinary life, he chooses to go forward down the hard road of discipleship, following Jesus. Bar-Timaeus has become bar-Theos (a son of God). As such, he provides us with the most winsome example possible of the beginning stages of discipleship.

XI. Long Day's Journey into Night, Part I (11:1–13:37)

The Markan passion narrative, if we include 16:1-8, makes up about 40 percent of the verbiage of this Gospel, and may well be the earliest portion of the Gospel put into some sort of written form.[1] It is the longest consecutive narrative in the Gospel and, for the most part, the one with the most time and scriptural references, perhaps because the author believed these events needed the most scrupulous documentation, explanation, and justification. The passion narrative proper could be said to begin with Mark 14, but it is probably better to see it as beginning with Mark 11.

TRANSLATION — 11:1–13:37

11 And when they came near unto Jerusalem, unto Bethphage and Bethany to the Mount of Olives, he sends two of his disciples and says to them, "Go unto the village opposite of you and immediately upon entering into it you will find a colt tied up upon which no one has yet set. Loose it and bring it. And if anyone says to you, 'What is this you are doing?' say, 'The lord has need of it.'" And immediately he sends them again there. And they went and found a colt tied to a door outside on the street, and they loosed it. And some of those standing there said to them, "Why do you loose the colt?" But they said to them just as Jesus said, and

---

1. This raises interesting questions about Mark 13:14, which, if there was a pre-Markan passion narrative, may only suggest that *this* portion of the Gospel was originally intended for a reader rather than a hearer. See the introduction, pp. 20-30 above.

they allowed them. And they brought the colt to Jesus and they put on it their cloaks, and he sat upon it. And many spread their cloaks upon the way, but others cut rushes from the fields and those going in front and those following cried out: "Hosanna. Blessed is the one coming in the name of the Lord. Blessed is the coming dominion of our father David. Hosanna in the highest." And he entered into Jerusalem into the temple precincts. And surveying everything, as it was already a late hour, he went out unto Bethany with the Twelve.

And the next day, when he was coming out from Bethany he was hungry. And seeing a fig tree from a distance which had leaves, he went to see if by chance he could find anything on it, and coming to it he found nothing except leaves, for it was not the time for figs. And answering he said to it: "May no one ever eat fruit from you," and the disciples heard him.

And they came into Jerusalem. And entering into the temple precincts he began to cast out those selling and those buying in the temple precincts, and the table of the money changers and those seats of those selling doves he overturned, and he did not let them carry vessels through the temple precincts. And he taught and said to them, "Is it not written that 'My house is to be known as a house of prayer for all the nations'? But you have made it a cave of bandits." And the high priests and the scribes heard, and they looked for a way to destroy him, for they were afraid of him, for all the people were astounded at his teaching. And when it was late, they went out, outside the city.[2]

And passing by early he saw the fig tree, withered from the roots. And Peter reminded, says to him, "Rabbi, behold the fig tree which you cursed has withered." And Jesus answering says to him, "Have faith in God.[3] Amen, I say to you that whoever says to this mountain 'Be taken up and cast into the sea,' and does not doubt in his heart but believes that what he says will happen, it will be for him. Therefore, I say to you everything which you pray and ask for, believe that you received, and it will be to you. And when you stand praying, forgive if you have anything against anyone, in order that your Father in heaven may forgive your lapses."[4]

And they come again into Jerusalem. And in the temple precincts as he was walking around the high priests and the scribes and the elders come to him. And they said to him, "By what sort of right do you do these things or who gave to you the authority in order to do these things?" But Jesus said to them, "I will ask you something, and you answer me, and I will tell you by what right I do these things.

---

2. It is hard to decide whether the singular "he went out" is original, or a later christocentric correction. See Metzger, *TCGNT,* p. 109.

3. Some important manuscripts read "if you have faith . . ." (A, D, Θ), but this is perhaps a later modification.

4. V. 26 seems to be rather clearly an addition based on Matt. 6:15. This verse is not found in many important manuscripts (A, B, L, W, Δ, and many others).

The baptism of John, was it from heaven or from human beings?" And they debated among themselves, saying, "If we say 'from heaven' he will say 'Why then did you not believe him?' But if we say 'From human beings . . .'?" They feared the crowd, for all regarded John being that he was a prophet. And answering Jesus say, "We do not know." And Jesus says to them, "Neither will I say to you by what right I do these things."

12   And he began to speak to them in parables: "A man planted a vineyard and put up a fence and dug a winepress and built a tower and let it out to cultivators. And he sent a slave to the cultivators at the time, in order to receive from the cultivators from the fruit of the vineyard. And taking him they beat him and sent him away empty-handed. And again he sent them another slave; that one they wounded in the head and insulted. And another he sent and that one they killed, and many others, whom on the one hand they beat or on the other they killed. He had still one left, a beloved son. He sent him last to them, saying, 'They will respect my son.' But those cultivators said to one another, 'This one is the heir. Come let us kill him, and we will be the heirs.' And taking him they killed him, and they cast him outside the vineyard. What will the lord of the vineyard do to the vineyard? He will come and put to death the cultivators, and he will give the vineyard to others. Have you not read this Scripture: 'The stone which the builders rejected, this one has become the head of the corner. By the lord this has happened and it is wonderful in our eyes.'" And they sought to seize him, and they feared the crowd, for they knew that he spoke the parable to them. And leaving him they went away.

And they sent to him some of the Pharisees and the Herodians in order to trap him in words. And coming they say to him, "Teacher, we know that truly it is not a care to you concerning anyone, for you do not regard the outward countenance of a person. In truth you teach the way of the God. Is it permissible to give the poll tax to Caesar — Are we to give it or are we not to give it?" But seeing the pose of theirs he said to them, "Why do you test me? Give me a denarius in order that I might see it." But they bring it and he says to them, "Whose image and inscription is this?" But they said to him, "Caesar's." But Jesus said to them, "The things of Caesar, give back to Caesar, and things of God to God." And they were utterly amazed at him.

And Sadducees come to him, who say resurrection is not to be, and quizzing him they were saying, "Teacher, Moses wrote us that 'If some brother dies and a wife be left behind and not having a child, that his brother must take the woman and raise up a seed to his brother.' There were seven brothers and the first took her, and he died and did not leave a seed. And the second took her, and died not leaving a seed and the third likewise. And the seventh did not leave a seed. Last of all the woman died. In the resurrection [when they are raised][5] which of these is she the

---

5. Some manuscripts add at this juncture the phrase "when they are raised." This could be original, considering Mark's pleonastic style. See Metzger, *TCGNT*, pp. 110-11.

wife of? For seven had her as a wife." But Jesus said to them, "Are you not misled knowing neither the Scriptures nor the power of God? For when from the dead they arise, they neither marry nor give in marriage, but are as angels in heaven. But concerning the dead that are raised have you not read in the Book of Moses [in the passage] about the bush how God said to him saying, 'I am the God of Abraham and the God of Isaac and the God of Jacob.' He is not the God of the dead but of the living. You are badly misled."

And one of the scribes coming hears him disputing, seeing that he answered them well, questioned him which is the first commandment. Jesus answered that "The first is 'Hear O Israel, the lord our God, the lord is One, and you shall love the lord your God from your whole heart and from your whole life principle and from your whole mind and from your whole strength.' The second is 'Love your neighbor as yourself.' No other commandments are greater than these." And the scribe said to him, "Good teacher, in truth you say that 'There is one and there is not another except him.' And the 'love him from the whole heart and from the whole understanding and from the whole strength' and the 'love of neighbor as self' more comprehensive is that than all the whole burnt offerings and sacrifices." And Jesus seeing that he answered intelligently said to him, "You are not far from the dominion of God." And no one dared to ask him anything.

And Jesus answering said while teaching in the temple precincts: "How is it that the scribes say that the Messiah is the Son of David? David himself said in the Holy Spirit, 'The Lord said to my lord, sit at my right hand, until I put your enemies under your feet.' David himself calls him Lord, and how then is he his son?" And a great crowd heard him eagerly.

And in his teaching he said, "Beware of the scribes who enjoy a walk in their long robes and greetings in the marketplace and first seat in the synagogue and first couches in the banquets. They devour the houses of the widows and for show offer great prayers. These will receive more abundant condemnation."

And he sat down opposite the temple treasury, he saw how the crowd cast copper coins into the temple treasury and many rich cast much. And one poor widow came and cast two lepta (which is a quadrans). And calling to himself his disciples he says to them: "Amen I say to you that the poor widow cast more than all of those throwing into the temple treasury. For all cast from their excess, but she from her want, all which she had she cast, the whole of her living."

13 *And coming forth from the temple precincts, one of his disciples says to him, "Teacher, see what sort of stones and what wonderful buildings." And Jesus said to him, "You see this great building? Not one stone upon another will be left here which will not be pulled down."*

And he was sitting on the Mount of Olives opposite the temple precincts, and Peter and Jacob and John and Andrew ask him privately, "Tell us when this is to be, and what are the signs when these future things will all be accomplished?" But Jesus began to say to them: "Look out lest someone mislead you. Many will come in my name saying that 'I myself am (he),' and many will be deceived. But when you hear of wars and reports of wars, do not be alarmed. It is necessary (that these things) happen, but the end is not yet. For nation will rise against nation and dominion against dominion, there will be earthquakes various places, there will be famine. This is the beginning of the birth pangs. But you look to yourselves. You will be given over to councils and beaten in synagogues, and will stand before governors and kings on my account as a witness to them. And unto all the nations first it is necessary to preach the Gospel. And when they bring you, handing you over, do not be anxious beforehand what you will say, but when it is given to you in that hour, this you speak, for it is not you speaking but the Holy Spirit. And brother will give over brother unto death, and father a child, and a child will rise up against parents and kill them. And you will be hated by all because of my name, but those holding out unto the end, these ones will be saved.

"But when you see the abomination of desolation standing where it ought not to be (let the reader understand), then those in Judea should flee unto the mountains, but those upon the roof should not come down nor enter a place to take anything from his house, and the one in the field should not turn back to get his robe. Alas for those in the process of having a child and those breast-feeding in those days. But pray in order that it not happen in winter. For there will be suffering in those days of such a kind that has not happened from the beginning of creation when God created until now and will not happen again. And unless the Lord cut short the days, no one would be saved of all flesh. But because of the elect, those whom he has chosen he cut short the days. And when ever some says to you, 'Behold here is the Messiah,' 'Behold there,' don't you believe it. For false messiahs and false prophets will rise up and they will give signs and wonders to mislead, if possible, the elect. But you watch out. I have told you all beforehand.

"But in those days after that persecution, the sun will be darkened, and the moon will not give its light, and the stars will be falling from the sky and the powerful ones those in the heavens will be shaken. And then they will see the Son of Man coming in the clouds with great power and glory. And then he will send the angels and he will gather together his elect from the four corners from the ends of the earth unto the ends of the heavens.

"But from the fig tree learn the parable: when the branch is already tender and it breaks into leaf, know that the summer (heat) is near. Thus also you, when you see these things happening, you will know it is at the door. Amen I say to you that this generation will not pass away until all this has happened. Heaven and earth will pass away but my words will not pass away.

"But concerning that day or hour no one knows, neither the angels in heaven nor the Son, except only the Father. See that you be alert for you know not when the time is. As a person going away from his home and gives his servants authority, to each his work, and to the doorman he orders that he be alert. Therefore, keep awake, for you know not when the Lord of the house is coming, whether late, or *midday, or at cock crow, or early, lest coming suddenly he find you sleeping. But I say to you what I say to all — keep awake!"*

A. A Grand Entrance? (11:1-11)

Mark 11 begins with Jesus coming into the region of Bethany and Bethphage, the former being about two miles outside Jerusalem, the latter we are unable to locate, though later rabbinic sources suggest it was near Jerusalem. One could say that the material in Mark 11–13 prepares us for the passion narrative proper, which begins in Mark 14. The major portion of Mark 11–12 falls into the category of what form critics would call controversy narratives, which transpire in Jerusalem and in particular in the temple precincts. Once again we have five controversy narratives, as we did in Galilee at 2:1–3:6, and deliberate selectivity must be said to be at work again here. The material in 11:27–12:25 seems to have been grouped together because of similarity of subject matter. Much depends on how long we think Jesus was in the area of Jerusalem prior to his crucifixion as to whether this material may be seen as stretching over the course of some weeks or must be all packed into one week.

D. Daube makes the intriguing suggestion that the last of the four controversy dialogues corresponds to four types of questions posed by rabbis which are only brought together in this order in the Passover Eve liturgy. These questions are posed in turn by a wise son, a wicked son, a son of simple piety, and finally the head of the household. The first is a question of wisdom concerning a point of Law (12:13-17). The second is a question of mockery which frequently bears on the resurrection (12:18-27). The third is a question of conduct centering on the relationship of God to humans (12:28-34). Finally there is a question of biblical exegesis which often amounts to an attempt to reconcile apparently contradictory passages.[6] If Daube is correct, this suggests that this material was arranged by an early Jewish Christian who was following a traditional form of a Passover liturgy, only now with the content being about Jesus. If there is a liturgical arrangement here, it is unlikely we can deduce any clear chronology from this section of material.

As Lane has pointed out, Mark 11 begins with several symbolic actions grouped together which have prophetic significance — riding into town on a donkey, cursing a fig tree, cleansing (or condemning) the temple — and are followed by the controversy dialogues.[7] There is a hint that the action of Jesus in

---

6. D. Daube, "Evangelisten und Rabbinen," *ZNW* 48 (1957): 119-26. The basis for this argument is found in several sources, with the order of the questions varying a bit; cf. *b. Nid.* 69b-71a; *y. Pesaḥ* X 37d; *Mek. Exod.* 13.8, sec. 4.

7. W. Lane, *The Gospel of Mark* (Grand Rapids: Eerdmans, 1974), pp. 390-93.

the temple prompts an attempt on Jesus' life and the controversies which ensue. In many ways, however, this first narrative in Mark 11 is enigmatic. Schweizer stresses: "The preparation for the triumphal entry and the great enthusiasm of the people come to naught. Shouts of joy ring out — but only outside the city. There is no announcement that the Messiah has come. . . . Finally all the excitement ends without anything being accomplished, since Jesus looks at the temple as a tourist might and then leaves."[8]

A great deal of controversy has arisen as to whether Mark is really suggesting that all the events of 10:46–16:8 took place in a single week.[9] Actually we can only trace to the fourth century A.D. the church tradition that all these things transpired during what came to be called Passion Week. We have already seen in Mark several examples of what looks like compressed chronology, and we may have another case of it here.[10] Hooker rightly argues that although Mark "links together the incidents in the temple as occurring on three successive days (11.12, 20), the teaching in the temple was not necessarily all given on the third day (cf. 14.49), while his dating in 14.1 gives no indication as to how long had elapsed since Jesus arrived in Jerusalem."[11]

It has even been suggested that Mark is recording events that happened during several festal seasons in Jerusalem. For example, in the month of Yishri (September-October) a festival was held called Tabernacles, involving cries of Hosanna as one entered the city; singing of the Hallel psalms (Pss. 113–18); waving of green branches,[12] even palm branches; traditions involving Zech. 9–13; and a focus on the Mount of Olives, on the temple, as well as on Gentiles.[13] All of these elements are found in the story of Jesus' triumphal entry, and this is hard to account for if in fact the entry in question took place during Passover.[14]

---

8. E. Schweizer, *The Good News according to Mark* (Atlanta: John Knox, 1971), p. 227.

9. Early on it was recognized that even Matthew and Mark do not present the same compressed account. Notice how Augustine's view that Matthew was the first Gospel written affects his analysis of Mark 11 in *The Harmony of the Gospels* 68.132.

10. One could suggest that the week framework came naturally to one saturated in the Hebrew Scriptures, only here it's the week in which God remade the world through the death of his Son. There are texts like Mark 14:49 which seem to suggest that Jesus was in Jerusalem for a more extended period of time. See Schweizer, p. 232.

11. M. Hooker, *The Gospel according to Mark* (Peabody, Mass.: Hendrickson, 1991), pp. 255-56.

12. According to *b. Sukk.* 37a-b, these branches were waved when the word "Hosanna" was shouted.

13. On the waving of palm branches as a political gesture conjuring up the Maccabean triumph, see 2 Macc. 10:1-9; 1 Macc. 13:52. W. R. Farmer, "Palm Branches in John 12,13," *JTS*, n.s., 3, no. 1 (1952): 62-66.

14. It has also been suggested that this event may have transpired in the winter, since the winter festival of Hanukkah (Dedication) celebrated the cleansing of the temple by Judas Maccabeus in 165 B.C.

John 12, of course, strongly suggests a one-week chronology of these events, but this may be a theological construct suggesting Jesus' reconstruction of the world in a week. More thought should be given to the suggestion that Jesus was deliberately summing up or coalescing elements of several feasts by his symbolic prophetic acts, though they all transpired at Passover. This in itself would constitute some sort of messianic gesture, like those of other sign prophets.[15]

Mark 11:2 speaks of a πωλος, which literally means a young animal and could be the young of an elephant, a gazelle, or a camel, to name but a few. When used alone in Greek sources, it means a young horse, but in the LXX it is used of the colt of an ass (cf. Gen. 32:15; 49:11; Judg. 10:4). On the basis of Zech. 9:9, the ass was understood to be the animal Messiah would ride, and in light of the echoes of that text in the Markan account, this is likely what is meant here. A second matter of vocabulary that is important in this story is the use of κυριος in v. 3. This word can of course mean something as simple as master. Thus it could be suggested that what is meant here is that the master (i.e., owner) of this colt has need of it. Then the question becomes: Was the master Jesus, or as Lane suggests, was the master of the colt with Jesus, having given Jesus the use of it?[16] If either of these conjectures is correct, it would certainly make this narrative far less enigmatic. The servants thought the owner had sent for his animal. In any case, we may or may not have a case of prophetic foresight here. Notice the close correspondence between the instructions and the disciples carrying them out.

In part because of some of the enigmas in the text, various scholars have concluded that this event likely did not transpire.[17] Perhaps the most plausible of these analyses, by D. Catchpole, nonetheless makes the mistake of misanalyzing the text of Zech. 9, and thus of Mark 11. A close examination of Zech. 9 shows that though the king who is coming to the city has had some victories over his foes, the final victory has not yet been achieved, as Zech. 9:10 makes clear. Thus Zech. 9 is not about a king being welcomed into a city already at peace, prepared for his coming. Nor does his coming inaugurate the era of peace. Thus it would be hard to argue that Mark 11 is created on the basis of Zech. 9, as it does not fit the preset Zecharian pattern.[18] Secondly, there is historical precedent for commandeering animals in Jesus' era following the rules for *angaria,* the impressing of a means of transportation for a

15. See my discussion in *The Christology of Jesus* (Philadelphia: Fortress, 1990), pp. 90-96.

16. Lane, pp. 395-97.

17. See, e.g., D. Catchpole, "The Triumphal Entry," in *Jesus and the Politics of His Day,* ed. C. F. D. Moule and E. Bammel (Cambridge: Cambridge University Press, 1984), pp. 319-24.

18. Notice how in the Markan form of this text Jesus is not hailed as Lord or King.

specific, limited period of time and for a specific purpose.[19] Perhaps the most striking part of Derrett's argument is his stressing that a ruler particularly had the right to impress something for emergency use, but even a text like Matt. 5:40-41 seems to suggest that soldiers and others could impress things if they needed to.

Mark does not in this narrative cite the text of Zechariah itself. His procedure in presenting Scripture fulfillment is different from the First Evangelist's, and more subtle. Thus, for instance, the reference to a colt tied and then loosed recalls Gen. 49:11 (cf. 49:8-12). Or again, the reference to the colt being unridden probably alludes to the fact that a sacred animal must not be put to ordinary use (cf. Num. 19:2; Deut. 21:3; 1 Sam. 6:7). Only the informed reader who knew his OT would recognize these sorts of subtle allusions. Mark depicts Jesus as deliberately setting out to fulfill the Zecharian vision of Messiah, which is a picture of a shepherd rather than primarily a warrior Messiah, and a humble one at that.

Notice that in Zech. 14:1-9 the Mount of Olives is designated as the place of future eschatological revelation of God's glory. The Mount of Olives is over 2,600 feet high, and from it one can see even to the Dead Sea. It is just possible that when Jesus speaks in v. 23 about "this mountain" being cast into the sea, he is referring to the Mount of Olives and the Dead Sea. Zech. 14:4, in fact, says the Mount of Olives is to be split in two and the whole land leveled when the Lord assumes his kingship. This suggests that v. 23 should not be seen as a general exhortation to prayer and faith, but prayer for and faith in the eschatological action of God in Christ.

A few other exegetical notes are in order on Mark 11:1-11. The end of v. 3 seems to involve an assurance that the colt will be returned; however, Matt. 21:3 seems to take it as part of the message itself.[20] At v. 7 the garments put on the colt were in place of a saddle. The spreading of the garments on the road is not unprecedented (see 2 Kings 9:12f.). The waving of the branches is similar to the response to Simon's triumphal entry (cf. 1 Macc. 13:51). Bear in mind that apparently there were no palm trees around or in Jerusalem in this era, the closest ones being in the subtropical city of Jericho. The Greek word στιβάς itself denotes leafy branches or even rushes, but John 12:13 specifically mentions palm branches.

The word "Hosanna" means "save we pray save now," if translated from the Aramaic, but in fact it had become something of a standard praise word (as it still is today) used in glorifying God. It may be significant that in 2 Sam. 14:4 and 2 Kings 6:26 this cry is used in addressing kings. Painter is probably right to

19. J. D. M. Derrett, "Law in the New Testament: The Palm Sunday Colt," *NovT* 13 (1971): 241-58.

20. On the textual problem here, see Metzger, *TCGNT,* pp. 108-9.

make something of the fact that the verb translated "were crying out" is in the imperfect, suggesting repeated cries.[21] Also, note that what is said in v. 9 is "blessed is he who comes in the name of the Lord, blessed is the kingdom of our father David that comes." The former sentence is a standard form of greeting, but even if taken literally, it does not mean "blessed is the Lord who comes." It implies that Jesus is an agent or prophet of God, one who comes in God's name, perhaps even the Messiah who does so. There was early Jewish messianic interpretation of Ps. 118:25-26 referring it to the final Davidide and the redemption wrought by him. The phrase "our Father David" is unknown elsewhere in early Jewish literature, and the reference to the coming kingdom of David may be meant to stand in contrast to the cry of bar-Timaeus about Jesus being the Son of David.[22] If so, then the cry here becomes ironic and perhaps, as in Matthew, should be seen as coming from the crowds, because the latter-day Son of David has already arrived and the coming kingdom has already in part come in the person of Jesus.

It is in any case not at all clear that we are to think the crowds understood that all this symbolized that Jesus was the Messiah, not least because Jesus is not conforming to the expectations of the warrior messianic figure of *Pss. Sol.* 17–18 and other early Jewish texts (*b. Sanh.* 98a). Lane suggests that what is happening here is the general enthusiasm of the pilgrims going up to Jerusalem and the feast with one they thought to be a great prophet and teacher, one who comes in the Lord's name.[23] In fact, Ps. 118:26ff. was one of the regular pilgrimage psalms used during the Feast of Tabernacles and Passover, and it may have been simply serendipity that Jesus rode into town when such a song was being sung, with the crowd quite unaware that it might have relevance in explaining the man riding on a colt with them.[24]

If Jesus did indeed ride into town on a colt, there seems little doubt that he associated himself with Zech. 9:9 or at least with traditions involving kings, and it needs to be noted that here alone in the Gospels Jesus chooses to ride rather than walk, so we need to see this as some sort of prophetic sign act. Notice that *m. Sanh.* 2.5 says no one else may ride a king's horse, and our text stresses that this is an animal which had not been ridden. Jesus' act seems to be a gesture of self-elevation — Jesus, so to speak, placing himself above the crowd of pilgrims. Yet if Jesus was the first to base messianic expression on Zech. 9:9, it may have escaped the notice of most of those around. This is all the more the case if we take the "those before and those following" to be the same as in 10:32, namely, his own followers, and if we conclude that they are the ones offering re-

21. J. Painter, *Mark's Gospel* (London: Routledge, 1997), pp. 155-56.
22. See Schweizer, p. 229.
23. Lane, pp. 397-98.
24. On the historical substance of this narrative, see my *Christology of Jesus,* pp. 104-7.

peated Hosannas.[25] But we have given a reason above to think that the cry came from the crowds.

V. 11 is interesting, as it appears Jesus makes an inspection tour of the temple precincts. Myers points out that this seems to be an act of reconnaissance because when he comes back, he immediately takes action, having sized up the situation on the first visit.[26] Is Jesus like the angelic figure in Ezek. 40–48, sizing it up for destruction or judgment? Whatever may be the case, Mark clearly wants to connect this episode closely with what follows for, as Painter points out, 11:12 will tell us that the events recorded there took place the "very next day." Jesus must quickly return to the temple to finish his unfinished business there.[27]

B. A Bazaar Situation and a Fruitless Tree (11:12-25)

L. Hurtado reminds us that in Mark 11–16 Jesus intimates that he himself replaces the temple as the center of the true worship of God, which is to say the place where God truly manifests his presence.[28] This is singular, not least because all the narratives right up to the death of Jesus keep revolving around or alluding to the temple, whether they entail prophetic acts or controversy and conflict in the temple, or oracles of destruction about the temple, or the rending of the temple veil. The very heart of Israel is being called into question, and the very presence of God in their midst is at stake. To reject Jesus is to reject the very presence of God in their midst. Temple worship could no longer go on with any divine imprimatur if the presence of God was rejected. Mark seems to be saying that Jesus brought an end to the validity of the temple and its ritual as the means of reconciliation and meeting between God and humanity. But in its place Jesus' death, through the rending of his body, becomes the sacrifice, the means of true meeting between God and humanity, and thus the means of coming into God's presence. Yet at the same time, the cry of dereliction becomes the ultimate irony in the story, for if Jesus is the locus where God's presence may be found on earth, and Jesus himself experiences God-forsakenness, then his death on the cross becomes the moment when it is made clear that all humanity and all the earth experiences God-forsakenness. This background prepares one to read the action of Jesus in regard to the fig tree and in the temple with more clarity.

---

25. C. Myers, *Binding the Strong Man: A Political Reading of Mark's Story of Jesus* (Maryknoll, N.Y.: Orbis, 1988), p. 296, stresses that 10:32 describes the disciples' approach to the city, and 11:9 uses the same Greek phrase.

26. See Myers, p. 299.

27. Painter, p. 156.

28. L. Hurtado, *Mark* (New York: Harper & Row, 1983), pp. 167-68.

In this section we see once more an example of Mark's "sandwich" technique, with one story used as a frame for another, and both stories meant to interpret each other. It is doubtful that we should see here some actual chronological sequence. Mark has created suspense by delaying not only the action in
the temple but also the withering of the fig tree.[29] The point of both the cursing
of the fig tree and the action in the temple is that they figure forth the coming
judgment of God on the heart of Israel. That which is appealing from a distance
(cf. Mark 11:13 to 13:1), on closer inspection has no real fruit to offer up to Jesus or God.

The story about the figs is prompted by a remark about Jesus' hunger
(v. 12). Are we to envision a Jesus so eager to get to the temple that he failed to
eat breakfast before he left Bethany?[30] Fig trees have leaves in the spring at the
end of March or the beginning of April. Early green figs appear before the
leaves, but they are not good to eat, and in fact often fall off, leaving only leaves.
Mark's reference that this was not the season for figs alerts the reader that this
likely transpired in Nisan, the month in which Passover falls. Lane suggests we
translate here "and the significant thing is that it was not even the season for
figs."[31] One needs to bear in mind how very important the fig tree was in everyday life in Israel, being the most fruitful of all trees, and as such it was often the
tree used to produce the firstfruits to be brought into the temple.[32] Later, at
v. 20, we learn that the fig tree is withered all the way from the roots (cf. 4:6), indicating total destruction, presumably a foreshadowing of what would happen
to the temple and Jerusalem in A.D. 70. This conclusion is likely supported by
13:28-32, where the fig tree is again a symbol of the end times.

Many have seen in Jesus' action something entirely uncharacteristic, a
negative action.[33] But in the first place, we seem to be dealing with a sterile
though leafy fig tree, in which case it was of no real use to anyone. Indeed, this
may be the very point. But the question must be raised whether 11:14 should be
seen as a curse or a prophetic utterance. Peter seems to take it in the former
sense later in the chapter. Thus I think Mark is portraying a symbolic prophetic
judgment act, like the action in the temple, which foreshadows what is to come.
Now it is a subtle thing because at this juncture Jer. 8:13 is not cited at all, but
surely it must be in the background — "when I would gather them, says the
Lord, there are . . . no figs on the fig tree, even the leaves are withered. . . ."

---

29. Painter, p. 156.

30. Painter, p. 157.

31. Lane, pp. 401-2.

32. See W. Telford, *The Barren Temple and the Withered Tree* (Sheffield: Sheffield University Press, 1980), pp. 193-96.

33. Some have seen Jesus' action as similar to some of the portrayals in the apocryphal
Gospels. See, however, Hooker, *Mark*, p. 261.

"Equally important is the expectation that in the messianic age the fig tree will bear fruit. The fig tree is an emblem of peace and prosperity: hope for the future is expressed in terms of sitting in security under one's vine and one's fig tree (e.g. Mic. 4.4; Zech. 3.10) and gathering fruit from them (Hag. 2.19)."[34] W. Telford urges that the fig tree would indeed have been understood as a symbol for Israel meant to bear fruit at the eschaton.[35] The point is that Jesus has come and is ready to gather in God's people, but they are bearing no fruit at all. Here we see judgment on Israel in general. In the succeeding story we see judgment on the temple priests and hierarchy who turn a place of worship into a bazaar. Then we have the parable of the vineyard, which is an oracle on all tenders of Israel's vineyard — the Pharisees, Sadducees, temple hierarchy, followed by condemnation of the scribes in particular. In short, we have a lot of bad news here as Jesus approaches the end of his life.[36]

It was S. G. F. Brandon who suggested that what actually happened on that fateful day when Jesus entered the temple was that he was followed into the temple by both disciples and the crowd, and that the crowd was incited to attack and pillage the temple when they saw Jesus' action.[37] The Gospels, however, say nothing about a violent riot by the crowd in the temple. Nonetheless, the story raises complex questions about attitudes of early Jews about the temple.

The Temple in Early Jewish Thinking

It can be said that Torah, territory, and temple are the three *T*s that represent the fundamental foci of early Jewish religion. It is clear that there were indeed mixed attitudes about the temple of Herod in early Judaism. For some it was precisely Herod's association with the temple and its building that made this temple problematic, for Herod was an Idumean by family heritage, which is to say his family descended from the Edomites. This coupled with his immorality, violent actions, Hellenizing, and self-aggrandizing activities (especially the building projects) made him an objectionable figure to many early Jews. It is not surprising, then, that in some parts of the Enochian and Qumranite literature we find views that this temple is hopelessly corrupt and will be judged or destroyed (cf. *1 Enoch* 89:73–90:29; 4QFlor 1.1-12; cf. for similar complaints about temple or the priests, *Pss. Sol.* 2:3-5; 8:11-13; 1QpHab 8.8-13; 12.1-10; CD 5.6-8; 6.12-17; *b. Pesaḥ.* 57a). S. Freyne has made a strong case that Galileans' views about the temple were generally different from Judeans' regarding Pharisaic regulations about paying the half-shekel temple tax (they preferred the Sadducean position on the matter); in addition, Galileans were not scrupulous

34. Hooker, *Mark*, p. 262.
35. For much more detail see Telford, *The Barren Temple and the Withered Tree.*
36. Myers, pp. 297-99.
37. S. G. F. Brandon, *Jesus and the Zealots* (Manchester: Manchester University Press, 1967), p. 333.

about tithing the firstfruits and the like, presumably in part because they were a goodly distance from the temple and could not always be going up to the temple when one crop or another ripened. Nevertheless, one should not conclude that the Galileans as a whole or in large part were antitemple, for both Josephus and the NT indicate that they made regular pilgrimages up to Jerusalem (cf. *Ant.* 118-20; Luke 13:1).[38] The crucial point here is that there was a range of views about the temple in Jesus' day, and a variety of people differed with either the Pharisees or the temple hierarchy or both within early Judaism. Jesus was one such person.

There is, in addition, evidence from early Jewish literature that some looked for a messianic figure to renew the temple. One may point to Josephus's mention of messianic figures who sought to do something about the temple *as a means of legitimating a messianic claim* (*Ant.* 18.85ff. and *War* 6.283ff.). But one would also want to consider a text like *1 Enoch* 90:28-30, which speaks of the reformation of the old House or the building of a new one. Finally, we have evidence that the sanctity of the temple was taken very seriously by many early Jews even when they might not be entirely happy with the current state and nature of the Herodian temple (cf. Acts 21:28-29; *m. Sanh.* 9.6). The Romans, of course, also took the sanctity of all sorts of temples throughout the empire very seriously, not least because sacrifices for, or in some cases to, the emperor were offered in them. Desecration of a temple was seen as a capital offense by the Romans.[39] It is very unlikely that the early church, while involved in evangelism and seeking acceptance at all levels of society, would make up a tradition about Jesus performing some sort of violent action in the temple.[40]

Jesus goes into the temple and immediately begins throwing out those selling and buying, and also overturns the tables of the money changers and the seats of those selling doves. Doves were usually the one item the poor could afford to buy to make an offering, and were used for the purification of women (Lev. 12:6; Luke 2:22-24) and the cleansing of lepers (Lev. 14:22), among other things.[41] Jesus' attack on those selling doves could be seen as an attack on those gouging the poor (see *m. Ker.* 1.7). Nor did Jesus allow people to carry utensils through the temple precincts, using it as a throughway. Was this the action of one trying to reform the corruption in the temple, perhaps especially in its economic activities,[42] or should we see all of this as a dramatic demonstration of coming judgment? Whatever was the case, in Mark it is certainly a symbolic prelude to his teaching. We must examine the prophetic actions first.

We know for a fact that animals and especially pigeons had been sold on the Mount of Olives for sacrifices for a long time, but apparently only in A.D. 30 did

---

38. See S. Freyne, *Galilee from Alexander the Great to Hadrian* (323 B.C.E. to 135 C.E.) (Notre Dame: University of Notre Dame Press/Michael Glazier, 1980), pp. 277-81.

39. See E. M. Smallwood, *The Jews under Roman Rule from Pompey to Diocletian* (Leiden: Brill, 1976), pp. 148ff.

40. See my discussion in *Christology of Jesus,* pp. 107-16.

41. See Myers, p. 301.

42. See N. Q. Hamilton, "Temple Cleansing and Temple Bank," *JBL* 83 (1964): 365-72.

the temple hierarchy authorize such sales in the temple precinct itself, perhaps so they could get a cut of the profits and have control over the procedures. There is reason to think it was Caiaphas who instituted this practice in the Court of the Gentiles.[43] Jesus' action would then have perhaps been an expression of divine indignation at this callous act which prevented true worship from going on in the Court of the Gentiles.[44] Remember, it would have been a major undertaking to actually clear the vast temple court. There is even a record that a single merchant once offered three thousand sheep for sale in the temple court.[45] Thus we must be dealing with some kind of symbolic action in the temple.

But perhaps the venue (the Court of the Gentiles) is not really the issue here. Jesus is interrupting sacrifices being made in the courts further within the temple than the Court of the Gentiles. The issue then becomes whether or not such activities at all within the temple as an act of worshiping God have become a sham, in which case we are dealing with a symbolic temple cleansing here.[46]

This is, of course, the only real act of violence or near violence recorded by Jesus. We must note, however, that Jesus did not burn anything, nor did he lead any troops or bandits into the temple; he simply interrupted the economic activities there temporarily, activities that presumably returned to normal afterward. This, then, cannot be seen as a real attempt to destroy the temple.[47] Far more probably it was a symbolic action or a played-out drama, not a power play to take over or do away with the temple. Rather it foreshadowed such a destruction. Perhaps we may see Mal. 3:1-5 in the background here, where the purging action of the Lord is the prelude to the judgment. If so, then Jesus, like the Baptist, comes as the forerunner attempting to cleanse the heart of Judaism before the great and terrible Day of the Lord dawns. This suggestion might be further supported by *Pss. Sol.* 17, in which Messiah is said to come and cleanse the land, making possible the conditions for redemption (cf. also Neh. 13:4-9, 12-13).[48] There is in fact no reason why the action in the temple could not be read both ways — as a symbolic purging, but a purging as a prelude to the com-

---

43. See V. Eppstein, "The Historicity of the Gospel Account of the Cleansing of the Temple," *ZNW* 55 (1964): 42-58.

44. Cf. 4QFlor, which suggests there were those in Jesus' day zealous to exclude Gentiles from the temple altogether. See D. Juel, *Messiah and Temple: The Trial of Jesus in the Gospel of Mark* (Missoula: Scholars, 1977), pp. 172ff.

45. Schweizer, p. 231.

46. See Hooker, *Mark*, p. 264. The case would be strengthened if it could be shown that this action actually took place during the Feast of Dedication, which celebrated the Maccabees' earlier cleansing and restoration of the temple. See 1 Macc. 4:36-59.

47. Against Painter, p. 157, who suggests: "Jesus' action was to overthrow this system forcefully and to prevent any business from taking place in the temple, at least for that day." But the text does not suggest an interruption that lasted anything like a day.

48. See C. Roth, "The Cleansing of the Temple and Zechariah," *NovT* 4 (1960): 174-81.

ing judgment and therefore a prophetic sign of that coming judgment. When the symbolic purging happens, the judgment cannot be far behind, much like the prophecy in Mark 13:28-29 about the fig tree.

As Lane reminds us, the turning over of the tables of the money changers could only have happened during a specific, limited period of time between Adar 25 and Nisan 1 when such tables would be there, which is to say this incident must have transpired at least two weeks before Passover itself.[49] This tax had to be paid by every adult Jewish male by Nisan 1 (cf. Exod. 30:11-16; *m. Shek.* 1.3). This strongly supports the contention above that Mark, as well as other Gospel writers, compressed the chronology here. There is evidence in later rabbinic literature that there were prohibitions not only of using the temple as a throughway (*m. Ber.* 9.5) but also of carrying one's wallet through the temple. Thus it may be ironic that these money changers were allowed to trade coins and that the Tyrian shekel or half-shekel could be used to pay the temple tax.

Once again, without Mark making it explicit, we may see Jesus fulfilling another text from Zechariah, in this case 14:21 — "and every vessel shall be sacred to the Lord . . . and there shall no longer be any trader in the house of the Lord." This follows Zech. 14:16, which spoke of God gathering Gentiles to his temple to worship him. Mark probably sees such a text as motivating Jesus, since he alone stresses that this is a temple meant for all peoples. V. 17 is a quote of Isa. 56:7 in combination with Jer. 7:11, probably following the LXX, which Mark's audience may have known. Gentiles had a right to pray in the temple as well as Jews. This quotation's significance would not have been lost on Mark's largely Gentile audience. It is thus possible to conclude that Mark wants us to see Jesus as not abolishing the temple but rather allowing Gentiles to worship at Passover. This, however, underplays the strong allusion to Jeremiah.

Jesus says they have made the house of God into a cave of robbers or brigands. The verb here, "had been made into," is in the perfect, suggesting a completed action. Probably this is not an allusion to the temple being a haven for Zealots,[50] but rather is a reference to Jer. 7:11, which serves as a warning that God is about to lay waste the Jerusalem temple (see 7:14).[51] It is important, of course, to understand the nature of such prophetic signs.[52] As Painter says, a

---

49. Lane, p. 405.

50. Mark may have deliberately chosen the term ληστης because he is writing as the Jewish War is going on and knows that in the winter of A.D. 67-68 a group of zealotic brigands had moved into Jerusalem, setting up headquarters in the inner part of the temple, where they stayed until A.D. 70 (see Josephus, *War* 4.151-57; 5.5). See J. Marcus, *The Way of the Lord: Christological Exegesis of the Old Testament in the Gospel of Mark* (Louisville: Westminster, 1992), pp. 117-18.

51. Lane, p. 407.

52. See now my discussion in *Jesus the Seer: The Progress of Prophecy* (Peabody, Mass.: Hendrickson, 1999).

"prophetic sign of impending destruction should be understood as a warning of disaster that may be averted by responding positively to the sign."[53] But the response to this action was hardly positive, and Mark seems to suggest that this action of Jesus was the straw that broke the camel's back. V. 18 becomes an important verse, for it indicates that God is rejecting not his people but rather their corrupt leaders, a point simply reinforced by the parable of the vineyard which follows in Mark 12. The upshot of Jesus' actions is said in v. 19 to be that the priests and scribes begin plotting Jesus' death. Gundry makes the following telling remark: Jesus "strikes fear even in the hearts of the hierarchs who are trying to destroy him. In fact they are trying to destroy him, *because* they fear him, *because* he has a powerful hold on the crowd. He will be crucified then, not because of any weakness in him. Quite oppositely, because of his power! Furthermore, the power for which he will be crucified is a power that he exerts for the benefit of all the nations, Gentiles as well as Jews."[54]

Mark concludes this entire episode by returning to the fig tree — now withered.[55] Jesus' exhortation to have faith in God,[56] if originally connected to this episode, seems to suggest that the withering happened due to Jesus' own faith in God.[57] Myers suggests a plausible connection between the mention of the fig tree and the exhortation to have faith in God. "The modern reader must remember that in the social world of the first century Middle East, a temple was closely identified with a deity's existence. This was supremely true for the Jew; one could not simply repudiate the temple without provoking the most fundamental crisis regarding Yahweh's presence in the world. Jesus directly challenges this identification, arguing that to abandon faith in the temple is *not* to abandon faith in God."[58] The logic of this connection may extend to the saying about forgiveness, for if the temple is to be destroyed and the sacrifices to be stopped, then forgiveness must be offered and received on some other basis, a basis which Jesus now enunciates.

---

53. Painter, p. 158.

54. R. H. Gundry, *Mark: A Commentary on His Apology for the Cross* (Grand Rapids: Eerdmans, 1993), p. 641.

55. The close verbal similarity between 11:21 ("Rabbi, look! The fig tree you cursed has withered!") and 13:1 ("Teacher, look! What wonderful stones and buildings!") has been rightly noted by Myers, p. 304. The destruction of the fig tree on the one hand and of the temple on the other are allowed to interpret each other, and the disciples are required to make a choice between accepting God's judgment (thus trusting God) and rejecting it by affirming the grandeur and durability of the temple and the temple cultus.

56. Hooker, *Mark*, p. 269.

57. This is probably the only place in the NT where the notion of faith in God is expressed by the genitival construction πιστις Θεου, though there is Rom. 3:3, where it is clearer that the genitive is a subjective one.

58. Myers, pp. 304-5.

Vv. 23-25 must be seen, because they appear elsewhere in other Gospels, as a collection of sayings about prayer and faith connected by a couple of shared common terms (*Stichwort* connection) — namely, faith and prayer. Mark seems to have placed this material here because of the reference to "this mountain," which may indicate that at least that saying originally was offered on this occasion.[59] If this is its proper *Sitz im Leben*, then the meaning might be that in "contrast to Jewish expectation that at the Last Day 'the mountain of the house of the Lord' would be exalted and 'established as the highest of mountains' (Mic. 4.1), Jesus now pronounces judgement on it and declares that it will be submerged in the sea . . . the place of destruction (cf. 5.13; 9.42)."[60] Notice that the sayings are introduced by the asseveration "Amen," affirming in advance the truthfulness and trustworthiness of what Jesus is about to say.[61] The idea of faith expressed here is of a basic trust or confidence in God's power to accomplish whatever his will is. V. 24, if an original saying of Jesus offered in Aramaic, will have meant something like whatever you ask for in prayer, believe and you will certainly receive it. V. 25 is reminiscent of the Lord's Prayer (cf. Matt. 6:12-15; Luke 11:4). For Jesus' followers, the willingness to forgive conditions the efficacy of their prayer.

C. Honor Challenges with the Titans, Part I (11:27–12:17)

Myers has noted a near identical five-step pattern to the two narratives which surround the parable of the vineyard in Mark 12:1-12. The pattern shared by the controversy narratives in 11:27-33 and 12:13-17 involves: (1) Jesus being approached by religious/political opponents; (2) they challenge him with a question concerning authority; (3) Jesus poses a counterquestion, challenging the opponents to reveal their own views and loyalties; (4) the opponents respond; (5) Jesus answers the original question accordingly.[62] Here we have another example of Mark's sandwich technique with the parable being meant to help us read each of the controversy dialogues that surround it, and vice versa.

What examining the material in 11:27–12:17 together makes most evident is that Jesus' primary clash is with the religious leaders of early Judaism, not with ordinary Jews per se. It is no accident that the three groups mentioned in 11:27 — the chief priests, the scribes, and the elders — were indeed the leaders of the Sanhedrin. The clash here, then, is with those who eventually would condemn Jesus on a fateful day Christians now call Maundy Thursday. Thus we

---

59. On this saying see p. 309 above, and cf. Hooker, *Mark*, p. 269.
60. Hooker, *Mark*, p. 270.
61. Painter, p. 160.
62. Myers, p. 306.

are meant to see here the playing out of the drama forecast by Jesus in the immediately preceding chapter at 10:33 and even earlier at 8:31.[63] The passion prophecies are already on their way to becoming true. But this is not all. We are now returning to the issue of Jesus' authority, an issue already raised by the Jewish authorities as early as 3:22-30.[64]

What is crucial about this first controversy dialogue which begins at vv. 27ff. is that Jesus links his ministry and the evaluation of it to John's. Hooker has reminded us that John is introduced in 1:2 with a quote of Mal. 3:1 about the forerunner, but that quote goes on to speak of the Lord suddenly coming into his temple thereafter.[65] Is Jesus being presented as that Lord in these episodes? I suggest he is, for only the Lord has the ultimate right to not merely pronounce but at least proleptically enact judgment on the temple.

The authorities want to know by what authority Jesus has been doing these things, presumably especially including his action in the temple. It was not uncommon in early Jewish discussions to answer a question with a question, as Jesus does here. Jesus' solidarity with John indicates that they both stand together as harbingers of the new eschatological action of God. The decision one makes about the forerunner will affect the decision one makes about the One who follows John. Jesus in a sense stakes his own authority on that of John.

The authorities are depicted here as a craven bunch, not wanting to alienate the crowds but nonetheless eager to get rid of Jesus. This indirectly suggests that the crowds support, at least superficially, John and Jesus. "Mark's purpose here is not to romanticize the 'masses' — for they will in this story also betray Jesus — but to suggest that the Jewish leadership is politically isolated, fearful of the very people it purportedly serves."[66] Thus they are both calculating and prepared to lie, for when they say they don't know whether John's baptism is of God or not, they are simply refusing to answer. Notice the reference to that authority being "of heaven," a Jewish circumlocution for "of God" which strongly suggests this discussion originated in a Jewish context. They are not really ignorant of John and his authority; they are simply unwilling to acknowledge it. The verb διαλογίζομαι has as a possible meaning "equivocate." It always is used in Mark in a setting of controversy and ideological confusion (cf. 2:6, 8; 8:16f.; 9:33).[67] Jesus thus refuses to play their game and reveal his source of authorization. What is indicated is that the authority John and Jesus had was bound up in their similar proclamation (see Mark 1), and their similar living out of the

---

63. Painter, p. 160.
64. See rightly Hooker, *Mark,* p. 271.
65. Hooker, *Mark,* p. 272.
66. Myers, p. 307.
67. See Myers, p. 307.

eschatological action and the dominion of God coming. This threatened the status quo, and as in the case of John, some authorities felt it necessary to eliminate Jesus in order to secure their own position.

I have argued elsewhere for the authenticity of the parable in Mark 12:1-9, at least in a simplified form (see *Gos. Thom.* 65),[68] a parable which suggests that Jesus saw himself as the final emissary sent by God to rescue Israel. Keep in mind that the evidence is slim that the Messiah was called God's Son in early Judaism, but note that the king was called this in the psalms (Ps. 2:7; cf. 2 Sam. 7:12-14). Even in its simplified form, however, it is clear that the story had certain allegorical elements.[69] It would appear that the parable implies that the Son was one who had authority over God's vineyard and its tenants, a claim rejected by the current tenants themselves.

The Markan form of the parable of the vineyard (contrasted with the *Thomas* form to some degree) has a background both in Isa. 5, where Israel is God's vineyard, and in the agrarian crises facing farmers in Jesus' day and venue (cf. Ps. 80:1-3; Jer. 2:21). The criticism in this parable is leveled against the cultivators, the leaders of Israel, not the vineyard itself, whereas the vineyard is critiqued in Isa. 5. One of the most volatile of all social situations in Israel was the phenomenon of absentee landlords holding property in the Jordan valley and elsewhere, something which had been going on to some degree for nearly three hundred years before the time of Jesus. It had been a bone of contention for a very long time. J. D. M. Derrett shows that the action of the tenants in this parable is explicable in terms of Jewish law, where possession was nine-tenths of the law when it came to land. If the possession of the current landholders had not been disputed for a period of time, they could claim to be the true owners.[70]

We must be careful not to overallegorize this parable, for it is a judgment saying with a particular point. God had sent Israel many servants (notice how "servant" is synonymous with "prophet" in Jer. 7:25f.; 25:4; Amos 3:7; Zech. 1:6), but Israel had abused them. There is a crescendo of violence in this parable with the first servant being beaten, the second wounded in the head and insulted, the next one killed, and finally the beloved (i.e., the only son, therefore the only heir) not only killed but shamed by not being given a decent burial, indeed even more shockingly shamed by being thrown over the vineyard wall and left for the carrion crow. The conclusion of the parable is deliberately eschatological — the owner will return and put to death the cultivators. There was indeed a sort of squatter's rights situation in Jesus' day such that if the only legitimate heir met his demise, it was possible for the land to be claimed by those

---

68. See my *Christology of Jesus*, pp. 213-15.
69. See rightly Hooker, *Mark*, p. 274.
70. J. D. M. Derrett, *Law in the New Testament* (Leiden: Brill, 1974), pp. 286ff.

who seized it.[71] The implication of the parable is that whoever has rejected the vineyard owner's son has rejected the vineyard owner. The vineyard owner will in turn reject these tenants and give the vineyard to others, among whom Mark's audience would have presumably seen themselves. The notable difference between this controversy material and that in 2:1–3:6 is that in the earlier chapters it is basically actions by Jesus or his disciples that are controversial, whereas here Jesus' teaching is objectionable.[72] We must at this juncture consider a few of the exegetical particulars.

Firstly, 12:1 refers to Jesus speaking in parables (though only one follows at this juncture) rather than in the plain speech he used to address the disciples in 8:32.[73] This is part of the strategy of Jesus all along according to Mark 4, part of his apocalyptic rhetoric, yet in this case the meaning seems all too clear to his interlocutors. Schweizer insightfully remarks that "Mark does not regard parables as pedagogical aids to illustrate what otherwise would be difficult to comprehend. For Mark a parable is a way of speaking about God, to which a mere intellectual response is not possible. The only person who can understand a parable is one who is willing to accept or to reject its message. It must produce either faith or disbelief."[74] At the beginning of the parable Mark's Greek is very close to the LXX of Isa. 5:1-2, and it is instructive to compare the Markan version to the simplified form not only in *Gos. Thom.* 65 but in Luke 20, where the echoes of Isa. 5 are scarce (though compare Luke 20:9).[75] I would suggest that we see in Luke and in *Thomas* two forms of the de-Judaizing of the tradition to make it more user-friendly for a more Gentile audience.[76] It is intriguing that in early Jewish handling of Isa. 5:1-2 the tower and the winepress were seen as figures for the temple and its altar (cf. 4Q500; Targum Jonathan and the Tosepta see *Me'il.* 1.16; *Sukk.* 3.15).[77]

Vv. 2-5 seem to draw on the popular notions about a string of rejected prophets in Israel (Matt. 23:29-35).[78] V. 6 assumes a setting where honor is considered more important even than life. The owner sends his son to the vineyard on the premise that even the scoundrels now running the vineyard will respect the owner's own child. There may also be the additional legal angle that the owner thought sending his son (who could most readily be his legal representa-

71. See J. Jeremias, *The Parables of Jesus,* 2nd ed. (New York: Scribner, 1963), pp. 74-75.
72. See Hooker, *Mark,* p. 273.
73. Hooker, *Mark,* p. 275.
74. Schweizer, p. 240.
75. Schweizer, p. 240.
76. See the discussion about the social situation referred to in this pericope by J. D. Hester, "Socio-Rhetorical Criticism," *JSNT* 45 (1992): 27-57.
77. See Marcus, *The Way,* p. 120. This may provide a further argument for the connection between Mark 12:1-9 and vv. 10-11 being original.
78. See Myers, p. 308.

tive) would provide his last chance to reestablish his legal claim on the land.[79] The tenants, in turn, could have assumed that the son was coming to claim his inheritance itself, not just fruit from the land, which would have implied that the owner was dead and, if the son were killed, the land would be ownerless and subject to being claimed by the tenants.[80]

Myers astutely points out that the accusation against the tenants (which is to say, the religious authorities) implicit in this parable is not merely that they failed to manage the vineyard properly but that they even had the arrogance to try and claim ownership of the vineyard.[81] Thus the killing of the son must be seen as an attempt to eliminate a rival claimant of the vineyard. In other words, the tenants knew very well that Jesus was a real threat to their control and authority over the temple and thus over the people of God. That Jesus would tell such a parable shows he was prepared to make such an implicit claim of "ownership" on the vineyard and at the same time deny such a claim was justified by the existing authorities.

It is intriguing to see what Matthew and Luke do with the end of the parable in vv. 7-8. They have the son cast out of the vineyard and then killed, rather than the reverse, as in Mark. This likely reflects a Christian rearranging of the story to fit the facts about Jesus' crucifixion outside of Jerusalem. This in turn speaks in favor of the primitiveness of the story in its Markan form.[82] V. 9 serves up a rhetorical question, inviting the audience to contemplate how the owner will respond to the shocking abuses of his servants and son. But the question then is answered directly by Jesus himself. It is not hard to understand why, on the basis of a parable like this and the teaching in Mark 13, the early church concluded that the judgment that befell Jerusalem in A.D. 70 was God's response to the rejection and death of Jesus by the Jewish leaders (see Eusebius, *Church History* 3.7.7-9).

Most scholars think 12:10-12 is an addition to the Markan parable,[83] though it may well be authentic Jesus material from another occasion and context.[84] The addition of the material at this location may however have come quite early, since we find it in the same location in *Thomas*, though there the two are not linked together.[85] Possibly the two traditions were linked together

---

79. See Derrett, *Law in the New Testament*, p. 288.

80. See Jeremias, p. 308.

81. Myers, p. 309.

82. Hooker, *Mark*, p. 276.

83. See the careful discussion of the tradition history in Marcus, *The Way*, pp. 111-14.

84. Hooker, *Mark*, p. 277, is representative when she points out that the point of the vineyard parable is not the vindication and restoration of the wounded messengers but rather the punishment of the wicked tenants. Thus vv. 10-11 seem out of place to most scholars.

85. Of course, if *Thomas* is dependent on Mark, then *Thomas* does not provide additional evidence for the early linkage of the parable of the vineyard with the keystone saying.

by the earliest Jewish Christians by catchword connection, since there may be a wordplay on *ben* (son) and *eben* (stone), a wordplay which at least M. Black thinks may go back to Jesus himself, as he sees these two traditions being originally only one tradition from Jesus himself.[86] The likening of Christ to a stone was a popular theme in early Christianity (Acts 4:11; Rom. 9:33; 1 Pet. 2:6-8; cf. Eph. 2:20; *Barn.* 6:2-4; Justin, *Dial.* 36.1). An allusion to the resurrection was found at some point in the Hallel psalm Ps. 118:22-23, as the psalm was interpreted eschatologically.[87] In Mark the citation is a verbatim quote of the LXX. It is possible that in the psalmist's context the reference is to one of the stones meant for Solomon's temple which was rejected in the construction of the sanctuary, but became the keystone in the porch arch (in which case we should definitely translate κεφαλην γωνιας as keystone, not cornerstone).[88] This metaphor makes even more apparent what was implicit in the parable, namely, that Jesus was referring to himself and his audience's rejection of him in the parable. It is interesting that the scribes or Torah lawyers were sometimes called builders, and may be alluded to here.[89]

V. 12 makes very clear that Jesus is understood to be speaking against his audience, but they are unable to lay hands on him because of their fear of the crowd. Notice, though, that they do understand quite well who Jesus is talking about. They are not completely imperceptive. In terms of Markan theology, we see here one more piece of evidence of how Jesus is presented as the new temple of God, replacing the old one. Just "as Jesus' action is a symbol of God's judgement on the temple, so the vineyard which is handed over to new tenants signifies the fact that true worship of God is now centred on the risen Christ, not in the Jerusalem temple" (cf. John 2:18-22).[90] In due course, this will lead us to the temple charges in Mark 14:58 and 15:29, which, though literally false, yet from another and more ironic point of view are true — the old temple will be destroyed, for a new eschatological temple, not made with human hands, will be raised up in the person of the risen Jesus.[91]

The next controversy story, which completes this Markan sandwich, is found in 12:13-17. While the form critics would call this a pronouncement story, from an historical and rhetorical point of view it needs to be seen as a *chreia* fo-

---

86. See M. Black, "The Christological Use of the Old Testament in the New Testament," *NTS* 18 (1971): 1-14.

87. See Marcus, pp. 114-15.

88. The phrase, of course, literally means the head of the corner, which could be a headstone joining two walls, but more likely means the headstone, the highest stone in an arch. In any case, the use of the term "head" makes it unlikely we should see a reference to some sort of foundation stone here. See rightly Gundry, p. 691.

89. See Marcus, *The Way*, pp. 124-25.

90. Hooker, *Mark*, p. 277.

91. This is in essence the thesis of D. Juel in his *Messiah and Temple*.

cusing on a famous saying of Jesus.[92] Its proper setting is surely Judea, where such a question would be most pressing because the Romans imposed the tax there in A.D. 6.[93] Here once more we have seemingly strange bedfellows juxtaposed, the Herodians and the Pharisees (see 3:6; 8:15). They come to try and trap Jesus (or snare him — αγρευσωσιν, used only here in the NT, elsewhere refers to the snaring of animals). They hope to trip him up in his words, and so find a way to get the people to repudiate him, or at least get him in trouble with the authorities. Thus we are meant to see the question asked as a malicious one, not one from a truth seeker. "Mark is heightening the political drama: Jesus is a hunted man."[94]

The function of the question in v. 14, then, is to make Jesus speak the truth. In fact, it is daring him to do so on the basis of his reputation of speaking the truth without regard to consequences.[95] He is not to evade the question or be devious. It is empty flattery when the interlocutors say Jesus speaks the truth and is no respecter of persons,[96] though of course, ironically, it is actually a correct analysis of Jesus' character. Notice also the use of the verb "permitted" at v. 14, by which is meant permitted by Mosaic Law (cf. 3:4) to pay the census coin to Caesar. The word κηνσον here means poll tax, a form of tribute imposed in A.D. 6 that elicited various reactions from Jews. The Herodians supported it in principle; the Pharisees seem to have resented it and even resisted it, but not violently; but the more zealotic Jews would not pay the tax on principle. Were Jesus to give a simple yes answer to the question, he would be seen as a traitor in the eyes of the people, while a negative response would suggest he was a revolutionary who would need to be dealt with for the crime of treason or sedition. In short, the question seemed to put Jesus in a no-win situation, but as we shall see, his response is so clever that he springs the trap, for he in fact avoids saying precisely what was owed to Caesar and what to God.[97]

V. 15 says Jesus saw their hypocrisy (or insincerity).[98] Thus he responds, "Why do you test me?"[99] That Jesus had to ask for a denarius to be brought to

---

92. On the authenticity of this narrative, see my *Christology of Jesus*, pp. 101-4. On Jesus' rhetoric see Gundry, p. 694: "In Jesus' universe of discourse, what counts as argumentatively persuasive is not logical validity, exegetical accuracy, or the like but cleverness, wordplay, oneupsmanship."

93. See F. F. Bruce, "Render to Caesar," in *Jesus and the Politics of His Day*, pp. 249-63.

94. Myers, p. 310.

95. Myers, p. 311.

96. The phrase literally is "to not look into a face," and Gundry, p. 693, suggests this may involve a play on words, namely, he does not look at coins with images of the emperor on them.

97. Painter, p. 164.

98. As Hooker acutely remarks, *Mark*, p. 280: "Since Jesus does not care for men's opinion, the attempt to flatter him by praising his sincerity seems ill conceived!"

99. Schweizer, p. 244: "Therefore, the story is a warning against the kind of discussion in which a person does not seek to learn but already has a closed mind toward Jesus."

him indicates that he does not have one, and perhaps would not carry one with him. This fact in itself would likely make a favorable impression on the crowd or common people, for it meant Jesus was not an obvious collaborator with the Roman oppressors.[100] It is not clear from v. 16 whether the Herodians or Pharisees had the coin on them (the former group were more likely to have carried denarii without qualms), but if they did, it would show their hypocrisy in asking such a question. It may also be the basis on which Jesus suggested to them that, in effect, if they were going to use Caesar's money, then they had to pay the price.[101] Presumably we are to think they had already settled the question in their own minds, and so were simply trying to draw Jesus out on the matter.

Jesus asks whose εικων is on the coin, and what the inscription says. In Jesus' day Tiberius was the emperor, and the inscription read "Tiberius Caesar, son of divine Augustus," implying at least Tiberius's quasi divinity. On the obverse side the coin read *pontifex maximus,* indicating that Caesar was the high priest, the highest religious figure in the empire. Tiberius reigned from A.D. 14 to 37, and during that reign it was the common understanding that the coins actually belonged to Caesar, since he minted them. The denarius was a small silver coin worth about fifteen or so cents. Hurtado has suggested an allusion to Gen. 1:27 in the use of the term "image."[102] If this is correct, the point of Jesus' reply would seem to be that we bear God's image and owe one sort of loyalty to God, while the coins bear Caesar's image and one owes a different degree and sort of loyalty to him (so Augustine, *Sermons on NT Lessons* 43; Tertullian, *On Idolatry* 15). On this reading, Jesus is very clearly not a revolutionary. Rather he thinks the state has certain limited though legitimate claims on its inhabitants, to which one must respond obediently and render the required goods or services. Some obligations imposed by the state were thus seen as not conflicting with one's obligations to God (cf. Rom. 13; 1 Pet. 2:13-17). This reading of the text would also suggest that Jesus was opposed to a reestablishment of a theocracy.

The problem with this reading is that when Jesus says "repay unto God the things that are God's," he can only be repudiating, at least implicitly, Caesar's claims to divinity. Divine honors belong to God alone, and God's claims are higher and prior to those of any earthly ruler. Indeed, Jesus does not imply a neat distinction between God and state, for in Mark 13 he is going to make clear that nations rise and fall under God's hand, for God is sovereign over all. Furthermore, it would appear that Jesus would certainly have agreed with the psalmist when he said that the earth is the Lord's and the fullness thereof, in which case nothing, properly speaking, belongs to Caesar! Myers

---

100. To use such a coin, much less to pay the tax, implied a recognition of the claims and authority of the one on the coin.

101. See Hooker, *Mark,* p. 281.

102. Hurtado, pp. 180-81.

puts it this way: "no Jew could have allowed for a valid *analogy* between the debt Israel owed to Yahweh and any other human claim."[103] On this reading Jesus' response could be seen as ironic, suggesting in effect: "o.k. give Caesar back these worthless pieces of metal he claims,[104] but know that we are to render to God all things since God alone is divine and to God belong all things."[105] "Rather than being a counsel of submission to earthly rulers, it is more likely to be a comment on the relative insignificance of the issue in light of the inbreaking dominion of God."[106] Whether or not one paid the tribute neither hindered nor helped the coming of God and the divine eschatological reign. Finally, the fact that Jesus is willing to handle the coins must count against the view that he was a zealot, for a zealot would not likely even touch a coin since it contained a "graven image." Whatever the precise nuances of Jesus' response, it could not be construed as seditious. Jesus might even have seen it as a religious duty to hand Caesar back his "unrighteous mammon."[107]

In closing the discussion of this pericope, it is worth asking how it helps us understand the middle part of the sandwich, the parable in 12:1-9. The answer must be that in the parable we saw those who were not prepared to render unto God, the owner of the vineyard, what was due to God, and here Jesus exhorts them about such a gross neglect of duty.[108] It is no wonder that the crowds are astounded not merely by the cleverness of Jesus' reply but by the authority it assumes to exhort even the leaders of Israel.

D. Honor Challenges with the Titans, Part II (12:18-44)

The material in 12:18-40 is closely linked with the immediately preceding pericope in that Jesus, in each case, deals with crucial questions with dialogue partners and teaching in the temple courts. We already noted the Jewish pattern of four questions,[109] which may link these stories together. But in the story in 12:35-40 we have gone beyond the point where Jesus is asked questions, having si-

---

103. Myers, p. 312.

104. Notice the small regard Jesus has for money elsewhere (in Matt. 6:24 and Luke 16:9), or indeed his warnings about the dangers of money as an obstacle to entering God's dominion (Mark 10:25; Luke 16:19-31).

105. See now the discussion by D. T. Owen-Ball, "Rabbinic Rhetoric and the Tribute Passage (Mt. 22.15-22; Mk. 12.13-17; Lk. 20.20-26)," *NovT* 35, no. 1 (1993): 1-14, who stresses the forensic character of this narrative, and analyzes it in terms of later rabbinic patterns of argumentation.

106. Witherington, *Christology of Jesus*, p. 102.

107. See Bruce, p. 262.

108. See rightly Hooker, *Mark*, p. 281.

109. See pp. 306-7 above.

lenced or verbally outmaneuvered his critics (see 12:34b), and here Jesus goes on
the offensive and himself asks a question, which is in turn followed by an example
story where the disciples are taught a lesson. In other words, the four stories involving questions do not really fit the rabbinic pattern very well, especially the last
one. What really unites the material in Mark 11–12 is the setting of the temple
courts, whether we are talking about actions (referred to at the beginning and end
of these chapters, 11:1-19 and 12:41-44) or teaching material.

12:18-27 has often been misread to suggest that Jesus expected an eschatological state of affairs that involved the transcending of human sexual differences and the cessation of human sexual activity, and indeed of marriage.[110] It
seems most unlikely that this passage is a church creation, in view of both the
nature of the discussion (levirate marriage) and the dialogue partners involved
(Sadducees).[111] Furthermore, in early church discussions about resurrection,
the focus was not on the state of angels so far as we can tell (see Rom. 8:29;
1 Cor. 15:49; Phil. 3:21).

The question raised by the Sadducees is deliberately puzzling, posed to
expose or even ridicule a belief they deemed erroneous. It is based on the requirements of the law listed in Deut. 25:5-10 (cf. Gen. 38:18). Both the question
and Jesus' response (which refers to angels, another thing, like the resurrection,
that Sadducees apparently didn't believe in) reflect a situation in the time and
location of Jesus, not later or elsewhere. Luke, however, has added to the
Markan pericope at Luke 20:34-36 and 38b-39 in a fashion that appears to reflect later concerns and issues. The Markan account, however, can be divided
into two major parts — the Sadducees' question (Mark 12:18-23) and Jesus' responses, first about the nature of the resurrection state (12:24-25), as well as
about the reality of the resurrection (12:26-27).[112]

It must first be seen that the Sadducees' question in vv. 18-23 is surely hypothetical. This can be surmised not merely because of the large number of
brothers and levirate liaisons referred to but also because levirate marriage
seems to have been largely in disuse in Jesus' day.[113] The function of levirate
marriage was to "raise up a seed" for the deceased brother who had died with-

---

110. See my discussion in *Women in the Ministry of Jesus* (Cambridge: Cambridge
University Press, 1984), pp. 32-34. For a recent argument that Jesus was an ascetic, see now
D. C. Allison, Jr., *Jesus of Nazareth: Millenarian Prophet* (Minneapolis: Fortress, 1999).

111. The Sadducees are mentioned only here by name in Mark, and they are so mentioned here because the issue touches on a particular belief of theirs, namely, that there will
be no resurrection (see Acts 23:8 and Josephus, *Ant.* 18.1.4; *War* 2.18.14).

112. Schweizer, p. 245, in fact argues that Jesus answers both the Pharisees' question
(about the nature of the resurrection) and the Sadducees' question (about the reality of the
resurrection).

113. See my *Women,* p. 152 n. 184. The similar material in Tob. 3:8; 6:9-12; 7:12-13
also suggests that we are dealing with a purely hypothetical question.

out a proper heir, in particular a male heir. Thus the family name and line would be enabled to continue. Once the levir had performed his duty with the brother's wife, he was under no obligation to treat her like his own wife. In other words, levirate marriage was not seen as on a par with real marriage, nor was it seen as resulting in a polygamous situation.

The case put forward by the Sadducees is particularly extreme. Not only had six brothers attempted and failed to impregnate the woman in question, but she had also outlived them all and was single when she died. It is perhaps this last fact which prompts the question: Whose spouse will she be in the resurrection? The Sadducees' question is predicated on the assumption that the life to come has significant continuity with this life, at least in regard to marriage. Apparently they thought it was impossible to believe in a notion like resurrection that led to the ridiculous situation of a woman having to choose between seven husbands!

Jesus' response, which begins at v. 24, suggests that the Sadducees are ignorant of both the content of the Hebrew Scriptures and of the power of God. Jesus stresses that in the age to come people will neither marry nor be given in marriage. Notice what Jesus does *not* say. He does not say there will be no *marriage* in the age to come. The use of the terms γαμουσιν and γαμιζονται is important, for these terms refer to the gender-specific roles played in early Jewish society by the man and the woman in the process of getting married. The men, being the initiators of the process in such a strongly patriarchal culture, "marry," while the women are "given in marriage" by their father or another older family member.[114] Thus Mark has Jesus saying that no new marriages will be initiated in the eschatological state. This is surely not the same as claiming that all existing marriages will disappear in the eschatological state.[115] Jesus, then, would seem to be arguing against a specific view held by the Sadducees about the continuity between this life and the life to come, a view involving the ongoing practice of levirate marriage.

I would suggest that Luke's expansion of his Markan source at Luke 20:36 understands quite well the drift of the discussion. In the eschatological state we have resurrected beings who are no longer able to die. Levirate marriage existed precisely because of the reality of death. When death ceases to happen, the rationale for levirate marriage falls to the ground as well. When Jesus says in v. 25b that people will be like the angels in heaven in the life to come, he does not mean they will live a sexless identity (early Jews did not think angels were sexless in any case; cf. Gen. 6:1-4!),[116] but rather that they will be like angels in that they are unable to

---

114. See my *Women*, p. 153 n. 191.

115. See, for example, Tertullian, *On Monogamy* 10, who specifically denies that God will separate in the next life those whom he has joined together in a holy union in this one.

116. Though there is, interestingly, evidence that some early Jews believed that angels

die. Thus the question of the Sadducees is inappropriate to the conditions of the eschatological state. I would suggest that Jesus, like other early Jews, likely distinguished between normal marriage and levirate marriage. In Mark 10 Jesus grounded normal marriage in the creation order, not in the order of the fall, which *is* the case with levirate marriage (instituted because of death and childlessness and the need to preserve the family name and line). Thus Jesus is intending to deny about the eschatological state "that there will be any natural relation out of which the difficulty of the Sadducees could arise."[117]

The argument, however, continues with Jesus supporting the reality of resurrection in vv. 26-27. Jesus' argument that the patriarchs are still alive, based on the use of the phrase "the God of Abraham, Isaac, and Jacob," is a fairly common example of the way early Jews would press the literal sense or what seemed to be a fundamental underlying assumption behind such a phrase.[118] Jesus refers to "the passage about the bush" because there was no division of texts into chapters and verses in his day, and thus texts had to be referred to topically. Jesus' belief that the patriarchs are still alive is also found in texts like 4 Macc. 7:19 and 16:25. Jesus does not cite a late Jewish text about the resurrection of the patriarchs, but rather focuses on a text from the Pentateuch the Sadducees would accept as Holy Writ.[119] The point is that the text seems to imply that the patriarchs were still alive, and more to the point, it implies something about God who is the God of the living. The biblical God had made promises to these patriarchs, and since they had not all yet been fulfilled, it must be assumed that they are still alive.[120] "It is absurd to assert that God pledges himself to a dead person unless this implies that the person is raised to life."[121] Underlying the entire discussion is a profound belief in the power of God, and God's ability to even overcome death or summon the dead back to life. Jesus in essence accuses the Sadducees not just of bad exegesis, but of a failure of nerve, a failure to believe in a God whose yes to life is louder than Death's no and whose power is great enough to create something out of nothing. In-

---

didn't marry — see *1 Enoch* 15:7. There was furthermore the belief that the dead became angels after the resurrection (cf. *1 Enoch* 51:4; 104:4; Bar. 51:9-10). On the discontinuity of this world and the world to come (including the assertion that there will be no begetting), see *b. Ber.* 17a.

117. J. Denny, "The Sadducees and Immortality," *ET*, 4th ser., 10 (1894): 401-9, here p. 403.

118. See Gundry, p. 704, on their creativity in handling the text and Hooker, *Mark*, p. 285.

119. See, e.g., Schweizer, p. 246: "The Sadducees were the priestly party i.e. the Jewish aristocracy. The only authority which they recognized was the 'Law' i.e. the first five books of Moses. Therefore they did not consider the doctrine of the resurrection to be scriptural since it does not appear until Isaiah 26.19 and Daniel 12.2. . . ."

120. See Painter, p. 166.

121. Schweizer, p. 248.

deed, as we shall see, "Power is so much a characteristic of God that the word is used instead of the divine name in Mark 14.62."[122]

Jesus' refutation of the Sadducees is punctuated at the end of this passage by a reiteration that they are totally wrong, reflecting apparently his strong feelings about resurrection and about the power and faithfulness of God to his people. Finally, we have in this story one more piece of evidence, though oblique in this case, that Jesus did not approve of patriarchal systems that left women bereft of social security or treated them merely as commodities or vehicles to fulfill men's desires for the propagation of *their* names.[123] The Sadducees believed in resurrection of a sort — raising up an heir for a brother. Jesus believed in a very different and more powerful sort of immortality — raising up of the dead.[124]

12:28-34 provides us with another dialogical narrative, but it is an open question whether we should class it with the preceding ones by calling it a controversy narrative. There is no air of hostility involved in this story, but rather we seem to have someone who is a genuine seeker of knowledge who admires Jesus' responses under pressure to the Sadducees and others, and responds well and wisely to Jesus' teaching. Thus Mark would seem to be indicating that the responses to Jesus, even during his last days of teaching in the temple courts, were varied, and sometimes were quite positive.

There was in early Judaism a great deal of dispute about how to rank the 613 commandments (248 positive commands, 365 prohibitions) in the Hebrew Scriptures in terms of importance, and even more debate as to which one was the most crucial or paramount of these commandments, which then could be used as a hermeneutical tool to interpret the rest. Thus the question the scribe raises in v. 28 is not merely hypothetical (unlike the question raised by the Sadducees), but an inquiry about the "first" commandment. Jesus responds with the Shema (Deut. 6:4-5), which is perhaps as close as one can get to a Jewish confession of faith.[125] It was the morning prayer for every good Jew from at least the second century B.C. Note too that Jesus combines Deut. 6:5 and Lev. 19:18, which also had precedent in early Jewish circles.[126] Notice that at v. 30 we

---

122. Hooker, *Mark,* p. 284.

123. See, e.g., E. Schüssler Fiorenza, *In Memory of Her* (New York: Crossroad, 1985), p. 144. Jesus does not claim that "sexual differentiation and sexuality do not exist in the 'world' of God, but that 'patriarchal marriage is no more,' because its function in maintaining and continuing patriarchal economic and religious structures is no longer necessary. . . . The Sadducees have 'erred much' in assuming that the structures of patriarchy are unquestionably a dimension of God's world as well."

124. See Gundry, p. 701.

125. Schweizer, p. 251, avers that a good Jew would recite the Shema plus Deut. 11:13-21 and Num. 15:37-41, though this conclusion seems to be based on dates from the post-NT era.

126. See Lane, p. 432 n. 49, and *T. Iss.* 5:2; 7:6; *T. Dan* 5:3; *T. Reub.* 6:9. Cf. the discus-

have the addition of the phrase "and with the mind," which is not in the Hebrew original. It is interesting that v. 31 mentions "these," but then the word "commandment" is in the singular. Possibly Mark wants us to think that for Jesus these two commandments are integrally related, love of God and neighbor being two expressions of the same basic impulse. On the other hand, we could translate "another commandment is not greater than these."[127]

Jesus' summary of the Law should be compared to that of Hillel (40 B.C.–A.D. 10): "what you yourself hate, do not do to your neighbor" (*b. Šabb.* 31a).[128] The scribe is impressed with Jesus' insistence on God's oneness and on the centrality of love. It is striking that this is the only example in the Gospels where a scribe actually agrees with Jesus![129] He pushes the matter a bit further by referring to the prophetic notion that God prefers loving actions more than any religious rite — whole burnt offerings or regular sacrifices (cf. 1 Sam. 15:22; Jer. 7:22; Hos. 6:6).[130] Jesus sees that the man has answered intelligently or wisely (νουνεχως), and tells him he is not far from the dominion of God. Notice that the scribe has assumed that what is being discussed is the heart of the Law, but Jesus' perspective on the Law, as on everything else, is eschatologically colored, such that he sees the discussion as being about entrance requirements to the eschatological realm of God, or to live therein.[131]

Note too that the scribe is not declared to be a disciple for his positive response. He must come and follow Jesus and recognize him, not just his teaching. Still, the man's openness to Jesus' teaching is a good sign. "By describing the scribe's enthusiastic response, Mark once again underlines the authority of Jesus' teaching — something he normally does by saying that Jesus silenced his opponents (cf. 11.33; 12.12, 17, 27). The final effect, however is the same: after

---

sion by J. B. Stern, "Jesus' Citation of Dt. 6.5 and Lv. 19.18 in the Light of Jewish Tradition," *CBQ* 28 (1966): 312-16.

127. Gundry, p. 712, suggests that Jesus is saying that there are no other commandments equal to, or greater than, these.

128. Compare the story about R. Akiba (d. A.D. 135), who died a martyr's death while reciting the Shema and stated, "To love your neighbor as yourself . . . this is a great general principle of the Law." See *b. Sifra* 89b and Schweizer, p. 251.

129. See Schweizer, p. 252.

130. The latter of which involved burning only a part of the animal, and in addition a portion of the animal would be eaten by the priest and the sacrificer.

131. On Jesus' hermeneutic and the love commandment, see V. P. Furnish, *The Love Commandment in the New Testament* (Nashville: Abingdon, 1972). See also Painter, p. 167: "From one perspective, all the detailed laws, of which there were over six hundred prohibitions and commands, were taken to be expressions of the way two principles of love towards God and neighbour were to be fulfilled. Alternatively, the two principles of love can be taken as the true meaning of all the commandments. From this point of view the love principles become the test of the applicability of the numerous specific commandments. The latter seems to be the understanding advocated by Mark." Similarly Hooker, *Mark*, p. 288.

that no one dared to ask him any question. . . ." In fact, the word order of the Greek makes the closure of this pericope emphatic — "no one, anymore, was daring to question him."[132] Thus Mark declares Jesus once and for all victorious or vindicated in all such debates and discussions with the Jewish authorities, and Jesus has accomplished this in their own domain, the temple courts.[133]

The dialogue with the scribes in a sense continues in vv. 35-40, though Jesus in fact goes on the offensive, merely quoting scribes who are absent and raising a question about their opinions about the Messiah.[134] This pericope reminds us once more of the biographical focus of Mark,[135] and thus of the great importance to him to answer in various ways the question of who Jesus was. Notice that here, as in 8:27-30, Jesus takes the initiative when it comes to the issue of his own identity.[136] Jesus comes closer to revealing his identity in public here than in any of the earlier chapters of Mark, and it is not incidental that he does so in the temple, which is to say in the place where people come to encounter their God and his truth and redemption. This episode, in fact, ends Jesus' public teaching, for from now on in 12:41ff., the teaching material is directed to the disciples.[137]

Jesus points out that the scribes insist that the Messiah will be David's son. But, says Jesus, on the face of it this seems to contradict Ps. 110:1, messianically understood.[138] The precise phrase "son of David" is apparently not attested before *Pss. Sol.* 17:23, but there is evidence from Qumran (4QFlor 1.11-13) where the promise to David (see 2 Sam. 7) is interpreted in light of Amos 9:11 (cf. CD 7.16; *b. Sanh.* 96b).[139] Here again Mark has followed the LXX with minor variations.[140] V. 36 is interesting for it indicates Jesus' clear belief in the inspiration of

---

132. See Gundry, p. 712.

133. See Myers, p. 318.

134. On the way Jesus frames the question, compare that of the disciples in Mark 9:11.

135. On the authenticity and details of this pericope, see my *Christology of Jesus,* pp. 189-91.

136. See Hooker, *Mark,* pp. 291-92.

137. See Schweizer, p. 254.

138. It is possible, though not certain, that Jesus introduces for the first time the notion of understanding Ps. 110:1 messianically. See Gundry, pp. 718-19. Against this conclusion is the fact that we may trace the beginnings of messianism back to 2 Sam. 7 and 22, which is to say it is traced back to David and his progeny. The author of Ps. 118 may have been looking forward to the ideal Davidic king, and called him *adonai* (not Yahweh), seeing him as being given the seat of executive power as God's right-hand man. It is not plausible to suggest that Ps. 110 dates from the Maccabean period, not least because it is found in early psalter collections such as the one at Qumran. We have independent evidence in Mark 14:62 that Jesus used this psalm messianically.

139. See also D. Flusser, "Two Notes on the Midrash on 2 Sam. 7.1," *IEJ* 9 (1959): 99-109.

140. It is not true, however, that the wordplay in regard to the word "lord" depends on the Greek, for it would work equally well in the Aramaic — *amar marya le mari.*

the Hebrew Scriptures, as well as in the Davidic authorship of this psalm. Marcus also points out that the reference to the Spirit in this fashion suggests that the psalm is to be understood eschatologically, prompted by the insight given by the eschatological Spirit.[141] The person in question is given the place of honor and power next to God, and the image of enemies being put under his feet is that of the victor placing his foot on the neck of the conquered,[142] a not uncommon ancient Near Eastern gesture to indicate total domination on the one hand and total capitulation and submission on the other. It suggests an absolute power of life or death over the one in the prone position. This tradition of citing Ps. 110 messianically and eschatologically is also found in 11QMelch.

The riddle is offered up in v. 37.[143] How can David's lord be David's son? Is Jesus here repudiating the Davidic origins of Messiah, as some have suggested? This seems unlikely, since elsewhere he doesn't repudiate the title Son of David,[144] but he may well have repudiated certain popular early Jewish notions about the Davidic Messiah, for instance, that he would simply be a normal, though God-empowered, human being like David himself. It is best to say that Jesus is repudiating the adequacy, not the accuracy, of assessing the Messiah by means of his Davidic descent. The point is that in Jesus' view the Messiah is more than, not other than, Son of David.

Notice that Jesus only raises but does not answer this question. The implication, however, seems to be that the scribes' notion of Messiah is far too mundane. He is a much greater figure than the original David, not merely a chip off the old block. Indeed, he is a transcendent figure, exercising lordship over even David.[145] The crowd is said to hear all this eagerly, loving to see Jesus poke holes in scribal balloons. We must indeed conjure with the likelihood that the Markan Jesus might be alluding to the fact that he himself was supernatural in dignity and origins and destiny.[146] The focus, however, is on the character rather than the identity of the Messiah in this pericope.[147] One may ask, how-

---

141. Marcus, *The Way*, pp. 132-33.

142. This text and its images were commonly predicated of Christ in early Christianity. See Acts 2:34-35; 1 Cor. 15:25; Heb. 1:13.

143. I have stressed in *Jesus the Sage* (Minneapolis: Fortress, 1994) that Jesus' public form of discourse was most often sapiential in character. Riddles were of course one form of wisdom speech. Mark informs us that a crowd is present to hear this discussion (12:37), which in turn means this is not private teaching for the disciples. See Painter, pp. 167-68.

144. See pp. 291-93 above.

145. For an interesting and perhaps independent treatment of this same Ps. 110:1 in Christian messianic fashion, see *Barn.* 12:10-11 and the discussion by Marcus, pp. 131-32.

146. See V. Taylor, *The Gospel according to St. Mark* (New York: St. Martin's Press, 1966), p. 493; I. H. Marshall, *The Gospel of Luke* (Exeter: Pater Noster, 1978), pp. 746-49.

147. See rightly F. Neugebauer, "Die Davidssohnfrage (Mark 12.35-37 parr.) Und der Menschensohn," *NTS* 21 (1974-75): 81-104.

ever, whether the complete citation is not of some relevance to Jesus' situation, in which case the motif of combat and victory may allude to Jesus' verbal victories over his scribal foes.[148]

Vv. 38-40, perhaps a later addition to the pericope, are a rebuke to scribes who love perks. They wore long white robes and loved the deference they received from the common people, including all rising when they came into their presence. In addition, they were given the seat in front of the Torah box in the synagogue, and it was considered good form to have such persons at one's banquets — indeed, they expected to be given the most honorable couch, next to the host. In addition, they expected certain titles of respect. Furthermore, they bilked widows of their living, an accusation that has echoes of Mal. 3:5. I share the view of Derrett that Jesus has in mind those who have been asked to be guardians of a widow's estate but who have taken more than their fair share of expenses.[149] Worse still, in order to drum up such lucrative business they made a show of their piety, praying long prayers. The connection, then, between this story and the one about the widow's mite becomes evident. The place where widows would encounter scribes praying and enlist their services would be in the temple courts.[150] The phrase "to devour a house" is a technical one in extrabiblical Greek, referring to the bilking of someone's property or funds.[151] The evaluation of scribes here seems unrelentingly negative. "This criticism makes sense if the scribes from Jerusalem were mainly aristocratic and rich Sadducees infamous for their exploitation of the poor (see Josephus *Antiquities* 20.180-181, 205-207)."[152]

The final pericope of this chapter is found in vv. 41-44. This is once again a *chreia* with a memorable saying in vv. 43-44 which is linked to a specific incident and place, the one described in vv. 41-42, and a specific person, Jesus.[153] The narrative begins with Jesus sitting across from the temple treasury in the temple court watching people file in to make their private offerings. There were many rich who threw much into the treasury, presumably referring to one of the thirteen trumpet-shaped receptacles found in this part of the temple.[154] But

---

148. See Marcus, *The Way*, pp. 136-37.

149. See J. D. M. Derrett, *Studies in the New Testament*, vol. 1 (Leiden: Brill, 1977), pp. 118-27.

150. See my discussion in *Women*, pp. 16-18, and H. Fledderman, "A Warning about the Scribes (Mark 12.37b-40)," *CBQ* 44 (1982): 52ff.

151. See my *Women*, p. 141 n. 53.

152. Painter, p. 169.

153. On the nature of *chreiae* and their specificity, see pp. 9-15 above. It is precisely when one recognizes the nature of this material as a *chreia* that the old form-critical assumptions about the adding of particulars to a generic and even universal maxim not originally spoken by Jesus are made to seem even more tenuous than they already appeared when I discussed this matter in *Women*, pp. 17-18.

154. It is not completely certain whether γαζοφυλακιον is meant to represent the trea-

there was also a poor widow who came to make her offering, an act made all the more impressive because it was a freewill offering. She gave two lepta, the copper coins of least monetary worth.[155] In all likelihood Mark found it necessary to explain the equivalent worth of these coins because his audience lived in a region where they were not in use, namely, in the West.[156] There were two lepta in a quadrans, which was only worth one-sixty-fourth of a denarius when Mark wrote his Gospel,[157] the pay of a day laborer. In other words, the widow's gift in actual monetary value was infinitesimally small. In Mark's account Jesus calls the disciples to himself (v. 43), thereby making the woman a model for his followers. Obviously it is not the amount given but the attitude and act of self-sacrificial giving that is being lifted up for emulation. The act is all the more notable because widows had few means in Jesus' culture to obtain money, and she could have chosen to give only half of her living (i.e., one copper coin).[158] The memorable saying which ends the pericope is punctuated in advance by the familiar phrase of Jesus, "Amen I say to you,"[159] with Jesus once more attesting to the truthfulness of his own words, a practice that seems to have been distinctive of his teaching in early Judaism. The woman is said to have given more than all the others combined, for she gave her whole living. Indeed, she gave out of her poverty and deficit,[160] while the rich gave out of their abundance.[161]

We may conclude this discussion by noting certain contrasts between 12:40 and 12:41-44. In the former there is a contrast between rich widows who trust their scribal managers and the deceitful male scribes, while in the latter a poor widow's behavior is contrasted to that of rich men. "In addition, the devotion and

---

sury itself or one of the offering receptacles. See Lane, p. 442 n. 83. Painter, p. 169, favors the receptacle view, as does Hooker, *Mark*, p. 296, who points out that these receptacles were in the Court of the Women.

155. See D. Sperber, "Mark xii.42 and Its Metrological Background," *NovT* 9, no. 3 (1967): 178-90. The reference to the quadrans, a coin not minted in the East, likely points to the western provenance of this Gospel. See pp. 31-35 above, and cf. the debate of an earlier age more concerned with such historical details: F. Blass, "On Mark xii.42 and xv.16," *ET* 10 (1898-99): 185-87, and also his "On Mark xii. 42," *ET* 10 (1898-99): 286-87; and W. M. Ramsey, "On Mark xii.42," *ET* 10 (1898-99): 232, and "On Mark xii.42," *ET* 10 (1898-99): 336.

156. Cf. Hooker, *Mark*, p. 296.

157. See Gundry, p. 729.

158. See Painter, p. 169.

159. On this phrase see pp. 231-32 above.

160. For a quite different reading of this passage which suggests that Jesus is lamenting a system of giving which impoverishes a widow in this fashion, see Myers, p. 321. This view is quite unconvincing since, in 12:43, Jesus makes a point of presenting the widow as a positive example to his disciples.

161. A point strongly stressed by the church fathers, who tend to focus on the woman's intention; see, e.g., Chrysostom, *On the Incomprehensible Nature of God* 6.12; Caesarius of Arles, *Sermons* 182.3.

self-sacrifice of the poor widow stand out against the dark background of the self-indulgence and false piety of the scribes and the easy and ostentatious giving of the rich. . . . Jesus' special concern and admiration for women is perhaps nowhere more strikingly juxtaposed with his disgust over certain groups of privileged and supposedly pious men than here. . . . Jesus' choice of the widow as a model reflects his view of how the advent of the Kingdom means just recognition of the truly godly, and just judgment of those who oppress the poor and disenfranchised (the widow being the prime example)."[162] The story reminds Mark's audience that even the poorest among them can make a worthy offering to God.[163]

E. Jesus and the Temple of Doom (13:1-37)

Mark 13 contains some of the most interesting and problematic material in the whole of Mark's Gospel, being the longest single discourse or block of continuous teaching. There "is perhaps no single chapter of the synoptic Gospels which has been so much commented upon in modern times as Mark 13."[164] There can be no doubt that this section is heavily indebted to the Hebrew Scriptures both by way of allusion and also brief quotation, and it should be seen as an example of late prophetic literature which includes some images and notions common in Jewish apocalyptic literature. It is not properly called an apocalyptic discourse because it does not involve: (1) an otherworldly mediator; (2) visions of heaven or otherworldly tours; (3) great quantities of apocalyptic verbiage or images or notions; (4) date setting.[165] There is, however, a partial indebtedness to Daniel in this material, but that characterizes some of Jesus' other utterances as well, including his own self-chosen moniker, Son of Man. Both the parenetic thrust and the address in the second-person plural distinguish this material from traditional Jewish apocalyptic material.

I agree with the complaint of W. S. Voerster that too much of the recent dis-

---

162. Witherington, *Women*, p. 18.

163. Hooker, *Mark*, p. 296.

164. L. Gaston, *No Stone on Another* (Leiden: Brill, 1970), p. 8. On the convoluted history of interpretation of this passage, see the review by D. M. Young, "Whoever Has Ears to Hear" (Diss., Vanderbilt University, 1994), pp. 277-81.

165. See, e.g., Hooker, *Mark*, p. 299: "the discourse lacks many of the features of apocalyptic writing: there is no heavenly vision, no use of bizarre imagery, no description of what happens after the parousia — no resurrection, no judgement, no punishment or reward — and the idea that one can pinpoint the time of the End is specifically denied. The writer is more concerned to warn his readers about the dangers in store and to urge them to be prepared for a long struggle than to encourage them by suggesting that the End is near: indeed he seems concerned to dampen down over-enthusiastic expectation of the End which can lead only to disappointment."

cussion of this discourse has focused on the literary history and origins of the material to the neglect of the actual exegesis of the text and the analysis of its meaning as an ancient communication.[166] Voerster is right that what we have here is a narrated speech, and that the overall impression left by this Gospel is of a "not too loquacious Jesus [and of] disciples who lack understand-ing."[167] It is also striking that for the most part, up to this point in Mark "the narrative was, with the exception of predictions and narrative commentary, told in the past tense (imperfect, aorist and historic present) and in the narrative mode. . . . The narrator returns to past events in chapter 14–16. . . ."[168] There is a sense that Jesus takes over the narrating role from the Evangelist. Furthermore, the predictions made in this chapter are not seen to be fulfilled within the narrative scope of the Gospel itself, unlike the passion predictions. This chapter makes clear that Mark is not merely concerned with the past of Jesus and his words and deeds. Then too, the effect of this long speech is that it slows down the narrative time just before the final narration of passion events, which do not have the breathless pace of what went before. "Before the trial, death and resurrection the reader is called to a halt."[169]

I also agree with N. R. Petersen that Mark 13 is Jesus' take on the conflicting eschatological interpretations of his time, and more importantly his giving his disciples the clues they need to sort out their own false expectations and assumptions from true ones.[170] Mark, of course, apparently thinks his own audience needs such sorting out as well, but he lets Jesus do the job for him here, with the one exception of his narrative aside. The net effect of the discourse is that the disciples are warned to be on alert, for while the "End" is seen to be not yet (indeed, it is coming at an unknown future day and hour), nonetheless the preliminary eschatological events are on the nearer horizon, within a generation. Part of what they must be on the alert for is apocalyptic fanatics who think that the End is already at hand and who point to false prophets, false messiahs, and various earthly upheavals to prove their point. In other words, this discourse to some degree de-apocalypticizes the eschatological discussion![171]

The detailed and careful efforts of J. Lambrecht, M. Hooker, and D. Young

---

166. W. S. Voerster, "Literary Reflections on Mark 13.5-37: A Narrated Speech of Jesus," in *The Interpretation of Mark,* ed. W. R. Telford (Edinburgh: T. & T. Clark, 1995), pp. 269-88.

167. Voerster, p. 272.

168. Voerster, p. 276.

169. Voerster, p. 278.

170. N. R. Petersen, "When Is the End Not the End? Literary Reflections on the Ending of Mark's Narrative," *Int* 34 (1980): 151-66, and his "The Reader of the Gospel," *Neot* 18 (1984): 38-51.

171. Which in itself makes it most unlikely that it had been Mark's narrative strategy all along to present Jesus as a hidden Messiah who would only be revealed after Easter. To the contrary, apocalyptic disclosure moments occur throughout the narrative, including even on the cross.

have shown that this discourse, far from being either an intrusion into this Gospel or a mere collection of bits and pieces of Jesus' eschatological teaching loosely joined together here, is closely connected with themes and ideas that occur elsewhere in the Gospel and is in itself a united and carefully integrated discourse, linking Jesus' Jerusalem ministry with the passion narrative proper which follows it.[172] The rhetorical unit proper begins at 13:1 and concludes with the end of the chapter, for 14:1-2 serves as a narrative transition to the next unit.

Rhetorically speaking, one must see this discourse as the final example of the sort of private explanation and inside information Jesus gave his disciples. One of its rhetorical goals is to get the disciples to focus less on the things that will happen and more on the one who will bring all things to a conclusion in due course — the Son of Man. This is why the discourse ends not with a return to the A' material (see below) but with the B' material, which deals with the Second Coming. Generally speaking, the A material deals with signs on earth (e.g., false prophets) while the B material deals with signs in heaven. The disciples seem to be falling into the same category as the Pharisees (8:11-12) in their request for a sign, or at least for an explanation of "the sign."[173] Jesus is presenting them an alternative to the Zealotic reading of Israel's future (which involved taking up arms and fighting the Romans), and indeed, is engaging in an ideological conflict for the hearts of his disciples.[174] "Against rebel eschatology, Mark pits the death/life paradox of his own narrative symbolics and the politics of nonviolence."[175] The discourse must be seen as deliberative in character, focusing on the future and on what sort of behavior will be useful and beneficial for the audience if they are to be prepared for this future. This entire discourse calls the audience to "look," "watch," and "be alert" (cf. 13:1, 2, 5, 9, 14, 23-26, 28, 32, 34, 35).

Jesus and the Rhetoric of Proclamation

Perhaps here is a good point to speak briefly about the cumulative effect of the rhetoric of Jesus in the major speeches in Mark, especially in Mark 4 and 13. First it needs to be noted that Jesus' rhetoric is ethos centered, which is to say it is grounded in his own authority and person and character and only secondarily depends on powerful arguments.[176] It is

---

172. See J. Lambrecht, *Die Redaktion der Markus-Apokalypse* (Rome: Pontical Biblical Institute, 1967); M. Hooker, "Trial and Tribulation in Mark XIII," *BJRL* 65, no. 1 (1982): 78-99; Young, pp. 280-85.

173. Myers, p. 330.

174. Myers, p. 332.

175. Myers, p. 333.

176. This is the sort of approach one would expect when speeches occur in biographies of particular individuals.

interesting, as Young has noted, that the Evangelist in fact portrays Jesus as a more adept and sophisticated rhetor than he himself seems to have been.[177] The "paratactic style of Mark's Gospel is an intentional act of simplicity in order to highlight through vivid contrast the rhetoric of Jesus, who speaks in fairly elaborate hypotactic style."[178] This, in turn, means that while Jesus seeks to persuade, much of his teaching is not open to debate. It is also fair to say that Jesus' discourses appear to be compact or succinct compared to the great rhetorical discourses of antiquity. There are no lengthy digressions or elaborations such as we find in the speeches of Cicero or as discussed by Quintilian. "Instead the discourses appear more like the chreia or the prosopopoeia of the schools than like the speeches of the great orators of the milieu. They are comparable with narrative speeches found in the historical, biographical, or romantic writings of the period in that they never take the readers of the work far from the narrator's own story."[179] It is true enough that we find Jesus using a variety of rhetorical devices — logical argument, chiasms, *inclusios,* emotive appeals, striking figures of speech, and he especially falls back on inartificial proofs in the form of Scripture citations. As Young has noted, Jesus uses enthymemes in his judicial speech material in this Gospel but relies on comparisons in the more frequently found deliberative material.[180] The most common forms of comparisons used by Jesus are of course the parables. What this means is that Jesus as a rhetor is portrayed in this Gospel as someone who relies more on the apt metaphor than on the syllogism; the vivid image is preferred over ironclad logic. This is not surprising since Jesus is portrayed as operating not in a Greco-Roman environment but in a Jewish one, and operating as something of a Jewish sage and prophet rather than a philosopher. Finally it should be said that while Jesus' rhetoric is often beguilingly simple, it is nonetheless often quite profound, as Jesus persuades by an aphorism here or a parable there.

Biographically speaking, the discourse in Mark 13 answers indirectly how Jesus could indeed be both the stone the builders rejected and at the same time the head of the corner in God's building of the new temple, the new people of God. Notice how it is only the coming of the Son of Man that triggers the "final" events of human history. From the standpoint of discipleship, the disciples are forewarned that they will be conformed to the image of the Son, for they too will be persecuted, despised, and rejected and will be made to testify before the authorities. But in the end, Jesus and his disciples will be vindicated and their judges will be judged at the return of the Son of Man (cf. 14:62).

177. See Young, pp. 372-73, and consider the tour de force argument about David's Lord in Mark 12.
178. Young, p. 373.
179. Young, p. 375.
180. Young, p. 373.

A Brief Guide to Those Perplexed about the Meaning of Mark 13 —————

This discourse deals with what can be called eschatological events, but bear in mind that Jesus believed he was already living in the eschatological age. Thus all future events, from his perspective, had an eschatological quality to them whether they were on the near horizon or on a more distant one. The majority of this discourse is taken up with the events leading up to and including the destruction of the temple in A.D. 70, but two brief passages deal with what will transpire after that destruction. Basically the discourse is about God's judgment on Jerusalem, on the temple, and on the Jewish leaders, and only after that (when the Son of Man returns), on the world. It is thus primarily not about the end of the world, but the end of a world — the world of early Judaism as a temple-centered faith.

This discourse is known as the Olivet discourse, due to its location or point of delivery, but it is widely believed that it contains material delivered on a variety of occasions.[181] In terms of the Markan context, Mark 13 is linked with what has been the focus of matters since Mark 11, namely, the fate of the temple and so of institutional Judaism as it was then known. It needs to be said that in a general way most of this prophecy did indeed come true during the generation after Jesus' death (A.D. 30-70), in particular during the Jewish war which climaxed with the destruction of the temple in 70. Vv. 1-23 and 28-31 fall into this category and are described as "these things" or what would happen in "those days." The material grouped after the chronological indicator "in those days *after* the suffering" (i.e., after the messianic woes) or described as "that day or hour," however, is describing the last day of judgment or the days that involve the end of human history. This subject is only discussed in vv. 24-27 and 32-37.

Thus the discourse as we now have it falls into an A, B, A′, B′ pattern with the emphasis falling on the A, as indicated by the length of the two A sections.[182] The A material basically deals with persons in a limited area which is called by Schweizer a war zone.[183] The pattern of exhortation we find here is a word of warning ("look out," "take care"), followed by a γαρ clause explaining why this is important. One of the problems in dealing with this passage in the Greek is that the Nestle text as well as the Metzger-Aland text inexplicably leave out some of these γαρs. They should, however, in all likelihood at least be read at the following junctures — vv. 6, 7b, 8, 9b, 11b, 19, 22, 33, and 35. L. Gaston has rightly noted that every eschatological element is attached to its parenetic context by γαρ. It is in order to also point out that Jesus' specific answer to the *when* question is not fully answered until vv. 32-37, and before that juncture the main discussion is about *what* will happen.

The major function of the Olivet discourse, then, is *not* to encourage eschatological forecasting, but rather to encourage watchfulness and diligence in Christian life and witness. In fact, there is a theme of discouraging forecasting (e.g., note the warning

---

181. Notice, for example, how Mark 13:9-13 is not found in Matt. 24 but rather in Matt. 10:17-22.

182. Young, p. 339, thinks we are dealing with a pattern such that the material at the end of the discourse answers the question first raised in 13:1 — namely, when will these things be — to which the answer is given: no one knows. On this reading the material I have called A and A′ deals with the signs indicating the beginning of the birth pangs, while the B and B′ material deals with the timing issue.

183. Schweizer, p. 263.

about the end being not yet, and of course the clear statement of 13:32). Careful attention must be paid when dealing with vv. 1-23 and 28-31 to the indicators that suggest these events do not usher in the End (cf. vv. 7, 8b — "but the beginning of the birth pangs"; v. 10 — "the gospel must first be preached to all nations"). Jesus is willing to speak of the nearness of the birth pangs and of the destruction of Jerusalem and the temple (within a generation). These are necessary precursors to the End, but they do not indicate or dictate the timing of the end of human history. Indeed, according to this discourse, no one, not even Jesus, can calculate the End, since it will break in at an unexpected time, accompanied but not foreshadowed by various cosmological disorders. The reason the disciples must always be prepared for the end (see v. 33) is because they cannot read from the course of human affairs any signs that it is near. Wars and rumors of wars, earthquakes and famines occur in every age of human history, and they do not necessarily carry any eschatological weight as signals.

It has been fashionable of late[184] to suggest that some, if not much, of this material represents the words of the risen Lord spoken by Christian prophets after the time of Jesus. I have elsewhere critiqued such a theory at length.[185] Here it must be said that almost every verse has an allusion to OT material and deals with common, much discussed eschatological topics, and as such it is possible that Jesus himself could have spoken such material. None of it clearly bears the marks of *ex eventu* prophecy either. L. Hartman has rightly urged that basically what we have in this chapter are meditations on a series of several passages from Daniel and some other relevant OT prophetic texts, but here they are applied in a new way. Dan. 7:8-27; 8:9-26; 9:24-27; and 11:21–12:13 seem to particularly lie in the background.[186] I also agree with the basic arguments of M. Hengel which suggest that the material in this discourse favors a pre–A.D. 70 date for this Gospel.[187]

We must not underestimate the import and relevance of this material for Mark's audience, a group of Christians under duress and facing, or having already faced, persecution during the reign of Nero.[188] This discourse would answer their questions about whether the disturbing events currently transpiring in Judea were the signs of the end of all things. Mark's answer to the question is no, but that it is the end of a world, the world of temple-centered Judaism, not to be confused with the day of the final judgment, the day of the return of the Son of Man, or the time of cosmological disturbances. In short, the Markan community lived during the age of the birth pangs, an age of suffering and persecution but not a time for stargazing. Rather it was a time for diligence and faithfulness to the word and to witnessing, even if one is persecuted. Hooker aptly sums things up this way: "What Mark has set out, then, are three false signs of the End which might mislead the faithful, and three signs that provide no real warning at all. Mark's purpose may perhaps be to discourage apocalyptic speculation. . . . If there is no timetable of events to lull us into the belief that there are still several events that must take place before the End, then there is no need for constant vigilance. But equally, since there will be no mistaking the End when it arrives, this vigilance means patient waiting at one's post, not speculation

---

184. See, e.g., E. Boring, *The Continuing Voice of Jesus* (Louisville: Westminster/J. Knox, 1991).

185. See my discussion in *Jesus the Seer*, pp. 320-27.

186. See Myers, p. 326.

187. M. Hengel, *Studies in the Gospel of Mark* (Philadelphia: Fortress, 1985), pp. 14-28.

188. See the introduction, pp. 31-35 above.

about how much longer the delay will be."[189] If Mark wrote this material around A.D. 68-69, one can only imagine the effect of the events in 70 on those who knew this Gospel. It would have confirmed to the audience that this was a book of true prophecy.[190]

One of the first things that becomes apparent from reading the discourse in Mark 13 in its entirety is that Mark is suggesting that Jesus believed that the destruction of the temple was seen as God's eschatological judgment, not merely a punitive action by the Roman authorities. This is in part why it can be connected to other, later eschatological acts of the Son of Man when he returns. In other words, this discourse involves a theocratic reading, not a zealot's reading, of the climax of the Jewish War. This judgment also applies to Mark's presentation in 11–12, where it is intimated that how Jewish officials reacted to Jesus determined their own fate with God.

The judgment they worked for in regard to Jesus is the judgment the temple leadership endured in 70. This is made especially clear by having the material in 13:1-4 follow immediately upon the temple controversy narrative of the previous couple of chapters. Hurtado suggests that Mark's purpose is to make sure his Roman Christians are not deceived by the events leading up to and including the temple's destruction. In particular, he seems especially concerned that they not listen to false prophets.[191] Lane is also correct to stress the hortatory character of this material. It is exhortation backed up by interpretation of eschatological events. What is not correct is to see this as a farewell discourse. As Painter avers, the parallels with farewell discourses break down not least because this discourse was not given on the night Jesus was betrayed, but *was* given in response to a specific question about eschatological matters.[192]

According to v. 1, the disciples emerge from the temple precincts (ιερου must refer to the temple precincts, while ναος is the specific word for sanctuary) and are commenting on the staggering size and beauty of the temple. This is hardly surprising when some of the stones were twenty-five by eight by twelve cubits — in other words, huge.[193] They were also bright white in color, and Josephus tells us they were ornate. The temple would have covered some

---

189. Hooker, *Mark*, p. 302.

190. There have been numerous studies of this chapter. Some of the more helpful ones include: D. Wenham's *The Rediscovery of Jesus' Eschatological Discourse*; G. R. Beasley-Murray's *Jesus and the Future* (1954) and his *A Commentary on Mark 13* (1957), and also his more recent general study, *Jesus and the Kingdom* (1984). To this should be added the work of L. Hartman, *Prophecy Interpreted* (1966), and the articles listed in Wenham on pp. 377ff., especially those by J. Dupont. One can also commend L. Gaston's *No Stone on Another* (1970).

191. Hurtado, pp. 200-208.

192. Painter, p. 173.

193. A cubit being about a foot and a half long.

one-sixth of the whole city's space. In the sunlight it would have appeared like a white mountain of marble decorated with gold. Though it has often been re-marked that the temple was unfinished in Jesus' day, Josephus indicates the building was begun about 20 B.C. and the sanctuary at least was finished within eighteen months and the outer buildings within eight years (*Ant.* 15.11.5-6), though he elsewhere refers to work being done on the building in A.D. 62. John 2:20 indicates that building went on for some forty-six years, so perhaps, as Hooker says, there was minor work continuously done well after the building was basically finished.[194] Nevertheless, Jesus says it will be pulled down without leaving one stone on another, a prediction that apparently Johanan ben Zacchai also made, forecasting the temple's destruction in forty years (*b. Yoma* 39b). There was, of course, a long-standing prophetic tradition of predicting the tem-ple's destruction (Jer. 7:14; 26:6; Mic. 3:12).

When Jesus arrives back at the Mount of Olives, the inner circle of the disciples (Peter, Jacob, John, and Andrew) ask him, while he is gazing on the temple from the nearby hill, when (ποτε) this will be, and what the sign will be when all this is to be accomplished. "Jesus was asked for '*the sign*' that her-alds the end. He began by speaking of *signs* that signalled 'the end is *not* yet.'"[195]

Notice that v. 5 begins with a δε, which may be significant. The disciples begin to ask him when and what will be the sign, *but* Jesus begins to warn them to watch out lest they be misled about false ones coming in his name saying εγω ειμι. This might mean that messianic pretenders are going to come claiming to be Jesus redivivus, perhaps even claiming divine status. Lane is likely right that we should see this as referring to various messianic pretend-ers in the age leading up to the temple's destruction, not in our own day. Un-fortunately though, many a Jew was to be misled by such people, including the Zealots, and ironically, rather than saving Israel, this was to lead to the de-struction of the temple.

Wars and reports of wars are not to disconcert the disciples. Notice the use of δει in v. 7, likely indicating that this is part of God's eschatological plan, and so the disciples should not be alarmed. They should also not be misled to think this is the End. Indeed, nation will rise up against nation (cf. Isa. 19:2), there will be earthquakes and famines. Yet all of this is but the beginning of the birth pangs. The word ωδινων should be examined in light of OT usage where the term is used in contexts which refer to judgment and Israel's sufferings, lik-ened to a woman in labor (cf. Isa. 13:8; 26:17; Mic. 4:9f.; Hos. 13:13; Jer. 4:31; 6:24). Notice that Jesus says this is only the beginning of the travail, suggesting some sort of extended process. The point is not to worry because all of this is

194. Hooker, *Mark*, p. 304.
195. Painter, p. 174.

within God's eschatological plan. It is striking how the various items mentioned here are the same as those mentioned in Rev. 6, and in the same order, beginning with false prophets. This, then, may be a stock list of disasters and travails.

The disciples are not to worry about what they can't control; they must concentrate, according to v. 9, on preparing themselves, for they can do something about how they will react when they are carted before (Jewish) judicial councils (συνεδρια) and beaten in the synagogues for heresy (the famous forty lashes minus one, which Paul says he endured on several occasions — 2 Cor. 11:24). In fact, three times in 13:9-13 the disciples are told they will be handed over, even by members of their own family. What is important about this last remark is that those who endured the lash did so in order to be able to *remain* a part of the synagogue.[196] Otherwise they would have simply left. Also they will be delivered up to Roman governors and rulers, and they will have to stand trial on Jesus' account. This last remark makes clear that the subject here is not general abuse but rather specific punishment for evangelizing. It is possible that the phrase εις μαρτυριον αυτοις means "for evidence against them." In any event, the point is that they will be witnessing in a hostile environment, and so be testifying against their accusers who reject their message.

The theme of witnessing even in a hostile situation is carried on in v. 10. While this verse has often been seen as prophecy after the fact, it need not be if Jesus even occasionally passed over into Gentile territory, as Mark suggests, and witnessed to non-Jews, thus providing a paradigm for his followers. Jesus adds that it is necessary that the gospel be preached to all the nations (which surely here means all the Gentile nations). The word "first" is important, for it indicates that human activity in some manner affects the length of the birth pangs.

There will be divine enablement when believers are delivered up to an authority (παραδωσει is a key repeated term in this section of the chapter). They will be given the right words to say by the Holy Spirit. As Schweizer remarks, the OT concept of the Spirit is implicit here, whereby "the Spirit is given to inspire especially marvelous utterances and is given only to special [persons] — the martyrs — in times of special need — in court proceedings (cf. 1.12)."[197] Again this does not suggest a Christian utterance from around A.D. 70; indeed, it does not suggest an utterance from after Pentecost. Witnessing for Christ can even cause family divisions, divisions in the closest of family relationships, so

---

196. This verse, as Schweizer, p. 270, rightly notes, suggests a time when the church was still intimately involved in the life of the synagogue. In other words, it suggests a time before A.D. 70, indeed before the Jewish War. It is a remark Jesus himself could well have made to his closest followers, anticipating that they would have the same response he got in the synagogues.

197. Schweizer, p. 271.

much so that the family members may even turn the Christian over to the authorities to be executed. Mark's audience would surely have been able to identify with this word about families with divided religious loyalties, a word about the cost of discipleship. Even in the extreme situation, the stress is still on faithful discipleship. V. 13b uses the word σωσεται, which could mean rescued, or even vindicated (cf. Job 13:16 LXX; Phil. 1:19, 28). It probably doesn't refer to eternal salvation. It is unlikely that Mark is enunciating a doctrine of salvation by endurance or martyrdom, a form of salvation by works.

Beginning with vv. 14ff., the discussion returns to the temple. What is referred to here can only be understood by referring to Dan. 9:27 and the LXX of Dan. 12:11, the latter of which may be a reference to the altar of Zeus erected by Antiochus Epiphanes in 168 B.C. (cf. 1 Macc. 1:54-59). The phrase in question likely means an abomination which results in desolation, that is, in abandonment of the temple by God. Less probably, one could translate it an appalling sacrilege. Though the gender of the word "abomination" is neuter, the word "standing" is a masculine perfect participle, which definitely suggests someone rather than something.[198]

Thus in Mark's text we are not talking about a heathen altar, but rather about someone who causes the temple to be desecrated and so abandoned.[199] This is in fact what happened to the temple. Josephus tells us how the Zealots took over from November 67 or the spring of 68, at which time they allowed criminals to roam the temple, including in the Holy of Holies, and even to murder others in the temple. As a sort of sick joke a man named Phanni was invested as high priest. It may be this last fact that Mark thinks Jesus was referring to, for he adds the parenthetical remark "let the reader understand." The phrase seems to mean "take note, you already know what this refers to." If Mark was writing in late 68, this note would be most germane. This may provide one significant clue to the dating of this Gospel.[200] It may be added that if Mark was writing at a time after the destruction of the temple, we might expect a clearer correlation between the disciples' initial question and Jesus' response, or in other words, an account here more nearly matching the historical events, such as we find in Luke 21. As it is, Mark's own theological perspective becomes clear

---

198. A point of grammar which seems to be lost on those who see an allusion to Titus's erection of the Roman standards in the temple which were then sacrificed to, coupled with an acclamation of Titus as emperor (*War* 6.6.1).

199. For a thorough canvassing of the six major interpretations of what Mark is alluding to here, see D. Ford, *The Abomination of Desolation in Biblical Eschatology* (Washington, D.C.: University Press of America, 1979).

200. Perhaps the most compelling case that the Jewish War serves as the backdrop for Mark's presentation of this Jesus material is that presented by J. A. Wilde, "A Social Description of the Community Reflected in the Gospel of Mark" (Ph.D. diss., Drew University, 1978), pp. 100-120.

here. For him, the destruction of the temple is confirmation not only that God has judged Israel but that God's designs and plans will henceforth be centered on Jesus and his followers.[201]

When the sacrilege takes place, then it is time to flee the city, for its destruction is imminent. This advice is in fact the opposite of usual Jewish and ancient Near Eastern advice, which thought of safety within the city walls, not least because Jews often thought that God would not allow his dwelling place to be destroyed. The point of v. 16 is that if you are on the roof praying and the time comes to flee, flee; don't even go into the house to get a cloak, simply go down the outside stairs from the roof and run.[202] Likewise, if you are working in a field, just run away. Jesus foresees that the time of destruction will be most difficult on those most vulnerable and immobile — those who are pregnant or those who have newborns.

They are to pray it doesn't happen in winter not just because of the exposure to the elements when camping out, but also because winter is the season when streams would be swollen and hard to ford, especially if one is in a hurry. The phrase "let him not turn himself to the rear" may allude to the famous case of Lot's wife, the paradigmatic example of why one should not look back when judgment is coming. V. 19 speaks of unparalleled suffering and persecution. Though the words "from the beginning of creation, when God created" seem redundant, they may not have been for a Gentile audience. The second phrase would be Mark's explanation of the first phrase to Gentiles who needed to be told that one God created it all.

It is interesting that Eusebius says there was a prophecy which warned the Jewish Christians to flee the city in time. They are said to have fled to the Decapolis, to Pella. This may be an authentic tradition, but it is not clear whether Eusebius is speaking about a prophecy of Jesus or a new prophecy of a Christian prophet in the 60s. Notice in v. 20 the ει followed by αν. When αν is present with past tense verbs in a conditional statement, it indicates an *unreal condition*. In other words, the elect are not really in danger from such circumstances. The Lord (here the Father may be meant) will cut short those days of severe distress, so some may be rescued. The sense of σῴζω here, as in 4 Ezra 6:25 and 7:27, is "rescued," "left alive," a common meaning of the term in Jewish and indeed Greco-Roman contexts.[203] The time has been cut short because of the elect whom God has chosen. Is this a reference to Christians or to godly Jews? Perhaps most likely it

---

201. K. E. Brower, "'Let the Reader Understand': Temple and Eschatology in Mark," in *Eschatology in Bible and Theology*, ed. Brower and M. W. Elliott (Downers Grove, Ill.: InterVarsity, 1997), pp. 119-43.

202. Schweizer, p. 273.

203. See my discussion of this matter in my *Acts of the Apostles: A Socio-Rhetorical Commentary* (Grand Rapids: Eerdmans, 1998), pp. 821-43.

is to the Jewish followers of Jesus, in particular, as it turned out, those who escaped with their lives from the final destruction of Jerusalem. We are not told on what basis the elect are chosen here, and notice that the author refers to an elect group, not to isolated elect individuals. In the OT the phrase "the elect" is often used of Israel in general (Ps. 105:6, 43; Isa. 65:9), but in Jewish literature from just before or during the time of Jesus "the elect" refers to the righteous few (*1 Enoch* 1:1; 62:8; 1QS 8.6; 1QH 2.13). During all these birth pangs the followers of Jesus are to keep their minds on the real task of witnessing to the authentic Christ, and not be distracted by false claims of a messiah appearing here or there. It is allowed that such false messianic and prophetic figures (cf. Deut. 13:4ff.) would arise and even perform signs and wonders, something Jesus himself refused to perform for the skeptics. V. 23 closes this section of the discourse. Jesus has warned his followers about all these birth pangs in advance so that they will be prepared and know what to do and how to interpret such events.

It is crucial to note that v. 24 begins with αλλα, a strong adversative. This certainly suggests we are to think that Jesus is now talking about a different subject, namely, what will happen "in those days, following that suffering."[204] The subject matter has turned to the real climax of human history. There will be heavenly phenomena accompanying the coming of the Son of Man. Bear in mind that the phrase "in those days" has clear eschatological associations, as texts like Jer. 3:16, 18; 31:33; Joel 2:28; Zech. 8:23 suggest. On the heavenly phenomena, one needs to compare Isa. 13:10; 34:4; Ezek. 32:7-8; Amos 8:9. Furthermore, signs in the heavens are commonly associated in the OT with the Day of the Lord (Isa. 13:10; 34:4; Ezek. 32:7-8; Joel 2:10, 31; 3:15; cf. Rev. 6:12-14; 8:12). The question, of course, is how literally one should take this language, since it is in most respects the traditional language used of a theophany, though now presented with a more apocalyptic flavor. The point of such language is clearly that creation reacts, that all heaven breaks loose when God comes down. There may also be something of the notion found in Rom. 8 which suggests that the fate of creation is bound up with the fate of humankind.

That something cataclysmic is being described is sure, but bear in mind that this same sort of language is used when describing the fall of Babylon, and we may be sure that all the stars did not fall from the sky on that occasion, nor is it likely that God only acts when there are eclipses! As Hooker says, the language here is "more than metaphorical, less than literal."[205] By this I take her to

---

204. Painter, p. 177, rightly points out that the discourse does not say how long the suffering will last, only that God has shortened it. This, in turn, means that the discourse does not assert a specific period of time after which the End must come. It only insists on the fact of the End and the reality of the preliminary events, the latter of which will transpire (including the temple's destruction) within a generation.

205. Hooker, *Mark*, p. 319.

mean the author is describing cosmic phenomena, but he is not giving an exact or scientific description of the phenomena. Nor is he merely suggesting that times were bad by hyperbolically employing heavenly metaphors. Nonetheless, the basic point is that the final coming of the Son of Man will be an earth-shattering event. What is described is seen as real, but the terms used are hyperbolic in character, indicating the significance of the event and the importance of the person referred to.[206]

The Son of Man riding on a cloud chariot is much like various OT descriptions of God's coming (cf. Ezek. 1 and various of the psalms), only in this case the function and role of the deity is taken by the Son of Man. The Son of Man will come to gather or rescue some from all parts of the earth, but to judge and condemn others. Actually, the angels will be the gatherers, collecting people from the four corners of the earth and from one end of heaven to the other, a theme found in texts like Deut. 30:4-5 and Isa. 60:4ff. (cf. the coming together of all nations in Mic. 4:1ff.). The point is that no one and no place will be overlooked in the search for the saved.

At v. 28 the message again shifts. Here Jesus is once more talking about some event for which there are signs and indicators that something is about to happen. This event can only be the destruction of the temple. Here we have Jesus' last parable in this Gospel, and it must be kept in mind that earlier the withered fig tree had been a symbol of God's judgment on Israel. This suggests that the same topic is being addressed here, in which case we are back to discussing "these things" and the days leading up to the destruction of the temple. The Mount of Olives would be a good place to tell this parable, since it was loaded with fig trees and at Passover in the spring the sap would begin to rise and the branches would grow tender and begin to break into leaf. This is the harbinger of summer's arrival. This is to be seen as a sign that judgment is near. The proper translation is "it is near," and the reference is not to the coming of the Son of Man but rather to the judgment of the temple.[207] In Luke 21:31 Luke supplies the subject "the dominion of God," which is said to be near.

V. 30 has been contorted in various ways and given various meanings (is it referring to this race?), but such exegetical gymnastics are unnecessary if the parable goes with vv. 3-23 rather than vv. 24-27. As Lane clearly demonstrates, elsewhere when Mark uses the phrase "this generation," it refers to Jesus' contemporaries (see 8:12, 38; 9:19) and is not a generic ethnic reference to a race of

---

206. It is interesting that some of the church fathers, such as Cyril of Jerusalem, in *Catechetical Lectures* 15.15, suggest that even the reference to the temple's destruction refers not to the events of A.D. 70 but to events which were yet in the future from the time Cyril lived, because he takes the abomination that makes desolate as a reference to the Antichrist's activity.

207. But see Schweizer, p. 281.

people.[208] From a biblical point of view, a generation was about forty years, and not coincidentally it was that length of time between Jesus' death and the destruction of the temple. Very clearly the ταυτα παντα of v. 30 should be related to the same phrase in the disciples' initial question (v. 4) and should also be related to the παντα in v. 23. Thus this verse was fulfilled quite literally around A.D. 70. V. 31 seems to be a way of Jesus saying that the world will fail before his words fail, or put another way, his word is more permanent and lasting than the universe.

Jesus thus alternates between describing events on the near horizon (these things) and those more remote (in those days after that suffering), and finally he concludes with a resumption in vv. 32-37 of the topic discussed in vv. 24-27. The clue that this is so is the εκεινης ημερας in both v. 24 and v. 32. Some later scribes, of course, had problems with v. 32, which asserts that there is something that Jesus did not know about matters eschatological, but the more difficult reading must be accepted here. Notice how various scribes tried to omit the key phrase at Matt. 24:36. The point of v. 32 is that no one except God the Father, who made the divine plan, knows the timing of the coming of the Son of Man.[209] Notice that those ignorant are listed in ascending order of closeness in knowledge to the Father — no humans know, neither do any angels, nor does even the Son. In view of the earlier indicators in Mark that Jesus is presented as a more than merely mortal figure, this saying is probably meant to suggest that Jesus saw himself as closer to God than the angels, at least in terms of knowledge of God's will and plan. The upshot of this is that if the Master does not know the timing of the parousia, neither do the disciples, and so they should not speculate. The use of καιρος here must be equivalent to the reference to the day or hour in the previous verse, since they are discussing the same subject. This rules out the artful and somewhat humorous dodge suggesting that while Jesus did not know the exact time of the parousia, he knew the general time it would transpire, namely, within a generation, if not sooner.

The discourse as a whole concludes with a parable, just as the section on "these days" had done with a parable about the fig tree. This parable involves a man who goes away from home, leaving his house in the hands of his servants, who are authorized to watch over it. Each one is left with a job, and the janitor or porter is left to watch the gate or door (remembering the use of the door in the previous parable as a symbol of the point of entry of a new thing). V. 35 makes explicit what v. 32 made implicit — Jesus is talking about when the Son of Man or Lord is coming.[210] Since no one knows the timing, one must be

---

208. See Lane, p. 480.

209. See my detailed discussion of this verse in *The Christology of Jesus*, pp. 228-33.

210. For an attempt to read Mark 13 as the record of the recent and continuing experience of the Markan community as it welcomes refugees from the Jewish War into its midst,

watchful or, more to the point, always doing the job God gave one to do, for blessed are those found doing such a task when the Lord returns. The allusion to the four watches of the night probably indicates that Mark has recast the parable to suit his Western and Roman audience, because doubtless Jesus would have referred to three watches.[211] The image of the thief in the night suggests a sudden coming at an unexpected time when most are likely to be unprepared. The discourse concludes with an exhortation Mark's audience needed to heed — don't be caught napping, be prepared for that sudden and unforeseeable coming.[212] The reference to the four watches of the night, coupled with the reference to sleeping, points the narrative forward to the Gethsemane story and what will happen to the disciples beginning at that juncture. As Myers says, it is as if Mark is saying to his own audience, "we all live in a Gethsemane moment in human history; we must not be caught napping like the first disciples were when the crucial moment arrived."[213]

Bridging the Horizons

Though it is true that the narrative time of Mark's tale slows down considerably when one reaches Mark 11, certainly the action and controversies do not slow down but rather pick up. The tone of the narrative also becomes more ominous, at least after the initial joy and excitement of the Palm Sunday account. It is worth pondering what sorts of persons would be prepared to say "Hosanna" in Jesus' presence on Sunday but turn around and say "Crucify him" on Good Friday. It is surely not just a matter of being quixotic. There is something fundamental about flawed human nature that Mark wants to make clear, not only in the passion narrative but in his entire portrayal of the disciples. His view could be summed up as follows — every human being is capable of having faith, but every human being is also capable of betrayal, of backing away from

---

see K. D. Dyer, "But concerning *That* Day . . . (Mk. 13.32): 'Prophetic' and 'Apocalyptic' Eschatology in Mark 13," in *SBL 1999 Seminar Papers* (Atlanta: Scholars, 1999), pp. 104-22. The attempt founders, however, on precisely the B sections of this discourse.

211. It is interesting that the passion narrative refers to events leading up to Jesus' death as taking place during these four watches — the Last Supper is in the evening, the Gethsemane events are in the middle of the night, Peter's denial is at cock crow, and the trial before Pilate is in the morning. See R. H. Lightfoot, *The Gospel Message of Mark* (Oxford: Oxford University Press, 1950), p. 53.

212. Cf. Hooker, *Mark*, p. 324: "The point of Mark's parable about the man who returns at night is not that his arrival is unexpected, but that his servants are given no warning about the precise time that he will come and must therefore be constantly vigilant."

213. Myers, p. 347.

commitments when the going gets rough, and indeed even of turning on the one that had been previously supported. In short, every human being has a heart of darkness, or to put it in Pauline terms, all have sinned and fallen short of the glory. So long as we naively view human beings as basically good but needing further enlightenment, we will never understand Mark's portrayal of the disciples, who had all the enlightenment one could ask for and yet still betrayed, denied, and deserted Jesus.

Mark's portrayal of the triumphal entry is considerably understated compared to those in the other Gospels. Jesus is not directly acclaimed by the shouting crowd in part because "for Mark it is the lowliness and humility of the entry into Jerusalem which matters not its triumphal nature. It is a kingship of hidden majesty, of humble power to save."[214] Perhaps the clearest evidence of the understated nature of Mark's portrayal is that the triumphal entry ends in Mark with a quiet surveying of the temple precincts by Jesus, and a return to spend the night in Bethany. Is Jesus sizing things up for the coming confrontation? This may be the case.

The term "Hosanna," which we find in Ps. 118:25 and literally means "save now," was certainly the cry of many Jews' hearts when they suffered from Roman domination. But Mark's account is laden with irony, for the crowd associated the triumphal entry with the promise of coming salvation, whereas, in Mark's view, Hosanna is what happens when the end of the week comes and there are no cries but Jesus' cry of dereliction. Salvation came in a manner no one expected, not during the ecstasy but during the agony, not when everyone was on Jesus' side but when he had been totally abandoned by humankind. This makes very clear that in Mark's view salvation comes in unexpected fashion and is a God-wrought thing, not the product of a human movement.

English aptly puts the matter this way: "Group spirit and movement can hold us in the initial period of belief, and can sustain us during difficult times. But it is no substitute for individual understanding and commitment. As such, group spirit can prevent us from making our own discoveries, and can hinder the truth from reaching the deepest areas of our personality. The more exciting the group experience whether in its free expression, sacramental mystery or corporate oneness, the more carefully do we need to ensure that our understanding is keeping track of our public activity, and our spiritual growth matching the group life."[215]

The story of Jesus cursing the fig tree needs to be seen as an acted parable, and, however uncomfortable this may make us moderns, it is a parable about God's coming judgment on his own people and their religious institutions. Those who have difficulty with this story often equate love and a loving God

---

214. D. English, *The Message of Mark* (Downer Grove: InterVarsity, 1992), p. 185.
215. English, p. 187.

with the absence of judgment, but this is a mistake, for the presentation of both God and Jesus in the Bible repeatedly stresses that their love is a holy love, and as such that love can and must be a refiner's fire on occasions where that is needed. Indeed, it is precisely because God *does* love his people that he judges them, for he wants them to repent and be a holy people. In other words, God's judgment in the case of his people is never purely punitive; it is also redemptive in character. Yet there is more to the fig tree story than this, for the fig tree is a symbol of the people of God, and thus a reminder that God expects his people to bear good fruit in due season. Those who do not do so face the judgment of God also enunciated in the parable of the talents. There are few things as frustrating to God as wasted abilities.

We should not waste our time worrying about the cursing of a barren fig tree, especially when we now know that when Mark says "it was not the season for figs," what he likely refers to is the edible female fruit of the tree, not the male fruit which appears earlier. The point is that the tree indeed was barren and had put all its energy into luxuriant foliage, but without fruit. It didn't even bear the male fruit and so was totally useless. How very like so many churches today that spend fortunes on their outward appearance and buildings but do not bear the good fruit of righteousness, and justice, and love.

The uniquely Markan story about Jesus' inspection tour of the temple, found in 11:11, is seldom preached on, but it deserves more attention. Here is how one expositor has approached the text. "This was an official visit of the King of Israel, an inspection tour at the heart of the nation. He went into the temple, where the very heartbeat of the nation was throbbing, represented in the worship that was lifted up to God. And he looked at *everything*. We know what he saw: commercialism, moneychangers, exploitation, corruption, and injustice. . . . But he did not say a word. He just looked around at everything. Nobody noticed him, because he had been there many times before. But they did not know this was an official tour of inspection by the King."[216]

How one teaches or preaches the story of Jesus' action in the temple will depend on whether one sees it as an acted parable of coming judgment or a symbolic attempt at cleansing the vicinity which represented the religious heart of Israel. This action is often seen as the litmus test to whether we should see Jesus as a reformer of Israel or as something more radical. Let it first be said that the story makes evident that Jesus (1) believes in God's coming judgment on Israel and (2) has a capacity for righteous anger. In regard to the second of these, it has been said that an essential requirement for any sort of ministry is a capacity for righteous anger about evil in the world. I would agree with this assessment, and would add that whatever else this story tells us about Jesus, it puts us

---

216. R. Stedman, "The King Is Coming," sermon preached June 1, 1975, p. 2 of his manuscript.

on alert to the fact that he was not merely "gentle Jesus, meek and mild." I would suggest that, considering when the temple action takes place during Jesus' ministry, it should probably be seen as an acted parable of coming judgment, for when Jesus goes up to Jerusalem to die, the die is cast. It is true enough that Jesus is very upset with the corruption in the temple, but he does not act like a reformer, he simply symbolically casts out those who are the objects of his wrath. Money changers and pigeon sellers are not treated in a redemptive way here! If this disturbs us, then we need to ask ourselves whether we have come to grips with God's capacity for righteous anger and Jesus' willingness to judge human sin and folly.

Beginning in 11:27-33 and continuing on through chapter 12, we have what amount to five or six challenges to Jesus' authority, and the stories present his responses. The issue of authority is a difficult one in any era, especially if its source is charismatic in nature, by which I mean if it does not come through the authorization of some human person or institutional process. It is interesting to see how Jesus asserts his authority without becoming defensive, which is a difficult art. Notice that Jesus chooses to refer to the authority of a figure to whom he has been closely linked, John the Baptist. This suggests that the more one can provide good analogies for one's actions and calling, the less likely people will be to question that calling and authority.

The parable of the tenants in the vineyard seems to have been originally directed against corrupt leadership in Israel. The original audience would likely have been familiar with Isa. 5 and the parable of the vineyard there. For those of us attuned to intertextual echoes, the difficulty today becomes how much we read the latter parable in light of the former, or how much we allow Jesus' parable to stand on its own. There is also the further issue of whether there is some abiding principle in this parable that could be applied today. I suspect there is such a principle, namely, that there is an enormous responsibility laid in the hands of those who tend God's vineyard. It is not, nor will it ever become, the tenants' own vineyard. Furthermore, if the vineyard workers are not open to correction and direction from God through his messengers along the way, not even from God's Son himself, they face a fearsome prospect of judgment.

It is an odd but nonetheless real truth that sometimes professional ministers are the first to reject the demands of the gospel, the fresh demands of God on their lives, because they think they already know what they are supposed to be doing and believe the vineyard is in their own hands and control. But the vineyard does indeed belong to the Father and will one day be claimed by the Son, and in the interim we are but stewards, not owners, of it. Chaucer once said, "If gold rusts, what then will iron do?" by which he meant if the leadership of God's people becomes corrupt and hard-hearted, one can hardly expect better of God's people.

All too often the pericope found in 12:13-17 has been used to urge a separation-of-church-and-state mentality, or a Christians-should-be-good-citi-zens-and-be-obedient-to-their-government sort of attitude. One needs to know that the question asked of Jesus is a trick question, and in a sense his answer is a trick answer as well. The word "hypocrisy" used in this story refers actually to playacting or, thinking of Greco-Roman drama, wearing a mask. Jesus' interlocutors are not honest questioners. Jesus' answer gets him off the hook.

In the first place, two things are quite clear: (1) Jesus is theocratic in his vision of things and believes all things belong to God. He is not suggesting here that the world is really divided up between things that belong to God and things that don't! (2) Jesus is equally clear in his critique of money. It is entirely believable that Jesus would say, give Caesar back his unrighteous coins with their graven images on them. This would be a very understandable early Jewish attitude. There may even be a critique here of those who choose to use Caesar's coinage. But it is also true that this saying makes clear that Jesus doesn't simply identify with the revolutionaries. He critiques the state without suggesting the taking up of arms, and calls his audience back to their ultimate allegiance, which must be first, last, and always to God.

We are made in God's image. We are God's common coin and belong to God. This being so, we owe no ultimate allegiance to the rulers of this world. If the rulers demand something of us that conflicts with God's demands or usurps God's place, we are under no obligation to obey such demands. It is possible that at the end of the day, Jesus' comment has to do with the growing cult of the emperor which was manifested on the coin, with the emperor being portrayed as a god and being called divine, a practice Jesus would clearly see as a violation of monotheism.

12:18-27 is a story in which once again someone tries to trap Jesus by means of a trick question. The aim of the Sadducees' question "is therefore to show what trouble you get into by believing in an afterlife."[217] Jesus' response is meant to show what trouble you get into when you don't believe in the entire witness of the Hebrew Scriptures which supports a viable positive concept of an afterlife.

This story has sometimes been used to comment on Jesus' view of marriage, suggesting that he was some sort of ascetic who saw marriage as something inconsistent with the realm of angels. This overlooks the fact that Jesus is only commenting on one particular kind of marriage, namely, levirate marriage, which, if death is abolished, has no more function (it being a means to raise up an heir for a deceased brother). Furthermore, what Jesus actually says about the eschatological state is that there will be no more acts of marrying. He does not say there will be no more marriage. One may and must also ask in what respect Jesus sees human relationships as like angelic ones, and on this

---

217. English, p. 197.

score it would appear he means to stress that it's a matter of living in a death-less, not sexless, existence at the eschaton.

The love commandment enunciated in 12:28-34, which is actually an amalgamation of two commandments, has been discussed and proclaimed so often that it has been trivialized and its radical edge blunted. In the first place, the very fact that Jesus *commands* love ought to immediately cause us to realize that something extraordinary is going on here that does not involve mere feelings. Feelings cannot be commanded, but decisions of the will and actions of the body can be. Notice also that one is commanded to love God with one's whole being; in other words, the cliché "it's the thought that counts" would not have been seen as the appropriate response to this command.

Early Judaism was in any case mostly a matter of orthopraxy, and Jesus would have placed the focus on deeds of love. There is offered, however, a contrast between loveless sacrifices which fulfill the letter but not the spirit of what God requires and a loving of God with one's whole being. This is not because Jesus was opposed to sacrifices offered in the right spirit, but because what God really wants is the wholehearted devotion of his people. But devotion without the horizontal component of loving one's neighbor as self is not merely selfish and self-centered, but it overlooks the fact that we are blessed to be a blessing to others. English rightly also notes that the one who enunciates this greatest commandment does so in the temple courts he has already pronounced judgment on, and he does so shortly before he becomes the ultimate sacrifice which at the same time is the ultimate example of a deed of love.[218] Jesus models the commandments he urges.

It is sometimes urged that Jesus commands us to love ourselves here. This, however, is incorrect. He assumes we will do so, and commands us to treat our neighbor in like fashion. But what could this commandment really entail? Is Jesus really suggesting that we should care as much about our neighbor's welfare, our neighbor's health, our neighbor's education, our neighbor's finances as we care about our own? It seems that the answer to this is yes, for the earliest followers of Jesus seem to have lived as if they had such an obligation (see Acts 2:43-47; 4:32-37). One can only wonder what the impact of the witness would be if Christians today lived as, and in community like, the earliest Christians.

The tale of the widow's mite in 12:41-44 rounds out the chapter on a much more sedate note. The message here is quite similar to the one at the base of the last pericope, namely, that total commitment is what God requires of his people, even in regard to their money. God measures a person not by the size of the gift but by the degree of commitment the gift, whether great or small in real terms, represents.

---

218. English, p. 199.

In his exposition on Mark 13, D. English rightly stresses that Jesus does not encourage "almanac discipleship," a kind of discipleship that behaves in certain ways according to the date on the eschatological calendar.[219] Though most of the events spoken of in Mark 13 have long since come and gone, being events that led up to the temple's destruction in A.D. 70, nonetheless much is to be learned from the discourse. For one thing, it shows how profoundly eschatological Jesus' message was, which is to say how historically focused it was. Jesus' message was about the present and the future, and in a sense about the future breaking into the present, unexpectedly and repeatedly. This explains the repeated call in this discourse for diligence, alertness, watching, for we do not ultimately know *when* the author of the human drama will bring the curtain down, but we do know *that* he will do so. And, as C. S. Lewis once put it, when the author himself comes on the stage, the play is over. It is too late to change the play or the players.

Jesus wishes to prepare his disciples both for the worst and the best of what is to come. D. Nineham aptly says, "When we remember that most of the early Christians were simple and unlearned people, for whom a speech in court would have been a terrible ordeal, we realize how much such a promise [of the Spirit being with them and giving them utterance] will have meant to them."[220]

In 1999 I had the privilege of preaching at the only Russian Protestant church that, even during the darkest days of Communism, Stalin was unable to close. The stories those Christians who attended this large Baptist church in Moscow had to tell sounded very much like parts of Mark 13. For example, there was the story of how during a Christian wedding the KGB came and took away the pastor, the bride, and the groom, for such weddings without the authorization of the state were completely illegal, as indeed were most kinds of church meetings outside the Orthodox Church. The couple and the pastor were apparently sent to Siberia to some gulag. Those Christians knew all too well the cost of discipleship, and the warnings of Mark 13 were not for them an idle threat. Further too, their life circumstances led them to place great hope in the return of Christ, the only one who ultimately could right such wrongs.

The prediction of the destruction of the temple is of course a central part of this discourse, and it will be remembered that this prediction was part of what got Jesus in hot water with the authorities, even though the report that reached them seems to have been garbled and distorted. The prediction seems to be accurate not only in regard to the timing of the event (exactly a biblical generation after the death of Jesus in A.D. 30), but also in some particulars as well. It is interesting that when Titus's troops burned the temple, there were apparently hidden reserves of gold in the treasury which had not been pilfered and that melted under the intense heat of the fire. The liquid gold apparently seeped through the cracks be-

---

219. English, p. 206.
220. D. Nineham, *The Gospel of St. Mark* (London: Penguin Books, 1963), p. 349.

tween various of the stones of the temple, leading the greedy Romans to pry the stones apart ("not leaving one stone on another") to retrieve the gold!

13:20 is a verse that deserves more attention. Jesus here promises that even during the darkest days of doom and gloom, the disciples should not assume that God has forgotten about their plight. To the contrary, Jesus says God has shortened those days so that God's people will survive. This reminds us that Jesus does not promise that his followers will be exempt from the final tribulation; rather the time will be shortened and the disciples will be strengthened so that they can endure it. Jesus offers no escape hatch called the rapture for believers who live in the last age of human history, and why should he? If his own immediate followers (and indeed, the next two thousand years' worth of his followers) were not to be exempt from persecution and suffering grisly forms of martyrdom, why should late Western Christians assume that the last generation of believers will be exempt from such forms of trial and tribulation? I see no exegetical reasons to make such an assumption. Indeed, even the reference to "one taken and one left" must be seen in the larger context as a reference to one taken away for judgment and trial and the other spared such a fate. Neither the one taken nor the one left behind is beamed up into heaven.

All Christians are called upon to live by faith, and none are promised exemption from suffering and trial, and possibly even death, for the sake of the gospel. One of the most compelling stories of martyrdom in the modern era is that of Jim Elliott, who ministered to the Auca Indians in South America and was killed by them. Not terribly long before his death he said, "He is no fool who gives up what he can not keep [his very life] to gain what he can not lose [eternal life]." Many of the earliest Christians lived by the wisdom of this motto, though they did not articulate it in this fashion.

In every era of human history there have been earthquakes, famines, wars, rumors of wars, and also false prophets and false messiahs. In this regard the prophecy in Mark 13 is generic enough when it speaks of preliminary events to always have had relevance to the people of God. What Mark 13 suggests about the false messianic figures is that they try to attract attention by their signs and wonders, something Jesus himself never did. His miracles were acts of compassion, not billboards trying to draw an audience. Indeed, the Markan account suggests that he was not best pleased when people showed up just for the miracles and ignored the teaching or preaching. "Jesus is restrained, not from performing signs and wonders as the need of people reaches him, but from using these to impose or compel faith. . . . He embodies the good news, and his death and resurrection are to be the heart of it. That is the gold in the bank, giving meaning to the notes and coins of signs and wonders. The false messiahs have only counterfeit money, impressive but with nothing to back it up."[221]

---

221. English, p. 208.

XII. Long Day's Journey into Night, Part II (14:1–15:47)

The passion narrative proper begins at 14:1 with a brief account of the plot to kill Jesus. This is followed by the anointing of Jesus, Judas's agreement to betray Jesus, the Last Supper, and the events in the Garden of Gethsemane. What is notable about the beginning of the passion tales in Mark is that Jesus is no longer involved in public activities. What is recounted are activities that take place offstage or out of the public eye or behind closed doors. As D. Juel points out, one-third of Mark's Gospel is devoted to an account of Jesus' last few days, and one-sixth to his last twenty-four hours.[1] While this might seem surprising in a modern biography, it is not so in an ancient one, especially in view of the widespread belief that how a person died revealed the person's true character.[2] Needless to say, there was much to explain about the demise of Jesus at the hands of the Roman authorities if a largely Gentile audience was to embrace the gospel and Jesus as their Savior.

---

1. D. Juel, *The Gospel of Mark* (Nashville: Abingdon, 1999), p. 139.

2. Nor is the lack of presentation of character development a surprise, since most ancients didn't believe in such a notion. They believed character was simply revealed over time. Juel notes the lack of character development in the case of Judas, and indeed we are not even told what happened to him in Mark. See Juel, p. 140.

TRANSLATION — 14:1–15:47

14 *It was the Passover and the Feast of Unleavened Bread was within two days. And the high priests and their scribes were looking how by some deceitful means seizing him they would kill him. For they said, "Not during the Feast lest there is a riot of the people."*

And he was in Bethany in the house of Simon the leper reclining with him. A woman came having a flask of expensive genuine nard perfume. Breaking the flask she poured the nard on his head. But some were indignant within themselves, [questioning] "Why did the waste of this perfume happen? For this perfume could have been sold for over three hundred denarii, and [the proceeds] given to the poor." And they were enraged. But Jesus said: "Let her be. Why do you give her trouble? She has done a good deed for me. For the poor you always have with you, and when you wish you will be able to do them good, but me you will not always have. She has done what she could, anointing my body in advance for burial. Amen I tell you, wherever the good news is preached in the whole of the world, what she has done will be spoken of as her memorial."

And Judas Iscariot, the one from the Twelve, came to the high priests in order to hand him over to them. But hearing they were glad and promised to give him silver. And he sought how he might opportunely hand him over.

And on the first day of the feast, when the Passover was sacrificed, his disciples say to him, "Where would you like us to prepare in order to eat the Passover?" And he sent two of his disciples and he says to them, "Go into the city and you will meet a person carrying a jar of water: follow him, and where he enters in say to the master of the house, 'The teacher says "Where is the guest room where I may eat the Passover with my disciples?"' And he himself shows to you an upstairs room with a great spread ready. And there you will prepare for us." And the disciples went out and came into the city and found it just as he said to them and they prepared the Passover. And when it became early evening he came with the Twelve. And reclining and eating Jesus said, "Amen I say to you that one from among you will hand me over, the one eating with me." They began to be distressed and they say to him one by one, "Not I." But he says to them, "One of the Twelve, the one dipping in the dish with me. The Son of Man, on the one hand goes just as it is written concerning him, but on the other hand alas to that person through whom the Son of Man is handed over. Good to him if that person had not been born."

And as they were eating, taking bread, blessed he broke it and gave it to them and he said, "Take, this is my body." And taking a cup, giving thanks, he gave to them, and all drink from it. And he says to them, "This is my blood of the covenant, the [blood] poured out for many. Amen I say to you that I will definitely no longer drink from the fruit of the vine until that day when I drink it new in the dominion of God." And singing a hymn they went out onto the Mount of Olives.

And Jesus says to them, "All will be caused to stumble, because it is written:

'Strike the shepherd, and the sheep will be scattered.' But with the raising of me, I will go before you into the Galilee." But Peter said to him, "Even if all are caused to stumble, but not I." And Jesus says to him, "Amen, I say to you that you, today, this very night before the cock crows twice you will disown me thrice." But with great emphasis he says: "Even if I must die with you, I will not disown you." But all of them also said likewise.

And they came into an enclosed field which was named Gethsemane, and he says to his disciples, "Sit here while I pray." And he takes with him Peter, Jacob, and John, and he began to be very dismayed and distressed, and he says to them, "Very sad is my spirit unto death. Remain here and stay awake." And going on a little way he fell upon the ground, and he prayed in order that if possible the hour might pass away from him. And he said, "Abba the Father, all things are possible to you. Take away this cup from me. But not what I myself will, but what you [will]." And he comes and he finds them asleep, and he says to Peter, "Simon, you are asleep? Were you not strong enough to stay awake one hour? Stay awake and pray, in order that you not fall into testing; the Spirit on the one hand is ready, but the flesh on the other hand is weak." And again going he prayed saying the same word. And again coming he found them sleeping, for their eyes were heavy, and they did not know what to answer him. And he comes the third time and says to them: "You sleep, from now on are even you resting? Is it distant? [No] the hour has come, behold the Son of Man is handed over into the hands of sinners. Arise, let's go. The one who hands me over is near."

And immediately while he was still speaking Judas, one of the Twelve, appeared and with him a crowd with swords and wooden clubs accompanying the high priests and scribes and elders. But the one handing him over gave them the agreed-upon sign saying, "The one whom I will kiss is him. Seize him and lead him away securely." And coming immediately he approached him saying, "Rabbi," and he kissed him with every show of affection. But they laid their hands on him and seized him. But one from among those present, drawing the sword struck the servant, taking off his ear. And Jesus answering said to them, "As if upon robbers you come out with swords and clubs to arrest me? Day after day I was with you in the temple teaching and you did not seize me; but in order that the Scriptures might be fulfilled." And leaving him they all fled. And a certain young man was following with him wearing a linen garment over his naked body, and they seized him. But abandoning the garment he fled naked.

And they led Jesus away to the high priest's house and all the high priests and scribes and elders came with him. And Peter followed him from afar standing right inside the courtyard of the high priest, and he was sitting with the attendants and warming himself by the light. But the high priest and the whole of the council sought testimony against Jesus with the object of putting him to death, and they could not find it. For many bore false witness against him, and the witnesses were not in agreement. And some rose up bearing false witness against him saying, "We heard him saying 'I will pull down this sanctuary made with human hands and after three days I will build another not made with human hands.'" And not even so were the witnesses in agreement. And rising in the middle the high priest asked Jesus saying: "You do not answer anything? What about these things they testify against you?" But he was silent and answered nothing. Again the high priest asks him and says to him, "Are you the Messiah, the son of the Blessed One?" But Jesus said: "Am I?" and "You will see the Son of Man seated at the right hand of the Power and coming with the clouds of heaven." But the high priest tearing his robe says, "Why do we still have need of witnesses? You have heard the blasphemy, what do you think?" But all those condemned him to be liable to death. And some began to spit on him and blindfold his face and cuff him and say to him, "Prophesy." And the attendants greeted him with slaps.

And Peter being outside in the courtyard one of the female servants of the high priests and seeing Peter warming himself looking straight at him says, "Even you were with the Nazarene, Jesus." But he denied it saying, "Neither do I know [him] nor do I understand what you are saying." And he went outside into the forecourt [and the cock crowed].[3] And the slave girl seeing him began again to say to the bystanders, "This one is from him." But again he denied it. And after a little while again the bystanders said to Peter: "Truly, you are one of his, for you are even a Galilean." But he began to curse and swear that "I do not know this man of whom you speak." And immediately the cock crowed a second time. And Peter remembered the thing that Jesus said to him that "Before the cock crows twice you will deny me thrice." And he burst into tears.

15   And immediately, early in the morning the high priest held council with the elders and the scribes and the whole Sanhedrin binding Jesus, he was led away and handed over to Pilate. And Pilate asked him, "Are you the king of the Jews?" But answering he says, "It is you who say it." And the high priests accuse him of much. But Pilate again asks him saying, "Do you not answer anything? You see how many things they accuse you of." But Jesus answered absolutely nothing, so that Pilate wondered.

But at each feast he freed to them one prisoner whom they begged for. But there was one called Barabbas in prison with the revolutionaries, having committed murder in the insurrection. And the crowd going up began to ask just as he used

---

3. A good number of manuscripts (A, C, D, K, X, and others) add at this juncture that the cock crowed. On the one hand, this could be seen as an original part of the text since 14:30 did promise two cock crows, and the omission of the reference here could be seen as an attempt to conform Mark to Matthew, which mentions only one cock crow. As Metzger, *TCGNT*, p. 115, says, copyists might also have reasoned that Peter could not have known that the later cock crow was the second one unless he had first heard this one. This would be an argument for the later insertion of the phrase. On the whole, from the point of view of the Markan outline, it seems reasonable that the sentence is original, but it is placed in square brackets due to considerable uncertainty on the matter.

to do for them. But Pilate answered saying to them, "Do you will that I would free to you the King of the Jews?" For he knew that it was because of envy the high priests had handed him over. But the high priests stirred up the crowd in order that he would rather free to them Barabbas. But Pilate again answering said to them, "What then do you wish me to do with [the one whom you call]⁴ the King of the Jews?" But again they cried, "Crucify him." But Pilate said to them, "What evil has he done?" But they all the more cried out, "Crucify him." But Pilate wishing to make satisfaction to the crowd released to them Barabbas, and he handed over Jesus when he had him flogged, in order that he be crucified.

But the soldiers led him inside the palace, which is the Praetorium, and they summon the whole of the cohort. And they clothed him in purple and put on him a twisted-together thorny crown. And they began to salute him: "Greetings, King of the Jews," and they strike him on the head with a reed and spit on him, and bending the knee bow down to him. And when they had made fun of him, they took off the purple robe and reclothed him in his own clothes, and they led him out in order that they might crucify him.

And they impressed, while he was passing by, a certain Simon of Cyrene coming from the fields, the father of Alexander and Rufus, in order to carry his cross. And they bring him upon the Golgotha place, which is translated Skull place. And they gave him myrrhed wine, which he did not receive. And they crucified him and divided his clothes, casting dice for them [to decide] who would take what. For it was the third hour when they crucified him. And there was the inscription of his charge inscribed "The King of the Jews." And with him was crucified two bandits, one on his right and one on his left.⁵ And passersby abused him wagging their heads and saying, "Well, well, the one destroying the temple and rebuilding it in three days. Save yourself coming down from the cross. Let the Messiah, the King of Israel come down now from the cross, in order that we might see and believe." And those being crucified with him taunted him.

And at the sixth hour there was darkness upon the whole of the earth until the ninth hour. And at the ninth hour Jesus called out in a loud voice, "Eloi, Eloi lama sabbachthani," which is translated "My God, my God, why have you deserted me?" And some of the bystanders hearing him said, "See he calls Elijah." But someone running fills a sponge of sour wine put on a reed offers him to drink, saying, "Let's see if Elijah comes to take him down." But Jesus letting out a great cry ex-

---

4. This phrase in square brackets is found in some good early manuscripts, including ℵ, C, K, X, and others, but it is also omitted by A, D, W, and others. On balance, in view of Matt. 27:22, it seems likely this phrase was in Matthew's Markan source. See Metzger, *TCGNT*, p. 118.

5. V. 28 is not found in most of our earliest and best manuscripts of both the Alexandrian and Western text types (ℵ, A, B, C, D, et al.) and probably is not original. See Metzger, *TCGNT*, p. 128. It was likely added by scribes because of Luke 22:37.

pired. And the inner veil of the temple was torn in two from top to bottom. But the centurion the one standing facing him when he expired thus said, "Truly, this one was the Son of God." But there were also women observing from a distance, who were even Mary Magdalene, and Mary [the wife] of Jacob the small and of Joses the mother and Salome. Who when they were in Galilee followed him and served him, and many other women who went up with him unto Jerusalem.

And it was already evening, it was the day of preparation which is before the Sabbath, Joseph from Arimathea an influential Sanhedrin member came, who was eagerly awaiting the dominion of God, plucking up courage came in to Pilate and asked for the body of Jesus. But Pilate was amazed if he was already dead, and calling to himself the centurion he asked him if he died long ago. And having learned this from the centurion granted the corpse to Joseph. And buying fine linen taking him down wrapped him in the linen and laid him in the tomb the one which was hewn from rock, and rolled the stone upon the door of the tomb. But Mary Magdalene and Mary of Joses saw where he was laid.

A. The Plot (14:1-2)

The framework that begins and ends the passion narrative in Mark's Gospel has to do with the plot against Jesus and its execution, resulting in the death of the man from Nazareth. In other words, there is a very dark border to the portrait that follows, and each episode that comes between the beginning of Mark 14 and the end of Mark 15 further highlights the gathering gloom.

The Feast of Unleavened Bread was originally a separate festival from Passover, but by Jesus' time they were both celebrated from Nisan 15 to Nisan 21, and thus the two festivals had in effect been combined (see 2 Chron. 35:17; cf. Josephus, *Ant.* 14.2.1; 17.9.3). There is debate as to whether in 14:1 Mark is counting in a Jewish manner or a Roman one (elsewhere he uses the Roman watches of the day), but it seems likely, since Mark affirms that Jesus was killed on Friday before sundown (i.e., before the Sabbath; see 15:42), that this verse is referring to what transpired on Wednesday of Passion Week. If Mark is counting in a Roman manner, as elsewhere, then a case can be made for a compatibility between the Markan and Johannine evidence about the timing of Jesus' death, for in the Fourth Gospel Jesus is said to die on the day of the slaughtering of the lambs (Nisan 14). This would mean that the Last Supper was not a Passover meal, or at least that Jesus and the Twelve celebrated the Passover before others in Jerusalem, perhaps slaughtering their own animal.[6]

It is puzzling, but intriguing, that according to most commentators, Mark

---

6. On the issues in John see my *John's Wisdom* (Louisville: Westminster/J. Knox, 1995), pp. 231-39.

seemingly records in 14:2 that the authorities resolve here *not* to do what in fact they end up doing, namely, seize Jesus during the festival. But if in fact the festival began on Friday, Jesus was actually seized just before the festival, on Thursday evening (if, that is, Nisan 15 began Friday at sundown).[7] He is taken by stealth at night (cf. 8:31; 9:31; 10:33; 11:18; 12:12), and so neither during a festival event nor in the presence of the festival pilgrims in the temple precincts (contrast what happens to Paul in Acts 21:27-40). The upshot of all this seems to be that Jesus was at least dead, if not also buried, before the festival properly began.[8] What this narrative suggests, as does the trial before Pilate, is that the authorities had good reason to fear the crowds, for apparently Jesus was quite popular with them. Notice also that Mark does not blame the Jewish people for Jesus' demise. The plot is between one disciple and the authorities (both Jewish and Roman). Once again we see Mark's sandwich technique, for the anointing story is set between the hatching of the plot in 14:1-2 and the description of Judas's treachery in 14:10-11 (an example of *inclusio*), and as elsewhere the story in between exegetes the brackets around it and vice versa. The death of Jesus is in the air wherever we go in this narrative, but there is deep irony here. What the plotters intended for evil, God intended for good, so that in effect, ironically the plotters cooperate in helping Jesus accomplish his mission of giving his life as a ransom for many.[9]

B. The Anointing for Burial (14:3-9)

How are we to relate Mark 14:3-9 and par. to Luke 7:36-50? Should we see them as two forms of the same story, or as two different stories which through cross-fertilization, probably at the stage of oral tradition, have come to look more like each other than they did originally? I have argued elsewhere that there were originally two distinct anointing stories, and that Luke's story has perhaps been influenced by his knowledge of the Markan story. Luke does not choose to include Mark's story in his Gospel since the two stories do have enough similarities that Luke believes only one story of this type is required in his selective narrative.[10] Especially telling for the conclusion that these are two different narratives are the facts that the woman in Luke's story is identified as a notable sinner and the story in Luke 7 is not about a proleptic burial ritual at all. Rather, unlike the Markan

---

7. Another suggestion by J. Jeremias, *The Eucharistic Words of Jesus* (London: SCM, 1966), pp. 71-73, is that Mark means "not in the presence of the festival crowd."

8. For another view see R. H. Gundry, *Mark: A Commentary on His Apology for the Cross* (Grand Rapids: Eerdmans, 1993), pp. 801-2.

9. See J. Painter, *Mark's Gospel* (London: Routledge, 1997), p. 180.

10. See my *Women in the Ministry of Jesus* (Cambridge: Cambridge University Press, 1984), p. 110.

tale, Luke's story is about forgiveness of sins. By contrast, even a cursory examination of the Markan, Matthean, and Johannine stories makes very apparent that we are dealing with the same story, for the similarities are of the very essence of the tale.[11] I would, however, suggest that Mark may have placed this story here for theological reasons (to help exegete the significance of the plot, the Last Supper, and Jesus' demise), for the Johannine placement of the story in Bethany prior to the triumphal entry seems historically more probable.[12] In fact, it appears that Mark presents us with a more generalized account, in *chreia* form, of the more primitive and detailed Johannine account.[13] Noteworthy is the contrast between the extravagance of this woman (like the extravagant gift of the widow with two lepta) over against the attitude of those who object to the act, presumably the male disciples, though Mark does not say so specifically. One could also say Mark has framed the discourse which focuses on judgment on the temple with two female examples of true piety.[14]

Remember that the *chreia* focuses on the central figure (in this case Jesus) and a memorable saying or deed of his.[15] Other persons involved in the narrative fall into the background and are not given personal attention in such a biographically focused *chreia*. The *chreia* form explains why on the one hand we are told that the woman's deed will serve as a memorial to her wherever the gospel is preached, but on the other hand she is no more named than is the disciple or disciples who objected to her extravagance. It is what she did for Jesus, on whom the personal spotlight shines, not who she is, that is of consequence in such a biography. All figures are mentioned only insofar as they contribute to our understanding of the central figure. The fact that the name of the host is mentioned (Simon the [former?] leper) simply helps fix the biographical story in a precise locale, which is also typical of such *chreiae*.

In early Jewish culture there were a variety of reasons for anointing a per-

---

11. On the historical substance of the Markan story, see my *Women*, p. 111 and the notes, and Gundry, pp. 809-14. As Painter, p. 180, says, the Matthean form of the story, as is usually the case, is an abbreviated version of the Markan account with the one further specificity of telling us it was the disciples who objected to the waste of the perfume (Matt. 26:8).

12. On the probable independence from the Markan account of the Johannine version of the story, see my *Women*, pp. 112-13.

13. I have argued in detail in my *John's Wisdom*, pp. 1ff., that the Fourth Gospel represents the memoirs of a Judean disciple of Jesus (not John the son of Zebedee) who was an eyewitness to the events that transpired in Jerusalem, Bethany, and in general the environs of the Holy City. Mark by contrast represents the account of someone who was not likely an eyewitness to the anointing, an account he retrieved from the Petrine preaching or teaching.

14. Painter, p. 181.

15. It may be a point in favor of the suggestion that the saying in Mark 14:9 is a later and Markan addition to the pericope that normally a *chreia* would have one climactic memorable saying, in this case the saying of Jesus about the poor, not two.

son. Anointing the scalp or skin with oil usually did not serve the same purpose as anointing someone with perfume, especially expensive[16] and fragrant perfume. The latter was saved for romantic or cosmetic purposes or for burial rites (cf. Song of Sol. 1:12; John 19:39-40; Luke 24:1). What the woman in 14:3 is said to pour on Jesus' head is μυρον, clearly not oil. Nard was a well-known eastern perfume with a very potent fragrance which came from a root found in India (cf. *b. Šabb.* 62a; *Mo'ed* 1; *Šabb.* 1.291).[17] The cracking of the vessel indicates that the woman intends to perform an extravagant act, not saving any of the perfume for later. The vessel itself, though called an *albastron,* was not necessarily made of alabaster. In fact, Painter suggests that the term only refers to the spherical shape of the container.[18] More importantly, the perfume was worth a year's wages of a day laborer, which leads Hurtado to suggest that "the substance may have been a family heirloom, something that could be sold in times of financial need."[19] If so, this woman is acting very much like the widow with the two lepta, using all her social security for an act of devotion.

Here we have a story about a dinner in a surprising place (the house of a leper)[20] where a surprising event transpired.[21] The locale says something about Jesus' views on ritual purity, unless Simon was a former or future leper. Even if he was a former leper whom Jesus healed, there would still be the stigma attached to and fear of such a person on the part of many, but not Jesus.[22] We

---

16. On the use of this term see 1 Tim. 2:9 — πολυτελες.

17. L. Hurtado, *Mark* (New York: Harper & Row, 1983), p. 216.

18. Painter, p. 181.

19. Hurtado, p. 216. It is interesting that C. Myers, *Binding the Strong Man: A Political Reading of Mark's Story of Jesus* (Maryknoll, N.Y.: Orbis, 1988), p. 358, suggests that this is a wealthy woman since she has this expensive perfume, and so stands in contrast to the widow in this respect. The point then becomes that women from various points on the social scale were devoted to Jesus.

20. Myers, p. 358, sees a link with the very first miracle story in Mark 1:41ff., where a leper is healed. If so, this might favor the suggestion that Mark saw Simon as someone Jesus had already healed.

21. M. Hooker, *The Gospel according to Mark* (Peabody, Mass.: Hendrickson, 1991), p. 328, says this story is yet another piece of evidence for an underlying Aramaic version of this Gospel's material, as it is full of awkward, even clumsy, Greek phrases. On this subject see pp. 18-20 above.

22. One can hardly imagine Simon the leper being Simon the Pharisee (Luke 7) in light of the Pharisaic concerns about ritual purity. Nor can one imagine if Simon the leper was healed by Jesus quite apart from ritual observance, that he then went on to become a Pharisee! Finally, if Simon the Pharisee contracted leprosy and was healed by Jesus and not by ritual cleansing, it would be hard to imagine that he would continue to be a Pharisee instead of becoming a disciple of Jesus. There are of course a plethora of Simons in the NT (ten) and in Josephus (nineteen or twenty). People regularly named their children after the Maccabean hero.

may perhaps see the act of hospitality by Simon as his grateful response to the healing by Jesus. Also we have here "another instance of the Jesus mission operating by household hospitality."[23] This was an important principle which carried over into the early church. The house became not only the place for hospitality and rest but the venue in which the gospel could be shared on any day of the week, and in-house teaching offered. The mention in v. 5 of giving to the poor may be because during the festival a gift to the poor was expected, even required.[24]

It is possible that Mark has changed a story originally about the anointing of Jesus' feet to one about the anointing of his head with expensive perfume, symbolizing the preparation of a royal figure for burial, and royal figures are anointed from the head down. The motive of the woman in any case seems to be devotional, and Jesus clearly interprets the act as preparation for burial. The Gospel writer, however, may see it as an example of a woman playing a prophetic or priestly role, for it was prophets or priests that performed royal anointings.[25] More to the point, the act is seen as a symbolic prophetic act which previews what will happen to Jesus. Mark describes this event as a beautiful deed, and so as a paradigm for his audience to emulate. Extravagant love in the service of Jesus is always to be commended.[26] Jesus' command to the objectors in Mark is clearly to the effect that they should leave her alone and not trouble her about what she has done.

14:7 should be compared with 2:19-20, for the remark is not meant to suggest that there should not be good deeds performed for the poor, but rather that the amount of time available to perform acts of extravagant love for Jesus, whose time is almost up, is limited. The poor, by contrast, will always be available to receive such acts of loving-kindness. Anointing for burial was an activity that women were regularly involved with in Jesus' age and culture, but in Jesus' case they would be unable to perform the task in the rush to get him into the tomb. V. 8 in the Greek seems to be a deliberate echo of 12:44, where the widow put in everything she had, for it reads literally, "what she had, she has done."[27]

14:9 alludes to the worldwide mission of preaching the good news, spoken of as well in 13:10. This has suggested to many commentators that the saying is unlikely to go back to Jesus, but perhaps the original saying was something like "Amen I tell you wherever the good news is proclaimed, what she has

---

23. Painter, p. 181.

24. See Hurtado, p. 217.

25. See my *Women*, p. 113; and E. Schüssler Fiorenza, *In Memory of Her* (New York: Crossroad, 1985), p. xiv.

26. Notice that the woman is not commended for her prophetic foresight, however, as she probably had no thought of her act being anything but an act of devotion. See Hooker, p. 327.

27. See Hooker, p. 330.

done will be told as her memorial," and Mark has more explicitly linked the saying to world evangelism by the church.[28] That the saying is a creation of the Evangelist seems unlikely, for in *chreiae* it is precisely the closing memorable saying which is the reason the story is told in the first place. It is not a mere redactional addition. It is interesting that the woman in effect unwittingly performs an act that amounts to a proleptic memorial to Jesus but the story is originally told as a memorial to her! However, in the context of the Gospel it becomes a memorial to Jesus and his character as well.

C. Sold for Silver (14:10-11)

These two important verses must be set with 14:1-2, which together sandwich the virtuous act of the woman with the treachery of both antagonists and a follower.[29] Thus Mark's audience is given examples to follow and to shun in quick succession.[30] It needs to be remembered that the plot, according to 14:1-2, was initiated by the Jewish authorities, not by Judas.[31] The issue of ease or convenience seems to be the reason the authorities chose to proceed against Jesus on the eve of the festival despite their earlier qualms. Apparently this was too good an opportunity to pass up, and Mark tells us they rejoiced at it. Mark does not really tell us what Judas's motives or driving forces were (unlike the other Gospels), though it has often been conjectured that he was a zealot[32] who had great hopes for Jesus, hopes which were dashed when he saw the way Jesus handled the entry into Jerusalem and the corruption in the temple, which is to say without taking up arms against Rome. There is a strong emphasis in Mark on the degree of Judas's betrayal — he was "the one of the Twelve" who did this.[33] We are meant to think of both tragedy and treachery here. Mark does nothing to exonerate Judas; to the contrary, he tells us that he was actively looking for an

---

28. See my *Women,* p. 114, and the notes.

29. See Hurtado, p. 217.

30. Which, as does Mark 13, suggests that some of Mark's audience was definitely under pressure and could be in danger of acting like a Judas when push came to shove.

31. See Painter, p. 183. But he is probably going too far in suggesting that they simply corrupted Judas. Rather, Judas himself takes some personal initiative to betray Jesus.

32. See, e.g., E. Schweizer, *The Good News according to Mark* (Atlanta: John Knox, 1971), p. 292, and cf. my discussion in *The Christology of Jesus* (Philadelphia: Fortress, 1990), p. 97. E. Stauffer, *Jesus and His Story* (New York: Scribner, 1960), p. 112, even suggests that Judas, who was apparently a non-Galilean (from Kerioth), was a plant of the Jerusalem authorities within Jesus' inner circle. This, however, contradicts the notion that Jesus had picked the Twelve, and did so at a time before the Jerusalem authorities would likely have known of or been interested in Jesus.

33. See Hooker, p. 331.

opportunity to hand Jesus over. That God uses Judas's action to fulfill the divine plan of salvation nonetheless does not make Judas's own self-initiated actions any less heinous.

D. Preparations for a Feast (14:12-16)

Several factors about this narrative seem anomalous. Firstly, there is the apparently clandestine nature of the preparations. The disciples are to follow a man who is occupied with an unusual task (for men; cf. John 4)[34] to a destination he, but not the disciples, will know.[35] Note also that the text says the man will meet them, not the reverse, which suggests that he will be looking for them. Secondly, the Master seems to be sending them to prepare for a Passover prior to the appropriate time. Lastly, Jesus remarks about "my room," as if he had a predetermined and familiar place in mind. Yet the disciples obey Jesus without question here, as if his orders are not cryptic.[36] It is interesting that while in the rest of Mark 14 we find references to the Twelve, the references in vv. 12-16 are only to the disciples, presumably including Judean disciples.[37]

Not surprisingly, various commentators have puzzled over this passage, and the usual conclusion is that we have here examples of Jesus' prophetic foresight.[38] But one must note the close similarity between this passage and 11:1-6, where Jesus sends two disciples into a village, telling them what they will find and do. There are eleven consecutive words in the Greek that are identical when one compares 11:1-2 to 14:13. Prophetic foresight may be what Mark is trying to suggest, but if so, nothing is made of the fact, and the disciples do not react with astonishment. Perhaps we have here an indication that Jesus had been to Jerusalem before and there was a familiar place where he took meals within the city (for the Passover had to be eaten, if at all possible, within the Holy City), and in fact arrangements complete with secret signal had been made in advance for him and his disciples to show up in a particular house on that night.[39] The likelihood that this is a correct conclusion is increased by a careful reading of the Fourth Gospel, which suggests not only that Jesus made repeated trips up to

---

34. Men might carry water in a skin, but not in a jar meant to gather water for household purposes, which was a woman's task. See Gundry, p. 821.

35. Myers, pp. 360-61.

36. Which in itself favors the clandestine explanation, with the disciples in on the secret plan, rather than the explanation of prophetic foresight, which only Jesus has.

37. See Hooker, p. 332.

38. See Painter, pp. 183-84.

39. See Hurtado, pp. 220-21: "Such secrecy was required, probably, because Jesus knew the authorities were looking for an opportunity to arrest him away from large public gatherings."

Jerusalem during his ministry, but also that he had a Judean disciple he was especially close to, the Beloved Disciple (not one of the Galilean disciples), in whose house he reclined as a guest at the head of the "table" during Passover week.[40] Since the Passover meal seldom finished before midnight and needed to be taken within the city walls of Jerusalem, this meant Jesus would have had to remain within the jurisdiction of the priestly authorities late into the night.[41] Indeed, if there is any validity to the tradition about the upper room being on Mount Zion, he would have been taking Passover within a stone's throw of Caiaphas's house.

A careful reading of v. 12, which has two temporal clauses, suggests that Mark is speaking to his audience in a non-Jewish way of thinking about days. The Jewish way, of course, was to reckon a day from sundown to sundown; the Roman way, from midnight to midnight. By the Roman way, the first day of Unleavened Bread (Nisan 15) and the day of the slaughter of the lambs (Nisan 14) were one and the same, for the former began on the evening of the latter.[42] There is much to commend in some of A. Jaubert's suggestions that the meal Jesus had with his disciples was a Passover meal, not celebrated on the normal day but rather earlier, perhaps following the calendar found in *Jubilees* and perhaps at Qumran. Though I disagree with her that this Passover day was Tuesday rather than Thursday, I think she is correct that Jesus was crucified, as John says, on the day of the slaughter of the lambs — Nisan 14. I further think part of the confusion comes from the fact that the Johannine account depicts a meal taken earlier in the week, which was not a Passover but a Greco-Roman–style banquet, complete with extensive symposium, which is to say with teaching.[43]

E. A Solemn Ceremony (14:17-26)

Passing Over the Passover? ─────────────────────────────────

It is all too easy to get embroiled in controversy as to whether the Last Supper was in fact a Passover meal. In my view it was, though it was celebrated early.[44] The earliness may be one good reason why it was celebrated in secret, for this would have meant that the

---

40. See my discussion in *John's Wisdom*, pp. 1ff., 235ff.

41. Hurtado, p. 221.

42. See Hooker, p. 334.

43. See my *John's Wisdom* on John 13, and cf. A. Jaubert, *The Date of the Last Supper* (New York, 1965).

44. For a fresh discussion arguing that the Last Supper was a Passover meal, see now M. Casey, *Aramaic Sources of Mark's Gospel* (Cambridge: Cambridge University Press, 1998), pp. 219-52, which includes a strong argument for an Aramaic substratum to this story.

disciples or their friends would have had to slaughter the lamb themselves, not have it done in the temple precincts. Yet they were in Jerusalem! This circumvention of the sacrificial protocol would itself have been an affront to the priestly authorities. Sacrificing animals for the feast outside of Jerusalem was of course not an unknown practice, for we find it at Qumran, at Mount Gerizim, in the Diaspora, and presumably in Galilee as well by those who were devout but unable to go up the ninety or so miles to the festival in Jerusalem.

It is, however, passing strange that neither the lamb nor the rite of purification is mentioned in the Markan verses that describe the meal. Is this because Jesus celebrated the meal with the other Passover elements but without the lamb? He was, of course, as we shall see, reinterpreting the Passover elements in a new way, and so one cannot argue that it is impossible that other innovations (e.g., no lamb) might have also been involved. Still it seems unlikely that the meal would have been held without the lamb, which was the main course, so to speak. Thus we must conjure with an "illegal" Passover meal, celebrated early and without the due process of the temple sacrificial rites, for the lamb had been slaughtered and dressed elsewhere.[45] This is yet another piece of evidence supporting the view that Jesus was a radical Jew, unafraid to alter tradition and even set aside portions of the Torah as no longer binding in the wake of the coming of God's eschatological saving activity.[46]

The story of the meal is told in telegraphic fashion in Mark. V. 17 says Jesus came with the Twelve in the early evening to take the meal, which may mean that the two sent ahead to prepare the way were disciples who were not among the Twelve, perhaps Judean disciples.[47] The first remark from Jesus' lips in this section (v. 18) is that one of the Twelve is going to betray him. It would appear that this meal was taken exclusively with the Twelve.[48] The "effect of this announcement for the reader is to isolate Jesus, not only from the Jewish authorities, but even from his own followers, making him seem totally alone though surrounded by others."[49] The announcement can only have had a chilling effect on the whole proceeding, for we are talking about the deepest sort of betrayal, as is made more evident by the citation of Ps. 41:9-10 in John 13:18, though one could just as well have cited Ps. 23 — "thou preparest a table before me in the presence of mine enemies." Here, as elsewhere, allusion to Scripture suggests in-

---

45. If Jesus indeed had relatives down the road in Bethlehem (where lambs were raised for sacrifice in Jerusalem), could he have relied on them to perform the sacrificial act?

46. See above, pp. 226-30, on Mark 7.

47. See Painter, p. 184.

48. It is my view that the meal portrayed in John 13, involving the beloved disciple himself, was taken earlier in the week, while this clandestine Passover was indeed taken on Thursday night and likely involved just the Twelve plus Jesus. There would likely also have been servers involved, perhaps the beloved disciple's family members if this meal transpired in the same spot.

49. Hurtado, p. 221.

directly that all is going according to the divine script for Jesus' life.[50] The story is full of irony, for despite all this celebrating and bonding over a meal, the participants are going to betray, deny, and desert Jesus very soon indeed. Yet Mark does not trouble to narrate either the fulfillment of the sign (dipping with the betrayer in the bowl) nor the exit of Judas. "The warning hangs in the air so that the reader is like the disciples at this point, not knowing whether the sign is fulfilled, not knowing whether Judas responded to the warning."[51] Apparently Mark assumes that at least some of his audience knows the outcome of these events.

According to v. 19, the disciples are extremely upset with Jesus' words, and notice how each one asks Jesus in turn what amounts to a question seeking exoneration — "You surely don't mean me, do you?" Notice that their perturbation comes from the accusation against one of the Twelve, not in the first instance from the horrible prospect of what this means for Jesus' fate. The Twelve continue to be a self-concerned bunch. "It is part of Mark's desire to emphasize again and again that even the disciples remain undiscerning to the very end (cf. 8.17-21)."[52] Jesus is to go forward to the cross without his inner circle, his closest allies and support group.

In the highly stratified world of male culture, the persons closest to the guest of honor or host at a meal were considered the most important guests. It is then a measure of the depth of the perfidy that Jesus says in v. 20 that it will be the one who dips the bread in the bowl with him that will betray him. Mark makes nothing of this, but there may be an implicit presenting of the story drawing on a text such as Ps. 41:9. V. 21 expresses aptly the horror of the matter. While it is true that it was part of the divine plan that the Son of Man must die as a ransom for many (10:45), nevertheless this does not exonerate Judas, who acts of his own volition to betray Jesus. About him, Jesus says, it would have been better if he had never been born, which echoes what Jesus said in 8:33-34.[53]

Vv. 22-26 provide the earliest Gospel description of the Last Supper meal itself. Scholars have often debated how much Mark himself has redacted his source in light of later Christian practice, especially in regard to the words over the bread and the cup. It is instructive to compare this primitive Gospel account to that found in our earliest source for this material — 1 Cor. 11:23-26. It has been often noted that the Lukan form of these sayings (Luke 22:19-20) is closer to the Pauline material than the Markan form,[54] which may suggest that

---

50. See Juel, p. 144.

51. Painter, p. 185.

52. Schweizer, p. 299.

53. Myers, p. 361.

54. In my view this is not merely because Luke had another source for some of his passion narrative material but because he was also a sometime companion of Paul. See the intro-

Mark has indeed done some editing for the sake of his largely Gentile audience. This would be consistent with the pattern of Markan editorial work we have found elsewhere in this Gospel,[55] and reminds us that the earliest Gospel does not always provide the earliest form of this or that saying or narrative. The matter is more complex than that.

The first thing that needs to be said about Jesus' reinterpretation of the elements of the Passover is that he does not reinterpret the lamb itself or the bitter herbs. Rather he focuses on the bread and the wine. Secondly, it is hard to make too many fine points about the words of institution on the basis of the Greek text, since Jesus likely spoke in Aramaic. Thus, for instance, this would mean that he said something like "this — my body," for the verb "is," found in the Greek, would not be in the Aramaic, and furthermore the phrase "my body for you" probably cannot be said in Aramaic any more than the phrase "my blood of the covenant" can.[56] What can be gathered from the reconstruction of the original is that Jesus was giving in advance to his disciples, in symbolic form, the benefits of his death, and asking his disciples to take them into themselves. Jeremias puts it this way:

> When at the daily meal the *paterfamilias* recites the blessing over the bread . . . and breaks it and hands a piece to each member to eat, the meaning of the action is that each of the members *is made a recipient of the blessing by this eating;* the common "Amen" and the common eating of the bread of benediction unite the members into a table fellowship. The same is true of the "cup of blessing" which is the cup of wine over which grace has been spoken, when it is in circulation among the members: *drinking from it mediates a share in the blessing.*[57]

It also seems clear that Jesus saw his death as the act which instituted or ratified the new covenant. Thus this meal, while it could be said to foreshadow the eschatological banquet (on which cf. Isa. 25:6; 65:13; *1 Enoch* 62:14; Bar. 29:8; Pirke Aboth 3.20), is actually about instituting a new covenantal relationship between God and God's people. This assumes that the old one was no longer in force or enforceable, or at the very least needed replacing. "For suddenly we realize that Jesus is *not* after all participating in the temple-centered feast of Passover (note that Mark never mentions the eating of lamb). Instead he is expropriating its symbolic

---

duction to my *Acts of the Apostles: A Socio-Rhetorical Commentary* (Grand Rapids: Eerdmans, 1998). But there is also evidence that the Lukan form has been influenced by the Markan version at Luke 22:20, where he combines the Pauline and Markan statements. See Schweizer, p. 300.

55. See, e.g., his treatment of the divorce material in Mark 10, pp. 274-80 above.

56. See Schweizer, pp. 301-3.

57. J. Jeremias, *The Eucharistic Words of Jesus* (London: SCM, 1966), p. 232.

discourse (the ritual meal) in order to narrate his new myth, that of the Human One who gives his life for the people."[58] The story is once again laden with irony, since the implication of the theological assertion about the expiating blood of Jesus poured out for many (v. 24) is that death (the ultimate pollutant in the Jewish purity system) is the means of ultimate cleansing.[59]

If indeed this story accurately represents Jesus' understanding of things (whatever the particulars about the authenticity of the words of institution), what astounding faith and trust must Jesus have had to have believed that his death would accomplish such a thing, and then to be so supremely confident that he could symbolically distribute the benefits of that death in advance of it happening! This high moment must be compared to his moment of struggle in the Garden of Gethsemane.

The words of institution would surely have been taken by the Twelve as symbolic, for that is how they would have understood the original interpretations of the elements of the Passover. But they must have had very grave difficulties accepting the "this is my blood" saying and then drinking the wine, since partaking of human blood was seen as abhorrent by early Jews, and indeed, would likely be seen as drinking someone's very life or life force (cf. John 6:52; *1 Enoch* 98:11). Even if the saying were seen as purely symbolic, it still would have surely offended the sensibilities of the disciples.

V. 25 is significant not least because it indicates that Jesus expects to be present at the messianic banquet in God's dominion. While the statement seems to echo some of the Passover liturgy, its sentiment should be compared to 1QSa 2, where we find the Qumranites looking forward to partaking of a meal in the last days in the company of an anointed priest and the Messiah of Israel (cf. 1QS 6). Notice that Jesus anticipates sharing in no more Passover meals, or at least not drinking any more wine, until the kingdom comes. This might be compared to traditional vows of abstinence while undergoing some holy process or period (cf. Num. 6:4; 30:2; 11QTemple 53-54).[60] Then he will drink it new, a statement on the discontinuity between Jesus' life at present and the eschatological state of affairs (cf. Isa. 25:6; *2 Bar.* 29:5-8; Matt. 8:11; Luke 14:15; Rev. 19:9). "Placed where it is, the saying suggests that Mark perhaps sees the death of Jesus as being in some way instrumental in bringing about the arrival of God's kingdom."[61]

V. 26 refers to the singing of a hymn, and it was indeed customary to sing

---

58. Myers, p. 363.

59. On which see J. Neyrey, "The Idea of Purity in Mark's Gospel," *Semeia* 35 (1986): 91-127, here p. 115.

60. One may raise the question as to whether Jesus' refusal of myrrhed wine at the cross and wine vinegar on the cross is part of this deliberate abstention. See pp. 396-400 below on these matters.

61. Hooker, p. 343.

some of the Hallel psalms at Passover celebration (Pss. 113–14 before the meal, Pss. 115–18 after it). This reference supports the view that Jesus partook of no ordinary meal on the last night of his earthly life, but rather of a celebratory and sacred one.

F. Repeated Denials and Desertion (14:27-31)

V. 26 serves as a transition to the next three scenes in the passion narrative, for the setting of those scenes is on the Mount of Olives. The scenes include prediction of denial, threefold implicit betrayal by a failure to watch with Jesus when he comes to the disciples three times wanting support, and finally the betrayal and arrest of Jesus. In short, these scenes become increasingly dark, with the relationship of Jesus and the disciples going from bad to worse to worst.

V. 27 deals with the general desertion of all the Twelve and links it to a prophetic Scripture — Zech. 13:7. Notice the difference between the way the verse is cited here and the way it is in the original, where it reads "strike the shepherd. . . ." Here we have "I will strike the shepherd," which stresses that it is by God's design and action that this happens to Jesus.[62] This means that once more we see the Markan theme that "even human weakness and hard-heartedness are part of the divine purpose. What takes place is both foretold in scripture and accepted in obedience by Jesus."[63] Notice that the statement of fulfillment of Scripture comes at those junctures where the story takes an unexpected turn — at Judas's betrayal, at the disciples' desertion, and at the arrest of Jesus through the perfidy of Jesus' "friend." The setting of this series of happenings is both natural and surprising. On the one hand, it was normal for pilgrims to camp on the Mount of Olives, and so Judas would know the vicinity where Jesus would likely be. Yet on the other hand, the same locale where Jesus had predicted the fall of the temple becomes the site of his betrayal — a far cry from the military victory predicted in Zech. 14 for the shepherd when he came to this locale. Or is it? In Mark's Gospel the road to triumph over all the forces of darkness leads through the cross, and thus ironically the darker the tableau becomes, the nearer Mark's narrative is to the dawn of victory, the rising of the Son. J. Marcus reads the data in the following suggestive fashion:

> The allusions to Zechariah 9–14 in Mark 14.22-28, then, may well be read by Mark and his audience in such a way that they provide a contrast to the inter-

---

62. As Hurtado, p. 232, points out, the whole context of Zech. 13 warrants close scrutiny, for it also speaks about a new people of God being created as a result of God striking the shepherd who stands next to him (13:7-9).

63. Hooker, p. 344.

pretation of those passages circulating in Jewish revolutionary circles known to them. Instead of seeing the arrival of the kingdom of God in the appearance of a triumphant Messiah figure on the Mount of Olives, a miraculous deliverance of Jerusalem from the Gentile armies that surround it, and a resanctification of the Temple through its cleansing from pagan influence, Mark would see the arrival of the kingdom of God, paradoxically, in the deliverance of Jesus to his Jewish enemies on the Mount of Olives, his humiliating death at the hands of Gentiles in Jerusalem, and the proleptic act of Temple destruction that accompanies that death (see 15.38).[64]

It is true that every time Jesus speaks of his passion in this Gospel, it provokes a crisis among the disciples and a flurry of verbiage.[65]

V. 28 is an exceedingly important verse from the point of view of Mark's theology, as it points to a positive conclusion beyond the cross and, some would say, makes it unlikely that 16:8 was the original conclusion of this Gospel.[66] The desertion of the disciples will not mean the end of their following of Jesus. Intriguingly, this verse is missing from the Fayyum Gospel fragment, a papyrus from the third century A.D. from Egypt. The verb here, προαγω, can either mean "go ahead of" (and thus go there before the disciples go) or "go at the head of" (and thus lead a group to Galilee). 16:7 needs to be compared at this juncture, and it suggests that the former interpretation is correct.[67] The verse also serves as a promise not only that Jesus' future will involve vindication by God, but also that the disciples will be regathered as a group.

As was true in Mark 8, Peter fixates on the part of Jesus' predictions that refers to the coming desertions and the death of Jesus, rather than on the promise of resurrection and regathering. In v. 29 Peter strongly affirms that though all others may be offended (or embarrassed) and so put off by Jesus' message (picking up on the prediction in v. 27), and so desert him, Peter himself will not do so. Peter's remark, however, provokes an even darker rejoinder, just as was the case in 8:33. Jesus' offers another "Amen" saying, testifying strongly that that very night Peter will deny Christ three times before the cock crows twice. V. 31 provides an equally strong rebuttal by Peter: "Even if I must die with you, I will by no means disown you."[68] The verb απαρνησομαι is a strong one and

---

64. J. Marcus, *The Way of the Lord: Christological Exegesis of the Old Testament in the Gospel of Mark* (Louisville: Westminster, 1992), p. 161.

65. W. Lane, *The Gospel of Mark* (Grand Rapids: Eerdmans, 1974), p. 511.

66. Noting Myers's (p. 365) judgment: "This first augury of the end of the story is arguably the single most important narrative signal in the second half of the Gospel, a kind of 'literary lifeline' that Mark throws to the reader."

67. See Hooker, p. 345.

68. This is about as strong a form of denial as is possible in Greek. See Hurtado, p. 232.

really means "to disown," i.e., to divest oneself of an association which one had previously. Interestingly, we are told that all the other disciples chimed in at this juncture affirming the same thing. But of course, all of them, including Peter, will do just the opposite of what they say, under pressure. Augustine put it well: "God knows in us even what we ourselves do not know in ourselves. For Peter did not know his weakness when he heard from the Lord that he would deny him three times" (*Tractate on John* 32.5).[69]

G. The Garden of Earthly Disasters (14:32-42)

At vv. 32ff. we are told that Jesus and the disciples go to a field in an estate called Gethsemane (which means oil press), and thus into a grove of olive trees. It is only John's account that calls it a garden (John 18:1). I agree with Lane that Jesus does not likely take the three with him because he is lonely and needs moral support (but cf. Mark 3:14a); rather he wants to help prepare them as he prepares himself for the events about to transpire.[70] Notice that Jesus does not spend time commiserating with the disciples but tells them to sit and pray, and stay awake, while he goes off to do the same.[71] This is the third time Mark portrays Jesus at prayer (once at the beginning of the ministry [1:35], once in the middle [6:46], and here).[72] It is interesting that in each case the hour is late and Jesus is basically alone. According to v. 33, Jesus becomes extremely distressed and dismayed, or to translate these verbs more literally, he is shuddering in distress and is appalled and anguishing.[73] He takes on the role of the righteous sufferer of the Psalms (Ps. 55:4-5). He says, "my spirit is very sad unto death." Surely there is an allusion to Ps. 42:6 here. Jesus is so sad he could simply die of a broken heart, not least because of how badly the disciples are going to fail him.[74] In v. 35 Jesus throws himself on the ground (a gesture suggesting utter

---

69. See T. C. Oden and C. A. Hall, eds., *Mark*, vol. 2 of *The Ancient Christian Commentary on Scripture* (Downers Grove, Ill.: InterVarsity, 1998), p. 209.

70. Lane, pp. 514-15.

71. Which, of course, raises the question as to who could have heard this praying of Jesus, since the disciples were both at a distance and also were nodding off. See Schweizer, pp. 309-10. Does Mark mean us to think of a postmortem transmission of such information? In any event, we have an independent witness to the essence of this event in John 12:27 (cf. 14:31; 18:11) and Heb. 5:7, and most scholars accept that the story has an historical basis. "It is difficult to believe that this scene would have been invented by Jesus' followers, for the tendency would have been to present him facing death serenely and calmly" (Hooker, p. 346).

72. See Myers, p. 365.

73. Myers, p. 366.

74. See Hilary of Poitiers, *On the Trinity* 10.36: "But a sadness even unto death implies that death is the completion, not the cause, of the sadness." See Oden and Hall, p. 209.

supplication and submission)[75] and speaks of letting the hour pass from him, and in v. 36 of letting the cup pass from him, both being ways of speaking of his coming death. The reference to the hour, however, reminds us once more of the apocalyptic language Jesus tended to use, for "the hour" is one appointed and determined by God, and indeed usually refers to the hour of the consummation of God's final judgment (Dan. 11:40, 45 LXX).[76]

Why does Jesus ask for this reprieve? Is he afraid? Is he simply a frightened human being or a reluctant martyr?[77] Two clues suggest another interpretation, one here and one at the scene on the cross. Here there is the reference to the "cup," that is, the cup of God's wrath.[78] At the cross Jesus speaks of being God-forsaken. It is, then, not so much the suffering itself that Jesus shrinks from, but rather facing abandonment by the one he has known as Abba all this time, and even more daunting, facing the wrath, the judgment of God on the cross. He dreads, as any human would, undergoing such judgment and punishment. As Garrett stresses, Jesus is undergoing a real and severe test or temptation, and the emotive language in the narrative is meant to indicate this fact. It requires great endurance for Jesus to pass such a test when his every natural inclination is to let the cup pass.[79]

Notice how even here he calls God Abba, another touch of irony in view of the fact that in the same breath he is accepting the drinking of the cup offered to him by Abba. This is the only place in Mark where we find the Abba address, the most intimate form of addressing God,[80] and it unveils for us something of the personal nature and intimacy in Jesus' relationship with the Father. The early church was to retain this form of intimate address for itself (Gal. 4:6; Rom. 8:15). Perhaps the most crucial part of this passage is the "nevertheless" clause — "nevertheless not my will but thine be done." As Schweizer says: "Jesus' sovereignty is that of one who has been victorious in temptation. And so Jesus' willingness to obey is more impressive because he walks this path consciously and deliberately."[81] There are several apparent echoes of the Lord's Prayer (which Mark does not include in his Gospel) in this prayer — the Abba

---

75. In fact, Gundry, p. 855, says it indicates panic.

76. See Schweizer, p. 312.

77. It is interesting how later church fathers (perhaps in part because of notions about God being impassible?) try to avoid the notion that Jesus suffered in regard to his own fate. For example, in Ignatius, *Eph.* 7.2 and *Pol.* 3.2, we find the comment that Jesus in himself is free from suffering, but suffers on our behalf. This seems to be an attempt to avoid the conclusion that Jesus might be concerned about himself and his own demise.

78. See pp. 377-78 above.

79. S. Garrett, *The Temptations of Jesus in Mark's Gospel* (Grand Rapids: Eerdmans, 1998), p. 89.

80. See my discussion in *The Christology of Jesus*, pp. 215-20.

81. Schweizer, p. 315.

address, the stress that God's will be done, and then after the prayer, Jesus' stress on the disciples not falling into temptation.[82]

Jesus himself prays three times to God, which was customary for a Jew to do when in distress (cf. 2 Cor. 12:8; Dan. 6:10, 13).[83] Jesus returns and finds the disciples asleep three times. Is this a parallel of Peter's threefold denial? In any case, it shows the lack of readiness of these disciples for what is about to transpire. They should have stayed awake and prayed not to fall into temptation. Notice that Peter is chided directly with his personal name, Simon. Yet despite protests, the disciples do fall and fail to pass the test. "Even at this delicate point in the narrative [Mark] does not relinquish his unrelenting criticism of the three 'leaders'!"[84]

The saying about the spirit being willing and the flesh weak in v. 38 refers not to the human spirit, but rather to the Holy Spirit, which is literally eager/ready (πρόθυμον). This conclusion is supported by the OT text to which Jesus here alludes — Isa. 31:3 and possibly Ps. 51:11-12. Human flesh, however, is oh so weak. V. 40 has the phrase "they did not know what to answer him," which was used earlier to describe the disciples' disorientation at the transfiguration (9:6). It is difficult to know what to make of the word απεχει in v. 41. On the surface it seems to mean "that's enough" (sleeping?).[85] Or possibly it means "that settles it" or "that does it," an expression indicating that things have been brought to closure.[86] Yet, in the other Markan occurrence of this verb (7:6), it refers to something being distant. If this translation is correct, then Jesus is being sarcastic, mouthing what the disciples are thinking about the end of these matters: "It's distant."[87] Jesus has said the betrayer draws near, but they, with their lack of battle readiness, are thinking it's far off.

There is no more time for pleading or cajoling the disciples, or even for warnings. The hour is upon Jesus. It is time for the Son of Man to be delivered into the hands of sinners, which could mean Gentiles, or possibly bad Jews and Gentiles. In either case, it is a negative comment on those he is handed over to, and there may be an allusion to Isa. 53 here. Thus Jesus rouses the disciples, saying, "Rise up, let's go, the deliverer of me is near." Jesus knows clearly what treachery is about to befall him. And his worst trial is yet to come. Gethsemane is "but the prelude to the final, most severe time of trial that he will undergo in his suffering and death at the hands of sinners."[88] It is no ordinary test he will

---

82. Hooker, pp. 348-49.

83. See Schweizer, p. 310.

84. Myers, p. 366.

85. Hooker, p. 350.

86. V. Taylor's translation aptly brings to the surface Jesus' incredulity over the disciples' behavior: "Still asleep? Still resting? The End is far away? [No] The hour has struck!" *The Gospel according to St. Mark* (New York: St. Martin's Press, 1966), p. 557.

87. See the detailed discussion in Gundry, pp. 856-57.

88. Garrett, p. 91.

face, but the eschatological test which involves evil at its worst, and God's very judgment on evil (cf. Rev. 3:10). The true and final confrontation with the powers of darkness actually comes on the cross when Jesus experiences our God-forsakenness, which at the same time entails our embracing of the darkness.

H. The Kiss of Death (14:43-52)

From the very beginning of this pericope in v. 43, we see the emphasis on Judas being one of the Twelve, thus making his act all the more inexplicable and treacherous. In fact, each time he is mentioned in this Gospel, he is mentioned as the one who handed Jesus over.

There is said to be a crowd with him with swords and wooden clubs, but it need not have been a large crowd. Nothing is said by Mark about Roman soldiers. Yet something more than a rabble is implied because this crowd came with the temple officials. With Judas are chief priests, scribes, and elders.[89] This is the same list of persons mentioned previously in Jesus' first passion prediction (8:31), but it is surprising that the elders are not mentioned in the reference to the plot in 14:1-2. That a prearranged signal is needed to indicate who Jesus is may mean that these officials, or at least the temple police (who were Levites), didn't know what Jesus looked like, or at least that in the dark a positive confirmation of identity was needed to make a quick arrest.[90] "The secret signal, the surprise attack at night, and of course the heavily armed contingent all imply that the authorities expected armed resistance."[91] A kiss was a normal form of greeting between a disciple and his teacher, a token of real friendship. Judas says that "the one whom I kiss should be grabbed and led away securely." The compound verb καταφιλεω used in v. 45 means to kiss with every show of affection, thus making the betrayal even worse. It is striking that after the betrayal by the kiss, Judas completely disappears into the night, never to appear again in Mark's narrative.[92]

V. 47 mentions the taking off of the high priest's slave's ear, but neither

---

89. As Painter, p. 191, says, the very group that made up the Sanhedrin.

90. Painter, p. 190.

91. Myers, p. 367.

92. The Fathers were often puzzled by the choice of Judas as one of the Twelve. For example, consider the remarks of Ephraem the Syrian answering why Judas was chosen: "To show his perfect love and his mercy . . . he therefore washed his feet, [those very feet] by means of which he had arisen and gone to [Jesus'] slayers. Jesus kissed the mouth of him who, by means of it, gave the signal for death to those who apprehended him. He reached out and gave bread into that hand that reached out and took his price, and sold him unto slaughter" (*Commentary on Tatian's Diatessaron* 2.219) (Oden and Hall, p. 216).

the victim nor the perpetrator is mentioned by name here,[93] and notably there
is no condemnation of the action in Mark, unlike in Matthew and Luke (Matt.
26:52-53; Luke 22:51).[94] Apparently it is unimportant to Mark as he focuses
biographically on his central character, Jesus. Jesus is incensed at the posse who
treat him as a common criminal, coming with armed troops, when he could
have been taken peacefully at any time while he was teaching in the temple.
"The night arrest out on the slopes of the mount of Olives is thus contrasted
with Jesus openly, freely, and daily teaching in temple."[95] Jesus sees in this rough
treatment a fulfillment of Scripture, and presumably Isa. 53 is in view.

It is at this juncture that we are told that all the disciples flee, and also a
young man who has nothing on but an expensive linen tunic flees. We do not
know who this young man is, but it is possible it was a young John Mark.[96]
There seems to be little other reason to include such a note, unless, as Lane has
argued, there is an allusion to Amos 2:16 — "even the valiant flee away naked in
that day" (i.e., the day of judgment).[97] Myers has suggested a connection with
the story about Jesus' burial and resurrection, since the only other place we find
the words "linen cloth" is at 15:46 and the only other mention of a young man
(νεανισκος) is at the tomb on Easter morning (16:5). He suggests that the
young man is a sort of allegorical symbol of the community or followers of Jesus first betraying and fleeing in shame, but then rehabilitated, reclothed, and
testifying.[98] But elsewhere the biographer Mark does not give way to allegory in
the narrative itself (unlike in some parables). It may be that we should see a
contrast between the young man who does not flee until grabbed, and so is
more stouthearted than the disciples, and the disciples, who flee without direct
provocation.[99] Notice that the posse is not interested in anyone but Jesus. There
is no hint that they chased the others, though they might have tried to grab the

---

93. One may think this is odd since, according to John 18:10-11, it was Peter, and Mark
is presumably relying on a Petrine source. But perhaps Mark wishes to spare the memory of
Peter at this juncture.

94. Myers, p. 367.

95. Painter, p. 192, who rightly adds that this description implies a considerable period
of time teaching in the temple.

96. See Gundry, p. 882. It is possible that Judas had led the posse to John Mark's house
where the Last Supper may have been held (cf. Acts 12:12-13), and not finding Jesus there,
went on to Gethsemane, being trailed by John Mark, who hastily threw some clothes on.

97. Lane, p. 527. In my view Schweizer, p. 317, is right to reject this suggestion.

98. Myers, p. 369.

99. On the supposed expanded version of Mark (secret Mark), which has a tale in
which Jesus raised this young man from the dead and then initiated him into the faith, teaching him the mystery of the kingdom of God, see Hooker, p. 353 n. 1. It must be said that only
Morton Smith, who published the story, has ever claimed to have seen the eighteenth-
century manuscript in which is found a purported letter by Clement of Alexandria which includes this tale.

young man. "The isolation of the Son of Man is absolute. Even the brief incident concerning the young man simply intensifies the atmosphere, which
seems to say 'Save yourself if you can.' Against this background, the quiet dignity with which Jesus calmly goes on his way stands out clearly."[100]

I. Trying Circumstances (14:53-65)

V. 53 begins the tale of the trial of Jesus, and it appears that Jesus was first led
away to the house of the high priest, Caiaphas.[101] This house had to have been
of some size, for we are told it had a courtyard and an outer gate where we find
Peter, trailing along at some distance. The quorum for the Sanhedrin was
twenty-three, so there must have been a banqueting or meeting hall of some
size if the trial actually took place at this locale. V. 54 tells us that Peter was
warming himself, which suggests it was a chilly spring night. Peter was apparently keeping company with some of the servants or hired hands of the high
priest, including the female doorkeeper who was to cause him some difficulties.
Jesus and Peter come to the place of their testing and trial, but the outcome in
each case is very different. Mark is quite frank at v. 55 in saying that both the
high priest and the whole Sanhedrin were seeking witnesses to testify against
Jesus so that they could have him killed. Though this is no doubt rhetorical hyperbole, it nevertheless means that the basic intent of this emergency meeting
called on the eve of the festival was prejudicial. Justice was not the aim of this
assembly.[102] The majority of the audience was surely not open to the possibility
of Jesus being exonerated. Indeed, they wished to see the opposite happen. The
members of this assembly would have included both the high priest and his
family; the elders, who were members of prominent families in the Jerusalem
area; and the scribes, some of whom would have been attached to Pharisaic
groups. Nonetheless, the dominant orientation of this group would surely have
been Sadducean and would have had a special concern for the temple. It is thus
no surprise, if Jesus was believed to have made some threatening remark about
the temple being destroyed, that this group would want to have seen Jesus out
of the way.

 Nor should we be surprised that only one charge is listed — "this fellow

---

100. Schweizer, p. 319.
101. Most of the supposed historical problems with the trial before the Sanhedrin
come from the assumption that the rules found in Mishnah tractate *Sanhedrin* (see *m. Sanh.*
4.1) applied in the time of Jesus. This is far from certain, especially if we are dealing with a
trial that is hastily arranged and breaks with various of the normal protocols in order to get a
job done prior to the festival.
102. See Myers, p. 375.

said, 'I will pull down the man-made sanctuary and in three days build another not made with human hands.'"[103] Notice that this charge is in the first person, whereas the remarks in Mark 13 merely refer to the fact that the temple would be destroyed, which in fact suggests God rather than Jesus would be the cause of its demise. As Hooker points out, Mark chooses the term ναος here, which, since it is not his usual term for the temple, may refer to the inner sanctuary, including the Holy of Holies. If so, the charge is even more grave.[104] Why does Mark mention only this charge? Because it helps to confirm his theology that Jesus' coming to Jerusalem does indeed precipitate the end of the temple, and furthermore, that he replaces it with his own resurrection body and the fellowship united to it, a building made without human hands.

The problem for the Sanhedrin is that the two witnesses had to agree, and in detail, before a guilty verdict could be pronounced. Add to this the consternation caused by Jesus' refusal to grace these false charges (cf. Pss. 27:12; 35:11) with a rebuttal (for he would be expected to answer the charges), and we have a very frustrated assembly. It may be that Mark is portraying Jesus as the righteous sufferer who suffers in silence (Pss. 38:13; 39:9; Isa. 53:7).[105] Thus, finally the high priest tries the direct approach[106] by asking, "Are you Messiah, the Son of the Blessed (One)?"[107] These two titles are in fact just two different ways of saying the same thing, but there is irony that the priest is so cautious about the name of God but quite careless about God's honor and justice in the way he adjudicates these proceedings.[108] One source for messianic thinking about Messiah as God's Son was Ps. 2, perhaps coupled with 2 Sam. 7:14. Though these texts do not really imply the divinity of the person in question, Jesus' response certainly appears to do so. The high priest is only asking "Do you claim to be Messiah?" not "Do you claim to be divine?" Thus the response of Jesus is shocking, suggesting that the Son of Man will fulfill the divine role as final judge, indeed as judge of the high priest and the Sanhedrin!

Jesus' response is unlike that recorded in Matthew. Here he simply says εγω ειμι, and since it is a direct answer to a direct question, it may not imply divinity, but what follows this answer certainly seems to.[109] But the remark of Je-

---

103. The expectation of the destruction of the old temple and the building of a heavenly one is found in early Jewish literature in *1 Enoch* 90:28-36 and *Jub.* 1:17, 27-28.

104. See Hooker, p. 358.

105. See Painter, p. 195.

106. On the likely authenticity of this dialogue with Jesus, see my *Christology of Jesus,* pp. 256-61.

107. "Blessed One" being a typical Jewish circumlocution for God.

108. See Hooker, p. 560.

109. Interestingly Myers, p. 376, suggests that we translate the words as a question with Jesus returning the priest's question with a question of his own — "Am I?" This interpretation is possible (and better explains the parallels in Matt. 26:64 and Luke 22:70) of εγω ειμι,

sus need not be taken as a statement; rather it can be seen as a question. Jesus goes on to quote a combination of Ps. 110:1 and Dan. 7:13.[110] Jesus, in short, says this august body will see the Son of Man both seated in the place of highest honor and authority (next to the Father's place of honor and authority)[111] *and also* coming on the clouds to judge. Both statements imply at least some sort of divine or quasi-divine status for the Son of Man.[112] The allusion to the clouds makes clear that a theophany is being spoken of, with the divine being riding on a cloud chariot said to be Yahweh's vehicle in the OT. Thus Jesus is boldly claiming a status even higher than the high priest has asked about.

The high priest's response to this is a sign of dismay and perhaps also of mourning. He tears his robe and asks why there is a need for witnesses since it is clear blasphemy has been spoken. "Perhaps the tearing of the high priest's garments points forward to the tearing of the sanctuary curtain in 15.38; certainly at this moment the fate of both Jesus and the temple is sealed."[113] As Myers suggests, there may be irony here, as in 3:29 Jesus said that one who blasphemes against God's Spirit is guilty of unending sin. By implication the high priest has accused the Spirit working in Jesus of blasphemy, and thus paradoxically he is the one guilty of blasphemy, not Jesus.[114] We are then told that all condemn him to death, which was the penalty for blasphemy (by stoning; see Lev. 24:10-16). This would presumably include even Joseph of Arimathea, who must not have believed Jesus was more than a divinely inspired human figure, perhaps a prophet. The reactions recorded in v. 65 are in fact ritualistic, meant to show disgust and abhorrence for what they had heard, and they seem to be echoing the description in Isa. 50:6. It is possible that the request that Jesus prophesy once he is blindfolded reflects a belief that a prophet or Messiah would be able to sense things about people through his sense of smell, a sign of miraculous powers. Jesus, however, refuses to play this game.

---

but it does not mean he is being evasive in light of the next clause. Rather, it would mean that, as in Mark 12:35-37, Jesus prefers to use his own term of self-designation over the traditional Davidic ones.

110. On how the judging scene in Dan. 7 informs Mark's presentation, see Marcus, pp. 166-67.

111. Matthew and Luke both add the phrase "from now on." Are they thinking of the immediate exaltation of Jesus to the right hand of God at death? Cf. Acts 2:33; 5:31.

112. See E. Boring's helpful recent study, "Markan Christology: God-Language for Jesus?" *NTS* 45 (1999): 451-71, who concludes: "The explicit use of God-language for Jesus by later NT authors and the classical creeds is in continuity with the Christology already present in Mark. . . . John, Nicea, and Chalcedon understood and developed Mark's Christology in a more profound sense than was done by either Matthew or Luke."

113. Hooker, p. 357.

114. Myers, pp. 376-77.

J. The Unkindest Cut of All (14:66-72)

The account of Jesus' trial is sandwiched between two halves of the telling of Peter's demise, with one story commenting on the other (not unlike the way the woman's anonymous loyalty contrasted with Judas's treachery earlier in Mark 14).[115] Jesus' faithfulness and truthfulness to the end is contrasted with Peter's unfaithfulness and dishonesty.[116] Once again we are dealing with a heavily ironic situation, for just as Jesus is being denounced as a false prophet, his prophecy about Peter's denials is coming true! Peter is accused by the high priest's servant girl of being an associate of Jesus. Peter's response is: "I neither know nor understand what you are saying." This might be seen as pretending not to understand the girl's Judean dialect, or perhaps what was meant by the accusation. In fact, however, Lane has shown how Peter is using the technical form for a legal denial of something (see *m. Sheb.* 8.3).[117] As we shall see, Peter is going to go to any length to deny this connection, including invoking a curse upon himself. We in effect see the situation of denial snowballing. The first lie leads to a more emphatic series of lies and denials in order to save face and appear to be consistent. But as Schweizer says,

> Peter's temptation came in a very unimpressive and incidental way. It was not the appropriate situation for confessing one's faith. The question he was asked did not really concern his faith at all. . . . Furthermore, there was no reason for him to vindicate himself publicly. The one who asked was simply a servant girl who probably had no idea what it really meant to be a "Nazarene," so neither a "yes" nor a "no" would have indicated anything about faith. Consequently, if Peter had replied in the affirmative, he would have risked his safety without giving any witness to his faith.[118]

Thus it was that Peter failed a much lesser test than Jesus faced, and in the process denied himself and his master, all the while Jesus was affirming his own identity. After the first denial Peter goes out into the forecourt, perhaps to make a getaway if need be. The reference to the cock crowing should likely be maintained in view of the reference in v. 72 to the second cock crowing, which has good manuscript support.[119] The servant girl is persistent, however, and tells the bystanders that Peter is definitely from among the crowd of Jesus' followers, a more specific charge of being a disciple of Jesus. Peter again denies the connection. The woman then plays a sort of trump card — "Truly you are from

---

115. See Lane, pp. 538-41.

116. Schweizer, p. 320.

117. Lane, p. 543.

118. Schweizer, p. 332.

119. See p. 362 n. 3 above.

them for you also are a Galilean." We are not told how the woman knew this, but it surely must be because of Peter's accent. Even in such a small country there were regional accents.[120]

The third time Peter denies he curses and swears: "I do not know the man." The irony is of course that he is right. He does not really know or understand Jesus. It is an awful thing to swear to God that one does not know God's Son. The cock crows again, and Peter then remembers what Jesus had said about the cock. Notice that Peter did not react to the first crowing of the cock. Peter then bursts into tears, realizing the magnitude of his sin and failure, which his master had correctly foretold.[121] It is not clear whether Mark is telling us he threw himself down and wept[122] or he broke down and wept,[123] but either way he is inconsolable over his moral failure at this point. This completes the Jewish side of the story. In Mark 15 we will hear of Gentiles and their various sorts of reactions to the demise of Jesus.

K. Justice — Roman Style (15:1-15)

If we are meant to see 15:1 as a reference to a second called meeting of the Sanhedrin, then the one mentioned in Mark 14 should likely be seen as a pretrial hearing meant to determine a viable charge against Jesus. But probably Mark's intercalation technique has required him to phrase things the way he does in 15:1.[124] Thus the chapter begins with a resumption of reference to the Jewish trial, only now the reference is to the making of a final decision on the matter. In many regards the trial before Pilate is simply a rerun of the trial before the Sanhedrin, but the charges which prompt action in each case differ.[125] Myers points out the following parallels:

---

120. A parallel from today would be the case of England, where there are still distinctive regional accents.

121. Eusebius and Chrysostom both make the valid point that Mark and his source must have had an extraordinarily high standard of truth telling to record this story. In fact, as Chrysostom suggests, Mark tells the story of Peter's denials more vividly and in greater detail than the others. "And it is for this very reason that he is called Peter's disciple" (*The Gospel of Matthew* 85.1; cf. Eusebius, *Proof of the Gospel* 3.5). See Oden and Hall, pp. 220-21. Schweizer's more modern verdict is similar: "The account of Peter's denial in vss. 66-72 probably corresponds to the historical facts. It is told in a very straightforward and credible manner" (p. 328).

122. The verb normally means "to throw over" or "to lay on."

123. See Painter, p. 197.

124. Hooker, p. 356.

125. It is worth noting that there is a further historical example of the Jewish authorities handing a troublesome prophet to the Romans in the case of Jesus ben Ananias, who also announced the doom of the temple after the time of Jesus (see Josephus, *War* 6.300ff.).

14:60-62	15:4-5, 2
. . . the high priest	And again Pilate
questioned Jesus saying,	questioned him saying,
"Have you no answer to make?	"Have you no answer to make?
What about the things	See what they
charged against you?"	are charging you?"
But he was silent	But Jesus answered nothing
and made no answer.	further at all. . . .
And again the high priest	And Pilate
questioned him and	questioned him,
said to him,	
"You are Messiah,	"You are the king
son of the Blessed One?"	of the Jews?"
And Jesus said,	And Jesus answered him and said,
"Am I!"	"You said!"[126]

Not only are there these parallels, but in each case the trial is followed by a consultation first between the high priest and the Sanhedrin, then between Pilate and the crowd as to what is to be done with Jesus. Both scenes end with a verdict and then a mocking and torturing scenario. Jesus is thus rejected and treated in similar manner by both Jewish and Gentile authorities.[127] A decisive point is that a Roman official would not crucify a man on charges of blasphemy against the Jewish God, for crucifixion was the punishment for crimes against the state such as insurrection or high treason.

We are told at 15:1 that the high priest was holding council early in the morning.[128] Was the official meeting of the Sanhedrin the night meeting, or was there a morning meeting preceded by an unofficial hearing at night? As Hurtado points out, if the night meeting had been official, there would have been no need for a morning meeting.[129] Lane, however, argues that the phrase in question (συμβουλιον ποιειν) cannot mean "hold a council" but rather has the sense of "take a decision" or "make a resolution" as it does elsewhere (cf. Mark 3:6; Matt. 12:14; 22:15; 27:7; 28:12).[130] Thus he argues that what we have here is the final

---

126. Myers, p. 370.

127. Myers, p. 370.

128. Sometimes the historical plausibility of the Jewish trial is questioned on the grounds of it being a night trial. These are insufficient grounds on two counts: (1) this may be an example of emergency proceedings to deal with a pressing situation on the eve of the feast; (2) Mark may mean to portray this trial as an example where legal constraints are jettisoned. See Myers, p. 372.

129. Hurtado, p. 245.

130. As the textual variants witness at this point, there is an ambiguity in the phrase.

phase of the night meeting.[131] We know for a fact that Roman trials were normally convened at dawn, so it was imperative for the Jewish proceedings, whatever they amounted to, to be done by then. Thus I think Lane is likely right. The phrase refers to the decision taken at the end of the Jewish proceedings. This notice should be seen as a resumption of 14:63-64, after the interlude about Peter's denials. Mark probably does not mean to suggest that there were two Jewish trial sessions. Mark is careful to divide the day of the crucifixion up into three-hour periods from morning to evening (cf. 15:1, 25, 33, 34, 42). As Painter suggests, this indicates the gravity and importance of the day, but in narrative time Mark is also saying in effect that this is the day the earth nearly stood still, for in Mark's view we are at the fulcrum of time and history.[132]

The decision in fact was to bind Jesus and lead him away. Notice the "handing over" terminology here and elsewhere in this chapter. This may have recalled for the Gentile audience their own being handed over to the authorities, and clearly the Roman trial would be the one they would most likely identify with. Thus Mark shows his audience how to behave by the example of Jesus (remembering the warnings in Mark 13 about one being summoned before the authorities). Since the Romans reserved the power of the sword for themselves, the most the Sanhedrin could do was hand Jesus over, unless they resorted to vigilante justice (e.g., by stoning him). But had they stoned Jesus, it would have been a more private affair, not sanctioned by the state or witnessed by a large crowd before the tribunal. If the point was to eliminate Jesus in the most public and shameful way possible so as to stamp out the Jesus movement, then the Romans must be involved. If they wanted a legal action which made Jesus a lawbreaker and troublemaker, the Romans must act. Thus the Jewish authorities proceeded as they did.

There is, however, considerable debate about where Jesus was led away to — the Antonia Fortress where the Praetorium of Pilate was, or the palace of Herod? We know that the latter is where Roman officials normally stayed when coming to Jerusalem for the feasts (cf. Josephus, *War* 2.14.8 and 15.5; Philo, *Leg.* 38), and this palace was situated in the northwest corner of the city, not next to the temple. Lane insists the palace must be the locale of this trial, which would mean that the traditional Via Dolorosa begins in the wrong spot and heads in the wrong direction.[133]

Who was Pontius Pilate? He was of the equestrian class (a knight), which means he had some property but was not a true patrician. Knights were used to govern the small and sometimes more troublesome areas of the empire. Prior to the reign of Claudius these governors were called prefects, not procurators,

---

131. Lane, p. 545.
132. Painter, p. 198.
133. Lane, p. 548.

due to the classification of the province. Mark, however, is writing for an audience of a later date, and so is likely using the term familiar to his own audience. Pilate ruled from A.D. 26 to 36, and both Philo and Josephus make clear that he was a rather cruel and vicious man, and his relationship with the Jews was far from cordial (cf. Philo, *De Legat.* 38; Josephus, *War* 2.9.2-4; *Ant.* 18.3.1-2).[134] This favors the view that the reason Pilate wanted to release Jesus was not because he was a fair-minded man, but because he wanted to spite the Jewish officials, whom he despised. There is, of course, nothing in our text that leads to the conclusion of the later Christian work, the *Acts of Pilate,* that suggests Pilate was so affected by Jesus' testimony that he later became a Christian (and indeed a saint in the Coptic Church). After Jesus' day Pilate was removed from office due to Jewish complaints directly to Rome.

Justice was carried out in different ways in the Jewish and Gentile systems of jurisprudence. The Sanhedrin was like a group of judges who heard witnesses against an accused man or woman, and if the testimonies agreed in detail they judged the accused. In the Roman system, however, judgment was the sole responsibility of the magistrate, and the judicial process mainly involved interrogation of the accused by the magistrate but also entailed the hearing of witnesses. Jesus, of course, save for basically one remark at each trial, does *not* in fact cooperate with such interrogation, and unlike so many in his position, he does not try to justify his actions or himself. This is likely what so puzzled Pilate.

Thus at 15:2 we must envision that the trial has gone through several stages perhaps, and Mark is only summarizing its conclusion. Here Pilate asks Jesus directly: "Are you the King of the Jews?" If this is an historical motif, then it is surely likely that Pilate was consulted in advance about what charge to ask Jesus about. The claim to kingship is the important thing, for such a claim would indeed constitute high treason and it is the title Jesus is labeled by for the rest of this chapter (cf. 15:9, 12, 18, 26, 32). Jesus' response here, unlike the final Son of Man response before the Jewish tribunal, may be seen as ambiguous. It can either be translated "that's what *you* say" or "you've said it." Note that Jesus' response (in what language — Greek?) is not so clear that it prompts Pilate's immediate order of execution.[135] Rather it prompts further questioning of the witnesses.

---

134. I am largely unpersuaded by the attempt of H. Bond to rehabilitate Pilate in *Pontius Pilate* (Cambridge: Cambridge University Press, 1998). True, the Gospel portrait is in some ways more sympathetic in its portraiture than Philo or Josephus, but this is only a marginal improvement. The truth is, he is depicted in the Gospels as a vacillating, self-serving anti-Semite who could be obstinate occasionally. The latter quality is more emphasized in Josephus and Philo.

135. Hooker, p. 367, says rightly: "Mark can hardly have understood it [i.e., Jesus' response] as equivalent to a straightforward 'Yes,' or Pilate would have had no choice but to convict Jesus straight away of insurrection. But neither can it be a straightforward denial; the response is non-committal."

At v. 3 we hear that the high priests accuse Jesus of many things. In other words, they try the buckshot approach, hoping something will eventually strike the target. Pilate again turns to Jesus for a response, but this time he doesn't answer anything (note the double negative in the Greek, which causes the second negative to be translated as a positive in English). Jesus' silence causes Pilate to wonder, and perhaps it is meant to cause Mark's audience to remember the description in Isa. 53:7-9. Now, of course, this is the sort of response Jesus' miracles had earlier produced. Pilate is surprised by Jesus' lack of defense and defensiveness, and this perhaps tips him off that something suspicious is going on.

At v. 6 we hear of a custom to release one prisoner at each feast. This custom, according to some scholars, is a fabrication of the Gospel writer. Lane was able to produce some evidence that on occasion a Roman magistrate would free someone on the basis of the clamor of the people for the freedom of that individual.[136] Josephus does not, however, mention such a custom. In Roman law there were two sorts of amnesties that could be granted. One was called *abolitio,* the other *indulgentia.* The former involved the acquittal of one not yet condemned, and Jesus would surely have fallen into that category at this juncture in the proceedings.

At v. 7 we are introduced to Barabbas, whose name according to a textual variant at Matt. 27:16 was Jesus Barabbas. This, in turn, has led to the suggestion that Pilate misheard the crowd when they were shouting for the release of Jesus Barabbas, thinking they were asking for Jesus of Nazareth. But there is no clear evidence for such a conclusion here, and most of the earliest and best manuscripts do not have the name Jesus appended to Barabbas. We are told that Barabbas was a revolutionary involved in some insurrection who committed murder in the process.[137] Here indeed was a proper candidate for crucifixion, and doubtless Mark wishes to play up the irony here. Jesus is going to be killed for the sort of crime that the man set free actually committed.

Pilate at some juncture brings the trial before the crowd. In v. 9 it seems clear that he is presenting Jesus as the candidate for release. "Do you wish me to release the King of the Jews?" is surely a leading question. As Schweizer stresses, Pilate's question implies that the people have not in fact asked for anyone in specific.[138] We are told at v. 10 that Pilate knows quite well that the Jewish officials don't like Jesus and want to get rid of him. The word used here is "envy,"

---

136. Lane, pp. 552-53.

137. Whether we should call him a zealot or not depends on one's analysis of the zealot movement. See my *Christology of Jesus,* pp. 81-88. In my view there was a zealot movement well before the Jewish War, as M. Hengel, *Die Zeloten,* 2nd ed. (Leiden: Brill, 1976), argued.

138. Schweizer, p. 337.

perhaps meaning they envy Jesus' following or his honor rating, or the large crowds' positive response to his teaching. The verse seems to suggest that Pilate know Jesus is innocent, in which case what follows reveals that Mark is not offering a positive portrayal of Pilate. What Mark is concerned about in the passion narrative is a rhetorically effective account that engenders pathos in the audience as the narrative climaxes.

Again at v. 11 we hear of the high priests being instigators of the action. They stir up the crowd to cry for Barabbas's release. At v. 12 Pilate in fact makes a dangerous move, turning over the final decision about Jesus to a volatile and hostile crowd. He asks, "What do you wish me to do with the King of the Jews?" The cry for crucifixion is a bloodthirsty one.

Notice at v. 14 that Pilate seems to indicate that he can't find any evil in Jesus or his deeds, or at least not sufficient evil for the extreme punishment being clamored for. Pilate, however, knows well he cannot afford to have a howling mob on his case at feast time, unless he wants to deal with a riot. Thus v. 15 says that Pilate, wishing to make "satisfaction" to the crowd, releases Barabbas and hands over Jesus to be crucified, after having him flogged, a normal prelude to Roman execution.[139] Flogging itself could produce death, for it was with the dreaded *flagellum,* which had bits of lead and bone tied to it, or even hooks which could tear the flesh off the bone of the victim. Since such torture could go on indefinitely, many a criminal died from the flogging. It was not an uncommon practice if the person to be dealt with was a non-Roman. The point was to inflict pain (punishment) and further humiliate the victim (cf. Acts 22:25). Possibly Isa. 53:12 LXX is in the background of this verse.

L. Adding Injury to Insult (15:16-24)

Where the soldiers led Jesus after the verdict is hard to say. V. 16 suggests it was to a place inside the palace called the Praetorium, but it might possibly mean in the courtyard of the Praetorium. Once there, the whole σπεῖραν, which may mean a cohort (600 men) or possibly a maniple (200-300 men), were present to escort him. Lane suggests these were the soldiers Pilate brought with him when he came to the city. In either case, it denotes a considerable number of soldiers (cf. John 18:3).[140]

Purple was of course the color of royalty, something the Phoenicians had originally been traders in, being the product of a shellfish leading to a murex dye. The soldiers twisted together a thorny crown. Then in further mockery they saluted Jesus as follows: "Hail, King of the Jews," a salutation that imitates

---

139. Hooker, p. 369.
140. Lane, p. 558.

one regularly offered Caesar. Hellenistic kings wore a laurel wreath on their heads, but Lane suggests that the crown of thorns (made out of the acanthus bush or of palm spines) was meant to emulate the famous many-pointed, or diadem, crown.[141] Jesus was then struck with a reed and spit on as an object of disgust (see Isa. 50:6), but at the same time they bent the knee to him. A Gentile audience would likely have read this with acute embarrassment, for many Roman Christians were likely proud of their Roman heritage. Having made fun of Jesus, the soldiers stripped off his robe, put his clothes back on him, and led him out to be crucified. But the mocking turns out, unbeknownst to the soldiers, to be a parody of the truth. It may be noted that in various places we see allusions to OT passages, especially the Psalms, but Mark does not make the allusions explicit usually.[142] But there are also parallels in this account to a similar incident that happened in Egypt a bit later in the first century. Philo (*In Flacc.* 36-39) tells us that when King Agrippa (who at the time was recognized by Rome as king of the Jews) arrived in Egypt, the populace ridiculed him by laying hold of a demented person named Carabas, and putting a crown and a royal robe on him, giving him a scepter, and addressing him as "lord."[143] Notice that in this ongoing narrative Jesus is disrobed twice, a clear shaming device in each case.

We are told at v. 21 that Simon of Cyrene was pressed into service to carry the cross,[144] an unusual occurrence, for Plutarch tells us that the prisoner was expected to carry the crosspiece himself (*Mor.* 554A). This likely means Jesus was so weak from the flogging that he was unable to carry the crosspiece all the

---

141. Lane, p. 559.

142. Various of the church fathers saw this whole chapter as irony laden. For example, Cyprian notes: "He was even covered with the spittle of his revilers, when, but a short time before, with his own spittle he had cured the eyes of the blind man. . . . he who has offered us the cup of salvation was given vinegar to drink. He the innocent, he the just, nay rather, innocence itself and justice itself is counted among the criminals, and truth is concealed by false testimonies. He who is to judge is judged and the Word of God, silent, is led to the cross" (*The Good of Patience* 7). There was, in fact, a whole history of interpretation devoted to spinning out the ironies of the passion narrative. Cf. Gregory Nazianzen: "He is given vinegar to drink and gall to eat — and who is he? Why one who turned water into wine, who took away the taste of bitterness" (*Oration* 29; *On the Son* 20). See Oden and Hall, pp. 226-28.

143. I agree with Myers, p. 379, that Mark is certainly not trying to portray the Roman authorities favorably here. This Gospel was not intended to fall into official Roman hands, and it is certainly not an apologetic to such officials. It is rather *kleinliterateur,* that is, literature meant for the Christian community in Rome, and portrays things from below and not by and large for those who are the elite of society. Indeed, Mark may be critiquing abusive Roman power here.

144. The text in fact says he was coming in from a "field," which would normally imply coming in from work. This would in turn imply that this happened not on the Day of Passover, but perhaps on the Day of Preparation. See Schweizer, p. 345.

way to the execution spot.[145] Apparently Simon was a Diaspora Jew who had come in from the fields (cf. 11:8) for the festival, and it is quite plausible that he would have been black, though he might have been a Jewish colonist in Cyrene.[146]

Only Mark mentions his children (cf. Matthew), and this seems to suggest their familiarity to Mark's audience. Interestingly, in 1941 a burial cave in Israel used for Cyrenian Jews was found, and there was an ossuary which read Alexander son of Simon. From Rom. 16 we read of a Rufus who is a Christian who lives in Rome. These three sources may well be talking about different people, but if they are the same person, we have some interesting light shed on our text. Perhaps the most important point to be made is that the reference to these two children of Simon strongly suggests that this Gospel had to have been written during those children's lifetimes, while they would be known by Mark's audience. All other things being equal, this favors a date for this Gospel prior to the destruction of Jerusalem.

Jesus was taken to a place called Golgotha, which, translated, says Mark, means the place of the Skull. That he has to translate again points to a Gentile audience. We are not sure where this place is, but the more likely of the two spots (Gordon's Calvary or the spot where the Church of the Holy Sepulchre is) is the one with the longest historical pedigree, which is to say the latter. The word "Calvary" comes from the Latin *calva* (skull). If the name of the place suggests a location, it suggests some sort of bare nob or hill. It was certainly both Jewish and Roman tradition to execute people outside city walls (cf. Lev. 24:14; Num. 15:35-36; 1 Kings 21:13; Acts 7:58; Plautus, *Mil.* 2.4.6-7). That the Holy Sepulchre is now within the third wall of "old Jerusalem" does not contradict the above suggestion, since that wall was built by Herod Agrippa I after Jesus' time. The locale of the Church of the Holy Sepulchre was outside the city wall in Jesus' day.

V. 23 simply says that someone gave or tried to give Jesus some myrrhed wine (i.e., drugged wine; cf. Ps. 69:21).[147] This was apparently a humanitarian act meant to ease the pain of what was happening and was about to happen, somewhat similar to the modern administering of morphine. This, then, would seem to have been the offer of some Jews, not the Gentile soldiers, for Prov.

---

145. For an attempt to analyze the story in terms of its rhetorical potential, see B. K. Blount, "A Socio-Rhetorical Analysis of Simon of Cyrene: Mark 15.21 and Its Parallels," *Semeia* 64 (1993): 171-98. I think he is right that the passage has an epideictic function, praising the action of Simon and holding him up for emulation. He is an example of cross-bearing discipleship.

146. Cyrene is in the country now known as Libya.

147. Notice how Matt. 27:34 substitutes gall for myrrh to better conform the story to Ps. 69:21.

31:6-7 may suggest that such an offer was a Jewish tradition (cf. *b. Sanh.* 43a). We know that myrrh in sufficient quantities would have a narcotic effect.

Jesus, however, would not take the drug, which suggests he wished to face his death without artificial aids. He wished to be alert and awake. It may also suggest he wished to die quickly, for such a drug (unlike morphine), while lessening the pain, would also prolong the agony, making a person more capable of enduring the pain for a longer period of time. In fulfillment of Scripture, we are told that the clothes of Jesus were divided by the soldiers (Ps. 22:18), who cast lots to decide who got what. It was ordinary Roman practice for a person to be crucified naked as a shaming device, but the Jewish practice of one about to be stoned was to permit a loincloth (*m. Sanh.* 6.3), which may have been the case with Jesus (though the Roman control of the process seems to suggest otherwise).

M. Death at Stake (15:25-41)

Crucifixion — the Extreme Penalty

Death on a cross was a horrendous way to die, for it was basically by means of suffocation that one expired, or possibly a combination of exhaustion and suffocation and exposure to the elements. Eventually the man could no longer hold up his chest cavity, and the result was suffocation, often after great gasps for breath. This practice was even considered barbaric by various of the great Roman writers, and of course Roman citizens were exempt from such a form of execution, which shows that the sentiment of horror was likely rather widespread. Cicero expresses the sentiment well. After calling crucifixion the grossest and most cruel and hideous sort of execution, he adds: "If we are to be threatened with death, then we want to die in freedom; let the executioner, the shrouding of the head, and the very name of the cross be banished from the body and life of Roman citizens, from their thoughts, eyes, and ears!" (*Verr.* 5.64, 66).

Nails were often used for crucifixion, and of course this means of impaling a person on a board also caused blood to flow and so hastened death. In all probability what Jesus was expected to carry was the crossbar of the cross, which, once one was impaled on it, was dropped into a slot in the vertical beam which was already set in the ground. At that point the person's feet would be secured either with nails or ropes. The reason for the nails seems to be the prevention of escape, for in noncelebrity crucifixions or during a war there would frequently not be a guard, and often persons lived for a good while, sometimes long enough to be taken down from a cross, especially under cover of darkness. The cross would sometimes be only a few feet off the ground, allowing friends to approach the victim and attempt a rescue. In Jesus' case, however, the reference to a pole on which was offered a drink in a sponge suggests he was rather high off the ground. Also, the scornful remark (v. 32) to come down may indicate some height. It was the Roman law that executioners had the right to the possessions of the one executed, but in Jesus' case there would have been precious little. Here Ps. 22:18 is seen as fulfilled.

H. R. Weber sums up some of the particulars not emphasized above: "If the con-

demned man was intended to be visible from afar, the high cross was chosen [see the reference to the sponge on the pole offered to Jesus]. Usually though, the pole measured no
more than seven feet. This meant that wild animals could tear the crucified man apart. The
feet of the victims were not supported by a footrest as Christian art has depicted it since
the seventh century, but were tied or nailed to the pole. Usually, the condemned man 'sat'
on a peg *(sedile* or *cornu)* which was fixed to the middle of the pole. . . . Generally, the crucified one died of gradual asphyxiation."[148]

V. 25 causes major problems for any biblical scholar, for it is apparently irrecon-
cilable with John 19:14, which says Pilate did not pronounce his verdict until
the sixth hour — i.e., noon. Besides this, one must allow some time for Jesus'
Roman trial after sunrise when the Sanhedrin had finished, and 9 A.M. seems
too early for Pilate to have been finished with Jesus. Neither Matthew nor Luke
includes this material, which suggests they saw its difficulty. Lane suggests this
verse was added later, though the textual evidence makes this a weak argument.[149] It is just possible that v. 33, which seems to try and fix the hour of Jesus' death at noon, may have caused someone to count backwards and insert
v. 25 here.

V. 26 speaks of the inscription nailed to the cross above the victim. This
would be a wooden board whitened with chalk on which letters were written
in ink specifying Jesus' crime. In Jesus' case it suggested he was executed as a
rebel, an insurrectionist. Now this inscription is important, for it indicates
clearly that Jesus had to have done or said something, however badly misinterpreted, to justify this charge of being King of the Jews. In other words, the
idea that Jesus was Messiah or King could not have been an invention of the
early post-Easter community. Doubtless the Jewish officials found this galling. Jesus was being ironically proclaimed to be who he was in public and by
Gentiles! But as we shall see, this becomes a verbal proclamation by a centurion in a moment.

V. 27 says Jesus was crucified with two "robbers." The phrase "one on the
right, one on the left" echoes what Jacob and John requested in 10:37, only here
they are positions of dishonor, not honor. The irony is that it is bandits, not disciples, who are prepared to be baptized with the baptism Jesus undergoes. The
disciples simply ran away, not being prepared to be reckoned with the trans-
gressors.[150] Theft, however, was apparently not a capital offense, in which case
"bandits" would probably be a better translation, suggesting insurrectionists
(cf. v. 7 and John 18:40). The word ληστας can be legitimately used of robbers

---

148. H. R. Weber, *The Cross: Tradition and Interpretation* (Grand Rapids: Eerdmans,
1975), p. 6.
149. Lane, pp. 566-67.
150. Myers, p. 387.

(cf. 14:48), but in Josephus it refers to zealots. Probably Mark also uses the term to suggest the fulfillment of OT prophecy (Isa. 53:12), but it is important that the term can have a double meaning.

Mark includes none of the mockery by the bandits we find in other Gospels, nor the conversation with the "penitent thief" that is unique to Luke. Yet as Painter stresses, mockery is at the heart of Mark's portrayal of Jesus' crucifixion, as attempt after attempt (by passersby, 15:29-30; chief priests and scribes, 15:31; those crucified with him, 15:32) is made to publicly shame Jesus.[151] V. 29 surely refers to Ps. 22:7, where the adversaries wag their heads at the psalmist's plight. This verse is pure taunt — the one who thought he would destroy the temple is now exposed as weak rather than powerful.[152] But once again there is latent Markan irony, for this is the one who will bring judgment on the temple and even be a temple raised up in three days. Thus ironically the true conclusions are found on the lips of the mockers.

V. 31, when it speaks of salvation, must surely mean people that Jesus had earlier healed or brought back from death.[153] But now Jesus is unable to save himself, but then, ironically, he didn't come to save himself or die for his own sins. Here it is admitted that he died for others. If Jesus wanted to save others, then it was true, he had to give up his own life as a substitute. Ergo, he was unable to save himself and still do God's will. V. 30 paves the way for this when the taunt is offered, "let him come down from the cross." In v. 32 Jesus is called King of Israel, and the taunt becomes "if you just come down from the cross we will see and believe." Of course, they had seen miracles before and not believed. This same verse indicates the ultimate in shaming humiliation — Jesus is taunted and reviled by those he is crucified with, apparently because of his delusions of grandeur.

At v. 33 we are told that darkness covers the face of the earth for three hours until the ninth hour (3 P.M.). The scene is meant to have apocalyptic overtones, as Myers stresses, indicating that the eschatological judgment of God is falling on Jesus.[154] This may be seen as a preliminary fulfillment of Mark 13:24, with God's final judgment happening on Golgotha.[155] Notice how in Amos 8:9-10 darkness expresses mourning for an only son, and the context of those verses also indicates that it signifies the judgment of God, as it does here. Jesus' death was an event with cosmic consequences. In the later apocryphal *Gospel of Peter* (15-27), it is said to have become so dark that many thought

---

151. Painter, p. 204.

152. Eusebius, *Hist. eccl.* 3.7.7, and Origen, *C. Cels.* 1.47, both assert that it was because of the crucifixion of Jesus that Jerusalem and the temple were destroyed.

153. Painter, p. 205.

154. Myers, p. 389.

155. See Schweizer, p. 353.

night had come and went to bed. It further states that when Jesus' body was laid on the ground, the earth shook greatly and this, coupled with the sudden reappearance of the sun, so shocked the nation that it perceived the wrong it had done and mourned the coming destruction of the city.[156] Notice, however, that unlike the earlier apocalyptic moments in this Gospel, there is no voice from heaven speaking to Jesus, answering his cry.[157]

The following chart shows how Mark anchors his narrative by having three apocalyptic moments that reveal the identity of Jesus at the beginning, middle, and end of the story.

Baptism	Transfiguration	Crucifixion
Heavens rent	Garments turn white	Sanctuary veil rent
Dove descends	Cloud descends	Darkness spreads
Voice from heaven	Voice from cloud	Jesus' great voice
"You are my beloved Son"	"This is my Son, the Beloved"	"Truly, this man was a/the Son of God"
John the Baptist as Elijah	Jesus appears with Elijah	"Is he calling Elijah?"[158]

The importance of the Elijah factor must not be minimized in these stories, for Elijah was thought to be the forerunner of the great and terrible Day of Yahweh (Mal. 3:1-2; 4:5-6). In other words, this punctuates that we are meant to see these events as signs that the end is at hand, and that God's judgment is falling on God's people, in the person of Jesus and in the place of the temple.[159]

At the ninth hour Jesus cries out in a loud voice, "My God, my God. . . ."[160] This is the only Markan word spoken from the cross, and thus must

---

156. A story which, unlike Mark, reflects knowledge of the destruction of the city itself.
157. Myers, p. 389.
158. Myers, p. 391.
159. Myers, p. 391, goes on to suggest that the threefold promise that the coming of the Son of Man would be seen (9:1; 13:26; 14:62) is fulfilled on the cross where disciples, the authorities, even the high priests see the moment when the Son is truly revealed for what he is — the suffering Savior of the world, the Human One. Parodoxically it is on the cross that the power and glory of God are revealed. There is some merit to the suggestion that God's power is made perfect in weakness; however, Mark 14:62 and 9:1 are surely not fulfilled on the cross, for this is not where Jesus is seen seated at the right hand of God. To the contrary, this is where he is seen forsaken by God.
160. Painter, p. 206, takes the reference to the loud voice as a sign that Jesus was neither exhausted nor at the point of death. Perhaps, however, we are to think that Jesus summoned up his last bit of energy for this cry.

be seen as important. In Ps. 22 it is an appeal to God to hurry up and intervene on the part of the one who is or at least feels God-forsaken. Yet this was precisely Jesus' position, abandoned to the fate of the sinner. "Jesus now experiences the most bitter blow which can befall the religious man: the sense of having been abandoned by God."[161] If one accepts the text *elwi, elwi lema sabaxthani,* the whole cry is in Aramaic, not part Hebrew and part Aramaic, unlike the Matthean version, which also suggests the Markan version is more primitive.[162] Mark is suggesting that Jesus experienced full alienation from God, the one he had just called Abba at Gethsemane, and had done so for "the many." Thus Jesus' cry is not seen as playacting, but rather as real agony articulated in scriptural terms of a person who apparently had never been so separated from or abandoned by God previously.[163] Schweizer puts it this way: "it is a radical expression of devotion to God which endures in every adverse experience — a devotion which continues to claim God as 'my' God and will not let him go although he can be experienced only as the Absent One who has forsaken the petitioner."[164] Notice that Mark once more must translate the Aramaic phrase for his audience. Some manuscripts tried to soften the harsh tone by rendering the text "why have you reproached me?"

V. 35 refers to popular expectations of Jesus' age. The crowd thinks Jesus is calling for Elijah. There was widespread belief that Elijah would come in times of need to protect the innocent and rescue the righteous.[165] Hurtado reminds us of the Elijah who did come before Jesus — John the Baptist, who had suffered a similar fate.[166]

The offering of sour wine to Jesus was actually not an act of cruelty, as wine vinegar was the Gatorade of its day, a real thirst-quenching drink. It was a common beverage for a soldier or a day laborer to drink. Jesus, however, does not drink it but expires with a shout. Mark's account is superb in its simplicity and starkness. He does not explain whether this expressed the intensity of his suffering or was a cry of triumph or defiance.

We are told that immediately the veil or curtain of the temple is rent from top to bottom, which suggests a divine act. The question is: Which veil? Is it the

---

161. Hooker, p. 375.

162. See Metzger, *TCGNT*, pp. 119-20.

163. See Ambrose, *On the Christian Faith* 2.7.56: "As human He doubts, He experiences amazement. . . . It was not as God He died, but as man. It was in human voice that He cried 'My God, my God why have you forsaken me?' As human, therefore, He speaks on the cross, bearing with him our terrors. For amid dangers it is a very human response to think ourself abandoned. As human, therefore, He is distressed, weeps, and is crucified." See Oden and Hall, p. 233.

164. Schweizer, p. 353.

165. Schweizer, p. 353.

166. See Hurtado, pp. 256-57.

veil between the Holy of Holies and the Holy Place, or the one between the sanctuary and the forecourt which could be seen in public? The Greek word καταπετασμα was used for both curtains (cf. Exod. 26.33, 37 LXX and Josephus, *Ant.* 8.3.3). We know that Herod the Great had hung a magnificent curtain in the main entrance to the temple that was visible from the forecourt (cf. Matt. 27:51, 54). Josephus, *War* 5.3, refers to a disturbance and some zealot activities but not specifically to the rending of the veil, yet he does indicate there was some sort of astonishing event in the temple about forty years before it was destroyed, which is to say in the year of Jesus' death. Heb. 6–9 may suggest the knowledge of a tradition that said the veil to the Holy of Holies was rent, meaning that God's presence would no longer be confined there now that Jesus had made it available everywhere.[167] In any event, I take καταπετασμα to mean inner veil, as is most natural if one takes ναος in its ordinary sense of inner sanctuary, not merely the temple precincts.[168] Painter makes the good point that at the beginning of Jesus' ministry the heavens are rent and the Spirit comes down upon Jesus. Here there is just about the opposite, for Jesus cries out that he is God-forsaken and the temple veil is rent, with the Spirit of God leaving the premises and thereby dooming it.[169]

A centurion saw Jesus die and exclaimed, "truly this man was a/the Son of God." Notice that the definite article does not appear in the Greek before the noun "Son," but normally predicate nouns which precede the verb omit the article. Yet it may still be that the word "Son" is indefinite, in which case the meaning would have originally been "truly this was a divine man" (a son of the gods), a conclusion drawn from Jesus' bravery even on the cross. Of course, Mark's audience would read more into such an exclamation, namely, that the Gentiles were going to recognize in Jesus the Son of God (cf. 13:10). Here, then, was the precedent for Gentiles to do so, even before Easter.[170] "At his baptism the heavenly voice proclaimed 'You are my Son' and at his death a Roman cen-

---

167. The later embellishment in *Gospel of the Nazarenes* 21 is also interesting. There the huge lintel of the temple is itself split, and a multitude of Jews are said to be converted on the spot.

168. Hooker, p. 378, makes the good point about the rending of the veil possibly being seen as the breaking down of barriers, and thus the confession of a Gentile immediately after signals that God's spirit is loose in the world and even Gentiles can be saved.

169. Lane, pp. 574-75; Painter, p. 207. E. Best, *The Temptation and the Passion,* 2nd ed. (Cambridge: Cambridge University Press, 1990), p. 191, rightly concludes that the rending of the veil, like the event on the cross, is a sign of divine judgment and wrath.

170. Juel, p. 146, however, suggests that we read the centurion's comment as sarcastic, and perhaps as a response to Jesus' cry of dereliction. This is possible, and would fit with the irony of the Gospel, but Mark is more concerned about correct Christology in regard to his central character than he is in being ironic. Perhaps we should simply say the centurion says more than he knows.

turion confessed 'Truly this man was [a] son of God.' Jesus's mission is framed by two voices which reveal his relationship to God. Recognition of this framing heightens the significance of the role of the centurion, raising the question of his symbolic function in relation to Markan Christianity."[171]

The references to the women at vv. 40-41 remind us that Jesus had female disciples while in Galilee, disciples prominent enough to be remembered by name. Furthermore, they seem to serve as the validating witnesses in Mark to the death, burial, and empty tomb, and Easter proclamation.[172] This is hardly a tradition Mark was likely to have made up, since he elsewhere does not give prominence to women disciples and in light of the general view in a patriarchal world of the lack of value of a woman's witness. "The irony of the absence of the disciples and the presence of the women has been carefully constructed and is heightened by the call to the women to be the first witnesses to the risen Jesus (16.7)."[173] But in fact, the women are disciples, for they are clearly described as those who both followed and served Jesus in Galilee, two things that characterize discipleship in this Gospel. Notice that it does not merely say they followed Jesus up to Jerusalem.[174] In fact, we may say that the three named women present the alternative to the three named men, the inner circle, for they are faithful to the last. "This is the last — and given the highly structured gender roles of the time, surely the most radical — example of Mark's narrative subversion of the canons of social orthodoxy. The world order is being overturned, from the highest political power to the deepest cultural patterns, and it begins within the new community. It will be these women, the 'last' become 'first,' who will be entrusted with the resurrection message."[175]

N. All Was Laid to Rest, or Was It? (15:42-47)

V. 42 indicates it was already evening on the Day of Preparation (i.e., Friday evening),[176] and thus there was need for real haste if Jesus was to be buried before the Sabbath (see Deut. 21:23). "In order for Joseph to be able to complete all that was necessary before the beginning of the Sabbath — his visit to Pilate, including all the questions Pilate would necessarily ask, the purchase of supplies, and the burial itself — Jesus' death would have had to occur rather early

---

171. Painter, p. 207.

172. See my discussion in *Women*, pp. 118-22.

173. Painter, p. 208.

174. See Myers, p. 396.

175. Myers, pp. 396-97.

176. Notice that Mark feels it necessary to explain what the Day of Preparation is, another clue that his audience is predominantly Gentile.

in the afternoon."[177] Hooker is quite right that it makes no sense for Joseph to hastily bury Jesus to avoid desecrating the Sabbath if in fact he is being buried on what is already another holy day, namely, Passover.[178] Taken with other evidence, this also favors strongly the view that Jesus was not executed after the Day of Preparation or after the day of the slaughtering of the lambs (which in this instance coincided, as did the onset of both the Sabbath and the Passover feast).[179] It must surely be significant that none of Jesus' family or close male disciples came for the body. Normally the Roman magistrate would only release the body to the nearest relatives. The contrast with the case of the Baptist, who was properly buried *by his disciples* (6:29), is noteworthy.

Here Joseph of Arimathea,[180] an influential Sanhedrin member eagerly awaiting God's eschatological reign and saving activity, plucked up his courage and went to Pilate and asked for the body so that he could bury it.[181] As Schweizer says, the mention of bravery suggests that Pilate was not really disposed to be that friendly toward Jesus and his sympathizers.[182] This act could have branded Joseph as a Jesus sympathizer, a dangerous condition to be in when the man had not merely died but had been publicly executed by the Roman authorities. Since he could not have carried the body alone, one must assume he had help, and the Gospel of John (John 19) suggests Nicodemus was that helper. It is possible, as Hooker suggests, that Joseph's main concern may not have been about Jesus, but rather about the curse upon the land if a corpse of one hung upon a tree was left unburied before the feast day, which would be a violation of the Law (see Deut. 21:23).[183]

Pilate had to check to see if in fact Jesus was already dead (for the very good reason that without official confirmation family or friends could take the body down before the man died), and seems amazed to find out he was. Εἰ πάλαι may well mean "even for a good while." Learning this, Pilate granted Joseph the corpse. It is important that we note that Joseph bought a "sindon," a cloth of fine linen, suggesting that he was a well-to-do man and also that it was

---

177. Schweizer, p. 361.

178. Hooker, p. 380.

179. Another point in favor of the Johannine chronology of these events.

180. One conjecture is that the town of Ramathaim, twenty miles from Jerusalem, is meant.

181. Painter, p. 209, suggests that the phrase "dominion of God" implies that Joseph had some prior knowledge of Jesus' teaching and perhaps some positive relationship with Jesus. This may be so, but the phrase was pretty common and generic, even though it is true it is at the heart of Jesus' preaching and teaching. In favor of Painter's suggestion is the fact that Joseph had undertaken a possibly risky and certainly difficult and expensive task on behalf of Jesus.

182. Schweizer, p. 362.

183. Hooker, p. 381.

not yet the feast day, for such purchases were not allowed on feast days.[184] Further, he had a rock tomb to bury Jesus in as well. We are simply told that Jesus was wrapped in the "sindon" and placed in the tomb hewn out of rock, with a stone rolled in front to prevent grave robbing, a major problem throughout this region before and during Jesus' time. The impression given is that this was a hasty affair to beat sundown and the arrival of the Sabbath.[185] None of the Gospels mention a washing of the body, which may have been omitted in the haste. John 19:40 may suggest he was buried according to Jewish custom, and also was buried with spices in the winding sheet. Rock tombs in the Jerusalem area were hewn out of an old quarry in Roman times. The stone was likely a disk placed in a slot that was on an incline so that it was deeper at the point where the stone would be in front of the door, thus making it more difficult to open than to close. This explains the women's query in Mark 16 about who would help them move this stone. Thus Jesus was buried in a rich man's tomb meant for Joseph and perhaps some of his family members.

Bridging the Horizons

The problem with teaching and preaching from Mark's passion narrative is that the stories are so familiar that many of one's listeners hardly hear the text or its exposition. One way of dealing with this dilemma is to focus on aspects of the text or themes that are not usually discussed or preached on in one's own circles. For example, very seldom does one hear a contrast between the woman's lavish devotion to Jesus as she breaks the alabaster jar and uses all the oil to anoint Jesus and the objection of the male disciples to the waste of money involved. One question raised by the story is whether there is a place for godly extravagance, the giving of a costly gift done to the glory of God, say, perhaps a church organ or stained-glassed windows, which are, strictly speaking, not necessities to the worship of God. The story, of course, should not be used to justify a pattern of lavish spending to the neglect of one's duties to the poor, but it does suggest that there is a time and a place for costly excess done to the honor of Jesus, who can never be honored too highly.

---

184. The later Mishnaic rules about it being okay to purchase things on the feast day so long as the financial arrangements were made later, probably come from the later period after Jamnia and during the time that such rabbinic rules began to come into play, but cf. *m. Šabb.* 23.1; *t. Šabb.* 17.13; *b. Šabb.* 151a.

185. Josephus, *War* 4.317, stresses how it was very important to Jews to get any deceased person, including a victim of crucifixion, buried before sundown. This is presumably because of the problems of ritual impurity associated with corpses, and also out of respect for the dead, lest the deceased body be further desecrated by animals or insects.

A valuable service can be done to the Christian community through clear and regular teaching about the nature of Passover and the Passover meal. This illuminates the way Jesus modifies this meal at the Last Supper to suit his own situation and purposes. The story becomes quite remarkable when one focuses on how Jesus interprets the elements prospectively in the light of his own coming death, whereas, of course, Passover was a retrospective celebration. But both meals were about celebrating the deliverance of God's people from oppression and death, which, in Markan perspective, is also what Jesus' death is about (cf. 10:45). But it is hard to convey the electrifying effect the original reapplying of the elements to Jesus himself must have caused. To an early Jew the idea of eating someone's body or drinking someone's blood was abhorrent. To us hearing the words of institution, the equations of bread with body and wine with blood seem commonplace and unsurprising. The problem with overfamiliarity with the material can perhaps be overcome by sharing about the symbolic interpretation of the Passover elements with a stress on how Jesus dramatically changes the referents.

It has been said that we live in a culture that is in denial about oh so many things — denial of death, denial of responsibility, denial of wrongdoing, and the list could go on. The story of Peter's denials of Christ always raises for us the question of the ways we may have betrayed, or at least been untrue to, Christ and the gospel. Self-knowledge in such matters can be a painful but nonetheless healing thing. It is perhaps true that few of us know in advance what we are capable of in a crisis situation. We may stoutly confess in advance that we will be true to the end, but put under pressure, how often do we bail out or back out or even deny we committed ourselves in the first place? While it is human nature to take the path of least resistance, Christ did not call us to do so. As D. Bonhoeffer stressed, Jesus called us to come walk with him down the road to Golgotha, being faithful unto death.

The story of Jesus in the Garden of Gethsemane is perhaps one of the most poignant stories in all the Gospels. Here we see Jesus in distress, needing his friends, needing to draw near to God, and being sorely tempted to avoid the way of the cross. It is a portrait of a truly human figure with which we can readily identify. Still, we must recognize that Jesus' temptations were not quite of the same ilk as ours. In this case Jesus is tempted not to die on the cross, submitting to the punishment for human sin, and so is tempted not to be our redeemer. While some humans have had messiah complexes, not many of us have wrestled with the temptation *not* to be the savior of the world.

It is perhaps worth comparing this story closely with the story of Adam in the Garden of Eden. In the story in Genesis a human being is sorely tempted and gives way to temptation. In the Garden of Gethsemane we see the new Adam, only he resists the severe temptation he faces. In Eden we see a person who does not wrestle in prayer with the decision he faces; in Gethsemane the man in question does do so, and prevails over sin. In Eden we see a man who relies too heavily on his closest companion and her judgment, while in Gethsemane we see a man who wishes to be able to rely on his disciples for moral support and prayer support, but is unable to do so. In Eden we see a man who runs from his God and hides from God's judgment, while in Gethsemane we see a man who faces up to and accepts God's judgment, having run to his God and sought answers from him in prayer. Yet it was not easy, and indeed it was against his natural inclinations, that Jesus went the way of the cross.

A pastor some time ago told me about a couple who had had a rancorous argument and the husband left the house angry and vowing never to go back. He went to see this pastor and said he hated his wife and his wife hated him. There was also a small child involved. The pastor pointed out his responsibility to obey God and be a faithful husband, even at times when he did not feel like it. So it was that, in spite of the fact that every fiber of his being dreaded going back to his wife, nonetheless he obeyed God's will and went. He was amazed to discover that God honored that decision; the couple was reconciled and forgave each other, and went on to have a strong marriage. There may well come a time when one's very soul rejects obeying God's Word and will. The Jesus who went through Gethsemane understands this feeling and attitude. Yet by a decision of the will one can obey anyway, and God will help those who honor his will.

The Gethsemane story also raises in an important way the whole question of the nature of prayer. Prayer is, of course, not a matter of informing God about something God does not know. The heart of Jesus' prayer is a petition — "let this cup pass." He is asking, not insisting, and he says, "if it is possible." Real petitionary prayer is whatever is the desire of a person's heart, whatever may be on the person's lips. Sometimes pious people think praying is about saying the right things, and indeed masking one's real desires or longings. This is certainly not the theology of prayer reflected in the Psalter, where we find every sort of petition imaginable, even horrible ones about dashing infants' heads on rocks because they are the children of one's enemies. The honesty of those prayers is stunning — heart and lips are one. Yet it must also be said that our weakness is also our strength, for it drives us to prayer and to reliance on God.

Thus Gethsemane teaches us to come to God without dissembling, without pretense, and quite literally pour out our hearts to God. Notice, however, that having done so, Jesus includes a proviso — "nevertheless not my will but thine be done." This should indeed be at least an implicit part of every prayer, a submitting to the will of God, for often we do not pray aright. Often we do not know what is best for us. Often we wrongly see God's job as fulfilling our every wish, as if God were some genie in a bottle. It has been said that if one signs Jesus' name to the bottom of one's prayer, one better make as sure as one can that what one asks is in accord with God's will. Just so, and this means praying is not just a matter of petitioning. It is also a matter of dialoguing with God and wrestling through to the point when one submits to God's will, having also made one's desires known. It needs to be kept steadily in view that the Bible suggests that God always answers prayer, but that sometimes the answer is no because we have not prayed according to or within the will of God.

About the case of Judas we have these sobering and sound words from D. English:

> We may all, and we all do, betray our Lord, though not as dramatically as Judas. It remains a heinous thing to do, and we are answerable. What Judas did not discover, though Peter did, and we now know, is that there is forgiveness even for such betrayals. (Judas took his own life, Mt. 27.3-5; Acts 1.16-20; while Peter was restored, Jn. 21.15-22.) And God can still take the broken and spoiled strands of life and weave them into the total tapestry (Rom. 8.28). We should never be complacent about sin, since all sin betrays Jesus: but nor should we be destroyed by remorse or guilt when sin overtakes us — there is forgiveness and restoration (1 Jn. 1.8-10).[186]

"Consider the source" is a phrase we often use. The Jewish trial of Jesus, as presented toward the end of Mark 14, is something of a travesty. The witnesses cannot agree, but so determined is the high priest to convict Jesus of some crime that he presses the matter. The high priest, were he a fair man, would have considered the source of the accusations against Jesus before pressing matters further. It is wise for us to do so also. We should not be accusing anyone of anything without proper and compelling evidence. While it is the task of every Christian to be his brother's or sister's keeper and hold him or her accountable for his or her actions, it is not the Christian's task to be anyone's final judge. That must be left in God's hands.

This is precisely why Christian advocates of capital punishment need to rethink the matter. In the first place we have no omniscient judges in any of our courts who can look into the human heart and discern without a doubt whether the person in question is guilty of the crime alleged against him. In the second place, if we insist on capital punishment for unsaved persons, we are placing them in the same position as Judas once he hanged himself — beyond the possibility of repentance and restoration. There is yet a third reason to oppose capital punishment. Capital punishment in most cultures is normally only exercised against those who cannot afford a good enough lawyer or a long enough judicial process. Those who are wealthy can normally either get off the hook or get a reduced sentence because of the skill of their legal representatives. This is unfair to anyone who is not wealthy, and more often than not it is doubtful justice is done in such capital cases against the nonwealthy. Further-

---

186. D. English, *The Message of Mark* (Downers Grove: InterVarsity, 1992), p. 223.

more, unlike some ancient Near Eastern situations, our modern penalties for perjury are not severe enough to really prevent lying from happening regularly in court. Then too, what if the person repents while in prison and does become a Christian and model citizen? Do we still execute that person?

Jesus himself is a perfect example of what happens when the legal process is manipulated. He was a victim of an act of capital punishment that should in all likelihood never have happened. "In the Sanhedrin the only totally innocent person is declared guilty by the religious leaders of the day!"[187] Furthermore, from a Christian point of view, Jesus should have been the very last victim of the extreme penalty, as he paid the price for all our sins past, present, and future, including the sin of murder. Unfortunately for us all, Jesus was not the last victim of capital punishment. Human life continues to be cheapened and seen as expendable, as less than of sacred worth, as a result. In the end, capital punishment probably says more about our lust for revenge than about a passion for true and equitable justice for all. God alone should be the final arbiter of capital cases.

Peter is depicted as weeping tears of remorse, having doubly shamed himself, not only because of his repeated disowning of Jesus but also because of his previous adamant insistence that he would never do so. Apparently he thought that his own strength and determination were enough to prevent him from such desertion. If he thought this, he was wrong. Only wrestling in prayer kept Jesus on track with God's will. But at least Peter deeply mourned and regretted denying Jesus, as his tears showed. It is often thought unmanly to weep, a sign of weakness. To judge from the Gospels and Heb. 5, just the opposite is the case, for Jesus frequently wept. It takes strong persons, whether men or women, to admit they are wrong and to deeply regret their sin and errors. The poet Charles Mackay put it this way:

> Oh you tears,
> I'm thankful that you run.
> Though you trickle in the darkness,
> you shall glitter in the sun.
> The rainbow could not shine if the rain refused to fall;
> And the eyes that can not weep are the saddest eyes of all.[188]

The trial before Pilate, as described to Mark's mostly Gentile audience, likely got their full attention. Early Christians knew that they themselves might well face a similar fate, as Jesus warned them in Mark 13. They would have seen the extreme irony in the account. C. F. D. Moule puts it this way: "Jesus, who is,

187. English, p. 226.
188. Cited by Ray Stedman in a sermon on September 21, 1975.

indeed, king of the Jews in a deeply spiritual sense, has refused to lead a spiritual uprising. Yet now, condemned for blasphemy by the Jews because of his spiritual claims, he is accused by them also before Pilate for being precisely what he had disappointed the crowds by failing to be — a political insurgent. Jesus refused either to plead guilty or to defend himself."[189]

The response of the crowd to Pilate's query about what to do with Jesus is chilling. It is not enough that they get an insurrectionist set free. They want the blood of an innocent man. We may well wish to ask what could so infuriate people about Jesus. Certainly one answer is that he had disappointed those who desired a military solution to Israel's problems, including the problem of the yoke of Roman rule. English also suggests that it was not merely what Jesus did not do, it is what he *did* advocate that also infuriated people — the suffering servant, nonviolent, dying-to-live approach to life.[190] I agree. Very few wanted to hear that it was better to lay down one's life willingly than to take a life, better to lose one's life by nonresistance than to go out as the Maccabean martyrs had done. In a violent world, armed to the teeth, this hardly made any sense. The heroes were not the humble, but the proud, not the meek, who were seen as weak, but the warriors. But Mark stresses that it is precisely through the absurdity of Jesus' self-sacrifice that the world was saved. The final solution came from God, not through human plotting and planning by the disciples or anyone else. Yet it is also true that had Jesus managed to save himself, he could not have saved us.

In various places in the passion narrative Jesus is depicted as having need of human help and support. We see this in the Garden of Gethsemane when he tries to enlist his inner circle to watch and pray with him. We see it again when Simon of Cyrene is pressed into service to carry the crosspiece. Such stories lead one to ask whether Jesus still needs our assistance? The answer, I think, must be yes. Mother Teresa, quoting earlier Catholic traditions, once said words to the effect that "Christ has no hands, but yours, no feet but yours." Unless God chooses to abandon the human experiment as it was originally set up, since God chooses to partner with human beings that have wills and minds of their own, there is indeed a need for us to do our part for the kingdom of God. Prayer, for example, can be a participating in the actualizing of God's will on earth. Like Simon, we may be called upon at an unexpected time and when we are quite unprepared to carry the cross for Jesus. Let us hope we will respond as he did. He may indeed have served as a positive example to fearful Roman Christians afraid of what would happen if Roman soldiers came and requisitioned their services for some task.

---

189. C. F. D. Moule, *The Gospel according to Mark* (Cambridge: Cambridge University Press, 1965), p. 124.

190. English, p. 230.

There is perhaps no more chilling spiritual experience than to go into a holy place, whether it be a synagogue, a temple, a mosque, or a church, and sense the "absence" of the presence of God. It is that absence that Jesus sensed at the end, which led him to cry out, "My God, my God, . . ." but the rending of the temple veil is also about the abandoning of that place by God's Spirit. Whatever else one may want to say about hell, it is the place where a person experiences the absence of the presence of God forever. One can then say that Jesus was indeed going through a personal hell, having never previously been so separated from the one he called Abba. But it was also God's people who had their religious center abandoned by God. Lest we think God would never do such a thing, it is well to remember the prayer of the psalmist: "take not thy holy spirit from me." When I was a young Christian, I once heard the question, "If you are apart from God, guess who moved?" But on the basis of the conclusion of the passion narrative, the implied answer to that question may not always be the correct one.

The passion narrative at its heart is about the cross, and it still holds true that how we react to the cross of Christ tells us a great deal about ourselves. Ray Stedman once called the cross God's great plowshare, ripping through the hypocrisy in our lives and laying us bare for all, including ourselves, to see.[191] I believe this to be true. It explains why, for example, Moslems insist that it was not Jesus but Judas on the cross, for God would never do that to Jesus. The cross is the great truth serum and litmus test. Our reaction to it shows what we really believe about God and about life. Sometimes it tells us more than we want to know about ourselves. Some are all too ready to wear the cross, but not to bear the cross. We often prefer a health-and-wealth gospel to one of suffering and service. We join churches because they meet our needs, not because they give us the most opportunity to serve and sacrifice for the gospel. Yet still, the cross beckons us to come and stand in its shadow. Whether we do so or not is the ultimate test of our discipleship.

---

191. In a sermon on September 28, 1975.

XIII. The End of the Beginning of the Gospel (16:1-8)

Since we have dealt at length in the introduction with the problems about seeing Mark 16:8 as the original ending of this Gospel, it only remains here to comment in detail on these last few authentic verses of Mark's book. While it is likely that Mark did go on to recount perhaps a couple of appearance stories, one to women and one to men, with the latter being in Galilee (as was promised earlier in Mark), there is a sense in which we have in 16:1-8 an end to the "beginning of the gospel" story. Once the ransom for many has been paid and the resurrection of Jesus has happened and the tomb is empty, we are already in a new era of God's dealings with humankind, even before Jesus appears to any of his followers. This is so because redemption is of God, and the appearances simply confirm and apply that truth to Jesus' disciples after the great supernatural work has been accomplished.[1]

Thus, if we concentrate on the fact of the empty tomb and the Easter message, we can see where the story will go next, even though initially the women were frightened and fled. The implicit suggestion of the account is that nothing less than an appearance of Jesus could serve to reform the scattered and frightened disciples, either the women or the men. This is to say, nothing less than an eschatological act of God, a miracle, founded or refounded the community of Jesus. And in a Gospel shaped by apocalyptic rhetoric, this is indeed an appropriate way to begin to round off one's account. The fact that we

---

1. For a good example of overreading the significance of Mark 16:8 as an ironical nonending, see J. D. Hester, "Dramatic Inconclusion: Irony and the Narrative Rhetoric of the Ending of Mark," *JSNT* 57 (1995): 61-86.

do not have the final tales or a sentence such as "and they saw Jesus and were re-united and strengthened to carry on as people of faith" does not prevent us from seeing where this story was heading and how it would turn out.

The empty tomb and the Easter message is the good news, and Mark leaves us with that, just as his Gospel began with such a persuasive proclamation. It is a pity, however, that we do not have his final account of the reunion between Jesus and his followers in which they finally accept the Easter message and become, in truth, Christians, believers in the risen Lord. Yet we know that God has not abandoned them, not even Peter, for the heavenly messenger stresses that the Easter message is for "his disciples and Peter" (16:7).

TRANSLATION — 16:1-8

And with the passing of the Sabbath Mary the Magdalene and Mary the mother of Jacob and Salome bought spices in order to come so they might anoint him. And very early on the first of the Sabbath they come unto the tomb when the sun had just risen. And they were saying to each other: "who will roll away the stone from the door of the tomb?"[2] And looking up they see the stone has been rolled away, for it was very large. And having entered into the tomb they saw a young man sitting on the right-hand side wearing a long white robe and they were utterly amazed. But he says to them, "Don't remain dumbfounded: You seek Jesus the Nazarene who had been crucified; he is risen, he is not here. Behold the place where they laid him. But go tell his disciples and Peter that 'I am going before you into Galilee.' There you will see him just as he said to you." And going out they fled from the tomb, for trembling and bewilderment was possessing them. And they said nothing to anyone, for they were afraid.[3]

---

2. In what is clearly a later addition, the Old Latin codex Bobiensis (itk) offers at this juncture a description of the actual resurrection of Jesus as follows: "But suddenly at the third hour of the day there was darkness over the whole circle of the earth, and angels descended from the heavens, and as he [the Lord] was rising in the glory of the living God, at the same time they ascended with him; and immediately it was light. Then the women went to the tomb. . . ." See Metzger, *TCGNT,* pp. 121-22. What is interesting about this later addition is not merely the desire to describe the resurrection event itself, but the fact that it appears to be equated with the ascension.

3. There are four versions of the ending of Mark. Our two oldest Greek manuscripts, A and B, lack vv. 9-20, as does Greek manuscript 304 from the twelfth century. These verses are also lacking from itk, the Sinaitic Syriac, and about one hundred Armenian manuscripts, as well as the two oldest Georgian manuscripts, one written in A.D. 897 and the other in 913. While Origen and Clement of Alexandria show no knowledge of vv. 9-20 (a silence which might be explained variously), more telling is the fact that Eusebius and Jerome both tell us these verses were absent from all *Greek* copies known to them. Thus the evidence for the

Mark has shown that apart from Jesus' women followers, Jesus has basically died amidst a host of detractors and enemies.[4] The women provide the continuity between the story of Jesus' death and burial and the story of Easter morning. Indeed, as E. L. Bode points out, the "only Easter event narrated by all four evangelists concerns the visit of the women to the tomb of Jesus."[5] The narrative begins by telling us at 16:1 that at least three women go to the tomb of Jesus in the early hours of a Sunday morning.[6] The fact that they bring spices to anoint the body makes very clear that there is no doubt in their mind but that Jesus is dead. They have come to lay another wreath on the tomb, so to speak, not to witness a revelation or a resurrection. They have also come only partially prepared, for while they have spices, v. 3 makes apparent that they have not brought anyone with them to help them move the

---

Greek text, as we have it, stopping at 16:8 is strong. There are four uncial Greek manuscripts (seventh–ninth century) as well as a few Old Latin, Syriac, Sahidic, Ethiopian, and Bohairic ones which simply add the following: "But they reported briefly to Peter and those with him all that they had been told. And after these things Jesus himself sent out through them, from east to west the sacred imperishable proclamation of eternal salvation." Both the style and the substance of this addition make clear that it is not Markan in character. But the same problems plague the pastiche of material that is given as the original ending (vv. 9-20) in the Textus Receptus and the vast majority of our manuscripts, including A, C, D, K, W, and numerous others. The earliest patristic support for this reading is Irenaeus. The fourth major form of the text is just a variation of the Textus Receptus with some additional material added after v. 14. It is attested in Codex Washingtonius. The most telling criticism against vv. 9-20 being original is that these verses are very non-Markan in style, including at least ten words not found elsewhere in Mark, words that he had an opportunity to use had he wanted to in various of his narratives. Furthermore, the connection between v. 8 and v. 9 is much too awkward, with the women being the subject of v. 8 and apparently Jesus the subject of v. 9. Notice too how Mary Magdalene is reintroduced at v. 9 and the other women disappear. This suggests that vv. 9-20 were not originally composed to add to Mark, but were perhaps a free-floating tradition before being added to this Gospel. As Metzger, *TCGNT*, 2nd ed. (1998), p. 105, says: "it is more likely that the section was excerpted from another document, dating perhaps from the first half of the second century." What vv. 9-20 *are* a strong witness for is the fact that it was felt very early on that 16:8 was not the original nor an appropriate ending. It is the judgment of Metzger's committee, while entertaining the possibility either that 16:8 is the original ending or that Mark did not finish the Gospel, that it is most probable that "the Gospel accidentally lost its last leaf [or column] before it was multiplied by transcription" (*TCGNT*, 2nd ed., p. 105 n. 2). With this judgment I concur, and would stress that the various additional later endings are all witnesses to the fact that many early Christians felt quite sure that 16:8 was not an appropriate ending, indeed not the intended ending of this work.

4. See D. Flusser, "The Crucified One and the Jews," *Imm* 7 (1977): 25-37, here p. 34.

5. E. L. Bode, *The First Easter Morning* (Rome: Biblical Institute Press, 1970), p. 5.

6. The way this is worded in the Greek suggests an original Hebrew idiom, and furthermore suggests the author is a Jew, for only Jews call weeks Sabbaths.

stone in front of the mouth of the tomb. Notice that v. 4 indicates that the women are not put off by the fact that the stone has been rolled away.[7] Rather they are curious and enter the tomb, and according to v. 5, it is only at this juncture that they receive a revelation. They see a young man in a white robe and they hear the Easter proclamation. Other early Jewish literature with similar descriptions understands the reference to be to an angel (see 2 Macc. 3:26, 33; Josephus, *Ant.* 5.277). The fact that the term νεανίσκος occurs here as well as at 14:51 probably does not suggest a connection, as the noun in question is not a technical term, and the young men are not said to have the same apparel.

V. 6 involves an angelophany, and in almost every passage in the Bible when a person or persons encounter God or God's emissaries, "it is necessary for God's first words to dismiss the person's fears. Man can't help being afraid when he realizes he is in the presence of the overwhelming majesty of God."[8] Mark wishes to stress in v. 6 that before anyone claimed to have seen the risen Lord, there was already the oral proclamation that he had triumphed over the grave. The way this verse is phrased makes clear that Mark wishes to stress the continuity between the earthly and the risen Jesus, and so confirm the value of the empty tomb tradition.

It was this very Jesus who was born in Nazareth, was crucified in Jerusalem, and now was risen from the dead. Confirmation of the proclamation comes from the ocular proof that the tomb is empty. This was the value of the empty tomb tradition. While by itself it could not demonstrate that Jesus had risen, in tandem with the revelatory proclamation and the appearances it could confirm the reality and truth of the resurrection. Thus the women are not just eyewitnesses of an empty tomb which by itself could be explained in various ways, but also earwitnesses of the Easter message according to v. 6.

According to v. 7, the task of the women is both specific and limited. They are to go and proclaim the Easter news to a specific audience, the disciples and Peter. It is in fact news about Jesus going to Galilee as he had previously told the disciples he would (14:27-28). Even death could not prevent Jesus from fulfilling his promises. Notice that the verb here is in the present tense, while it was in the future in 14:28, perhaps suggesting that Jesus is on the way there as the angel speaks.[9] Galilee perhaps signals a new beginning for those who deserted or

---

7. Bede's remark at this juncture is interesting. The stone is rolled back not because such an act was necessary to allow Jesus to come out of the tomb, but rather to let the witnesses in to see it was empty and to encounter the angel. See Bede, *Homilies on the Gospels* 2.7; T. C. Oden and C. A. Hall, eds., *Mark*, vol. 2 of *The Ancient Christian Commentary on Scripture* (Downers Grove, Ill.: InterVarsity, 1998), p. 242.

8. E. Schweizer, *The Good News according to Mark* (Atlanta: John Knox, 1971), p. 372.

9. Schweizer, p. 365.

denied Jesus.[10] Their restoration requires of them a journey to go and meet Jesus and see him in Galilee.[11]

The women's reaction to the entire experience in the tomb is to flee. Since it is unlikely that v. 8 is the original ending of the Gospel (see below),[12] not too much weight should be placed on this last verse.[13] An ancient biography of one's hero is most unlikely to end in this fashion.[14] It probably does not imply a total and eternal silence of these women, disobeying the command of the angel. If we note the parallel construction of v. 8 in the Greek, it suggests that we should take seriously the imperfect verb tenses and relate the two sentences, which each follow καί, as well as the two γάρ clauses. The implication would be that, for the circumscribed period of time the women were in terror and fled from the tomb, they said nothing to anyone.[15] Naturally the fear would at some point subside, and the women would cease to be tongue-tied at that juncture. D. Catchpole makes the following observation: "Mark 16.7 and 8b do not have to be related as command and disobedience . . . to command, but as command and an obedience . . . which brings the message to certain specified persons

---

10. See J. Painter, *Mark's Gospel* (London: Routledge, 1997), p. 211. He is also right that the focus does not seem to be on Galilee symbolizing Gentile territory, for in Mark Jesus goes outside of Galilee to have contact with Gentiles (see 5:1-20; 7:24–8:10).

11. Painter, p. 213, goes on to suggest that Mark's focus on Galilee, coupled with his dark portrayal of Jesus' family and of the failures of Peter, indicates he is critiquing the central authority of the Jerusalem church, and represents the Pauline point of view not only of the Jerusalem church, but also of the radical nature of Jesus' teaching and practice which broke down walls between Jew and Gentile. In and through Jesus the curtain separating Jew and Gentile has been rent, and the presence of God loosed upon the world. There is much to commend in this suggestion, but one wonders if Galilee is really such a symbol of critique. Rather the emphasis seems to be on it being a symbol of restoration and renewal for the disciples.

12. See rightly Schweizer, p. 366.

13. Contrast, for example, the study by A. T. Lincoln, "The Promise and the Failure: Mark 16.7, 8," *JBL* 108 (1989): 283-300. Lincoln, however, stresses that vv. 7 and 8 are the ending, with the promise taking precedent over and overcoming the human failure, which is such a theme in this Gospel. But the question is whether silence and the lack of faith is an appropriate post-Easter response to the gospel, and if there is no record of the failure being overcome, why should we assume it happened?

14. The comparison with Greco-Roman tragedies is quite beside the point. Mark's Gospel is about tragedy transfigured and transformed into triumph. It is about good news triumphing over and through the suffering and resurrection of Jesus and over and even through the disciples' desertions and misunderstandings. Mark's narrative is not a play to be enacted but a story to be read about the good news of Jesus. "They fled in fear and said nothing to anyone" may suit the ending of a tragedy, but not a laudatory biographical Gospel.

15. See R. H. Smith, "New and Old in Mark 16:1-8," *CTM* 43 (1972): 518-27, and cf. my *Women in the Ministry of Jesus* (Cambridge: Cambridge University Press, 1984), pp. 118-19.

while at the same time realizing correctly that the public at large are not meant to be brought within its scope. Of course this indicates indirectly that the disclosure to the world at large is going to happen by means of the preaching of the disciples rather than through the women."[16]

It will be worthwhile to bring this commentary to a close by dialoguing with two recent commentators who have thought long and hard about the ending of Mark, M. Hooker and R. Gundry.[17] Hooker opts for the view that 16:8 is probably the original ending of the work, while Gundry offers a host of reasons why this argument is not cogent.[18] His view, like my own, is that one can find shards of the original Markan ending not only in Matt. 28 but, he would add, perhaps also in Luke 24. One of the difficulties with Hooker's view is that she fails to notice that silence about Jesus is no longer the order of the day after the resurrection in Mark's scheme of things. Rather speech is required, and indeed the angel demands speech of these women at 16:7. She is, however, quite right that Mark 16:9-20 is a patchwork quilt of material taken from Matthew, Acts, and other sources. These additional verses do not in fact resolve the dilemma raised by the fright and flight of the women, nor do they explain how the male disciples came to hear the news from the empty tomb.

Hooker's argument that the witness of the women would have been useless anyway misses the point that Mark is writing to a largely Gentile audience in Rome for whom the testimony of women would not be simply dismissible. A good deal of her interpretation seems to be based on the notion that Mark is recording the beginning of the gospel, which is true enough, but the appropriate ending of the beginning of the gospel according to Mark himself is the appearance of Jesus in Galilee to his disciples. The suggestion that the author is inviting the audience to go to a metaphorical Galilee (i.e., the land of the Gentiles) where they will see the risen Lord is weak, since 16:7 is related to 14:28 and involves a specific and quite geographical statement meant for the first disciples, not Mark's audience. We have two different and likely independent traditions that tell us that such an encounter in Galilee did in fact transpire (cf. Matt. 28 to John 21). As Gundry says, it is the Eleven, not the audience, who are being invited to Galilee. While Hooker is right that a paragraph might end with γαρ, and perhaps even some kinds of documents, this one ends with fright, flight, and a γαρ, which is asking too much. Notice

---

16. D. Catchpole, "The Fearful Silence of the Women at the Tomb — a Study in Markan Theology," *JTSA* 18 (1977): 3-10, here p. 6.

17. On this whole matter see also my discussion in the introduction, pp. 40-49 above, and on what follows see M. Hooker, *The Gospel according to Mark* (Peabody, Mass.: Hendrickson, 1991), pp. 382-88, and R. H. Gundry, *Mark: A Commentary on His Apology for the Cross* (Grand Rapids: Eerdmans, 1993), pp. 1009-21.

18. On the older debate and discussion of this matter, see my *Women in the Earliest Churches* (Cambridge: Cambridge University Press, 1988), pp. 162-63, and the notes there.

that elsewhere Mark uses this or a very similar construction, but never to end a story (cf. 5:15; 6:50; 9:6).

Gundry's discussion is much more satisfactory. He stresses, rightly, that Mark goes to great lengths in the passion narrative to reveal fulfillment of early promises and predictions, especially those of Jesus, and this leads us to expect the same with the prediction of the resurrection appearance. He points out that the women are awestruck and temporarily dumbstruck, but that if the author had wanted to suggest that they disobeyed the command given to them, he would have introduced their activity with an adversative such as δε, not with και, for every other place we have disobedience as a response in Mark it is introduced with δε (cf. 1:45; 7:36; 10:14, 22, 48; 15:23, 37).

Gundry also stresses how closely Matthew follows Mark, and of course, Matthew does go on to relate appearances. He suggests that Matthew modifies Mark to say the women fled with joy, drawing this from the second commissioning account found now in Matt. 28:9-10. But Mark's account especially needs such a second commissioning story to overcome terror and the possible disobedience suggested in 16:8, since there is no note of joy suggesting obedience in Mark. Gundry thus concludes that Matthew found the second commissioning story in Mark, and added the note of joy at the tomb, perhaps to make the story have more continuity. In any case, the resurrection appearances, as 1 Cor. 15 shows, were clearly a part of the earliest Christian confession, and as such it is unlikely that Mark would have simply left them out.

Gundry also stresses that γαρ does not turn up as the very last word in any other ancient source, with the possible exception of Plotinus, *Enn.* 5.5 (but cf. the way a discourse rather than a narrative ends with γαρ in Plato, *Prt.* 328c; Musonius Rufus, *Twelfth Tractate*). It is not enough to provide examples where it ends a paragraph (e.g., Gen. 18:15 LXX). Gundry suggests that we find the lost ending in Matt. 28:9-10, 16-20 and Luke 24:9b-12. One further suggestion is that we should compare Mark 16:7-8 to Mark 1:44 and the response of the leper where he is commanded to say nothing to anyone except the high priest, to whom he is to tell his tale. This would suggest that the women were to be silent to the general public, but to communicate with the disciples. Silence in general does not characterize Mark's redaction, especially when speech is commanded by a divine figure. Nor is there any good reason to think Mark silences the women to make the men the first witnesses of the empty tomb and the risen Jesus. To the contrary, he has just portrayed the women disciples in a more positive light than the male ones in Mark 15.

Finally, in regard to the suggestion that the Gospel of Mark begins abruptly and so it is apropos that it end abruptly, one may say that while abrupt at the outset, Mark's narrative begins with the gospel, and we may expect it to end in like fashion, however smoothly or abruptly it concludes. Between 15:40 and 16:8 Mark has carefully built the case for the women to be valid witnesses to the death, burial, empty tomb, and Easter message. He cannot have wished to undermine this case by finishing with "they fled in terror, saying nothing to anyone." The latter remark is not the gospel, nor apparently a record of faithful response to the heavenly vision. More would be required for Mark to end with the gospel and with the means by which it was carried forward to other audiences, including Mark's own. Thus we have an authentic verse in 16:8 which is likely not Mark's true ending. This reminds us that any religion founded on historical events and carried forward by means of historical processes is subject to the accidents of history. The final portion of Mark's Gospel has been subject to such an accident, unfortunately. While this is a cause for regret, it also can be a stimulus to humility, making clear that there is much yet to be discovered and learned about early Christianity, and it reminds us to be thankful for the authentic good news we do have. The "existence of the Gospel *implies* a positive fulfillment [of the women's quest and the angel's command] beyond failure."[19] Or, to put it in the memorable words of Schweizer: "In the entire tradition, even in the accounts of Jesus' appearances to his disciples, we can sense that the truth of Jesus' resurrection had to prevail against men who were very critical and who did not anticipate that such a thing would ever occur. . . . So man's continued inability to understand is contrasted with Jesus' promise to go before them and accomplish what human hearts cannot do; despite every failure he would call the disciples again to discipleship and would encounter them in a way that would enable them to see him."[20]

Bridging the Horizons

One of the most endearing things about this Gospel is that it does not spare the disciples from the searchlight of honesty. Though Mark goes out of his way to stress the faithfulness of the women disciples at the cross and at the burial, he does not spare them when he recounts their shocked and fearful reaction to the angelic presence in the tomb. Sometimes it is possible to see some of the figures in the Gospel story as supermen and superwomen of faith, but Mark never allows us to indulge that illusion. Indeed, as English says, "Our first century forebears in the faith were not naturally superior (or inferior) to us. Neither did faith and discipleship come any easier for them. Yet despite all, they went on believing and laid the foundation for us."[21] Just so, and it reminds us that even our Gospel role models are all fallible sinful human beings, with the exception

---

19. Painter, p. 210.
20. Schweizer, p. 373.
21. D. English, *The Message of Mark* (Downers Grove: InterVarsity, 1992), p. 242.

of Jesus. This Gospel warns us time and again about idolizing the early Christians, placing them on some sort of pedestal they can only fall off of once we look at them more closely. We can appreciate their witness and their moments of strong faith, but we are not called upon to imitate all their mistakes and sin. Sometimes their lives cry out "Go and do likewise," like the story of blind bar-Timaeus, but sometimes their lives cry out "Go and do otherwise," like the story of Peter's denials of Christ. But lest we judge the women at the tomb too harshly, we would do well to ask ourselves: How would we have reacted to a close encounter of the first kind with an angelic being in a place where all we expected was death and honoring the dead?

It is interesting that the present ending of Mark's Gospel places us in most respects in the same position as the women (with the possible exception of the angelic presence). We can go and experience the empty tomb where perhaps Jesus once was and we can hear the proclamation that he is risen and gone before us, but it still lies in our hands as to how we will respond to such evidence. Is the visual evidence enough, is the oral testimony enough to convince, convict, and convert us? Or do we as well need to have an encounter with the risen Lord? I would suggest that Mark is telling us that the empty tomb and the oral witness are necessary, but by themselves are insufficient to create faith. A real encounter with the divine is required.

Recently I had the privilege of taking twenty-five of the leading pastors in North America to Israel and Greece. We saw the sites, heard the witness, but it was interesting where we actually had the encounter — in a little chapel where we had communion near Gordon's Calvary, at Dominus Flevit when we sang the great hymns of the faith, on the last day of the trip when we prayed and thanked God for what had happened and shared what the trip had meant to us. God meets us in unexpected places and at unexpected times. God often comes unbeckoned, and sometimes in spite of what we expect. The Gospel of Mark, and especially its ending, tells us to expect the unexpected from God. In the place of death the women found the harbinger of life as well as the word of life. And they were surely never the same thereafter. Hopefully this may be said of all of us as we have worked our way through this amazing Gospel about the beginning of the good news. The great thing about this good news is — it never ends. Not even death or the malice of human opposition or supernatural evil or even the misunderstanding of believers can stop it. Thanks be to God for his incredible gift of his crucified and risen Son.

Appendix:
Mark's Perspective on the Disciples

The very first act Mark records of Jesus setting up the dominion of God on earth is his choosing of disciples, in this case two pairs of brothers (1:16-20). Even more interesting is the fact that three of these first four (Andrew excluded) were to become the inner circle within the Twelve (cf. 5:37; 9:2ff.; 13:3f.). We are told that Jesus would make them fishers of human beings. This phrase uses the occupation of these disciples as a way to describe their future vocation. Three things should be noted: (1) the call is to follow and be with Jesus, which is perhaps the primary characteristic of a disciple (cf. 1:16-20; 2:14; 3:14); (2) it is Jesus who will make these disciples what they will become ("I will make you . . ."); (3) their task of a new sort of fishing is yet in the future and involves dealing with other human beings, in particular fishing them out of the chaotic waters which are dark and dangerous.[1] However, the term μαθητης is not yet applied to any of these first four selections. This label is first applied to these four and apparently others at the selection of Levi (2:15).[2] Notice, however, that the story is told in such a fashion that already at 1:36 a leader begins to surface from among the group of disciples — Peter (Σιμων και οι μετ αυτου).[3] Furthermore, Jesus seems to take up residence, possibly, in Simon's

---

1. See the detailed study by R. P. Meye, *Jesus and the Twelve: Discipleship and Revelation in Mark's Gospel* (Grand Rapids: Eerdmans, 1968), pp. 99ff. This appendix is very much in the debt of this important study.

2. See R. P. Lightfoot, *The Gospel Message of St. Mark* (Oxford: Oxford University Press, 1950), pp. 108-9.

3. V. Taylor, *The Gospel according to St. Mark* (New York: St. Martin's Press, 1966),

house in Capernaum or to have used it as a base for operations early on (cf. 1:29; 2:1).[4] In any case, he makes himself at home where his first disciples live.

The call of Levi (2:13-17) reveals a distinction Mark uses increasingly from this point on in the Gospel — that between the "crowd" or any other on-lookers and the disciples. At this juncture the distinction only begins to appear. Jesus teaches the crowd that gathers (2:13), but he does not choose a disciple from among them. Rather he chooses Levi as he is passing and sees the tax col-lector sitting at the tax office, or perhaps more likely, the toll collector sitting at the toll booth. It is not clear that Levi is Matthew, but this possibility cannot be ruled out. If he is not then already in the narrative, we have the calling of a dis-ciple who is not one of the Twelve. Yet clearly the focus is on the calling of the Twelve up until 3:13. In any case, the stress is on the fact that Jesus calls people as individuals, not as members of a crowd, or even as members of some other discipleship group, such as John's disciples.

An important point about the structure of 2:13-17 needs to be noted. 2:15-17 is primarily about tax collectors and sinners, not about disciples. It is the former two groups on which the scribes comment. The scribes question the disciples about why Jesus eats with these other groups of people. Very clearly, in v. 16 the disciples are distinguished from the sinners and tax collectors. Is there a similar distinction in v. 15? Note that the "many" tax collectors and sinners are the subject of the verb in 15a. The main point is that they are dining with Je-sus, and apparently the disciples are present as well, but the scribes do not seem to be particularly concerned that the disciples are dining with these two groups of people. The question then becomes, who is being referred to in the γαρ phrase "for they were many and they followed him"? Does this refer to the dis-ciples or to the tax collectors and sinners? Is the verb ακολουθεω used in a semitechnical sense denoting discipleship here or not? If we take the phrase "and his disciples" at the end of v. 15b as parenthetical or an afterthought, it is possible that we do not have a reference here to many disciples but a repetition of the notion of many sinners and tax collectors that followed Jesus. The verb "to follow" does not settle the issue, since Mark can use it of the crowd in a non-technical sense (cf. 3:7; 5:24). Thus it is not only possible but grammatically a more natural conclusion that there is not a reference to many disciples here, but rather again to many sinners and tax collectors who followed Jesus.[5]

---

p. 183; C. E. B. Cranfield, *The Gospel according to St. Mark* (Cambridge: Cambridge Univer-sity Press, 1972), p. 89.

4. It is not clear that this house is Simon's, but see A. Plummer, *The Gospel according to St. Mark* (Cambridge: Cambridge University Press, 1914), p. 73; H. B. Swete, *The Gospel ac-cording to St. Mark* (London: Macmillan, 1909), p. 31.

5. See R. H. Gundry, *Mark: A Commentary on His Apology for the Cross* (Grand Rapids: Eerdmans, 1993), pp. 128-29.

In 3:7 it is mentioned that Jesus withdraws with his disciples and presumably away from the multitude who, undeterred, follow him anyway. There seems to be here a Markan distinction between the small group of disciples and the larger group of those who follow Jesus to be healed, hear him, or see wonders. 3:7 prepares us for the important passage in 3:13-19, to which we now turn.

3:13-19 is to be seen as the second of three programmatic statements about some or all of the Twelve and their role and task (the first being 1:17). This becomes apparent when we notice its close verbal links with two other programmatic statements about the Twelve (1:17 and 6:7-13, 30). These links consist in the following factors: (1) the four mentioned in 1:16-20 are mentioned first among the Twelve in 3:16ff.; (2) the verb ποιεω is used to describe the activity of Jesus toward those mentioned in both 1:17 and 3:14; (3) the description of the activity of Simon and Andrew in 1:17 is expanded on in 3:14-15.[6] As we shall see, the tasks mentioned to the four will be carried out by the Twelve, and indeed, 6:7-13, 30 features these tasks (preaching, exorcism) as almost the entire scope of their work, though anointing the sick (6:13b, the only activity of the disciples not also predicated of Jesus) and teaching (6:30) are mentioned in passing. Thus 1:17; 3:13-19; and 6:7-13, 30 all serve as Markan summaries of the activities of the Twelve. There are some particular features of 3:13-19 which we must concern ourselves with at this point.

Mark tells us that Jesus went up unto the mountain and called to himself those he wanted and they came to him. In light of 3:7, where we saw the distinction between the crowd and the disciples, we may agree with Lane that "While it is possible to think of a larger company of disciples from whom Jesus appointed Twelve to remain with him . . . [i]t seems preferable to hold that only Twelve disciples were involved from the beginning."[7] I would have one caveat about this remark. It would be better to say that only twelve were involved *at* the beginning. In any case, Mark does not stress, as Luke does, the choice of the Twelve from a larger group of disciples, for they are individuals handpicked by Jesus from the start. Nevertheless, the phrase "as he wished" makes clear that Jesus could have chosen others at the beginning of things.

We read at 3:14 that Jesus "makes Twelve" and are reminded that Jesus is the initiator of discipleship and that the collective entity the Twelve is not simply the sum of its parts, but a new thing. Mark uses the phrase "the Twelve" several times more than any other Gospel writer (cf. 3:16?; 4:10; 6:7; 9:35; 10:32; 11:11; 14:10, 17, 20, 43). Some have suggested the verb εποιησεν be rendered less literally as "appoints," but the sense in either case is that Jesus forms the group. Why twelve? Obviously there is some relationship with the twelve tribes of Israel, but of what sort? Is this the new Israel? Are they merely representatives

---

6. See Meye, pp. 106-8.

7. W. Lane, *The Gospel of Mark* (Grand Rapids: Eerdmans, 1974), p. 132.

to the new Israel sent out by Jesus? Lane's answer is: "Through the choice of the Twelve, Jesus made visible his claim upon the whole people in their several divisions. The Twelve reflect backward on the prior history of the people of God as the people of the twelve tribes. In proleptic form they represent the final form of the Messianic community, the eschatological creation of God."[8]

The Twelve, however, are not merely the representatives of the old or new Israel, they are representatives to Israel, and thus their missionary task is mentioned first in 3:14b. We are told at this juncture and not before that they were also called αποστολους.[9] If we have a Markan redactional phrase here, then what would seem to be implied is that while the Twelve were apostles, the two terms do not connote precisely the same thing, even though in this case they refer to the same person. It seems likely that the term *shaliach* or its Aramaic equivalent stands behind the term αποστολος and means that Jesus appointed the Twelve as his agents, those who would be extensions of himself and carry out the tasks he had come to do — preaching, teaching, healing, and the like.[10] It may be significant that the first three among the Twelve also have special nicknames (Rock, Sons of Thunder). This suggests their special intimacy with Jesus, and thus that they had a closer ongoing relationship with Jesus than the other nine did (cf. 3:16; 5:37; 9:2). It is possible that the nicknames indicate that the three were given special tasks, or that Jesus had conferred a promise on these three through a naming ritual, as was sometimes the case in early Judaism when surnames had symbolic significance.[11] Most probable is the suggestion that these names are eschatological, reflecting roles these three will assume in the dominion, and so not symbolizing their present attributes or tasks.[12]

Besides the primary task of being a disciple of Jesus, the Twelve are also sent out to preach and given εξουσια to cast out demons. In this description we see something of what the apostles do, but also what it means to be an apostle — one authorized, empowered, sent with a specific commission by Jesus. Notice that the description of their work could just as well be predicated of Jesus' work (cf. 1:14 and 1:34). Thus, in effect, the disciples are called to be like Jesus, and are given the authority and power to do so. Mark records no similar commission to any other group of men or women in his Gospel. This must be kept steadily in view as this discussion continues.

---

8. Lane, p. 133.

9. This is textually somewhat in doubt. We may have an assimilation to Luke 6:13; however, Metzger, *TCGNT,* pp. 80-81, is, rightly I think, unconvinced this is so.

10. See C. K. Barrett, *The Signs of an Apostle* (London: Epworth, 1970).

11. H. Bietenhard, "ονομα," *TDNT,* 5:253-61, 81, suggests that the name Cephas speaks to Simon's destiny to be the foundation of the community, and that Boanerges may imply the unbreakable fellowship or mighty witness of these two.

12. Barrett, p. 27. This is all the more likely since the disciples labor in obscurity during the ministry and often misunderstand things.

After relating the parable of the sower to the crowd that had gathered around Jesus by the lake, Mark tells us he was questioned by οι περι αυτον συν τοις δωδεκα (4:10). This awkward phrase has often caused difficulties to exegetes. The most common interpretation is that it refers to a group besides the Twelve that were given access to Jesus' private instructions, and usually the commentators call these others disciples.[13] R. P. Meye challenges this view and argues that this phrase means "those associated with or belonging to the Twelve." He understands this to mean a group within the Twelve.[14] Several points favor the traditional view: (1) in 3:34 we have the phrase τους περι αυτον to refer to those women and men who do the will of God, and thus become part of Jesus' family of faith; (2) the phrase in question should likely have read οι εν τοις δωδεκα (those among the Twelve) if Mark was suggesting what Meye argues; (3) the phrase in 4:10 speaks of those surrounding Jesus but with the Twelve. It is possible, as Barrett once pointed out to me in personal conversation, that the Twelve may exemplify the sort of people that were surrounding Jesus, but apparently do not exhaust the group. Perhaps we should reflect back to 3:34, which refers to insiders, including the Twelve. I would suggest that both in 4:10 and in 3:34 Mark may have in mind the faithful women who, he later says, followed Jesus in Galilee (15:41), though of course he may also have in mind some additional men as well.

Jesus, when he is alone with the Twelve and this wider group of followers, says these two groups are given the secret (το μυστηριον) of the dominion of God, not just of the parables which those outside this group receive. Perhaps in light of 4:13-34, "the secret" involves a revelation of what the dominion is like and how it comes, explained through a private interpretation of the parables and other teachings of Jesus (see 4:34b). It then seems likely that the phrase "his own disciples" in 4:34 involves the Twelve and those others to whom the secret is given in 4:10. Thus again, the Twelve epitomize the disciple group in Mark; they do not exhaust it. When discipleship is the theme, the spotlight is clearly on the Twelve, but others can be seen standing just outside this spotlight.

We find an instance of private instruction for only the three among the Twelve at 5:37. Jesus purposely takes only Peter, Jacob, and John into Jairus's house, and only they plus the parents go into the room and witness the raising of the daughter. Since none of this larger group perform any service during the miracle, one can only assume that Mark sees the three as witnesses in this case. Yet notice that the time for proclaiming what has been seen is not yet (5:37), though later Jesus will indicate that there would be an appropriate time to relate such things (see below on 9:9).

---

13. So Cranfield, p. 152; Taylor, p. 255; Lane, p. 156, and numerous others.

14. Meye, pp. 154-55. It is interesting that the Talmud has a tradition that Jesus had five disciples, one of whom was named Mathai (*b. Sanh.* 43a). Could this relate to Mark's mention of five being especially called by Jesus?

The one extensive instance in Mark where we are told of the mission of the Twelve during Jesus' ministry is found at 6:6b-13. Some have judged this tradition to be inauthentic since it is said that there is no further indication of such a mission.[15] This, however, is not quite correct. When Jesus descends from the mountain of transfiguration (9:14-29), he finds the other disciples trying to perform an exorcism. There are thus hints elsewhere in this narrative that the disciples were given ministry tasks during Jesus' earthly ministry (cf. also 11:2; 14:13). It would appear that the earthly ministry of Jesus may have been a time for the Twelve primarily to be with Jesus and so to be prepared for their future ministry. Thus 6:6b-13 should be seen as a summary statement of the sort of ministry the Twelve had during Jesus' life, and as an extension of Jesus' own ministry.

Both in number and in extent, these trial runs or forays of the Twelve into the countryside were likely quite limited, and may have been examples of on-the-job training in Galilee more than anything else.[16] Since we have already seen a larger group of disciples, the fact that Jesus apparently sent only the Twelve on such forays may be significant. Nonetheless, we should not likely see in this a creation of a missionary office at this point, but rather some sort of special commission involving special requirements suitable to that location and point in time in Jesus' ministry (e.g., taking of only a staff, one tunic, etc.).[17]

The Twelve are sent out two by two with the authority/power ($\varepsilon\xi o \upsilon \sigma \iota \alpha$) Jesus had over unclean spirits. This delegation of authority seems to imply that the Jewish concept of agency is in operation — sent ones authorized and empowered by the sender to carry out specific limited tasks, who are to be treated as if they were the sender himself.[18] They may have been sent out two by two because of the Mosaic provision that a true testimony must be established by two witnesses (Deut. 17:6; Num. 35:30). The practice of traveling in pairs was common among Jews in any case (cf. Luke 7:18; 24:13; John 1:37).[19]

This ministry of the Twelve seems to have borne the character of the preaching of John the Baptist, just as Jesus' early preaching seems to have done. The preaching was about preparing for the coming of God's dominion by means of repentance (6:12; cf. 1:4, 15). Yet the work of the Twelve was not without its aspect of fulfillment, for "they drove out many demons and anointed many sick people with oil and healed them" (6:13). The Twelve were like Jesus in their words and deeds, and also in their reliance on the existing system of ancient Near Eastern hospitality (vv. 10-11). In these various ways the Twelve were

---

15. See, e.g., R. Bultmann, *History of the Synoptic Tradition* (Oxford: Blackwell, 1963), pp. 31-33.
16. See Swete, p. 109; Lane, p. 206.
17. Lane, p. 207.
18. Lane, pp. 206-7.
19. See Taylor, p. 303; Cranfield, p. 198.

Jesus' representatives to Israel. To this point in Mark's narrative, the portrayal of the disciples is basically positive. They are called and they respond to the call. They are commissioned and successfully carry out the commission.

Mark connects the narrative of the mission of the Twelve with the feeding of the multitude via the linking material in 6:30, in which the "apostles" give Jesus a report of the results of their mission just prior to the feeding of the five thousand. It is good Markan technique to join these two stories together so that they may be seen to exegete each other. There is also perhaps an implied contrast between John's disciples, who have just completed the last rites on John (6:29), and Jesus' disciples, who have just completed the first rite of duty for Jesus (6:30). They are likely called "apostles" here because they have just functioned as such, as missionaries or "sent ones" of a sort, for the first time.

Notice that after reporting back about their deeds and teaching, the Twelve are invited by Jesus to withdraw with him to a private place and get some rest. Again the Twelve are singled out from the larger group for this privilege. They are, however, unable to do this because the crowds see them leave and end up beating them to their destination (6:33). As Meye points out, it is interesting that just here, after the Twelve completed their first mission, they are treated as being one with Jesus by the Gospel writer.[20] It is also important to recognize that throughout these first six chapters, Mark has left the definite impression that Jesus sees his primary task as preaching or teaching, and only secondarily and in response to need does he do miracles, except for exorcisms, in which Jesus and the Twelve seem to go on the offensive.

Having been treated as extensions of Jesus' ministry in the material immediately prior to the feeding of the five thousand, the Twelve are, not surprisingly, found ministering with Jesus to the crowds (v. 34), though this proves to be an unusual event. Jesus uses this occasion to teach the Twelve that their ministry must be to the many even if it is costly or wearisome, or even seemingly impossible (10:45). Jesus instructs the Twelve, despite their desire for some peace and quiet, and their longing to be rid of the multitudes and the responsibility they involved, to give them something to eat (vv. 35-37). He desires that they be as compassionate as he is (v. 34). It appears "the one mission of the twelve is a point of beginning for Jesus' instruction in the full meaning of their mission."[21] Put in a different way, the first mission of the Twelve is but a prelude to a period of instruction concerning Jesus' mission, their mission, and the foundation of both — namely, Jesus himself.

The identity of Jesus is the key to understanding these two missions, as 8:27–10:45 will make clear through an extended discussion about mission. That Jesus doesn't give up on the Twelve as he prepares them for their role as leaders

---

20. Meye, p. 101.
21. Meye, p. 112.

among his disciples, even though they fail to have compassion, fail to understand, fail to recognize who Jesus is, indeed fail almost totally, tells us something of Jesus' design, but also of his mercy toward them. The Twelve have apparently been chosen not because of their outstanding wisdom or compassion
or suitability or other outstanding attributes, but in fact in spite of the absence
of such attributes.

Mark will emphasize, through the feeding miracles, perhaps especially
the second one (see 8:19-21), that Jesus uses such events as moments to instruct
the Twelve, though they completely miss the point. It is precisely in these stories
and the sea stories connected to them that the theme of the disciples' incomprehension begins to come to the fore. Notice how they are terrified when they see
Jesus walking on the water. The problem seems to be that they do not recognize
who Jesus is and what his presence means (6:49-50). This, of course, is the chief
problem or question with which this Gospel in biographical format seeks to
deal.[22] Mark says succinctly: "They were completely amazed," and then he adds
a final γαρ clause to explain why — "for they had not understood about the
loaves; their hearts were closed." The lesson in the miracle of the loaves had
been lost on them. After that miracle they should have expected most anything
from Jesus. The problem was not a lack of revelation; it was a lack of receptivity
to it — "their hearts were closed." There is irony here because, according to
v. 54, the crowd immediately recognized Jesus and knew they could expect miracles of him. It is at this juncture that Mark breaks off the initial account of the
Galilean ministry, ending with an ominous contrast between the crowd and the
Twelve in terms of understanding. The obtuseness of the Twelve will be a theme
that receives ever louder emphasis as the Gospel progresses.

Mark especially gives us an opportunity to judge whether the Twelve are
making any progress by giving us in 8:1ff. a story closely parallel to the one in
6:35ff. Mark stresses that this feeding is clearly after the feeding of the five thousand.[23] 8:1 tells us that Jesus calls the Twelve together and speaks to them about
meeting the crowd's need for food. The title "the apostles" in 6:30 suggests it is
the Twelve who are doing the ministry task of feeding the people, and this must
be remembered as one reads 8:1-10, for in the related story in 8:11-14 Jesus is
rebuking a group which was involved in ministering to both crowds.

Once again the Twelve make the same excuse as before for not being able
to feed the crowd — they are in a remote place (cf. 8:4 to 6:35). While in 6:37
they objected to how much money would have to come out of their pockets for
such an undertaking, here in 8:4 they feebly question whether they can get

---

22. See the introduction, pp. 36-39, on the structure of Mark.

23. Εν εκειναις ταις ημεραις; see Cranfield, p. 255, and Plummer, p. 194, on how this
phrase relates to 7:31. Moreover, the order of the feedings as mentioned in 8:19-20 gives us
clear evidence of Mark's intentions.

enough bread in such a remote location. In both cases Mark's point about the Twelve is evident — they utterly fail to recognize who is asking them to perform these tasks and what his powers are. They think in purely human terms and make typically human excuses. Indeed, even after both feedings they are still able to worry that they have brought only one loaf of bread with them into the boat as they proceed elsewhere (8:14)! Thus both miracles were meant to teach the Twelve something about Jesus' identity but fail to do so. Even stilling a storm or walking on water only leads the Twelve to again raise the question of who Jesus is, but they still fail to discern the answer or exercise faith (cf. 4:41; 6:51-52; 8:14-17). Herein we seem to have an implicit commentary by Mark that while miracles may help one raise the question of who Jesus is, they do not in and of themselves provide the answer or create the faith necessary to discern the truth. Jesus' actions and teaching and even the disciples' own actions are parables of who Jesus is, but until they discern who Jesus is, they cannot be taught, much less take in, what Jesus' real mission is in life.

To this point in the Markan narrative we have seen Peter as one of the three, as part of the inner circle within the Twelve — eminent but not preeminent. From 8:27 on Peter begins to be set apart from the rest of the Twelve, primarily as the representative of and spokesman for them, whether Jesus or the crowd is the audience. No doubt Mark writes with a knowledge of Peter's later importance and brings out his prominence here, but with a telling honesty. He presents Peter as the embodiment of all the best and the worst of the Twelve. He does not spare even Peter, even though he surely knew Peter's later importance.

8:27-30 is one of the climaxes of this Gospel, one of its key disclosure moments. It is indeed a narrative with a difference, for up to this point Jesus has attempted to teach the Twelve who he is by parables and their interpretation, by parabolic actions both of his own and of the Twelve in conjunction with him. Here in Caesarea Philippi, rather than the Twelve asking themselves who Jesus is (cf. 4:41), he asks them concerning the general human and popular opinion of him. As the narrative soon reveals, Jesus is not simply taking an opinion poll. This is a leading question, and it produces one of the pivotal moments in Mark's narrative so far as the Twelve are concerned. The dialogue in 8:14-21 and the healing of the blind man in 8:22-26 (perhaps to be seen as a parable of the healing of those who lack comprehension) have paved the way for this revelatory moment.[24]

The introductory question in 8:27 and its answer show how well the messianic secret has been kept. Jesus then asks point-blank what the disciples think. The "you" (υμεις) is placed at the beginning of the question to make it emphatic. "But *you*, what do you say?" The "you" here is plural. Jesus, of course, is not just asking for information; he is hoping the light will dawn so

---

24. See Meye, p. 71.

there will be a breakthrough in insight. Peter's response is equally emphatic — "*you* are the Messiah." This is not the whole truth, but it is the truth. As one sees quickly thereafter, the question then becomes what sort of messiah Jesus is, and Peter clearly is not thinking of a suffering and dying one.[25] Perhaps because of the political implications of such a claim, but perhaps also because of the lack of full comprehension even by the disciples, Jesus warns them not to tell anyone about him.[26] Jesus seems to know that the title *mashiach* used without qualification and addition can give rise to grave misunderstandings. "Thus the silence of Jesus, as Mark presupposes it in our passage . . . has theological significance."[27]

Once the disciples, as personified in Peter, have realized something of who Jesus is, Jesus is able to turn to a new stage in his instruction and say something about what his mission is. 8:31 indicates a decisive new phase in Jesus' teaching of the Twelve (και ηρξατο διδασκειν αυτους . . .). He is able to begin to tell the Twelve what his future is, and in this way explain what the implications of their following him mean for the future. They must be prepared for the way of the cross if they are to follow Jesus and lead his followers at some later time. This new teaching is no longer couched in parables or their explanations. It is said to be clear and plain teaching (παρρησια), and it elicits a clear response from Peter. It is a prophecy of Jesus' suffering, rejection, and death, but also of his resurrection after three days. The introduction of the suffering and death motif is accompanied by a stress that it is the Son of Man who is involved, and indeed that divine necessity is involved (δει). "The distinctive feature in the N.T. use of the term [Son of Man] is the combination of the term . . . with necessary suffering and death; and nowhere is this combination more strongly emphasized than in the last half of this Gospel. Between 8.27 and 16.8 the term occurs in twelve contexts, in nine of which it is connected with service, suffering, and death, and only in three with a future coming in power and glory."[28]

We have seen Peter in 8:27-30 at his best, but in 8:31ff. we "immediately" see him at his worst. When Jesus begins to speak of his suffering and death, Peter begins (in both cases ηρξατο) to rebuke Jesus. The verb επιτιμαω is a strong word meaning to censure or rebuke.[29] If Peter speaks in strong words to Jesus, Jesus then returns the favor (cf. επιτιμαν in v. 32 to επετιμησεν in v. 33). We are told that Jesus turns and looks at the disciples, for he realizes that Peter has spoken for

25. On Peter as the representative and archetypal disciple, see R. E. Brown et al., *Peter in the New Testament* (Minneapolis: Augsburg Press, 1973), pp. 62-63, and cf. O. Cullmann, *Peter: Disciple, Apostle, Martyr* (London: SCM, 1953).

26. Taylor, p. 377, says the prohibition is credible as a council of prudence in view of the political repercussions of such a claim.

27. Cullmann, p. 179.

28. Lightfoot, p. 42.

29. BAGD, p. 303.

them, but he rebukes Peter specifically because he speaks for them all as their leader and representative. Indeed, he calls him "Satan," being a person who has in mind something other than the things of God. Despite this, paradoxically it is in this same text that Peter's leadership position in relationship to the Twelve becomes evident, and is built upon in the narrative which begins at 9:2.

Notice that Jesus' anger at Caesarea Philippi continues over into the next story in 8:34-38. Instead of continuing to teach the Twelve alone about the way of the cross, Jesus summons the crowd (but from where?) along with his disciples in 8:34 and says, "If *anyone* wishes to come after me he must deny himself and take up his cross and follow me." Here it is probable that ακολουθεω is used in its more theological sense. This entire phrase makes clear that the Twelve cannot cling to their favored special position. They must act like Jesus is acting and will act. Jesus can call others even from the crowd to follow him. It is significant that this is the first occasion that such an appeal is made to them. If the Twelve reject Jesus or his mission, then Jesus can reject them and call others to follow him on the *via crucis*.

This stern warning is, however, followed by the narrative in 9:2-10, where the education of the Twelve and its leaders in who Jesus is and what he is about continues. Mark offers a precise chronological note at 9:2 (after six days), which is without parallel in this Gospel prior to the passion narrative. It has been suggested that the precise time note indicates that we must connect the prior language about suffering with the discussion of glory and triumph which follows in 9:2ff.[30] One could perhaps speak of the reinstatement of Peter and the three into Christ's good graces here, though one must note that Peter gets another rebuke! Nonetheless, the three share a revelation and personal communication with the divine. It seems to serve in the Markan scheme of things as a preview of coming attractions, but is it a preview of the risen Christ or of Christ coming in glory? Furthermore, some have even suggested that this is a predated or retrojected resurrection appearance.[31] Various features of the account must tell against this last suggestion: (1) the presence of Moses and Elijah, (2) the voice, (3) the cloud, (4) Peter's words. In short, virtually all the distinctive features of the story tell against such a view.[32] Further, all the resurrection accounts begin with Jesus being absent, unlike here.[33]

---

30. So Lightfoot, pp. 42-43.

31. Bultmann, p. 259.

32. See E. L. Bode, *The First Easter Morning* (Rome: Biblical Institute Press, 1970), pp. 45-46 n. 2.

33. Cranfield, pp. 292-96; Lightfoot, pp. 43ff. Cf. C. H. Dodd, "The Appearances of the Risen Christ," in *Studies in the Gospels: Essays in Memory of R. H. Lightfoot*, ed. D. E. Nineham (Oxford: Oxford University Press, 1955), pp. 9-35, who notes that this tale has none of the formal features that the postresurrection appearances have, and this is not likely an antedated or displaced resurrection story.

We thus must see this as a story of Jesus foreshadowing his being in some sort of state of glory. One could argue that the mention of the high mountain and the bright raiment suggests Christ as he was being taken up into heaven — the exalted Christ.[34] This on the surface makes better sense than seeing this as a parousia preview, for Mark views that as involving the return of the Son of Man unaccompanied by Moses and Elijah. The point of this event seems to be to convey to the three that Christ indeed will be vindicated and exalted beyond suffering. But it also involves an exhortation for them to listen to Jesus' subsequent teaching. Thus this is not just about an experience the three have; it is about the expression of God confirming the identity and authority and words of the Son.

Here we have an event which takes place from first to last solely for the benefit of Jesus and the three (κατ ιδιαν μονους). The story raises numerous questions. For example, if Peter is so spiritually obtuse at this point, how does Mark think he recognized that the two other figures with Jesus were Moses and Elijah? Peter may be giddy from the experience, but he is not portrayed as totally spiritually obtuse. But once again we see the schema of revelation to a small group come into play. Various features make clear that this is a visionary and revelatory experience — the verb "transfigured," the verb "appeared," the cloud overshadowing, the voice from heaven (cf. the baptismal account in 1:11), and the sudden disappearance of Moses and Elijah.[35] Again, the function of this revelation seems to be to make clear to the three the identity of Jesus so that they will listen to him about his coming suffering and vindication.

As for Peter, he seems to be both perceptive and yet not perceptive enough. He seems to want to place Jesus on the same level with Moses and Elijah, making tabernacles for each one.[36] The problem with this is he fails to recognize the uniqueness of Jesus. As Lightfoot says, "The heavenly voice corrects his error."[37] Only Jesus is God's beloved Son. Peter again represents the other disciples. While he alone speaks, the voice from heaven responds to all of them — ακουετε αυτω.

Perhaps the most crucial feature of this narrative for an analysis of the Twelve comes in v. 9, where it says, "as they were coming down from the mountain, Jesus gave them orders not to tell anyone what they had seen until the Son of Man had risen from the dead." This indicates a limited period of time in which silence is appropriate.[38] "The clear implication of this statement is that

---

34. See G. H. Boobyer, *St. Mark and the Transfiguration Story* (Edinburgh: T. & T. Clark, 1942), p. 23.

35. See Lightfoot, p. 44.

36. Lightfoot, p. 43.

37. Lightfoot, p. 43.

38. See Swete, p. 181.

the period of concealment is to be followed by a time of open proclamation when his status as the transfigured Son and eschatological Judge is to be announced to all (cf. Ch. 13.10; 14.9)."[39] As this is the only clear instance in Mark where he indicates a limit to the "don't tell yet" and the silence it requires, we must pay close attention to these words. By implication, they commission the three to proclaim such things after the resurrection of Jesus. Perhaps, then, we are to see this scene as a recommissioning of the three for a future ministry. Let us compare it to 3:13-18.

As in 3:13, we are told that Jesus and his intimates ascend a high mountain (9:2), though in the former text Jesus goes up the hill and calls the others to follow him. In both cases a selective process is entailed. Secondly, the three are mentioned by name in the order listed in 3:16-17, the only difference being that in 9:2 Simon is only called by his nickname. This may reflect his changed status since 3:16-17. In 9:9 the future task of the three is revealed, while in 3:14-15 we have a similar commissioning, only later fulfilled (6:6bff.). The difference in the nature of the future mission and its content in each case reflects the fact that in the earlier text we are on one side of the Caesarea Philippi event and by 9:2 we are on the other. In both cases we appear to still be in Galilee (but see 9:30), which may have significance for 16:7. Notice that 9:9 is not a simple repetition of 3:14-15. And 9:2ff. is a further development of the *didache* in 8:31ff., though the teaching about the resurrection is not understood (9:10). Notice that Jesus is not deterred by this. Instead he launches into more teaching, this time about the coming of Elijah as the forerunner (9:11-13), but he also repeats the facts about the Son of Man's suffering (9:12b).

After the rarefied air of the Mount of Transfiguration, we come back to earth with a jarring impact in 9:14-30. Once again we see at least nine of the disciples in a negative light. The distinction of these disciples from the crowd is clear again (9:14). It is the nine who are in an argument with the scribes.[40] Here the nine fail to fulfill the commission originally given them in 3:15. They were asked to drive a demon out of a man's child, but they were unable (9:18). Jesus' response is strong, as he classes the nine with the "unbelieving generation."[41] They continue to be απιστος and hard-hearted (cf. 4:40; 6:50, 52; 8:17-21). They appear virtually indistinguishable from unregenerate humanity (cf. 8:12, 38).

In distinction from these disciples, Jesus is a man of faith for whom all things are possible (9:23). The boy's father realizes that by implication he is called to believe in this man of faith. The note in v. 29 about prayer indicates that had the disciples had faith and asked the Father, the situation could have

---

39. Lane, p. 13.

40. Note the parallel construction that highlights this with both phrases ending with αυτους referring to the nine.

41. On this remark being directed to the nine, see Lane, p. 332; Cranfield, p. 301.

been different. The whole scene, but especially v. 29, indicates that Jesus' inner circle are the inner circle because of Jesus' choice and plan, and for no other reason. They have authority over spirits only because Jesus has given it to them, and they have it only if they exercise it in dependence on God and not as an independent personal power. Here their failure is contrasted with the success of the unknown exorcist in 9:38, whom, perhaps in frustration, they have tried to stop "because he is not one of us." In short, these disciples are what they ought to be only if they deny themselves (8:34) and their unbelieving natures and rely on Jesus through faith. V. 19 implies both Jesus' frustration and his tolerance. Even now he does not abandon the Twelve: this indicates the designs of the Master, not the deserts of the disciples.

In v. 28 we have the Markan theme once again of private instruction of the Twelve. Jesus wishes it to remain this way despite the απιστος reflected in 9:14ff. This silence and privacy is important, for it shrouds the future of Jesus, the Son of Man, from the crowds. We are told explicitly that he doesn't want anyone to know he is traveling on, for he is teaching the disciples (9:30-31). Once again at a point where the rejection of the obtuse disciples seemed possible, Jesus' continued teaching of them as a private enterprise is emphasized. They must be prepared by him, for "the Son of Man is going to be betrayed in the hands of human beings. They will kill him, and after three days he will rise." But even after these seemingly clear remarks, the disciples do not understand and are even fearful to ask Jesus about the matter. Perhaps we are to deduce that they fear Jesus' wrath if they reveal their lack of perception again. Some have deduced from this text that they do understand Jesus' words but are afraid to ask further about a painful subject. But the verb αγνοεω seems to suggest otherwise.[42]

To this point in Mark's narrative we have seen basically three reactions of the Twelve to Jesus. They have in the first instance responded positively to his call for them to join him, travel with him, minister with him, be with him, and be his "learners," which is of course what μαθητης means. This said, however, the other two major reactions of the Twelve to Jesus' teaching and miracles are either misunderstanding or lack of faith or the former based on the latter (cf. 4:13, 40; 6:52; 7:18; 8:17; 9:10), even though we are to understand that they have been with Jesus all along, hearing his teaching from the beginning, even at times when they do not really participate in the action in the narrative (cf. 1:21, εισπορευονται; 3:20, 5:1, ηλθον; 6:1).

From 9:33 on we see all sorts of wrong attitudes of the Twelve about their roles and unique place in Jesus' ministry. In 9:33-37 it is pride and vying for position. In 9:38-40 it is jealousy.[43] In 10:13-16 it is perhaps prejudice or a feeling that

---

42. See Taylor, p. 403.

43. Interestingly for a change, it is John, not Peter, who represents and speaks for the disciples in this story.

they or Jesus should not have to be troubled with children, or that children could not be followers of Jesus. At 10:28 it appears that the concern is for compensation, or at least a desire for a guarantee of salvation. In 10:35ff. it is a desire for a special place in Jesus' coming dominion. Having seen now the large and rather grim picture of where the story is going, we must turn to the first of these episodes.

The setting of 9:33-36 is Capernaum, perhaps in Peter's house again. The disciples, while on the road to Capernaum, have been arguing about who is the greatest. Jesus proposes to give them a lesson in humility. Once again they receive a prophetic teaching "in-house." V. 35 is important, for here we find Jesus' definition of leadership. The task of the first is to be last and the servant of all. Leading in Jesus' community is not a matter of striving after or debating greatness. This is very important teaching for the Twelve to hear. Notice that Jesus does not say they should not be first. Rather, he tells them how to be first in a way that conforms to Jesus' own example and his intentions for the Twelve. This is not an expression of a nonhierarchical vision of leadership; rather, what being first means is redefined so that in fact expected roles are reversed. Nor is Jesus giving them the secrets of how to be great in their own or the world's eyes. Indeed, the world was likely to see this sort of leadership as contemptible slavelike behavior. Jesus speaks of a greatness that requires the first to have no concern over status or importance. True greatness involves forgetting the whole matter of having greatness and getting on with humble service. This is Jesus' teaching to the Twelve about how they are to lead. It does not question the appropriateness of their doing so. Unfortunately, 10:35ff. shows that the Twelve, or at least its inner circle, do not soon forget their own aspirations.

At almost every opportunity Mark reveals that Jesus applies to the disciples even teaching originally directed at someone else. For instance, in 10:23ff., after Jesus has taught the rich man the one thing he did not wish to hear, we are told: "and looking around he says to his disciples, 'How hard it is for a rich man to enter the dominion of God.'" The disciples' reaction to this teaching is amazement. They are totally nonplussed (vv. 24, 26 — εξεπλησσοντο — the strongest of the two verbs here, meaning "totally dismayed"). The teacher, however, goes on to say that salvation is a free gift of God, for whom all things are possible (v. 27). Nonetheless, Peter is still thinking in terms of material or personal sacrifice and its possible relationship to salvation when he says in desperation, "We have left everything to follow you!" This is apparently an attempt to compare the disciples favorably to the rich young man who would not give up his wealth to follow Jesus. He seems to convey the feelings and hopes of all the Twelve. Taylor's remark at this point bears repeating: "The distinction of tenses in αφηκαμεν and ηκολουθηκαμεν is noteworthy; the decisive renunciation in Peter's mind stood out against the permanent following."[44]

---

44. Taylor, p. 433. Following is ongoing; renunciation is a punctiliar act.

Apparently in concession to their weakness, Jesus reveals the rewards for those who follow him with undivided loyalty. They involve in this age having a new family, the family of faith, and this family includes women, who are one's sisters in faith. The definition of who Jesus' followers are in Mark's perspective must be large enough to include such women, even though the focus of the bulk of the narrative is on the Twelve or some part of that group. Jesus also suggests that the disciples will have their material needs provided for. These sorts of benefits are seen as both present and future, but along with them come persecutions for what they have done and are doing. This pericope closes with a warning lest these benefits go to the disciples' heads. "But many who are first will be last, and the last first." This cautions the Twelve not to rely on their present status as if it were some sort of guarantee of present and future benefits. One can fall from the place of first, for reversal can happen at any time.[45] Perhaps there is an intimation here of the reversal we shall encounter in the passion and resurrection narratives involving the Twelve and the women.

Jesus begins his trek up to Jerusalem at 10:32. Those who are with him have mixed emotions, none of which are positive. Though we are not told specifically who the "they" are who are amazed, it seems likely that Mark means the Twelve, perhaps identifiable by their typical reaction to such things (cf. 10:24). It says rather clearly, "but those who followed were afraid." Who are these who follow behind Jesus? It is possible to contrast those who are amazed with those who follow behind Jesus (the women? — cf. 15:41; 16:8), but it seems more likely that both verbs apply to the Twelve or the disciples in general, including the Twelve and the women. Here we are meant to see their reluctance to go down this road. They are now literally following behind Jesus, for they are afraid. Though Jesus' action may correspond to the Jewish custom of a teacher preceding his disciples, previously the disciples seem to have not done this, and the motive for their doing so here is given as fear.[46] In any event, we have a picture of Jesus leading his disciples to the confrontation awaiting in Jerusalem, and the followers are astounded and apprehensive about what will come to pass. Later Jesus will lead them away from Jerusalem to Galilee, again preceding them to the destination and commanding them to follow. Here we have a picture of Jesus consciously accepting his destiny.[47]

The motif of private instruction comes to the fore again in 10:32b. Jesus takes the Twelve aside and gives them a third or fourth teaching about the Son of Man and his betrayal, death, and resurrection (cf. 8:31-38; 9:9, 12; 9:31). The word "again" is important here, for it likely implies that it was the Twelve, perhaps exclusively the Twelve, who had been previously given the prediction

---

45. See Swete, pp. 218-19; Plummer, p. 244.

46. But cf. G. Kittel, "ακολουθεω," *TDNT,* 1:213-14.

47. Taylor, p. 437.

about the Son of Man.[48] Perhaps Jesus is to be seen as trying to prepare the leaders of his community of followers to guide and prepare his other followers for what is to come. This is their task, and in preparation for it Jesus gives his most explicit explanation of what will happen to him (vv. 33-34). Furthermore, he identifies the Twelve with himself in his inescapable movement toward Jerusalem (αναβαινομεν). They too must share in Jesus' destiny to this extent, but it is only the Son of Man who will be betrayed, condemned, handed over, mocked, flogged, killed, and finally raised.

As we begin to move toward Jerusalem, the narrative moves toward a climactic utterance in 10:45. Juxtaposed as it is with the most explicit prediction of Jesus' passion, the request of Jacob and John is concerned with their self-glorification. They ask for the seats of honor on either side of Jesus when he comes into his glory (cf. 1 Kings 2:19; Ps. 110:1; 1 Esd. 4:29; Josephus, *Ant.* 6.235). This probably implies that they expect Jesus, once he enters Jerusalem, to restore its former glory and reestablish David's throne. They understand Jesus' messiahship as royal and political. This is the most likely interpretation of Jacob and John's aspirations, though the term "glory" may suggest that they have in mind the places of honor at the messianic banquet (cf. 8:38; 13:26). But 9:1 and the mention of Jerusalem as the destiny likely implied to these two a nearer and more earthly glory.[49]

Jesus makes one last effort at teaching the Twelve the meaning of the words he has just spoken. He speaks of his baptism and the cup he must drink — both images of overwhelming calamity and even of the wrath and judgment of God.[50] What are we to make of the disciples' apparently glib answer in v. 39a, especially when Jesus seems to agree with them that they will be sucked into the maelstrom? The Sons of Thunder will indeed in some sense endure the fury of the storm that hovers over the head of Jesus. Notice that Jesus does not speak of the crowd sharing his destiny. He endeavors once more to correct the attitudes of the Twelve. He desires that they lead as he leads — proceeding down the road of self-sacrifice.

Though the ten are indignant at the request of Jacob and John, Jesus speaks to them as if they had no right to be angry, for they likely shared similar hopes and ideas. Jesus feels he must address them all to remedy the problem. In 10:41-44, as in 9:35, he proposes to explain what true leadership in his community must mean. Again he does not dismiss the notion that the Twelve should lead; rather he tries to refine and reorient their thoughts. The Twelve are not to be like the Gentile rulers or the "great ones."[51] If they are to follow their Lord

---

48. See Meye, pp. 163-64.
49. Cf. Lane, pp. 278-79; Taylor, p. 440.
50. Cranfield, p. 338.
51. On Jesus' knowledge of petty rulers of Palestine and Syria, cf. Lane, p. 382.

and then lead his followers, they must renounce any thoughts or tendencies to want to be lords in a worldly sense. They can only be great paradoxically by being servants. Whoever wants to be first must become the slave of all. The final crushing blow against all human ambition and desire for personal greatness is expressed in 10:45.

The one person who truly had a claim to all the world had to offer in the way of greatness chose to be a servant. In this he shows the way of true greatness. The final proof of Jesus' message is to be found in his mission. Unlike worldly rulers, Jesus as the Son of Man did not come to be served, but rather to serve and to give his life as a λυτρον αντι πολλων.[52] In the face of this rebuttal there can be no claims, indeed not even any requests, for seats of honor. The disciples' greatness must be found in renouncing worldly greatness and personal aggrandizement and advancement and being the servant of many, just as their master had been and would be doing. The και which begins v. 45 should likely be translated "even" and is emphatic — "*Even* the Son of Man came to serve."[53]

The contrasts in this passage are many and notable. There is the contrast in the context between what is said in 10:32-34 and 10:35-37. There is the contrast between Jacob and John's desires and Jesus' mission. There is the contrast between the worldly great ones who lord it over people and the Lord who reveals that true greatness comes from humble service. After this point in the narrative, the same familiar themes keep recapitulating themselves without the Twelve coming any closer to understanding Jesus or his mission. But we must note that right to the end Jesus never gave up attempting to teach them (cf. Mark 13 and 14).

At 10:46 we have the familiar distinction between the disciples and the crowd. Jesus continues to rely on the Twelve, and at 11:2 he sends two of them on a brief mission to get a colt and prepare the way for his entrance into Jerusalem. At 11:9 we seem to have two groups, those who go before and those who follow (the Twelve and the women?). And they both shout, "Hosanna. Blessed is the one who comes in the name of the Lord."

After entering Jerusalem and going briefly to the temple, Jesus takes the Twelve along and goes to Bethany (11:11). In 11:21 the prominence of Peter surfaces again in the fig tree incident, and Jesus exhorts him to have faith. The crowds and the disciples are once more distinguished in 12:41, 43. In the same story we find the motif of private instruction of the Twelve. In this case a poor woman and her generosity are used as an object lesson for the Twelve, so that they too might be self-sacrificial.

---

52. "A ransom in place of the many"; on the meaning of this phrase see pp. 288-92 above.

53. Cf. Taylor, p. 444; Swete, p. 226.

There is an intimation that the disciples are still thinking in terms of human and material greatness at 13:1, and Jesus challenges this notion of greatness with a prophecy at 13:2. Here Peter, Andrew, Jacob, and John ask for and receive special private (κατ ιδιαν) instruction about the time and signs of the end. Once again we have the motif of private revelation on the mountain, as at 9:2ff., and special instruction for the inner circle of the Twelve.[54] In the course of this revelation Jesus lets his audience know that they will share his fate. Just as he will be dragged before the authorities, so will they be (cf. 10:33 to 13:9). Just as some will abuse Jesus, so likewise this will happen to the disciples (cf. 10:34 to 13:9). What they will experience is no more than what Jesus experienced first (cf. 13:11 to 14:46). 13:13 in a sense describes both Jesus' fate and that of those who seek to be like him, but Jesus had warned the disciples before that such would be the case (10:30 — persecutions). The discourse is revealed specifically to the inner circle so they will be prepared both for the birth pangs and the end whenever it comes. They have been given the full explanation, but Jesus also gives a warning to all (13:37).

The telltale signs that Jesus' end is at hand begin at 14:10ff. Here we find the beginning of a pattern present in all the Gospels of the complete failure of the Twelve and their desertion of Jesus. Nonetheless, Jesus continues to call on the Twelve for small missions. In 14:13, as in 11:1, two are called on to prepare the way so that Jesus may share a meal with his disciples. Mark stresses that this meal was shared with the Twelve (14:17), though others were likely there as well, including the owner of the home. Jesus reveals that he knows that it is one of the Twelve who will betray him (14:20). Further, he predicts that all the Twelve will fall away (14:27) and yet promises that, after he is raised, "I will go before you into Galilee." This promise, introduced by reference to the resurrection, seems to suggest the reversal of the smiting of the shepherd and the scattering of the sheep.[55] The Twelve, however, in essence follow Jesus no farther down the *via crucis* than engaging in a symbolic partaking of his death in the meal. Probably the Last Supper should be seen as one last attempt through signs to teach the disciples about Jesus' death. It is not to be overlooked that Jesus points out that his blood is to be poured out for the many (cf. 10:45).

Jesus points to the nature of his ministry and thus sets the example for what the Twelve's ministry is to be like: self-sacrifice for the many. Peter, once again representing the best and worst of the disciples, vows not to fall away (14:28), but Jesus in turn foretells his denials (14:30). Though Peter insists emphatically that he would rather die than disown Jesus, once again we have a profession (cf. 8:27-30) that will later prove a sham, in this case because of a nega-

---

54. See Meye, pp. 133ff.

55. So C. F. Evans, "I Will Go before You into Galilee," *JTS* 5, no. 5 (1954): 3-18, here p. 9.

tive sort of insistent confession before another audience (14:66ff.). Mark makes evident that Peter in his vows and insistence speaks for all the disciples (14:31). But they too will prove false (14:50).

The inner circle of the Twelve are called upon for one final duty — to watch with Jesus in his hour of need and sorrow. He needs their presence and ministry. Yet even then they fail him and have no answer when he confronts them with this failure (14:40b). Jesus has had enough and says so (απεχει, v. 41) of disciples who will not serve him or others, no matter how much he teaches them. His fellowship with them and his time of waiting have come to an end. He must go to the cross alone. Adding insult to injury, it is one of the Twelve who betrays him into the hands of his enemies (14:43). Were it not for 14:28, we might assume that the Twelve are permanently abandoned by Jesus.

During the passion narrative Mark gives no indication that the Twelve are present or with Jesus. 14:50 says they have all fled, presumably from Gethsemane to some safe haven within or near Jerusalem (Bethany?). Though Peter follows Jesus to the courtyard of the Sanhedrin after Jesus is arrested, this tentative venture ends in disaster and denial. And thus it is at this juncture that we discover that only the women who followed Jesus in Galilee are present at the crucifixion and the empty tomb (15:41; 16:1-8).

When we come to the women's visit to the tomb at 16:1ff., what we find is surprising. Here a young man commands the women to go say to the disciples and especially Peter that Jesus is going before them into Galilee. The term "disciples" here seems to mean the remnant of the Twelve.[56] Peter is singled out, and that is in keeping with what we have seen on various other occasions in Mark. He particularly needs to be reinstated after his denials, but also because he will be the leader of the disciples again.[57]

Though the focus is on the Twelve here, bear in mind that it is the women who have been last at the cross, present at the burial, and first at the tomb. They have heard the Easter message, received the commission to speak authoritatively to the male disciples. We must assume that the promise that Jesus will see the disciples in Galilee includes them as well.[58] After all, it is stressed in Mark 15 that they were Jesus' followers in Galilee, and Galilee is now the place where Jesus will start over again with his followers. It is where the disciples were first called and commissioned, and where they first ministered. It is where they were first taught, and experienced Jesus' miracles. 16:8, of course, leaves us with a report of at least temporary disobedience by the women, but this is the only place in this Gospel where they are portrayed in a negative manner, and since we are meant to think of the restoration of the male disciples, it seems likely that we

---

56. See Meye, pp. 80-83, 194-95.
57. See Cullmann, pp. 24-25; Brown, p. 71 n. 65; Meye, pp. 182-83.
58. But see Meye, p. 182, who sees the "you" as referring only to the Eleven.

should think this was the case with the women. The reader will in any case know this was the case presumably (see Acts 1:14). In other words, too much should not be made of 16:7-8 in assessing Mark's evaluation of women as disciples. They seem less fallible than the Twelve, and if the latter can be restored in Galilee, so can the former.

There is, however, a further important point. Mark does want to leave us with the impression that at the end of the day, true discipleship, based on true understanding of Jesus and his mission, was only possible after Easter. Only Jesus' death and resurrection finally overcame the disciples' resistance to him and his message. There is also a paradoxical message of hope for future generations of disciples who likewise fail under pressure. The message is that there can be forgiveness and restoration.

Mark's approach to the Twelve and the other disciples is a study in contrasts. Mark does not exalt or exonerate the Twelve; he makes their faults painfully obvious. Nonetheless, he features them prominently as the ones who Jesus has called, equipped, commissioned, and sent out. In the first half of the Gospel they are presented as responding for the most part in the right way, though their comprehension level is low. It is striking that members of the Twelve are virtually the only persons mentioned by name in this Gospel (other than Jesus and the occasional person Jesus healed) up to the passion narrative.

The focus on the Twelve is especially clear in the various places where there is a stress on Jesus privately teaching them or some subset of that group. Peter frequently comes to the fore as the representative (for better or worse) and spokesman of the group. There are several revelatory moments where it appears that the light has broken through to them. When they go out on a mission and return and are called apostles for just about the only time in this Gospel, some progress seems to have been made (6:6b-13, 30). Peter's confession, though limited, is correct so far as it goes, and it proves to be a watershed in regard to Jesus' teaching of the Twelve. Thereafter he can tell them about the Son of Man's mission to go up to Jerusalem and die (8:31; 9:31; 10:32-34; 10:45). The transfiguration likewise reveals that Peter understands a little of the nature of Jesus' mission and is perceptive enough to recognize the other two prophets present, even if he does not understand Jesus' uniqueness.

These high moments are counterbalanced by Peter being called Satan, and his denial of Christ three times after he had sworn emphatically never to do so and never to abandon Jesus even if it meant death. In this, Peter is only revealing the lack of faith and comprehension and thus the misunderstanding which is a theme that runs like a red thread through Mark's presentation of the disciples. The two themes of Jesus' teaching and the Twelve's misunderstanding clash again and again, so that there are even points at which it seems Jesus might reject the Twelve (8:31f.; 9:19; 14:41), just as they implicitly and finally explicitly reject him and what he stands for. That Jesus does not abandon the

Twelve reflects God's mercy and grace, not the Twelve's personal indispensability or unique gifts.

Mark recognizes that there are other disciples, and among them he mentions especially a group of women from Galilee (4:10; 10:32; 11:9; 15:40-41). There are in addition other figures, such as bar-Timaeus or the anonymous anointer in Bethany, which makes clear that Mark believes there were other male and female followers of Jesus. The spotlight is not on these other disciples, but then, remember that the spotlight in this ancient biography is primarily on Jesus and only secondarily on the disciples. If one forgets this fact, one can easily take a very dim view of the possibilities of true discipleship or of Mark's evaluation of the earliest disciples, especially if one thinks this Gospel ends at 16:7-8. However, there are enough clues and enough positive remarks about both male and female disciples that we should not come to such a conclusion. Even when the disciples abandon Jesus in his hour of greatest need when he experiences our God-forsakenness on the cross, Jesus has not abandoned them. Rather he will go before them into Galilee, and reconfigure and recommission them there.

The great message in this Gospel is that God in Christ is not finished with us yet, and that God's yes, in the end, is much louder than our no. His grace is greater and overcomes the scope of our sin. And thus we must not be too hard on Jesus' fallible followers as they are presented in this Gospel, not only because we are like them, but even more so because Mark is right. True discipleship is only possible after Easter when the full significance of the life, death, and resurrection of Jesus can be known.[59] We have then even less excuse than those first followers if we do not take up our crosses and follow Jesus down the *via crucis.*

---

59. See D. English, *The Message of Mark* (Downers Grove: InterVarsity, 1992), p. 21: ". . . the people in the story are not able to come to proper discipleship because they do not yet know the full story. They are faced by Jesus before his death and resurrection. If true discipleship is, as Jesus keeps on making clear, to carry our cross after him, and to discover God's care for us as we do, then they are bound to be unable to perceive its total meaning before he dies and rises. . . ."

Index of Modern Authors

Dalman, G., 165n.81, 180n.139
Daube, D., 124n.50, 275, 306
De Bruyne, D., 22n.71
Denny, J., 329n.117
Derrett, J. D. M., 182, 183n.147, 226,
    232n.103, 272n.48, 309, 320, 322n.79,
    334
Dewey, J., 36, 109, 110nn.3-4, 135,
    136n.90
Dibelius, M., 184, 191n.191, 278
Dittenberger, W., 69n.7
Dodd, C. H., 78, 431n.33
Doudna, J. C., 17
Drury, J., 165n.78
Dubrow, H., 2n.4
Dunn, J. D. G., 41, 121, 130n.73, 158, 228
Dyer, K. D., 349n.210

English, D., 92n.17, 95, 140, 196, 198,
    247, 247n.154, 251n.156, 254n.157,
    293, 294, 295n.148, 297, 298n.150, 351,
    351n.214, 354n.217, 355, 356,
    357n.221, 406, 407n.187, 408, 418,
    442n.59
Eppstein, V., 315n.43
Evans, C. F., 439n.55

Falk, Z. W., 226n.85
Farmer, W. R., 307n.13
Farrar, A., 48
Fiorenza, E. Schussler., 275, 276n.62,
    330n.123, 368n.25
Fish, S., 57
Fitzmyer, J. A., 226n.85
Fledderman, H., 334n.150
Flusser, D., 332n.139, 413n.4
Ford, D., 345n.199
Fowler, R. M., 14, 37n.111, 37, 56n.164,
    59n.169, 132
Freyne, S., 33n.101, 313, 314n.38
Furnish, V. P., 331n.131

Gamble, H. Y., 48n.136
Garrett, S., 76nn.26 and 29, 241,
    242n.141, 243n.147, 379, 380n.88
Gaston, L., 336n.164, 340, 342n.190
Gnilka, J., 61, 180n.139, 214n.44

Goodman, M., 33
Grasser, E., 194n.203
Guelich, R., 22n.73, 38n.114, 97nn.3-4,
    103n.17, 104n.19, 121n.38, 124nn.51-
    52, 133, 136n.95, 141nn.1-2, 144,
    145n.1, 151n.11, 152nn.17, 20,
    159nn.48, 50, 161n.58, 165n.76,
    168n.89, 169n.92, 173n.110, 175,
    180n.139, 182n.144, 184n.156,
    188n.178, 192n.194, 201n.2, 202n.4,
    211n.30, 213n.41, 214n.42, 218n.57,
    219n.60, 221n.63, 222n.68, 229,
    234nn.114, 116, 237, 239n.132
Gundry, R. H., 20n.68, 24n.79, 25n.80,
    38n.114, 70n.11, 87n.1, 90n.10, 92n.15,
    114, 115, 116n.23, 119n.34, 127n.62,
    135, 136n.94, 140n.98, 171n.98,
    175n.119, 177n.128, 187n.174,
    192nn.193, 196, 210n.28, 212n.36,
    216nn.50-51, 234, 235n.117, 242,
    243n.143, 244, 261, 263n.18, 266n.29,
    277nn.72-73, 280nn.86-87, 282n.96,
    282, 284nn.105, 107, 317, 323n.88,
    324nn.92, 96, 329n.118, 330n.124,
    331n.127, 332nn.132, 138, 335n.157,
    365n.8, 370n.34, 379n.75, 380n.87,
    382n.96, 416-17, 422n.5

Hamilton, N. Q., 314n.42
Harrisville, R. A., 231n.98
Hawkins, J. C., 18n.61, 19n.63, 180n.141
Head, P., 19n.64, 40n.118
Hengel, M., 8, 20, 21, 25n.80, 66, 70,
    86n.11, 211, 341, 391n.137
Hester, J. D., 321n.76, 411n.1
Hoehner, H. W., 215n.46
Hooker, M., 2n.7, 38n.14, 102, 104,
    104n.19, 110n.6, 116, 118, 119n.30,
    123n.47, 126n.61, 132nn.78-79,
    136n.91, 137n.96, 143, 143n.8,
    154n.29, 155n.31, 157, 160, 164n.74,
    165n.79, 166, 167n.83, 169, 170n.94,
    172n.104, 174, 175n.116, 176n.123,
    180n.141, 183, 185n.157, 187nn.170,
    172, 189n.181, 191, 195n.204, 203n.7,
    208, 210n.26, 212n.35, 215, 216n.54,
    218n.58, 221n.66, 223n.74, 228n.91,

Index of References